Saints and their Cults

Saints and their Cults

Studies in Religious Sociology, Folklore and History

Edited with Introduction and
Annotated Bibliography by

STEPHEN WILSON

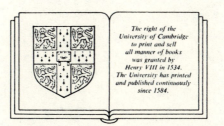

The right of the
University of Cambridge
to print and sell
all manner of books
was granted by
Henry VIII in 1534.
The University has printed
and published continuously
since 1584.

CAMBRIDGE UNIVERSITY PRESS

Cambridge

London   New York   New Rochelle
Melbourne   Sydney

Published by the Press Syndicate of the University of Cambridge
The Pitt Building, Trumpington Street, Cambridge CB2 1RP
32 East 57th Street, New York, NY 10022, USA
10 Stamford Road, Oakleigh, Melbourne 3166, Australia

First published 1983
Reprinted 1985

Printed in Great Britain at the
University Press, Cambridge

Library of Congress catalogue card number: 82-25296

British Library Cataloguing in Publication Data

Saints and their cults.
1. Cults
I. Wilson, Stephen
291   BP603
ISBN 0 521 24978 3

TM

'meminerint cum affectu pio parentum meorum in hac luce transitoria . . .'
(St Augustine, *Confessions*, Book IX)

Contents

Illustrations

MAPS

FIGURE

Acknowledgements

The article by Robert Hertz first appeared under the title 'Saint Besse, Etude d'un culte alpestre' in *Revue de l'Histoire des Religions*, LXVII (1913), pp. 115–80; and subsequently in Robert Hertz, *Sociologie religieuse et folklore* (Paris, 1928 and 1970), pp. 110–60, published by Presses Universitaires de France.

The article by Evelyne Patlagean first appeared under the title 'Ancienne hagiographie byzantine et histoire sociale' in *Annales*, 23 (1968), pp. 106–26; and subsequently in *Structure sociale, famille, chrétienté à Byzance, IVᵉ–XIᵉ siècle* (London, 1981), Ch. V, published by Variorum Reprints.

The article by Patrick Geary first appeared under the title 'L'humiliation des saints' in *Annales*, 34 (1979), pp. 27–42.

The article by Gabrielle M. Spiegel, 'The Cult of Saint Denis and Capetian Kingship', originally appeared in the *Journal of Medieval History*, I (1975), pp. 43–69, published by the North-Holland Publishing Company.

The article by Michael Goodich, 'The Politics of Canonization in the Thirteenth Century: Lay and Mendicant Saints', originally appeared in *Church History*, 44 (1975), pp. 294–307, published by The American Society of Church History.

The article by Pierre Delooz first appeared under the title 'Pour une étude sociologique de la sainteté canonisée dans l'Eglise catholique' in *Archives de Sociologie des Religions*, 13 (1962), pp. 17–43, published by the Centre National de la Recherche Scientifique.

The article by Albert Soboul first appeared under the title 'Sentiment religieux et cultes populaires pendant la Révolution, saintes patriotes et martyrs de la liberté' in *Archives de Sociologie des Religions*, 2 (1956), pp. 73–87, published by the Centre National de la Recherche Scientifique; and subsequently in *Annales Historiques de la Révolution Française*, 29 (1957), pp. 193–213; and in Albert Soboul, *Paysans, sans-culottes et Jacobins, Etudes d'histoire révolutionnaire* (Paris, 1966), Ch. VII, pp. 183–202, published by

Librairie Clavreuil; a translation appeared in Jeffry Kaplow (ed.), *New Perspectives on the French Revolution: Readings in Historical Sociology* (New York, 1965), pp. 338–50.

A version of the article by Stephen Wilson, 'Cults of Saints in the Churches of Central Paris', originally appeared in *Comparative Studies in Society and History*, 22 (1980), pp. 548–75, published by Cambridge University Press.

The article by Pierre Sanchis first appeared under the title 'Les Romarias Portugaises' in *Archives de Sciences Sociales des Religions*, 43/1 (1977), pp. 53–76, published by the Centre National de la Recherche Scientifique.

The article by Marc Gaborieau first appeared under the title 'Le culte des saints chez les musulmans au Népal et en Inde du nord' in *Social Compass*, 25 (1978), pp. 477–94.

We gratefully acknowledge the permission of the publishers, editors and authors mentioned to republish this material either in its original form or in translation. Patrick Geary kindly supplied the English original of his article.

The preparation of the Bibliography was facilitated by the ever-efficient service provided by the staff at the British Library, and by Ann Wood and her staff in the Inter-Library Loan department of the University of East Anglia Library.

Marjan Bhasvar and Christine Aldiss helped with the typing of the translations, and Marjan typed the Bibliography.

Finally, the editor would like to extend personal thanks to colleagues and friends who provided him with information and encouragement, and particularly to John Gordon and John Thompson.

Notes on contributors

PIERRE DELOOZ was born at Namur, Belgium, in 1921, and holds a doctorate in the social sciences from the University of Liège. He is Professor of Sociology at the Faculté Universitaire Catholique of Mons and consultant at the International Research and Information Centre, Pro Mundi Vita, in Brussels. He is the author of *Sociologie et canonisations* (The Hague, 1969).

MARC GABORIEAU is the author of several studies on Nepal, and is attached to the Centre d'Etudes de l'Inde et de l'Asie du Sud, Ecole des Hautes Etudes en Sciences Sociales, Paris.

PATRICK GEARY comes from Louisiana. He received his doctorate at Yale University, and taught at Princeton before taking up his current position at the University of Florida. His publications on medieval society and culture include *Furta Sacra, Thefts of Relics in the Central Middle Ages* (Princeton, 1978).

MICHAEL GOODICH is Associate Professor in Medieval History at the University of Haifa, Israel. He is the author of two books: *The Unmentionable Vice: Homosexuality in the Later Medieval Period* (Santa Barbara, 1979); and *Vita Perfecta: The Ideal of Sainthood in the Thirteenth Century* (Stuttgart, 1982).

ROBERT HERTZ was one of the most distinguished pupils of Emile Durkheim. Born at Saint-Cloud near Paris in 1881, he graduated in first place as *agrégé* in philosophy at the Ecole Normale Supérieure in 1904. After two years' research work in the British Museum, he taught at the *lycée* of Douai, and, from 1907, at the Ecole Pratique des Hautes Etudes in Paris. His main works, in addition to that published here, are two essays: 'La Représentation collective de la mort' (1907); and 'La Prééminence de la main droite' (1909), which have appeared in English translation under the title *Death and The Right Hand* (London and New York, 1960), edited by

xi

Rodney Needham. Hertz was killed in action at Marcheville on the Western Front in 1915.

EVELYNE PATLAGEAN is Professor of Late Antique and Byzantine History in the University of Paris-X (Nanterre). She is the author of *Pauvreté économique et pauvreté sociale à Byzance, 4ᵉ–7ᵉ siècle* (Paris and The Hague, 1977), and most of her papers up to 1979 have been collected in *Structure sociale, famille, chrétienté à Byzance, IVᵉ–XIᵉ siècle* (London, 1981).

PIERRE SANCHIS took his doctorate at the Ecole des Hautes Etudes en Sciences Sociales in Paris in 1976, and is now Associate Professor in the Department of Sociology and Anthropology of the Federal University of Minas Gerais, Brazil.

ALBERT SOBOUL was Director of the Institut d'Histoire de la Révolution Française in Paris and editor of the *Annales Historiques de la Révolution Française* until his death in 1982. His first major work was his doctoral thesis: *Les Sans-culottes parisiens en l'An II, Mouvement populaire et gouvernement révolutionnaire 1793–1794* (1958). He was Professor at the Sorbonne (now University of Paris-I) from 1967 to 1982, and was the author of many books and articles on the French Revolution. These include, in English: *The Parisian Sans-culottes and the French Revolution, 1793–4* (Oxford, 1964), an abridged edition of his thesis; and *The French Revolution 1787–1799, from the Storming of the Bastille to Napoleon* (London, 1974).

GABRIELLE M. SPIEGEL was educated at Bryn Mawr, Harvard and Johns Hopkins, where she received her doctorate in 1974. She currently teaches history at the University of Maryland. She is the author of a number of articles on medieval history and historiography, and of a book: *The Chronicle Tradition of Saint-Denis: A Survey* (Leiden and Boston, 1978).

STEPHEN WILSON was born in 1941. He received his doctorate from the University of Cambridge in 1967 with a thesis on 'The Historians of the Action Française', and he currently teaches European history at the University of East Anglia, Norwich. He is the author of over twenty articles on history, historiography and religion, and of a book: *Ideology and Experience, Antisemitism in France at the time of the Dreyfus Affair* (Rutherford, London and Toronto, 1982). He is at present engaged on a study of feuding in Corsica.

Introduction

STEPHEN WILSON

In recent years there has been something of a revival in the study of saints or hagiology. Not that the subject has ever been neglected – indeed, it has attracted more scholarly attention over the centuries than most – but, rather, new methods and approaches have forced it to yield new fruits. Where a scholar of an older generation could assert that most Breton saints' Lives, for example, were 'entirely devoid of historical value',[1] his successors in France and elsewhere, taking a wider view of what is 'historical', have shown that saints' Lives and other material related to their cults can reflect important features of the societies in which they occur. These include not only modes of religious perception and feeling but also social relationships and political structure. At the same time, social anthropologists, religious sociologists, folklorists – the label is unimportant – have begun to apply to the study of 'popular Catholicism', notably in Latin America and the Mediterranean world, the same methods of analysis that had previously been reserved for that of non-Christian and particularly 'primitive' religions. This book gathers together a number of studies in each of these now overlapping genres, most of which are presented to English readers for the first time. To these, two studies of non-Christian saints, 'secular' and Islamic, have been added for comparison. A special mention should be made of the study of St Besse by Robert Hertz. It exemplifies both the historical and the sociological trends to which we have referred, but what is more surprising about it is that it was written in 1913 and has been comparatively neglected despite its brilliance.

I

By way of introduction, a brief account of the history of the cult of saints in Christianity is here provided, together with some analysis of its various manifestations and functions, in an attempt to give an idea of their scope. Most religions, including monotheistic Judaism[2] as well as Islam,

1

distinguish in practice if not in strict theory between a higher god or gods and lesser divine beings. The former are remote, concerned with origins and things cosmological, while the latter are more familiar, in closer touch with mortals, and are concerned with mundane matters, such as the well-being of a village, clan or family, or the health and fertility of humans, animals and fields. Whether specifically regarded as local or ancestral spirits or not, such 'godlings'[3] fill the void between the everyday human world and the distant rulers of the cosmos. In the Christian world, belief in non-human spirits, angels and devils, exists and has sometimes been important – and some angels are regarded as saints, notably St Michael[4] – but such lesser divine beings have more often been humans, living and dead, whose special virtues and circumstances have made them suitable and powerful mediators between the two spheres.

The history of these Christian saints has aroused much controversy, and a 'straight' account of it is not, therefore, easy. Many writers, from contemporary pagans themselves to Protestants and anticlericals later, argued that the cult of the saints was of pagan origin. The saints were 'the successors to the gods', in Saintyves's phrase, and to the pagan heroes. Striking similarities existed in the form of their respective cults, and dates of festivals and sites of worship were identical. According to Lucius, for example, the shrine of St Cosmas and St Damian at Cyrrhus in Syria, which flourished from the fifth century, was a continuation under another name of a shrine devoted to Asclepius, and was characterized by the same methods of healing, notably 'incubation', while others identified the pair of saints with Castor and Pollux, the heavenly twins of Greek mythology.[5] While anxious to refute the general thesis involved here, Catholic scholars have accepted that pagan sites and festivals were Christianized via the cult of saints, but see the process as one of opposition rather than osmosis, at least in the first instance. Constantine, for example, dedicated the temple of Poseidon at Constantinople to St Menas, 'having driven out the idols',[6] while the cult of St Babylas was introduced at Daphne in the mid-fourth century in order to oust the oracle of Apollo, which indeed fell silent as a result.[7] Many saints' Lives, moreover, from that of St Martin in fourth-century Gaul to that of St Stephen of Perm in fourteenth-century Russia, represent the saint as a missionary battling with and triumphing over the old religions. And even where it was agreed that pagan elements were present in the cult of the saints, this was very often seen as a necessary compromise with mass converts or gross peasants and as a departure from an originally purer and more exclusively Christian practice. 'What we teach is one thing', declared St Augustine, 'what we tolerate is another; and what we are obliged to put up with is yet another.'[8]

The Greek or Latin equivalents of the term 'saint' were initially applied in the Early Church to baptized church members and to the faithful departed, usages later revived among some Protestants.[9] Only gradually did the term come to be reserved for a special category of holy person: the martyr. This lends particular weight to the view that the Christian cult of saints, far from originating in paganism, arose rather from veneration for those who had died precisely because they refused any compromise with the established Roman religion. The martyrs were regarded as precious witnesses to the truth of the faith for which they had died, and they were commemorated and honoured accordingly at their burial places. St Augustine was at pains to point out that Christians did 'not in those shrines raise altars on which to sacrifice to the martyrs but to the one God, who is the martyrs' God and ours',[10] but, as his disclaimer indicates, many of the martyrs' tombs quickly became important shrines, with special churches or *martyria* built over them, and simple commemoration gave way to a cult of miracle-working saints.

When the era of persecutions ended and Christianity became publicly established in the Late Roman Empire, new concepts of sainthood emerged. Asceticism was assimilated to martyrdom, and sanctity was also ascribed to those who spread the gospel among the heathen or who governed the Church with piety. These notions were exemplified and proclaimed in the Lives of St Anthony of Egypt by St Athanasius and of St Martin of Tours by Sulpicius Severus, which provided the models for centuries of hagiography. Anthony was the classic ascetic, pushing human life to its limits of endurance in solitariness, fasting, sleeplessness, and wrestling with the temptations of innumerable demons. But this deprivation, as we shall see in other cases, was a source of power, and Anthony and the other Desert Fathers were miracle workers, sought out by sick and anxious pilgrims. Martin was an ascetic and a miracle worker, too, but, more significantly, he was a missionary, an uprooter of paganism, and a bishop, a member albeit reluctant of the regular government of the Church. St Martin also represents another category of saint which was very important at this stage of the Church's history. He was the Apostle of Gaul, known sometimes as the Thirteenth Apostle, and many other local churches in Late Antiquity and the Early Middle Ages also rested their prestige and their authority on such apostolic claims. Rome, of course, had as founders St Peter and St Paul, Apostles and martyrs, over whom none boasted precedence. Alexandria had St Mark, later assumed by Venice. The Church of Georgia had been founded, it was claimed, by St Nina, 'the Equal of the Apostles',[11] while Compostela later claimed St James, Vézelay St Mary Magdalene, and Limoges St Martial, allegedly the child who had brought Christ the loaves and fishes in the Gospel story.[12]

Together with these extensions of the notion of sanctity went a number of developments in the cult paid to saints. The clear distinction drawn by St Augustine between worship of God and veneration of the saints was elaborated into a clear theological stance by other Early Fathers, particularly St Jerome, and then by the Scholastics. Worship proper (*latria*) was due to God alone; the saints were to receive only veneration (*dulia*); while the Virgin Mary was to be honoured with *hyperdulia*. Neither veneration of the saints nor of the Virgin Mary was held to be absolutely necessary to salvation. The saints, moreover, were to be venerated, not in themselves but only as possible 'channels of grace' from God.[13] Of course, in practice such distinctions were not always heeded or understood by the faithful or by the clergy.[14]

The cult of the early martyrs had been an essentially local cult centred on the tombs which contained their remains. While tomb cults remained, and remain, characteristic of Christianity, other forms developed from them. First, some cults ceased to be purely local, and were spread more or less deliberately by the distribution of 'relics' from the original site. This was a feature of the spread of Roman influence, and in the West the 'relics' concerned were, until the sixth century at least, substances or objects which had been placed on or near the tomb; oil from its lamps for example, or, most prized, cloths assimilated to those which had actually been dipped in the martyr's blood.[15] These relics were regarded as extensions of the saint's body and shared its sacred quality.

Secondly, since Constantinople, the new and Christian Rome, had no martyrs of its own to match those of the old Rome, the bodies of important saints were brought there from outside, starting with those of St Timothy, St Andrew and St Luke in 356–7.[16] This encouraged further 'translations' in the East and also the practice of discovering the hitherto unrecognized remains of saints, known as 'invention'. The best-known inventions of this period were those of the martyrs Protase and Gervase at Milan in 386 and of St Stephen at Jerusalem in 415. At the same time, holy bodies were divided or dismembered, and parts of them were deposited in churches and enclosed in costly reliquaries. Both translation and dismemberment offended against Roman law and burial custom as well as against original Christian sentiment, and they were resisted in the West, notably by Pope Gregory the Great. This resistance seems eventually to have been broken down during the later barbarian invasions. It was in the eighth and ninth centuries that the remains of the Roman martyrs were moved from the Catacombs into the churches of the city itself to prevent their desecration or neglect, and Dark Age chronicles are full of accounts of monastic communities moving to flee from the invaders and taking the bodies of their saints with them.

After this the religion of the Middle Ages in the West was certainly one which paid special devotion to the relics of the saints, in this sense, and which moved and divided, stole and threatened, swore by and bargained with them in ways that we will discuss. Meanwhile, three further aspects of medieval and later relic 'worship' should be mentioned. First, it was a requirement from early in the history of the Church and reiterated by the Seventh General Council of Nicaea in 787, that every consecrated church should have a relic placed in its altar.[17] This means that relics were incorporated into formal worship in an important way. Secondly, relics were by no means exclusively associated with the cult of saints. Indeed, many of the most revered relics of Christendom, such as the 'True Cross' and its fragments, the Virgin's robe or the 'Holy House' were associated with Christ and his mother.[18] Moreover, as we shall see, the pilgrimage *par excellence* from Late Antiquity onwards was to Jerusalem and the Holy Land, the 'loca sacra' where the events of the Old and New Testaments had actually occurred.

In the East, the precocious development of corporal relic devotion gave way from the seventh century, if not earlier, to icon worship. As the Frankish *Libri Carolini* expressed the divergent evolution at the end of the eighth century: 'They place almost all the hope of their credulity in images, but... we venerate the saints in their bodies or better in their relics... in the ancient tradition of the Fathers.'[19] Used at first in private devotion and deriving probably from boxes made to contain relics,[20] icons became the focus of public worship in the East, emerging from the Iconoclastic attack on them in the eighth and ninth centuries better-established than ever. Although related to the veneration of the saints, icons came to be much more central to Orthodox worship and theology than relics or images ever were in the West. A parallel Western development, but still significantly divergent, was the spread of the three-dimensional statue. Originating perhaps in part from certain kinds of reliquary in the form of effigies or busts,[21] the statue like the icon represented Christ and the Virgin Mary as often as it did the saints, and its increasing importance in the Later Middle Ages may be linked to the spread of Marian devotion in particular. Both trends continued to run together through the Counter-Reformation period, which was characterized by the 'invention' of statues and by cults of miraculous statues and images, both imitating aspects of the cult of relics.

This period also saw the culmination of two other developments. Where the saint of Late Antiquity and the Early Middle Ages had been the martyr, the ascetic or the bishop, the saint of the Later Middle Ages and the Early Modern period tended to be a member of a religious order, and the orders were in the forefront of propagating new cults. This reflected the progress of a certain channelling of sanctity into specialized ecclesiastical institutions. At another level of control, the whole process of designating saints had been formalized. The sanctity of the early martyr had been evident from the mode of his death, and the same spontaneous local attribution remained primary for centuries. From the Early Middle Ages, however, the control of bishops and synods became normal, and canonization was signalled by ritual 'translation'. In the Western Church, the approval of the papacy was then added. The first papal canonization was that of St Ulric of Augsburg in 993. Papal intervention was at first solicited as a means of enhancing the proposed cult rather than being imposed by authority, but it did coincide with the general revival and growth of papal power from the eleventh century, and it came in due course to be decisive and exclusive, ousting episcopal canonization altogether from 1234. An elaborate bureaucratic procedure was established in the thirteenth century, and this was placed in the hands of the Congregation of Rites in 1587 and further codified later. In the acephalous Eastern Church, canonization by synod or council remained the rule, although few canonizations appear to have been made in the modern period. Criteria were established, but no elaborate procedure was followed.[22] Although it is correctly maintained that the initiative in making saints remained in the West with the faithful, the slow and complicated procedure meant that only well-established pressure groups, and particularly, the religious orders, could in effect have saints made (see Goodich in Ch. 5 and Delooz in Ch. 6), and that the papacy and its bureaucracy could powerfully influence the selection of those who were ultimately canonized, that is, of those who were entitled to a public cult. This did not, of course, prevent the existence of 'unofficial' cults which had been neither absorbed nor successfully suppressed by the ecclesiastical authorities, but these undoubtedly became rare or marginal phenomena.

Both Sorokin and Mecklin have claimed that the saint as a social type is in the decline in the modern period, being incompatible with a materialist and secular society.[23] Delooz has pointed out from the formal canonization statistics that this is not the case and that new saints are being produced at a steady rate, while the studies by Wilson (in Ch. 8) and Sanchis (in Ch. 9) illustrate that devotion to saints is very much alive in Western Europe today. Any simple thesis of the modern decline of the saint, moreover, takes a very narrow view of sanctity, ignoring the whole phenomenon of secular 'martyrs', from those of the French Revolution studied by Soboul (in Ch. 7) to Lord Byron, Alfred Dreyfus[24] and Che Guevara, to mention only a few more recent examples. It ignores, too, the way that so many popular heroes are assimilated to the saints with their tomb or grave cults, the cherishing of their relics[25] and the erection of statues of them.[26] And, on occasions, such assimilation could be quite explicit, recalling the old amalgamation with paganism, but in reverse. When Lampedusa's Father Pirrone returns to his native village in Sicily in 1861, it will be recalled, the cart in which he travels has been newly painted with 'patriotic pictures... culminating in a rhetorical presentation of a flame-coloured Garibaldi arm in arm with an aquamarine Santa Rosalia'.[27]

The point is that saints belong to and reflect the societies which produce and honour them, and no one would expect late-twentieth-century believers or non-believers to have the same saints necessarily as the contemporaries of St Simeon Stylites or St Francis of Assisi, or to regard them in the same way. The history of saints' cults is thus of a complexity that can only be hinted at here, and reflects the profoundest changes in mentality and social structure.

We have mentioned changing notions of sanctity and in the preferred types of saint. Further important variations here were the saint as reformed sinner[28] and the saint as 'alter Christus'.[29] Also telling in this context are the changing avatars of particular saints over time, seemingly superficial but representative of fundamental transformations. Gibbon wrote of the Apostle James, with reference to the legends associated with his shrine at Compostela, for example, that 'from a peaceful fisherman of the lake of Gennesareth, he was transformed into a valorous knight, who charged at the head of the Spanish chivalry in their battles against the Moors'.[30] St Joseph, the husband of the Virgin Mary, was ignored by the Early Church and was generally represented in the Middle Ages as 'a decrepit old widower',[31] if not as a buffoon and a cuckold. It was not until the Later Middle Ages, and more particularly the Counter-Reformation period, that his cult was promoted and developed, so that by 1940 it could be said that his 'incomparable mission . . . raised him far above all other saints'.[32] In the same way, cults could decline after a period of widespread popularity. During the fourteenth and the first half of the fifteenth century, St Louis of Anjou was regarded as one of the greatest Franciscan saints 'ranking. . . next after the founder and St Anthony of Padua' and enjoying an extensive cult, but by this century his name had become 'practically unknown outside his own order'.[33] Or new saints could displace old ones, much as some early saints had displaced pagan deities. The chapel dedicated to St Brune or St Victoire at Rochefort in the diocese of Nîmes was placed instead under the invocation of Notre-Dame-de-Grâce in the mid-seventeenth century.[34] Again, at Traoun-Mériadek in Brittany, the cult of the local Breton saint, Meriadoc, was replaced by that of St John in the fifteenth century, and an important pilgrimage developed there, encouraged by the Dukes and centring on the claim of the shrine to possess the Baptist's index finger.[35] Such changes clearly reflect the growth of centralization in Church and states, as well as changes in religious feeling proper and, in the case of St Joseph, in attitudes towards the family. Moreover, the whole phenomenon of this constant renewal of saints, of new canonizations, of the growth of new cults and the decline of old ones, is itself of significance. Despite assertions to the contrary at the theological level, the power of saints was not eternal but might ebb and flow over time, and, as in other areas where fashion prevails, the cult of the saints set its own premium on novelty.

A geographical dimension is also present here – some societies, some countries, some regions producing and honouring many saints, others few or none at all. Delooz (in Ch. 6) has pointed to the overwhelming Latin preponderance among Western canonized saints, and to the Italian preponderance in particular. This is clearly related to Italy's proximity to the canonizing authority, a usually Italian pope, but this is not the whole explanation. Italians have also been more prone to perceive sanctity, especially in the second Christian millennium, and to attach importance to it. But, even here, there are further complications, with differential patterns in time and space. Sallmann has noted that 'on the map of medieval sanctity south Italy is a depressed zone. Neapolitan sanctity only makes its début in a sudden burst during the Counter-Reformation, reaching its full flowering in the years 1550–1850 when it becomes a massive cultural fact';[36] and south Italy has remained in our own time a zone where popular cults have persisted in strength.

Before we leave the history of saints, mention should be made of the opposition which their cults aroused. The doubts of many early Christians were echoed with more or less force by 'heretics' through the Dark and Middle Ages, and were amplified, of course, to form an important element in the programmes of the sixteenth-century Reformers. Luther was not altogether opposed to the veneration of saints and the Virgin Mary, although he objected strongly to the theology of indulgences which had been attached to it. Nor did the Church of England remove all saints' festivals from its liturgy. But the opposition of Calvin and of Calvinists was more thoroughgoing and, even in England, the triumph of Protestantism meant the destruction of the medieval shrines and their relics, and the extirpation of established cults, notably that of St Thomas of Canterbury.[37] Similar attacks were made later by secular revolutionaries in France, Spain, Russia and elsewhere. The vehemence of some iconoclasm is an indication of the power, religious but also social and political, associated with shrines and their cults. Such violent opposition, moreover, can be seen as only the extreme pole of a wider spectrum in which a purer unmediated religion is contrasted with a religion cluttered with saints and images. As we shall see, this contrast is by no means necessarily one simply between learned and 'popular', or even clerical and lay. Although some peasants seem to have been reluctant to neglect the saints or, more certainly, to destroy their images,[38] others associated the saints with a venal clergy and broke without difficulty with both.[39]

II

But if saints' cults have their specificity and their complex history at a variety of levels, they also display certain structural features which may be seen across cultures and across time, and to these we now turn, looking first at the different manifestations of devotion to the saints.

Although officially-recognized public cults in the Christian world might only be paid to the dead, there as elsewhere the cult of the dead saint usually sprang, save in the case of martyrs, from a reputation for sanctity in life. Indeed, the practice of heroic virtues and the accomplishment of miracles before or after death are required criteria in canonization procedures, and this reflects the general view, although popular opinion may place more emphasis on miracles. The Lives of the saints as well as more objective documentation, such as that relating to canonizations, are full of examples in which sanctity is clearly attributed to living persons. Sulpicius Severus wrote of St Martin that, in his lifetime, 'he was already regarded by everyone as a saint'.[40] Thomas of Celano relates of St Francis that, after the miracle of the swallows, people, having seen the sign, 'were filled with great admiration and they hastened with deep reverence to kiss the hem of the saint's garment, and they praised God, saying: "Truly, this man is a saint and a friend of the Most High!"' On other occasions, people sought 'to touch him in their devotion ... [and] they laid hands on him, pulled his habit and even cut pieces from it so as to keep them as relics'.[41] Recluses who fled from the world were frequently besieged by visitors and supplicants, seeking advice, cures or edification: for example the Desert Fathers, the Stylites or pillar saints of Syria and Asia Minor, and St Cuthbert on Farne Island. Such living saints were credited, as we have seen, with special powers, of healing, of clairvoyance, of protection. Some were consulted almost like oracles, or later as confessors, a speciality of the Curé d'Ars and of Padre Pio. Their sanctity might be further demonstrated by a proneness to states of ecstasy, or by a light or warmth about them or some other emanation of power. St Bonaventure relates that the Bishop of Assisi once disturbed St Francis at prayer and 'was shaken with sudden fear [so that] his limbs became rigid and he was incapable of speech ... [Then] he felt himself being pushed outside and fled'.[42]

We have already referred to the orientation of saints' cults around their tombs or relics, but some further aspects of this require elucidation. First, in such a context, the death of the saint assumed special significance. At death, in one perspective, the saint joined the ranks of the blessed in paradise and his intercession became fully effective; in another, his body, which despite his holiness had been marked in life by sin and human weakness, became a wholly sacred relic. People were therefore especially anxious to have contact with or to gain possession of the corpse of reputed saints. Before the funeral of St Ambrose, according to Paulinus, 'crowds of men and women kept throwing their handkerchiefs and aprons at the body of the saint in the hope that they would touch it'.[43] When St John Baptist de La Salle died in 1719, 'everyone hastened to obtain a last glimpse of the face of a man whom all revered as a saint ... In their anxiety to secure a memorial, people seized his poor clothes and tore them to shreds and laid hands on anything within reach. Some even cut locks from his hair.'[44]

There was also a danger that the corpse might be mutilated or dismembered, which led to burials in secret and other precautions. After the death of St Daniel the Stylite on his pillar in 493, the ecclesiastical authorities, after 'kissing the blessed body' themselves, had it cased in lead before bringing it down, afraid that it might otherwise 'be torn asunder by the crowd'.[45] In a compromise with such popular necrophilia, the veins of the corpse of St Gerard Majella were opened after his death in 1755 to allow people to dip handkerchiefs in his blood while it was still warm.[46] More frequently, the corpse as a whole was coveted. St Francis was not the only saint to be guarded by armed men on his last journey and on his death-bed lest his body be stolen, and many conflicts are reported over the possession of the corpses of reputed saints.[47]

But why was sanctity thus concentrated in bodily remains? A clue would seem to lie in the often-noted relationship between asceticism and miraculous powers. As the functions of the body were denied and overcome, so supra-corporal power accrued to the saint: 'the powers of the body made way for the power of the spirit', in the words of St Hilary.[48] And this process reached its culmination at death, the final denial of the body. Brown has noted a connection between the torture and bodily mutilation suffered by the early martyrs and their peculiar posthumous healing power,[49] and the same link may be detected in later cults, for example, that of Simon de Montfort whose body was dismembered on the battlefield at Evesham.[50] Moreover, extreme asceticism, such as that of St Theodore of Sykeon, could turn the living saint into the equivalent of a corpse, with its stench, its infestation with worms, its burial in the ground.[51] But, if the living saint resembled a corpse, then the dead saint did not. Incorruptibility of the corpse was usually, and still is, taken to be a sign of sanctity,[52] and it is a commonplace of hagiology that saints' bodies give off sweet odours.[53] Recognized saints, too, are not buried in the ground like ordinary mortals but are raised above it in shrines, cases and caskets. As we have seen, their solemn 'translation' to such elevated places was often the means of proclaiming their sanctity, and the taboo on disturbing the remains of the dead and dismembering their bodies did not apply to the saints, or rather was deliberately flouted where they were concerned. So the cult of the saints was a form both of the cult of the dead and of victory over death, and the paradox existed at both the theological and the 'popular' level. This is reflected in the practice of burial 'ad sanctos' or by the bodies of the saints, to which St Augustine gave hesitant approval and whose popularity has recently been re-emphasized by Ariès.[54] By being buried close to the saints or their relics, one's chances of ultimate bodily resurrection were increased or even guaranteed. St Bernard, for example, asked to be buried with relic of St Jude, 'trusting that he would be sure to rise from the grave with our Lord's Apostle on the Last Day'.[55]

It was commonly believed, too, at the 'popular' level that, far from inhabiting any distant heaven, the saint remained present in his shrine. Delehaye wrote that, for those who followed his cult, St Menas 'resided, invisible, in his basilica' in the Mariut, near Alexandria, and where a saint had several shrines, like St Thecla, she or he moved from one to the other in circulation.[56] The saint, moreover, was especially present and powerful on the day of his festival. At Tours, for example, most miracles occurred on 11 November, the main feast of St Martin, and such miracles were seen as 'irrefutable signs of the presence of the saint'.[57] Concomitantly, where the relics were absent, it might be difficult if not impossible to perceive any link with a saint. When the Bishop of Spoleto told his flock early in the fifth century that they enjoyed the protection of St Peter, they were incredulous, given that the saint's body did not reside in their city but in Rome.[58] A further indication of belief that the saint was present in his remains is to be found in the numerous legends of 'automobile' relics, or of relics choosing their own resting place, of which Hertz (see Ch. 1) provides an example.

Though cults centred so often on saints' remains, public cults were characterized at the formal level by their incorporation into the liturgy of the Church. From earliest times, the cult of saints had been associated with the celebration of the Eucharist, which had been performed on martyrs' tombs at their anniversaries, and this had led to the custom of placing relics in altars, to which we have referred. Later, 'the petitioning of the saints' became an important part of the Eucharistic liturgy itself, taking the form of a lengthy litany,[59] and special votive masses were introduced. Special liturgies were developed for saints' festivals, which included readings from their Lives (*legenda*), panegyrics and homilies. Litanies of the saints were also prominent in other liturgical forms, such as the *Laudes* used to acclaim bishops, kings, emperors and popes.[60] Placing saints in the liturgy followed from canonization in the West in later centuries, but was itself a mode of canonization in the East.

When saints were placed in the liturgy of the Church, they also entered its calendar, alongside the great feasts. In the Early Church, such festivals were scarce and strictly local, but over the centuries separate lists of saints honoured locally (martyrologies) became exchanged, and then amalgamated into a general calendar. This had reached a point of saturation when it was formalized in the West in the Roman Martyrology of 1584. Every day of the year was then associated with one or more saints, when it was not an important feast associated with Christ himself or the Virgin Mary. At the same time, and more indicative of the way in which the cult of the saints had entered into the fabric of social life, the calendar of ordinary people, by which they set dates for the tasks of the agricultural year, for leases and payments, and, of course, for celebrations, became one of selected saints' days.[61]

A further formal manifestation of saints' cults is the dedication of churches to them. Church dedications have been used by historians to trace patterns of settlement and conquest, but of course they most obviously reflect patterns of 'religious enthusiasm',[62] though these are not always easy to interpret. Like Celtic churches, early Roman churches were named after founders who were not necessarily saints. Such founders might then *ipso facto* be granted the status of saints, an important Celtic phenomenon, or churches might be rededicated, or both. And although dedications might in the first place represent the wish to place a sacred building under a particular protection and reflect a living 'popular' cult, dedication was an official act which above all reflected the preferences of the clergy. Especially where rededications occurred, as in Celtic Wales, wide discrepancies might emerge between official dedicatees of churches and saints who were in practice venerated there and in the district. To take another example, Fournée provides many cases from Normandy where the official dedicatee is eclipsed in his own church by devotion to the statue of another saint, and where the patron of the village or parish honoured at the annual festival is different from the patron of the church.[63] Mention should also be made here of the naming of places after saints,[64] which was frequently an extension of the naming of churches, as in Wales, but could also be an indication of the importance of particular shrines and of pilgrimages to them, to which we now turn.

The term 'pilgrimage' covers a wide variety of phenomena, most of which involve visits over a greater or lesser distance to shrines or holy places associated with saints. Here it should be noted that shrines of different Virgins or manifestations of Christ, such as the Mexican shrine of the Black Christ at Chalma or that of Bom Jesus da Lapa in north-eastern Brazil,[65] were regarded as shrines of distinct divine beings, and may for most purposes be treated as saints' shrines. As a song sung by devotees of Our Lady of the Pillar of Saragossa put it: 'There is no Virgin like ours. The rest are merely paper.'[66] Pilgrimage could be a wandering without specific mundane object, such as that practised by some Celtic saints,[67] but this was rare. The most common form of Christian pilgrimage was the local one. This might take the form of a visit to a shrine or chapel on the territory of the village but distant from the main inhabited place. Also common was the pilgrimage to a site shared by several villages, like that of Saint-Besse (see Ch. 1). At another level were regional pilgrimages like the Breton *pardons* or the Portuguese *romarias*, studied by Sanchis (see Ch. 9).[68] At yet another level were national and international pilgrimages, typified by those to the great shrines of Late Antiquity and the Middle Ages: that of St Menas in Egypt, or Tours, Saint-Maurice, Compostela, Vézelay, Canterbury in Europe; and by the modern ones to Lourdes, Fátima or the Virgin of Guadalupe in Mexico. The pilgrimages to Rome, the 'capital' of

Christendom, and to Jerusalem and the Holy Land, were in a special category again, the Christian equivalents of the pilgrimage to Mecca in Islam or to the Ganges in Hinduism. It should be noted here that the 'national' connotation of some modern pilgrimages was absent in earlier centuries.

Pilgrimages may also be distinguished by the type of site visited. At one end of the scale may be a wayside statue in a niche, a spring with a tiny pool or a country chapel; at the other an elaborate complex of multiple churches, shrines, relics, statues, as at Rome, or at Jerusalem, where every detail of the life of Christ, the Virgin and the Apostles as well as that of many Old Testament events had been minutely localized.[69]

Pilgrimages were usually annual events, for both shrine and pilgrims, but some were undertaken on demand in circumstances of immediate distress. In many parts of Europe, proxies might be used here, especially where help was being sought for sick children. The bigger pilgrimage sites were in continuous use, though activity reached a high-point during the festival of the saint, and they were usually visited by individual pilgrims only once in a lifetime. Some pilgrims went to Jerusalem, Rome or elsewhere hoping to die there, a special means of achieving burial 'ad sanctos' that has analogies in Hindu practice.[70] Proxy pilgrimage was also a feature of the big pilgrimages, pilgrims going on behalf of family, community or religious house. A related phenomenon was the ordering of posthumous proxy pilgrimages in wills, in much the same way that masses were ordered for the salvation of testators' souls.[71]

As this begins to indicate, the reasons for going on pilgrimage were also very diverse. Though largely devotional, the pilgrimage of Jerusalem, for example, was obligatory in some Christian communities,[72] and it was also imposed in the Middle Ages by lay and ecclesiastical authorities as a punishment for certain offences. Such penal pilgrimages were also made to Rome and to other places. It was the custom, for example, in both medieval Scandinavia and Scotland for those who had committed vengeance killings to go to Rome in expiation.[73] Sometimes, pilgrims imposed penance on themselves, often following a vow. The pilgrimage itself usually involved considerable hardship and expense, and some pilgrims added mortifications to this, for instance, walking barefoot, going part of the way on their knees, fasting, keeping silent, or even carrying stones round their necks.[74] Some pilgrimages were collectively organized as pilgrimages of penance, notably that to St Patrick's 'purgatory' on Lough Dergh. However, most pilgrims seem to have sought cures, and the shrines which they visited have, above all, been healing shrines, though the recreational element, which merges in later centuries with secular tourism, should not be ignored.

The pilgrimage phenomenon indicates again, and perhaps better than anything else, the ambiguous nature of the cult of the saints. As saints are persons possessed of a charisma that is potentially dangerous and anarchic, and which the authorities thus seek to control by channelling it via monasticism, canonization procedures, formal liturgies and emphasis on the post-mortem cult, so pilgrimage cuts across geographical and social boundaries, takes people out of their established places, mixes social strata and the sexes, allows individuals to wander like vagabonds, and focuses, not on the Church's formal rituals though these may be present, but on a whole range of para-liturgical and unorthodox practices (such as touching tombs, kissing relics, making circuits and processions, bathing, imbibing, feasting) which the clergy can only partially control. However, while of the utmost importance, the potentially chaotic and liminal aspect of pilgrimage should not be over-emphasized. Even medieval pilgrims followed well-worn routes with guide-books in hand and bought standardized souvenirs. In many cases, the clergy were able to control pilgrimages adequately and to their own benefit, as we shall see, and pilgrimages were incorporated into the social and economic structure, providing occasions for match-making and other contacts, for markets and fairs. The pilgrimage route, moreover, became a regular vehicle for cultural exchange, as historians of medieval art, architecture and literature have stressed.

Pilgrims' souvenirs – relics, badges, medals – might provide the focus for personal cults. In a similar genre were domestic images of different kinds: statues, paintings, prints and icons. In the Orthodox world, prayer before the domestic icons was enjoined by the clergy and closely paralleled the public liturgy, but in the West there could be divergence between the two. The members of the poor urban Mexican family, whose story has been recounted by Oscar Lewis, went frequently on pilgrimages and some were keen devotees of religious images, but they did not attend mass or go to confession. 'I am satisfied to have my pictures', says Marta, 'and to pray at home.'[75] A related, more public, manifestation of a similar extra-ecclesiastical type is the placing of statues in niches built into the external walls of houses, or in streets and squares, a practice very common still in Mediterranean Europe.

More universal is the practice of using saints' names, often to invoke protection thereby. We have seen that churches and chapels are named after saints, but so are bells, boats, schools, colleges, clubs and associations, and people, the last two being particularly important. Confraternities were a prominent feature of European societies from the Middle Ages until the nineteenth century, and fulfilled a variety of functions, devotional, charitable, sociable and professional. It is of great significance that they were placed very often, though not exclusively, under the patronage of a saint, and that many of them played a leading role in communities as organizers of the saint's festival. It is significant, too, that confraternities, like pilgrimages, were the field for latent or open conflict between clergy and people. Christian confraternities rarely had the kind of exclusive access to their saint found in the Sufi orders, but they could be important expressions of particularisms within the community.

The practice of naming children or converts after Apostles and martyrs existed in the Early Church. Later, Canon Law required that children be named with saints' names, but the custom does not seem to have become general until the Later Middle Ages, when clerical control over baptism may have become stricter. Children might be named after the saint on whose day they were born, and who then became their special patron. They might also be named after saints to whom their parents had a particular devotion, especially if they had been conceived after special invocation. Local cults might also have an impact on naming customs or fashions.[76] However, the explanation of onomastic patterns remains generally problematic. Michaëlsson points out, for instance, that while St Giles was a popular saint in medieval Provence, where he had an important pilgrimage site, his name was very rarely used there as a personal name. Moreover, the general correlation between church dedications and Christian names is often poor.[77]

We have referred to the general importance of images in the cults of saints, and to domestic images in particular. In any discussion of the different manifestations of cults, the place which saints' images occupy in the painting and sculpture of Christendom in the period up to the end of the eighteenth century, and the impact which the 'worship' of these and of relics has had on church architecture, can hardly be exaggerated. Equally important, though less often acknowledged, has been the cults' influence on literature, taking the term in its widest sense. Halkin has written that 'during the ten or twelve centuries of the Byzantine Empire's existence, no literature was more in demand or more appreciated at all levels of society, lay as well as clerical, than hagiography',[78] and a book like Sulpicius Severus' Life of St Martin was a multi-secular best-seller in the West. Hagiography is, of course, a complex genre that has evolved over time. It includes both learned, sophisticated Lives akin to secular biography, and 'popular' Lives incorporating folk tales and fantasy. It embraces some of the most precious autobiographies which we have, those of St Augustine, St Teresa of Avila and St Teresa of Lisieux, and it also comprises the liturgical texts, to which we have referred, and popular songs like the Breton *gwerz*.

The earliest Lives, of course, were written in Latin and Greek, but vernacular Lives appeared in the West quite early in the Middle Ages and remained very popular until recent times. Collections of Lives existed in earlier centuries, notably the Lives of the Desert Fathers, but the sub-genre did not find its classic form until Voragine's *Golden Legend* in the thirteenth century. With the establishment of a universal calendar, this form tended to ossify, but hagiography generally was revitalized by the persecutions of the Early Modern period, which produced material for new Lives of martyrs both Catholic and Protestant. Hagiography of these different kinds fulfilled a similar variety of functions. Lives were written to stimulate devotion and provide examples of piety; they were written to boost particular cults, to promote canonizations, and thus to further the interests of particular groups or institutions. An interesting example of the last is provided by the different Lives of St Francis. Here there were two 'official' Lives, and other unofficial accounts which the orthodox wing of the Franciscan Order tried to suppress. There were also collections of popular legends, the well-known *Fioretti*. On the 'popular' level, saints' Lives could fulfil functions similar to those fulfilled later by serial stories or *romans-feuilletons*,[79] and, one might add, with the Passions of the martyrs in mind, by horror films. Saints' Lives also performed other functions. 'Reading a saint's Life aloud was considered to be a kind of prayer', Chauvin writes of medieval Poitou; 'to facilitate a woman in labour, the Life of St Margaret was chosen'.[80] Hagiography rarely promoted cults independently of anything else, though it is suggested that the cult of St Alexis in France was of wholly literary origin.[81] Inversely, saints' cults had their impact on secular literature from the *chansons de geste* and Chaucer to Flaubert and T. S. Eliot. Finally, it should not be forgotten that saints' Lives are among the oldest documents existing in Western culture; and that their critical editing by Bollandus, Mabillon, and others in the seventeenth century helped to lay the foundations for modern historical scholarship.

III

Cults of saints fulfilled an extraordinary variety of functions. These may be broadly grouped under the headings of universal assistance, patronage, and political functions, though all three overlapped.

Like supplicants at Asian and African shrines[82] or those of Antiquity, Christians had recourse to their saints in all circumstances of adversity, in the hope of securing help from them. The saints were looked to to make women, the land and animals fertile, to prevent or cure sickness of all kinds, to ward off pests and storms, and to bring general good fortune. Some aspects of this universal function were specific to societies without modern technology and communications but others were not, or not entirely. In the first category, for example, one may place the match-making saints. Certain shrines were visited by girls seeking marriage, and certain saints were known as 'marrying saints'.[83] This should be related to the fact that marriages were frequently arranged at saints' festivals, which were times of general social interaction, and that festivals and pilgrimages might provide the only opportunities for courtship, supervised or unsupervised, in traditional societies. Freer patterns of social intercourse and migration in modern societies have largely removed this saintly function, or it has been taken over by the marriage bureau and the agony column, although a residual element remains. Again, the very high level of infant disease and mortality in traditional societies and the inadequacies of medicine explain the frequent recourse to saints by parents of young children. Shrines specialized in different infantile ailments, and a particular class of shrine was resorted to in France, and doubtless elsewhere, at which still-born babies were 'resuscitated' so that they could be legitimately baptized.[84] None of this suggests a society indifferent towards the lot, material or otherwise, of young children, such as some historians have mistakenly imagined, but it does reflect a society where more practical means of preserving them were not available.

A more problematic area is that in which saints encounter demons. Many, but not all, saints' Lives are dominated by constant combats with devils, and many living saints, including the Curé d'Ars and Padre Pio in our own times, were engaged in similar struggles. This reflects a view that the middle ground between humans and the higher gods was inhabited by both malign and benign beings, and that the latter did battle with the former on the behalf of humans. Here it is significant that infertility, sickness, crop failure, storms, the misfortunes against which the saints were invoked, were often believed to be caused by devils or their agents. Natural forces were thus personified and 'explained' in the absence of a modern 'scientific' framework of explanation (see Patlagean in Ch. 2).

In the second or non-specific category would be recourse to the saints by individuals in times of distress or crisis, for which modern society has no better 'solutions' than had medieval. In a prayer to St Margaret, John Lydgate invited

> folken alle that be disconsolat
> In your myschief and grete adversite
> And alle that stonde of helpe desolate

to pray to the saint for relief,[85] which is different only in externals from the prayers collected by Bonnet from French shrines in 1975.[86] Detailed discussion will suggest that the first category predominates, although the functions of the cults were multiplex and adaptable to a very wide range of social situations.

Like Hindu gods or 'godlings', or those of Antiquity, Christian saints were often specialists, giving aid in particular circumstances, as St Margaret or St Leonard did in childbirth, or protecting against and curing particular diseases (the association of St Sebastian and St Roch with the plague is well known), or finding lost or stolen objects like St Osyth and St Anthony of Padua, or lending protection and patronage to particular professions and occupations, as did St Nicholas to the *avocats* and law students of Paris, or St Catherine to the *midinettes*. Long lists could be compiled in most of these categories, forming a system of astonishing complexity. This in itself led to further complications, since, save in the obvious cases, people had to resort to the advice of lay specialists and/or divination in order to know which saint to consult or invoke in any given situation.

Where saints' avocations were in general currency, they seem often to have been arrived at by a process of association akin to divination. Thus, for example, St Agatha, whose breasts were cut off during her martyrdom, was invoked by nurses and nursing mothers who were short of milk, and by women with breast troubles; while in France, St Clare was invoked for eye disease, since she enabled one to see clearly (*clair*). Specialization also cut across localism, which we have seen was an essential feature of the early martyr cults and remained extremely important later, but it did so in surprising ways. With a few exceptions, the more important medieval shrines were non-specialist and were often advertised by their monastic guardians and beneficiaries as able to cope with every ill imaginable. Specialized shrines tended to be regional and district ones visited only by local people, though it was considered necessary to travel some distance for cures.[87] Specialization may also have occurred within towns and cities in response to the multiplicity of shrines available there. Furthermore, several historians have detected a trend from the time of the Counter-Reformation and associated with Marian cults, towards non-specialization generally. A process of concentration may be traced here, but where secular society moved at the same time towards specialism and the division of labour, the cult of saints did not. This is nowhere more obvious than in the case of disease and illness, to which we now turn.

As we have noted, the shrines of the saints were, above all, shrines of healing. This is true of the great shrines of Late Antiquity and of modern ones like Lourdes and San Giovanni Rotundo, with their hospital annexes, and it has been demonstrated over recent years that it was true also of medieval shrines. For example, 73 per cent of the miracles reported at Norman shrines in the Middle Ages relate to cures.[88] Nearly all those performed by St Gibrien at Reims were cures, and Sigal has written that the saint was regarded above all as a 'doctor'.[89]

A variety of beliefs about the nature of illness was involved in such 'medical' recourse to saints. Most obviously, disease was frequently seen as a consequence of collective or individual sin, or of demonic possession, and recourse to religious help was therefore appropriate. But this belief was not always present and, as we shall see, many of the modes of cure which were current lacked any moral or spiritual element. Again, saints were commonly associated with the complaints which they cured to the extent of lending their names to them. A medieval Norman miracle account refers, for example, to the 'morbus sancti Laurentii';[90] while, in nineteenth-century Berry, the cattle disease against which St Posen gave protection and remedy was known as the 'disease of St Posen'.[91] What is more, the saint was often believed to send or cause the disease which he subsequently might cure, a pattern also found in African and Asian beliefs about the relationship between disease and divine beings. All this raises again the question of specialisms. Some saints were believed to cure particular diseases, either generally or in association with specific shrines. Two examples in the latter category are St Anthony of Egypt, associated with the cure of ergotism or 'St Anthony's fire', and St Hubert, associated with the cure of rabies. All or part of St Anthony's relics were translated in the eleventh century to Mota in the French district of the Viennois, an event which coincided with local outbreaks of ergotism, a disease produced by eating a poisonous fungus which grows on rye and whose symptoms include burning sensations, convulsions and gangrene. The saint's shrine gained the reputation of affording a remedy for this disease, and a special Order of Hospitallers of St Anthony of the Viennois was founded to administer it and to care for the sick who attended it. The shrine remained important throughout the Middle Ages and beyond, though its efficacy was extended in this later period to other diseases.[92] The shrine of St Hubert was at the town of the same name in the Belgian Ardennes. Its origin seems to have been medieval, and it was still active in the later nineteenth century and still devoted to its speciality.[93] The rationale behind such specialisms is often hard to find. That of St Hubert was probably an extension of his patronage of hunting and hunting dogs. In another case, that of the Blessed Bonaventure of Potenza, who died in 1711, it is suggested that his posthumous healing specialism was related to the malady of the bowels which he had himself suffered in life.[94]

Cures were effected by a wide variety of procedures. First were those which involved contact with the saint, living or, more often, dead. So people touched the saint's clothes, the ground on which he had stood, the straw on which he had slept, his tomb, his relics, his images. Tombs were scraped or chipped and the dust or fragments consumed, and the same was done to statues, crosses, walls and floors of shrines. Oil or wax from the lights of shrines was used to anoint the body or to place against affected parts of it. Water was drunk that had been used to wash the saint's corpse or relics or tomb. At the shrine of St Anthony, wine was poured over the relics and administered to patients in tiny amounts. Where springs or wells were associated with the cult, the water might be drunk, but people also washed or bathed in it, or dipped in it clothing belonging to the sick. An unusual variant, practised at the shrine of St Hubert until modern times, involved making an incision in the patient's forehead and placing in it a thread from the stole of the saint, which had to be kept there until the wound healed. More common were the customs of passing or being passed under the relics of the saint while they were being carried in procession, and various procedures which entailed measuring the statue or the tomb of the saint. In parts of Portugal, for example, 'pieces of red thread the exact length of a particular saint's height' were used as amulets.[95]

In another category are cures involving trance, sleep or unusual mental states. Trance seems to have been little used at European shrines, though some south Italian examples have been noted,[96] and Gerald of Wales reports a very interesting twelfth-century case at the church of St Eluned near Brecon. At her festival, people sang and danced until they collapsed into trances. They then acted out the sins which they had committed and were cured of their illnesses.[97] The practice of 'incubation' customary in some shrines of Antiquity, whereby patients slept in the shrine and received visits in their sleep from the healing god or hero, seems to have been continued at some Christian shrines in the East. Western examples may be cited, too, in which patients slept on or by tombs and shrines, or in which the healing saint appeared to them in dreams. According to Aelfric, for instance, a man who was blind, dumb and near to death was taken to the grave of St Swithun at Winchester 'to keep the vigil'. He watched 'until it was becoming day, then he fell asleep, and the worshipful tomb as it seemed . . . was all rocking, and to the sick man it seemed as if someone was dragging one of his shoes off his foot; and he suddenly awoke . . . healed by the holy Swithun'.[98] More commonplace were exorcisms, which are related to the struggles with demons, to which we have referred, and to the idea that disease could be caused by demonic intervention. A further category of cures comprises those effected by rituals related only peripherally if at all to shrines, for example, spells and incantations using the names of saints. Some procedures relating to contact with the shrine also had additional 'magical' elements. For instance, pilgrims to a statue of St Martin in the church of Crosville-la-Vieille (Eure), which was supposed to cure stomach disorders, 'brought two ribbons with them, one of which was left hanging on the statue, while the other, having also touched the saint, was worn for nine days, then burned and its ashes buried in the ground'.[99]

All such cures are 'non-medical' in the modern sense, and, indeed, saints often proscribed recourse to ordinary doctors. On the other hand, some saints' cures were clearly consistent with contemporary medical practice, and no line was necessarily drawn between the two. The saints who visited patients in dreams in the great Eastern shrines passed among them like doctors applying balms and poultices,[100] and it has been pointed out that therapy by exorcism, such as that practised by St Martin, was a form of 'the classical treatment by evacuation', in which demons were expelled by vomiting or defecating.[101] By contrast, purely spiritual modes of cure through prayer and penance seem to have been unusual, at least before the modern period.

Somewhere between the two, perhaps, comes the vow, or the promise to the saint to perform certain actions, nearly always including a visit to the shrine, if he effected the desired cure or other favour (see Sanchis in Ch. 9). In one of the posthumous miracles of St Francis, for example, the mother of the youth of Suessa, killed when a house collapsed on him, 'made a vow that she would cover the altar of the Blessed Francis with a new linen cloth, if he would recall her son to life for her'.[102] In Lewis's *The Children of Sánchez*, Roberto in prison vowed that if he got out he would walk barefoot all the way from the prison to 'the Villa of Guadalupe', and also that he would go to Chalma.[103] Collective vows were also common, particularly, it seems, in the Mediterranean world from the sixteenth to the eighteenth centuries. In 1656, for example, the municipal authorities of Ajaccio signed a legal document whereby they placed the city under the protection of Our Lady of Mercy, so that she might preserve it from the plague, and promised in return to honour her with processions and masses.[104] Such vows often promised, too, that chapels or churches would be built in honour of the saint invoked. Probably the most famous votive building of this kind is the palace of the Escorial, built by Philip II to honour a vow to St Lawrence. Gifts and services, moreover, were an essential part of all vows, the *quid pro quo* for the favour requested. They ranged from pins, ribbons, candles, wax, incense and small amounts of money, to clothing, jewelry, livestock, land and buildings, as we have seen. Such gifts formed an important income for shrines, and might be sold or redistributed in alms. In some cases, patients or supplicants vowed themselves or their children to the service of the saint, becoming servants and attendants at the shrine, or joining the religious house which administered it.

Gifts to shrines following vows cannot always be distinguished from the category of objects known as 'ex-votos'. These included wax models of parts of the body that had been cured, crutches, the chains of released prisoners, model ships given by those who had survived shipwreck, horseshoes, and shirts of successful sportsmen, as well as written messages, printed notices in newspapers, plaques at the shrine and paintings illustrating the circumstances of the favour received. The last are found in Bavaria, Switzerland, the northern Mediterranean area and Latin America, and have recently aroused much interest among scholars, particularly in France and Germany, where many paintings have been rescued from neglect, dispersal or destruction. Ex-votos continued a tradition dating back to Neolithic times, and clearly had a propitiatory function and served to advertise the shrine concerned, as well as simply expressing gratitude. Some connection may be posited, too, between the accumulation, on the one hand, of ex-votos in the form of parts of the body, made of wax, silver, gold and other metals, and, on the other, of actual bodily relics of the saints, which were frequently encased in precious metals or wax effigies. Are the simulated and the real bodily parts, which are so similar in appearance, complementary or alternative aspects of the same basic cult? What is their relationship with other 'magical' practices and notions, and with general ideas about the body and its functioning? Further investigation of these problems would be of great interest.

Historians studying some of the later medieval shrines have noted the growing importance of the vow and the decline of actual contact with the tomb or relics as the principal mode of cure, and have sometimes explained this in terms of an increase in sophistication. But both procedures could be, and often were, used together. St Charles of Sezze, for example, in the mid-seventeenth century, effected the cure of the General of his order by signing him with the relics of St Salvator of Horta and of St Lidano, and by vowing to go on pilgrimage to the shrine of the latter saint at Sezze.[105] Moreover, the complementary practice of punishing saints who did not perform the required favours highlights the vow's 'magical' and unsophisticated features as well as the element of bargaining or negotiation. According to Sébillot, 'when the harvest is bad the peasants of the Quercy run to the churches, pull down the statues of the saints and beat them' for having allowed the calamity to occur, while in the Ain 'girls praying to St Blaise tell him that they will throw his statue in the Rhône if they are not married within the year',[106] examples that could be multiplied. Saints, on their side, punished vows that were not fulfilled by reversing cures.

It is perhaps more profitable to look at the vow in the context of relationships within the social milieu, as social anthropologists have done. Here it can be seen as a utilization of idioms taken from gift exchange and notions of transaction and reciprocity among equals,[107] or from quite inegalitarian debt relationships,[108] or from a variety of forms of patronage somewhere between. Moreover, the religious vow may be regarded as a sacralization of such secular ties and the structures to which they belong, or the whole transactional, bargaining mode, which the Catholic Church has to some extent imitated and encouraged with its own system of indulgences, may be regarded as an invasion of the sacred sphere by wholly inappropriate considerations, a stance, of course, taken up in classic form by Luther.

Vows, therefore, lead us to patronage. The analogy between the cult of the saints and patterns of secular patronage has been pointed out by many writers. 'The link joining the saint to the faithful', writes Sallmann for example, 'reproduces, transposed into the supernatural domain, the link of clientship which joins the powerful' in society to their dependents.[109] Nor was the analogy only implicit, waiting to be drawn out by the ingenuity of observing scholars. The faithful themselves perceived saints as patrons.

Lydgate called St Giles 'chief patron ... of pore folk', while St Edmund was the 'cheef patroun' of his monastery at Bury and of the surrounding district.[110] Boissevain notes that in Maltese the same word is used for both 'saint' and 'patron'.[111] The same significance can be attached at one remove to the practice of addressing saints with the titles of deference used for lay patrons and the great of this world. Thus an early-sixteenth-century document announcing the indulgences to be gained through pilgrimage to his shrine in the Viennois refers to 'the glorious saint My Lord St Anthony'.[112] The same conceptualization is present in the notion of the saints and the Virgin Mary as intercessors, proclaimed in the official theology of the Church and variously adapted or understood by the faithful. Here saints might be seen as advocates pleading causes before a stern divine judge, as mediators, as go-betweens, as intriguers or wire-pullers at the court of Heaven — all metaphors were used. It is significant also that the saints themselves were arranged in a hierarchy, in both the liturgy and official iconography, with the Virgin Mary as the arch-intercessor through whom petitions of other saints were directed.

As this shows, such patronage took many forms, corresponding to some extent with the historical evolution of the cults. Living saints could have clients like other leading figures in society; these could be casual supplicants, more regular followers tied to the saint as confessor or adviser, or members of a permanent entourage. Necessarily, the patronage of the dead saint was different, though the model of the living saint, the saint still present, mitigated this difference. So Brown has written that the martyr took on the 'distinctive late-Roman face [of] ... the good *patronus*', generous, strong but not violent, and inspiring complete loyalty.[113] He notes also that the invisible patronage of the martyr was directly related to that exercised on earth by the bishop, a connection which continued into the medieval period, when it was paralleled by a similar link between the patronage of saint and of monastery. In the early feudal period, moreover, men commended themselves to the saints and their churches, as they did to lay seigneurs.

From another angle, patron saints may be classified by their type of client. First, there are personal patrons, after whom their clients are often named, and to whom they pay special devotion. So St Theodore of Sykeon was devoted to St George, who appeared to him in visions and some of whose relics he later acquired.[114] St Charles of Sezze's mother, he relates, 'was especially devoted to St Francis and recited the hours which his lay brothers say', while Charles himself was devoted to the Virgin Mary and to St Joseph, whom he calls his special 'advocates', as well as to St Anne and to St Salvator of Horta.[115] At another level was the saint of the family or the clan. In the Balkans, for example, the main saint's festival was often that of the patron of the clan and not of the village,[116] a reflection of the clan's importance in local social structure. Rather different is the devotion to a particular saint on the part of an aristocratic or royal dynasty, to which we will return in the context of political cults proper. We have seen, too, that saints were patrons of associations or confraternities, but probably the most important form of saintly patronage was that of the locality: village, ward or city.

Once Christianity became established, every place came to have its patron saint or saints. These fulfilled the functions of the local gods or tutelary spirits found elsewhere in the world. First, the local patron provided general protection. 'Tolve is mine and I will protect it', declared St Roch, the patron of this south Italian village, in a popular print.[117] Such protection involved ensuring the fertility of fields and animals and saving the place from disease, storm and flood, our 'universal' function again. For example, St Genevieve, the patron of Paris, was not only resorted to continuously by the sick of the city, but, in times of crisis, her relics were taken out in solemn procession, as in 1206 when they caused a raging flood of the Seine to subside.[118] The link was expressed and renewed via the annual saint's festival, of which Hertz (see Ch. 1) provides a good description. The festival usually involved special ritual, official and unofficial, in honour of the saint; a procession in which the saint's relics or statue would be carried between significant points of the village territory, often marking its boundaries; and a banquet in which all the inhabitants participated, followed by further merrymaking. Special bread or cakes might be baked and consumed, and some kept to ensure good fortune in the coming year. Relatives who had left the village returned on the occasion of the festival, thus retaining their links with their native place. This is a particular feature of festivals in Corsican villages today, which are conveniently held in August when the émigrés return. The saint's festival, in effect, is a classic Durkheimian expression of community. Festivals also provided the means for peaceful communication between neighbouring, and often rival, villages, and peace was usually though not always maintained under the aegis of the saint.

More dramatically, the patron might defend his or her fief against external enemies, as St Demetrius defended his city of Salonika against the Avars and the Slavs in the seventh century,[119] as St Tropez protected his city in Provence against Spanish naval attack in 1637,[120] or as Our Lady of Divine Love is supposed to have saved Rome from bombardment and destruction in 1944.[121] The importance of such supernatural protection is further indicated by the fact that those wishing to subdue towns and cities commonly attacked their patrons. A sixth-century inscription relates that, when the Goths devastated the northern suburbs of Rome, 'they first waged a shameful war on the saints' and desecrated the tombs of 'the holy martyrs'.[122] Similarly, the Bulgarians, at war with Salonika in the eleventh and twelfth centuries, tried to appropriate the support of St Demetrius, claiming that he had abandoned his old clients. Rivalry for the possession of particular patrons could also exist between cities, again providing the idiom through which more secular competition was expressed. Promotion by Benevento in the Early Middle Ages of the cult of St Michael at Monte Gargano, for example, was a means by which that city sought to maintain its own influence in the area and keep out that of Naples.[123] More directly, the city of Bari acquired the remains of St Nicholas from Myra in the later eleventh century by theft, in order to boost its own prestige and thus its economy vis-à-vis the Venetians.[124] This operation was also related to factionalism within the city, a reminder that patron saints could also reflect and serve rivalries within the community. At the same time, the promotion of civic patrons directed against external threats and natural disasters could often be a means of dampening down internal conflict.

The same may be said of regional and of national patrons. Czarnowski has argued that St Patrick 'incarnated the national unity of the Irish', because as an outsider he was able to transcend the clan and local loyalties served by other Irish saints.[125] Regional patrons could be simple centres of loyalty, often associated with dynasties, or their patronage could have a more positive connotation. The district of Tours, for example, in the turbulent Merovingian period was seen as the territory of St Martin, and as such was a non-combatant area.[126] Similarly, the inhabitants of the lands of the bishop of Durham in the tenth and eleventh centuries 'were regarded as St Cuthbert's people, as Haliwerfolc or holy men's folk', who should not be molested.[127] The designation of medieval Novgorod as 'the Republic of St Sophia' had something of the same significance.[128]

Although the roles could overlap, a distinction may be made between the saint as patron and the saint as mediator. Like the former, the latter might begin in his lifetime. Brown has emphasized this aspect of the role of the holy man in Late Antiquity, which he sees as similar to that played by the Islamic saints of the Atlas studied by Gellner.[129] These were members of holy lineages, geographically situated at strategic points among warring tribes, and regulating their transhumance and political arrangements as well as settling their disputes. Christian saints fit rarely if at all into this exact pattern. For one thing, outside the Celtic world, where the term 'saint' extends to the clergy in general,[130] families or dynasties of saints were unknown.[131] Indeed, one of the signs of the saint's peculiar indifference to worldly matters was his abandonment of family and kin. However, secular lineage could to some extent be replaced by the saint's belonging to a monastery with which he became identified, and by the practice of passing on the mantle of sanctity to a favoured disciple, which is found in both East and West.[132] Nevertheless, the social 'engagement' of saints was often very limited, and saints, living and dead, were frequently outsiders in the communities where they were honoured, or they had withdrawn, in the case of the living, into unoccupied and neutral space: the desert, the forest or mountains. As outsiders and disengaged neutrals, often with supernatural powers, they were able to act as mediators in disputes and as peacemakers. The Life of St Theodore of Sykeon relates that 'when men were at enmity with each other or had a grievance one against another he reconciled them, and those who were engaged in law-suits he sought to bring to a better mind, counselling them not to wrong each other'.[133] The internecine warfare in and between the city states of medieval Italy is punctuated by truces engineered by saints,[134] while the pacification of vendettas was an important part of the pastoral and missionary activity in Corsica of St Alexander Sauli and St Leonard of Porto Maurizio.[135]

As the example of mediation shows, 'patronage' did not necessarily imply a wholly hierarchical relationship. Clients could choose among patrons and, by having several, play one off against another. The sheer multiplicity of saints available for service as patrons is most significant in this context. A village or town might be placed under the patronage of two or more saints, the least effective of which might be relatively neglected. Again, pilgrims visited several shrines before they lighted on the one which met their needs and received their gifts and lasting devotion. Churches were full of images, and the faithful might select among them or pay some attention to them all, 'just in case'. In none of these instances does the cult of the saints provide a reflection of, or a sanction for, the dutiful client relationship. Brown has pointed out, too, that, while using the idiom of patronage, the cult of saints might be a means of asserting independence vis-à-vis lay patrons or masters.[136] This was most obviously so where the unfree sought emancipation at the saint's shrine, or where the offender sought sanctuary from arrest.[137] It is important to note, too, for the element of patronage has received much emphasis, that the cult of saints used other social idioms – those of friendship, kinship, community – and encompassed such anti-social and anarchic ideals as the 'alter Christus' and the 'holy fool'.

Patronage frequently had a political element, and we now turn to what may be called the political uses or functions of saints' cults. These fall into a number of categories. First, within the Church, cults were used to promote and defend the interests of individual monasteries and churches, of religious orders, of dioceses and of the papacy. They could also be an adjunct to the secular power of dynasties in traditional states, and they could be used by opposition groups, as well as for other purposes, in both traditional and modern societies.

Important shrines were nearly always kept by monasteries, and the fortune and well-being of the monastery depended on the prestige and success of the shrine. Local cults were therefore promoted by monasteries in divers ways, and with varying degrees of success. As we have seen, relics might be 'invented', bought or stolen, and then solemnly and publicly 'translated', or relics already in place might be reactivated. Thus Sigal concludes that the translation of the relics of St Gibrien at Reims in the twelfth century was aimed 'at attracting back pilgrims and their offerings' to the abbey of Saint-Rémi, where the saint's body had lain since the sixth century.[138] Cults might also be promoted around images. St Charles of Sezze tells quite guilelessly how he and his fellow-friars encouraged devotion to a picture of St Anne at their convent church at Carpineto by organizing a procession to instal it and having a special mass sung. He goes on to recount that 'once devotion to St Anne was established... the Father Guardian wanted devotion to the Blessed Salvator of Horta to be introduced also, for he was famous for his miracles. He told me what he had in mind and asked me to have a picture made.'[139] Again, existing shrines might be taken over and developed by a religious house: the shrine of Notre-Dame-des-Lumières near Goult in Provence, for example, enjoyed 'a striking boom' after a Carmelite house had been installed there in the 1660s.[140]

The promotion of cults could also be a gambit in rivalries between monasteries. When the monastery of Conques was threatened in the ninth century with suppression or take-over by its rival at Figeac, the monks determined to acquire the relics of an important saint in order to strengthen their position. They finally secured the relics of St Foy, which were 'translated' (and probably stolen) from Agen around 865, and the miracles which supervened made the situation of Conques then unassailable.[141] A similar rivalry underlay the translation of St Bavon at Ghent in the tenth and eleventh centuries. Ghent had two abbeys, that of St Bavon and that of Saint-Pierre-au-Mont-Blandin, one of which may earlier have been subsidiary to the other. During the Norman invasions, the monks of St Bavon emigrated with the body of their saint, and lost all their lands. The monks of Saint-Pierre fared much better during this troubled period, and by the mid-tenth century had the lion's share of local lay patronage and donations. The monks of St Bavon solemnly translated the relics of their saint, therefore, in 946, in order to increase their prestige and to try to divert gifts in goods and land in their own direction. Their rivals put it about that the relics were not genuine, a story that may have gained some credence, since the 'long-disadvantaged' abbey of St Bavon carried out two further 'translations' in 1010 and 1058, which were accompanied by miracles.[142]

As these and other cases indicate, the successful and attractive shrine was one where miracles occurred with adequate frequency. Miracles, of course, were interpreted by the 'enlightened' clergy in the Augustinian tradition as attestations 'of the faith which proclaims that Christ rose from the flesh',[143] and as 'demonstrations that the intervention of God continues in the present as in the past'.[144] They were also seen as an important means of converting both heathen and Jew. But, above all, as the careful recording of the Miracle Accounts of particular shrines and the display of ex-votos make abundantly clear, miracles were the essential signs of the power of the saint, and the magnet which drew pilgrims and income to the monastery which guarded his shrine. Another important requirement from the Later Middle Ages was to ensure that one's local patron saint was 'properly' canonized, and individual monasteries, as well as religious orders, took the initiative in promoting procedures at Rome. The cause of St Edward the Confessor, for example, was promoted in the twelfth century largely by the abbey of Westminster.[145]

The motivation of cult promotion is reflected in its association with building programmes, and this also provides some measure of how far such promotion achieved its ends. The translation of St Gibrien at Reims was related to the need to complete the reconstruction of the abbey of Saint-Rémi. One of the most striking examples of this association, however, is provided by Vézelay. The abbey there acquired the relics of St Mary Magdalene in the mid-eleventh century, and subsequently enjoyed a period of fame and fortune lasting two hundred years. A new abbey church, the present magnificent structure with its rich sculpture, was built between 1096 and 1135, at the height of the cult's success.[146] Mention may also be made of the cult of St William at Norwich, a cult again promoted in order to complete a building programme, but which was relatively unsuccessful, perhaps because of the existence in the vicinity of two other important shrines, at Bury St Edmunds and at Walsingham.[147]

But successful cults brought their own difficulties, too, for the monasteries or other bodies responsible for them. The prestige and income of the flourishing shrine aroused envy and greed. The abbey of Vézelay was in incessant conflict with the citizens of the town which had grown up around it, with the abbots of Cluny, with the bishops of Autun, and with the counts of Nevers. The enormous increase in the importance of the shrine of Notre-Dame-de-Rochefort in the early seventeenth century, and the consequent influx of donations, aroused the interest of no fewer than four religious houses and led to litigation among them for its control, as well as to violent encounters between their respective supporters at the shrine itself.[148] Conflict could also focus on the possession of relics, as we have seen. In a further well-known example, the abbey of Saint-Denis and the chapter of Notre-Dame-de-Paris were in dispute over the relics of St Denis. The abbey claimed to possess the whole body of the saint, and thus exclusive rights to his prestige, while the chapter claimed to possess the top of the saint's head. Lengthy litigation, coming eventually before the Parlement of Paris in the fifteenth century, failed to decide the issue, though the claims of the chapter seem to have been generally accepted (see Spiegel in Ch. 4).[149]

Successful shrines made monasteries vulnerable, but, particularly in times of disorder and war, all monasteries were vulnerable, as we have seen they were during the Dark Age invasions. Here, the identification of the monastery with its protective saint could be a crucial means of defence, especially when that identification could be extended to its property and lands, as we have noted that it frequently was. After the death of St Wilfrid, his Life relates, 'his abbots and their subjects were afraid [that] their old enemies might take up the attack again', but they fortified themselves with the thought that they now had 'an intercessor in Heaven', guarding and defending them unceasingly.[150] But such psychological reassurance among the saint's clients might not be enough. How could monks persuade enemies or potential enemies that the saint was indeed their powerful protector?

First, they cultivated the general idea that saints were to be feared. St Gregory the Great told the Empress Constantina, for example, that 'the bodies of the Apostles Peter and Paul shine with such great miracles and terrors in their churches, that one cannot even go to pray there without great fear'.[151] We have seen, too, that saints were believed to send the diseases which they cured. 'We worship saints for fear', wrote William Tyndale, 'lest they should be displeased and angry with us and plague us or hurt us... Who dare deny St Anthony a fleece of wool for fear of his terrible fire, or lest he send the pox among our sheep?'[152] Monasteries also preserved more specific evidence in hagiography and in Miracle Accounts of saints' power and willingness to punish as well as to give aid. Those who expressed scepticism about the authenticity of the saint's relics or about his miraculous powers, those who violated his shrine, those who failed to respect his pilgrims, those who failed to attend his festival or prevented others from doing so, those who neglected his service, those who left vows unfulfilled, and, of course, those who stole from his shrine or destroyed it, all could expect to suffer the saint's vengeance in due course, and this might mean serious illness, incapacity or death. According to a fifth-century Miracle Account, for example, the Lestrygonians, who pillaged the shrine of St Thecla at Seleucia, were struck blind by the saint, while the bishop of Tarsus who forbade his people to go to the shrine on pilgrimage died a few days later.[153] In a medieval example, the abbot of Saint-Vanne suffered a paralytic stroke when he planned to sell a relic of the saint in order to pay the abbey's debts.[154] All such punishments had the function of maintaining the prestige and integrity of the shrine, and the last example is an interesting indication that its guardians might themselves need to be reminded of their own self-interest here. In another such instance, recounted by Aelfric, the monks of Winchester came to resent rising several times every night to sing Te Deums in celebration of St Swithun's miracles, but, when they stopped doing so, they were warned by the saint that 'if they will not perform the hymn, straightway the miracles shall soon cease',[155] an object lesson in the value of publicity.

The punishment of the saint was also invoked in defence of the secular property of monastic houses. Those who refused to pay tithes, those who took the monks' goods or who cheated them, and, above all, those who usurped the property of the Church, all were or could be punished. One of a number of such stories told by Gerald of Wales, for example, relates that a certain man laid claims to lands that had been donated to the abbey of Margam. 'He pressed his claims by various acts of violence', and finally set fire to 'the best barn belonging to the monks, which was piled high at the time with corn'. Soon afterwards, he went mad, ran to the abbey 'baying like a dog and shouting that, thanks to the monks, he was being burnt up inside', and died some days later.[156]

Several recent studies have demonstrated how monasteries, exposed in times of weakness or collapse of the public authority to the depredations of lay seigneurs or of their own recalcitrant agents, might have recourse to specific defensive rituals. These included excommunication and solemn malediction of their enemies,[157] and, when these had failed, the relics of the patron saint or saints of the monastery and thus of the district might be brought directly into play; these could be sent out to places where conflict was occurring to intimidate would-be usurpers, or – the ultimate recourse – they might be publicly humiliated in the ways described by Geary (in Ch. 3),[158] thus depriving both monastery and district of their protection and inviting retaliation from them. A less formal example is found in the *Chronicle* of Jocelin of Brakelond. The bishop of Ely, who was then justiciary and chancellor, refused in 1187 to accept a complaint from the abbot of St Edmund's relating to a dispute with the monks of Canterbury.

Some time afterwards, when he was come on a visitation . . . he made a speech at the shrine of the holy martyr. The abbot, seizing the opportunity, said to all present: 'My lord bishop, the liberty which the monks of Canterbury claim for themselves is the right of St Edmund, whose body is here present; and because you do not choose to render me assistance to protect the privileges of his church, I place that plaint between him and you. Let him henceforth get justice done to himself.' The chancellor deigned not to answer a single word; but within a year from that time was driven from England, and experienced divine vengeance.[159]

Belief in the power of saints to punish their offenders reflects a more fundamental belief in an immanent justice that also underlies the contemporary institution of trial by ordeal,[160] and all are related to other social and political factors, most obviously the availability of other kinds of sanction. Belief in the punishing saint is also another example of the religious cult using the idiom of its social context. As Gerald of Wales very perspicaciously observed, 'both the Irish and the Welsh are more prone to anger and revenge in this life than other nations, and similarly their saints in the next world seem much more vindictive'.[161] The punishing saint, in effect, belonged to the same society as the feud and the curse.[162]

If saints and the awe which they inspired were a crucial instrument or expression of the power of individual monasteries, so they were at another level of that of religious orders. Aigrain has referred here to 'the celestial families' of the orders,[163] their advocates in heaven and their glory in this world, and we have alluded to the overwhelming importance of founders and members of orders in the Roman calendar of saints. The same monastic preponderance is found in the Orthodox world, although laymen are much more numerous among Russian saints than is common elsewhere.[164] In the West, this reflects the fact that the religious orders were zealous creators, promoters and defenders of cults of their own members. Bollandus complained of the inveterate tendency of orders to swell the ranks of their saints simply by adding the names of deceased brethren to existing lists.[165] As Goodich illustrates (in Ch. 5), the orders acted as the most effective pressure groups in canonization procedures, being uniquely placed to pursue causes over the years. Religious orders were also very well-placed to promote cults among the faithful. The Franciscans, for example, having contributed to procuring his canonization in 1317, played a leading part in fostering the cult of St Louis of Anjou in Italy in the following century, only one instance of Mendicant activity of this kind at the time. More recently, the Capuchins promoted the cult of Padre Pio in the face of hostility from the secular clergy. Religious orders might also adopt prestigious saints from outside their ranks and foster their cults, as the Carmelites did with St Joseph in the Counter-Reformation period. Hagiography was an important mode of propaganda here, and attacks on it might be vigorously defended. When the Bollandist Papebroch cast doubts in 1668 on the historicity of the Carmelites' 'succession' from the prophet Elijah, the order riposted with a fundamental attack on the whole Bollandist enterprise and obtained a judgment of the Spanish Inquisition against it.[166] Sometimes orders were very closely involved in one cult in particular, as was the Order of Hospitallers of St Anthony. Not only did it administer his shrine in the Viennois, as we have seen, and raise income from it, but this was augmented by begging expeditions, on which much play was made of the saint's punishing powers. Cults might also be involved in conflicts within orders. We have seen that the Franciscans sustained two hagiographic traditions relating to the founder, and the General Chapter of 1260, which commissioned the 'official' Life by St Bonaventure, at the same time ordered that 'by holy obedience all legends previously written about the Blessed Francis should be destroyed'.[167] Moreover, the cult of St Louis of Anjou was fostered by 'the extreme Zealot party [who] fastened upon him as the type of Holy Poverty in their war with their laxer brethren'.[168]

We have seen that there was a tendency in the Early Church for the local saint to be identified with the bishop, and later for saints to be identified with the territory of dioceses. The existence of local diocesan cults and the promotion of the cults of local saintly bishops by their successors, for instance, the fourteenth-century cult of St Thomas Cantilupe studied by Finucane,[169] all testify to the importance of saints to the prestige and standing of dioceses. In an earlier example, the invention of the relics of St Protase and St Gervase increased the authority of St Ambrose, bishop of Milan, and strengthened his hand against the local Arians who were supported by the Empress Justina. Saints might also be used in attempts to improve the status of sees. The early Lives of St Samson of Dol, for example, seem to have been composed with a view to advancing the diocese's metropolitan claims.

Saints' cults were also significant for the ties which they could establish between local churches and Rome. German and Anglo-Saxon hagiography of the Carolingian period, for example, stressed the relations of bishops with the papacy. The dissemination of relics served a similar function through Late Antiquity and the Dark Ages, and again in the nineteenth century Roman relics became an important expression of ultramontane piety at a time when centralized authority in the Church was being very greatly strengthened in terms both of organization and of ideology. The same process is reflected in liturgical forms, dedications and types of cult. Perdrizet has noted that the cult of St Peter and St Paul 'characterized the countries and religious orders most susceptible to Roman influence and obedience'.[170] Much the same may be said of the cults of other Roman saints, and particular significance attaches here to their promotion in newly Christianized territory, such as medieval Poland, and to the substitution of Roman for local saints where the faith was already well established, as in Wales and Brittany.

Punishment by saints could also be invoked in support of papal power. When King Aldfrith of Northumbria refused to carry out the instructions of a papal brief, he was 'stricken down by the power of the Apostles for his defiance of Rome', and a subsequent vow 'to God and St Peter' to make amends did not prevent his swift demise.[171] This episode, recounted in the Life of St Wilfrid, was part of a much wider struggle between Church and monarchy over the appointment of bishops and the creation of dioceses and between the Celtic and Roman forms of Christianity, in which St Wilfrid played a leading role as the champion of Rome. The rapid canonization of St Thomas of Canterbury after his murder in 1170 is a further example of the assertion of papal versus royal power by means of a saint's cult. Papal power and patronage were also expressed and enhanced by the ever popular pilgrimage to Rome, which was promoted by the periodic proclamation of new indulgences and jubilees, and by the control exercised from the thirteenth century, as we have seen, over canonization.[172]

Given the power of the saints, it is not surprising that secular authorities and groups should also have sought to utilize it to their own advantage. Monarchies added cultivation of the saints to other symbolic modes of enhancing their prestige and power. So the Carolingians with their imperial ambitions seconded the spread of the cults of Roman saints, and the Byzantine Emperors consulted and honoured living holy men. More particularly, ruling dynasties had their own special cults. As Spiegel shows (in Ch. 4), the cult of St Denis was promoted both by the monks of the abbey near Paris and by the Capetian kings. In the words of Bossuat, 'the glory and the virtues of the saint cast reflected glory on the ruling house', and it is significant that the legend of the saint was reactivated through the production of new Lives during succession crises in both the thirteenth and the fourteenth centuries.[173] Less successful examples of the same process at work are provided by the attempt of Boleslas the Valiant of Poland to advance St Wenceslas as the patron of his family and the duchy in the tenth century, and by the curious concoction of an imaginary St Napoleon during the First Empire.

Such cults cast special glory on the dynasty concerned, if the saint was actually a member of it. This was the case with St Louis of Anjou, who had renounced his rights to the throne of Naples in 1296 in order to become a Franciscan. When he died a few years later in Provence, a popular cult sprang up around his tomb, and his father Charles II at once pressed for his canonization, which was promulgated, as we have seen, in 1317. Aided by the Franciscans, the saint's royal relatives then successfully propagated his cult in both Provence and Italy, and shrines were built at Marseille and Naples. Though he also aroused genuine family and popular devotion, St Louis was clearly treated as a valuable political asset, and, as a 'Guelph saint', in the words of Bertaux, he became a rallying-point for the Angevin and anti-imperial cause.[174]

More directly, rulers or their spouses could themselves become saints. This seems to have been a phenomenon especially characteristic of Western Europe in the eleventh and twelfth centuries, when examples from England, Scotland, Hungary, Portugal, the German Empire and the Scandinavian countries can be cited. But it was also found in other periods and other cultural areas. King Louis IX of France was canonized in 1297; saintly princes like St Alexander Nevsky were not uncommon in medieval Russia; while Henry VII's chapel in Westminster Abbey is a lasting monument to his attempt to have his uncle Henry VI canonized. As this last

example shows again, medieval rulers might see the attribution of sanctity
to their forebears in a distinctly political light and were prepared to go to
considerable time, effort and expense to obtain it. The prestige of one
dynasty might thereby be enhanced vis-à-vis another. The 'canonization'
of Charlemagne, contrived by Frederick Barbarossa in 1165, was clearly
intended to strengthen the Empire and to weaken the French monarchy
with its rival claims to sacredness.[175] Paradoxically also, the canonization
of a royal saint might strengthen the hand of a monarch vis-à-vis the
Church and the papacy. Scholz concludes that the canonization of Edward
the Confessor in 1161 enabled Henry II to appear to display religious zeal
and fidelity to the pope, 'while he was actually preparing to curtail the
independence of the English Church and to limit the rights of Rome in
England'.[176] The more positive advantages of such cults were mixed.
Some royal cults were genuinely popular and must have buttressed loyalty
to the crown, but others, like that of St Edward the Confessor, attracted
little enthusiasm. The qualities required of contemporary saints might also
be unsuited to monarchs and could thus cast doubts on the authority of the
latter. Folz has pointed out that many people found the model of humility
represented by St Louis of France inappropriate in a king, and thus
disturbing.[177] The attitude of the Church towards royal saints was
ambiguous. On the one hand, the canonization of dead monarchs was a
means of exercising some control over their living successors, and of
countering the notion that all monarchs were sacred. On the other, it might
give an advantage to monarchs who were enemies of the Church, as we
have seen, and it could debase the currency of sanctity.

It has been plausibly suggested that the phenomenon of royal saints
marks an important stage in the development of states in Europe,[178] and
here it is significant that royal saints occur very rarely after the end of the
Middle Ages, when states began to develop bureaucracies and armies and
to have less need of supernatural focal points. However, dynastic saints do
sometimes develop into national patrons – the English cult of St George
promoted by Edward III or the cult of St Casimir in Poland would fall into
this category. National patrons are of special importance in the modern
period for nations lacking full independence; for example, St Patrick in
Ireland or Our Lady of Czestochowa in Poland, where the cult provides a
focus that is otherwise lacking and allows an expression of patriotic feeling
in religious guise that might not be possible in more direct form.

This leads us to the use of saints' cults as a form of political opposition.
Aware of the power of saints, rulers were often anxious to monopolize or
to neutralize it. Thus the Byzantine Emperors absorbed or suppressed the
cults of city patrons in their domains, and that of St Demetrius of Salonika
was one of the few to survive into the Later Middle Ages. Brown has
suggested that the Iconoclastic movement should be seen as part of this

process, a centralizing reaction against the cult of civic saints and their icons, following the success of the Arab raids of the late seventh century; while Magdalino has argued that the Emperor Manuel I, in the twelfth century, actively discouraged the contemporary holy man, because 'he derived his charisma independently of the imperially dominated hierarchy' and was 'potentially a subversive weapon in the hands of ambitious princes of the blood'.[179] And it is certainly the case that movements of opposition to monarchs and monarchies often coalesced around the cult of saints or would-be saints. This is true of resistance to the Přemyslids in tenth-century Poland and to the Paleologi in thirteenth-century Byzantium, but seems to have been peculiarly prevalent in medieval England, where the cults of St Thomas of Canterbury, St Hugh of Lincoln and St Edmund of Abingdon, as well as those of the uncanonized Simon de Montfort, Thomas of Lancaster and Archbishop Scrope, to mention only the most prominent, all served as vehicles for anti-royal sentiment and activity.[180] Such opposition could be aristocratic, clerical and/or 'popular'. St Thomas again became a symbol of opposition during the Reformation period, and his cult was proscribed in 1538, the prologue to the destruction of his shrine. Here reasons of state coincided with Protestant ideological objection to saints' cults generally.

The cult of St Thomas points to another element. Living saints could be outspoken critics of rulers, and, unlike him, some enjoyed a kind of saintly immunity. So St Theodore of Sykeon rebuked the Emperor Phocas for 'his murderous ways' and threatened him with God's wrath.[181] The 'holy fools' of Russian tradition could play the same role. Both St Basil and St Nicholas of Pskov were said to have dared to criticize Ivan the Terrible, while Giles Fletcher related in 1588 that a holy fool in Moscow 'inveyeth commonly against the state and government, especially against the Godonoes [Godunovs] that are thought at this time to be great oppressours of that commonwealth'.[182]

Saints could also be vehicles of opposition within the Church. A number of modern Marian apparitions – La Salette, Fátima, Garabandal – have been used to criticize papal policy, while La Salette, in particular, has been the focus for dissident and schismatic groups.[183] There may be overlap here with the support given to cults by modern politico-religious movements of opposition. The cult in the west of France in the later nineteenth century of Louis Grignion de Montfort, founder of the Company of Mary, fell into both categories; while the campaign to have Joan of Arc canonized and declared France's national patron in the years before the First World War became a mainly Right-wing and anti-Republican affair, despite the existence of a wider sympathy.[184]

Before leaving the topic of political uses, we may mention other categories, most of which belong clearly to pre-industrial society. Perhaps most important is the oath. In a society where public authority is weak and legal institutions rudimentary, the oath assumes special importance as a means of making agreements binding and of enforcing group responsibility for the behaviour of individuals, and it requires supernatural sanctions in order to be effective. Gellner has shown how the saints of the Atlas sponsored collective oaths made to purge offences, and parallel institutions existed in medieval Europe. More characteristic of Christendom, however, was the oath on the relics or the images, or in the name of dead saints. Novices taking their vows, in the Rule of St Benedict, signed a document which was 'drawn up in the names of the saints whose relics' were present.[185] Gerald of Wales reported that the Celtic people and clergy revered bells, crooks 'and other similar relics of the saints', and believed that they would be severely punished if they swore oaths on them which they failed to keep.[186] In Wales, 'solemn compacts' were still being ratified on the relics of St Teilo at Llandaff in the seventeenth century;[187] while oaths in the name of the saints were still functional rather than just expletives in northern Greece in the 1950s.[188] A particularly important use of swearing by the saints was in the ratification of public treaties in the early medieval period, and the councils which met to proclaim the Peace of God in the late tenth and early eleventh centuries assembled the relics of the saints 'to provide guarantors of men's own pledges of mutual peace and justice'.[189]

Saints' cults also provided networks for political and cultural influence, as we have seen in the case of pilgrimages and festivals, and for the developing power of the papacy. But these ties went beyond such 'religious' confines. Foreville, for example, has shown how the diffusion of the cult of St Thomas of Canterbury reflected but also strengthened links between England and south-western France in the twelfth and thirteenth centuries;[190] while Obolensky has noted the important role played by the cult of St Demetrius in the spread to Slavonic lands not only of Byzantine Christianity but of Byzantine influence generally.[191] On a more local level, one may note the way in which urban shrines attracted peasants from the surrounding districts, thus reinforcing rural–urban dependence. So the Sabine peasants still came down to Rome in the nineteenth century to celebrate Ascension there, concentrating their devotions, according to Stendhal, on a bronze statue of St Peter in his basilica.[192]

If saints were here expressive of harmonious social and political interaction, they could also serve conflict. We have seen that saints' cults could relate to rivalries between monasteries or cities. Saints were also used as emblems in warfare. Otto I, for example, carried the lance of St Maurice into the battle of the river Lech in 955, in which he defeated the Hungarians. Icons were commonly carried or invoked in battle in medieval Russia, against both heathens and Christians;[193] and medieval warriors like

Roland placed relics in the hilts of their swords. Many of the most popular saints, moreover, were soldiers: St Maurice, St Demetrius, St Martin, St George; while, in modern times, St Anthony figured on the rosters of at least two Portuguese regiments.[194] All of this must have lent some legitimacy to military activity (and to the knightly and other élites engaged in it), though, on the other hand, cults could be given an anti-military slant. St Besse was not the only saint invoked by those wishing to avoid conscription (see Ch. 1), and it may be noted that the Curé d'Ars had been a deserter in his youth. As we saw in discussing local patrons, saints could also become the focus of local conflict. Neighbouring villages could pursue rivalries via rival cults or disputes over shared ones, as in the case of St Besse.[195] Groups within villages could become hostile to the patron as the symbol of an established élite, as in Republican Spain,[196] or rival saints' cults could express an endemic factionalism, as in Malta.

This brings us to the wider question of the social meaning of saints' cults. Those who have examined the sociology of saints are agreed that they reflect the structure of the societies which produce and honour them. This is true of early medieval saints, of the canonized saints of the West, of the saints of Byzantium and of Russia; and two features stand out. First, saints are of overwhelmingly aristocratic or upper-class origin, and hagiographers place great emphasis on this, if only by pointing to their subject's renunciation of the privileges of high status. Thus St John the Almsgiver is said to be 'descended not from ignoble or ordinary ancestors, but from . . . an illustrious family of brilliant renown';[197] while St Patrick was provided with a more speculative genealogy, sacred and profane, 'something of the utmost importance in the aristocratic society of Ireland'.[198] Patlagean has noted that such 'aristocratic references' not only added to the prestige of the saints concerned but also reflected advantageously on their families or lineages as well as on their 'class',[199] a parallel to the royal saints which we have discussed. This general phenomenon relates again to a feature of some canonization procedures, where the saint's cult is clearly promoted by a local aristocratic group.[200]

Secondly, saints are also overwhelmingly male. The 'canon' of Russian saints includes fewer than a dozen women;[201] while among saints canonized in the West, the proportion of women, as Delooz demonstrates (in Ch. 6), never rose above 20 per cent until this century and was often considerably below this. The imbalance is to a considerable extent offset by the importance of devotion to the various manifestations of the Virgin Mary, but nevertheless remains a bias of very great significance, the more so in that women seem always to have participated fully in saints' cults, and that in modern European peasant societies, at least, religion is something of a female speciality. A further feature is also revealing. In the Western Church – the same is not true of Russia – female saints are nearly always virgins and not married women with children. Although saints were associated with fertility and resorted to by barren women, maternity as such was presented as a religious ideal only in the ambiguous figure of the Virgin Mother of God.

Does this mean that the cults of saints were a means by which a certain social order was legitimized or sacralized? Were they in some way instruments of social control, as some writers have suggested?[202] In order to answer these questions, some further features of the cults must be considered, which, taken together, suggest that these notions, like that of patronage, illuminate the functions of the cults but by no means exhaust them.

Students of medieval cults and pilgrimages in East and West have stressed that they cut across classes, involving rich and poor, clergy and laity. Hagiography, we have seen, appealed again at all social levels, and, though of course it was written by a learned and literate minority, it would be hard to show that its authors were not acting in complete good faith. Providing another indicator, Tamplin argues that the importance of references to saints in 'a courtly poem such as *Sir Gawain and the Green Knight*' points to 'a widespread approval of popular cults' among the élite.[203] *Bona fide* aristocratic involvement in cults was of course maintained until recently, especially in southern Europe. Stendhal claimed that the aristocracy of Naples still believed in the liquefaction of the blood of St Januarius in 1828,[204] and the Salina ladies in Lampedusa's *Leopard* are avid relic collectors.

We have discussed the political aspects of royal involvement in saints' cults, but this reflected more than mere calculation. Kings, princes and emperors followed the major medieval pilgrimages in greater style than ordinary pilgrims but in the same spirit and for similar reasons: to ensure success in battle, to obtain cures and good health, and to get heirs. The last seems to have been particularly important and outlived the medieval period. The long childless Anne of Austria, later mother of Louis XIV, visited the shrine of Saint-Fiacre-en-Brie to ask for the birth of a son, while James II and Mary of Modena visited Holywell in 1686 for the same reason. Like their subjects, some kings were more superstitious than others in this respect. The passion of Louis XI of France for pilgrimages, relics, medals and living holy people has become legendary. Others in perhaps the same category are Frederick the Wise, Elector of Saxony, the display of whose relic collection provoked the posting of Luther's theses at Wittenberg in 1517,[205] and Philip II of Spain who had a collection of over seven thousand relics in the Escorial.

However, despite the existence of much common ground across classes as far as the cults of saints were concerned, one can also detect significant distinctions. Vauchez, in his study of fourteenth-century cults in southern France, suggests that, while all classes participated equally, the perception of what was involved was different for each;[206] in particular, the noble laity and the clergy were more likely than other groups to embrace a moral and spiritual notion of the saint's intercession. On slighter evidence, Dunin-Wasowicz states that cults of different saints in medieval Poland appealed to different social strata: St Giles to the princely élite, St Lawrence to the knights, and St Adalbert to the 'masses', an adaptation, it seems, of the patronage principle to a society of 'estates'. More certainly, as we have seen, the cults of military saints in Western Europe in the Early and Central Middle Ages appealed particularly, and were directed by the clergy, to the knights, while ideals of sanctity often reflected or expressed an aristocratic ethos.[207] To take another example, the Walsingham cult in Norfolk enjoyed aristocratic promotion and support, and, for a later period, Barbin and Duteil demonstrate that three French pilgrimages of the seventeenth century appealed to three different social strata.[208]

The 'popular' or folkloric element, moreover, has been an obvious feature of many saints' cults from the earliest times. We have come across it in various connections, but it deserves further consideration. Here some distinction should be made between semi-ecclesiastical elements, such as festivals, processions, cults of wayside chapels and confraternities, and others, where pagan features are more marked, as in cults associated with mountains, trees or springs. From the earliest times also, the clergy, or its more 'enlightened' and 'puritanical' members, had condemned the 'immorality' and 'indecency' which often accompanied the former as well as the unorthodoxy betrayed by the latter. But the fact that such condemnations were reiterated down the centuries suggests that the practices themselves were very well established. Writing of the Brittany of his youth, Renan noted that the clergy 'far from encouraging the old popular devotions [to the Breton saints at their chapels], merely tolerated them; and would have suppressed them had they been able to ... but the saints of the chapels were too strongly rooted in the countryside for anyone to think of trying to get rid of them'. And legends told of the dire consequences attending the few clerics rash enough to make the attempt.[209] An actual contemporary example illustrates the same gap between 'popular' cult and clergy. It concerns the church of Notre-Dame-de-Cléry in the Loiret in France, which possessed an ancient and miraculous statue of the Virgin. The *curé* and the parish council decided in 1836 to replace this with 'a new Madonna in plaster, freshly decorated in the modern style', which prompted violent scenes in the church. The *curé* was jostled after mass, and told: 'Give us back our good Virgin ... ours is the only one which will work miracles. Take a look at it and you'll see there's not a worm hole in it!' The old statue was eventually recovered and put back in its usual place, to applause and the singing of a Te Deum.[210]

All of this sufficiently indicates that the cult of the saints was an important ingredient of a 'popular' religion which was conceived of as belonging to the 'people' as against the clergy, or to the locality as against the outside world and its regulatory powers, and, as the bias of our evidence suggests, this feature seems to have become more prominent in the post-medieval period in Europe in the face of changes which tended to marginalize certain regions and certain parts of the population. Here the association of saints' cults with a vestigial folklore is no accident, and the enduring importance of saints' cults in southern Italy or the Alpine region is no surprise. However, the cults are not only a feature of regional 'underdevelopment', they also have a class dimension in industrialized societies. In his analysis of prayers at French shrines, Bonnet found that only 10–20 per cent were written by well-educated middle-class people.[211]

This brings us back to the notion of social control, which has sometimes been used to explain such phenomena. It is a type of explanation which we have applied to particular cults, but even on this level the argument presupposes a willingness to believe, a need to have a shrine, a supernatural patron and miracles, which no clergy, however enterprising, can wholly create. At the general level, moreover, explanations must accommodate the full range of phenomena which we have sketched in this introduction. This includes the promotion of cults by the clergy and the secular powers for their own purposes, but it also includes the practice of cults by the poor and the uneducated in ways of which the clergy wish and try to deprive them. The saints serve, too, as vehicles at the 'popular' level for hopes and beliefs that look beyond the established order of things, in this world as well as in the next. A number of saints were 'justiciars' and 'righters of wrongs', for example St Theodore of Pontus, St Gerald of Aurillac or St Yves in Brittany, and were invoked by the poor against the mighty, much as monasteries mobilized their saints against lay usurpers. Browning has plausibly argued that the saint in much 'popular' Byzantine hagiography was 'the counter-hero of the dispossessed',[212] and the observation surely applies more generally. Again, there is no doubt of the appeal of St Francis, 'the little poor man', to the poor of his day. Perhaps more telling, however, is the scepticism implied in the warning issued to the saint by a peasant near Mount Alverna: "You must take great pains to be as good as all people think you are, for many have great faith in you...I warn you, do not be different from what people hope you are.'[213]

As we have occasionally noted and as the study by Gaborieau (Ch. 10) illustrates, many features of the Christian cults of saints have analogies in other religious cultures: Buddhism, Jainism, Hinduism, Islam and others. Martyrdom was at the origin of cults of saints among the Sikhs, for example, and the Shahidganj at Lahore was the equivalent of a Christian *martyrium*.[214] Burial 'ad sanctos' accompanied tomb cults in Northern

India, and funerals 'ad sanctos' were the rule in nineteenth-century Cairo.[215] The Buddhist saints in their struggle against Bonism in Tibet engaged in the same feats of miracle-working as St Patrick in pagan Ireland or St Martin in Gaul, and the same syncretic compromise was eventually arrived at.[216] The holy hair of the Hazratbal mosque in Kashmir aroused the same passionate devotion as any relic of the medieval West, and its theft or disappearance in December 1963 became an international incident like the removal of the body of St Louis of Anjou from Marseille in 1419, and triggered off riots reminiscent of Byzantium at the height of the Iconoclastic movement.[217] The phenomenon of automobile relics or corpses is also found in Islam. Lane relates that the corpse of a dead saint not uncommonly indicated in the course of its funeral procession where it wished to be buried. Tombs of Islamic saints, as Gaborieau notes, were regarded very differently from those of ordinary mortals to the extent of being given a distinct name, and Lane again relates that, at the funerals of saints or holy men, the usual laments were replaced by hymns of joy,[218] all of which parallels the Christian notion that the dead saint had transcended death. The faithful made vows, and touched the tombs of the saints in modern Islamic Egypt, moreover, 'as if they were collecting...an emanation from the saint himself',[219] which could as well be said of medieval and later Christian practice. Muslims, Buddhists, Jains and Hindus venerated and venerate images of saints; and saints everywhere, via images, tombs, relics, or in the flesh, are implored and petitioned for good health, fertility and prosperity. The local saint and patron was of special importance here, as in Christendom, while shrines brought pilgrims, wealth, prestige and power to an equal if not a greater degree to monasteries.

A more systematic comparison would be of great value, and it would have to take account of significant differences as well as of structural similarities in the cults themselves and in their social context. In Islam, for example, the principle of descent from the Prophet or founder is an element that is absent in Christianity, and lineages of saints are correspondingly important. Again, most religions lack the centralized authority of a church, and control of cults is therefore lax in comparison with the Christian situation. If this book serves to encourage the pursuit of such comparative analysis, as well as emphasizing what has been so universal a mode of religious and human expression, it will have served its purpose.

NOTES

Where full references are not supplied in the notes, items will be found in the Bibliography, which also provides the Introduction with general reference and acknowledgement. Figures in heavy type refer to the Bibliography.

1 Ferdinand Lot, *Mélanges d'histoire bretonne* (**928**), p. 97.

2 See Joshua Trachtenberg, *Jewish Magic and Superstition, A Study in Folk Religion* (New York, 1939 and 1970).

3 A term used by O'Malley, *Popular Hinduism, The Religion of the Masses* (**1296**), Ch. 5.

4 On the important medieval cult of St Michael, and especially the pilgrimages to Mont-Saint-Michel and Monte Gargano, see Rojdestvensky, *Le Culte de Saint Michel* (**94**); Mâle, *Art et Artistes du Moyen Age* (**438**), Ch. VII, 'Le Mont-Saint-Michel'; Elena Cassin, *San Nicandro, The Story of a Religious Phenomenon* (London, 1958), Chs. VII and VIII; Musset, 'Recherches sur les pèlerins (**655**), pp. 128–32; Delaruelle, 'L'Archange Saint Michel dans la spiritualité de Jeanne d'Arc' (**95**); Rintelen, *Kultgeographische Studien in der Italia byzantina* (**96**), Pt I, 'Der Kult des Erzengels Michael in Süditalien'; and Labande, 'Les Pèlerinages au Mont-Saint-Michel' (**659**).

5 See also J. Rendel Harris, *The Dioscuri in the Christian Legends* (Cambridge, 1903); Rendel Harris, *The Cult of the Heavenly Twins* (Cambridge, 1906), Ch. XI; and Deubner, *Kosmas und Damian* (**1014**). To take another example, an epigram in the Greek Anthology even made 'a statue of Herakles pathetically deplore his enforced transformation into an image of St Luke'; see Lewis Richard Farnell, *Greek Hero Cults and Ideas of Immortality* (Oxford, 1921), p. 151.

6 Delehaye, 'L'Invention des reliques de Saint Menas' (**1024**), p. 120.

7 Delehaye, *Les Origines du culte des martyrs* (**186**), p. 467; and Vacandard, *Etudes* (**140**), p. 170.

8 St Augustine, *Contra Faustum*, XX, 21, cited by Marignan, *Etudes* (**234**), p. 8.

9 The credal clause, 'the Communion of Saints' (*sanctorum communio*), probably also reflects this usage, though its interpretation has aroused much controversy, and Protestants generally prefer to see it as a reference to common participation in the sacraments or 'sacred things'; see H. F. Stewart, *Doctrina Romanensium De Invocatione Sanctorum Being a Brief Enquiry into the Principles that Underlie the Practice of Invocation of Saints* (London, 1907), esp. pp. 96–107; Benko, *The Meaning of Sanctorum Communio* (**148**); and J. N. D. Kelly, *Early Christian Creeds* (London, 1972), pp. 388–97.

10 St Augustine, *Concerning the City of God against the Pagans* (Harmondsworth, 1972), p. 1048.

11 Timothy Ware, *The Orthodox Church* (Harmondsworth, 1980), p. 177.

12 Apostolic saints became later the objects of more general devotion, and New Testament saints remain among the most popular. Old Testament figures were rarely regarded as saints in the Catholic West, though they were in the East, where St Elijah, for example, had an important cult. Some Protestants have also had a special veneration for Old Testament figures.

13 Vitricius, *De laude sanctorum*, cited by Kemp, *Canonization and Authority* (**49**), pp. 4–5.

14 The *Pilgrim's Guide to St James of Compostela*, for example, declared that St Giles 'should be venerated, adored and loved' at his shrine in Provence; see Dunin-Wasowicz, 'Saint-Gilles et la Pologne' (**1157**), p. 126.

15 Such objects were most commonly called *brandea* or *eulogia*, it appears, though other terms were used; for this and the practice generally, see in particular Grabar, *Martyrium*, II (**198**), pp. 343–3; and McCulloh, 'The Cult of Relics' (**328**).

16 The first 'translation' recorded was in fact, it seems, that of St Babylas to Daphne, to which we have referred and which took place around 350, according to Delehaye, *Les Origines du culte des martyrs*, p. 65.

17 See Braun, *Der Christliche Altar in seiner Geschichtlichen Entwicklung* (**312**), esp. II, pp. 545–73. Protestant opposition to stone altars probably derives from dislike of this practice, though this is not made explicit; see G. W. O. Addleshaw and Frederick Etchells, *The Architectural Setting of Anglican Worship, An Inquiry into the Arrangements for Public Worship in the Church of England from the Reformation to the present day* (London, 1948), pp. 25ff. and 135–6.

18 For a catalogue of these, see Boussel, *Des Reliques* (**324**), Chs. 5–8.

19 Cited by Geary, 'The Ninth-Century Relic Trade' (**371**), p. 13.

20 This is the suggestion of Grabar, *Martyrium*, II, Ch. VIII.

21 An early Coptic Life of St Menas refers to a wooden statue being made for the Prefect Atnasis and being placed on the body of the saint 'in order to obtain his intercession', after which it was used to give protection 'at sea and in battle'; see Delehaye, 'L'Invention des reliques de Saint Menas', p. 125. The best known early Western reliquary-statue is that of St Foy at Conques dating from the late tenth century; see Mâle, *L'Art religieux du XIIe* siècle (**427**), pp. 201–3 and Figs. 146 and 147; and Hanns Swarzenski, *Monuments of Romanesque Art, The Art of Church Treasures in North-Western Europe* (London, 1974), p. 33 and Plate 7; and, for other examples, *ibid.*, Plates 163–5; and Geneviève Moracchini and Dorothy Carrington, *Trésors oubliés des Eglises de Corse* (Paris, 1959), Plates III and 34–35 (a thirteenth-century head of St John Chrysostom from Sisco in Corsica).

22 See Peeters, 'La Canonisation des Saints dans l'Eglise russe' (**41**); J. Bois, 'Canonisation dans l'Eglise russe' in Vacant and Mangenot (eds.), *Dictionnaire de Théologie Catholique* (**8**), II, cols. 1659–72; 'The Canonization of Saints' (**42**), *The Christian East*, XII (1931), pp. 85–9; and Behr-Sigel, *Prière et Sainteté dans l'Eglise russe* (**80**), pp. 24–35.

23 See Sorokin, *Altruistic Love* (**29**); and Mecklin, *The Passing of the Saint* (**28**). A similar incompatibility is implied in the observation of Stendhal that 'the quality of *saint*, which was once the height of honour, today detracts from St Paul. This man has had a far greater influence on the world than Caesar or Napoleon.' Stendhal, *A Roman Journal* (1829) (New York, 1957), p. 13.

24 See, for example, Patrick Leigh Fermor, *Roumeli, Travels in Northern Greece* (London, 1966), p. 172; and Stephen Wilson, *Ideology and Experience, Antisemitism in France at the time of the Dreyfus Affair* (Rutherford, London and Toronto, 1982), p. 93.

25 Napoleon's toothbrush was displayed in London in 1965 and his hat was sold for a large sum in 1969 (Boussel, *Des Reliques*, p. 231); Lord Byron's shoes and other belongings were preserved as 'sacred relics' at Missolonghi (Fermor, *Roumeli*, pp. 160–7); while clothes belonging to Marilyn Monroe were sold amidst much publicity in 1981.

26 See Agulhon, 'La "statuomanie" et l'histoire' (**489**), pp. 145–72.

27 Giuseppe di Lampedusa, *The Leopard* (London, 1963), p. 155.

28 'Have mind, daughter', Margery Kempe was told by Christ, 'what Mary Magdalene was, Mary of Egypt, St Paul, and many other saints that are now in Heaven, for of unworthy I make worthy, and of sinful, I make rightful.' *The Book of Margery Kempe, A Modern Version* by W. Butler-Bowdon (London and Toronto, 1954), p. 64.

29 The most obvious example is the stigmatized St Francis, but the notion was also applied to the early martyrs and to Byzantine saints; see Delehaye, *Les Passions des martyrs* (**191**), p. 19; and Han J. W. Drijvers, 'Hellenistic and Oriental Origins', in Hackel (ed.), *The Byzantine Saint* (**231**), pp. 26–8.

30 Edward Gibbon, *The History of the Decline and Fall of the Roman Empire* (London, 1825), I, Ch. XV, p. 301.

31 Graef, *Mary* (**1173**), I, pp. 90–1.

32 Mâle, *L'Art religieux de la fin du XVIᵉ siècle* (**424**), pp. 313–25; and Cabrol, *The Year's Liturgy* (**534**), II, p. 138.

33 Toynbee, *St Louis of Toulouse* (**265**), p. 1 and *passim*.

34 Sauzat, 'Pèlerinage panique' (**681**), pp. 377–9.

35 Le Braz, *Au Pays des Pardons* (**684**), pp. 172–200.

36 Sallmann, 'Image et fonction du saint' (**61**), pp. 856–7.

37 Despite their overt rejection of the cult of saints, Protestants retained some of its features, notably the veneration of martyrs; and an early English Protestant referred to Lollard tracts in 1532 as 'holy reliques'; see Margaret Aston, 'Lollardy and the Reformation: Survival or Revival?', *History*, 49 (1964), p. 154.

38 See, for example, Cassin, *San Nicandro*, pp. 20–2; and Gerald Strauss, *Luther's House of Learning, Indoctrination of the Young in the German Reformation* (Baltimore and London, 1978), p. 304.

39 See, for example, Emmanuel Le Roy Ladurie, *Montaillou, Cathars and Catholics in a French village 1294–1324* (Harmondsworth, 1980), esp. Chs. XVIII and XIX; and Carlo Prandi, 'Religion et classes subalternes en Italie, Trente années de recherches italiennes', *Archives de Sciences Sociales des Religions*, 43 (1977), p. 120, citing Moscato.

40 Hoare (ed.), *The Western Fathers* (**757**), p. 21.

41 Karrer (ed.), *St Francis of Assisi* (**755**), pp. 41 and 49.

42 *Ibid.*, p. 166.

43 Hoare (ed.), *The Western Fathers*, p. 184.

44 J. B. Blain, *La Vie de Monsieur Jean-Baptiste de La Salle* (1733), cited by W. J. Battersby, *De La Salle, A Pioneer in Modern Education* (London, 1949), p. 211. The same enthusiam for relics meant that the habit on the corpse of St Charles of Sezze, who died in 1670 at Rome, had to be replaced nine times; see Perotti (ed.), *St Charles of Sezze* (**822**), p. 214 (note by Severino Gori).

45 Dawes and Baynes (eds.), *Three Byzantine Saints* (**728**), pp. 69–70.

46 See De Rosa, 'Sainteté, clergé et peuple' (**58**), p. 262, citing the canonization procedure.

47 For example that over the body of the Welsh saint Teilo, which seems eventually to have been divided into three to satisfy all claimants; see G.

Hartwell Jones, *Celtic Britain and the Pilgrim Movement* (London, 1912), *Y Cymmrudor*, XXIII, pp. 352–3.

48 Cited by Hoare (ed.), *The Western Fathers*, p. 253.

49 Brown, *The Cult of the Saints* (**146**), pp. 82–3.

50 See Hole, *English Shrines and Sanctuaries* (**650**), pp. 99–103.

51 Dawes and Baynes (eds.), *Three Byzantine Saints*, pp. 100–1.

52 It was one of the criteria for canonization in the Russian Church. For a recent Western example, see the report in *The Observer* (20 September 1981) on the Irish cult of Mary Therese Collins, who died in 1929 and whose body was accidentally found to be perfectly preserved fifty years later. However, such preservation was not necessarily taken to be a sign of sanctity; in the Middle English poem *St Erkenwald*, an incorrupt corpse is found to be that of a pagan judge, and after it has been baptized, it then decays, which completely reverses the connection between sacredness and incorruptibility; see Henry L. Savage (ed.), *St Erkenwald, A Middle English Poem* (**804**).

53 This is usually the property of dead saints, but is sometimes reported of the living, for example Padre Pio.

54 St Augustine, 'On Care to be had for the Dead', *Seventeen Short Treatises* (Oxford, 1847), pp. 517–42; and Philippe Ariès, *L'Homme devant la Mort* (Paris, 1977), Ch. 2.

55 Webb and Walker (eds.), *St Bernard of Clairvaux* (**762**), p. 126.

56 Delehaye, 'L'Invention des reliques de Saint Menas', p. 135; and 'Les Recueils antiques' (**1026**), pp. 48 and 54. Le Braz notes a related Breton belief that saints visit each other on the days of their respective 'pardons', *Au Pays des Pardons*, pp. 301–3.

57 Delaruelle, 'La Spiritualité des pèlerinages à Saint-Martin de Tours' (**656**), p. 498. The same phenomenon has been noted in non-Christian contexts; see, for example, Gilsenan, *Saint and Sufi* (**1288**), pp. 57 and 63.

58 Dufourcq, *La Christianisation des foules* (**137**), p. 41.

59 Klauser, *A Short History of the Western Liturgy* (**512**), pp. 51–3.

60 See Ernst H. Kantorowicz, *Laudes Regiae, A Study in Liturgical Acclamations and Mediaeval Ruler Worship* (Berkeley and Los Angeles, 1946 and 1958).

61 A most interesting example of this is provided by the small Jewish community of L'Isle-sur-Sorgue in the Comtat in the eighteenth century, whose members, of course, kept their own Jewish religious festivals, but employed the calendar of saints' days in legal and business transactions; see J. A. Kohnstamm, 'Family Structure and Behaviour and Ghetto Life in the Jewish Community of L'Isle-sur-Sorgue 1680–1760' (unpublished Ph.D. thesis, University of East Anglia, 1982), p. 89.

62 Robert Brentano, *Two Churches, England and Italy in the Thirteenth Century* (Princeton, 1968), p. 230; see also Richard Hooker, *Of the Laws of Ecclesiastical Polity* (1597), Fifth book, Ch. XIII (London, Everyman, no date), II, pp. 44–7; and Delehaye, 'Loca Sanctorum' (**544**), pp. 5–40.

63 Fournée, *Enquête sur le culte populaire de Saint Martin* (**113**).

64 See, for example, Isaac Taylor, *Words and Places or Etymological Illustrations of History, Ethnology and Geography* (London, 1909), pp. 9–11 and 239–44; Auguste Longnon, *Les Noms de lieu de la France, leur origine, leur signification,*

leurs transformations (Paris, 1920), Chs. LXIX and LXX; Allen Mawer, *Place-Names and History* (Liverpool and London, 1922), pp. 16–17; and Delehaye, 'Loca Sanctorum', pp. 43–64.

65 On these cults, see Turner, *Image and Pilgrimage* (**594**), pp. 53–7; and Gross, 'Ritual and Conformity' (**691**).

66 Carmelo Lison-Tolosana, *Belmonte de los Caballeros, A Sociological Study of a Spanish Town* (Oxford, 1966), p. 301.

67 See also Hans Lietzmann, *The Era of the Church Fathers, A History of the Early Church*, IV (London, 1953), p. 172. The concept was also applied, metaphorically of course, to human life generally or the Christian practice of it, a usage given its classic expression by Bunyan; see also Delaruelle, 'Le Pèlerinage intérieur' (**249**).

68 See also Rodney Gallop, *Portugal, A Book of Folk-Ways* (Cambridge, 1961), Chs. VI and VII.

69 See Halbwachs, *La Topographie légendaire* (**616**); and Delaruelle, 'Deux guides de Terre Sainte' (**620**). Places associated with non-Biblical saints could also become 'loca sacra', to be visited by pilgrims, for example, the cell of St Thomas Aquinas in the Dominican convent at Naples; see Jacob Burckhardt, *The Civilization of the Renaissance in Italy* (London, 1951), p. 89.

70 See O'Malley, *Popular Hinduism*, pp. 125–6.

71 See, for example, Ariès, *L'Homme devant la Mort*, Ch. 4; and Pierre Chaunu, *La Mort à Paris, XVIe, XVIIe et XVIIIe siècles* (Paris, 1978), Chs. XI, XIII and XIV.

72 'Pilgrimage to Jerusalem the Copts hold to be incumbent on all who are able to perform it...', Edward William Lane, *The Manners and Customs of the Modern Egyptians* (1860) (London, Everyman, no date), p. 547. This attitude may have been modelled on Muslim attitudes and practice vis-à-vis pilgrimage.

73 See Otto Springer, 'Mediaeval Pilgrim Routes from Scandinavia to Rome', *Mediaeval Studies*, 12 (1950), pp. 96–9 and 102; and Denis McKay, 'Parish Life in Scotland 1500–1560', in David McRoberts (ed.), *Essays on the Scottish Reformation 1513–1625* (Glasgow, 1962), pp. 108–9.

74 For the last, see Cassin, *San Nicandro*, pp. 121–2. All the others were very common.

75 Oscar Lewis, *The Children of Sánchez, Autobiography of a Mexican Family* (Harmondsworth, 1964), p. 324. However, devotion to domestic images was sometimes encouraged by the Catholic clergy; see Michel Albaric, 'Images consolatrices, Textes du Père Etienne Binet, S. J., *Ethnologie Française*, XI (1981), pp. 243–6, for a seventeenth-century French example.

76 For example, in the Balagna district of Corsica girls are commonly named after St Dévote and St Restitude who are venerated in that locality; while at Ars 40 per cent of girls were called after St Philomena in the period 1835–55, when her cult was being promoted by the *curé*; see Boutry, 'Un Sanctuaire et son saint' (**303**), p. 371.

77 Michaëlsson, *Etudes sur les Noms de Personne*, (**574**), pp. 69–71; and Delaruelle, 'La Piété populaire en Ombrie au siècle des Communes' (**249**), pp. 56–8; see also Georges Duby, *The Chivalrous Society* (London, 1977), pp. 62–3.

78 Halkin, 'L'Hagiographie byzantine' (**864**), p. 1.

79 Van Gennep, 'Vie des Saints et roman-feuilleton' (**832**).

80 Chauvin, 'Le Livre des Miracles de Sainte-Catherine-de-Fierbois' (**1021**), p. 294.

81 See Mölk, 'La Chanson de saint Alexis' (**924**).

82 See, for example, M. J. Field, *Search for Security, An ethno-psychiatric study of rural Ghana* (London, 1960).

83 For example, St Gonçalo, St Anthony and St John in Portugal (Gallop, *Portugal*, pp. 133, 140 and 153); St Pancras in Corsica (J.-M. Filippi, *Recueil de Sentences et Dictons usités en Corse avec traduction et lexique* (Paris, 1906), p. 21); and St John and St Anne in Brittany (Le Braz, *Au Pays des Pardons*, pp. 105, 218–20, 348–9 and 365–8).

84 See, for example, Saintyves, 'Les Résurrections d'enfants morts-nés et les sanctuaires à "répit"' (**998**); and J.-Ch. Didier, 'Un Sanctuaire à "répit" du diocèse de Langres, L'église de Fayl-Billot, Haute-Marne, d'après des actes notariés du XVIIᵉ siècle', *Mélanges de Science Religieuse* (1968), pp. 3–32.

85 Henry Noble MacCracken (ed.), *The Minor Poems of John Lydgate*, I (Oxford, 1911 and 1962), Early English Text Society, 107, p. 192.

86 See Bonnet, *Prières secrètes des Français d'aujourd'hui* (**1244**).

87 This point is emphasized by Dupront ('Anthropologie du sacré' (**593**), p. 250), who writes: 'La puissance thérapique est exogène', and who notes the common belief that a community which harboured a particular curing saint would be free of the disease with which he was associated. Le Braz notes the same phenomenon in Brittany, but also the precaution taken of paying a special visit to the 'home' saint before embarking on a pilgrimage elsewhere; see Le Braz, *Les Saints bretons* (**1217**), p. vii.

88 Gonthier and Le Bas, 'Analyse socio-économique de quelques recueils de miracles' (**1033**), p. 20.

89 Sigal, 'Maladie, pèlerinage et guérison' (**1032**), pp. 1526, 1534 and *passim*.

90 Cited by Gonthier and Le Bas, p. 16.

91 Mellot, 'Un "complexe" original de cultes berrichons' (**1007**), p. 356. For further French examples, see Kraemer, 'Les maladies désignées par le nom d'un saint' (**987**).

92 Chaumartin, *Le Mal des ardents et le feu Saint-Antoine* (**983**).

93 Gaidoz, *La Rage et St Hubert* (**972**). As we shall see, the mode of cure at Saint-Hubert was peculiar, and involved the saint's stole, which was supposed to have descended miraculously from heaven; on this category of relic, see Saintyves, 'Talismans et reliques tombés du Ciel', in *Les Reliques et les Images* (**311**), pp. 185–332.

94 See Sallmann, 'Image et fonction du saint', pp. 853–4 and 863–4.

95 Gallop, *Portugal*, p. 60.

96 See particularly, Ernesto De Martino, *La Terra del rimorso* (Milan, 1961). Canziani describes a dramatic representation of curing at the festival of St Vincent de Paul at Villamagna in the Abruzzi: 'Peasants who pretended to be ill lay on... beds, imploring grace from the saint, while other peasants dressed as sisters of charity [and as doctors] nursed them and gave them medicine.' Later the devil appeared in the hope that they would die, but was

vanquished by the saint. Canziani, *Through the Apennines* (**1055**), pp. 49–50.

97 Gerald of Wales, *The Journey through Wales and The Description of Wales* (Harmondsworth, 1978), pp. 92–3.

98 Skeat (ed.), *Aelfric's Lives of Saints* (**798**), p. 449. On incubation generally, see Defrasse and Lechat, *Epidaure* (**162**); L. Deubner, *De Incubatione* (**973**); and Hamilton, *Incubation* (**978**).

99 Coutil, *La Chapelle Saint-Eloi* (**685**), p. 217.

100 See Delehaye, 'Les Recueils antiques', pp. 24–7.

101 Rousselle, 'Du sanctuaire au thaumaturge' (**996**), p. 1104. Similarly, it has been argued that St Hildegard was in effect an early female medical practitioner; see Gertrude M. Engbring, 'Saint Hildegard, Twelfth-century Physician', *Bulletin of the History of Medicine*, VIII (1940), pp. 770–84.

102 Kaftal, *St Francis in Italian Painting* (**442**), p. 100, citing St Bonaventure's Life.

103 Lewis, *The Children of Sánchez*, pp. 216, 218, and 238.

104 See François Maestroni, *Ajaccio et la Madunnuccia* (Ajaccio, 1978), pp. 19–24. For further examples, see Février, 'Fêtes religieuses de l'ancien diocèse de Fréjus (**1060**), pp. 177–80; Lison-Tolosana, *Belmonte de los Caballeros*, p. 306; and Christian, *Local Religion* (**293**), Ch. 2.

105 Perotti (ed.), *St Charles of Sezze*, p. 145.

106 Sébillot, *Le Folk-Lore de France* (**1252**), IV, pp. 167–8.

107 See Riegelhaupt, 'Festas and Padres' (**1065**), p. 847.

108 See Gross, 'Ritual and Conformity', pp. 140–6.

109 Sallmann, 'Image et fonction du saint', p. 871.

110 *The Minor Poems of John Lydgate*, pp. 125, 167 and 171.

111 Boissevain, *Saints and Fireworks* (**1074**), pp. 120–1.

112 'Monseigneur Sainct Anthoyne'. Chaumartin, *Le Mal des ardents et le feu Saint-Antoine*, p. 73.

113 Brown, *The Cult of the Saints*, pp. 38 and 41.

114 Dawes and Baynes (eds.), *Three Byzantine Saints*, pp. 91–2, 101 and 154.

115 Perotti (ed.), *St Charles of Sezze*, pp. 4, 9, 56, 67, 104, 114, 123–5 and *passim*.

116 See Joel Martin Halpern, *A Serbian Village* (New York, 1958), pp. 238–40; also Canziani, *Through the Apennines*, p. 200, on Albanian communities in Italy.

117 Carlo Levi, *Christ Stopped at Eboli* (London, 1948), p. 33.

118 See Perdrizet, *Le Calendrier Parisien* (**532**), p. 71; and Achille Luchaire, *Social France at the Time of Philip Augustus* (New York, 1967), pp. 2–3.

119 See Delehaye, 'Les Recueils antiques', pp. 59–60; and Obolensky, 'The Cult of St Demetrius' (**1162**), pp. 5ff.

120 See Février, 'Fêtes religieuses de l'ancien diocèse de Fréjus', p. 173.

121 See De Lutiis, *L'Industria del santino* (**1201**), pp. 39–40.

122 Cited by Barker, *Rome of the Pilgrims and Martyrs* (**187**), pp. 294–5.

123 See Cassin, *San Nicandro*, pp. 106–8.

124 See Geary, *Furta Sacra* (**370**), pp. 115–27.

125 Czarnowski, *Le Culte des héros* (**114**), p. 313 and *passim*.

126 Marignan, *Etudes*, pp. 24–5.

127 Craster, 'The Patrimony of St Cuthbert' (**1114**), p. 199. For additional examples, see Duby, *The Chivalrous Society*, pp. 44–5.

128 See Fedotov, *The Russian Religious Mind* (**79**), II, Ch. V.

129 See Gellner, *Saints of the Atlas* (**1284**); and Brown, 'The Rise and Function of the Holy Man in Late Antiquity' (**144**).
130 The 'saint' in John M. Synge, *The Well of the Saints* (Dublin and London, 1912) is a wandering friar, though he has thaumaturgical powers; more generally, see Hartwell Jones, *Celtic Britain and the Pilgrim Movement*, pp. 345–6; and Bowen, *The Settlements of the Celtic Saints* (**572**), p. 1.
131 There are traces of lineage notions in relation to sanctity, however; for example, in France families with the gift of healing commonly claimed descent from a saint; see Thiers, *Traité des Superstitions* (**306**), I, Book 6, Ch. IV, pp. 497–519; Gaidoz, *La Rage et St Hubert*, pp. 118–19; Dubuc, 'Le Culte de Saint Hubert' (**989**), pp. 68–9; Fournée, *Enquête sur le culte populaire de Saint Martin* (**113**), pp. 51–2; and Bloch, *The Royal Touch* (**1120**), pp. 171–6; and, despite saintly antipathy towards kinship ties, the relatives of saints often came to be regarded as saints, too; for example, the mother, a brother and a sister of St Bernard, and the mother and a brother of St Dominic, were honoured with cults (see Delooz, *Sociologie et Canonisations* (**33**), p. 345).
132 For example, St Daniel was the 'successor' and heir to the sanctity of St Simeon Stylites and was given his tunic to indicate this (Dawes and Baynes (eds.), *Three Byzantine Saints*, pp. 11 and 18–20 – presumably on the Old Testament model of Elisha assuming the mantle of Elijah); while St Francis on his death-bed is said to have passed on his charismatic leadership of the order to Brother Bernard, as he had earlier conveyed guardianship of its 'true' tradition to Brother Cesar of Speyer (Karrer, *St Francis of Assisi*, pp. 119 and 146–7).
133 Dawes and Baynes (eds.), *Three Byzantine Saints*, p. 184.
134 See Cabrol, *The Year's Liturgy*, II, pp. 119, 125–6 and 291.
135 In the sixteenth and the eighteenth centuries respectively; see François J. Casta, *Le Diocèse d'Ajaccio* (Paris, 1974), pp. 94–5 and 125–6.
136 Brown, *The Cult of the Saints*, p. 64.
137 On sanctuary, see Cox, *The Sanctuaries and Sanctuary Seekers of Mediaeval England* (**1098**); McGoldrick, 'The Medieval Right of Sanctuary' (**1099**); and Hole, *English Shrines and Sanctuaries*, pp. 20–37.
138 Sigal, 'Maladie, pèlerinage et guérison', p. 1538 and *passim*.
139 Perotti (ed.), *St Charles of Sezze*, pp. 123–5.
140 Cousin, 'Deux cents miracles en Provence' (**1035**), p. 231.
141 See Bouillet and Servières, *Sainte Foy* (**279**), pp. 100–5 and 417–21; Gaillard, 'Une abbaye de pèlerinage (**657**); and Geary, *Furta Sacra*, pp. 70–6.
142 See Coens, 'Translations et miracles de Saint Bavon'(**1110**); also B. de Gaiffier, 'Les Revendications de biens' (**1106**), pp. 137–8.
143 St Augustine, *Concerning the City of God*, p. 1047.
144 B. de Gaiffier, 'Miracles bibliques et Vies de Saints', *Nouvelle Revue Théologique*, 88 (1966), p. 380.
145 See Scholz, 'The Canonization of Edward the Confessor' (**1139**).
146 See Charles Porée, *L'Abbaye de Vézelay* (Paris, no date); Francis Salet, *La Madeleine de Vézelay, Etude iconographique* (Melun, 1948); and Saxer, *Le Culte de Marie Madeleine* (**255**), I, Part II.
147 See Anderson, *A Saint at Stake* (**1104**). The case of St William is also of

interest since it is one of a number of cults of child-martyrs at the time who were reputed to have been ritually killed by Jews; see Vacandard, 'La Question du meurtre rituel chez les Juifs', in *Etudes de critique*, 3rd series, pp. 328–41; and Léon Poliakov, *The History of Antisemitism* (London, 1965), I, pp. 56–64.

148 Sauzat, 'Pèlerinage panique', pp. 383–6.

149 Also Bossuat, 'Traditions populaires relatives au martyre... de saint Denis' (**259**), pp. 500–1.

150 Webb (ed.), *Lives of the Saints* (**766**), pp. 205–6.

151 Cited by Barker, *Rome of the Pilgrims and Martyrs*, pp. 32–3; see also McCulloh, 'The Cult of Relics', pp. 148–9.

152 Cited by Keith Thomas, *Religion and the Decline of Magic, Studies in Popular Beliefs in Sixteenth- and Seventeenth-Century England* (Harmondsworth, 1973), p. 29.

153 Delehaye, 'Les Recueils antiques', p. 53.

154 See Luchaire, *Social France*, p. 231.

155 Skeat (ed.), *Aelfric's Lives of Saints*, p. 457.

156 Gerald of Wales, *The Journey through Wales*, p. 127.

157 On malediction, see Lester K. Little, 'Formules monastiques de malédiction aux IXe et Xe siècles', *Revue Mabillon*, LVIII (1975), pp. 377–99; and 'La Morphologie des malédictions monastiques', *Annales*, 34 (1979), pp. 43–60.

158 See also Platelle, 'Crime et châtiment à Marchiennes (**1108**), and, more generally, Southern, *The Making of the Middle Ages* (**1183**), pp. 133–4.

159 Ernest Clarke (ed.), *The Chronicle of Jocelin of Brakelond: A Picture of Monastic Life in the Days of Abbot Samson* (London, 1903), p. 79.

160 See Rousset, 'La Croyance en la justice immanente à l'époque féodale' (**1112**); and John W. Baldwin, 'The Intellectual Preparation for the Canon of 1215 against Ordeals', *Speculum*, XXXVI (1961), pp. 613–36.

161 Gerald of Wales, *The Journey through Wales*, p. 189.

162 Here it is significant that the 'cursing well' was also a significant phenomenon in medieval Wales; see Jones, *The Holy Wells of Wales* (**1255**), pp. 71–2 and 117–23.

163 Aigrain, *L'Hagiographie* (**839**), pp. 102–6.

164 Fedotov gives a figure of about a quarter, 'a proportion impossible in Greece or in the Latin West'. Fedotov, *The Russian Religious Mind*, I, p. 276.

165 See Delehaye, *Sanctus* (**142**), pp. 134–5.

166 This prohibited the sale or the reading of the volumes of the *Acta Sanctorum* for March, April and May, and was not lifted until 1715 and then only partially; see Delehaye, *L'Oeuvre des Bollandistes* (**833**), Ch. 5.

167 Karrer, *St Francis of Assisi*, pp. 66–7.

168 Toynbee, *St Louis of Toulouse*, p. 217.

169 See Finucane, *Miracles and Pilgrims* (**1037**).

170 Among the latter, he singled out Cluny in the High Middle Ages, the Dominicans in the Later Middle Ages, and, from the sixteenth century, the Jesuits. Perdrizet, *Le Calendrier Parisien*, p. 163.

171 Webb (ed.), *Lives of the Saints*, p. 196.

172 Though clearly a field for the exercise of papal patronage, canonization was

rarely used in a crude or nepotist way, though Delooz notes that Urban V canonized his uncle Elzéar of Sabran; Leo IX, who came from Alsace, three fellow-countrymen; and Sixtus IV, a Franciscan, six of his own order (Delooz, *Sociologie et Canonisations*, pp. 174–6).

173 Bossuat, 'Traditions populaires relatives au martyre... de saint Denis', pp. 480–4.

174 Bertaux, 'Les Saints Louis dans l'art italien' (**264**), p. 636 and *passim*.

175 Although this 'canonization', in which the Antipope Paschal III was involved, is not regarded as valid by the Church, the cult of Charlemagne is tolerated locally, on the grounds that public veneration had existed earlier, when papal sanction was not absolutely necessary; see Dom Prosper Guéranger, *The Liturgical Year* (**521**), II, pp. 467–83; Robert Folz, *Le Souvenir et la légende de Charlemagne dans l'Empire germanique médiéval* (Paris, 1950), pp. 203–22; and Peter Munz, *Frederick Barbarossa, A Study in Medieval Politics* (London, 1969), pp. 242–5.

176 Scholz, 'The Canonization of Edward the Confessor', p. 56.

177 Folz, 'La Sainteté de Louis IX' (**1145**), p. 37.

178 See Bernard Guenée, 'Etat et Nation en France au Moyen Age', *Revue Historique*, 237 (1967), p. 22; see also Gorski, 'Le roi-saint: Un problème d'idéologie féodale' (**1143**).

179 Paul Magdalino, 'The Byzantine Holy Man in the Twelfth Century' in Hackel (ed.), *The Byzantine Saint*, p. 64. In a very different context, Bell writes that: 'After their defeat of the Gurkhas [in the late eighteenth century], the Chinese used their increased power in Tibet to regulate the appearance of the high Incarnations. They were especially perturbed at so many of those in Mongolia appearing in princely families, thereby increasing the power of chiefs who, from the Chinese viewpoint, were more than powerful enough already.' Charles Bell, *The Religion of Tibet* (Oxford, 1931), p. 156.

180 One of the first to draw attention to this phenomenon was J. J. Jusserand, *English Wayfaring Life in the Middle Ages* (London, 1892), pp. 339–44.

181 Dawes and Baynes (eds.), *Three Byzantine Saints*, pp. 175–6.

182 Cited by Fedotov, *The Russian Religious Mind*, II, pp. 338–40.

183 See Emile Appolis, 'En marge du catholicisme contemporain: Millénaristes, Cordiphores et Naundorffistes autour du "secret" de La Salette', *Archives de Sociologie des Religions*, 14 (1962), pp. 103–21.

184 In addition to the study by Sanson, see Lucien Thomas, *L'Action Française devant l'Eglise (de Pie X à Pie XII)* (Paris, 1965), p. 70; and Stephen Wilson, 'Catholic Populism in France at the time of the Dreyfus Affair: the *Union Nationale*', *Journal of Contemporary History*, 10 (1975), pp. 691–2.

185 Justine McCann (ed.), *The Rule of Saint Benedict* (London, 1952), pp. 131–3 (Ch. 58).

186 Gerald of Wales, *The Journey through Wales*, p. 87; see also the oaths by the bodies of the saints sworn by the protagonists in the epic *Raoul de Cambrai* in David Herlihy (ed.), *The History of Feudalism* (Brighton, 1979), pp. 146, 147, 153, 156, 158, 165 and 167.

187 Hartwell Jones, *Celtic Britain and the Pilgrim Movement*, p. 352.

188 See Leigh Fermor, *Roumeli*, p. 36.

189 H. E. J. Cowdrey, 'The Peace and the Truce of God in the Eleventh Century', *Past and Present*, 46 (1970), pp. 44–9; and see Duby, *The Chivalrous Society*, pp. 123 and 130.

190 See Foreville, 'La Diffusion du culte de Thomas Becket' (**1163**).

191 See Obolensky, 'The Cult of St Demetrius of Thessaloniki' (**1162**).

192 Stendhal, *A Roman Journal*, p. 60.

193 In the battle of Novgorod in 1169, for example, the city fought under the protection of its own icon of the Virgin, while the Russian princes fought under that of Our Lady of Vladimir; see Fedotov, *The Russian Religious Mind*, I, pp. 295–8; also *ibid.*, II, pp. 176–8.

194 See Gallop, *Portugal*, p. 132.

195 Pilgrimage to the chapel of Notre-Dame-de-la-Chiapella in the Cap Corse, for example, was the focus for endemic conflict between the villages of Tomino and Rogliano until well into the nineteenth century; see also Verga's Sicilian example in 'Guerra di Santi' (**1072**).

196 See Lison-Tolosana, *Belmonte de los Caballeros*, p. 303.

197 Dawes and Baynes (eds.), *Three Byzantine Saints*, p. 199.

198 Czarnowski, *Le Culte des héros*, p. 78.

199 Patlagean, 'Sainteté et Pouvoir' (**867**), p. 100; see also Laious-Thomadakis, 'Saints and Society in the Late Byzantine Empire' (**230**), pp. 86–9 and 104–6.

200 For an early-eighteenth-century south Italian example, see Sallmann, 'Image et fonction du saint', pp. 835–43. Here the fact that the Blessed Bonaventure of Potenza was the son of a tailor matters less than that his cult was sponsored by the local nobility.

201 Fedotov, *The Russian Religious Mind*, I, p. 389, gives a figure of 12; Kologrivof, *Essai sur la Sainteté en Russie* (**82**), pp. 274–88, mentions only 5.

202 Marvin Harris, *Patterns of Race in the Americas* (1964) (Westport, Conn., 1980), writes, for example, that 'the fiesta complex [in Latin American societies] was a direct expression of the attempt by the Church to maintain control over the highland Indian populations and to derive wealth from them'; see also De Lutiis, *L'industria del santino*.

203 Ronald Tamplin, 'The Saints in *Sir Gawain and the Green Knight*', *Speculum*, 44 (1969), p. 418.

204 Stendhal, *A Roman Journal*, p. 43.

205 See Roland H. Bainton, *Here I Stand, A Life of Martin Luther* (New York, 1955), pp. 53–60.

206 See Vauchez, 'La Religion populaire dans la France méridionale' (**60**).

207 See also Duby, *The Chivalrous Society*, pp. 107 and 121; Karl Bosl, 'Der Adelsheilige, Idealtypus und Wirkchlichkeit' (**901**); and Friedrich Prinz, 'Heiligenkult und Adelsherrschaft im Spiegel merowingischer Hagiographie' (**907**).

208 See Barbin and Duteil, 'Miracle et pèlerinage au XVIIe siècle' (**682**).

209 Ernest Renan, *Souvenirs d'enfance et de jeunesse* (Paris, 1883?) pp. 80–1. According to Le Braz, *Au Pays des Pardons* (**684**), pp. 20–3, for example, the rector of Trédarzec, who had the shrine of St Yves at Porz-Bihan demolished and the statue of the saint put in the presbytery attic, died soon afterwards, having being warned by three supernatural visitors.

210 *La Gazette des Tribunaux*, 6 May 1836, No. 3317, p. 662. Note that the old statue's miraculous powers are related to its resistance to pests and decay, an interesting parallel to the connection made between sanctity and the incorruptibility of the corpse.

211 The same phenomenon is found in Egypt, where the Sufi orders appeal to the marginalized lower class; see Gilsenan, *Saint and Sufi*, pp. 34–5.

212 Robert Browning, 'The "Low Level" Saint's Life in the Early Byzantine World', in Hackel (ed.), *The Byzantine Saint*, p. 127.

213 Karrer, *St Francis of Assisi*, p. 247, citing the *Fioretti*.

214 Ganda Singh, *History of the Gurdwara Shahidganj, Lahore, from its origin to November 1935* (Amritsar?, 1935).

215 Lane, *The Manners and Customs of the Modern Egyptians*, p. 526.

216 See Bell, *The Religion of Tibet*, esp. pp. 36–9 and 80–94; Lobsang P. Lhalungpa (ed.), *The Life of Milarepa* (London, 1979); Giuseppe Tucci, *The Religions of Tibet* (London, 1980), esp. Chs. 1,6 and 7; and W. Zwalf, *Heritage of Tibet* (London, 1981), Ch. 3.

217 See Ved Mehta, *Portrait of India* (Harmondsworth, 1973), pp. 139–81.

218 Lane, *The Manners and Customs of the Modern Egyptians*, pp. 523–4.

219 A. M. Hocart, 'From Ancient to Modern Egypt' (1942), in *The Life-Giving Myth and other essays* (London, 1970), p. 230.

1

St Besse: a study of an Alpine cult

ROBERT HERTZ

Every year on 10 August, at the head of a remote valley in the Italian Graian Alps, a devout and joyful crowd gathers right up in the mountains at a height of more than 2,000 metres: this is the festival of St Besse, the protector of Cogne and of the Soana valley. To the rare outsiders who witness it, it offers a picturesque and poetic spectacle. Inside and around the little chapel, built against a steep rock, throngs a motley band of pilgrims. The bright colours of the costumes of the Canavese region stand out against the grey of the rocks and the monotonous green of the pastures. As soon as the procession and the service are over, animated groups spread themselves out, eating, drinking and singing as they relax after the morning's hard climb. Their noisy revels, however, barely manage for these few hours and within a small space to disturb the silence and peace of the immense mountains.

But neither the grandeur of the surroundings nor the especial charm of this ceremony can make the historian of religions forget the problems posed by the festival of St Besse. What meaning do the faithful give to their annual presence in this place, and to the rites that they carry out here? And, beyond the perhaps illusory reasons provided by the believers themselves, what is it that brings together every year in this solitary spot, at the cost of a painful climb and often a long journey, a whole host of men, women and children, who come from the neighbouring valleys and even from the plain of Piedmont?

Simple observation of the festival did not provide an adequate answer to these questions; and thus it proved to be the point of departure of a long and complicated enquiry. First of all it was necessary to interview a large number of those devoted to St Besse, or rather to let them talk freely.[1] Then, several educated people, who know the region well from having been born there or from having resided there for some time, kindly agreed to reply to the questions which I put to them.[2] Finally, if St Besse has up to now been the object of no monograph, one can glean some information, at least indirect, about him from the historical and hagiographical literature.[3] It is from these three sources that the information analysed in the present study has been drawn.

I THE ENVIRONMENT OF SAINT-BESSE

Before we penetrate inside the shrine of our saint, let us cast a quick glance at the region which surrounds it and at the people who have frequented it over many generations.

Monte Fautenio where the devotees of St Besse gather every year is situated in the mountains which dominate the upper Soana valley (see Map 1), that is to say at the eastern extremity and on the southern slope of the Gran Paradiso chain. Here, the formidable mountain wall which

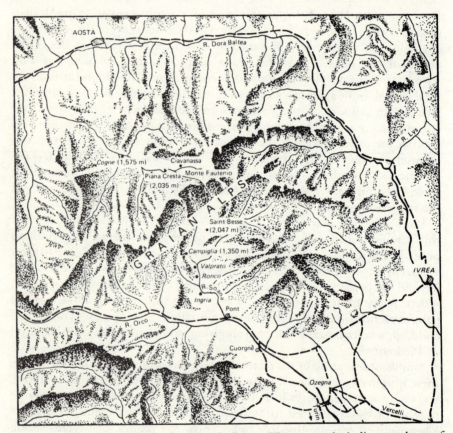

Map 1   The diffusion of the cult of St Besse (The names in italics are those of places where the saint is honoured.)

separates the basin of the Dora Baltea river from that of the Orco falls to a
level of around 3,000 metres, and several cols, which are relatively easy to
cross, at least in summer, allow one to pass from the Cogne valley, a
tributary of the Aosta valley, into the Soana valley, which goes down to the
plain of Piedmont. But these routes are hardly used today, save by a few
mountaineers and by the people of Cogne on their way to the shrine of St
Besse.[4]

We know very little about the primitive inhabitants of this part of the
Alps. It is only in the second century BC that they emerge from the night of
prehistory. Classical authors describe for us under the name of the Salassi a
collection of pastoral tribes, warlike and plundering, who occupied the
mountainous region between the Dora and the Orco and who put up an
obstinate resistance to the invasions of those wishing to 'civilize' them.
Their devastating incursions into the rich Cisalpine countryside gave the
Romans the opportunity to intervene in a district which was important
both for its geographical location and also for its mineral wealth. But it was
not until the time of Augustus, at the end of a hundred and fifty years of
struggle, after the foundation of the two colonies of Ivrea and Aosta and
after the campaign of extermination conducted by Terentius Varro, that
the Salassi were obliged to accept the law of their conquerors. Then, during
the period of peace provided by Rome, people from the plain, attracted by
the deposits of iron and copper in the valleys, installed themselves in the
mountains as if these had been a conquered country, and they taught the
original occupants of the soil the Latin speech from which the present
dialects derive.[5] But, when the power of Rome collapsed, the hold of these
masters from below was loosened, and the mountain tribes fell back into
isolation and oblivion, from which they scarcely emerged before the
fourteenth century. We know that the Soana valley was one of the main
centres of that savage *jacquerie* known as the 'Tuchinaggio'. As in the time
of the Salassi, the birds of prey from the mountain swooped down to the
opulent plain; they destroyed the crops and burnt the castles, to put an end,
it was said, to the exactions and to the usurping tendencies of the
seigneurs.[6] But, at the dawn of modern times, it was in vain that the
mountain people so tragically manifested their desire to remain their own
masters. As a strong State was gradually constituted on the plain so by a
slow, peaceful, but sure penetration, it extended its domination as far as the
high valleys of the Alps.

It is remarkable that the most obvious manifestations of these people in
'history' should be acts of aggression or of defence against the people of
the flat region below them. It seems as if the mountain-dwellers at certain
times feel the need to avenge themselves upon their privileged neighbours
of the plain for the harshness and difficulties of their Alpine environment.

Not long ago, the formalities involved in drawing lots for military conscription used to lead every year to veritable pitched battles on the streets and squares of Pont between the lads from 'above' in their felt hats and those from 'below', who wore berets. Although today it takes less serious forms, the conflict still continues. In the eyes of the people of the Soana valley, the plainsman is always a foreigner whom they call by a special name, 'maret', and towards whom they harbour, if not hostility, then at least distrust. Indeed, they experience so intense a need to cut themselves off psychologically, that they have invented a special jargon, which even their closest neighbours cannot understand.[7] Of course, this little mountain society cannot live entirely turned in on itself, without any relationship with the outside world, however much it might want to; it is obliged to seek from the plain, by pillage, trade or emigration, the complement to the meagre resources which the mountains provide. But, even when they offer their products or their labour to the masters of the plain, the mountain-dwellers endeavour to lose none of their independence. The many men from the Soana valley who go to work in Paris during the winter are all engaged in the same occupation as glaziers and, as far as possible, they live together, forming within the great city little closed and homogeneous villages. Moreover, if any of the men are tempted to let themselves be influenced by city ways, the women, who never leave the valley, are always there to react against this and to maintain local custom.

Thus, throughout the course of history, the same struggle has gone on, sometimes silent, sometimes open and violent, between the little Alpine tribe, which, by dint of cohesion and tenacity, has defended its threatened autonomy, and the wider society of the plain, which has wanted to impose on the former its own ideas and its law. The obstinate particularism, the gregarious instinct, the passionate attachment to local tradition, which above all characterize the votaries of St Besse, explain why, in the face of strong contrary influences, they have retained down to our own times habits of thought and a way of life that are centuries old.[8]

As soon as one enters the Cogne valley, one could believe oneself transported back into the Middle Ages. Almost without exception, the women still wear the costume of their forebears; with their hair tied at the back under pointed bonnets and cut in fringes on their foreheads, with their glass bead necklaces and wide muslin collars, with their stiff bodices and their short skirts curiously puffed out, with their hieratical bearing and slow gait, they look, on festival days, like so many holy images come down from their niches. Most of the houses are still made of wood; people usually sleep in the byres 'because it is warmer there in winter and to keep an eye on the animals'. The economy is almost entirely pastoral. Their only wealth consists of livestock, large and small, and of the pasture on which it feeds.

The nature of the terrain and the rudimentary state of the existing technology impose a crushing burden of labour on the men and, above all, on the women. The latter do all the field work: one sees them bringing back to the village barns from far away huge bales of hay which they carry directly on their heads. Bread is baked in each house once a year with wheat grown by the family. Despite the purity of the air, the general state of health is poor because of bad sanitary conditions; but the people of Cogne have their own explanations for the 'fevers' that kill so many youngsters: they were brought this year by 'the big black clouds which come up the valley'.

These few scattered traits will perhaps be sufficient to give some idea of the social and mental state associated with the cult which we are studying.[9] Our description will proceed from its fixed and most constant elements to those which are more elusive and variable. We will examine in turn the role played by St Besse in life today and in the ritual practice of his worshippers – that is, the organization of the cult devoted to him – and then the legend, which explains and justifies the modern devotion by reference to past events.

II THE DEVOTION TO ST BESSE

If you ask local people who St Besse was, when he lived and what he did, you will usually obtain from them only vague and incoherent replies. However, as far as the status of the saint at present is concerned, they will answer you with unanimity and precision: St Besse is a saint who has 'great powers' and who performs 'many miracles'. His name arouses in them above all, not intellectual curiosity, but feelings of tender veneration, gratitude and hope. To honour their great patron, they will vie with each other in telling you stories in which his power is conspicuously manifested. Some of these are drawn from everyday life and concern their close relatives: the sister of one is sure to have been cured by St Besse 'alone' of an old and chronic illness; the child of another, who had gone on the pilgrimage hobbling on his crutches, had left them at the shrine. Other stories touch on the marvellous, the fabulous: in the mountains, a man could not free himself from a snake which held him prisoner, he vowed to carry out a novena in honour of St Besse, and at once the snake slipped away. What the saint has done for so many others, he will surely accomplish for us, if we worship him as we should. Anyone who has a favour to ask must participate in the festival of 10 August. Anyone whom misfortune strikes or threatens 'makes a vow' to St Besse: he promises to attend his festival the following year or even for nine years in a row. Anyone who fails to fulfil a vow should beware: some 'accident' will certainly befall him! But if he perseveres in his devotion, he will not be disappointed.

The power of St Besse is not limited to any particular category of favour:

he is a saint who 'gives firm protection in all circumstances'. He is invoked against sickness in people,[10] and in livestock, as well as against the spells of witches; for there are still very evil witches in the valley. Nevertheless, according to some, there is a class of things which is the particular province of St Besse. As the images represent him in the guise of a warrior, he is, in a special way, the patron of soldiers. No man who has to leave for the wars, or simply for the barracks, would fail to attend the festival and to bring away from it a 'stone of St Besse', which he will wear on his person constantly. This is why none of the men from Cogne, who have taken part in wars from those of the First Empire to the African campaign, has ever been killed in battle, so far as anyone can remember. Yet, since the institution of compulsory military service, the main task of the warrior saint has not been to protect his devotees against shot and shell but rather to exempt them from being soldiers altogether. Youths about to draw lots for the annual conscription contingent have only to attend the Saint-Besse festival: they will not then be chosen and will not have to join the regiment![11] But this tendency of St Besse to specialize in military affairs is, as we shall see, a secondary phenomenon, and one that is perhaps peculiar to Cogne.

The stream of favours, which the patron of the two valleys pours out over his worshippers, originates in a precise point in the landscape, which is the setting for the annual festival. The chapel of St Besse is attached to the side of a huge block of shale, an enormous natural standing-stone, which sticks up in isolation in the middle of the high pastures, its face forming a vertical or overhanging cliff thirty metres high.[12] On top of this rock, called St Besse's Mount, is a cross and a tiny oratory. It is to this place that the faithful come each year to draw on the precious virtue which helps them to vanquish life's misfortunes.

Although the saint's protection of his own is effective throughout the year, it is only on the day of his festival that he communicates the benefit of his power to the faithful assembled around him. Doubtless one can anticipate the salutary effusion of his grace or favour by means of a vow; but the vow, far from dispensing one from visiting the shrine, by realizing its benefits in advance makes the visit absolutely obligatory. It is on 10 August that the debts contracted towards the saint during the past year are paid;[13] and it is on 10 August that one goes to be provided with a fresh supply of grace for the year to come.

In every festival, each party must have his due. The saint has his, and the faithful have theirs. And first of all, St Besse receives from his visitors the homage of their presence. The greater the gathering of pilgrims, the 'finer' the festival is judged to be and the more the saint is honoured. Beyond this, the pilgrimage itself represents a real sacrifice. It is no light thing in the mountains where the summer season is so short to set aside one or two days, not to field work but to the cult of the saint. To reach Saint-Besse, moreover, from Cogne means a journey of eight to nine hours over a difficult route which crosses a col at an altitude of over 2,900 metres.[14] From Campiglia, the nearest village, there are 700 metres to climb on a rough track, which takes two hours; the stages of this route are marked by small chapels and some people increase the merit of the ascent by making it in bare feet. The pilgrims who assemble for the festival, therefore, braving bad weather and fatigue, have brought the saint a precious offering of their time and their trouble by the mere fact of their coming.

The celebration of mass in the little chapel, sumptuously decorated and brilliantly lit, renews and augments the sanctity of the place. The sermon given by the priest exalts the greatness of St Besse, his glory and his power, as well as reminding his worshippers of their religious duties. But the central event of the festival is the procession. In good order, the whole community of the faithful leaves the chapel, grouped according to sex, age and religious dignity; they only return to it after having 'done the round of the Mount', that is to say having made a complete circuit of the rock, proceeding, of course, from left to right and reciting the prayers of the rosary as they go.[15] To add to the lustre of the ceremony, the parish of Campiglia, on whose territory the shrine is situated, provides St Besse with an accompaniment of all kinds of banners and holy images; but these are only accessories. By contrast, two other elements are essential to the procession. These are, on the one hand, the two *fouïaces*, ornaments composed of ribbons and fabric in bright colours, mounted on wooden frames, and almost entirely covering the faces of the young girls who carry them on their heads; these *fouïaces*, regarded today as the 'trophies' of St Besse, in the past contained consecrated bread which was distributed after the procession.[16] On the other hand, and above all, there is the massive statue of St Besse, dressed as a Roman soldier and holding the palm of martyrdom in his hand. Four or eight young men carry it on their shoulders carefully and seriously, as befits those entrusted with a trying but honorific and praiseworthy task. Is it not right that the emphasis in this ritual promenade should be placed above all on the hero of the day, on the master of the 'Mount', on glorious St Besse himself? Back in the chapel, alone, he receives the adoration of the faithful, who prostrate themselves before his statue and devoutly kiss his feet.

Beyond these personal or liturgical prestations, the faithful send or bring material offerings to the shrine. On the Sunday preceding 10 August, in all the parishes participating in the festival, a collection is taken after mass, known at Cogne as a 'picking', and the proceeds of this are given to the treasury of the chapel. But many of the faithful prefer to bring the gift which they have promised the saint in their own hands and in kind. Each one of them offers at the shrine his or her most precious possession, for a man a calf or a lamb, for a woman her finest shawl or even her wedding dress.[17] It is true that this sacrifice is not necessarily definitive. At the end of the service, the president of the festival auctions all the objects which have been offered to the saint. If the pilgrim is really attached to the 'gift' which he has given, there is nothing to stop him from recovering possession of it, provided that he pays the price for it.[18] An ingenious procedure this, which assigns to the saint the essence of the offering, that is its money value, while allowing the devotee to buy back the cherished object of which his devotion had temporarily deprived him. Giving up the spirit in order to keep the substance, is this not, in the last analysis, the very basis of religious sacrifice?

The gathering of people, the rituals and the procession, the pious offerings have all raised to its highest pitch and fully activated the sacred energy that emanates from the shrine. Before abandoning themselves entirely to the joy of being together and of happy feasting, the faithful have set their hearts on obtaining for themselves their share in the festival, by drawing on the abundant and lively source of grace that is offered to them. In the past, consumption of consecrated bread, which used to be carried in the *fouïace* and was distributed after the procession, incorporated the benefits of the ceremony in their flesh. Some people, men and women, still, it seems, rub their backs against the rock to cure themselves from pains or from sterility.[19] But it is also necessary to take home visible tokens of the protection of the saint, which will extend over space and prolong through the whole year the efficacy of the festival. So, at the doors of the chapel, several stalls are set up, where a mixture of sweetmeats, musical toys and objects of devotion is displayed; one can buy there small images of the saint, crude little pictures or medals, which are like small change to the gold reserve of the great statue in the shrine. At one time, when the cross on top of the rock was of wood, people went to scrape it in order to collect a little dust, to be used as a remedy in case of illness. The faithful today do not have this resource; for the old cross was blown down in a storm and has been replaced by an iron one. But they still have a means of remaining in communion with the saint that is more direct and more certain.

We have seen that the chapel of St Besse is an integral part of the great rock which dominates it. A ladder set up behind the altar gives access to the heart of the Mount itself. The faithful go up the ladder and chip the rock with their knives, detaching small pieces which they piously carry home with them. These are the 'stones of St Besse'. They are regarded as if they were relics of the saint. At ordinary times, they are simply kept in the house like a talisman; but, at times of special danger, such as a war, for example, people wear them on their persons. If a member of the family is ill, the stone is put into the water that he is given to drink; he is even made to swallow a few particles of it.[20] It is a sovereign remedy; but, in the words often on the lips of the faithful, 'it mustn't be mocked, *you've got to have faith and trust*'. When the festival is over and the gathering breaks up, when the pilgrims in small groups get back to their scattered hamlets, bearing with them a few fragments from the mighty rock and imbued with its special power, one could say that St Besse himself goes down with them to their settlements and that, dispersing himself while retaining his being, he takes up his place for the year to come in each of the houses where he is adored.

The festival thus profits both the faithful and their patron. It exalts the prestige of the saint; it maintains and increases the honour of his name and the renown of his shrine. Without the festival, it would be as if St Besse did not exist and he would quickly lose his place in this world. As for the faithful, they bring away from their visit to the Mount a little of that fortifying and tutelary sanctity which is necessary to them in order to live their hard lives. Just as the deep valleys breathe out towards the sky a soft warm vapour which, after being condensed on the mountain side, falls back on the valleys in life-giving drops, so the humble parishes of men send up towards the venerated shrine the living breath of their devotion, which, transfigured in that holy place, returns to them in a rain of blessings.

III THE COMMUNITY OF SAINT-BESSE

The continued existence over time of the shrine and of the festival of St Besse is assured by a small association, which comprises five distinct parishes, Campiglia, Ronco, Valprato, Ingria and Cogne. Of these five places, it is said that they have 'the right to Saint-Besse'. They have all contributed in the past to the building and then to the enlargement of the chapel; they still contribute to its upkeep and its embellishment. Each of them in turn[21] has the responsibility, or rather the honour, of giving the festival, of ensuring its material organization and its success, and of nominating its main actors, who are, on the one hand, the bearers of the *fouïaces* and of the saint, and, on the other, the president.[22] This last person is a layman, qualified by his piety and by his wealth; his function is to ensure the good order and the splendour of the proceedings, to collect the offerings and give them to the treasury, to proceed to an auction sale of the 'gifts' made to the saint, to pay the singers and the musicians, and, finally, to entertain the presidents of the other parishes and all the members of the clergy who happen to be there.

It would appear at first sight that nothing could be more tranquil or harmonious than the life of this little religious federation, all of whose members seem to be on a strictly equal footing. But this is an illusion. Closer observation reveals that the devotees of St Besse are torn by wranglings, by conflicts of ambition, by struggles sometimes concealed, sometimes open, violent and even bloody.

Simple differences of geographical situation have the effect of determining differences in rank among the five associated parishes. It is clear that
Cogne, which is situated on the other side of the Graian Alps, is in a far less
advantageous position as far as Saint-Besse is concerned than the other
four parishes, situated in the Soana valley where the shrine itself is located.
But Cogne does not only belong to a different fluvial basin, it belongs also
to a different political and religious region. While the Soana valley, like the
whole Canavese district, belongs to Piedmont, is part of the diocese of Ivrea,
and shares in Italian language and civilization, Cogne is a dependency of the
duchy and the diocese of Aosta, whose historical links dating back several
centuries still attach it to French language and culture.[23] Between the
people from Cogne and the other worshippers of St Besse, therefore, there
is a profound mental divide; they are almost foreign to each other. This
distance is not attenuated, as it often is on frontiers, by frequent commercial
dealings. If economic relations were more active in the past between the
Cogne and the Soana valleys, today they are non-existent: the people of
Cogne only cross the mountain wall which bounds their basin to go to
Saint-Besse: they do not even bother to go as far as Campiglia.[24] So, at
the festival, they feel a little out of place and isolated; for fear of being made
the objects of ridicule, the women of Cogne do not wear their outland-
ish Sunday costume on that day; they do everything possible to remain
unnoticed.[25] One can understand consequently that the people from the
Soana valley should regard their associates from the other side of the
mountains as intruders. 'Let them come to pay their devotions at Saint-
Besse, if that is what they want, but let them do so as so many other pilgrims
do, on an individual basis; why should they claim to direct our festival, to
administer our shrine and to carry our saint? Do we, on our side, interfere
and want to lay down the law in the many holy places of which the diocese
of Aosta boasts?'

It is the people from Campiglia, above all, who nourish such thoughts.
And if they dream of rejecting Cogne from the community of Saint-Besse
altogether, it is perhaps because they hope thereby to remove the main
obstacle to their own pre-eminence or even to their exclusive domination
over the shrine. It is a fact that Campiglia enjoys special prestige in the
Soana valley, despite its small population;[26] it is said to be the oldest
settlement in the valley, and the first Christian parish through which all the
others were converted. What is more, since the people of Campiglia live in
close proximity to the shrine, they feel attached to the saint by the most
intimate of ties and they tend to regard him as their own special patron.
Many men from Campiglia are called Besse. It is true that when they
emigrate, which they frequently do, they appear to be rather embarrassed
by their patron, who does not figure in the official church calendar and
whose name is redolent of the sticks; they therefore take another,[27] as if to

mark their change of status, their uprooting. But, when they return home, they are more than happy to place themselves again under the protection of the saint, who is at once their personal patron and the guardian of their home country. Finally, by force of circumstance, the other parishes have been brought to entrust the care and upkeep of the shrine to the nearest church, and to have recourse to the latter also for the ornaments and accessories of the festival. And it is thus that the people of Campiglia have come to regard the chapel of the Mount as a simple dependency of their parish and to conceive the desire to convert the mortgage which they hold on Saint-Besse into complete and total possession.

But will they succeed? They have tried more than once in the past, and have met with effective opposition. The people of Cogne, the first in line, have seemed little disposed to give up the right which has come to them from their ancestors. Let us hear the testimony here of one of the heroes of those Homeric struggles, an old man of 77, who having for years been a mason, now looks after bees in his retirement. As I was showing him one day the photographs which I had taken of the shrine and of the festival, he said to me with a smile: 'Ah! Saint-Besse! I got a pretty knife-wound there once.' I was surprised. 'To explain that to you, I will have to take you very far back.' And he told me the legend of the saint, which, as we shall see, attributes to the people of Cogne an important role in the origin of the cult, thus establishing their right to take part in the festival. Then he arrived at times closer to our own, though still fairly indeterminate.

One year when it had become necessary to enlarge the chapel, the rector of Campiglia, in order to inspire his parishioners with a greater ardour for the task, promised them as a reward that from then on, in each procession, of the four bearers of the saint's statue, two should always come from Campiglia. The following year, it was Cogne's turn to run things. When the youths from Cogne who had been chosen to carry the statue tried to place it on their shoulders, those from Campiglia opposed them, citing the promise of their *curé*. A discussion ensued and soon hand-to-hand fighting broke out. The interior of the chapel was all confusion and tumult; people were pushing in all directions; it was like a cornfield in a thunderstorm. Already, some people had their knives out. The priests and the presidents finally calmed everything down; but, that year, the procession could not take place.

The following years, the Campiglia people lay low and the festival took its normal course; but when, five years later, Cogne's turn arrived again, we were absolutely determined to uphold our rights. So that year, eight well-built youths were picked to hold the bars of the statue; I was one of them. In the chapel, the rumpus began again and throughout the entire procession the Campiglia people subjected us to violent assaults; it was only with great difficulty that we prevented the statue from being overturned. During the attacks, the people of Ronco, Valprato and Ingria kept us going by shouting: 'Come on, people of Cogne; if you weaken, we are lost too.'[28] It was in the course of this battle that I received a knife-wound in the right thigh, which did not stop me from going right on to the end. When we arrived at last at the chapel door again, the people from Ronco, Valprato and Ingria commiserated with us, saying: 'Look at the poor people from Cogne! What a sweat they are in!'

Poor St Besse! Was it really worth his while to come to settle so high up and so far from humankind, in the mountain wastes, only to become mixed up in the petty riots of his worshippers? Should we pity him or congratulate him for having devotees so furious and so jealous in their zeal to serve him? At least we can admire the unyielding tenacity of the people of Cogne in their defence of 'the honour of their parish' and of the cultural patrimony which they held from their fathers.

That time, the resolute attitude of the lads from Cogne had the upper hand over the pretensions of the people of Campiglia. When the case was eventually put before the bishop of Ivrea, he decided, in order to satisfy to some extent the imprudent promise made by the *curé*, that the people from Campiglia could in future carry in the procession as many banners as they liked; but, as far as the *fouïaces* and the statue of the saint were concerned, they would continue to be carried by each parish in turn as was customary. This wise decision did not, however, end the debate. It appears that the people of Campiglia renewed their attempts to encroach on the rights of the others, for there were further battles during the festival, so that the government decided to send a few gendarmes there every year. Sobered by this intervention from outside and tired perhaps of the struggle, the devotees of the festival of St Besse decided a few years ago, 'for the sake of peace', to reform the ancient constitution which governed them. Henceforth, the bearers of the saint will not be nominated successively by the various parishes; the honourable function will be allocated every year to those willing to pay most for it, from which ever parish they may come. Thus, for ten or twenty francs according to the year, any man can buy his share in the sacred responsibility. This is a dangerous innovation, which may provide the treasury of the chapel with a new source of revenue, but which introduces a dissolving principle into the ancient community. And, of course, each year the men of Campiglia never fail to outbid their competitors, thus monopolizing all the bars of the precious statue: 'They are too proud', people say, 'to allow their St Besse to be carried by anyone else!'

One can foresee without being too rash in which direction the present trend will continue. The old local culture, which formed the natural atmosphere of the Saint-Besse festival, is already very much weakened; it will not long resist the invasion of townspeople and of modern ideas and habits. If the passions of old have died down, it is because people's faith has faltered. When the king is at Cogne for the ibex hunting, or when the weather is bad, the contingent which crosses the mountain from Cogne to go to Saint-Besse dwindles sometimes to the parish president alone.[29] The people from Campiglia could doubtless in time realize their dream; but, when they had become sole masters of the shrine, it would have lost much of its value. St Besse would no longer be in danger of receiving blows in the fray or of being knocked to the ground. People would no longer compete for the honour of bearing him; who knows whether anyone would still be prepared to bid for the job? The statue would have become very heavy for shoulders no longer fortified by faith. The 'Mount of Saint-Besse' would still offer the people of the valley a reason for an excursion on 10 August, where they would go to picnic and to dance without really knowing why.[30] All that would be left to the saint to do would be to emulate so many of his past devotees and to go to settle in the distant city: the cathedral of Ivrea has a place kept for him. But who would recognize the old dweller in the wild rock in this well-dressed townsman, lost in the crowd of official saints? The 'St Besse of the mountain' would no longer exist. He would not have long survived the old local organization, of which his shrine was the centre and which straddled in so bizarre a fashion natural barriers, political frontiers and the regular lines of church administration.

IV ST BESSE IN THE PLAIN

The name of St Besse is not among the most famous in the Christian world. Outside the district surrounding the shrine of Monte Fautenio, he is only known and honoured in the village of Ozegna and in the chief city of the diocese to which the Soana valley belongs, in Ivrea. This town flatters itself that it possesses the relics of the saint; for several centuries at least, a very popular cult has been devoted to him there,[31] and he has been raised to the dignity of 'co-patron of the diocese'. But this official cult and the local cult appear to be completely unconnected with each other: the festival of 'St Besse of the plain' takes place, not on 10 August, but on 1 December, at a time of the year when the 'St Besse of the mountain' would often have been prevented from receiving visitors by snow covering his shrine.[32]

The discordance between the dates of the festivals, the almost complete autonomy of the mountain cult, could lead one to suppose that we are here confronted by two different saints, with only their name in common. But it is very hard to admit that two saints called Besse should be found within so limited a territory, when there is no other in the entire Church; moreover, the ecclesiastical authorities of the diocese declare that the protector of the Soana valley and the co-patron of Ivrea are one and the same saint.[33] But of these two cults, the one urban and official, the other rural and slightly unorthodox, which gave birth to the other? Is St Besse a child of the mountains, whom the diocesan capital has adopted and magnified? Or rather, is he a big man from the town, who has not disdained to take up residence, for the benefit of a few rough mountain-dwellers, in a little chapel beneath a vast overhanging rock?

According to a most erudite and shrewd Italian historian, Father Savio, the cult of St Besse at Ivrea would appear to be the original and may be traced back to the first centuries of Christianity in Piedmont.[34] But this hypothesis, which rests solely on a reading of texts relating to Ivrea itself and which, as its author admits, cannot be positively supported by any direct evidence, seems hardly compatible with the present diffusion of the cult of St Besse.

If the propagation of the cult was effected, as Father Savio appears to admit, from the centre to the periphery of the diocese, why then has this spread occurred in one direction only? Why have the people of Ozegna and of the Soana valley, and they alone, adopted as a direct protector the glorious co-patron of the whole diocese? And above all, if the mountain community has borrowed its knowledge of St Besse from the diocesan capital of Ivrea, how is it that this cult has been established and perpetuated at Cogne, which, since the twelfth century at least, has belonged to the see of Aosta[35] and has no connection with Ivrea? These difficulties disappear, if one admits the inverse hypothesis, according to which the cult of St Besse originated in the mountains, and was spread first from Campiglia to Ozegna, and then from Ozegna to Ivrea. Now, this hypothesis has some foundation, according to a tradition, unknown at Cogne but very much alive in the Soana valley, and whose earliest literary expression dates back to the fifteenth century.[36]

This tradition relates that the body of St Besse had rested for many years in the little chapel built against the Mount, where the faithful from the district came to adore it. But, in the ninth century, pious robbers from Monferrato, resolved to lay hold of it and carry it back to their own country.[37] They put the precious remains in a sack, which they loaded onto a mule. When they arrived at Ozegna, where they had to spend the night, they told the innkeeper, so as not to arouse his suspicions, that their sack only contained lard[38] and they put it in a corner of the room. But while they were asleep, the innkeeper, passing by the room, noticed that it was all lit up. Looking for the cause of this mysterious light, he opened the sack and saw the bodily remains. He was persuaded that these must be the relics of a great saint, and, deciding to keep them for his own village, he put them in a safe place and filled the sack instead with some old bones taken from the cemetery. It is not known what happened to the Monferrato robbers, who were themselves robbed; but the mule returned straight away to the shrine on the Mount.[39] The inn which housed the relics was transformed into a chapel, from which the present church at Ozegna, still dedicated to St Besse, derives. For a long time, the sacred body remained in this spot, attracting the devotion of the people of the Canavese district and working many miracles. But at the beginning of the eleventh century, Ardoino, King of Italy, wanted to enrich the cathedral of Ivrea with this treasure and ordered it to be transported there with great pomp.[40] The journey was not without incident. According to my informants in the Soana valley, who are doubtless echoing the tradition as maintained at Ozegna, as it left the village, the waggon carrying the relics would not move forward; to get it to continue on its way, one of the saint's little fingers had to be cut off, and this has stayed at Ozegna. According to Baldesano, who himself gleaned the story from oral tradition in Ivrea, before it reached its destination, and just as it was crossing the bridge over the Dora, the sacred body halted its vehicle again; the citizens of Ivrea had to solemnly vow to place it in a crypt below the main altar of the cathedral. As soon as they had done so, the extraordinary weight which the relics had acquired was lightened, and St Besse took possession of his new domain.

The learned Bollandist, who relates this story, following Baldesano, severely chides the poor canon for having so willingly accepted these wretched popular traditions, 'populares traditiunculas':[41] how could he not have perceived their historical improbability, their immorality and the 'odious consequences' that followed from them? For the substitution by which Providence so poorly rewarded the zeal of the pious robbers must have meant that in Monferrato some people had been induced to adore as holy relics what were just ordinary human remains. These scruples of an enlightened conscience could not be more foreign to the legendary hagiography of the Middle Ages, to which our story belongs. Nothing is more common in this literature than the theme of the theft of relics[42] or the episode of a translation interrupted by a prodigious resistance put up by the holy corpse itself.[43] The intervention of King Ardoino is scarcely likely to enhance the credit of this collection of commonplaces. Some Italian historians of our time still like to salute as 'a champion of Latin independence against German tyranny', this restless marquis whom the Italian counts twice invested with a precarious kingdom in order to check the imperial power, and who was twice excommunicated as a 'killer of bishops'. With all the more reason has legend taken hold of this Piedmontese Charlemagne to make a national hero of him and to attribute to him the honour for everything in the region which is beautiful, great or sacred.[44] The city of Ivrea, which thanks to him was promoted in the first years of the eleventh century to the rank of the capital of Italy, is only repaying a debt of gratitude in tracing back to Ardoino the origin of the cult which it has vowed to St Besse.[45]

But it would be an abuse of the critical method to refuse to recognize the basic reality hidden beneath these inconsistent fictions. Generally speaking, the familiar stories about the 'invention' or the 'translation' of relics prove nothing by themselves about the authenticity or even the existence of the relics in question; but they do inform us very exactly about the location and the mutual inter-dependence of the cult centres. In this sphere, the imagination of the makers of legends does not have the free scope which it enjoys in connection with mythical or distant events; for it is subject, here, to inescapable facts in the present and, above all, to the jealous control of local passions and susceptibilities. If the townspeople could have made St Besse's peasant and mountain worshippers believe that the object of their crude devotion had been borrowed from the city, they would surely not have failed to do so. Since this was impossible, they were content to claim for their cathedral possession of the holy body, leaving Ozegna with only the consolation of a little finger and the shrine in the Soana valley with the honour of having originally housed the relics of the saint. The mountain herdsmen, for their part, were in no position to protest against such a share-out, which, if it deprived them of the mortal remains of their protector, cast them at least in an essential role in the establishment of the sacred treasure of the diocese.

Perhaps it will appear surprising that a religious centre as important as Ivrea should have been reduced to going to look so far away and so late in the day for the relics which it required; but the case of St Besse is not here exceptional. None of the three patrons, who especially protect the city and the diocese of Ivrea and whose relics are kept in the cathedral, is a native saint; each one of these three sacred bodies, according to the ecclesiastical tradition, has been imported from outside at a relatively recent date. The body of St Tegulus remained unnoticed until the end of the tenth century, when, they say, it was discovered by the bishop, St Veremund, at a place situated some distance to the north of Ivrea and moved into the cathedral a little before that of St Besse.[46] As for St Sabinus, former bishop of Spoleto, his relics were only brought to Ivrea towards the middle of the tenth century, at a time when there were very close relations between the dukes of Spoleto and the marquises of Ivrea.[47] If political reasons led the people of Ivrea to adopt a foreign bishop as their main patron, it seems probable that similar considerations may not have been absent from their choice of St Besse as their 'co-patron'.

The political horizon of Ivrea in the Middle Ages was strictly hemmed in, on the one side by the mountain wall of the Alps and, on the other, by a circle of powerful neighbours, Vercelli, Monferrato and the county of Savoy. Only the Canavese district, a rich agricultural region extending to the west as far as the mountains, could offer Ivrea the complementary resources and the power base which it so desperately needed. So the dominant preoccupation of the politics of Ivrea from the eleventh to the fourteenth century was always to extend its influence over the Canavese, to fend off rival claims, by war if need be, and to pacify the incessant quarrelling of the local nobility so as to unite them in a federation under the hegemony of the city. In addition, the bishops of Ivrea carved out properties for themselves in the labyrinth of fiefs and sub-fiefs that existed in the Canavese, and used these to extend their influence in the district.[48] It is thus that we see in a charter of 15 September 1094 that Count Hubert of the Canavese makes a gift to Bishop Ogier and to the canons of Saint-Mary of Ivrea of several estates that belong to him, and in particular of that of Ozegna.[49] At a time when religion and politics were intimately linked, when the principal temporal power in the territory of Ivrea was that of the bishop,[50] when the ties of religious community were the most effective social links, Ivrea could not have demonstrated more clearly its wish to annex the Canavese than by according a place of honour in its cathedral to the saint whom the people of the area venerated with a fervent devotion and whose shrine was situated in the bishop's territory. It is very likely that the naturalization of St Besse at Ivrea took place at this time: it prefigured and prepared for that solemn undertaking of 15 March 1213, by which the counts of the Canavese became citizens of Ivrea in perpetuity and promised to defend the cause of the city both in peace and in war.[51]

But, in order to play a role in the politics of Ivrea, St Besse would first have had to descend from his mountain and establish himself in the Canavese. He could not have chosen a better place than Ozegna. This large village, as described by Casalis, is situated in the middle of fertile country, where trade is important; it is surrounded by an almost continuous ring of other villages and small towns; it controls a bridge over the Orco, which is of capital importance for the traffic of a vast region; finally, it is located at the junction of three main roads, which lead, one to Ivrea, another to Vercelli and Monferrato, and the third to Turin.[52] Crossroads, which are the nexus, one might say, of social circulation, have always been an intense focus of religious life. Now, among the human currents which intersected at Ozegna, there was one which issued forth every autumn from the little closed valley of the Soana on its way towards the industrial centres of Monferrato and Vercelli.[53] On this first stage of their migration, still full of St Besse, the mountain-dwellers must have taught his name, his power and his benefits to those who gave them shelter. As often happens, in the struggle for supremacy, it is the roughest and strangest god who triumphs over his more orderly but less interesting rivals. And it was thus, as the tradition rightly says, that the old inn of Ozegna was set apart for the cult of St Besse.[54] By dint of giving hospitality to the emigrants from the mountain, the peasantry of the Canavese had appropriated their patron saint.

Thus, the hypothesis, according to which the St Besse of the mountain came to Ivrea via Ozegna fits in with the present pattern of the diffusion of the cult, with the testimony of the tradition, and with historical fact. The chapel in the Alpine pastures, the church in the rich countryside of the plain, the cathedral in the city, these three abodes of St Besse mark the successive stages of a development which has not allowed him to remain confined to an obscure little valley, but has brought him out to occupy a modest but honourable place in the regular company of saints.

V THE LEGEND OF ST BESSE

We have been able to describe the devotion to St Besse and the organization of his cult almost without reference to the legend which justifies it; so true is it that religious practice is, in large measure, independent of the reasons which are supposed to underlie it. Not that these reasons are not available to the faithful: they are abundantly furnished with them both by the teaching of the Church and by popular tradition.

In the official legend of the diocese,[55] St Besse is presented to us as a martyr who 'ennobled the region with his precious blood' after having had to suffer tortures of extraordinary cruelty. He was a soldier of the Theban Legion, which was massacred in 286 on the orders of the Emperor Maximian. Having managed to escape, Besse sought refuge in the mountains of the Soana valley. It was from there that he instructed the inhabitants of the valley in the faith, and particularly the people of Campiglia, who were the first to accept the salutary influence of the Gospel. But the pagan soldiery, avid for Christian blood and anxious to satisfy their Emperor, had set off in pursuit of St Besse and eventually found him among the rocks of Monte Fautenio.[56] This is how they came to discover him. Some mountain herdsmen had cooked a lamb which they had stolen from their master's flock; having come across Besse in the area, they invited him to share in their feast. But he refused to eat a lamb which he knew had been stolen and he began to tell them off in no uncertain terms for their reprehensible action. Afraid of being reported to their master, or simply angered by his reprimand, or rather perhaps moved by hatred for the Christian faith which he was not ashamed to confess,[57] the herdsmen threw the apostle off a high rock. The saint, however, was not killed by his terrible fall.[58] While all this was going on, the soldiers who were pursuing St Besse arrived on the scene. They recognized Besse and, having made sure that he was still obstinate in his confession of the faith of Christ, they brutally stabbed him to death. Some people claim, the narrator adds with some disdain, that, after having been thrown from the rock, Besse managed to leave the Soana valley and went to live for a while in the mountains closer to the Dora Baltea, that is to say in the direction of Cogne; and that the martyrdom took place there.[59] What is certain in any case is that the faithful, and especially those from Campiglia, through devotion towards the glorious martyr, gathered up his remains and buried them in a hole in a rock; it was over this tomb that the little chapel was erected, which, after many transformations, still exists and which is visited by many pilgrims on 10 August each year.[60]

Such was the glorious career of St Besse, as it is told from the pulpit by the *curés* and as one can, it seems, 'read it in the books'. It would be astonishing if this legend, legitimized by the Church and by the printed word, should not have had some impact on the faithful. In fact, it seems to have been unanimously accepted in the Soana valley, which is placed, we have seen, under the direct authority of the city of Ivrea.[61] But things are not the same at Cogne; for this parish is free from the influence of Ivrea, and the ecclesiastical authorities of Aosta are doubtless not particularly interested in a saint who does not come within their competence. Only a very few people from Cogne can give a more or less accurate account of the official legend, and they do so with difficulty like schoolchildren reciting a set lesson which they have barely understood. Moreover, the legend as they tell it has certain variants. All of them make the saint die from his fall off the Mount; the pagan soldiery do not need to intervene. In addition, it is before he went to live on the heights above the Soana valley that Besse resided at Cogne. Finally, people do not know what happened to his body, nor do they seem to care.

These changes or corrections bring the official legend closer to the popular tradition which is much more widespread among the simple faithful of Cogne. According to this, St Besse was a herdsman who took his sheep to pasture around the Mount. He remained all the time at the top of the rock. He was a very holy man, a true man of God; the only work he did was to pray.[62] Moreover, his sheep were the fattest to be seen and they all stayed grouped around him, so that he never had to chase after them. Two other shepherds from the same mountain could not stand the fact that Besse's sheep looked after themselves and were always the finest ones, so they threw him down from the top of the Mount.[63] A few months later – it was in the middle of winter, near Christmas – some people from Cogne passed by the place and they noticed at the foot of the rock a flower of marvellous beauty and brilliance, growing out well above the snow. Surprised by a sight so unusual for the season, they went to fetch others. When the snow had been removed from the place marked by the miraculous flower, the corpse of the saint was discovered, intact! In falling, the body had been imprinted on the rock, at the very place where people still go to find the stones of St Besse. It is for that reason that a chapel was built in the place and that people go to pay their devotions every year. Cogne has the right to the festival, because it was the people from Cogne who first discovered the body of the saint.

Such is the notion which nearly all the people of Cogne still have today of

the life and death of St Besse, despite sermons and pious brochures to the
contrary. If one points out to them that their version does not agree with
the teaching of the Church, most seem troubled and do not know what to
say. If one insists, if one asks them why, on the images and medals which
they all have in their possession, this herdsman is shown in the guise of a
warrior, either they answer that they don't know or they say: 'That's true;
he was still a young man . . . ; he had done his military service.' They seem,
in general, to be totally unconcerned by the discordance which exists
between the form of the saint, as the Church presents it to them, and the
representation given to him by the local tradition. A few of them, however,
more worried by considerations of logic, have found a way of reconciling
the two rival images: when the Christian soldier, fleeing from his persecutors, took refuge above Campiglia, he 'became a herdsman' and began
keeping sheep. Thanks to this metamorphosis, the legendary hero can
become someone else while remaining himself – an easy procedure, which
costs little, and to which the popular imagination never hesitates to have
recourse in order to adjust one incongruous element to another. But,
whether linked or not to the local legend, the image, represented in pictures
and statues, lives its own life and reacts back on the devotion. By dint of
seeing St Besse the herdsman dressed as a soldier, many people from Cogne
have come to believe that he must have a particular interest in the affairs of
soldiers in the field – or defaulting conscripts.

It is not surprising that the people from Cogne should have remained so
obstinately attached to the popular legend of St Besse: they are at home in
it, all mountain-dwellers together, while they feel out of place and
constrained in the context of the Emperor Maximian, the Theban Legion
and the glorious martyr. They feel respect, but little sympathy, for a tale in
which the best part is played by a foreigner, who has come from the plain to
instruct and moralize them, and in which herdsmen are portrayed as
miscreants, robbers and murderers. How much more attractive is the other
St Besse: a simple local boy, the best shepherd of the finest flock that has
ever been seen on the mountains! What strong and varied emotions are
aroused by the different tableaux of which the legend is composed! There is
first of all the idyllic and charming image of the herdsman constantly at
prayer, surrounded by his blessed flock. Then follows the sombre drama,
the foul deed of the other envious herdsmen, the pitiful end of poor Besse.
But what pride and delight when it is *our own folk* who discover the
marvellous flower! And what joyful confidence must lie in being able to tell
oneself that the divine herdsman, in falling, was as if compounded with the
rock, to rest there, eternally present in the midst of his protégés; for the first
miracle is the foundation and the guarantee of all those which the saint
accomplishes daily or that people hope that his power will perform. The
official legend teaches the faithful the origins of their faith; it reminds them

of some of the duties of a good Christian, and that they should not wrong their masters or murmur against their *curés*. Useful lessons, of course, but which have the drawback of being lessons! The other legend, *theirs*, takes hold of their being and transports them into a world that is at once familiar and sublime, where they find themselves again, but transfigured and made noble.

Of these two traditions, the one learned and edifying, the other naïve and poetic, the older is certainly the second. The first, in effect, brings us no original information about St Besse: that part of the story which refers to him personally consists of generalities so poor and so banal that they could just as well apply to a host of other saints.[64] St Besse is really for the Church only a unit in a legion; his only individuality resides in his name. The only features contained in the official legend that have anything special about them have been borrowed from the oral tradition, though even then they have been touched up; the local image of the saint, having been reflected through the minds of the literate clergy, returns to its point of departure, corrected and deformed.[65]

Let us recall the single theme that the popular tradition develops: a holy herdsman is thrown by envious rivals from the top of a rock to which he imparts his sacred quality. This theme appears in the other legend, but in a different place and under a different guise. First, it has seemed out of the question to the authors of the new version that Besse should be placed on the same level as his executioners and that he should only surpass them by the beauty and the docility of his flock. For the people of Cogne, sanctity is a singular power which comes from intimate communion with the divine world and which is manifested in temporal effects. For the clergy of Ivrea, sanctity is a spiritual and moral virtue which presupposes a religious qualification of a definite kind. The inefficient and envious herdsmen became hardened sinners, in rebellion against their spiritual director; the exemplary herdsman became a victim of the duty incumbent professionally on all ministers of religion. In the second place, St Besse could not die from his fall, because his death had to be an authentic martyrdom, in order to have its full sanctifying quality. The fall from the top of the Mount thus becomes a simple episode, which explains, though how is not quite clear, that the pagan soldiers were able to lay their hands on their victim. Finally, in the learned legend, the rock from whose height the saint is thrown is not the Mount of Saint-Besse; it is just some rock or other; the chapel where the festival of 10 August is celebrated was built near another rock, in a hole inside which the body of the martyr had been placed. In effect, for the Church, the only sanctity which does not emanate directly from God, proceeds from the remains of persons who have perfectly realized the Christian ideal; the Mount could only be regarded as sacred on condition that it had served, at least for a time, as the burial-place of a martyr. What is more, the official legend has its eye always on Ivrea, and not on Cogne or on Campiglia. It wishes, above all, to exalt the glorious 'co-patron' of the diocese and to justify the cult which the diocesan capital renders the relics kept in the cathedral. This being so, it became necessary to detach the sanctity from the Mount and to concentrate it in the body of the saint; for the rock remains eternally fixed in the same place, but the body, real or supposed, is mobile and can very well serve as the vehicle for the same beneficial energy, should the powers that be decide one day to 'enrich' their sacred treasury with it. All the interest of the people of Cogne is concentrated by contrast on the Mount; once the body of Besse, in imprinting itself on the rock had impregnated it with its own properties, that body could disappear without causing any trouble. It is the rock, henceforth, which is the real body of the saint: is it not the rock which inexhaustibly dispenses to the faithful those saving 'relics', the stones of St Besse?

Thus, just as the pious robbers, it seems, stole the body of the saint and brought it down to the plain, so too the pious arrangers have transformed a simple shepherd into a Theban legionary and they have imputed his death, not to envious comrades, but to Caesar's pagan soldiers. Should we then severely condemn them for having done violence to the local traditions upon which they worked and for having substituted a 'fiction' which suited them better for the 'true' image of the saint? This would be a very unreasonable application of the rules of historical criticism. The people of Ivrea have not subjected St Besse to treatment any different from that to which we still subject the mountain-dwellers who are attracted to the cities; in adopting him as their 'co-patron', they imposed on him the dress and the characteristics that seemed to them decent. If it is true that words change their meaning when they pass from the countryside to the town,[66] why should not the name of St Besse take on a new, more abstract, more conventional significance in the mouths of his new devotees? The popular tradition is no more and no less 'true' than the other. From the moment that all the essential elements of the cult find themselves transposed to an ideological level which suits the intelligence and the emotions of the believers, it does not matter that the two legends contradict each other or diverge; they are equally legitimate for the different milieux which accept them.

The story of this Theban Legion is both curious and very instructive, for the cult, which originated at Saint-Maurice-en-Valais, was propagated along the roads which come down from the Alps, into Switzerland, into the Rhineland, into Burgundy, into Savoy, into Dauphiné and into Italy. St Eucherius, who is writing about one hundred and fifty years after the terrible massacre is supposed to have taken place, only gives the names of four of the martyrs; but he affirms that the 6,600 Christian soldiers who

comprised the legion all perished in the fields of Agaunum, save perhaps
for two of them, Ursus and Victor, who were martyred instead at
Soleure.[67] Eleven centuries later, Baldesano, who was apparently much
better informed, could reproach St Eucherius for having appeared too
reserved or too stingy in exploiting the blood of the Thebans. At the
summons of the canon of Piedmont, a whole host of little saints, all dressed
as legionaries – and among them our St Besse – sprang up in the depths
of the Alpine valleys and in the Italian countryside and claimed to be
parading under the banner of St Maurice, the glorious patron of the House
of Savoy. Perhaps, had his faith been less robust, Baldesano might have
been worried by this multitude of heroes whom he had called forth.[68] At
the end of the day, the Thebans, who were reputed to have escaped the
collective massacre in order to be able to suffer martyrdom individually in
places very far away, had come perhaps to exceed in numbers the total
complement of the legion as St Eucherius defined it.[69] It is true that a little
erudition can be adduced to dissipate this scruple. It is possible to call in as
reinforcements the two Theban Legions which St Eucherius does not
discuss, but which are known to the *notitia dignitatum* (the Imperial list of
civil and military offices): the Thebans, who enlightened so many parishes
with their evangelism as well as sanctifying them with their blood, really
belonged to *three* legions, all of which were Christian, and all of which were
persecuted by pagan emperors.[70] But, when one considers that each one of
these apostles was pursued by 'Caesar's soldiers', one is alarmed to think
that the main occupation of the Roman armies, towards the beginning of the
fourth century, must have been hunting for Thebans dispersed
throughout the valleys of the Rhône and the Rhine and in every fold of the
Italian Alps. Beyond this, inspection of the roster of the Legion produces
some surprising findings. Several names figure there very many times;[71]
and, what is more, most of the Thebans do not have individual and
personal names; they are called after their attributes or their functions.[72] So
one finds there men called Candidus, or Exuperius, or Victor, or Adventor,
or Solutor, or even those with the name Defender who protect their
devotees against avalanches and floods.[73] It appears that the Theban
Legion is a legion of local gods and personified epithets.[74]

Moreover, the period of expansion and luxuriant multiplication for the
companions of St Maurice was followed by a period of retrenchment and
brutal cut-backs. A first decimation occurred in the middle of the
eighteenth century, when the Bollandist, Father Cleus, declared his strong
suspicion that many of the presumed Theban martyrs had usurped their
titles.[75] But the nineteenth century was to prove itself even more cruel. A
Catholic historian reduced the Legion of St Maurice to the limited
dimensions of a *vexillatio* or a miserable auxiliary cohort.[76] In vain a
German doctor tried to save the four martyrs whom St Eucherius named

personally;[77] this last handful of survivors was attacked in its turn[78] and Father Delehaye sees no reason not to relegate the Passion of the Martyrs of Agaunum to the category of 'historical novels'![79]

St Besse was one of the first victims of this new massacre of the Theban Legion. Already, Father Cleus, having dubbed the account of Baldesano 'an eminently fabulous history', expressed the view that, for lack of ancient and certain evidence, one should agree to remove the name of St Besse from the list of military martyrs.[80] The only response which came from Ivrea was to cite a legend from a manuscript breviary, preserved in the archives of the cathedral and dated 1473.[81] It is not very likely that this document, coming more than a millennium after the events which it describes, would satisfy the requirements of the Bollandists[82] and persuade them to go back on their declared intention, made known in 1875, to present St Besse in the Acts of the saints of December, not as a Theban martyr, but indeed as a bishop of Ivrea.[83]

If St Besse really was the predecessor of St Veremund and the poet Ogier, then it must be admitted that the mountain people of Cogne and of the Soana valley have altered his true features in the most remarkable way. But Father Savio has no difficulty in demonstrating that the historical identification proposed by the eighteenth-century Bollandist, and provisionally maintained by his successors, rests on no serious foundations.[84] It is true that Ughelli, in his *Italia sacra*, having related that the cathedral of Ivrea possesses the relics of 'the glorious martyr St Besse', then includes in the series of bishops of the diocese, for around the year 170, a certain Bessus 'whom F. Bergomense mentions in his chronicle calling him a saint'.[85] However, this chronicler, in his book published in 1485, tells us only that 'the inhabitants of Ivrea hold in great veneration the relics of St Besse, a bishop of their city'.[86] One must agree with Father Savio that this late and imprecise testimony, which contains no chronological indication, in no way proves the existence of a bishop of the Church of Ivrea called Besse, at a period quite arbitrarily chosen by Ughelli, and on which we possess no historical information.[87] The only conclusion which may be drawn from the text of Filippo Bergomense is that in 1485 – that is to say twelve years after the first known compilation of the legend of St Besse, the Theban martyr[88] – the adopted co-patron, who had arrived two or three centuries earlier from one of the episcopal estates, was regarded at Ivrea, at least by some of the faithful, as a former bishop of the city. This version which doubtless flattered the civic pride of the people of Ivrea, remained current until the eighteenth century, when we see Canon Dejordanis place side by side in the inventory of the relics of the cathedral 'the body of St Besse, third bishop of Ivrea and confessor' and 'the body of St Besse, martyr of the Theban Legion'.[89] A strange duplication, when one considers that the church of Ivrea has only ever honoured one St Besse, whose festival falls on 1 December. But the legend of the Theban martyr was soon to impose itself generally; and, when in 1591 the glorious leader of the Legion, represented by part of his relics, emigrated in great pomp from the abbey of Saint-Maurice to the cathedral of Turin, he found to welcome him at the doors of the church of Ivrea two of his former soldiers, Besse and Tegulus, in the form of two painted panels.[90] Today, thanks in part to Baldesano's book, the image of St Besse, the Theban martyr, has so completely supplanted that of St Besse, bishop of Ivrea, that the faithful of the diocese would doubtless be left unmoved were they to see their co-patron disappear from an expurgated list of their former bishops.

The adventure of St Besse is not encouraging for the mountain herdsmen who might be tempted by the honours of the plain. Having enticed him into their midst, the townsmen have dressed him up to suit their tastes, without even being able to agree among themselves: for some of them have put a bishop's crook in his hands, and others the legionaries' sword and the martyrs' palm. When the latter had succeeded in winning acceptance for their preference, yet other citizens arrived, who, like the envious herdsmen of the legend, cast down the saint from the glorious pedestal on which he had been perched. And now after so many transformations, the historical personality of St Besse seems very pro-blematical and very uncertain, since even in the small society of his earliest devotees, two disparate traditions have been able to survive down to our own time. Neither of these tell us anything about the real identity of the hero which they have in common; but both shed a sharp light on the habits of thought and on the psychology of the profoundly different social groups in which they were elaborated.

In the small closed circle of his native land, St Besse is a herdsman, closely related to the abrupt rock which dominates the high pastures, themselves the basis of the district's wealth. Surrounded by his fat and docile sheep, he fully exemplifies the idea which the mountain-dweller still possesses today of what constitutes terrestrial goodness and happiness: a faithful shepherd, who puts all his trust in God and whose beasts, as a result, 'look after themselves'. But, when St Besse emigrates to Ivrea, among the learned canons of the cathedral, he has to transform himself radically in order to continue to incarnate the ideal of his worshippers. He becomes, on the one hand, a soldier, fighting in his place in a holy militia, under the orders of a powerful leader; and he is, on the other hand, an apostle who faces the worst sufferings and death for the defence, the propagation and the glory of his faith. The divergence and the mutual im-perviousness of the two legends of St Besse reflect the huge distance, moral and cultural more than physical, which separates Cogne from Ivrea even today. Here, we have a small community of rough and simple mountain people, devoted to their livestock and persuaded that the highest virtue consists in abandoning oneself completely to God's care; there, a circle of churchmen, nourished on a culture of books, more erudite perhaps than discerning, but very keen to enlighten the illiterate villagers and to moralize, actuated, moreover, by priestly duty and by a centralizing urge.

VI THE GENESIS OF ST BESSE

The local cult of St Besse poses three distinct problems for the historian. First, how is one to explain the special organization of the community grouped around the shrine and, in particular, the participation of Cogne in a festival of the Soana valley? Secondly, why is the cult centred on a steep rock on the mountain with which the name of Besse is connected? And thirdly, where does the belief in a mysterious and protective power, radiating from the shrine over the whole district, stem from? Each of the two legends which are current among the mountain people offers a different solution to these problems, which are equally satisfactory to the faithful to whom they address themselves. But we, who inhabit a different spiritual atmosphere, cannot rest content with either of these traditional 'explanations'. Is it possible to conceive of a third explanation which would account for the same facts without introducing elements other than those supposed to operate in history, according to the received scholarly opinion of today? This is what we shall try to do for each of the three problems which we have outlined.

We have seen that the organization of the cult of St Besse runs counter to, or ignores, the regular ecclesiastical divisions, since it straddles two dioceses. Among the five parishes which have the right to the festival, there is one which enjoys a kind of primacy which it aspires to convert into an exclusive domination; the other four are in a subordinate or precarious position: this is the case, especially, for Cogne, whose participation in the festival is regarded as an intrusion by the people from Campiglia and appears indeed to be paradoxical. One is tempted to try to figure out this very odd organization by supposing that St Besse must once have been the patron of a single community, established not far from his shrine, which later split up into several segments; the latter, having become independent, would have continued to participate in the cult of their old protector, with differences in their rank or status corresponding to their distance, greater or lesser, from the centre of the cult. This hypothesis is verified as far as Valprato, Ronco and Ingria are concerned; for we know positively that the parish of Campiglia gave birth to the other three parishes of the Soana valley in a series of successive dismemberments,[91] as the population of the valley became less exclusively pastoral and as the centre of its economic life tended to draw closer to the plain. But how can one accept any link based on dependence or on common origin between the population of Cogne and that of Campiglia, when we see them separated the one from the other by a thick wall of mountains and by a yet more formidable psychological frontier?

But, as geographers know well, it is a serious mistake to imagine that mountains are always and everywhere barriers between peoples, made to divide rather than to unite, while valleys remain necessarily the easiest and the oldest means of communication. Downstream from Cogne, the valley contracts and becomes a narrow gorge with precipitous sides; when a road had not yet been cleared through this defile, or when it had fallen into disrepair, it was infinitely more trouble to penetrate the Cogne basin by going straight up the Aosta valley than by crossing the cols from the Soana valley on the other side. The earliest inhabitants of Cogne certainly took this latter route, if a tradition is to be believed that is still alive and unanimously accepted in the district: everyone agrees that their ancestors came into the valley from above, coming from the Canavese. For a long time, it is said, the herdsmen of Campiglia confined themselves to taking their animals to graze in the rich pastures of Ciavanassa on the other side of the mountain in the summer only. But, one day, they decided to winter there, and founded the village of Cogne on the bastion of Piana Cresta (see Map 1), situated some kilometres up the valley from its present site and, thus, much closer to Saint-Besse. It was only after many years that the little colony from Campiglia moved down into the meadows of Saint-Ours where the chief settlement of the valley is now placed. But it took a long time for the new swarm to detach itself completely from the mother-hive and to lead a life of its own. Cogne was at first only a 'fraction' of a parish, a simple hamlet, without church or cemetery: the living, in order to pray, went up on the mountains from where they could hear the sound of their dear bells, while the dead, for their long sleep, returned to the consecrated ground where they had left their ancestors. More material links continued to attach the people of Cogne to their distant home: all their economic relations were with the Canavese; can one not still be shown at Cuorgnè, a small town in Piedmont, the 'Cogne market', that is to say the square where the people from Cogne came to sell their cheeses? There is every reason to regard this tradition as the legendary expression of historical facts; for it is confirmed by several indications which seem conclusive,[92] and it is certainly the case that from the point of view of physical type, of customs and of costume, the inhabitants of Cogne stand out among the people of the Aosta valley as a completely isolated island.[93]

But, as time went by, the frontiers between human groupings tended to be displaced and to become identical with the watershed line. When roads were cleared or re-established along the valley, the economic and religious life of Cogne became oriented more and more in the same direction as its river. A new population from Savoy, attracted by the fine pastures and by

the iron mines, came to be mixed with the old inhabitants who had come
from the Soana valley. While Campiglia came more and more under the
influence of Piedmont and was drawn into the orbit of Ivrea, Cogne
became a direct dependency of the bishopric of Aosta;[94] so much so that
soon there remained nothing of the moral or temporal ties which had for so
long bound the ancient emigrants to their former home. However, one
single link remained that nothing until now has been able to break – not
the length and the difficulty of the journey, not the attraction of new
sanctuaries more brilliant and easier of access, not even the hostility of the
people of Campiglia, treating as intruders their kinsmen from across the
mountains. This link, which stretched but never snapped, is the religious
one, the fidelity of the people of Cogne to their old patron.

St Besse must have had an extraordinary power of attraction and
cohesion to hold in check the centrifugal forces that were tending to break
up the little community of his worshippers. What then is the real nature of
this focus of so intense and so persistent a devotion?

We have seen that the legends, popular and semi-learned, of St Besse are
mainly intended to account for the mysterious quality attributed to the
Mount: they both seek, via different symbols, to introduce the sanctity of a
holy man, more or less intimately, into the heart and substance of the rough
stone. The real basis of the cult, even today, is the belief in the sacred
character of the rock, around which the cult gravitates. Is it not likely that,
in very ancient times, this fundamental belief was still free of the layers of
representation that have come successively to cover it over and that it stood
out clearly and directly in the consciousness of the faithful? It is certain that
the ancient inhabitants of a great part of Europe practised rock cults;[95] it is
probable that they practised them, as so many primitive peoples still do, in
complete good faith, without feeling the need to justify themselves in their
own eyes, and without seeking at all costs to make the power of the rock
which they venerated issue from the ideal perfection of a holy man. It
would be easy to produce a crowd of examples taken from simpler societies
in order to support such a conjecture.[96] But there is no need to look in the
Antipodes for what we can find close at hand without even leaving French
territory. In 1877, Messieurs Piette and Sacaze were able to observe, almost
intact, in the far Pyrenean valley of the Larboust, this cult of rocks against
which several church councils fulminated from the fifth to the seventh
centuries; these writers listened to 'respectable old men' expressing with
feeling their 'great faith' in the sacred stones, which the people of the valley
went to 'touch' with all reverence in order to obtain fertility for their fields
and for themselves. Here, the rocks are still the immediate and the avowed
objects of devotion; or, if people feel the need to represent their power in
concrete form, they do so in the guise of special spirits, 'half angels, half
serpents, inhabiting the sacred rocks'. According to Messieurs Piette and

Sacaze, the priests of the Larboust valley were rigorously combating this persistent paganism, as the Council of Nantes in 658 already prescribed; they had the sacred stones destroyed secretly and scattered the smallest fragments far away, thus running the risk of provoking disturbances among their parishioners who were scandalized by such sacrilege.[97] In general, and particularly in the Alpine region, the Church has adopted a less rigorous attitude towards the 'worshippers of stones': it has not razed to the ground the sacred rocks, but has simply placed crosses on top of them, flanked them with little chapels and associated them in one way or another with Christian belief and practice.[98]

If we were able to compare at leisure the cult of St Besse with that of the many other saints of the region, male and female, who are adored and celebrated in the immediate neighbourhood of a rock, we would find, on the one hand, an astonishing uniformity in the ritual practice and in the elementary representations which it implies, and, on the other hand, an almost infinite diversity in the legends which are supposed to explain the existence of the cult and to define the sacred being to whom it is addressed. So many shrines, so many different justifications for a devotion which is always and everywhere the same. Here are employed the themes, familiar to us, of a mortal fall or of a burial-place; but, elsewhere, a holy bishop, finding the gates of Ivrea closed one evening, went to sleep on a rock, leaving the imprint of his body on it for ever.[99] This stone is sacred because the Theban Valerian made it his oratory and left the mark of his knees on it,[100] while that one is sacred because the Theban Solutor was martyred there and sprinkled it with his blood.[101] If rocks are the goals of the two most frequented pilgrimages of Piedmont, it is because St Eusebius once hid his miraculous Black Madonna at one,[102] while at the other a pious local woman at the start of the eighteenth century hollowed out a niche in which she placed a statue of the Blessed Virgin.[103] But how can one accept that 'causes' so particular and so contingent could have produced an effect so general and so constant? How can one see in these 'explanations' anything but superficial and variable translations of the ancient fundamental belief which saw in certain rocks the seat and focus of a divine power?[104]

Perhaps some readers will reproach us, not with this conclusion, which will seem to them only too obvious, but with the roundabout ways which we have followed to arrive at it. Since history is silent about St Besse; since the legends, which are thin, recent and contradictory, have no documentary value; since, finally, the only certain information which we possess about St Besse is his name, why not, from the outset, seek in the name the revelation of the true identity of the supposed Theban martyr? Certainly, such a method would have been more direct and more rapid; but would it have been more certain? So many elaborate constructions, founded on resemblances between names, have lamentably collapsed, so many 'erudite legends' have gone to join the popular ones that they were meant to replace, that one must be bold indeed to base a religious theory on the etymology of a sacred name.[105] However, at the end of this study, we do not wish to take prudence to the length of evading the enigma of the name Besse, when this mysterious name is an essential element of the cult of which we are trying to give an account. But let it be clear at the start that our etymological hypothesis adds nothing to the force of our other conclusions, from which, on the contrary, it derives any value which it may have.

The name Besse[106] is found fairly frequently either as a family name or as a place-name in central and southern France, in Switzerland and in Italy. But as a first name it is extremely uncommon. In Antiquity, it occurs only very occasionally in inscriptions of Illyrian provenance.[107] In the Middle Ages, it appears that 'Bessus' was sometimes used as a diminutive for Bertericus.[108] But what is certain is that outside the diocese of Ivrea, Besse does not exist as a baptismal Christian name and that even inside the diocese, the people of Campiglia are almost the only ones to take the name of their patron. What is more, as we have seen, something close to shame makes them adopt another name when they leave their native district.[109] To explain this rather doubtful name, some historians have suggested that the real St Besse came originally of a Thracian people called the Bessi,[110] or rather from a part of Piedmont which is still called 'La Bessa';[111] history, it is claimed, would have retained no memory of such a person had the name by which he is known not been an ethnic description. Such a hypothesis is not inherently absurd; but it is entirely arbitrary, and it seems very difficult to accept that a strange and impersonal name, having no links with the district where the cult developed, should have been able, in the absence of any historical tradition, to serve as the core of several legends and as the denomination of a local cult of such fervour and tenacity. Let us attempt another procedure which will not oblige us to suppose, quite gratuitously, that behind this name, which is not really a name, there lies a person with no historical individuality. Since everything, in the legend and in the ritual, takes us back to the Mount of St Besse, the centre of the local devotion, the point of departure of the cults of Ozegna and of Ivrea, let us see whether the name Besse may not designate some attribute of the great sacred rock which sticks up in the middle of the Alpine wilderness.[112]

The name *Munt della bescha* is found frequently in the canton of the Grisons to designate the high sheep pastures or the peaks which overlook them.[113] *Bescha* is the plural of the masculine noun *besch*, which most Romance linguists relate to the Latin word *bestia*; in the language of the mountain herdsmen, the general term has taken on a restricted meaning and designates simply livestock, and in particular sheep.[114] In the speech of the Soana valley, following the rules of local phonetics, the term corresponding to the Romansh *besch* would have the form *bess*. But we are not reduced to dragging in an imaginary word in order to support our argument. If, in the speech of the valley today, *bess* no longer exists in the meaning of 'animal' or 'sheep',[115] it is still used metaphorically: it is a term which people apply to the simple-minded.[116] The strange resemblance between this unflattering epithet and the name of their patron doubtless goes some way to explain the haste with which men from Campiglia who are called Besse 'dechristen' themselves when they go down to the plain. But perhaps there is more to this than an unfortunate coincidence.

The designation *Mont-bess*,[117] 'mountain or rock of the sheep', perfectly suits an eminence situated in the middle of an Alpine pasture and which legend represents to us as always surrounded by flocks. Then, when the word *bess*, for unknown reasons, stopped being used by the people of the valley to mean 'sheep',[118] it became a proper name, free from vulgar connotations, and could serve as the core of two or three different mythical personalities. The 'rock of the sheep' saint first became an exemplary shepherd, then a missionary, was then cast from the top of the Mount for having been unwilling to eat a stolen sheep, and finally became a bishop of Ivrea. Only this last legend, formed in the atmosphere of the town and amounting as far as we are concerned to no more than two words and a date, has lost all memory of the original meaning of the word, which designated the sacred stone cherished by the shepherds.[119]

I must admit that this argument, taken in isolation, did not appear at all convincing to the perspicacious linguist who was kind enough to examine it. Monsieur Meillet agreed that the Latin *bestia* could have engendered a word meaning 'sheep' in the Soana valley; but, he added, 'a phonetic possibility is not a proof'. One could not make the point better, and, if I knew the name Besse simply from the literary texts, I would beware of trying to establish its etymology. But study of the legends and of the diffusion of the cult and, above all, observation of local religious practice have singularly restricted the field of possible hypotheses and, taken together, they perhaps add an extra cogency to a simple 'phonetic possibility'. Coming in support of a complex of facts that are not linguistic but religious, will the proposed etymology perhaps appear less unsound to competent judges like Monsieur Meillet?

But, even were this hypothesis and every other of the same kind to be deemed inadmissible or undemonstrable, even were we constrained to accept this remarkable name as that of a quite indeterminate saint who happened to serve to christianize the local cult of a sacred stone, our conclusions would still stand. The sacred rock, having for a long period been worshipped for itself, was later adored because it bore the imprint of a model shepherd or because it had sheltered the remains of a Christian martyr. But, over the centuries, it is always basically the sanctity of the rock, expressed in various ways, which has attracted the pious crowd of pilgrims to this mountain site. Where then does the diffuse sanctity of the Mount stem from?

It is hardly credible that the dimensions of this block of stone, or the relative strangeness of its situation and of its form, should themselves be sufficient to explain a devotion so tenacious and so rich in psychological significance. One must look elsewhere, and in the direction which has already allowed us to account for the changes which the organization of the festival and the content of the legend have undergone – and are still undergoing. If it is true that the contingent and variable elements in the local cult of St Besse are directly related to the nature and behaviour of the various groups of devotees, if they are determined in the last analysis by the changing structure and composition of the social context, then we have to admit that the most profound and essential element of this cult, that which has remained immutable through all the vicissitudes of history and right down to the present, must also be explicable in terms of some feature of the collective existence that is equally fundamental and permanent. This feature, this necessary condition, which has allowed the small tribe of St Besse to remain in existence down to our own day and to maintain its originality in the face of a hostile environment and of powerful forces tending to undermine it, is the faith that this obscure mountain people had in itself and in its ideal, and its will to survive and to overcome temporary setbacks or the hostility of men and of things. As the legends indicate in their own way, the divine principle, that the devotion upholds and exploits, was never at any time inherent in the dead rock, but exterior and superior to it, animating it by being incorporated with it. If the men of today, despite all the obstacles, persist in coming to enrich themselves and to acquire new strength beside the Mount, it is because their forefathers, over the generations, have put there the best of themselves and deposited their successive notions of human perfection; it is because their distant ancestors had made this eternal rock, which survives all storms and which the snow can never entirely cover, the emblem and the focus of their collective existence. Those people from Cogne were not mistaken, therefore, who saw a brilliant flower shining one day close to the Mount in the winter gloom, illuminating the thick fog and melting the snow around it. But they did not realize that the marvellous flower had sprung from the depths of their ancestors' soul. It was their loftiest thought, their liveliest hope, which had taken root on the side of the rock that stood among the life-giving pastures; and it is that flower which, from on high, still continues to enlighten and to warm hearts frozen by the suffering, the anguish, and the dull hardship of everyday life.

We townspeople should not exult too much over the impending

disappearance of these 'gross superstitions'. Over the centuries, St Besse has taught his devotees to rise above the restricted horizon of their daily life, if only for a few moments, by loading on to their shoulders with joy the heavy burden of the ideal, and to retain even in times of distress 'the faith and the trust' that overcome evil. In communicating to them little pieces of his substance – the small stones brought out each year from the immense rock – he made them understand, in the concrete language which they alone could grasp, that each one of them derived his strength and his courage from a superior being, who included all individuals present and to come and who is infinitely greater and more durable than all of them. When the sacred rock becomes once more an ordinary rock, quite empty and purely physical, who will there be to remind the people of the valley of these truths, which are as substantial as the stone of which the Mount of Saint-Besse is made?

CONCLUSION

Perhaps it was superfluous to spend so long discussing these rustic stories and this little saint, hidden in the recesses of the Alps. But the least celebrated saints are sometimes the most instructive. And, if it is true that the religious life of a people is a manifestation of its profoundest being, the cult of St Besse has the merit at least of taking us inside the consciousness, otherwise so distant and so closed, of the mountain people. Beyond this, St Besse, however limited his domain, is not confined to one or two Alpine valleys: one finds him transplanted into the capital of a vast diocese, into Ivrea where for several centuries he has been honoured with a very popular cult. Now, as all experienced critics confess, the personality of the saint of Ivrea is a mystery that scholars have tried in vain to elucidate by searching in the episcopal archives or by comparing late and contradictory texts. Have we perhaps been more fortunate by taking as our point of reference, not the sumptuous cathedral of the town but rather the humble chapel of Monte Fautenio? If this attempt has succeeded, in part at least, then one must conclude that every time circumstances are right, the hagiographer will do well not to neglect those precious instruments of research, a pair of stout shoes and a walking-stick.

What is more, the local cult of St Besse allows us to study the formation of a religious legend, in conditions that are particularly favourable. Nearly everyone agrees today that the Lives of the saints are the product of two distinct forces, the inventive spontaneity of the people and the work of learned compilers. Critics, working to recover the historical truth beneath the jumble of legends and concerned above all to purge the belief of the faithful of all adventitious elements, have in general been very severe on popular legends and on the writers who have echoed them. Even in a book as temperate and as sophisticated as that of Father Delehaye, the collective imagination figures as a kind of gremlin, intervening only to mix up dates, to confuse names and to alter events and get them out of proportion.[120] These scornful judgments might be well-founded, if it were a question of the 'people' emerging from a condition of mythological innocence into a sort of semi-civilized state and setting out to write history. But would it be fair to assess 'the imagination of the child' by simply considering the more or less fantastic historical compositions of primary school children? Moreover, since the anonymous author of the legend is not the person who writes it down, one is nearly always obliged to imagine what the 'popular' narrative was like from the literary version given by the compiler. And by what signs can one tell that the latter, in any particular part of his work, is just retailing what is authentic to the people, that he really is 'the echo of the popular voice'?[121] Any verification is usually impossible, because no element for comparison exists. Even the oral traditions of the countryside today, when they are closely connected with the cult of Christianity, are so saturated with representations of ecclesiastical origin that it is quite chimerical to regard them as 'popular'. However, it happens that by rare good fortune, some of the devotees of St Besse have retained in a pure state the original tradition on which the learned have set to work. In this privileged example, where we are able to collate the model and the copy, the popular legend appears indeed to be indifferent to historical truth and to Christian morality; but it lays no claim to either, since it exists on a totally different level of thought; yet, in its own sphere, it is perfectly coherent and perfectly adapted to its milieu. On the other hand, we see the compilers of the various literary versions recasting and reconstituting the oral tradition in an attempt to make it fit into a Christian framework. If the official legend of St Besse offends common sense, logic and the truth of the facts, the blame does not lie with the 'people', but with those who have sought to 'correct' them. Of course, it would be rash to draw general conclusions straight away from the results of this particular comparison; but the experiment which St Besse allows us to make should put us on our guard against the temptation of regarding hagiographical texts as the faithful reflection of the popular beliefs on which they are based.[122]

Finally, there is a very good chance that observation of an Alpine cult reveals to us very ancient forms of religious life. As has often been said, the mountain is a marvellous preserver, on condition of course that the tides of the plain have not yet swept over it. The Italian Graian Alps are a paradise in this respect; they form a kind of reserve where the ibex, which has disappeared from the rest of the Alps, is found in large numbers and where the rarest Alpine plants abound. In the pastures around the shrine of St Besse, the edelweiss is about as common as the daisy in our lowland meadows. Nor is the sociologist less fortunate here than the zoologist or the botanist. In the same way that in the Alps the primitive rock emerges sometimes from the accumulation of more recent strata which cover it elsewhere, so one can see standing out here, in a few small islands, and for only a little longer, vestiges of Europe's most ancient civilization. At the extremities of the high valleys, beliefs and ritual gestures several thousand years old are perpetuated, not in the form of survivals or of 'superstitions', but in the shape of a real religion with its own life and which is publicly celebrated beneath a transparent Christian covering. The main interest of the cult of St Besse is without doubt that it offers us an image, fragmentary and slightly veiled, but still distinct and very much alive, of the religion of prehistory.

NOTES

1 I spent about six weeks at Cogne (from 20 July to 1 September 1912); I was therefore able to question the people of the valley at leisure, speaking with herdsmen, game-keepers, guides, etc., and by preference with old men and women who are most in touch with local legends. It will become apparent later why Cogne was found to be the most favourable field of observation. I spent only two days in the Soana valley, during the festival itself; but Monsieur Guazzotti, the pharmacist at Ronco, has kindly interviewed the rectors of the parishes of Ronco and Campiglia for me; I have also been able to gather a certain amount of information from emigrants from the Soana valley now living in Paris.

2 These are Dr Pierre Giacosa, professor at the University of Turin, who has been visiting the region for many years; Canon Fruttaz of Aosta; Canons Gérard, Ruffier and Vescoz, all natives of Cogne, who have kindly communicated instructive accounts to me through my friend P. A. Farinte; and Professor Francesco Farina of Turin, who knows the Soana valley very well and has devoted an excellent little work to it which we shall have more than one occasion to cite. May I here express my gratitude to all these gentlemen, and ask them to excuse me if I have seen fit to derive from the facts which they have taught me and from my personal observations conclusions to which they do not subscribe and for which, of course, I am solely responsible.

3 Monsieur Jean Marx, archivist and palaeographer, and above all Monsieur Paul Alphandéry, Assistant Director of Studies at the Ecole des Hautes Etudes and Director of the *Revue de l'Histoire des Religions*, have kindly furnished me with precious bibliographical references for which I thank them warmly.

4 One can find a description of these cols in Martelli and Vaccarone, *Guida delle Alpi occidentali* (Turin, 1889), II, pp. 224ff. The most frequented is the Colla della Nouva (2,933 m).

5 See E. Aubert, *La vallée d'Aosta* (Paris, 1860), pp. 9ff.; Carlo Promis, *Le antichità di Aosta* (Turin, 1862), pp. 11ff. and 192ff.; Florian Vallentin, *Les*

Alpes cottiennes et graées, Géographie galloromaine (Paris, 1883), pp. 58ff.;
Mommsen in *C.I.L.* [*Corpus inscriptionum Latinarum* (Berlin, 1863–   ).
S. W.], V, pp. 736, 750ff. and especially 769.

6 On the *Tuchinaggio*, which lasted on and off from 1383 to 1423, see T. Tibaldi,
La regione d' Aosta attraverso i secoli (Turin, 1900), II, pp. 359ff.; and III, p. 10;
and F. Farina, *Valle Soana* (Ivrea, 1909), pp. 17ff.

7 On this language, see C. Nigra, 'Il gergo dei Valsoanini', *Archivio glottologico
italiano*, III (1878), pp. 53ff.; cf. Farina, pp. 73ff.

8 This is particularly true of Cogne: despite its admirable situation which
attracts many tourists every year, and despite the importance of its iron mines,
it is still not linked to the Aosta valley by a carriage road! One has existed for
twenty years now in the Soana valley: so the people there no longer deserve
the epithet of 'savages' applied to them around 1840 by G. Casalis in his
Dizionario geografico-storico... degli Stati di S. M. il Re di Sardegna (Turin,
1836–   ), VIII, p. 489; and XVI, p. 590. The paragraph which follows
applies only to Cogne.

9 Compare with the monograph which Monsieur Jean Brunhès has devoted to
the inhabitants of the valley of Anniviers (Valais) in his book, *La Géographie
humaine* (Paris, 1910), especially p. 601.

10 According to Canon Ruffier, St Besse is invoked especially for back pains and
lumbago.

11 A few people from Cogne have disputed this, doubtless believing that it does
not redound to the credit of their saint; but the fact has been affirmed to me by
several trustworthy informants, some of whom had themselves benefited
from St Besse's powers of exemption.

12 The other side of the Mount is much less steep and is covered with turf; a
small path allows one to climb up to the summit.

13 However, it sometimes happens that, following a vow, people pay the *curé* of
Campiglia to go up to say a mass in the chapel at some other time during the
year.

14 To arrive in time for the festival which begins at nine o'clock in the morning,
the pilgrims from Cogne spend the night before either in the chalets of
Ciavanassa or at the shrine itself, in a small building next to the chapel and
intended for this purpose. They return home by the evening of 10 August.

15 The most pious, it seems, or those who have made a vow, must climb up to
the summit after the procession to complete their rosary there. According to
Canon Gérard, as soon as the pilgrims from Cogne arrive on the eve of the
feast 'they form a procession and go nine times round the huge rock'; at the
completion of each rosary, 'they clamber up the rock in order to kiss the iron
cross placed at the summit, right on the edge of the precipice'. On the ritual of
'going round the stone', see Paul Sébillot, 'Le culte des pierres en France',
Revue de l'Ecole d'Anthropologie, XII (1902), pp. 205ff.

16 The custom of carrying consecrated bread in processions is widespread in the
Canavese; the bread is offered by the faithful, having been prepared in a
special way (with saffron), and it is distributed after the festival to the
officiating clergy and to all the participants. The consecrated bread is given
the name *carità*, which also applies to the pyramid of multicoloured ribbons

which covers it. For a young girl it is a great honour to carry the *carità*, and guarantees a prompt offer of marriage. (See Casalis, *Dizionario*, VIII, p. 596; and F. Valla in *Archivio per lo studio delle tradizioni popolari*, XIII (1894), p. 122.) The word *fouïace* no longer has any meaning in the dialect of Cogne; it does not figure in the *Dictionnaire valdôtain* of abbé Cerlogne, or in the *Dictionnaire savoyard* of Constantin and Desormaux. But it is easy to recognize it as akin to the old French word *fouace*, derived from the Latin *focacia*, which is found in Rabelais and in La Fontaine, and which is still in use in various forms in several regions of France to mean a girdle-cake, cooked in the oven or under the ashes of the fire; it certainly referred therefore to the consecrated bread which was carried in the procession of St Besse. The name of the contents, which have disappeared, has remained attached to the container; but, since the original meaning of the word is not understood, efforts have been made to find a new one for it, connected somehow with the image of the saint; hence the idea of a military trophy. (Canon Gérard assures me that the *fouïace*, or festival cake, is still carried in the procession; but this claim is contradicted by every other testimony that I have been able to gather.)

17 According to Canon Gérard, the ribbons, handkerchiefs, scarves, embroideries, etc., offered at the chapel, are hung on the *fouïaces* during the procession.

18 The offering of gifts in kind and the sale by auction of objects dedicated to a shrine are characteristic of a number of pilgrimage sites in the Val d'Aosta, notably at Notre-Dame-du-Plou and at Notre-Dame-de-Guérison (near Courmayeur). The object bought back is not, it seems, subject to any taboo, and possesses no special virtue.

19 I was not able to observe this phenomenon with my own eyes, nor was I able to have it confirmed by the 'natives' whom I questioned; they did not deny that it took place, but always said that they did not know anything about it, afraid perhaps of seeming too 'superstitious'. The authenticity of the phenomenon has been guaranteed for me by the doctor at Ronco and particularly by Professor Farina, who knows the Soana valley very well and whose wife comes from there. The custom, so widespread, which consists of 'touching' a sacred robe in order to have children, may be currently observed still at the shrine of Oropa in Piedmont; see Paul Sébillot, *Le Folk-lore de France* (Paris, 1904), I, pp. 338ff.

20 One can find analogous phenomena described in Sébillot, *Folk-lore*, pp. 342ff. He relates the practice to 'the custom of detaching fragments from the tombs or statues of saints' in order to use them as remedies.

21 Many people from Cogne told me that 'the turn of Cogne' came round every *seven* years. This obvious mistake made on the subject of a periodic event to which they are very much attached is doubtless to be explained by the general chronological imprecision characteristic of the popular mind, and also by the prestige of the number seven.

22 In theory, it is the priests and choir of the parish presiding over the festival who officiate in the chapel. But the present *curé* of Cogne does not seem to concern himself about this prerogative.

23 During the whole of the Middle Ages, the valley of Aosta (as far as the Lys)

formed a kind of French march, dependent successively on the kingdoms of
Burgundy and of Provence and on the county of Savoy, and opposed to the
Italian march of Ivrea. It was only from the fourteenth century that Aosta and
Ivrea became united under the domination of the House of Savoy; but even
then the Aosta valley did not become Piedmontese territory: it continued to
belong to the court at Chambéry. See Tibaldi, *La regione d' Aosta*, especially II,
pp. 317ff., on the war of 1229 between Aosta and Ivrea; and III, pp. 14ff.

24 The man from Cogne who has for many years carried out the functions of
president of the Saint-Besse festival and who is obliged to go there every year,
told me that he had never travelled beyond the site of the shrine.

25 It seems that at one time the children of Campiglia used to put pebbles on the
humps formed by their huge bustles.

26 In 1901, the population of Campiglia was 209, that of Valprato 1,355, that of
Ronco 3,105 and that of Ingria 1,280. Ronco is today the economic centre
and the administrative capital of the valley. See Farina, *Valle Soana*, pp. 24,
36ff., 49 and 59.

27 Usually Lawrence, because he is the official saint honoured on 10 August. As
a man from the Soana valley working in Paris, explained to me, 'Lawrence is
the French for "Besso"'. One senses that St Besse could easily merge
completely with the more illustrious figure of St Lawrence.

28 'Couragi, Cougneis; si teñi nen boun, noi autri soma pers.' Professor Farina,
who has kindly provided me with the correct orthography of this historic
saying (uttered in all seriousness), tells me that it is in the dialect of Piedmont
and not of the Soana valley. This is not too surprising, for the dialects of
Cogne and of the Soana valley have almost nothing in common.

29 This year [1912] there were a little more than a dozen people from Cogne at
the festival; this, it appears, was less than the current average. It is said that
once, especially in years in which Cogne 'led' the festival, 100 or even 200
pilgrims used to come from across the mountains.

30 This is already the case for the numerous Piedmontese who have settled in the
valley, especially at Ronco. Of course, it would not be impossible, under the
influence of favourable circumstances, for the shrine of St Besse to enjoy a
renaissance and to become the centre of a famous pilgrimage, like many other
sacred sites of the same kind; see p. 83 below. But, were this to happen, the
mountain cult, isolated and relatively autonomous, would cease to exist.

31 The ancient Statutes of the city of Ivrea, which go back to around 1338,
already mention the festival of St Besse among its legal holidays and as one of
the three great annual fairs of the place; see *Historiae patriae monumenta, Leges
municipales*, I, col. 1164 and col. 1184. On the date of this document, see E.
Durando, 'Vita cittadina e privata nel medio evo in Ivrea', *Bibl. Società Storica
Subalpina*, VII, pp. 23ff.

32 People say in the Soana valley that the 'real' feast of St Besse is on 1
December, but that the bishop of Ivrea through a decree authorized the
mountain-dwellers to celebrate their festival on 10 August. The people of
Cogne seem to know nothing of the feast of 1 December.

33 A small brochure, published with ecclesiastical approval, bears the title: *Vita*

e miracoli di San Besso, martire tebeo, compatrono della diocesi d'Ivrea (Turin, Artale, 1900). It is, I believe, a reprint, and will be referred to from now on as *Vita*. A portrait of the saint appears on the cover with the legend: 'Protector of the Soana valley'.

34 See Fedele Savio, S. J., *Gli antichi vescovi d'Italia dalle origini al 1300. Il Piemonte* (Turin, 1889), pp. 180ff. In a luminous exposition to which we will have to return in connection with the legend, Father Savio begins by establishing that in the fifteenth century the people of Ivrea had no solid information about the life and death of St Besse; then he adds: 'Consequently, St Besse must have been venerated at Ivrea from the earliest times and perhaps from the first centuries of Christianity.' This conclusion seems to us a little forced. In support of his hypothesis, Father Savio cites a funerary inscription, copied at Ivrea, it seems, towards the end of the ninth century and which Gazzera assigns without proof to the end of the sixth century; a certain priest Silvius declared that he had deposited in a monument there the relics of some holy martyrs beside which he himself wished to be buried and whose protection he invoked for his native place; see C. Gazzera, *Delle iscrizioni cristiane antiche del Piemonte* (Turin, 1849), pp. 80ff. Gazzera wonders whether the 'holy martyrs' of this inscription may not be the saints Sabinus, Besse and Tegulus, who are honoured at Ivrea. Father Savio declares that such a hypothesis is false as far as St Sabinus is concerned; but he admits that the epitaph of Silvius could well refer to Besse and Tegulus. This is indeed possible; but there is nothing to prove it and one would have to begin by demonstrating that the two saints in question were 'indigenous to Ivrea'; and this is precisely what is at issue.

35 This follows from two papal charters (of 15 January 1151 and of 6 May 1184), confirming the privileges and possessions of the bishop and of the canons of Saint-Ours of Aosta in the Cogne basin; see *Historiae patriae monumenta*, I, pp. 795ff., 931, 981 and 1091.

36 This is found in a manuscript breviary, preserved in the archives of the cathedral of Ivrea, dating, it seems, from 1473; cf. Savio, *Gli antichi vescovi*, p. 181. [The text of this document was communicated to Hertz while his study was being printed, and he added it as a short Appendix to the original article. It has been omitted in this version. S. W.] The oldest printed account of this tradition is found in G. Baldesano di Carmagnola, *La sacra historia thebea . . . Opera non meno dilettevole che pia* 2nd edition (Turin, 1604); the first edition of 1589 contains no reference to St Besse, pp. 269ff. In the list of sources, placed at the start of his book, Baldesano mentions a *Historia di S. Besso*, which is perhaps the breviary of 1473, a copy of which may have been sent to him from Ivrea after the first edition of his book had appeared. Cf. *Vita*, pp. 8ff.

37 Tibaldi, *La regione d'Aosta*, I, p. 375, n. 3, reproduces a 'legend from Aosta', published by E. Duc in the *Annuaire du Diocèse d'Aoste* in 1893, which recounts the story of the translation of the relics of St Besse. In this version, the theft of the relics is attributed to the people of Cogne who, going down 'at the end of the autumn to Monferrato where they worked as distillers . . . took with them the body of the saint with the intention of making a gift of it to some place along the way'. This version, which I can confirm has never been

collected at Cogne in this form, results from a combination of the information given by Baldesano and the tradition of Cogne relating to the discovery of a holy body, which is recounted below (p. 73).

38 An oral tradition. Baldesano says simply 'rubbish'.

39 This feature of the local legend is not found in Baldesano.

40 The oral tradition, at least as told me by people from the Aosta valley now living in Paris, provides no precise dates or proper names.

41 *Acta SS.*, Sept., VI (1757), p. 916.

42 See P. Saintyves, *Les Saints successeurs des dieux* (Paris, 1907), pp. 41ff.

43 See H. Delehaye, *Les Légendes hagiographiques* (Brussels, 1905), pp. 35ff.

44 On this general phenomenon of 'cumulation', which is very common, see Delehaye, pp. 20ff.

45 On the historical role of King Ardoino and on the legends which formed around his name, see L. G. Provana, *Studi critici sovra la storia d'Italia a tempi del re Ardoino* (Turin, 1844), esp. pp. 252 and 307; F. Gabotto, 'Un millennio di storia eporediese (356–1357)', *Bibl. Soc. Stor. Subalp.*, IV, pp. 19ff. and 118; and Preface to 'Studi eporediesi', *ibid.*, VII (1900), p. v; B. Baudi di Vesme, 'Il re Ardoino e la riscossa italica contro Ottone III', *ibid.*, pp. 1ff. It is to be noted that Ferrari whose *Catalogus sanctorum Italiae* is cited in this context by the Bollandists [*Acta SS.*, Sept., VI. S. W.] (p. 917) disputes whether Ardoino ever actually played the role ascribed to him by the 1473 breviary.

46 C. Boggio, 'Le prime Chiese cristiane nel Canavese', *Atti della Società di archeologia e belle arti per la provincia di Torino*, V (1894), p. 67.

47 Savio, *Gli antichi vescovi*, pp. 182ff. Why does this author accept the historicity of the tradition about the foreign origin of the cult of St Sabinus and brush aside the quite analogous tradition concerning St Besse? On the relations between Ivrea and Spoleto in the ninth and tenth centuries, see Gabotto, 'Un millennio', pp. 14ff.

48 This account is based on the work of Gabotto, already referred to; see esp. pp. 46ff., 56ff., 81ff. and 118ff.

49 F. Gabotto, 'Le carte dello Archivio vescovile d'Ivrea fino al 1313', *Bibl. Soc. Stor. Subalp.*, V, p. 13. Ozegna remained under episcopal control for a long time – we see the bishop of Ivrea in 1337 ceding various territories, including Ozegna, to Count Aymon of Savoy; see Gabotto, 'Un millennio', p. 207.

50 On the historical importance of Ogier and on the temporal power of the bishops of Ivrea, see Gabotto, 'Un millennio', pp. 38ff.

51 On this, see Casalis, *Dizionario*, VIII, p. 647; and Gabotto, 'Un millennio', pp. 81ff. Among its signatories figure the counts of a number of small towns situated in the vicinity of Ozegna – Agliè, Valperga, Pont, etc.

52 See the article 'Ozegna' in the *Dizionario* of Casalis, XIII (1845), pp. 751ff. ('località centrale').

53 The allusion to Monferrato in the legend of the theft of the relics seems of some significance. Vercelli was much richer and more populated than Ivrea in the Middle Ages, according to Gabotto, 'Un millennio', p. 119.

54 The ruins of a very old chapel of St Besse were still extant at Ozegna in the time of Casalis (*Dizionario*, XIII, p. 755). It should be noted that the church of Ozegna is the sole church actually dedicated to St Besse, for, in the Soana

valley, the saint only 'possesses' the little chapel of the shrine in his own name, while at Ivrea he is only a guest in the cathedral which is dedicated to the Blessed Virgin.

55 An authorized version of this may be found in the *Vita*, pp. 5ff. (see n. 33 above). The anonymous author of this brochure reproduces almost word for word the version in *Memorie storiche sulla chiesa d'Ivrea* by Canon Saroglia (Ivrea, 1881), p. 16; I am acquainted with this thanks to the kindness of Canon Vescoz who copied this passage for me (henceforth cited as A). But, when he comes to the account of the martyrdom, he intercalates Baldesano's narrative, *La sacra historia*, p. 129 (henceforth B), though not without touching it up a bit. Another version of the legend has been provided by Saroglia in *Eporedia sacra* (Ivrea, 1887); Canon Boggio has kindly copied p. 146 of this work for me (henceforth C). Finally, Ferrari in his *Catalogus sanctorum Italiae* supplies a fourth version, composed 'ex antiquis lectionibus quae in ecclesia Eporediensi recitari consueverant'; this is cited in *Acta SS.*, Sept., VI, p. 917 (henceforth D).

56 The *Vita* leaves A to follow B at this stage.

57 This third explanation is added to B by the *Vita*.

58 Baldesano is far less affirmative; he simply says: 'Some people add that this fall was not the cause of his death; God preserved him miraculously so that his martyrdom might be more spectacular.' However, D certainly makes Besse die as a result of his fall, which conforms with the local tradition. By contrast, in C, the role of the herdsmen is reduced to denouncing Besse to the pagan soldiers, who put him to death, 'by throwing him down from a high mountain'. Finally, in A, the herdsmen disappear altogether, being supplanted by Maximian's ruffians, who, having thrown the saint down from the height of the rock, cut off his head.

59 This last statement is found only in the *Vita* itself. In C, it is said that Besse, coming from the Aosta valley, arrived in the Soana valley via the mountains of Champorcher and of Cogne. This version is also that reproduced by Mgr Duc in vol. I of his *Histoire de l'église d'Aoste* (according to the extract kindly supplied me by Canon Ruffier). From this point, the *Vita* takes up A again, only adding the special mention of Campiglia.

60 While A, followed by the *Vita*, makes no connection between the rock from which the saint was thrown and the Mount overhanging the chapel, C specifies that 'in conformity with the custom of the Romans', the martyr was buried at the very place of his persecution.

61 However, the oral tradition of the Soana valley adds that St Besse, while preaching the Gospel to the local inhabitants, also practised the shepherd's calling. This information, whose importance will become clear later, has completely disappeared from all the literary compilations.

62 Some narrators omit all allusion to the piety of Besse; they pass straight away to the description of his flock, adding the remark: 'it was a miracle'.

63 According to some, the fall was repeated three times.

64 The following illustrates well the abstract and impersonal character of the official St Besse. The wife of the president of Cogne one day showed me several medals, all the same, which were souvenirs of the festivals in which

her husband had participated. I was surprised to note that these medals bore the inscription: 'Saint Pancras'. When I expressed my astonishment, I obtained the sharp response: 'No; it is the portrait of St Besse.' And, in effect, the image was of the standardized 'soldier-martyr' type.

65 Even at Ivrea, as we have seen, it tends to vanish altogether leaving only a wholly schematic image, in which the 'confessor of the faith' confronts his 'pagan persecutors'; see nn. 55 and 58 above.

66 See A. Meillet, 'Comment les mots changent de sens', *Année Sociologique*, IX, pp. 1–38.

67 *The Passion of the Martyrs of Agaunum* has been edited by Krusch, among others, in *Monumenta Germaniae Historica, Scriptorum rerum merovingicarum*, III, pp. 32ff. Abbé Lejay has provided a good critical account of the question in the *Revue d'Histoire et de Littérature Religieuse*, XI (1906), pp. 264ff.

68 On the contrary, he expresses his satisfaction that the number of Theban saints in Piedmont should have more than doubled between the appearance of the first and second editions of his book.

69 According to Canon Ducis, *Saint Maurice et la légion thébéenne* (Annecy, 1882), pp. 31ff., in addition to the 6,000 Thebans decimated at Agaunum, there were about 1,000 in the German lands – Cologne alone claims 318, 300 in Switzerland, and an innumerable host in Italy.

70 This is the explanation put forward by abbé J. Bernard de Montmélian, *Saint Maurice et la légion thébéenne* (Paris, 1888), I, pp. 225ff.

71 See *ibid.*, pp. 336ff.

72 This has been noted by H. Dümmler, 'Sigebert's von Gembloux.... Passio Sanctorum Thebeorum', *Abhandlungen der Königlichen Akademie der Wissenschaften zu Berlin*, Philosophisch-historische Classe (1893), p. 20, n. 2; cf. Krusch, *Monumenta Germaniae Historica*, p. 21. He is even suspicious of the name 'Mauricius' (= 'Niger').

73 On the last, honoured in several places in the Aosta valley, see Tibaldi, *La regione d'Aosta*, I, p. 379.

74 On the general phenomenon of the substitution of martyred saints for the ancient local gods, see Albert Dufourcq, *La Christianisation des foules* (Paris, 1903), pp. 44ff.

75 *Acta SS.*, Sept., VI, p. 908.

76 P. Allard, *La Persécution de Dioclétien* (Paris, 1890), II, pp. 354–7.

77 F. Stolle, *Das Martyrium der thebäischen Legion* (Breslau, 1891), pp. 82ff.

78 Notably by Dümmler and Krusch.

79 Delehaye, *Les Légendes hagiographiques*, pp. 129, 135ff. and 245.

80 *Acta SS.*, Sept., VI, pp. 915ff.

81 G. Saroglia, *Memorie storiche*, p. 16; cf. Savio, *Gli antichi vescovi*, p. 181. [The Latin text of these breviary lessons was added to Hertz's original article as an Appendix, as we have noted. S. W.]

82 Although it appears fully to satisfy certain Piedmontese historians. Professor Farina has kindly shown me an extract from the work of the Salesian Father A. M. Rocca, *Santi e beati del Piemonte* (Turin, 1907), in which the 'official' legend of St Besse is affirmed without qualification, save that the rock from which the martyr was cast and that which served as his burial-place are

expressly said to be identical. The critical spirit does not yet seem to have ravaged the diocese of Ivrea. 'It would be hard to find in Piedmont a town which is more attached to its local beliefs and to ecclesiastical traditions', writes C. Patrucco in *Bibl. Soc. Stor. Subalp.*, VII, p. 269.

83 This hypothesis had already been put forward in *Acta SS.*, Sept., VI, p. 917; cf. *Ad Acta SS Supplementum* (Paris, 1875), p. 400.

84 Savio, *Gli antichi vescovi*, pp. 180ff.

85 Ughelli, *Italia sacra* (ed. Coleti, 1719), IV, col. 1064.

86 Filippo Bergomense, *Historia novissime congesta, Chronicarum supplementum appellata* (Brescia, 1485), fol. 97 v. The same affirmation is found in almost the same terms in Alberti, *Descrittione di tutta Italia* (1553), cited by Savio, p. 180, n. 2.

87 This is also the view of Gabotto, 'Un millennio', p. 7, n. 3.; Bima, *Serie cronologica degli arcivescovi e vescovi di Sardegna* 2nd edition (Turin, 1842), p. 123, mentions 'Besso called saint' with the date 730 (*sic*). But his list, as Savio says (p. 176), is 'completely imaginary'. The name Besse does not figure among the bishops of Ivrea in Gams, *Series episcoporum ecclesiae catholicae*, p. 816.

88 Of course, there may have been older ones which we know nothing about. E. Dümmler has published a series of fourteen liturgical poems, written according to him by a priest of Ivrea in the time of Bishop Ogier, and perhaps by the bishop himself; these include a poem in honour of St Tegulus, martyr, and a poem in honour of the Theban Legion, in which only St Maurice is named. The absence of any poem or any allusion to St Besse is probably significant and seems to confirm the hypothesis that the cult of St Besse was not introduced to Ivrea before the end of the eleventh century; see E. Dümmler, *Anselm der Peripatetiker nebst andern Beiträgen zur Literaturgeschichte Italiens im elften Jhdt* (Halle, 1872), pp. 83ff. The authors of the *Voyage littéraire de deux religieux bénédictins* (Paris, 1717), I, p. 244, saw at the abbey of Talloires 'a poem on the martyrdom of the Theban Legion, composed by Ogier, Bishop of Ivrea'. This manuscript has never been rediscovered; cf. Savio, p. 202.

89 This inventory, dating from 1775, is cited by Savio, p. 181.

90 Baldesano, *La sacra historia*, pp. 326ff.

91 The parish of Ronco detached itself from that of Campiglia in 1280, and that of Valprato in 1609; Ingria was only separated from Ronco in 1750; see F. Farina, *Valle Soana*, pp. 25, 40 and 49.

92 In particular, the traces still existing of two paved roads which run from Cogne to Pont; they have, it is said, been partially destroyed by the build-up of granular ice and glaciers since the Middle Ages; see Casalis, *Dizionario*, III, p. 382 ('Campiglia'); and V, pp. 309ff. ('Cogne'); and abbé Vescoz, *Notices topographiques et historiques sur la vallée de Cogne* (Florence, 1873). In the thirteenth century, the bishops of Ivrea still possessed lands in the Cogne valley; see Gabotto, 'Un millennio', pp. 79ff.

93 The view expressed here accords with that of Dr Giacosa and the other scholars of Aosta whom I was able to consult; all agree that the local tradition is based on a historical foundation.

94 See n. 35 above.

95 See Déchelette, *Manuel d'archéologie préhistorique*, I, pp. 379ff, and 439ff. Of course, we would not dream of affirming that the ancient people of the Soana valley practised this cult alone. It is probable that, like the mountain-dwellers of the Gévaudan about whom Gregory of Tours informs us (*P.L.*, LXXI, col. 831), they also knew the cult of lakes: the shores of Lake Miserin are still the theatre every year of a great festival, dedicated to Our Lady of the Snows and frequented by the people of the valleys of Champorcher, Cogne and the Soana.

96 One may find particularly instructive information in A. C. Kruijt, *Het animisme in den indischen Archipel* (The Hague, 1906), pp. 205ff. ('the stone is the seat of an impersonal spiritual force'); and in Fathers Abinal and La Vaissière, *Vingt ans à Madagascar* (Paris, 1885), pp. 256ff. ('a power, endowed with a physical and moral influence over men as well as over other creatures... resides in the stone').

97 Edouard Piette and Julien Sacaze, 'La Montagne de l'Espiaup', *Bulletins de la Société d'Anthropologie*, 2nd series, XII (1877), pp. 237ff.

98 Cf. Salomon Reinach, 'Les Monuments de pierre brute dans le langage et les croyances populaires', *Revue Archéologique*, 3rd series, XXI (1893), pp. 333–7ff. Monsieur Reinach is careful to warn (p. 196) that these beliefs apply to sacred stones in general, and not just to monuments made by men.

99 This is St Gaudentius, first bishop of Novara. A church was built in this place around 1720; see Savio, *Gli antichi vescovi*, p. 247; and C. Patrucco, 'Ivrea da Carlo Emanuele I a Carlo Emanuele III', *Bibl. Soc. Stor. Subalp.*, VII, p. 283. See in *Archivio per lo studio delle tradizioni popolari*, from vol. XIII(1894), pp. 65 onwards the interminable series of 'Miraculous imprints in Italy'; and cf. Sébillot, *Le Folk-lore de France*, I, Chs. IV and V, especially pp. 320ff., 359ff., and 402ff.

100 Baldesano, *La sacra historia*, p. 130.

101 J. Bernard de Montmélian, *Saint Maurice*, I, pp. 238ff.

102 On the famous shrine of Oropa, see Casalis, *Dizionario*, II, p. 312 ('Biella').

103 The shrine of Notre-Dame-de-Guérison, above Courmayeur, is still called locally 'La Croix du Berrier', *berrier* meaning 'rock' in the Aosta dialect; see the instructive booklet *Le Sanctuaire de Notre-Dame-de-Guérison à Courmayeur*, 3rd edition (Aosta, 1909).

104 If the cult of sacred stones has given birth to a certain number of local Thebans, it may also have contributed, to some extent, to the birth of the cult of the martyrs of Agaunum themselves. Notre-Dame-du-Scex or 'of the Rock' is still honoured today at Saint-Maurice with a very popular cult; see J. Bernard de Montmélian, *Saint Maurice*, I, pp. 126ff. The shrine is situated 100 metres above the town, on top of a rocky ledge and near a spring; cf. *Dictionnaire géographique de la Suisse* (Neuchâtel, 1902) (Sex).

105 See the judicious remarks of Delehaye, *Les Légendes hagiographiques*, Ch. VI, especially pp. 194ff.

106 Some educated people from Aosta write 'St Bès'. Some people from Cogne have told me that 'in French, you must say Bisse'. The name in the Soana valley is 'Bess', and the Italian name 'Besso'.

107 *C.I.L.*, III, s. 8312; cf. W. Schulze, 'Zur Geschichte lateinischer Eigennamen', *Abhandlungen der Königlichen Gesellschaft der Wissenschaften zu*

Göttingen, Philologisch-historische Klasse, NF V (Berlin, 1904), p. 39, n. 6.
As for the famous Egyptian God Bes, nothing, as far as I know, could lead one
to suppose that his cult or his name might have been introduced into the
region with which we are concerned.

108 Giulini in Savio, *Gli antichi vescovi*, p. 183.

109 See pp. 64–5 above.

110 See the article 'Bessoi' in Pauly-Wissowa. [Pauly and Wissowa, *Real-Encyclopädie der classischen Alterthumswissenschaft* (Stuttgart, 1893–   ). S.W.]
Their conversion to Christianity took place towards the end of the sixth
century.

111 This district, which forms part of the diocese of Vercelli, borders on that of
Ivrea, according to Savio, p. 183. There used to be a monastery there called
'della Bessa', to which G. Barelli refers in *Bibl. Soc. Stor. Subalp.*, IX, p. 271.
Perhaps these facts would account for the assertion made uniquely by Ferrari
that 'St Besse, having given up his arms, lived for some time the life of a hermit
in the region between Vercelli and Ivrea'; *Acta SS.*, Sept., VI, p. 917. The
similarity in the names may have prompted the idea that St Besse played a role
in the foundation of the monastery 'della Bessa'. But I have been unable to
gather any further information on this point.

112 The name 'Besse' crops up quite frequently in Swiss toponymy: 'Lo Besso', a
peak in the valley of Anniviers; 'Pierrebesse', 'Crêtabesse', etc. According to
Jaccard, *Essai de toponymie, Origine des noms de lieux... de la Suisse romande*
(Lausanne, 1906), pp. 34 and 548, this word comes from the low Latin *bissus*
meaning 'double', 'twin', or 'forked', and thus always designates a mountain
with two peaks, or a block made up of two rocks joined together, etc. Since, at
least to my knowledge, the Mount of Saint-Besse has no such dual feature,
this particular epithet does not apply to our rock. I was tempted to connect
the name 'Besse' with *becca*, which is found currently in the toponymy, alongside *becco*, to designate a rocky peak in the form of a beak. Such an etymology
would have fitted in well for the context, given the shape of the Mount; but it
seemed to be ruled out by the phonetic conditions of the dialect of the Soana
valley. According to these, *becca* must either remain as it is, or give the form
beči, but never *bess*. (I owe all this information to Professor Farina and to
Monsieur Terracini, an Italian linguist, who has made a special study of the
dialects of the mountains of Piedmont.)

113 *Dictionnaire géographique de la Suisse* ('Bescha'). The German equivalent is
'Schafberg'. Under this name, and under those of 'Schafhorn', 'Schafstock',
'Schafthurm', etc., the same *Dictionnaire* gives a long list of rocky summits,
dominating sheep pastures.

114 See Palliopi, *Dizionari...* (Samaden, 1895) ('besch'); and cf. Canello and
Ascoli, in *Arch. Glottol. Ital.*, III, p. 339; G. Paris, in *Romania*, IX, p. 486;
Körting, *Lateinisch-romanisches Wörterbuch*, 2nd edition (1901); and Meyer
and Lübke, *Romanisches Etymologisches Wörterbuch* (1911) ('bestia' and 'be-
stius'). The forms *biscia, bessa, bisse* are found in Italian and in old French to
mean 'serpent'.

115 Professor Farina tells me that in the Soana valley dialect, 'sheep' is *bigio*, and
'lamb' is *feia*. *Bestia* exists meaning 'animal' in general.

116 Cf. in Italian *biscio* or *besso*.

117 This formation is quite normal in the toponymy of the region. Monsieur
    Terracini draws my attention in particular to: 'Pera-čaval' (near Usseglio),
    'Monte-Bo' (in the Sesia valley) and, in several places, 'Pian-fé', which means
    'plateau of the lamb or of lambs'.

118 As for *bess* meaning 'imbecile', the sanctity of the Mount rules out any close
    connection between two names belonging to mental spheres so widely
    separated. [This 'coincidence' is perhaps too hastily dismissed by Hertz?
    S.W.]

119 Monsieur Terracini, to whom I expounded this hypothesis, believes that it
    does not raise any difficulties of a phonetic nature and that it is plausible.
    Bestia, he adds, 'in the Soana valley as in the other valleys, seems really to be a
    newcomer; the word is also Piedmontese. *Bigio* is a slang form, which is or
    was very commonly used in the valley.'

120 Delehaye, *Les Légendes hagiographiques*, pp. 12ff.

121 *Ibid.*, p. 67.

122 Cf., on the same lines, A. Van Gennep, *La Formation des légendes* (Paris, 1910),
    pp. 128ff.

2

❖❖❖❖❖❖❖❖❖❖❖❖❖❖❖❖❖❖❖❖❖❖❖❖❖❖❖❖❖❖❖❖❖❖❖❖❖

Ancient Byzantine hagiography and social history

EVELYNE PATLAGEAN

Any attempt to investigate the humblest forms of social life in the early Byzantine period[1] must encounter the seductions of the hagiographical literature. This is abundant, and it is eloquent when archival documents are practically non-existent, outside Egypt, and when other sources are silent or laconic. So, at the outset of his or her enquiry, the historian must adopt a critical position vis-à-vis hagiography. In this perspective, we have attempted a structural analysis, since we found the usual positivist method insufficient and wasteful.

Two approaches have contributed towards its elaboration. The first to examine hagiographical works, as we know, were clerics anxious not to profane the cult of saints by doing honour to apocryphal persons;[2] to this precise concern corresponds a rigid and limited preoccupation with assessing authenticity. Later, when historians decided to exploit the whole mass of texts, authenticity came to be seen in a new light; from this point of view, it was sufficient to establish the date of a work and, if possible, the place where it was written in order to take from it topographical, economic, social, and even historical data.[3] But both types of approach are all too often based on the supposition that the texts were 'popular' in content just as their production and consumption were reserved for the lower orders of society.[4] Scholars therefore felt free to manipulate the texts, to pluck concrete information from a hagiographical context, which was itself ignored; the latter was seen, it seems, as a mere stringing together, with some variations in their order, of a limited number of legendary themes, among which the authors, who were both stupid and truthful, had inserted certain facts which were the only elements worthy of attention.[5] Such a method of picking and choosing certainly seems to be the only one feasible for amassing a series of facts on a specific point; but, when used to the exclusion of any other, it substitutes for the dynamic coherence of a living work a fictive chimera in which cock-and-bull stories and reliable

101

observations are inexplicably mingled. Should not the latter also be suspect in such a context? Quite the opposite, it appears; for paradoxically the critical approach in question takes them quite literally, precisely because it does not examine the criteria by which the hagiographical authors selected and classified the facts which they present.

Moreover, the hagiography of the early Byzantine period is not simply 'popular' literature. It was written by monks, and it was addressed to the whole of society.

The Bollandists, again, were the first to classify medieval Byzantine hagiography into types and periods. Father Delehaye has shown that it evolved with the history of the Church.[6] As the militant period receded into the past, accounts of martyrdom lost their attraction and were replaced by ascetic Lives which became more and more fantastic. Greek hagiography of the sixth and seventh centuries, in effect, is that of a powerful Church, which was wealthy, had established institutions, and was omnipresent. Hagiography diversified in response to needs that had become complex, and divided into two main genres: collections of exemplary stories, on the one hand, and saints' Lives proper on the other. The related Miracles of a saint were sometimes incorporated into the Life, as in that of Simeon the Younger Stylite; but there were also highly legendary saints, such as St Artemius, concerning whom we have only a collection of Miracles centred on a shrine, without any biography.[7]

The two genres have a certain number of themes in common, and the same types of miracle and anecdotal illustrations of moral, religious or scriptural truths occur in both. But the Lives and Miracles were usually linked to a region, or to a micro-region, generally the zone of influence of the monastery where they were written; for example that of Mount Admirable for Simeon the Younger Stylite. The scene of the story hardly changes, unless the saint travels to Constantinople or to Jerusalem. With this exception, the monastery or the shrine remains the centre of the account, with the saint moving so little that he even works his miracles from a distance or through bilocation;[8] and people from the district or further afield come rather to him to be healed or advised. On the other hand, the collections of edifying tales have no local roots. They are usually located in regions especially associated with the practice of ascetic virtues: Palestine, Sinai, or Egypt, and they sometimes also take the reader to the cities of Alexandria, Antioch or Constantinople.

Each type has its own public. The poor and the simple play an important part in the Lives and in the Miracles, as they did in real society, and in accordance with certain tendencies of Christian thought. But the authors emphasize the social diversity of the people who have dealings with the saints: peasants from the monastery's lands or round about, citizens of all social conditions from neighbouring towns, courtiers and high functionaries, and even sometimes the emperor himself. The hagiographers wanted to be read by all social classes, for their aim was to instil into the whole of society veneration for the monastic 'order' as a whole, and, locally, for a particular monastery or shrine; and indeed, in one way or another, the whole of society had dealings with them. By contrast, the spiritual anthologies seem to have been designed for a less clearly defined, more extensive public, which was at the same time very similar wherever it was found. This comprised the monks themselves, and other people leading more or less ascetic lives.[9]

This group of monks, to which the writers of both hagiographical types belonged, was less homogeneous than one might think, and had mixed social origins. Certain themes in accounts of both types show how rash it would be to explain the peculiarities of hagiography in terms of the 'popular' origin of its authors. The saint is often born of well-to-do or rich parents, or even of dignitaries.[10] His poverty is always voluntary, even if he is of more modest origins.[11] The poor man who has no recourse, no choice, figures only as 'the other'; monks of humble origin are confined to minor roles. Hagiographical accounts are built – if only to repudiate them – on the values of those milieux where poverty is alien. Affirmation and then immediate denial: the authors' attitude is complex and seems to us to confirm the social complexity of their public.

Even more conclusively, the authors never fail to praise their heroes' intellectual merits, and, in the first place, their education, either in their families,[12] or in monasteries.[13] Those who take early to the hermit's life always receive miraculously the education which they would otherwise have lacked:[14] an indication of how important education was. And, though its contents were strictly religious, this was neither singular nor inadequate in sixth- and seventh-century Byzantine society. Adult characters always read, write and sing psalms; even in the poorest huts in the Egypto-Palestinian desert, there are the Scriptures or spiritual books.[15] Saints are praised for their knowledge of theology, exegesis and dialectics;[16] the aims here are twofold, however, the main one being to illustrate with what humility they hide their knowledge from monks of 'popular' background or from mere laymen.[17] These few facts show the danger involved in supposing hagiography to be confined to ignorant authors and audiences. Finally, we must stress that hagiography is not isolated, that contemporary historiography is close to it, sharing certain themes and categories, and sometimes even borrowing directly from it.

It is not legitimate, therefore, to submit hagiography to the criteria of a classical historical and literary tradition, whose path may be followed through medieval obstacles down to our own time. Hagiography will always resist this type of analysis, for its underlying structure means that it cannot be reduced to such a tradition, even if certain trimmings and occasional references help to mask its foreign character.

These are the reasons which have led us to attempt structural analysis, in the hope of understanding the mental categories of ancient Byzantine hagiography.[18] It is the only way by which we can account for each text as a whole and correctly assess these sources which social history and indeed history in general can no longer afford to overlook.

The idea sprang from the obvious resemblance between certain fields of contemporary anthropology and the subject matter of the hagiographies. It also seemed an opportunity for special collaboration between history and anthropology.

The series of oppositions by which Lévi-Strauss defines both history and anthropology is also to be found in the field of hagiography, but it is incomplete and forms a variant, which is neither plain history nor plain anthropology. To use Lévi-Strauss's terminology, our hagiography is akin to anthropology in that its models are on a mechanical and not a statistical scale,[19] and in that the unconscious model is of great significance. Byzantine society in the Early Middle Ages fits almost entirely, and certainly with regard to the present field of study, into a mechanical model, partly because it intrinsically possesses its characteristics and partly because the elements of a possible statistical model have not been preserved; but this fault in transmission cannot be imputed entirely to chance. On the other hand, the richness of the unconscious level, which is to be expected in this type of society, explains why scholars using traditional critical methods have found themselves at a loss regarding hagiography. We will search out the unconscious level beneath the conscious model of the saint's Life, and attempt to explain the totality of the hagiographical account through the way in which the different models fit one over another.

However, the main opposition between anthropology and history, as we know, is not here; it lies in the time dimension which the historian has at his disposal but of which the anthropologist is deprived for reasons which are again accidental but nevertheless significant. This difficulty disappears when the object of study is a coherent body of literature, from a relatively homogeneous cultural area, and written over less than two centuries. The evolution of time can hardly be felt in these works, which differ rather according to the author's personality and degree of culture, and in some respects also according to his region of origin; but we have been able to neglect these differences without prejudicing the analysis of their common structure, which we will now describe.

Our hagiographical accounts portray men who feel totally insecure in a world that is heavier with menace than it is rich in promise. Their structure defines the relationship between these men and this world. The texts, moreover, are rich enough to provide the basis for a historico-anthropological study,[20] along the lines of certain recent studies of societies which, making all due allowances, are comparable to the one with which we are here concerned. Knowledge of these contemporary studies – while not essential in the presentation of results – will be of great assistance in the course of the investigation.[21]

The hagiographical accounts reveal three superimposed models whose articulation forms the structure with which we are concerned. They correspond to three levels of relationship between men and the world, which is always seen in terms of an attack which men fight off thanks to an intermediary with superhuman powers. Working from the unconscious to the conscious level, we find first the *demonic model*, in which the attack is perpetrated by demons, operating beyond any moral values; next follows the *scriptural model*, in which the terms of the relationship closely follow the characters and events of the Gospels or occasionally of the Old Testament; lastly comes the *ascetic and moral model*, which differs from the previous one in that the terms of the relationship are consciously transposed on to a plane of asceticism, virtue and sin.

Demonic attack comprises every possible negative relationship between men and the world. Most immediately, the individual's own personality is seen as a value, a finite perishable quality which can be taken away from him. This is what happens when he is possessed by a demon. Hagiography provides us with a harvest of rich, detailed observations of the behaviour of the possessed, which deserve special study. A demon takes over the possessed person entirely and reveals itself in aggressive, incongruous behaviour, and through the violent negation of social rules; the possessed person attacks strangers, utters obscenities and even does injury to himself, since his normal personality is no longer carrying out its function of self-preservation. When a saint casts it out, the demon at first resists and insults him, then comes out through the victim's mouth, usually in the form of a snake. The victim, emptied, falls to the ground as if dead, and sometimes does actually die some days later.[22] People are vulnerable in their bodies as well as in their personalities: demons attack them with blows or by throwing stones at them,[23] or via poisonous or harmful animals,[24] or , finally and most commonly, through illnesses of all kinds. Demons can also attack a man's possessions: his house, his crops.[25] They are personal, negatively oriented forces, which manifest themselves either directly through their actions, or else in the guise of animals, which may be purely illusory.[26] However, these negative interventions do not affect more fundamental matters: subsistence, climatic phenomena, natural disasters, or the control of life and death.

In this model of the relationship between men and the world, the demon is an immediate presence and has no development, whereas the human intermediary defending men against demons has a history. His power of riposte is not an innate gift; it is acquired by an ascetic training which eventually sets him apart from other men and takes him beyond the natural limits of the human condition. His origins show themselves, however, in the fact that he takes no initiative, confining himself to restoring the proper desirable relationship between men and the world wherever demons have destroyed it. Consequently, the miracle worker's power does not stem from and is not manifested in positive extremes of human behaviour, as in other cultures,[27] but is related rather to an absence. Ascesis begins with two modes of separation: the saint leaves human society at an early age to go into the desert, and he abstains from sexual relations. In other words, he leaves the field of culture to rejoin that of nature, whose limits he then reaches and at which he carries on his struggle;[28] sexual abstinence is usually combined with abstinence from food. Detailed description of the ascetic's extraordinary fasts is an obligatory feature of the Lives and also of the accounts in the spiritual collections. The Life of Simeon the Younger Stylite preserves the ultimate version of the model, in which the ascetic no longer eats at all.[29] Many texts explicitly stress the opposition between nature and culture in the food of the ascetic.[30] This consists as a rule of plants which are not cultivated and which are consumed without being cooked, whereas cultivated or cooked foods – civilized products like wine and often bread – are forbidden.[31] Abstinence from meat should be noted: it is a well-known prohibition in similar contexts in other societies; but, additionally, in the Romano-Byzantine world, meat was associated with life in urban society, and, for this reason, besides any economic considerations, was never part of an ascetic's diet. The only people who consumed meat in the desert, in a state of nature, were the Barbarians who hunted wild animals and who sometimes killed their own beasts when forced to do so.[32] The return to nature and the abandonment of culture may also be seen in the saint's near or total nudity, in his lack of concern for hygiene or bodily welfare, and in the absence of shelter against winter weather.[33] This whole way of life, in its deprivation, was conceived by people whose values lay with culture and whose non-values lay with nature.

The presence of this underlying model, which is outside Christianity and alien indeed to any moral orientation, is attested by a passage in Procopius' *Anecdota*, which has not yet, it seems, been properly appreciated: the famous description of Justinian as a demon prince.[34] His way of life is exactly like that of the ascetics; he neither sleeps nor eats to speak of, increasing his self-denial before Easter to the point of having only one hour of sleep and of eating wild plants with a little water to drink. Only his sexual activity is excessive, though marital. The power that he has won over his human nature is identical to that of the saints; for example, he seems like them to be capable of supernatural travel. But his powers have the opposite significance to theirs: he uses them only in the cause of evil. Procopius illustrates this by turning upside down the scene, common to hagiography, of the demon who retreats, terrorized, before the saint; here it is the pious hermit who takes fright at the entrance to the throne room, because he perceives the demonic personality of the Emperor.

The future miracle worker must dominate in himself the nature which he finds all round him. He braves the biological limits of nutrition, sleep, pain, the laws of equilibrium and of motion. The first stage of ascesis ends when demons attack him openly after a stay of varying length in the desert. In this first model, at the deepest level, the demons are not symbols of moral temptation; like other men, the ascetic suffers their tangible or phantom attacks, but in his case, they are more serious, because he is a declared adversary and not a mere victim. Thus, they push Sabas into the Dead Sea;[35] as a child, Simeon is assailed on his column by fantastic birds, by a hand pulling him into the shadows, and in other ways too, all of which must have rich symbolic meanings.[36] The first part of a Life ends in fact when the first miracle is wrought. This division into two of the Lives of saints has not been sufficiently taken into account: first, the acquisition and the inaugural demonstration of miraculous powers, then the exercise of this power in human society, without it ever being endangered or weakened.

The second part of a saint's Life begins with the interruption of solitude, the return among men of a human being who has become stronger than they are.[37] Miracles now occur one after the other. The first often function as signs; they show that the saint has broken free of the human condition, of the shackles of time[38] and space,[39] that he can command the elements,[40] demons, illness, hunger and wild beasts.[41]

However, this underlying model is not in fact found here in its entirety; it has been eroded by Christianity. Birth, death, great collective catastrophes, are never attributed to demonic aggression. To look for the reason for this would be to introduce the historical dimension into our analysis; let us simply acknowledge that our fundamental model can only be seen in a less than perfect form, since the course of history has irrevocably modified the original complete version. On another level, the scriptural model is more nearly complete, but not entirely so.[42]

We will deal more briefly with the other two models which we have discovered in the texts, and will be content merely to summarize the results of our analysis. The scriptural model shows the similarity between the saint and Christ, with secondary reference to other figures, such as Moses.[43] In itself, it contains no moral explanation for the misfortune of men or for the merits of the saints, but makes only a formal reference, the highest, in order to guarantee the effectiveness of the miracle-working saint. This convinces the reader and leads him to believe any circumstantial details which the hagiographer may add, particularly those concerning the monastery to which he belongs. The first part of saints' Lives, the ascetic conquest of miraculous powers, does not, of course, have a detailed model in the Scriptures. The authors, nevertheless, recall Christ's withdrawal into the desert and his encounter with Satan,[44] and also John the Baptist's experience as a hermit. The scriptural model is more obvious in the second part of the Lives: the exercise of the saint's powers. One has the impression that the whole of the human condition is included here – birth and death, famine and epidemics – as well as the kinds of misfortune attributed in the previous model to demons – attacks on the personality, on the body and on property. But, in reality, the series of miraculous actions is chosen according to a rigorous criterion of scriptural reference. The saint heals the illnesses and infirmities mentioned in the Gospels, including demonic possession; he raises people from the dead, as Christ did Lazarus; he calms storms; multiplies the provisions of the faithful; and provides miraculous draughts of fishes.[45] To benefit from his activity, only faith is necessary.

The moral model is the only entirely conscious one, the only one, too, in which man plays an active part beside his mediator. A moral fault explains all the setbacks of individual or collective existence, physical or mental illness,[46] material damage, disasters of all sorts.[47] A man attacked by a demon often turns out to be a sinner.[48] The saint acquires his power through ascesis in which his bodily deprivations have spiritual value and in which he is tried by purely moral exploits of humility, obedience, etc.[49] His superhuman power consists of discovering the fault which has led to the evil, and in determining the right redress; it is only after this that he works his restorative miracle. The orientation is always the same: the saint confines himself to putting things right; he never spontaneously adds a superabundance of good in a deserving case. This model, however, is not complete either: the saint predicts catastrophes brought on by some collective fault, but he can never change their course; when he brings a dead man back to life, as Christ did, it is never a man who died in punishment for his sins. In a word, in the same way that the unconscious model was influenced by Christianity, the moral model, already specifically Christian, is hemmed in by theological notions which undermine it.

These then are the three levels on which the hagiographical account presents first the conquest of superhuman power through ascesis and then the beneficial exercise of that power. We can see how such a structure accounts for the wealth of specific, concrete information contained in hagiography. In the first place, some of the information serves the structure itself. Here we shall take the example of health, which is related to research which we have undertaken. On this subject, of such importance in social history, the hagiographical texts offer an apparently plentiful documentation, but one which is full of traps and lacunae that only structural analysis can perceive and, to a certain extent, overcome, given the definitive absence of any possibility of direct observation of the facts. The underlying model is on the whole rather poor if one is aiming to establish a general picture of health with modern clinical definitions. On the other hand, the demonic interpretation offers wide possibilities for the study of illness in more general cultural terms; mental troubles, psychological echoes of organic disease, appear fairly clearly. The scriptural model, as we have seen, imposes strict limits on factual information here; so, when saints heal crowds of blind men and paralytics, are we dealing with the Gospel model quite simply, or with a feature of oriental life that had remained unchanged between the time of the Gospels and the sixth and seventh centuries? Certainly with both, but the all-powerful references often impoverish the descriptions, robbing them of details and making them useless to the historian.

The moral model should have been the freest; but eventually it, too, became fixed in traditional themes which also impoverish the documentary aspect of the account through their lack of precision. However, the information remains significant, even at the level of stereotype. The shorter the account, the less illustrative detail it contains. Concomitantly, a long work, such as the Life of Simeon the Younger Stylite, resembles a chronicle of a monastery and its district, and the hagiographer is able not only to illustrate the model but also to record particularly striking case histories.

The structure that we have described does not, one may object, account for all the socio-historical data to be found in our accounts; but, as we shall see, it does account for forms of space and time which hagiography preserves but which historiography lets escape. We may thus observe not so much a definite separation between historical and hagiographical works as the possibility of a common classification along a continuum at either end of which, at almost theoretical extremes, are the work of pure hagiography and that of pure history.[50] In this perspective, a socio-historical study can consider the two groups as complementary rather than divergent sources.

The space in which an author places his work determines his choice of facts. Early Byzantine mentality is dominated by an urban and civic image of space conforming to a specific organic definition which must be briefly discussed here. A town was any agglomeration, big or small, which had the distinctive features of civic, that is to say urban, life: not only the hippodrome and the theatre, but also the forum, the *stoa*, the public baths, the basilicas, all places where the citizens could assemble. This definition had been handed down from Classical Antiquity, along with the ideology of the monumental donation.[51] It applies particularly to Constantinople or to a big town like Antioch, but it can also raise to the rank of a city a distant garrison like Dara, which was transformed by Anastasius and renamed

Anastasiopolis.[52] Churches and religious establishments had been integrated into the classical scheme and had taken on a significance similar to that which other public buildings had, but they were not in themselves sufficient to mark the urban dignity of an agglomeration.[53] At the heart of the urban image, the hippodrome reflects in itself the city, the Empire and the world;[54] a structural study of it would certainly throw light on the political life of the early Byzantine city. For the present, we will simply emphasize the importance of the urban image for the problem with which we are now concerned. Several easily deduced cultural reasons explain the fact that all types of historical work are confined for this period to the urban space; indeed, all events originate in and lead to towns. In its internal history, the whole Empire appears as a collection of juxtaposed urban spaces with historical voids between them. What is more, the force of the definition is such that it determines the selection of data within the urban space itself. Authors search out civil and political expressions of social facts; they choose from the economic and social background only what determines or threatens the equilibrium of a town in its traditional definition: monetary devaluations, crises of food supply, agitations and disorders. Even plagues and earthquakes are mainly described and their damage evaluated with respect to towns.

Hagiography's originality is that it breaks free of urban space. It presents the same material image of it as do the historians, but only to deny it any value. We have already seen that the repudiation of secular civic life marks the beginning of the ascetic life. Later, when the saint comes back to the world of men, he still does not enter the town; he lets the town-dwellers come to him and seek the benefit of his power outside their own space. The exceptional case of Simeon Salos, the voluntary fool, who enters Emisa incognito in order to take up a secret ministry there, is significant in itself, for the whole story is constructed on an ascetic reversal of the values of ascesis. Simeon lives in town and becomes a waiter in a back-street restaurant, in the same way that he gorges himself on meat although he has vowed not to eat bread, or that he goes into the women's public baths. The depravity of the town is symbolized by the evil haunts where a monk who has left the desert will succumb to temptation;[55] or by the hippodrome and the theatre from which the converted mime must tear himself away;[56] or by the baths themselves, the hiding places of demons of temptation.[57] However, hagiography is deeply marked by the urban image which it is trying to exorcize; the hippodrome, the seat of the Basileus, may be forbidden in earthly towns, but in the spiritual world it provides an ambiguous setting for combat and victory;[58] even the cheering heard there may be similarly transposed.[59]

What are the consequences of this freedom? There are urban scenes in hagiography; and sometimes they are of some importance. The Life of Simeon the Younger Stylite describes the trials of Syrian towns, and of Antioch in particular, during the plague, the Persian invasion and earthquakes. Similarly, Cyril of Scythopolis dwells on the damage caused in Palestinian towns by the Samaritan revolt of 529.[60] Elsewhere, on the other hand, in the Life of Theodore of Sykeon, or of Marcellus the Sleepless, even the capital is not the object of any special attention. And in all Lives, the towns are no more than a part of one single unlimited space, one material setting. Thus, hagiography can record the humbler facts of urban life, show the poor who have set up home in front of a church or who go to warm themselves in a glass-blower's workshop. History prefers not to include such scenes in its traditional townscape, although certain historical works were nearly as free as hagiography: the *Anecdota* of Procopius, the *Chronicle* of John Malalas, the *Ecclesiastical History* of Evagrius. Moreover, the towns are no longer the places outside which nothing important in internal history ever happens. Hagiography does a lot to help us reconstitute the organic limits of the territory around each of them.[61] The desert of the first part of the Lives, the inhabited area of the second, can be located anywhere at all, even right at the gates of towns; the first is a wild space and the second a rural one, and both are the setting for social facts which are not included in the urban space of historiography.

Like that of space, the form of time demands a different choice of social facts in historiography and in hagiography. Historians have in common their use of linear, irreversible time, expressed according to points of reference recognized by the community itself: the year of Creation, or of the foundation of the city, more rarely consular years. Successive internal events seem in fact to be limited to repetitions of certain types: riots, catastrophes, constructions. We saw above how the choice of these is explained by the urban form of space, but they must also, according to the old classical tradition, be exceptional in order to merit recording. This criterion can vary according to the genre and the author's intelligence, but it is sufficiently respected on the whole to deprive us of ordinary events.[62]

Hagiography seems also at first sight to employ historical time. The account refers to well-known events, even to a system of dates by the years of an emperor's reign. However, facts are ordered, in reality, according to internal requirements which are quite independent of chronology or the measurement of duration. Hagiography provides a timeless acount of the passage of men beyond the human condition: or, alternatively, we could place it in the *reversible* time of myths. This is why authors often situate their saints' Lives fictively in some far-off moment of the past, if a deliberate anachronism of this kind can serve their purposes; for example, to prove the apostolic antiquity of an episcopal seat. In fact, most Lives mentioned here happened not long before the hagiographer was writing or were contemporary with him.

So what is the role of events in hagiography? Some are those which also form the subject matter of the histories. For example, the successive disasters in the Life of Simeon the Younger Stylite are part of a well-known chronology. But each of these exceptional events is merely the setting for one of the saint's miracles, whose extraordinary quality is emphasized by the gravity of its circumstances; thus historical selectivity is also used in the specific perspective of hagiography. But, liberated in time as well as space, the Lives of the saints, which thus appear to be historical although their structure is foreign to historical time, can include without discrimination those humble incidents so precious to social history, because they too provide opportunities for the demonstration of the saint's power. In one sense, indeed, these incidents will carry more weight with the public described above, and will be the more appreciated in that they are directly familiar. Here, at last, we have the explanation for the abundance of concrete information in hagiography. Its function requires, as we can see, that it be exact within certain limits which are perceptible when the texts are closely studied. For example, the authors had no reason to manipulate prices, whereas the food rations which they mention may for the good of the cause be made bigger or smaller than the real average; this ruse is usually executed with an artlessness that betrays it, and we are always left with a rough kind of measurement and with a quantity of examples unequalled in any other Eastern source.

We have now outlined the oppositions in the categories of space and time in historical and hagiographical works, and pointed to their relevance and value for socio-historical investigation. Here perhaps lies the surest means of distinguishing between the two genres when they appear to be sliding into each other to form a single register, when, as rarely happens, the hagiographer becomes a historian, or, much more common, when the historian borrows general schemes or whole episodes from the hagiographer; and here we can cite not only John Malalas,[63] Evagrius,[64] or Theophylact Simocatta,[65] but also Procopius himself.[66] There must be a logic to these borrowings, and it could be a subject worth studying.

But that is not our object here, and it only remains for us to conclude. We have aimed in our defence and illustration of ancient Byzantine hagiography to highlight a structure in which social history can find a justifiable and solid source of information instead of a heap of interesting but fortuitous details. Strict structural analysis, used up to now only by anthropologists, may well find here in the field which we have all too briefly introduced, a privileged means of access to the study of religious structures in process of historical change, and recorded, moreover, in writing in the

very society in which they occurred. We very much hope so. For, by this
method, the historian of the Middle Ages can recover – with respect to a
past which despite himself he grows used to – that feeling of total
strangeness or alienation without which he cannot totally apprehend his
object of study.

NOTES

1 Without going further into a question which is irrelevant here, let us simply say
   that by this term we mean the period between the last quarter of the fifth and
   the middle of the seventh century.
2 P. Peeters, 'A travers trois siècles, l'oeuvre des Bollandistes', *Mémoires de
   l'Académie Royale de Belgique*, Classe des Lettres, 39/4 (Brussels, 1942).
3 The first steps in the field of Greek hagiography were taken in A. Tougard,
   *Quid ad profanos mores dignoscendos augendaque lexica conferant Acta Sanctorum graeca
   bollandiana*, and *De l'histoire profane dans les Actes Grecs des Bollandistes* (Paris,
   1874). This method has been practised from the later nineteenth century,
   particularly by Russian Byzantinists. We were unable to gain access to A. P.
   Rudakov's book, *Očerki vizantijskoj kultury po dannym greč. agiografij* (Moscow,
   1917): only one volume yet published.
4 This notion is clearly expressed in H. Delehaye, *Les Légendes hagiographiques*
   (Brussels, 1905). It is maintained in A. J. Festugière, *Les Moines d'Orient, culture
   ou sainteté, Introduction au monachisme oriental* (Paris, 1961), though his argument
   is mainly based on the previous period and in particular on the *Lausiac History*;
   see also by the same author, *Antioche païenne et chrétienne, Libanius, Chrysostome, et
   les moines de Syrie* (Paris, 1959), on the indigenous and primitive character of
   fifth-century Syrian anchoretic life. E. Stein, finally, takes as self-evident the
   exclusively low 'popular' nature of Oriental hagiography, starting with the
   Life of St Anthony, *Histoire du Bas-Empire*, II (Paris, 1949), pp. 698–700; and I
   (Paris, 1959), pp. 146–50; see also H. I. Marrou, 'Le Bas-Empire vu par un
   élève de Mommsen', *Journ. Sav.* (1964), pp. 47–58; he allows that Cyril of
   Scythopolis was an exception but does not mention any other hagiographical
   work from the same period. For a contrast, see the fair and measured pages by
   F. Halkin, 'L'Hagiographie byzantine au service de l'Histoire', *Thirteenth
   International Congress of Byzantine Studies*, Main Papers XI (Oxford, 1966),
   pp. 1–10.
5 See the treatment of the Life of Simeon the Younger Stylite in P. Van den
   Ven's otherwise remarkable edition, *La Vie ancienne de S. Syméon Stylite le Jeune
   (521–592)*, I (Brussels, 1962), Introduction and Greek text.
6 H. Delehaye, Lectures at the Collège de France (6–10 May 1935), 'L'Ancienne
   Hagiographie byzantine, origine, sources d'inspiration, formation des genres',
   Byzantion, X (1935), pp. 379–80.
7 The appendix gives a list of works cited here; it is far from exhaustive of the
   period, and we have chosen only the most fertile examples. The reader is
   referred to the *Bibliotheca Hagiographica Graeca*, 3rd edition, ed. Fr. Halkin

(Brussels, 1957), listed as BHG 3 plus inventory number; a few further chronological details may be found in H. G. Beck, *Kirche und Theologische Literatur im byzant. Reich* (Munich, 1959). The present study is mainly limited to Asia Minor, Syria, and Palestine as far as the Sinai desert.

8 See the examples given in n. 39.

9 See the prologue of the alphabetic-anonymous Collection of the Apophtegmata studied by Guy, *Apophtegmata*, pp. 13–15, cited in the Appendix.

10 *V. Joh. Silent.*, 1; *V. Sampson.*, fol. 198; *V. Sabae*, p. 86; *Apopht. Arsen.* 36; *Joh. Eph. V. Sanct. Orient.*, 12, 21, 44.

11 Simeon the Younger Stylite was the son of a master perfumer, and Theodore of Sykeon the illegitimate son of the landlady of an inn but also of a high functionary.

12 Texts cited above; John of Ephesus explains the importance of Greek literature in the studies of these young men. For popular education, note the little country schools grouped around hermits, *Joh. Eph. V. Sanct. Orient.*, 5, 16.

13 *V. Gerasim.*, 1; *V. Alyp. Styl.*, 3; *V. Sabae*, p. 87 (Sabas finished his education in a monastery). Two authors add their own examples: Cyril of Scythopolis tells how his father entrusted him when he was a child to Sabas (*V. Sabae*, p. 180); George of Sykeon, from a different, less cultured background, tells how he was taught the rudiments in a monastery (*V. Theod. Syk.*, fol. 227 v), and how Theodore did not really approve of his being engaged in literary work even if its subject was someone else (*V. Theod. Syk.*, fol. 271 v).

14 Theodore of Sykeon, who could not learn the Psalter on his own, prayed to an image of the Saviour in a church; honey-like sweetness came from the latter's mouth, and, when he tasted it, the saint immediately became learned (*Vita*, fol. 162); Nicon the Higumene appeared to Simeon Salos and his companion while they were in the desert and taught them (*Vita*, p. 138).

15 *Apopht. Agathon*, 22; *Ammoes*, 5; *Gelasios*, 1; Nau, 541; *Prat. Spir.*, 55, 134.

16 Simeon Salos, the Voluntary Fool, was able to settle a discussion about Origen that two monks came from far away to submit to him – he interrupted his simulated madness for a moment to do so (*V. Sym. Sal.*, pp. 152–3). Arsenius, a contemporary of Theophilus of Alexandria, received a thorough education at court before becoming a monk (*Apopht. Arsen.*, 5, 6, 36).

17 Arsenius, in the texts cited above, depreciates culture in comparison with the spiritual virtues that the 'Egyptian bumpkins', who were in the desert with him, had acquired through practical effort. Learning is only a preparation for ascetic practice and yields to it (Nau, 541). Simple men and even laymen are quoted as examples, but less for their ignorance than for their way of life (Eulogius, the stone-cutter, BHG 3, 618; the old wood-cutter, Nau, 628; the market gardener, Nau, 67).

18 The following pages assume that the reader is familiar with Claude Lévi-Strauss, *Structural Anthropology* (London, 1977) and particularly the Introduction, 'History and Anthropology', pp. 1–27; chapter XI, 'The Structural Study of Myth', pp. 206–31; chapter XII, 'Structure and

Dialectics', pp. 232–41; and chapter XV, 'Social Structure', pp. 277–323; see also n. 42 below.

19 'A model the elements of which are on the same scale as the phenomena will be called a "mechanical model"; when the elements of the model are on a different scale, we shall be dealing with a "statistical model".' Lévi-Strauss, *Structural Anthropology* (1977) p. 283.

20 Michel Foucault, *Madness and Civilization: A History of Insanity in the Age of Reason* (London, 1971) discusses the Middle Ages only in his fairly short first chapter and then only in the Western world.

21 Obviously, one would only retain those mental structures which corresponded exactly to those in the texts, or which at least gave rise to no significant opposition. One would therefore leave on one side not only non-Christian societies but also Christian societies of colonial origin, in which other factors come into play – see the evocative descriptions of A. Métraux, *Le Vaudou Haïtien* (Paris, 1953). There remain, in particular, the backward Christian societies of the Mediterranean; those of southern Italy have the advantage of a history with no great cultural upheavals since the Middle Ages, when Byzantine culture was itself present in the region. E. De Martino has recently carried out two valuable investigations, the first in Lucania: *Sud e Magia* (Milan, 1959), Fr. trans. *Italie du Sud et Magie* (Paris, 1963), the second in the Terra di Bari: *La Terra del rimorso* (Milan, 1961), Fr. trans. *La Terre du Remords* (Paris, 1966). The first assembles precious data on supernatural attacks, the invasion of personalities rendered vulnerable and unstable by rural poverty, and the resort to human intermediaries between men and the [supernatural S.W.] world. The other studies a particular cultural model of mental illness present in the region since the Middle Ages: the troubles that are attributed to the bite of the tarantula.

22 Here are two examples, the first from the Life of Simeon the Younger Stylite (para. 147), the second from the Life of Theodore of Sykeon (fol. 196): 'He was brought before the saint [Simeon] and at once remained hanging head downwards with the demons inside him, and they were punished during five days and five nights. And the saint questioned them with these words: "Why have you dared to do all this to this man?" the demons wept and replied, "We were sent to cast him into the fire or to make him perish in water." Having chastised them in the name of Our Lord Jesus Christ, the saint ordered them to come out of him and not to return; and with much clamour, they left him.' The woman delivered by Theodore of Sykeon suffers from a thousand pains, which stem from 'the activity of the spirits' inhabiting her; she comes to the door of a church where the saint is presiding over a ceremony; 'the spirits moved her to action and she threw off her cloak and the cloth from around her head; she howled and parted the crowd in her path; and then she began, with much groaning, to bark at the blessed Theodore, while the demons blasphemed as if they were confounded by his arrival. Seeing this, the whole crowd began to chant the *Kyrie Eleison*. The woman, as if suspended above the ground, with her hands bound and pointing upwards, came through the air from the ambo to the railings of the gallery, while the demons clamoured, as if the blessed one were

interceding against them with God.' A great variety of similar cases could be assembled; for example from the same Life of Theodore of Sykeon (fol. 229), the demon is visible under the patient's skin like a mouse, and runs away down his limbs when the saint appears; or (fol. 265 v), a collective deliverance in which the patients lacerate their clothes which are then buried, etc.

23   *V. Theod. Syk.*, fols. 181, 220 v, 233.

24   *V. Theod. Syk.*, fol. 229 (a poisonous lizard gets into a pot of vegetables); *V. Sabae*, p. 95 (snakes and scorpions), etc.

25   *V. Theod. Syk.*, fol. 220 v (attacks against villagers). The demons often haunted places with pagan vestiges – around a marble sarcophagus used as a watering place (*V. Theod. Syk.*, fol. 224 v), or a desert place full of old tombs (*V. Alyp. Styl.*, para. 8).

26   *V. Theod. Syk.*, fols. 216 v and 251 (two separate incidents in which a black dog appears to travellers who are then struck with some infirmity).

27   See the Lucanian personality of the old peasant seer with special powers over young women, De Martino, *Sud e Magia*.

28   On this opposition, see Claude Lévi-Strauss, *The Elementary Structures of Kinship* (New York, 1969, Chapter I).

29   *V. Sym. Styl. jr*, para. 256. The hagiographer felt that he should give some explanation of this apparently absolute fast, and says that an angel came every Sunday to give Simeon a miraculous dish of a sort of rice (*oryza*), which is not usually included in ascetic diets.

30   On the opposition between nature and culture in diet, see Lévi-Strauss's notes, 'Le Triangle culinaire', *L'Arc*, 26 (1965/1), pp. 19–20.

31   Among numerous texts, let us mention Nau, 517 ('abstinence from food, from bread made with corn, in a word from any food cooked by fire'); and *V. Sym. Styl.jr*, para. 3 (Simeon as a child 'will not consume his portion of meat, nor of wine, nor of anything prepared by human skill'). The material explanation of the absence of fuel in desert hermitages, far from weakening the structural explanation, provides a basis for it.

32   *Anast. mon.*, X; *Nili Mon. Narrationes*, III (PG, 79, col. 612). This text may be earlier than our period.

33   *V. Alyp. Styl.*, para. 14; *V. Sym. Styl.jr*, para. 23; *V. Theod. Syk.*, fol. 172. We are told that in this respect Bessarion led a beast-like life (*Apopht. Bessarion*, 12); and he is one of the rare characters in the texts whose activity as a miracle worker is quite fully described.

34   *Procopius, Anecd.*, XII, 20–30 and XIII, 28–30. B. Rubin, 'Der Antichrist u. die "Apokalypse" des Prokopios von Kaisareia', *Zeitschr. D. Morg. Ges.*, 110 (1960), pp. 53–63, keeps to a fairly formal study of the Oriental origins of the Antichrist theme.

35   *V. Sabae*, p. 106.

36   *V. Sym. Styl. jr*, para. 39.

37   The obligation to return is debated in the Life of Simeon Salos (the dialogue between Simeon and his companion Johannis, who chooses to remain in the desert, *V. Sym. Sal.*, pp. 142–4); and in the Life of John the Silentiary, who prefers total solitude to monastic life in the monastery (*laura*) of St Sabas. Communities often demand the protection of saints; see the account in Nau,

491, in which an ascetic dies at the gates of a town which mourns him, because his prayers used to obtain water, bread and salvation for everyone. When the saint is a stylite, the crowd comes to him.

38 The saint foretells his own death (*V. Theod. Syk.*, fol. 273 v); the destiny of illustrious visitors (*V. Sabae*, p. 146; *V. Theod. Syk.*, fol. 187; *V. Alyp. Styl.*, para. 22); and the misfortunes of the people as a whole – invasions (*V. Sym. Styl. jr*, para. 57), plague (*V. Sym. Sal*, pp. 159–60), earthquakes (*V. Sym. Styl. jr*, paras 78 and 104–6). In this last series, the imagery has an apocalyptic beauty which deserves more attention.

39 The saints travel great distances in spirit: Simeon the Younger Stylite goes to heal Justin II in his palace (*V. Sym. Styl. jr*, paras. 208–11); Simeon Salos goes to talk with his mother in Edessa (*V. Sym. Sal.*, pp. 138–9). Julian the Stylite knows from a distance that Simeon the Younger Stylite has died (*Prat. Spir.*, 57). Ammonas goes to Constantinople and returns in one night, bringing back tax exemption for the monks of the region of Pelusium (*Apopht. Patr. Ammonas*). For miracles at a distance for people who invoke the saint, see *V. Sym. Styl. jr*, paras. 68, 79; *V. Sabae*, p. 119.

40 The first miracle is often to do with water, which figures at some point in most Lives: a spring in a dry place (*V. Sabae*, p. 101; *V. Alyp. Styl.*, para. 8); or rainfall ending a drought (*V. Theod. Syk.*, fol. 163 v; *V. Sym. Styl. jr*, para. 96; *Prat. Spir.*, 174); *V. Sabae*, p. 167 (a cloud appearing over his monks' heads). See also various examples in *V. Theod. Syk*: Theodore's region had a harsh climate.

41 Simeon the Younger Stylite gets rid of all sorts of beasts who are devastating the countryside (*V. Sym. Styl. jr*, paras. 51–2, 68, 79, 178, 182–3). More often than not, this power is used symbolically over lions; a lion is defeated (*V. Sabae*, p. 119), enslaved (*V. Sym. Styl. jr*, paras. 182–3), kills a boar which is devastating the monastery's crops (*Prat. Spir.*, 18, 163), leads the monastery donkey out to graze (*Prat. Spir.*, 108; *V. Geras.*, 7). The importance of this theme of the tamed lion is shown by its presence in the late-sixth-century *Itinerary of Antoninus* (*Itineraria Hierosolymitana*, ed. P. Geyer (Vienna, 1898), para. 34).

42 On the historical transformation of structures, see in addition to Lévi-Strauss, cited in n. 18, by the same author, 'Les limites de la notion de structure en ethnologie', in Roger Bastide (ed.), 'Sens et usage du terme structure dans les sciences humaines et sociales', *Janua Linguarum*, XVI (The Hague, 1962), pp. 40–5.

43 The parallel is rarely explained because the episodes on which it is based are sufficiently recognizable; there is an example in the eulogy at the end of the Life of Marcellus the Sleepless. We must add that the authors also refer to certain great hagiographical models: St Anthony; Simeon the Elder Stylite; or the Voluntary Fool, one of the most interesting types: see S. Murray, *A Study of the Life of Andreas, The Fool for the sake of Christ*, Inaugural Dissertation, 1908 (Leipzig, 1910).

44 Satan disguised as an old man nearly succeeds in throwing Theodore of Sykeon off a cliff (*V. Theod. Syk.*, fols. 160 v and 161).

45 Numerous examples are found in all the Lives; though for the draught of fishes

there is only one example – in *V. Theod. Syk.*, fol. 256 v. Miraculous food supplies are also interesting for the details which they sometimes include about the monastic economy. They occur in two forms: the inexhaustible supply (*V. Theod. Coenob.*, p. 39), which can be of some produce other than corn or bread (oil, *Anast. mon.*, IX; *V. Georg. Chozib.*, 37); or the empty granary, which is miraculously filled at the last moment and which has not had to be replenished since (*V. Sym. Styl.*, paras. 122–3; *V. Marcell.*, fol. 240 AB; *Prat. Spir.*, 28; Nau, 281).

46 *V. Theod. Syk.*, fol. 203 v (to effect a cure, a priest has to make peace with his higumene); *V. Sym. Styl.*, para. 101 (a girl is ill because her mother has done something wrong), etc.

47 *V. Sabae*, p. 159 (an offence against the Archbishop of Jerusalem provoked in succession drought, a plague of locusts, famine and an epidemic). The predictions cited above (n. 38) always illustrate a moral explanation of the misfortunes foretold, with, if possible, a Biblical reference; the idea obviously exceeds the limits of hagiography, see the *Novella* of Justinian, 28 (N. 77), A. 535, on blasphemers and homosexuals, and historians such as Evagrius and Malalas, *passim*.

48 *V. Sym. Styl. jr*, para. 214 (blasphemer). This naturally leads on to the idea of demons possessing people in order to force them to do evil (*Prat. Spir. Add. Marc.*, 8, where a demon makes a woman living in ascesis follow beauty treatments and go to the baths).

49 See Nau, 461 (moral merit gives the power to work miracles through mortification dedicated to God); Nau, 528 (animal food is suited to men who have acted like animals); and many other texts.

50 The historiography of the early Byzantine period has been judged even more inflexibly than hagiography on its merits or demerits according to the classical tradition of the great Greek and Roman historians (see the extreme attitude of Stein, *Histoire du Bas-Empire*, II, pp. 702–23). This may explain why no one has studied all its forms, or gone beyond a convenient but superficial classification into traditional court histories, ecclesiastical histories and 'chronicles' at the bottom of the scale, not far removed from the saints' Lives, of which the most significant surviving example is that bearing the signature of John Malalas; see E. Gerland, 'Die Grundlagen der byzant. Geschichtschreibung', *Byzantion*, VIII (1933), pp. 93–105; and in similar vein, G. Moravcsik, *Byzantinoturcica*, I, *Charakteristik der Quellen*, 2nd edn (Berlin, 1958), pp. 71–4.

51 See the late-fourth-century eulogy of Antioch in Discourse XI by Libanius, and for the fifth century the monuments of the same town in the border of the mosaic found in Yakto, in the suburbs of Antioch, in a villa which may have belonged to a high-ranking functionary: in the centre, framed by a hunting scene, is an allegorical figure of Generosity (Megalopsychia), making the gesture of *sparsio*; see D. Levi, *Antioch Mosaic Pavements*, I (Princeton, 1947), pp. 326–45 and plates LXXVI–LXXX. In the sixth century, the same definition of a town appears throughout Procopius, *De Aedif.* For this whole period, see also the epigrams gathered by L. Robert, 'Epigrammes du Bas-Empire', *Hellenica*, IV (1948). The urban model even crossed the frontiers of

the Empire, into Persia; see *Chronicle of Joshua the Stylite*, transl. W. Wright (Oxford, 1882), 19 and 75; Procopius, *Belli Pers.*, II XIV, 1.

52 *Chron. Pasq.* (ed. Bonn), pp. 608–9; *Chron. Malalas* (ed. Bonn), p. 396.

53 Procopius, *De Aedif.*, *passim*; and the inscriptions and epigrams (*Anth. Pal.*, IX, *passim*), celebrating the generosity of church builders; see also Paul the Silentiary's Description of Hagia Sophia (particularly 68–73).

54 See A. Grabar, *L'Empereur dans l'art byzantin*, Pub. Faculté de Lettres, Strasbourg, 75 (Paris, 1936).

55 *Prat. Spir.*, 97. The theme is developed at length in the account of the Life of Abraham and his niece Maria, which may antedate our period (BHG, 3, 585).

56 *Prat. Spir.*, 32; *Joh. Eph. V. Sanct. Orient.*, 52.

57 *Prat. Spir.*, see n. 48.

58 Here are two examples taken from the Sayings of Marcellus of Scetis (*Prat. Spir.*, 152): 'When I was in my own country (Apamea), there was a charioteer named Phileremos (Desert-Lover). One day, when he had been beaten in a race, his faction stood up and shouted at him, "Desert-Lover doesn't win races in town!"' From then on, Marcellus used to repeat the words to himself each time temptation assailed him. He then speaks of the effectiveness of the Psalms in warding off demons; no other part of the Scriptures 'afflicts them as much as the Psalter. Just as in an assembly of factions, if one praises the king, the other is not troubled and will not attack, but when one side begins to shout insults, the other will reply with much excitement, in the same way, the demons are not troubled and stirred to riot by the rest of the Scriptures as they are by the Psalms.'

59 Simeon the Younger Stylite is cheered at his spiritual coronation in solitude (*V. Sym. Styl. jr*, para. 47). Simeon Salos dances wearing a leafy crown with a branch in his hand, crying out Νίκα τῷ βασιλει καί τῇ πόλει, the first meaning 'spirit' (νους), the second, 'soul' (ψυχή).

60 *V. Sabae*, pp. 171–3.

61 On this important notion, see L. Robert, *Villes d'Asie Mineure*, 2nd edn (Paris, 1962), pp. 367–74.

62 To take an example which is becoming classic, the historiography of this period only takes note of prices in times of famine.

63 Conversion of the mime (see above, n. 56), ed. Bonn, pp. 314ff. On Malalas and his 'work for a public as wide as it was ignorant', see Stein, II, pp. 703–5.

64 Evagrius, *Ecclesiastical History*, ed. by Bidez-Parmentier (London, 1898), I, 13–14 (on Simeon the Elder Stylite); IV, 33 (on Barsanuphios); IV, 34 (on Simeon Salos, the Voluntary Fool); IV, 36 (the Jewish child saved from a furnace); V, 21 (visions and miracles heralding the coming of Maurice, predictions of Simeon the Younger Stylite); VI, 20 (citing of the Life of Golinduch by Stephen of Hierapolis).

65 *Theoph Simoc.*, ed. by De Boor (Leipzig, 1887), I, 2 (a young man clothed in white with an image in his hand appears to the Emperor Tiberius); I, 11 (the sin of Paulinus and the miracle of the relics of St Glyceria); V, 12 (story of St Golinduch); VII, 12 (an ascetic predicts the murder of Maurice and his children); VIII, 14 (miracle of St Euphemia).

66 Procopius, *De Aedif.*, I, VI, 5 (Justinian is cured by a vision of Sts Cosmas and Damian, and thanks them by building a shrine); VII, 7–15 (Justinian is cured by the relics of the martyr, Irene); II, III, 4 (a vision sent from on high inspires in Justinian a plan against the floods of Daras). The text analysed above (n. 34) also contains many significant examples.

APPENDIX

List of hagiographical accounts quoted in the present study:

BHG 3, 1448 p-pb. *Anast. mon. Narrationes XXXVIII vel XLII de Patribus Sinaitis.* (Sinai peninsula; mid-seventh century), F. Nau (ed.) *Oriens Christ.*, 2 (1902), pp. 60–83.

BHG 3, 1448 q. *Anast. mon. Narrationes* (identical to the above?), F. Nau (ed.), *Oriens Christ.*, 3 (1903), pp. 61–77.

BHG 3, 65. Anon., *Alypii Stylitae Vita premetaphrastica* (Hadrianopolis in Paphlagonia; died in the reign of Heraclius), H. Delehaye (ed.), 'Les Saints stylites', *Subs. Hagiogr.*, 14 (Brussels, 1923), pp. 148–69.

BHG 3, 693–696e. Anon., *Gerasimi mon. Vita* (Jordan desert; died 475). Papadopoulos–Karameus (ed.), *Analect. Hierosol. Stachyol.*, IV (St Petersburg, 1854), pp. 175–84.

BHG 3, 1072. Anon., *Marcelli Acoemetorum archimandritae Vita* (the monastery of the Akoimetoi (sleepless) near Constantinople; died after 469). Cod. Paris, gr. 1491, s. IX–X, fols. 230 v–45 v.

BHG 3, 1614 z. Anon., *Sampsonis presb. xenodochi Vita* (the Life claims that Sampson founded the great St Sampson's hospital in Constantinople under Justinian, but Justinian only restored an existing hospital, and the Life seems to date from after his reign; see Procopius, *De Aedif.*, I, II, 14–16).

BHG 3, 669. Antonio A., *Georgii Chozibitani Vita* (George was a monk in the Choziba monastery, south of Jericho; died *c.* 625). Cod. Paris. Coisl. gr. 303, s. X–XI, fols. 135–71, (see *Anal. Boll.*, 7 (1888), pp. 97–144, and 8 (1889), pp. 209–10).

BHG 3, App. VI, 5a and s. *Apophtegmata Patrum* (collected stories from the Scetis desert between Palestine and Egypt and elsewhere, probably for the most part assembled before the seventh century; a multi-faceted collection, partly unpublished, only samples of which are as yet available for study). See J. C. Guy, 'Recherches sur la tradition manuscrite des *Apophtegmata Patrum*', *Subs. Hagiogr.*, 36 (Brussels, 1962).

1. PG, 65, 71–440 (cited as *Apopht.*, followed by the ascetic's name and his serial number).

2. Nau, *Rev. Or. Chrét.*, 12 (1907), pp. 48–69 and 171–81; 13 (1908), pp. 45–57; 14 (1909), pp. 357–79; 17 (1912), pp. 204–11; 18 (1913), pp. 137–46, (cited as Nau followed by number).

3. Cod. Paris. Coisl. gr. 126, s. XI, fols. 158–353 v, (cited as Nau, followed by number, numbering continued by Guy).

BHG 3, 1689–91c. Arcadio A., *Symeonis Stylitae Iunoris Vita* (Mount Admirable monastery near Antioch), A. 517–592. P. Van den Ven (ed.), I, Introduction and Greek text (Brussels, 1962).

Cyrillo Scythopolitano A. (Cyril of Scythopolis, born 524 in Scythopolis in Palestine). Schwartz (ed.), *Texte u. Untersuch z. Gesch. der altkirchl. Literatur*, 49, 2 (Leipzig, 1939): BHG 3, 897. *V. Iohannis Sabaitae hesychastis*, (pp. 201–22); BHG 3, 1608. *V. Sabae mon. hegum* (pp. 85–200).(Sabas, died 532, founded the St Sabas monastery, or *laura*, south of Jerusalem. John the Silentiary, died 559, was a member of the same *laura*.)

Joh. Eph. V. Sanct. Orient. – John of Ephesus, *Lives of the Eastern Saints* (trans. Brooks, *Patr. Orient.*, XVII (1923); XVIII (1924); XIX (1925).

BHG 3, 1440z–1442w. *Johannis Moschi Pratum Spirituale* (*Prat. Spir.*) (PG 87, 2851–3112). (Collection of religious stories gathered from the East, Egypt and Italy, whose author died *c.* 620.)

BHG 3, 1442a. *Additamenta Marciana* (new fragments). E. Mioni (ed.) *Orient. Christ. Per.*, 17 (1951), pp. 83–94; *Stud. Biz. e Neoell.*, 8 (1953), pp. 27–36.

BHG 3, 1748. Georgio Syceota A., *Vita Theodori Syceotae* (Theodore was a monk in the Sykeon monastery, near Anastasiopolis, in Asia Minor; died 613). Cod. Patm. 254, s. X–XI, fols. 155–278, more trustworthy than the only existing edition, see F. Halkin, *An. Boll.*, 72 (1954), pp. 15–34.

BHG 3, 1677. *Leontio Neapol A., Vita Symeonis Sali seu Stulti* (Simeon Salos from Emisa in Syria, late sixth – early seventh century; a 'salos' is a voluntary fool). L. Ryden (ed.), *Acta Univ. Uppsal.*, Stud. Gr. Uppsal., 4 (Uppsala, 1963).

3

Humiliation of saints

PATRICK GEARY

Monastic communities performed two religious functions vital to medieval society at large. First, the religious prayed for the salvation and well-being of the local population, particularly their benefactors and supporters. Inclusion in the prayers of the religious during one's lifetime and after one's death was a vital concern to a population obsessed with the insecurity of this life and the uncertainty of the next. Second, through the divine office, the mass, and the cult of the saints whose relics were honoured in the community's church, the regular clergy fulfilled the ritual actions necessary to keep the spiritual powers benevolently disposed towards human society. The relationship between saints in particular and the communities in which their bodies or relics lay was perceived as reciprocal: the saint was the protector and patron of the human community which responded to this protection and in fact earned the right to it through the veneration it accorded the saint.[1]

Since, unlike secular clergy, monks and regular canons had no means of forcing lay co-operation or fair dealing through excommunication or interdict, and because they frequently lacked effective political or military force, they naturally turned to these two services for their leverage on the rest of society. Specifically, they manipulated their 'salvific' function by ceasing to pray for their opponents and, in an inversion of the normal course of their prayers, cursed them. As Lester Little has recently shown, curses were solemn rituals performed by monastic communities to ensure that the malefactor was damned rather than saved.[2] The ceremony closely resembled that of excommunication but, since the monks did not have the power, reserved to the bishop, of casting the offender out of the Church, they could only associate themselves as closely with this power as possible and invoke Biblical curse traditions while praying that the offender be damned. The second religious function, that of continuing the proper cult of Christ and the saints, was manipulated in a more subtle and varied way through the ritual of the *clamor* (clamour) and the accompanying

humiliation of relics and images.[3] These measures were based on the
physical control which the religious had over the most important sacral
objects in the Christian tradition : the body of Christ – the Eucharist – and
the bodies of the saints. Again, unlike bishops, the religious could not
legally suspend the Christian cult in a given area as retaliation against some
opponent, but they could mistreat cult objects and prevent popular access
to them, thus disturbing the proper relationships between the human and
the supernatural orders and involving not only the alleged opponent but all
of society which depended on these powers.

The clamour and the humiliation thus formed a part of the spiritual
arsenal which religious communities could command in their disputes with
their neighbours. Moreover, in their varying forms, these two mechanisms
provided the possibility of an escalation of force not available in curses. A
curse called on God to damn an individual; it was in itself an absolute act
not permitting levels of damnation. The clamour and humiliation could be
performed in a variety of ways depending on the gravity of the situation :
the clamour could be made alone, or it could be accompanied by a
temporary humiliation of the church's relics and sacred images lasting until
the completion of the clamour, or in extreme cases the humiliation could
continue after the completion of the clamour until the dispute had been
settled. The rites of clamour and humiliation are extremely rich in
fundamental symbolic juxtapositions and gestures which clearly illuminate
the monastic preoccupation with *humilitas* and *superbia* so well described by
Little in another article.[4] They are worthy of study not simply to illustrate
monastic symbolics, but also because their use illuminates the relationships
between religious and secular communities which were determined by each
group's attitude towards these sacred objects. Moreover, although these
rituals are rich in verbal articulations of Christian traditional prayers in time
of affliction and are quite orthodox in their stated theology, they
simultaneously incorporate systems of multivalent symbolic gestures
which resemble on a structural level other purely popular rites designed
to coerce saints to aid their *famuli* (or servants). The ways in which
these two sets of rites, monastic and popular, were used in specific
historical circumstances, and the contemporary descriptions of the effectiveness of these rituals, demonstrate the fundamental unity of religious
perception and experience which, in the eleventh and twelfth centuries,
cut across categories of lay or clerical, illiterate or literate, popular or
élite.

We shall examine these practices first through their liturgies, and then
through the ways in which they were actually used and functioned in
specific historical circumstances. Finally we shall consider how contemporaries perceived and interpreted the results thus obtained.

THE LITURGY OF HUMILIATION

The clamour and the humiliation are closely related and appear in a variety of combinations in liturgical manuscripts from the tenth until the thirteenth century. Although specific references to humiliation are rare, the rite's inclusion in the so-called *Consuetudines Farfenses*, which are actually from Cluny, strongly suggests that in the eleventh and twelfth centuries the practice was known in Cluniac houses throughout Europe.[5] Most simply and frequently, the clamour was a cry to the Lord for help made during the mass between the *Pater noster* and the *Pax Domini*. At that time, while the priest held the newly consecrated host, a prayer was recited asking the Lord's help. The prayer could be either a short prayer, the 'lesser clamour', or a longer, 'greater clamour', of which the latter seems to have been the most common. For further effect, during the recitation of the clamour the religious might prostrate themselves before the Eucharist as a form of humiliation.

The clamour could also be accompanied by the humiliation of relics and/or images. At the same time as the monks descended from their choir stalls to the floor of the church (*ad terram*), the most important relics and images of the church could be placed on the ground before the altar to join the monks in their humiliation. After the recitation of the clamour the relics and images could be returned to their proper place. The most serious form of humiliation occurred in a separate ceremony, after which the relics continued in their humiliated circumstances until the dispute was terminated.

The ritual of humiliation is preserved in two forms: one is the temporary humiliation as a part of the clamour from the above-mentioned customary of Cluny; the other is the liturgy for the separate humiliation as practised at Saint-Martin of Tours.[6]

At Cluny the ritual of humiliation was an expansion of the clamour and occurred at the principal mass between the *Pater noster* and the *Libera nos quaesumus Domine*. The officiating clergy open on the floor before the altar a piece of coarse cloth such as would be used for a hair-shirt. On it they place the crucifix, the gospel books, and the relics of the saints. All of the religious then prostrate themselves on the floor and sing Psalm 73 *sotto voce*. Then two bells are rung and the celebrant genuflects before the 'newly consecrated body and blood of the Lord and before the above mentioned relics' and sings in a loud voice six other psalms and the clamour, the text of which we shall examine shortly. After the clamour is completed the relics are returned to their places and the priest recites *sotto voce* the collect, *Libera nos quaesumus Domine*.

At Tours, the humiliation has a ritual which takes place outside of the mass. After Prime, when all the bells of the tower have been rung, the canons enter the choir. They sing seven psalms and a litany (unfortunately lost). Then the most important members of the community and the ministers place on the ground before the subdean's seat a silver crucifix and all of the reliquaries of the saints, and put thorns on top of and all around the tomb of St Martin. In the centre of the nave they place a wooden crucifix likewise covered with thorns, and they block all but one of the church doors with thorns. At dawn, Matins is rung for, and the office of the day begins in a subdued tone. The canons (the clergy of Saint-Martin were regular canons, not monks) descend from their stalls and follow the office on the ground. Everything about the hours is muted: antiphons are not neumed, the choir sings *in cappa*, candles are not brought up around the altar in the usual way. The mass of the day is celebrated as though it were a private mass. After the *Pater noster*, the clamour is recited in much the same way as at Cluny: the deacon says the great clamour while the celebrant stands before the altar holding the Eucharist and the canons lie prostrate on the ground. After the clamour, all say Psalm 51, the bells of the church are rung, and the service continues in a loud voice.

The major humiliation differs in two significant ways from the minor: first, although the clamour is recited later, the physical humiliation is performed in a separate ceremony. Secondly, the ritual humiliation continues until the humiliation caused by the injustice has been ended.

The ceremony at Prime is essentially private, announced to the rest of the world only by the ringing of the bells. The most important members of the community are charged with placing their most precious objects, the silver crucifix and the relics, on the ground, although they remain before the subdean's seat and hence still in the choir. Thorns are placed on St Martin's tomb since it could not be moved and had to be humbled in place.

By dawn, the arrangements are complete. The ceremony of the clamour is included in the mass in much the same way as at Cluny. The divine services continue but in a reduced way. Again, the physical association of the humiliated canons and the humiliated saints is emphasized by the canons joining the relics on the floor before the Eucharist.

The prayers and psalms sung during the rite of humiliation and clamour elucidate the situation and articulate the community's official interpretation of the nature of the injustice and the necessary conclusion of the affair. Essentially drawn from the rich psalm literature of cries to the Lord in times of oppression, the primary prayers are Psalms 73.1, 'Utquid, Deus reppulisti'; 84.8, 'Ostende nobis Domine misericordiam tuam'; 105.4, 'Memento nostri, Domine'; 7.7, 'Exsurge Domine'; 101.2, 'Domine, exaudi orationem meam et clamor meus ad te veniat'. The theme is clear – the monks and canons cry with the psalmist to the Lord that he may deliver them from their enemies: 'Remember this congregation which you gathered of old', 'aid us in this time of persecution'. The enemy is characterized as acting out of pride, the vice which, Little has shown, was seen in monastic literature as the cardinal sin: 'the pride (*superbia*) of those who hate you rises' (73.23); 'They have burned by fire your sanctuary, they have polluted on the earth the sanctuary of your name' (73.7). The religious call on the Lord to destroy the proud, to eradicate them from the land of the living.[7]

The clamour itself, in its longest and most complete form, is found with only slight variations across a wide geographical area from the tenth until the fifteenth century, although most of the manuscripts do not include rubrics for its use.[8] The prayer elaborates the same themes found in the psalms in a more precise way: 'In spiritu humilitatis et in animo contrito, ante sanctum altare tuum, et sacratissimum Corpus et Sanguinem tuum, Domine Jesu Redemptor mundi accedimus.' The opening sentence recognizes the ritual moment at which the clamour is recited: the deacon or priest reciting the prayer as well as the entire community are before the altar and before the newly consecrated bread and wine. It also establishes the spiritual disposition of the community – a spirit of humility which is proper to a human community. 'Et de peccatis nostris pro quibus iuste affligimur, culpabiles contra te nos reddimus.' They acknowledge the justice of their suffering for their sins. 'Ad te, Domine Jesu, venimus, ad te prostrati clamamus. Again, the literal and figurative prostration of the community is recalled. 'Quia viri iniqui et superbi suisque viribus confisi undique super nos insurgunt, terras huius sancti atrii tui ceteramque tibi subjectarum ecclesiarum invadunt, depraedantur, vastant.' The enemies of the community are acting out of pride, the cardinal vice in the monastic tradition, and the crime they commit is not primarily against the religious but against the house of the Lord. 'Pauperes tuos cultores earum in dolore et fame atque nuditate vivere faciunt, tormentis etiam et gladiis occidunt; nostras etiam res, unde vivere debemus in tuo servitio, et quae beatae animae huic loco pro salute sua reliquerunt, diripiunt, nobis etiam violenter aufferunt.' The damage to the community is presented as evil primarily because it removes those necessities of life the religious must have in order to render the divine cult. 'Ecclesia tua haec, Domine, quam priscis temporibus fundasti et sublimasti in honore et nomine sanctorum tuorum [here are mentioned the patrons of the community] sedit in tristitia. Non est qui consolitur eam et liberet, nisi tu Deus noster.' The saints, whose relics lie humiliated before the altar, are mentioned but not addressed directly. Rather, they too, along with their servants, make their clamour to the Lord. 'Exsurge igitur, Domine Jesu, in auditorium conforta nos, et auxiliare nobis. Expugna impugnantes nos – – [here space is left for the insertion of the opponents' names]. Frange etiam superbiam illorum qui tuum locum et nos affligunt.' Again, the sin of *superbia* is contrasted with the *humilitas* of the community. 'Tu scis, Domine, qui sunt illa, et nomina eorum et cordia antequam nascerentur tibi sunt cognita.' This second reference to the names of the malefactors, known to the Lord since before their birth, recalls the importance attached to the ritual use of names in blessing or cursing. 'Quapropter eos, Domine, sicut scis, iustifica in virtute tua, fac eos recognoscere prout tibi placet, sua malefacta; et libera nos in misericordia tua. Ne despicias nos, Domine, clamantes ad te in afflictione sed propter gloriam nominis tui et misericordiam qua locum istum fundasti, et in honore sanctorum tuorum [again are mentioned the patrons' names whose relics are being humiliated] visita nos in pace et erue nos a presenti augustia. Amen.' The final lines of the prayer repeat the plea for justice, for divine intervention which will make the evil recognize their sins, and for divine mercy on the monastery which the Lord had raised up to the glory of the saints.

In conclusion, the ritual of humiliation establishes both physically and liturgically three interrelated structures: status reversal in the proper human–divine hierarchy; interdiction of access to cult objects; and injury to the saints through mistreatment of their images.

The lesser and the greater humiliations ritually and physically represent the injustice done to the community. The clamour and humiliation occur just after the most solemn part of the principal and therefore public mass. The community has just prayed in the *Pater noster* to be delivered from evil. The Eucharist is still present on the altar. Before it the most sacred objects of the church are humiliated, as are the members of the community. The verbal clamour is preceded by the clamour of the bells, and the prayer is addressed to the Eucharist as it is held above while the community, saints and monks alike, lie below. The saints have been humiliated by injustice. Hence they are placed in a humbled position along with the monks who share in the harm done the saints.

At Tours and elsewhere, the thorns are reminiscent of the crown of thorns, the mocking humiliation of Christ. But they serve a second purpose: they prevent people from approaching the tomb, touching it, or otherwise being as close to the sacred object as was usual in the medieval devotion to saints. The wooden cross covered with thorns in the nave (probably at the position from which the Eucharist was distributed) is in close proximity to the laity who, as will be seen, are selectively admitted into the church to witness the humiliation. Likewise, the thorns in the doorways both call attention to the plight of the community and deny access to the shrine.

The aggression against the church has inverted the proper hierarchy of human and divine relationship. The physical rite actualizes this inverted hierarchy: the crucifix, relics and monks are on the ground, the *humus*; the church is obstructed with thorns. Likewise, the liturgy emphasizes the lowly circumstances of the monks and saints who, prostrate, cry up to the Lord: 'Submissa voce'; 'officium altum' (abandoned); 'missa quasi privata'; 'in suppellicis'; 'in cappa', etc. The psalms and the clamour exhort the Lord to reverse this situation: 'Leva manus tuas'; 'Exsurge Domine', etc., while the *superbia*, the pride of the offender, is constantly emphasized. After the conclusion of the clamour proper, the bells are rung and the service continues in a loud voice anticipating the ultimate restoration of the proper order.

The ritual also juxtaposes public and private by removing from public access the primary objects of devotion. The actual humiliation is performed in private before dawn; the clamour is done publicly at mass. The location of the humiliated objects, indicated in Fig. 1, shows a division between

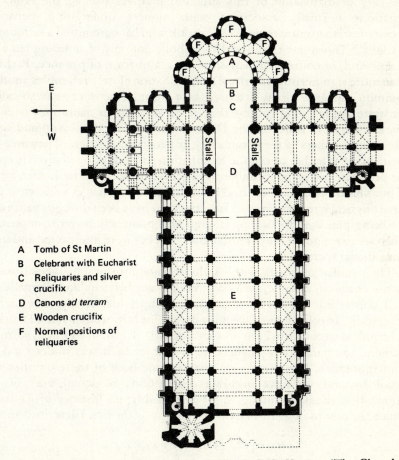

A Tomb of St Martin
B Celebrant with Eucharist
C Reliquaries and silver crucifix
D Canons *ad terram*
E Wooden crucifix
F Normal positions of reliquaries

Fig. 1   Saint-Martin of Tours *c.* 1100. After Carl K. Hersey, 'The Church of Saint-Martin at Tours (903–1150)', *The Art Bulletin*, 25 (1943), pp. 1–39.

those objects publicly humiliated and those privately humiliated: St
Martin's tomb and the wooden crucifix remain in the parts of the church
permitted to the public, although they are surrounded and thus isolated by
thorns. The other reliquaries have been removed from their normal public
places in the apsidal chapels and are, along with the silver crucifix,
separated from the faithful by the chancel wall.

Finally, the relics and other sacred objects are not only humiliated but
they are punished. Obviously such an interpretation is not found in the
articulated prayers of the liturgy. But ritual is always susceptible to a variety
of levels of interpretation by participants and spectators alike, and the ritual
of humiliation is no exception. At one level the monks are simply
dramatizing what has happened to the saints at the hands of the *superbi*, but
the very dramatization of this situation involves placing the saints in
situations normally associated with sinners undergoing penance.
Prostration is a gesture required of a monk who has committed a serious sin
at Cluny.[9] Thorns are traditionally symbolic not only of suffering but also
of sin. And, of course, the hair-shirt is a major form of penance. Perhaps
even more significantly, the ritual of humiliation closely resembles another
common monastic ritual practised as a form of penance: the so-called
prostrate psalms sung during the season of Lent in many monasteries.
These psalms are added to the Divine Office during the season and sung
while the members of the community lie prostrate as a sign of penance for
their sins.[10] Whether or not the humiliation ritual developed directly from
the prostrate psalms, the similarities necessarily recalled the Lenten ritual
of punishment and penance. And since the relics and images underwent this
same physical humiliation, they too appear to have been doing penance and
are being punished for wrong-doing. This point will be most important
when we examine the ways humiliation of relics were interpreted and used
in medieval society.

The humiliation ritual, with its physical and liturgical juxtapositions of
humus, humilitas, superbia, sublimatio, etc., is aesthetically and dramatically
well conceived. However, it must be judged historically, not merely
liturgically. In other words, we must determine how well this ritual worked
in historical circumstances to protect monastic claims. In addition, we must
examine the perception of the ritual's efficacy as it was understood by
contemporaries. Fortunately we can examine both of these questions in
detail because we have accurate descriptions of actual uses of the
humiliation ritual, including, most remarkably, an instance at Tours in
which the canons of Saint-Martin used precisely the ritual described above.

HUMILIATION IN PRACTICE

In late 996 or early, 997, Count Fulk Nerra of Anjou and Touraine entered
the cloister of Saint-Martin of Tours with armed retainers and did damage

to the house of one of the canons, the treasurer. This incident probably took place during Fulk's siege of the city of Tours. The canons took the attack as a gross injustice and an atrocity of the first order, since the monastery was in theory immune from the count's jurisdiction. Having no other recourse against the powerful count, they decided to humiliate the relics of their saints, and the humiliation's description accords well with that of the liturgy we have just examined: 'They placed the bodies of the saints and the crucifix on the ground, and they placed thorns on the sepulchre of the confessor Martin and around the bodies of the saints and the crucifix. They kept the doors of the church closed day and night, refusing admission to the inhabitants of the castle, only opening them to pilgrims.'[11] Thus, after humiliating the relics, the canons refused the count and his men access to the church. Outsiders, however, were allowed to enter, no doubt in order to witness the pitiable condition of Martin and the other saints and to spread the word of this situation far and wide.

The count, whose family had maintained a close relationship with the monastery in which at least five of his ancestors were buried, was eventually softened by the action, for the account continues:

The count, regretting his actions not long after, and seeking forgiveness, by his own free will entered the cloister and went to the house of Secardus, the master of the students. From there, barefoot, he humbly entered the church with some of his followers. Stopping first before the sepulchre of Blessed Martin, after giving sureties, he promised to God and to Blessed Martin through the hands of Bishop Rainald of Angers never to do such a thing again. Then he made satisfaction before the bodies of the saints and finally before the crucifix.[12]

Apparently, then, the humiliation had precisely the results desired by the canons and asked for in the liturgy. The count, in his pride, had caused the humiliation of Martin and the other saints. In order to make satisfaction, he had to humiliate himself physically. Thus, barefoot, he entered the church and went in turn to each humbled sacred object, starting with the most important. The ultimate results of the humiliation, then, were exactly what the canons had wanted. The monastery had been violated and its patrons humiliated. The canons had then placed themselves and their most sacred objects in the position of humility implied by the count's action. This humiliation caused the noble to humble himself, undergoing a humiliation rite of his own to restore the proper hierarchical relationship between human and divine. Neither the humiliation of the saints nor that of the count resulted in permanent loss of status. As Lothar Bornscheuer has pointed out, the necessary result of humiliation is sublimation,[13] and so the saints are raised up in a joyful rite and returned to their proper places and the count is returned to his proper position of honour among men. The subsequent good relations between Fulk and the monastery of Saint-

Martin indicate that the count had acquired the monastery as an ally in Tours.

The description of Fulk's humiliation is quite similar to one which occurred in 1152 at the monastery of Saint-Amand.[14] A noblewoman, Gisela, and her son Stephen attempted at the death of their husband and father, Heriman, to usurp as their inheritance rights those things which Heriman had enjoyed in fief from the monastery. The description of what followed, reported by Bishop Gerald of Tournai, emphasizes the same mechanism of hierarchical inversion as we saw at Tours. The injustice had inverted the proper relationship between the monastery and the lay community represented by Gisela and Stephen. The monks then physically represented the resulting humiliation of the saints in the humiliation ritual. The monks took the reliquaries 'in which Sts Stephen, Cyrinus and Amand had been placed to be honoured and, lowering them from the place of their lofty and honourable sanctuary, they humiliated them on the ground before the altar. The monks, their souls likewise humiliated in the dust, poured out their prayers in the sight of the highest majesty'. The last sentence is an obvious reference to the clamour before the Eucharist. The two evil-doers were so terrified, that like Fulk, they approached the monks asking for mercy. Again, the final reconciliation of the two was in the church before the humiliated relics where Gisela and Stephen bound themselves by 'a terrible oath' taken on the relics of St Amand. Immediately after the oath, the monks, 'in a voice of exaltation and praise, raised the relics up from the ground and replaced them in their proper locations'. Again, this final act was accompanied by a liturgy which has not yet been rediscovered.[15]

Obviously then the humiliation worked. We must ask why it did so. Were the offenders simply terrified into repentance by the solemnity of the ritual? Probably not. First, the final reconciliation often came quite a while after the humiliation – sometimes more than a year after.[16] Moreover, in spite of the monks' contentions, the actions of the nobles were frequently not as clearly evil or unjust as one might at first believe. In numerous cases, the nobles seem to have acted out of a different concept of the rights of the monastery and of their own rights, a concept which responded to other widely held social norms.

Typical here is the case involving the inheritance of Gisela and her son. The rights they demanded at Heriman's death were perfectly natural in a society in which offices and duties were normally hereditary. A similar case involving a disputed succession occurred around the same time at the monastery of Meung-sur-Seine.[17] A certain Erunus had held a piece of land of the monastery and had regularly paid the dues owed the monks. Upon his death his son Odo claimed the land as his own property. This time the humiliation of St Lifard's relics did not convince Odo of the justice of the monks' cause, and he paid for his *superbia* with his life. Thus, the disputes settled by humiliation of relics were often conflicts between two opposed traditions of right: legal rights defended by the religious, and customary rights claimed by the laity. Viewed from this perspective, the balance of justice is not and was not as clear as the canons and monks would have wished.

If the humiliation did not directly appeal to the alleged wrong-doers, it did act on others and helped to force public opinion on the issue. At Tours, for example, the Bishop of Angers, probably eager to end a dispute that was causing grave difficulties not only to the principals but also to the local population who depended on the power of St Martin, finally seems to have arbitrated the dispute. Similarly, Gisela and Stephen did not just give in to the monks' claims. After the humiliation they agreed to submit the case to arbitration by eight laymen and eight clerics. Likewise, at Saint-Jean-d'Angély, the humiliation of St Lucinius's relics against the local duke so disturbed the bishop and the count that they pressurized him into a reconciliation.[18] Thus the ritual of humiliation, while directed at the evil-doer, was actually most effective in gaining support and sympathy, or at least concern, from third parties who could put pressure on the offender to negotiate. In a sense, the monks or canons went on strike from their primary task of providing local access and proper veneration to Christ and the saints. They dramatized their work stoppage by the humiliation, and thus caused enough disturbance in society at large to have their opponent forced to the bargaining table for binding arbitration.

Humiliation was thus excellent propaganda for the ecclesiastics' cause. But within the context of medieval society, it would be superficial and anachronistic to dismiss it as nothing more. Its efficacy rested on a universally shared sense of the importance of supernatural intervention in human affairs, common to the monks, their opponent, and society at large. Regardless of the justice of the monks' cause, their critical role as those responsible for maintaining supernatural favour gave them an extra advantage. Right or wrong, their opponent and the rest of society could not endure the mistreatment of its defenders and patrons for ever. Thus, eventually, the opponent was forced to come to terms, not necessarily out of any sense of personal wrong-doing or guilt, but, as in the words of Bishop Baldwin of Noyon describing the compromise agreed to by one Gerald with the monastery of Saint-Eloi of Noyon, 'exceedingly terrified and advised by his wiser friends'.[19]

Gerald and others in his situation quite probably were terrified of supernatural retribution. But, although the liturgy of the humiliation called upon God for deliverance, all parties apparently looked not to God but to the humiliated saints for this retribution, even though, as we have seen, the saints seemed to be participants with the monks in the clamour rather than objects of it. This apparent contradiction deserves close examination.

HUMILIATION AS COERCION

The liturgy, we saw, essentially involved placing the monks and the saints together in the same humiliated position and then raising the clamour to the Lord for help. Except for the litany, which probably included the invocation of the community's patrons, all of the prayers are directed to God alone. Physically, the saints shared the floor with the monks. Moreover, they lay between the monks and the Eucharist, thus holding a proper, intermediary position between the community and the Lord. However, when help did come, it was almost always credited to the direct intervention of the saint on behalf of the community. This perception leads us to reconsider the third element of the humiliation liturgy, the punishment of the saints.

This aspect of the ritual, not the cry to the Lord for help, is emphasized most frequently in descriptions of the humiliation. Bishop Baldwin, for example, explained that the monks 'had deposited the bodies of the saints from their positions on to the ground'. Orderic Vitalis, describing the humiliation of saints which took place at Le Mans in 1090 said only that the clerics 'deposed images of the Lord and the saints, and crucifixes, and reliquaries on to the ground, and blocked the doors of their church with thorns, and ceased the ringing of the bells, the chanting of the liturgy, and the solemn celebrations, just like a mourning widow'.[20] These descriptions are only natural since, as we have seen at Saint-Martin of Tours and elsewhere, the humiliation did not end with the conclusion of the clamour, but continued until the dispute had been ended. With the clamour liturgy, the humiliation was justifiable as a physical representation of the saint joining the monks in the cry for help to the Lord. But when the humiliation continued beyond the liturgy, it became an act of coercion and of punishment directed against the saint himself.

Heinrich Fichtenau was the first to notice that humiliation of relics was directed not only against the perpetrator of the offence but against the saint as well for allowing it to happen.[21] The monks and canons had an obligation to render their patrons proper liturgical service. In return, the saints were obliged to protect the community from harm. Thus, while the human offender was at fault for abusing the community, the saint was also at fault for allowing the abuse to have happened in the first place. The ritual humiliation then had two levels of meaning. The first was the orthodox, verbalized clamour with and through the saints to the Lord, which physically represented the humiliation to which the saints had been subjected. Since the liturgy was developed from the psalms and perhaps from the Lenten practice of the prostrate psalms, it was natural that the prayers were all directed to God. However, simultaneously, in the physical act of humiliation, the saints themselves were humiliated, punished in order to force them to carry out their duties. This second focus of humiliation as coercion did not differ greatly from a popular ritual designed to force saints to protect their followers, that of beating saints' relics.

Humiliation was practised chiefly by ecclesiastics because they were, as we have seen, the people with primary access to saints' bodies. However, occasionally laymen had unsupervised access to the saints and were known to practise a ritual clamour of their own characterized by physical attacks on the relics. From Saint-Calais-sur-Anille, for example, we have a fairly detailed account of such a practice. Serfs living on a distant piece of monastery land had long been mistreated by a local noble. After suffering from his injustice for a long time and seeing no relief in sight, they decided to travel to the tomb of the saint and to seek his protection. They set off carrying gifts for the saint and arrived late at night after a two-day journey during which they had fasted. The custodian of the church was at first hesitant to allow them to enter alone so late at night, but they finally convinced him with their gifts and with the story of their oppression.[22]

Once alone within the church, they began their 'clamour'. First, they lay before the altar praying and crying. Then they rose and two of the peasants stood on either side of the altar, removed the altar cloths, and then began to strike the altar stone containing relics of St Calais all the while *clamantes*: 'Why don't you defend us, most holy lord? Why do you ignore us, sleeping so? Why don't you free us, your slaves, from our great enemy?', etc. The guards heard the commotion and came running to the altar. On seeing what was happening, they expelled the peasants from the church. Needless to say, a short time later the evil noble fell from his horse and broke his neck – the classic end of the sinner puffed up by pride.

The description need not be taken as strictly historical (no names or specific details are given) and the conclusion, 'Let no one dare to disturb the possessions of the Venerable Calais or of his monastery', clearly shows that the story is designed as a cautionary tale and not as history. However the detailed description of the peasants' clamour, which was neither necessary for the moral lesson of the tale nor approved of by the author, is probably not pure fiction.[23] Moreover, the story is not the only known example of this practice. The Miracles of St Benedict at Fleury tell of a certain Adelard who persisted in mistreating peasants on monastic lands. Once he stole something from a woman who then ran to the saint's church. There she threw back the altar cloths and began striking the altar crying to the saint, 'Benedict, you sluggard, you sloth, what are you doing? Why do you sleep? Why do you allow your servant to be treated so?'[24]

Because the serfs of these monasteries were the *famuli*, the slaves, of the saints to whose monasteries they belonged, they felt that the saints were obliged to protect them. Thus the oppression was the fault of the saints. The ritual by which they attempted to rectify the situation was an inversion of their usual relationship with the saint, just as the monks' ritual was an inversion of theirs. The peasants arrived and entered the church as they normally would to pray to the saint. Before entering into contact with the sacred object, they had prepared themselves through the journey, the fasting, and the gifts. In the church, they prostrated themselves, but this prostration should not be seen as the same as in the monks' humiliation. *Superbia* and *humiliatio* are vices and virtues of the aristocracy, lay and ecclesiastic, not of the peasantry. Hence this rite of coercion, even if sharing the purposes of the clerics' rite, used a different set of symbols. The prostration is rather the incubation which, since Antiquity, was a normal means of coming into contact with the supernatural in a holy place. That the peasants' position was an incubation and not a humiliation is clear from the description of their actions: 'Verum illi cum orationibus diutius incubuissent...'. Likewise, the physical action against the saint was one most appropriate within a peasant culture and not a monastic one. Punishment in lay society comes not in the form of hair-shirts, thorns or prostration, but rather in the form of blows. Thus the peasants beat their saints, just as they would beat a reluctant beast of burden, to awaken him and force him to do his job.

Allowing then for variations between two cultural systems with their own sets of symbols, and omitting the intellectualization of the monastic liturgy, we find a fundamental similarity between the two rituals. The saint as protector of the community has not provided the protection which he is obliged to provide, in return for veneration and offerings. Therefore the saint is punished, differently in each case, but conforming to the norms for punishment within the cultures of the different communities. The saint is then stirred to action and begins to perform his duty. Since the actions of the humiliation were directed against the saint even if the words of the liturgy were directed to the Lord, it is not surprising that when help does come, it is the saint who is credited with the victory, just as St Calais was seen to have intervened on behalf of his serfs. In the mid-eleventh century, for example, the monastery of Saint-Médard of Soissons humiliated its relics against Duke Goscelin of Lorraine because he had received from Henry I the village of Donchéry, claimed by the monks.[25] The relics were placed on the church floor for an entire year while the duke remained obstinate. Finally he returned the village, according to the monks, after a vision in which the monastery's patrons, Sebastian, Gregory, Médard and Gilderd, were discussing in his presence what was to be done with someone who abused their property. They then began to beat the duke on the head and he awoke bleeding from his mouth and ears. After a year of humiliation, the saints had finally taken matters into their own hands. Similarly, when Odo, the son of the vassal of Meung-sur-Seine who had attempted to turn his fief into an allod, suffered a stroke after the humiliation of St Lifard, the punishment was attributed by the monks as well as by Odo's family to the saint himself.

We can conclude then that, while expressed in different symbolic systems, monks, lords and peasants in the eleventh and twelfth centuries shared the same understanding of the mutual rights and responsibilities between the supernatural and the human worlds. Their focus, in times of crisis, was on the patron saints of their communities with whom they had a special bond, and when one party failed to live up to his obligations the other could force compliance, in the one case through miraculous intervention, in the other through humiliation or beating.

THE DECLINE OF HUMILIATION

We began our examination with the observation that humiliation of saints was a means by which otherwise powerless communities could obtain redress of grievances. For monks and canons as for serfs, it was a form of self-help – going directly to the supernatural powers and begging or bullying them into doing their job. The popular clamour with its ritual beating was never condoned by the Church – access to the divine was to be through the intermediary of the clergy. Although initially considered blameless, the ecclesiastical humiliation rite fell into disfavour as alternative means of redress appeared – means which operated through the channels of an increasingly centralized and hierarchical Church. Humiliation had often been accompanied by other forms of sanctions such as curses and appeals to bishops for excommunication. In 1049, for example, Abbot Remigius of Saint-Eloi asked Bishop Baldwin of Noyon to excommunicate the monks' opponent against whom they had humiliated their relics. But by the thirteenth century the episcopal and papal hierarchy was becoming increasingly unhappy with the tendency of communities to humiliate their relics and images and to discontinue services without canonical grounds. This practice, particularly frequent among canons, was contrary to the increasingly legalistic organization of the Church and was hence unacceptable. Such action taken without formal public notification of the causes, and the attempt at adjudication, went outside the hierarchy by appealing directly to the supernatural powers. The Second Council of Lyon in 1274 thus condemned humiliation within the context of condemning arbitrary cessation of the liturgy – wild-cat strikes as it were.[26] Simultaneously, the Fathers seem to have reacted strongly to the implicit mistreatment and punishment of the saints implied in the humiliation, since they termed it a 'detestable abuse of horrendous indevotion'.[27] Thus, at the same time as the hierarchy was converting the Church from a ritual system to a legal one, it condemned the close reciprocal relationships between men and saints which had belonged to an earlier sort of Christianity, one in which both men and saints could honour or humiliate, reward or punish each other, depending on how well each did his part in a mutually beneficial relationship.

NOTES

1 I am grateful to the Departments of History and Religion and the Social Science Committee of the University of Washington with whose members I discussed a preliminary draft of this article, and to Professors John Bossy and Karl F. Morrison for their advice.

2 Lester K. Little, 'Formules monastiques de malédiction aux IXe et Xe siècles', *Revue Mabillon*, LVIII (1975), pp. 377–99.

3 Virtually all discussions of humiliation of relics in recent years have been based on the collection of examples of this practice published by Du Cange in his article 'Reliquiae', *Glossarium Mediae et Infimae Latinitatis*, V (Paris, 1845), p. 690, cols. 1–3. The brief discussion of the subject in Nicole Herrmann-Mascard's *Les Reliques des saints: Formation coutumière d'un droit* (Paris, 1975), pp. 226–8, does not go beyond the article of Du Cange. Recently H. Platelle has written an excellent article in which he presents the humiliation of saints within the context of monastic reform and judicial procedures: 'Crime et châtiment à Marchiennes: Etude sur la conception et le fonctionnement de la justice d'après les Miracles de sainte Rictrude', *Sacris erudiri*, XXIV (1980), pp. 155–202.

4 L. K. Little, 'Pride goes before Avarice: Social Change and the Vices in Latin Christendom', *American Historical Review*, 76 (1971), pp. 16–49.

5 Bruno Albers (ed.), *Consuetudines Monasticae*, I (Stuttgart–Vienna, 1900), II, XXXVII, 'Pro adversa preces faciendam', pp. 172–3. The true origin of these *Consuetudines* was demonstrated by Ildefonse Schuster, in 'L'Abbaye de Farfa et sa restauration au XIe siècle sous Hugues I', *Revue Bénédictine*, 24 (1907), pp. 17–35 and 374–402, especially, pp. 374–85.

6 Martène (ed.), *De Antiquis Ecclesiae Ritibus*, III (Rouen, 1702), pp. 431–2; 2nd ed, II (Antwerp, 1737), cols. 898–9.

7 The prayers of clamour, the psalms, and the collects, closely resemble those which Little found in the malediction liturgy ('Formules', esp. pp. 378–80). The collect *Hostium nostrorum* appears in the Roman Missal among prayers against persecutors and in time of war. P. Bruylants, *Les Oraisons du missel romain*, II, *Orationum textus et usus iuxta fontes* (Louvain, 1952), no. 628, p. 174.

8 V. Leroquais, in *Les Sacramentaires et les missels manuscrits des bibliothèques publiques de France*, 4 vols. (Paris, 1924), lists eleven manuscripts containing clamours beginning 'In spiritu humilitatis'. The earliest is in a tenth-century sacramentary of Saint-Martin of Tours ((B)ibliothèque (N)ationale nouv. acq. lat. 1589) and was the text used by Martène in his edition. If the manuscript is

from Saint-Martin the prayer must have been copied from a manuscript of Saint-Maurice of Tours, since the saints named in the clamour are the Virgin and Maurice. Other early copies of the clamour are likewise written in at the beginning or end of earlier manuscripts, like the text on fol. 3 v of the Pontifical of Langres (Dijon, Bib. mun. ms. 122) added in the eleventh century. In the twelfth and thirteenth centuries clamour was frequently placed among prayers for protection from invasion or for the Holy Land, as in Valenciennes, Bib. mun. ms. 108, a twelfth-century collectionary of Saint-Amand, fol. 50 v; or it is found among excommunications as in a thirteenth-century missal of Sainte-Courneille de Compiègne, BN ms. lat. 17319, fol. 216. In the latest manuscript, a fifteenth-century missal of Riermont (BN ms. lat. 14283, fol. 81 r), the clamour has been included as a prayer to be said immediately after the *Pax Domini*. In this version, like that of Sainte-Courneille, no place is left for including the names of the malefactors and the prayer seems more a regular part of the ordinary than a special invocation in times of difficulty. This change may be the result of condemnation of the humiliation in the Later Middle Ages.

9 *Consuetudines Monasticae*, I, II, xi, p. 149.

10 As for example in Rabanus Maurus, *De Universo*, XXII, 19, *PL*, CXI, col. 518: 'Spina vero est omne peccatum, quia dum trahit ad delectationem quasi pungendo lacerat mentem'. On the prostrate psalms, see for example the *Decreta Lanfranci*, in David Knowles (ed.), *The Monastic Constitutions of Lanfranc* (London, 1931), pp. 19–20.

11 The original version of this paper incorrectly identified the Fulk of the document as Fulk V, following the examination by Mabille, *La Pancarte noire de Saint-Martin de Tours* (Paris, 1866), p. 206. For the correct dating, see Olivier Guillot, *Le Comte d'Anjou et son entourage au XIe siècle*, II (Paris, 1972), C 12, p. 27. The document was published by Louis Halphen, *Le Comté d'Anjou au XIe siècle* (Reprint, Geneva, 1974), pp. 348–9. I am grateful to Professor Bernard Bachrach for this correction. The doors of the church were closed day and night, 'castrensibus etiam non introeuntibus, solis peregrinis patuere'.

12 Note the progression (Fig. 1) from the periphery of the basilica to the nave to the choir. On the relationship between the counts of Anjou and Saint-Martin of Tours, see L. Halphen and R. Poupardin (eds.), *Chroniques des comtes d'Anjou et des seigneurs d'Amboise* (Paris, 1913), *passim*. Since earlier relatives including Enjeuger, the founder of the family, were buried at Saint-Martin of Tours, by excluding the count from the church, the canons had also cut him off from his ancestors.

13 Lothar Bornscheuer, *Miseriae Regum, Untersuchungen zum Krisen-und Todesgedanken in den herrschaftstheologischen Vorstellungen der ottonisch-salischen Zeit* (Berlin, 1968), pp. 76–93 and esp. 194–207.

14 BN nouv. acq. lat. 1219, pp. 170–4 (nineteenth-century copy of the cartulary of Saint-Amand, Arch. Dép. Nord, 12H 1, fol. 99 v–102). A partial copy of the latter appears in Martène, *Thesaurus*, I, 429–33.

15 A twelfth-century manuscript from Saint-Amand (Valenciennes, Bib. mun. ms. 121, fol. 89 r) contains an ordo,' Quo modo fit clamor pro tribulatione', which calls for the prostration of the community and contains some of the same psalms and collects as the Tours and Cluny liturgies. However, no mention of

the relics' humiliation appears. Valenciennes, Bib. mun. ms. 108, a twelfth-century collectionary which contains the clamour 'In spiritu humilitatis', fol. 50 v, does not give rubrics describing its use or mentioning the humiliation.

16 As when Saint-Médard of Soissons humiliated its relics against Duke Goscelin of Lorraine for a year. Léopold Delisle (ed.), *Recueil des Historiens des Gaules et de la France*, XI (Paris, 1876), pp. 455–6.

17 *Acta Sanctorum ordinis S. Benedicti* (AASSOSB), I, p. 161.

18 Du Cange, *Glossarium*, V, 690. Similarily, an *advocatus* of Saint-Eloi of Noyon was convinced to reach a settlement after a humiliation by 'amicis suis sapienter consultus' (BN ms. lat. 12669, fol. 109 v).

19 *Ibid.*

20 *PL*, CLXXXVII, col. 1090.

21 'Zum Reliquienwesen im früheren Mittelalter', *Mitteilungen des österreichisches Institut für Geschichtsforschung*, 60 (1952), p. 68.

22 *Miracula S. Carilefi ad ipsius sepulcrum facta*, *AASSOSB*, I, pp. 650–1.

23 For an excellent general examination of the value of *miracula* and, more specifically, of *exempla*, for the study of popular culture, see Jean-Claude Schmitt, '"Jeunes" et danse des chevaux de bois. Le folklore méridional dans la littérature des *exempla* (XIIIe-XIVe siècles)', *Cahiers de Fanjeaux*, 11, *La Religion populaire en Languedoc du XIIIe siècle à la moitié du XIVe siècle* (Toulouse, 1976), pp. 127–58.

24 E. de Certain (ed.), *Les Miracles de Saint Benoît*, (Paris, 1858), pp. 282–3.

25 Delisle, *Recueil des Historiens*, pp. 455–6.

26 Hefele-Leclercq, *Histoire des conciles*, 6 (Paris, 1914), Can. 17, p. 195.

27 'Ceterum detestabilem abusum horrendae indevotionis illorum, qui crucis, beatae Virginis aliorumve sanctorum imagines, seu statuas, irreverenti ausu tractantes, eas in aggravationem cessationis huiusmodi prosternunt in terram, urticis spinisque supponunt, penitus reprobantes: aliquid tale de cetero fieri districtius prohibemus.' *Ibid.*

4

The cult of St Denis and Capetian kingship

GABRIELLE M. SPIEGEL

Bernard Guenée noted recently that the emerging states of Western Europe invoked God as their patron less frequently than their own national saints.[1] While God might be seen as favouring certain lands at particular times, He could not be monopolized. The inherent universalism of Christian religious thought potentially militated against the growth of national feeling. To find unfailing support for national causes, the peoples of Europe turned instead to local saints. In Guenée's opinion, the first stirrings of national sentiment among the young states of Europe are expressed, strengthened, and given specific content through the choice of a protective saint whose special responsibility is to oversee the destinies of his people and to preserve the realm from threat. In particular, Guenée called attention to the status of St Denis as the principal protector of the French realm under the Capetians. Yet the interaction between the cult of the saint and the development of the Capetian monarchy has never been fully explored.

Throughout its history, the monastery of Saint-Denis sought to establish a tie with the ruling house, to make the abbey indispensable to the crown as the chief and privileged guardian of the royal presence. But beyond that, as the home of the principal Apostle to Gaul and the first Bishop of Paris, it had a symbolic importance for the whole of France, independent of the monarchy itself. This article will attempt to investigate the growth of the cult of St Denis, its progressive alliance with the monarchy, and the possible function of the cult within the context of French royal, and ultimately national, history.

Although the material for a full history of the cult is not yet available, what we do know is highly suggestive. If a firm determination of the role of St Denis in Capetian history must await the completed study of his cult, an indication of its probable meaning can at least be proposed. While the conclusions drawn at the end of this article are for the present hypothetical, they nevertheless seem warranted by the abbey's writings. It is hoped that they will have some value for the history of the role of political and national saints in the development of Western European states which remains to be written.

I

The earliest writings relating to St Denis date from the end of the fifth century. As far as can be gleaned from the confusion and complexity of the early texts, it appears that the historical Denis was one of seven bishops sent from Rome in the third century to preside over the cities of Gaul. St Denis was sent to Paris and became its first bishop. According to Gregory of Tours, he was beheaded during the persecution which occurred under Decius and Gratus, suffering his martyrdom in 251.[2] Conforming to Roman custom, he was executed outside Paris, in all likelihood in the Roman village of Catulacum, now identified as the present settlement of Saint-Denis.[3] Apart from these salient facts, early histories of the saint supply little authentic information concerning his mission or martyrdom.

The oldest extant life of the saint, the *Passio sanctorum martyrum Dionysii episcopi, Rustici et Eleutherii*, written at the end of the fifth century at the monastery of Saint-Denis, already sets forth the primary elements out of which the legend of the saint was fashioned. According to the *Passio*, St Denis came to France in the first, not the third, century at the instance of Pope Clement I. The *Passio* thus establishes the apostolicity of his mission and, by implication, of Parisian faith.[4] At the same time, the *Passio* provides Denis with two companions, Rusticus and Eleutherius, who share his martyrdom. After their execution, the *Passio* records, a certain pagan woman secreted away the holy bodies from their Roman persecutors and buried them in a field which she had prepared for sowing. With the passing of the persecution that claimed the saints' lives, a tomb commemorating the martyrs was built, later enhanced by the construction of a basilica.[5] Although the *Passio* does not name this woman, later texts designate her as Catulla, out of evident confusion with the site of the tomb. These additions to the saint's life are already incorporated into the *Vita Genovefae*, composed *c.* 520, which goes on to describe the church built by St Genevieve in honour of the holy martyrs and the miracles associated with its construction.[6]

The most important additions to the legend, however, appear in the ninth-century writings of Hilduin and Hincmar, which fix the history of the saint in the form in which it continued to be known for the rest of the Middle Ages. While Hilduin's primary purpose was to confirm the apostolic date of St Denis's mission, and hence of the monastery's origin, he also embellished the legend with a series of details that evolved into its most distinctive characteristics and added charm and persuasiveness to his fabrications.

As related by Hilduin,[7] the legend stated that St Denis had been born in a suburb of Athens called Areopagus, hence the toponym, the Areopagite. He was converted to Christianity by St Paul, who baptized him and instructed him in Christian doctrine and later appointed him Bishop of Athens. Upon learning that Paul had been imprisoned by Nero, Denis hastened to Rome but arrived too late to help his friend or share his fate. Instead, Pope Clement commissioned him as Apostle to Gaul. Arriving in Gaul, Denis established a church at Arles and then journeyed north to Paris. Although Hilduin does not explicitly say that Rusticus and Eleutherius accompanied him, they appear later in the account of proselytizing activities in the environs of Paris.[8]

Among Denis's converts was a nobleman, Lisbius, who gave Denis his house and land adjacent to it on which to build a church. There Denis established a community dedicated to propagating the word of God, which served as a centre for missionary efforts in the region of Paris. The success of his efforts aroused both the envy of the Devil, who directed neighbouring pagans against him and, more importantly, the ire of the Roman authorities. In the general persecution ordered by Domitian, St Denis and his companions were made the object of a special attack led by the provost Sisinnius as agent for Domitian. Arrested by Sisinnius, Denis was commanded to abjure his faith; when he refused he was tortured and cast into prison. Dionysian writings portray the saint's steadfastness in the face of innumerable tortures, which were commemorated in the twelfth century by the chapel of Saint-Denis-du-Pas, located just behind the chevet of the cathedral of Notre-Dame in Paris.[9]

The night before the execution, Christ appeared outside the cell window and administered mass to the martyr and his holy companions. The next morning the saints were led to the top of Montmartre and executed. It is Hilduin who first mentions Montmartre as the site of the decapitation, explaining that formerly it had been called 'Mons Mercurii' but now takes the name of 'Mons martyrum' from the popular memory of the saints' passion.[10]

There then occurred the famous miracle with which St Denis is so particularly associated. For no sooner had the severed head fallen to the ground than St Denis reached down, picked it up and, accompanied by a host of angels singing God's praises, walked five miles to his chosen burial place, the site of the present church dedicated to him.[11]

Like so many other elements, the introduction of this miracle is the work of Hilduin and rests, as Levillain has shown,[12] on a misreading of a passage in the *Passio*.[13] Despite this, it became the most dramatic and best-known episode of the saint's life.

An important debate arose several centuries later, over whether or not the head of St Denis had been cut off whole at the neck or whether it had received an additional blow, severing the top of the cranium. In the twelfth century, the monk Rigord reports that the canons of Notre-Dame claimed to possess this partial relic as a gift from Philip Augustus.[14] The monks, for their part, insisted that they retained the head intact, and the matter so threatened the abbey that it decided to exhibit the head separately for a year in refutation of the Parisian rumours.[15] In addition to describing this event, Rigord offered the supporting testimony of Haimo, whose *Detectio corporum Macharii Areopagitae Dionysii* had been written in 1053 on the occasion of an opening of the saint's tomb.[16] At that time, the monks were defending their possession of Denis's relics against the pretensions of the monks of Regensburg, who claimed to have discovered the saint's body under their church. The invention of St Denis in 1053 had similarly uncovered the saint's relics intact.[17]

Debate over the fate of this capital relic persisted well into the fifteenth century. In 1410 the case appeared before the Parlement of Paris. The proceedings of the trial have survived but do not reveal the outcome.[18] Popular legends of the fifteenth century indicate, however, that many sided with the canons, believing the relic to be in the possession of Notre-Dame.[19] Even then, the monks felt it necessary to oppose such notions.

To Hilduin, too, is due the identification of St Denis as Dionysius the Areopagite. In seeking to strengthen the theory of St Denis's apostolicity, it was highly convenient to confuse him with the author of the famous writings attributed to the Areopagite, a Greek manuscript of which had, in fact, just been sent to Louis the Pious in 827 by the Byzantine Emperor, Michael the Stammerer. When Louis commissioned Hilduin to write a Life of Denis, in 834, he requested him to base his account on all available Greek and Latin sources.[20] Included among them were the Areopagite's writings, and Hilduin devoted several chapters of his work to summarizing their contents. The identification of St Denis with Dionysius the Areopagite became, like the miracle of the decapitation, a primary and characteristic part of the legend, contributing greatly to the fame and prestige of the abbey.

The historical sleight of hand involved in this identification was discovered by none other than Abelard during his stay at the abbey after his mutilation. As he tells us in the *Historia calamitatum*, he 'happened one day across a statement of Bede's in his Commentaries on the Acts of the Apostles in which he said that Dionysius the Areopagite was Bishop of Corinth, not of Athens'.[21] True to form, Abelard did not tactfully refrain from pointing out this contradiction to the monastery's claim that its Dionysius was the Areopagite. In response, the monks threatened to turn him over to the king who they believed, Abelard says, 'would wreak vengeance upon me as one who would take from him the glory and crown of his kingdom'.[22] Rather than face such consequences, Abelard fled in the middle of the night to the neighbouring county of Champagne, placing himself under the protection of Count Thibaut.

That the doubts raised by Abelard did not disappear can be seen from a letter of Innocent III in 1216. While ostensibly declining to determine whether the body of the blessed Dionysius resting at the monastery was that of the Areopagite, 'qui mortuus fuit in Graecia', or another's, Innocent nevertheless promised to send 'true relics' of the Areopagite's body so that, in having both, the monastery would necessarily have the authentic one.[23] Despite these lingering suspicions, only Abelard seems seriously to have questioned Hilduin's theory of Areopagitism and even Abelard later retracted his claim in a letter to Abbot Adam.[24]

But such troublesome questions arose only later. In the meantime, a local cult of the saint soon flourished. The *Passio* already speaks rather vaguely of a church elevated by the faithful gathered around the primitive tomb of the saint shortly after his martyrdom,[25] suggesting that a shrine of St Denis existed possibly as early as the fourth century.[26] The first clear evidence of a church constructed to serve the needs of a religious community comes from the *Vita Genovefae*, which records the foundation of a basilica by St Genevieve sometime around 475. The earliest miracles appear in connection with the building of Genevieve's church, and they refer to the cult of St Denis as an established fact.[27] In the sixth century, Gregory of Tours speaks of *custodes* or guardians of the cult in connection with a pillage by the soldiers of Sigebert in 574. Although *custodes* is a vague term whose usage is not fixed in the sixth century, its application to those serving the cult of the saint permits the assumption that by the 570s there already existed an embryonic congregation of monks and other lay members attached to a basilica, that is, a church containing relics as distinct from an *ecclesia* or place of liturgical assembly. The cult, while still local, was steadily gaining prominence, for Gregory recounts two miracles relating to the saint's capacity to protect his tomb from attack.[28] At this time, the objects of veneration were the relics of St Denis alone; the relics of his companions Rusticus and Eleutherius were added only in the seventh century, when a special chapel was built to house them.[29]

The fame of the saints and the growth of their cult were sufficient by the seventh century to attract larger and larger numbers of pilgrims to an annual celebration of Denis's feast on 9 October. The grant of the Fair of Saint-Denis by Dagobert in 635 or 636, the first royal concession of its kind, testifies to the growth of the cult in Merovingian France and to the increasing homage paid to the saint.

The greatest infusion to the treasury of Dionysian miracles resulted from the ninth-century work of Hincmar. In his *Gesta Dagoberti I regis Francorum,*

Hincmar not only recorded with almost obsessive concern the marks of
favour conferred upon the monastery by this benign prince, he elaborated a
series of miracles involving saint and monarch that added a significantly
new dimension to the legend of St Denis. In addition, it was Hincmar who
compiled the *Miracula sancti Dionysii*, which detailed in one convenient
place the saint's miraculous acts beyond those already set forth in the
history of Dagobert's reign.[30]

The miracles described by Hincmar in the *Gesta Dagoberti* serve to
explain Dagobert's extraordinary devotion to the monastery of Saint-
Denis, which subsequently expressed itself in a series of privileges and
donations given to the abbey, recounted at the end of the *Gesta*. At the same
time, they establish the saint's protective capacity over all those who seek
his aid in times of difficulty. In this, Hincmar struck a theme that was to
resound throughout the rest of Dionysian literature.

Two miracles reported by Hincmar exemplify this point. In chapters
2–4, Hincmar narrates the story of how the young prince Dagobert chased
a hart which, in seeking to escape the pursuing dogs, took refuge in the
little household sheltering the relics of the holy martyrs, which Hincmar
describes as that constructed by Catulla. The dogs, which had followed the
hart to the spot, were unable to enter the shrine, as if restrained by a
supernatural force, although the door was open. When the news of this
miracle reached Dagobert, he greatly wondered at it and, according to
Hincmar, this incident marks the beginning of Dagobert's special love and
devotion for the holy martyrs.[31]

A short time afterwards, as Hincmar explains in chapters 6–11,
Dagobert himself had occasion to seek the saint's protection. In order to
avenge an affront which the governor Sadrigesilus, Duke of Aquitaine, had
inflicted upon him, Dagobert had the Duke whipped by his servants and
shaved his beard. Clothar, informed of this attack, ordered his son's arrest,
and Dagobert, to escape his father's vengeance, took refuge in the house
sheltering the martyrs' bodies.

Although Clothar dispatched his sergeants to pursue the fugitive, they
too, like the dogs, were prevented from entering the shrine. Meanwhile,
Dagobert fell asleep and saw in a marvellous dream a vision of the three
saints whose abode he had entered. One, clearly St Denis himself, stepped
forward and promised their support in all circumstances, if Dagobert in
return promised to honour their memory by refurbishing their tombs.[32]
Once king, Dagobert kept his promise, exhumed the bodies and founded
nearby another church which he adorned with great beauty.[33] After
describing the translation of the saints' relics to their new church, Hincmar
continues with an account of the miracles performed by St Denis as
evidence of his unfailing efficacy and concern towards those devoted to
him.[34]

The two miracles obviously aim at providing a fabulous background to explain and make plausible the history of the translation and new foundation of the abbey church which Hincmar actually invented. Despite this pragmatic purpose, they also constituted a dramatic episode in the saint's legend and signalled his protective alliance with a Frankish monarch. In this, Hincmar brought to the fore a theme which had been only briefly suggested before and gave it a central place in subsequent Dionysian tradition. More immediately, he promoted the cult of the saint by showing his concern for the lowliest as well as the most exalted among his followers. By means of Hincmar's work, St Denis's fame grew steadily and the monastery increasingly became a centre of pilgrimage in northern France.[35]

In all this, there is nothing particular to differentiate the cult of St Denis from a number of others in France. Every saint exercised miraculous powers on behalf of his devotees, and by the ninth century most had well-developed local traditions which recounted their beneficent actions and exalted their religious utility. Even the story of the 'céphalorie' – the saint's decapitation and miraculous journey – which we associate especially with St Denis is attributed to at least four other local saints of France and probably stems from the early custom of representing a beheaded martyr holding his head in his hands.[36] What does distinguish the cult of St Denis is his subsequent elevation as a national saint of France and, more specifically, as the patron saint of the monarchy.

To a certain extent, St Denis's position as the first Bishop of Paris and the principal Apostle to Gaul logically entailed a special degree of veneration. Nevertheless, it remains true that St Denis's position as the patron saint of the monarchy was not a necessary conclusion. In every age, under each successive dynasty, the monks of the abbey consciously sought to present its saint as the special guardian of French kings in whose hands lay the fate of the nation.

II

There were, roughly speaking, two types of document and two stages in which the monks of Saint-Denis promoted their special relationship to the throne. One was by means of false charters, common until the twelfth century, which were designed to support legal claims to territories, restore lost or precariously held economic privileges, and authenticate relics. Saint-Denis was not alone in this practice, although the prolific nature of the monks' falsifications and the magnitude of their claims does set it apart. In such charters, assertions concerning a special bond between the abbey and the king were set forth incidentally, as cause for the confirmation of territorial, legal, or religious privileges.

The other more broadly based type of document relied instead on the persuasion of historical propaganda. For the thrust of the entire magnificent historiographical tradition of the monastery of Saint-Denis was to establish the interpenetration of the history of the monarchy and the history of the abbey, each conducted under the aegis of the blessed martyr. While this type of document dates from as early as the ninth century, its most important examples are found in the twelfth.

Taking the latter first, it is clear, in terms of the historiographical traditions of the monastery, that the monks sought, from the twelfth century onwards, to present St Denis as the supreme patron of the royal house by consistently underlining his protective role in all circumstances when Capetian kings found themselves in danger. The theme is so pervasive that it functions almost as an organizing principle of the abbey's vast historical works, both Latin chronicles and the vernacular *Grandes Chroniques*. But in addition to these texts, which dealt with the history of the monarchy as such, the monks also recorded the life of the saint. And in these smaller works, the tie between the monastery and the king, their bond under the patronage of the saint, and the numerous occasions on which his miraculous intervention had been exercised for their mutual benefit, were made clearer still.

There are three distinct groups of works emanating from Saint-Denis which deal with the saint's life. The first, and least important from our perspective, consists of mere hagiographical collections, or legendaries, in which the life of St Denis is treated among many others. Although these collections retain the distinctive features of the saint's legend, they contribute only minimally to the historical theme of his actions in support of the monarchy. They are important only peripherally as a source for other works, supplying details in the saint's history.

A second group is composed of illuminated manuscripts, intended as picture-books, which tell the story of St Denis by word and image equally. Of these, the mid-thirteenth-century manuscript (BN nouv. acq. Fr. 1098) is an outstanding example. While these works incorporate the 'historical' contributions of Hilduin and Hincmar, their primary focus remains the legend of St Denis, to which the illuminations are directed.

A final group consists of true historical works, chronicles in their own right. In them the life of St Denis, while only a part, is nevertheless the principal part.[37] Their distinguishing characteristic is the fusion of the life of the saint and his monastery with the history of France. The first work in this tradition is the *Vita et Actus beati Dionysii*, written in 1223.

The *Vita et Actus* is important for the history of the cult of St Denis because it is the first work to utilize both Hilduin and Hincmar and to project, in its totality, the new version of the legend of St Denis that had been in the process of fabrication since the ninth century. At the same time, the life of the saint is inserted into the history of France, and, throughout, the underlying intention of the work is to set forth the history of the protection extended by St Denis to the kings of France from the time of Dagobert to 1223.

The royalist character of the work intrudes even into such unexpected passages as those dealing with the abbey's relics, whose translation to Saint-Denis is usually recorded as an act of royal devotion to the monastery in recognition of the saint's special relation to the kings of France.[38] These stories were original to the *Vita et Actus* and underlined royal involvement in all aspects of the cult objects worshipped at the abbey.

Shortly after the *Vita et Actus*, a French version of the saint's life appeared, including thirty miniatures which represented his legend and the origins of the abbey as narrated in the text. This manuscript (now BN nouv. acq. fr. 1098) dates from around 1250 and is divided into three parts. A first part, consecrated to the life of St Denis and a history of the abbey's origins, is based on Hilduin and Hincmar and incorporates elements of the text of the *Vita et Actus*. The second part is made up of thirty miniatures depicting scenes from the preceding text, captioned in Latin verses below the illuminations. A final section deals principally with liturgical pieces and includes parts of the history of the relics taken from the *Vita et Actus*. The relative brevity of the *Vie de Saint Denis* and its utilization of the vernacular suggest that it was written for the instruction of visitors to the abbey who might wish to learn, in abridged form, the principal circumstances of the saint's life and the acts of protection which he had performed for the king and the realm of France.[39] As such, it testifies to the growth of the cult in the thirteenth century and to its increasingly popular character.

The *Vie de Saint Denis* in turn became the model for what is probably the most important of this series of works, the *Vita et Passio Sancti Dionysii* of Ivo of Saint-Denis, written at the request of Philip the Fair and presented after 1317 by Gilles Pontoise, Abbot of Saint-Denis, to Philip the Long, at which time a French translation of the original Latin text was added.[40] Like its forerunners, Ivo's work was not simply a Life of the saint but a true historical collection comparable, in smaller proportions, to the *Grandes Chroniques* in its desire to collect into one place the material concerning the history of the monarchy in relation to the cult of St Denis.

Ivo's text is divided into three parts. It is more of a chronicle than the earlier works and possesses a certain logical superiority over the *Vita et Actus* in its strict adherence to chronological order in the treatment of the diverse miracles and relic histories which had become a standard part of Dionysian tradition by the fourteenth century. The first part contains a history of St Denis from his birth until the period of St Paul's preaching at Athens; the second, an account of the acts of St Denis from the time of his conversion until his death; a final historical section serves as a summary of

French history from the legendary Trojan origins of the Franks down to
the death of Philip the Fair (1314), viewed principally in relation to the
cult of St Denis.[41]

In the introduction to the third, historical section, Ivo emphasizes that
he will treat specifically those instances in which St Denis, through his
protection, had brought victory to French kings who fought under his
banner.[42] 'For', he concludes,

> St Denis was the illustrious patron of the realm and of the kings of the Franks, a watchful
> guardian who concerned himself with deeds which affected the very persons of the kings
> themselves. The miracles he performed have a special place, and among his miraculous
> deeds the most marvellous is the fact that the Frankish kings and people, who formerly
> among all the nations were most fervently bound in pagan error, by him were made the most
> Christian people and were set apart by abundant signs in the form of earthly goods and
> heavenly honours, and even more importantly, became determined and energetic defenders
> of the Christian faith and its soldiers in war.[43]

Throughout, Ivo's overriding preoccupation is to supply evidence to
support his claim that St Denis is indeed the patron saint of French kings
and that Frenchmen everywhere owe a large measure of their prosperity to
his miraculous protection. In effect, what all these works have in common
is a desire to develop and spread the cult of St Denis while at the same time,
as Delisle remarked, 'imposing upon it a national and patriotic character'.[44]
By furnishing concrete, specific examples of the saint's intercession on
behalf of the monarchy and people of France, they sought to persuade the
reader that the history of the saint and that of the kingdom were
inextricably linked.

III

Although the texts just discussed are the most pointed in their effort to
interweave the cult of St Denis with royal history, they are not alone. The
same motif is discernible in almost all Dionysian texts, and the chronicles,
both Latin and vernacular, provide significant additional testimony which,
because of the more restricted scope of the *Vitae*, could not have been
included in them.

The chronicles offer two general types of acts performed by St Denis in
service to the crown. The first, and less numerous, are miraculous cures or
acts of deliverance of the royal person himself. The importance of this
genre is that it reiterated and expanded upon Hincmar's theme of St Denis's
direct concern for the kings of France. It also implicitly bespoke the king's
inherent worthiness to be the recipient of such grace and thus contributed
to the image of French kings as devout and holy men.

An interesting example of the abbey's jealous solicitude in reporting St
Denis's curative powers is Rigord's account of the recovery of Philip

Augustus after an illness incurred during a hunting expedition in 1179. As Rigord explains, Philip had become separated from the main hunting party; fearing for his safety, he prayed to God, the Virgin Mary, and St Denis, 'regum Francorum patrono et defensori',[45] inscribing the sign of the cross upon his forehead and commending himself to their care. Finally discovered by a serf and returned home, Philip fell ill from the experience. According to Rigord, Philip was then cured by the incessant prayers of his father, Louis VII, and miraculously restored to health. What Rigord fails to mention is the pilgrimage that King Louis made to the tomb of Thomas Becket at Canterbury to obtain his son's recovery, the first voyage of a French king to English soil and one universally reported by English chroniclers.[46] Indeed, in recognition of the English saint's response to his prayers, Louis placed gold on the altar of Canterbury and granted the monks a rent of 100 hogsheads of wine from the lands of Poissy, a grant which Philip Augustus confirmed the following year.[47] Clearly, the intervention of St Thomas was viewed by Rigord as an incursion on the privilege of St Denis, as the official patron and protector of French kings, to cure the king,[48] a status Rigord had carefully mentioned in his description of the hunting incident.[49]

If the hunting incident afforded Rigord only an ambiguous opportunity to report St Denis's curative powers, a better occasion presented itself in 1191, when the young prince Louis fell seriously ill while Philip Augustus was away on crusade. When all the physicians despaired of the child's life, the queen, Adèle, taking council with the prelates and barons of the court, decided that relics should be brought from Saint-Denis and a procession held in the streets of Paris to pray for divine aid. Rigord contends that this was the first time the saint's relics had been taken outside the village of Saint-Denis. Moreover, while Rigord states only that the queen and her counsellors decided on this course of action, the *Grandes Chroniques* interpolate the text by adding that 'il fu acordé de commun conseil que on eust recors et refuge à celui qui est garde et defense du roiaume; c'est li glorieus martyrs Saint Denis'.[50] Both texts, of course, attribute the ultimate cure to the power of the exhibited relics.

Similar instances of St Denis's compassion for kings in sickness are reported by Guillaume de Nangis in 1244 and by the second continuator of his *Chronicon* in 1321. In the case of Louis IX's illness in 1244, even invocations to God throughout all the churches of the realm were unable to ameliorate the king's condition. Louis lay perilously close to death when Blanche ordered Eudes Clement, Abbot of Saint-Denis, to take the bodies of the holy martyrs out of their tombs and exhibit them at the abbey. This was done, Guillaume explains, because 'the king found his surest hope after God and his most blessed mother, the Virgin, in these [Denis, Rusticus and Eleutherius] as the protectors and advocates of his affairs and of his realm'.[51] Guillaume further emphasized the particularity of the tie between saint and monarch by explaining that the opening of Denis's tomb was never done 'except for the safety of the king or in cases of danger to his realm'.[52] The saint's efficacy proved itself again and within a few days Louis was cured.[53]

In Philip V's case in 1321, the relics were actually brought to his bedside for him to see and touch. In this instance, St Denis provided only temporary relief, for Philip died shortly afterwards. Nevertheless, the chronicler reports that Philip's last words confirmed Denis's powers, for in dying Philip proclaimed: 'I know that I was cured by the merits and prayers of St Denis and that I have fallen into the same sickness meanwhile through the operation of my own evil'.[54] Even St Denis, it seems, could not prevail against individual royal unworthiness.

While these few cases are not in themselves of great importance, they do indicate (if the evidence of the chronicles is to be trusted) that the monks and those kings and queen mothers who requested the saint's intervention believed that St Denis was peculiarly the patron of the monarchy and could be counted upon to give his support in times of great need. The intimate, almost familial, relationship between the monarchy and the abbey is perfectly expressed by Rigord, who speaks of Philip Augustus as entering Saint-Denis 'as if descending into his own chambers'.[55] And it is instructive that the *Couronnement de Louis*, a *chanson de geste* composed between 1131 and 1137,[56] already speaks of the king of France as 'li reis de Saint Denis'.[57] Similarly, the Anglo-Norman chronicler, Jordan Fantosme, writing in 1174, addresses Louis VII as 'Gentil rei de Saint Denis'.[58] Of all the saints invoked by the *chansons de geste*, St Denis is mentioned most often; by the twelfth century the position of St Denis as the special benefactor of French kings is already part of popular legend.

The second and more interesting type of miraculous act reported in the chronicles of Saint-Denis deals with the saint's general protective role over the realm as a whole. The significant aspect of this genre is the relationship which the chronicles project between the saint and all the peoples of France.

The tradition of calling upon St Denis to protect the realm from danger goes back as far as Merovingian times. It was in keeping with the general practice of this religious age, for as the *Vita et Actus* reminds us, it was customary to turn to the saints in times of urgent necessity, of death, pestilence, and war.[59] Under the Capetians, this general practice was, in the case of war, focused on a ritual assumption of the banner of St. Denis, accompanied by prayers for his support before the opening of military engagements. The most significant moments when French kings besought their patron's support and recognized his endeavours on behalf of the realm are therefore involved with the removal and return of the abbey's standard in times of national emergency.

The practice of depositing a royal flag at the monastery of Saint-Denis began with Hugh Capet. This flag was not the abbey's own, but one which had belonged to Charlemagne. Legend, history and poetry described it as a gift from Pope Leo to Charlemagne, in recognition of his status as Emperor of the Roman people, for which reason it was sometimes called 'Romaine'.[60] The *Chanson de Roland* describes it as an 'orie flambe' and gives 'Munjoie' as its preferred name. Throughout Carolingian times, until at least the end of the eleventh century, the banner retained something of the religious overtones of its origins, while taking on more and more of a national character.[61]

The standard of Saint-Denis, however, was that of the Vexin. It had devolved to the king when the Vexin was added to the royal domain in the reign of Philip I, the county being held by the kings of France in fee from the monastery. The standard was in origin, thus, feudal and seigneurial, without previous royal associations. In the hands of the king, however, it soon acquired royal dimensions. Its fame and importance as a royal standard were sealed when, in 1124, Louis VI, threatened by the invasion of Henry V of Germany, approached the altar of St Denis and pronounced him 'the special patron and, after God, special protector of the realm'. Taking the banner from the saint's altar, Louis 'invited all France to follow him'.[62] Suger's account of these events vigorously asserted the saint's privileged position as protector of the realm; he emphasized that Frenchmen considered it their prerogative that, 'if the subjects of any other realm dare to invade their own, the relics of this saint, this admirable defender, be, with those of his companions, placed on his altar to defend it'.[63] Although Suger is the first to report this practice, Odo of Deuil, describing Louis VII's departure on crusade in 1148, already speaks of it as customary.[64]

In his account of Philip Augustus's war with Flanders in 1184, Gervais of Canterbury designates the flag carried by Philip as the 'signum regis Karoli'.[65] It was but a short step to the identification of the banner of Saint-Denis with Charlemagne's Oriflamme. Both Rigord and Guillaume le Breton describe the banner of Saint-Denis in this way, and from their time onwards the confusion of the two flags is complete, as is clearly reflected in the dual battle cry of the French: 'Montjoie Saint Denis'.[66]

The significance of the Oriflamme was two-fold. As the flag of Charlemagne, it recalled the tie between the Capetians and this illustrious ancestor and was a physical embodiment of the imperial pretensions which French kings inherited from their Carolingian predecessors.[67] Further, like any flag, the Oriflamme had the quality of a corporate image. In handing it over to Louis VI, Suger gave the monarchy a symbol of corporate unity hitherto lacking, but one which retained its distinctive association with the cult of St Denis. As the special ensign of St Denis, the Oriflamme represented his spiritual leadership, as Suger declared, over 'all France' (*tota Francia*) which followed it into battle.

Time and again, the chroniclers record the victories won under the saint's banner as a consequence of his intercession. During Louis IX's attack on the port of Damietta, the Oriflamme preceded even the holy cross carried by the papal legate.[68] On leaving for his second crusade, Louis took up the Oriflamme and devotedly recommended the French realm to the 'garde et en la protection du martyr Saint Denis'.[69] Philip III, forming his battle lines against the King of Tunis, aligned them behind the saint's standard, 'so that its divine power might grant it to them to triumph over their enemies with swift victories'.[70] Again, when seeking to avenge the rights of Blanche, daughter of Louis IX and widow of Fernando of La Cerda, whose children were disinherited by the King of Castile, Philip went to Saint-Denis to receive the banner and seek assurances of victory against his proud enemies.[71] Philip the Fair, as well, attributed the success of his armies against the Flemish in 1304 to St Denis, under whose banner they had fought. He gratefully recognized the saint as 'Franciae specialis patronus, quorum patrociniis confitebatur praecipue se protectum.'[72] Lest he seem neglectful of the grace extended to him by the saint, Philip presented the abbey with 100 *livres* of rent from the royal treasury.[73] The accumulated force of these reports was to fix the image of St Denis above all others as, in Guillaume de Nangis's words, 'defender of the Frankish realm and Gallic people'.[74] Beyond his curative and protective functions for kings and ruling dynasties, St Denis played a critical defensive role in the history of the French realm and in the life of its people.

IV

Perhaps more telling even than the historical writings of the abbey were the works of outright forgery, devised by the monks to authenticate relics and vindicate claims to lands and privileges. Freed from the restraint of historical truth and endowed with more than sufficient historical imagination, the monks advanced propositions concerning the relationship between monastery and throne that sometimes reached outrageous proportions. While the fabulous backgrounds with which these charters were supplied were in a sense ancillary to the original intention of the documents, they set into motion traditions that came to have a life of their own.

Of these forgeries, one is of particular relevance for this enquiry, namely the false charter of Charlemagne, published in the *Monumenta Germaniae Historica* as *Dip. Kar.* no. 286 and known as the 'Donation'.[75] According to this charter, Charlemagne called a council at Saint-Denis, wishing to recognize the saint's aid in protecting the realm from danger against its enemies. He therefore decreed that all kings, archbishops and bishops should venerate the monastery as the 'caput omnium ecclesiarum regni' and its abbot as Primate of France, whose consent was to be sought in the election of bishops and abbots. Further, he declared that he himself held France in fief from God and the holy martyr – 'quod a deo et a te regnum Franciae teneo'. In acknowledgement of this dependency, he placed four *besants* of gold upon the altar of St Denis and directed that his successors should do so also, bound not by human but by divine servitude. Henceforth the kings of France should be crowned at Saint-Denis and leave the insignia of their office at the abbey.[76]

By this single act the monks asserted a territorial right to France, a right to the consecration of French kings as against that of Reims, a position as treasurer of the royal insignia (ultimately achieved), and a commanding status of primacy over the French Church. The leading idea of the charter, that the King of France was in essence the vassal of the saint, can be seen translated into stone in the iconography of the monastery's Porte des Valois, dated shortly after 1175, which depicts thirty-six voussoir figures paying homage to St Denis.[77]

The language of the charter is feudal in tone and closely resembles Suger's account of Louis VI's assumption of the Oriflamme in 1124, at which time Louis had also declared himself a vassal of the saint, calling the abbey the 'caput regni nostri'.[78] But, in effect, the claims of the Charlemagne charter are larger still. For in relating that Charlemagne placed four *besants* of gold upon the altar of St Denis, the charter framed not an act of devotion, nor even an act of vassalage, but a virtual act of serfdom.

Four pieces of money, usually four *deniers*, ordinarily constituted the *chevage*, the *capiti proprii*, paid by serfs to their seigneur, and these were, as a consequence, often called 'homines quatuor nummorum.'[79] Where Suger carefully explained that Louis VI would have done homage for the Vexin, 'si non rex esset', lest it derogate from his royal majesty, the charter did not shrink from inscribing the king of France on its lists of spiritual serfs. The author of the *Grandes Chroniques* was so taken aback by the implications of the charter that he hastened to add that the practice should not be considered a token of servitude but a command of freedom. To support this interpretation, he recalled that Alexander the Great, when he conquered the East, excused those who rendered him four *deniers* from all other exactions. When French kings placed gold on the altar, it signified only that they held the realm from St Denis, 'que il ne feissent en nule maniere, se ce fust en nom de servage'.[80] Despite this demurral, the meaning of the charter remained clear, and it was incorporated, without interpolation, into later Dionysian histories.

Surprisingly, Louis IX was to re-enact literally the conditions of the Charlemagne forgery. The anonymous *Gesta Sancti Ludovici*, written by a monk of Saint-Denis, informs us that Louis annually visited the monastery on the saint's feast day and, kneeling with his son before the great altar, head bared and on bended knee, offered four *besants* of gold to the holy martyr as token of the dependence he wished to recognize towards the saint who was protector of his person and his realm.[81] Further, the fact that he brought along his son suggests that he felt the ceremony was creating or recognizing a hereditary obligation.[82] The same story is told by the chronicler known as the Confessor of the Queen Margaret, who adds that when Louis returned from crusade in 1254, he made a collective offering of twenty-eight *besants*, four for each of the seven years he had been absent from France.[83] The Confessor's chronicle invites belief as a faithful summary of the inquiry, now mainly lost, conducted for the purpose of Louis's canonization.[84] If the monks of Saint-Denis had invented the story, other churches surely would have challenged such extraordinary testimony.

That Louis IX was capable of a servile act of devotion towards a revered saint of the realm no one doubts. If evidence of this obeisance were confined to him alone, it would be possible to question its importance among the ritual practices of Capetian kings. But new evidence, recently discovered in the Vatican Library, reveals that Louis IX was only following a custom that can be traced back to the reign of his grandfather, Philip Augustus. The section of an accounting of royal jewels in Philip's Register A contains a final entry which reads: 'Dominus Rex quando ivit ad sanctum dyonisium iiii bizantios'.[85] Palaeographical evidence suggests that the entry was inserted into Register A between 1204 and 1211. At the time of Louis IX's return from crusade in 1254, then, the practice was already of half a century's standing. Not only had the monks of Saint-Denis persuaded the kings of France to accept their banner as the national standard, they had convinced them to perform an act of servitude to the saint. No clearer evidence of the status of St Denis as the patron saint of the monarchy can be imagined.

v

It is easy to ascertain the motives which lay behind the monks' efforts. From a purely economic point of view, a tie with the royal house was a lucrative and important business connection. It led to such obvious economic privileges as the Fair of Lendit, granted to the monastery by a grateful Louis VI in 1124, continuous donations of lands, rents, and the like. Even less directly remunerative marks of favour, such as the fact that Saint-Denis became the normal burial place of Capetian kings, could be turned to profit. And one should not, of course, underestimate the importance to men of this age of purely honorific signs of prestige and status.

But it is perhaps less clear why kings both as practical and as protective of the royal dignity as Philip Augustus and Louis IX co-operated in this enterprise. Literary and documentary sources overwhelmingly confirm that the Capetians consciously promoted the cult of the saint, identified the abbey's interests with their own, and accepted the saint as their benefactor. What did they hope to gain by acknowledging their debt to St Denis, by symbolically placing themselves in the position of his vassal and servitor, and by addressing him as their patron and protector? Why, in the simplest terms, did Philip Augustus and Louis IX make royal policy out of the fantasies of the false Charlemagne charter?

Bossuat has suggested that the history of St Denis as written at the monastery, with its emphasis on the special concern of the martyr for the king, furnished French kings with a defensive arm at times when the legitimacy of their power was contested, and this explains their interest in advancing the cult.[86] Certainly, in a period when royal power was only newly won, the patronage of France's leading national saint buttressed the sense of royal legitimacy and contributed to the creation of a mystique of kingship with enormous potential for the future of the monarchy.

Similarly, the Polish historian, Karol Gorski, has lately proposed that the notion of a 'Roi-Saint', a holy king, be used as a comparative measure of royal power.[87] In those lands where kings successfully portrayed themselves as devout (and the rendering of obeisance to a saint was one means of doing so) we can expect the emergence of strong state organizations, reinforced by the devotion and loyalty of subjects who share the religious ideals embodied in the figure of the holy king.[88] Strayer's recent article provides a case study of this principle.[89] He argues convincingly that the position of the French king as the 'most Christian' in Europe, combined with the union of the ideas of the 'sacred king' and the 'holy country', accelerated the emergence of the French state at the end of the thirteenth century. At the same time, it enabled Frenchmen to identify the king – and through him the kingdom – as an object worthy of loyalty, even love, and thereby immeasurably strengthened the ability of the state to confront the crises of the coming centuries. As Schramm once remarked, belief in the state and the people means in the High Middle Ages belief in the king.[90] And it might be added that this is especially true in France, which lacked the territorial cohesion of England and the ideological legitimacy of the Empire.

To be sure, royal sanctity functioned as a step in the building of national loyalties. But a problem still exists in understanding how the king, in this case the French king, came to acquire a national identity through which the sentiments of his subjects could be channelled. As Strayer himself pointed out, the thirteenth-century Capetians 'had to invent the France which they claimed to rule . . . they had to expand the idea of France to make it match the expansion of their own power'.[91] France in the thirteenth century was no longer the feudal monarchy of Louis VI, nor yet the absolute monarchy of the Ancien Régime, but something in between, 'still medieval but already modern'.[92] It was, essentially, a developed bureaucratic state with claims to national loyalty, and the question still remains: how was this transition effected? How did the king shed his more limited identity as feudal overlord and become a national leader?

It is worth at least making a hypothesis that one of the things French kings sought in allying themselves with the cult of St Denis was the enlargement of the royal personality. As the monks progressively stamped a national character on the cult, they created a ritual vehicle by means of which the kings of France could reach out and tap a significant reservoir of national feeling. By identifying themselves with a revered national saint, Capetian kings could hope to transfer to themselves the affections of their subjects already directed to the saint.

The whole tenor of Dionysian writings suggests that the cult of St Denis served not only French kings but, as Guillaume de Nangis had said, all the 'regnum et populi Franciae'. The language of the chronicles is filled with references to 'France' and 'li Franceis' which reveal a new consciousness of the nation as a historical personality, bound together in devotion to a national saint. Precisely because of his position as both national saint and patron of the monarchy, the cult of St Denis could bind together king and people, 'rex et regnum'. Where other national saints might become the focus of opposition to the monarchy, in France saint and monarchy co-operated to endow the realm with a religious character, following the tendency so brilliantly traced by Kantorowicz of the spiritualization and sanctification of the secular state in the twelfth and thirteenth centuries.[93] While the cult of St Denis is not solely responsible for this development, it made its contribution.

Further, the cult had a specific importance for the monarchy as such, and for the transition from feudal forms of rulership to a more expansive concept of the state. If one considers the claims of the false charter seriously for a moment, St Denis ruled all France. It is possible that rulers as different in character as Philip Augustus and Louis IX saw in this claim an ideological justification for shared aspirations. By adhering strictly to the terms of the false charter, their actions framed the conviction, or at least the pious hope, that they too ruled all France and, as the charter stated, recognized no superior except God and St Denis. The putative origin of the charter added historical legitimacy to its precepts, and the implicit contention that France was not included in the Carolingian imperial legacy fuelled Capetian efforts to assert their independence from imperial hegemony.

From Louis VI on, the kings of France carried the banner of St Denis into war with them and exhorted their followers to battle with the cry 'Montjoie Saint Denis'. In taking the saint's symbols as their own, were they not seeking to demonstrate that they, like him, bore the responsibility for the preservation and protection of the entire realm? The image of the king as the defender of the realm was a critical component in royalist theory, during both the Early and High Middle Ages. By allying themselves with a saint whose principal function was the defence and protection of the French realm, Capetians emphasized the national scope as well as the religious character of their royal mission.

The utilization of the cult of St Denis by Capetian kings for the creation of a national identity parallels the development of France as a legal personality, a process marked by increasing references to the crown, the *corona regni*, as a juristic entity throughout the twelfth and thirteenth centuries. Yet it can be argued that the cult's significance results from the relatively weak juristic notion of the crown in France, compared at least to England. Precisely because France failed to achieve a national legal community comparable to its English neighbour, it was necessary to look to other sources of cohesion.

The absence of a legal, political, or constitutional community of the realm, as Langmuir has argued, radically tipped the balance of power in favour of the monarchy, which 'emerged as the sole symbol of unity in the kingdom, far above the many communities it ruled'.[94] In France, personal kingship dominates the crown as the principle of French unity. There is no tension between dynastic patriotism and popular nationalism, and the cult of kingship, of the king as *pater patriae*, evolved naturally and without strain into a patriotic cult of the kingdom of France.[95] As a Venetian ambassador remarked at the beginning of the sixteenth century, 'there are states more fertile and richer than France, such as Hungary and Italy. There are greater and more powerful states, such as Germany and Spain; but none is so thoroughly unified'.[96]

The history of this evolution is not the concern of this article. But it can be said that the achievement of a national identity by the Capetian monarchy marked its beginning. In that process the cult of St Denis played a part. The success of French kings in representing themselves as national leaders, responsible for the defence and direction of the whole realm, owed something to those small acts of devotion and obedience which they performed at the altar of the saint. By them Capetian kings claimed not only the saint's exalted position as national patron and protector, but also a community of feeling with all Frenchmen who similarly recognized the role of St Denis in their well-being.

By the end of the thirteenth century the king of France had become the object of intense devotion on the part of his subjects. With Louis IX's canonization in 1297, France produced the perfect type of the sacred king. His relics, lying in state at the abbey of Saint-Denis, became the focus of a cult of kingship, an appropriate culmination to the monastery's efforts to fuse its history with that of the monarchy. Here Frenchmen worshipped a national saint and the nation's sainted king; royal sanctity, national loyalty, religious personality and historical identity all drew easily together, to collaborate in the construction of a French state whose distinctive feature was the commanding position of the king in the life of the nation. If the monks promoted the kings of France for their own economic benefit, perhaps the return to the king on his investment in the monastery was, in the end, though different, no less profitable.

NOTES

1 A shorter version of this article was presented in May 1974 at the Ninth Conference on Medieval Studies, Western Michigan University, Kalamazoo, Michigan. B. Guenée, *L'Occident aux XIVe et XVe siècles* (Paris, 1971), p. 121. See also his 'Etat et nation en France au moyen âge', *Revue Historique*, 237 (1967), pp. 17–30.

2 'Huius tempore septem viri episcopi ordenati ad praedicandum in Gallis missi sunt, sicut historia passiones sancti martyres Saturnini denarrat. Ait enim: sub Decio et Grato consolibus, sicut fideli recordationem retenitur, primum ac summum Tholosana civitas sanctum Saturninum habere coeperat sacerdotem. Hii ergo missi sunt...Parisiacis Dionysius episcopus...De his vero beatus Dionisius Parisiorum episcopus, diversis pro Christi nomine adfectus poenis, praesentem vitam gladio inminente finivit.' W. Arndt (ed.), 'Historia Francorum', *MGH, Scriptorum Rerum Merovingicarum*, I (1885), p. 48.

3 S. Crosby, *The Abbey of Saint-Denis 475–1122* (New Haven, 1942), p. 39.

4 'Igitur sanctus Dionysius, qui tradente sancto Clemente Petri Apostoli successore, verbi divini semina gentibus eroganda susceperat... ac Parisius Domino ducente pervenit...' M. Félibien, *Histoire de l'abbaye royale de Saint-Denys en France* (Paris, 1706), p. clxiv.

5 *Ibid.*, p. clxv.

6 B. Krusch (ed.), 'Vita Genovefae virginis Parisiensis', *MGH, Scriptorum Rerum Merovingicarum*, III (1896), pp. 215–38.

7 J. Migne (ed.) 'Areopagitica sive Sancti Dionysii vita', *PL*, 106 (1864), pp. 14–50.

8 The *Vie de Saint Denis*, written in the mid-thirteenth century, does explicitly mention that Rusticus and Eleutherius accompanied Denis to Paris. (B)ibliothèque (N)ationale nouv. acq. fr. 1098, fol. 8 v.

9 Crosby, *The Abbey of Saint-Denis*, p. 25.

10 'Quorum memoranda et gloriosissima passio e regione urbis Parisiorum in colle qui antea mons Mercurii, quoniam inibi idolum ipsius principaliter colebatur a Gallis, nunc vero mons martyrum vocatur... qui ibidem triumphale martyrium perpetrarunt, celebrata est VII idus Octobris.' 'Areopagitica', p. 50. Cf. L. Levillain, 'Etudes sur l'abbaye de Saint-Denis à l'époque Mérovingienne', *Bibliothèque de l'Ecole des Chartes*, 82 (1921), p. 40.

11 'Et facta est comes multitudo coelestis exercitus exanimi ejus corpori, caput proprium ab ipso monte, ubi fuerat decollatus, per duo fere millia deportanti usque ad locum in quo nunc Dei dispositione et sua electione requiescit humatum, sine cessatione hymnis dulcisonis Deum laudans. 'Areopagitica', p. 47.

12 Levillain, 'Etudes sur l'abbaye de Saint-Denis', p. 49.

13 The *Passio* says only: 'In hac ergo fidei constantia permanentes, reddentes terrae corpora, beatas coelo animas intulerunt: talique ad Dominum meruerunt professione migrare, ut amputatis capitibus, adhuc putaretur lingua palpitans Dominum confiteri.' Félibien, *Histoire de l'abbaye royale de Saint-Denys*, p. clxiv.

14 H.-F. Delaborde (ed.), *Oeuvres de Rigord et de Guillaume le Breton* (Paris, 1882), 2, pp. 114–15.

15 The theory that Denis had lost a portion of his cranium had a certain iconographic life in thirteenth-century France. L. Demaison discovered two seals of the abbey of Saint-Denis-de-Montmartre which depict St Denis with his head cut above the eyebrows, carrying the remnant between his hands. The oldest extant example seals a charter of the month of June 1216, which is the earliest date that can be established for these figures of St Denis amputated at the cranium. ('Les Statues du portail de gauche de la cathédrale de Reims', *Bulletin de la Société Nationale des Antiquaires* (1916), p. 185). In a supporting discussion, H.-F. Delaborde pointed out that there existed at Notre-Dame of Paris a relic from Saint-Etienne-des-Grès which purported to be the top of St Denis's head, a fact which explains why the figure of St Denis on the portal of Notre-Dame carries only this part of his head. ('Relique du crâne de Saint Denis à Notre-Dame de Paris', *Bulletin de la Société Nationale des Antiquaires* (1916), p. 190.)

16 Félibien, *Histoire de l'abbaye de Saint-Denys en France*, pp. clxv–clxxii.

17 Haimo actually makes no specific mention of the head, being more concerned to authenticate the identity of the saint. Rigord, in his review of this incident, however, explicitly adds: 'et aperto vase Beati martyris Dionysii, totum corpus ipsius cum capite inventum est, exceptis duobus ossibus de collo...' (Delaborde (ed.), *Oeuvres de Rigord*, 2, pp. 61–2). The *Grandes Chroniques de France*, a ten-volume vernacular history of France written at Saint-Denis from 1274 on and based on the abbey's collection of Latin histories, uses the original text of Haimo but follows Rigord in this interpolation. J. Viard (ed.), *Les Grandes Chroniques de France* (Paris, 1930), 6, p. 145.

18 H.-F. Delaborde, 'Le Procès du chef de Saint Denis en 1410', *Mémoires de la Société de l'Histoire de Paris et de l'Ile-de-France*, 11 (1884), pp. 297–409.

19 R. Bossuat, 'Traditions populaires relatives au martyre et à la sépulture de Saint

Denis', *Le Moyen Age*, 11 (1956), pp. 479–509. Compare the fifteenth-century text of the Religieux of Saint-Denis, BN MS. lat. 5949A, fol. 319 r.

20 J. Migne (ed.), 'Epistola XII Ludovici ad Hilduinum Abbatem S. Dionysii anno 835', *PL*, (1864), col. 1328.

21 J. Muckle (ed.), *The Story of Abelard's Adversities* (Toronto, 1964), p. 53.

22 *Ibid.*, p. 55.

23 'Abbati et conventui monasterii Sancti Dionysii in Francia scribitur, et, quia ab aliquibus dubitabatur an corpus beati Dionysii quod in eodem monasterio requiescit fuerit corpus beati Dionysii Areopagitae, qui mortuus fuit in Graecia, vel alterius, domus Papa mittit eis de veris reliquiis, sive corpus illius beati Dionysii Areopagitae, et concedit omnibus visitantibus quadraginta dies.' J. Migne (ed.), Innocent III, 'Registrum', *PL*, 216 (1891), col. 993. While the Register seems to conclude that the relics sent by Innocent were those of Dionysius the Areopagite who, having 'died in Greece', could scarcely have been the Apostle to Gaul, the account of this transaction in the *Vita et Actus Beati Dionysii*, written shortly afterwards in 1223, states that the gift made by Innocent III was the body of St Denis, Bishop of Corinth, not that of the Areopagite; see C. Liebman, *Etude sur la vie en prose de Saint Denis* (New York, 1942), p. 209. Moreover, the *authenticum* of Innocent, copied into the *Vita*, retains a great deal more ambiguity over which body Innocent thought he was sending than the Register's version implies (*ibid.*, p. 210). The Religieux de Saint-Denis, in the fifteenth century, describes this affair under the rubric *De corpore sancti Dionysii Corynthiorem episcopi ad ecclesiam Sancti Dionysii translato*, reaffirming the Dionysian position that St Denis of Corinth was not the Areopagite (fol. 375 r). A feast of St Denis of Corinth was celebrated at the abbey on 18 April; see Félibien, *Histoire de l'abbaye royale de Saint-Denys*, p. 219.

24 Abelard's letter to Abbot Adam is clearly authentic. Since Benton has raised doubts about the authenticity of the *Historia Calamitatum*, it is possible that Abelard's stated position there is forged. See John Benton, 'Fraud, Fiction, and Borrowing in the Correspondence of Abelard and Heloise', Communications presented on 4 July 1972 at the Colloque International Pierre Abélard–Pierre le Vénérable at the Abbaye de Cluny, *Colloques Internationaux du Centre National de la Recherche Scientifique*, 546 (1975), pp. 471–511.

25 Félibien, *Histoire de l'abbaye royale de Saint-Denys*, p. clxv.

26 It seems logical that had the *Passio* intended to refer to the church erected by St Genevieve it would have mentioned her role in the foundation. The passage must therefore refer to an earlier shrine, possibly even a small church which later became dilapidated, since the 'Vita Genovefae' gives as the reason for Genevieve's foundation the terrible condition of the saint's shrine; see 'Vita Genovefae', p. 222.

27 *Ibid.*, p. 224.

28 W. Arndt (ed.) Gregory of Tours, 'Liber in gloria martyrum', *MGH, Scriptorum Rerum Merovingicarum*, I (1885), pp. 535–6.

29 Crosby, *The Abbey of Saint-Denis*, p. 44.

30 It was Levillain who established Hincmar as the probable author of the *Miracula* in 'Etudes sur l'abbaye de Saint-Denis', pp. 58–114. See also A. Luchaire, 'Etudes sur quelques manuscrits de Rome et de Paris. Les *miracula*

Sancti Dionysii', Bibliothèque de la Faculté des Lettres de Paris, 8 (1899), pp. 20–9. The *Miracula* are published in J. Mabillon (ed.), *Miracula Sancti Dionysii, Acta sanctorum ordinis S. Benedicti, saed. III* (Paris, 1772), 2, pp. 343–64.

31 B. Krusch (ed.), 'Gesta Domini Dagoberti Regis Francorum', *MGH, Scriptorum Rerum Merovingicarum,* II (1888–9). pp. 401–2.

32 *Ibid.,* pp. 402–4.

33 The story of Dagobert's vision was incorporated into all subsequent legendaries of the saint. Compare the accounts in the *Vita et Actus* (Liebman, *Etude sur la vie en prose de Saint Denis,* pp. 187ff.), the *Vie de Saint Denis* (BN nouv. acq. fr. 1098, fol. 20 v–21 r), and the *Grandes Chroniques de France* (Viard (ed.), 2, pp. 103ff.).

34 'Gesta Domini Dagoberti', p. 411.

35 Crosby, *The Abbey of Saint-Denis,* p. 44.

36 *Ibid.,* p. 38.

37 Liebman, *Etude sur la vie en prose de Saint Denis,* p. 10.

38 See, for example, *ibid.,* the translation of St Hilary of Poitiers by Dagobert (p. 202); the translation of Sts Patroclus and Romanus and Hilary of Toulouse (pp. 202–3); and the translations of Sts Cucphatus and Hypolitus by Charlemagne (pp. 204–5).

39 Such, L. Delisle believed, was the origin of the piece. 'Notice sur un livre à peintures... exécuté en 1250 dans l'abbaye de Saint-Denis', *Bibliothèque de l'Ecole des Chartes,* 38 (1877), p. 444.

40 On Ivo see *ibid.,* pp. 455ff.; and Delisle's earlier article, 'Notice sur un recueil historique présenté à Philippe le Long par Gilles de Pontoise, abbé de Saint-Denis', *Notices et extraits des manuscrits de la Bibliothèque Impériale,* 21, 2 (1865), pp. 249–65. See also H. Martin, *Légende de Saint Denis, Reproductions du manuscrit original présenté en 1317 au roi Philippe le Long* (Paris, 1908); and B. Haureau, 'Ives, moine de Saint-Denys'. *Histoire littéraire de la France,* 31 (1899), pp. 142–51.

41 See Ivo's *Vita et passio Sancti Dionysii.* BN MS. lat. 5286, fol. 3 v.

42 'In rebus que bellicis pugnatores victoriossimi eiusdem patronum sui Dyonisii protegente eos in omnibus ea qua apud Deum praecellit potencia dum nec ad bella quicumque solliti sunt praefati reges procedere quin primus ad eiusdem peculiaris patronum sui Dyonisii venerabile monasterium humiliter accedentes extractis de locis suis... commune totius francorum exercitus vexillum... sperantes per sanctorum suffragia praedicorum et hostium superbiam deprimere ac de ipsis victoriam obtinere.' BN MS. lat. 5286, fol. 117 r.

43 'Verum sanctus ipse Dyonisius regni regumque Francorum patronus praecipuus, custos vigil et sollicitus ex nonnullis quae circa regum ipsorum personas gestas sunt, miracula per eum exhibita praecipuum tenent locum interque facta per eum mirabilia mirabilius existit quod Francorum reges et populi praecaeteris olim nationibus gentilitatis erroribus ardentius astricti, per eum facti sunt Christianissimi amplioribusque divitiarum terrenarum et coelestium honorumque tytulis dilatati sed quod majus est fidei Christianae assidui defensores et strenui, in rebusque bellicis pugnatores.' BN MS. lat. 5286, fol. 117 r.

44 Delisle, 'Notice sur un livre à peintures', p. 454.

45 Delaborde (ed.), *Oeuvres de Rigord*, p. 11.

46 W. Stubbs (ed.), Benedict of Peterborough, *Gesta regis Henrici Secundi Benedicti Abbatis*, Rolls Series (London, 1867), pp. 240–2.

47 Delaborde (ed.), *Oeuvres de Rigord*, p. 12, n. 1.

48 *Ibid.*, p. 12, n. 1.

49 The *Grandes Chroniques* qualify Rigord's phrase by adding a reference to the kingdom: 'patrons et défense des rois et dou roiaume de France' (Viard (ed.), *Les Grandes Chroniques de France*, 6, p. 93). Thomas himself recognized the greatness of St Denis and in his dying words, reported by Herbert of Bosham, commended the cause of his church to the French martyr: '...et beato Dionysium Francorum apostolo commendans, ut illi inter martyres potissimum Deo inspirante sic commendaretur ecclesiae causae, cui ipse in ecclesia per martyrium simile jam assimilabitur in poena, isto sicut et illo decalvato. Se itaque exposito mox causam ecclesie quam egerat patronis commendavit, et pro suis oravit.' J. Robinson (ed.), *Vita Sancti Thomae archiepiscopi et martyris auctore Herberto de Boseham*, Rolls Series (London, 1877), p. 499.

50 Viard (ed.), *Les Grandes Chroniques de France*, 6, p. 203.

51 'Rex siquidem post Dominum et sacratissimam Virginem matrem ejus, in ipsis [i.e. Denis, Rusticus and Eleutherius] utpote in suis et regni sui advocatis et protectoribus, confidentius sperabat.' Guillaume de Nangis, 'Vita Sancti Ludovici regis Francorum', in M. Daunou (ed.), *Recueil des historiens des Gaules et de la France*, 20 (1840), p. 344.

52 'solummodo pro salute regis Franciae, vel regni sui periculo.' *Ibid.*, p. 344.

53 Viard (ed.), *Les Grandes Chroniques de France*, 7, pp. 106ff.

54 'scio me meritis et precibus beati Dionysii curatum fuisse, et malo meo regimine iterum in eamdem aegritudinem incidisse.' H. Géraud (ed.), *Chronique latine de Guillaume de Nangis de 1113 à 1300 avec les continuations de cette chronique* (Paris, 1843), 2, p. 38.

55 'Quadem autem die, dum, pro negotiis regni agendis, rex per villam Beati Dionysii transitum facerat, in abbatiam Beati Dionysii, sicut in propriam cameram suam descendit.' Delaborde (ed.), *Oeuvres de Rigord*, p. 65. Compare the *Grandes Chroniques* on the death of Philip Augustus: 'Il garda et defendi l'eglise de Saint Denis en France sor totes autres, come sa propres chambre...' Viard (ed.), *Les Grandes Chroniques de France*, 6, p. 370. The passage in the Latin chronicle of Guillaume le Breton on which this text is based omits the reference to the chamber (Delaborde (ed.), *Oeuvres de Rigord*, pp. 320–4). Suger paints a similar picture of Louis VI's native affection for St Denis and his hope and confidence in the martyr's concern: 'Altus puerulus, antiqua regum Karoli Magni et aliorum excellentiorum, hoc ipsum testamentis imperialibus testificantium, consuetudine, apud Sanctum Dyonisium tanta et quasi nativa dulcedine ipsis sanctis martyribus suisque adhesit, usque adeo ut innatam a puero eorum ecclesie amiciciam toto tempore vite sue multa liberalite et honorificentia continuaret et, in fine, summe post Deum sperans ab eis, seipsum et corpore et anima, ut, si fieri posset, ibidem monachus efficeretur, devotissime deliberando contraderet.' H. Waquet (ed.), *Vita Ludovici Grossi Regis* (Paris, 1964), p. 6.

56 The *Couronnement*, while concerned with the coronation of Louis the Pious, was probably directed towards the coronation in 1131 of the infant Louis VII at the age of ten. The poem makes Louis the Pious an infant, although in reality by 813, the date of his coronation, he was already thirty-five or thirty-six years old. For this and other arguments, see A. Lanly (ed.), *Le Couronnement de Louis, Chanson de Geste du XIIe siècle* (Paris, 1969), pp. 8ff.

57 E. Langlois (ed.), *Le Couronnement de Louis* (Paris, 1920), pp. 46 and 112.

58 R. Howlett (ed.), Jordan Fantosme, *Chronique de la guerre entre les Anglois et les Ecossois en 1173 et 1174*, Rolls Series (London, 1886), p. 206.

59 'Antiquitus solebant fieri, sicut et nunc quoque fiunt, processiones ab ecclesiis ad ecclesias a religiosis pastoribus sancte matris ecclesie, subsequente eos humillima devotione populi. Et hoc fieri consueverat quotiens aliqua urgens necessitas compulisset, videlicet si mortalitas hominum, si late vagans pestilentia, si aeris inequalitas, aut si inter reges aut principes bellorum immanitas desevret.' Liebman, *Etude sur la vie en prose de Saint Denis*, p. 205.

60 The principal source of this legend is the *Chanson de Roland*, lines 3094–5, which explains that: 'Saint Piere fut, si aveit num Romaine/Mais de Munjoie iloec out pris eschange'. See M. Sepet, 'Le Drapeau de France', *Revue des Questions Historiques*, 17 (1875), p. 516. The *Nova gesta Francorum*, written at the abbey of Saint-Denis in the early twelfth century, reiterates this legend: 'Mox et Leo in eius loco successit missis legatis ad pium Karolum clavis confessionis Sancti Petri simul et vexillum romane urbis direxit'. BN MS. lat. 11793, fol. 27 v.

61 Sepet, 'Le Drapeau de France', p. 516.

62 Suger, *Vita Ludovici Grossi*, p. 220.

63 *Ibid.*

64 'Dum igitur a beato Dionysio vexillum et abeundi licentiam petiit, qui mos semper victoriosis regibus fuit.' V. Berry (ed.), Odo of Deuil, *De profectione Ludovici VII in orientem* (New York, 1948), p. 16.

65 A. Cartillieri, *Philip II August König von Frankreich* (Leipzig, 1899), p. 145, n. 3.

66 Historians such as Sepet have claimed that the confusion of the two standards dates from as early as the reign of Louis VII ('Le Drapeau de France', p. 518). No clear-cut evidence exists before the chroniclers of Philip Augustus (see Delaborde (ed.), *Oeuvres de Rigord*, pp. 98–9). By the time of the *Grandes Chroniques* (1274), the original banner of the Vexin is described as the Oriflamme at the moment of Philip I's acquisition of the county of the Vexin and the obligation to carry it in battle is considered to be part of the service of the fief. For additional references to the Oriflamme see Philippe Contamine, *L'Oriflamme de Saint-Denis aux XIVe et XVe siècles* (Nancy, 1975).

67 For the political uses of the dynastic tie between Carolingians and Capetians see G. M. Spiegel, 'The "reditus regni ad stirpem Karoli Magni": A New Look', *French Historical Studies*, 7 (1971), pp. 145–74. For the flag's connection with the cult of Charlemagne during the reign of Philip Augustus see P. Schramm, *Der König von Frankreich* (Weimar, 1960), 2, pp. 139–40. The fourteenth-century *Traité du Sacre* by Jean Golein emphasizes the Oriflamme's imperial connotation for Charlemagne and, through him, for all French kings: 'Si veulent aucuns dire que celle banniere baillée par la vision de l'empereur de

Constantinople à Charlemaine pronostiquoit qu'il devoit estre empereur du peuple romain, si comme il fu apres, et appelé patrician et empereur; et celle enseigne imperial voult laissier en France en signe de Empire perpetuel par succession de hoir masle.' Cited by M. Bloch, *Les Rois thaumaturges* (Strasbourg, 1924), p. 486.

68 Guillaume de Nangis, 'Vita Sancti Ludovici', p. 370.

69 N. de Waill, (ed.), Primat, 'Chronique Latin', *Recueil des Historiens des Gaules et de la France*, 23 (1876), p. 40.

70 'donec divina potentia concessisset eis ex hostibus victrici dextera triumphari'. Guillaume de Nangis, 'Gesta Philippi regis Francorum, filii sanctae memoriae regis Ludovici', in M. Daunou (ed.), *Recueil des Historiens des Gaules et de la France*, 20, p. 474.

71 *Ibid.*, pp. 502–5.

72 Géraud (ed.), *Chronique latine de Guillaume de Nangis*, p. 345.

73 Félibien, *Histoire de l'abbaye royale de Saint-Denys*, p. 262.

74 'regni Franciae et populi Gallici defensoris.' Guillaume de Nangis, 'Vita Sancti Ludovici', p. 468.

75 The dating of this charter is uncertain and it bears an ambiguous relation to the comparable passage in *Pseudo-Turpin*. Schramm dates it later than the *Pseudo-Turpin*, which he believes was written c. 1140 (*Der König von Frankreich*, p. 135). Van de Kieft believes it could not have been written before 1156 and awards Odo of Deuil a principal part in its fabrication ('Deux diplômes faux de Charlemagne pour Saint-Denis au XIIᵉ siècle', *Le Moyen Age*, 13 (1958), p. 432). Barroux, on the other hand, attributes it to Suger and dates it shortly after 1124. He sees it as a result of the same impulse that guided Suger's account of Louis VI's assumption of the Oriflamme, namely a desire to depict France as a vassal of the abbey ('Suger et la vassalité du Vexin', *Le Moyen Age*, 13 (1958), p. 15). Least likely is the opinion of M. Buchner, who dates it in 1149 and considers it a response of Suger to the rebellion of Robert of Dreux after the failure of Louis VII's crusade ('Das gefälschte Karlsprivileg für St Denis. BM² nr. 482 und seine Entstehung, zugleich ein Beitrag zur Geschichte Frankreichs im 12. Jahrhundert', *Historisches Jahrbuch*, 42 (1922), pp. 12–28 and 250–65). Since the leading idea of the charter, that the King of France is the vassal of St Denis, appears to underlie the iconography of the abbey's 'Porte des Valois', which was constructed shortly after 1175, this latter date would seem to constitute a *terminus ad quem* for the date of the charter. On the 'Porte des Valois' see G. Sommers, 'Royal Tombs at Saint-Denis' (Ph.D. dissertation, Columbia University, 1966), pp. 70–1. The passage in *Pseudo-Turpin* to which the charter should be compared can be found in H. Smyser's edition of the *Pseudo-Turpin* (Cambridge, Mass., 1937), p. 106.

76 E. Mühlbacher (ed.), Charter no. 286, *MGH, Diplomata Karolinorum*, I (1906), p. 429.

77 Sommers, 'Royal tombs at Saint-Denis', pp. 70–1. Other iconographic features of the thirteenth century emphasize the bond between king and abbey. According to Robert Branner, the presence of royal coats of arms among the ornaments of the Gothic work reflects a desire to express the abbey's relationship to the crown. *Saint Louis and the Court Style* (London, 1965), p. 46.

78 Suger, *Vita Ludovici Grossi*, p. 220.

79 H.-F. Delaborde, 'Pourquoi Saint Louis faisait acte de servage à Saint Denis', *Bulletin de la Société Nationale des Antiquaires* (1897), p. 256.

80 'Partant, si ne doit-on pas cuider ce soit servages, ainz est droiz establissemenz de franchise : car ensi fist Alixandres li Granz, quant il ot conquis tout Orient, que tuit cil qui il rendoient 1111 deniers fussent quites de touts autres costumes. Dont li roi de France paient chascun an 1111 besanz d'or et les offrent desus lor chiés aus marty-s en recognoissance que il tienent de Dieu et de li le roiaume de France; que il ne feissent en nule maniere, se ce fust en nom de servage.' Viard (ed.), *Les Grandes Chroniques*, 3, p. 289. The charter is also reported in Guillaume de Nangis's *Chronicon*. For all the Mss. in which it appears, see Delisle, 'Mémoire sur les ouvrages de Guillaume de Nangis', *Mémoires de l'Académie des Inscriptions et Belles-Lettres*, 27, 2 (1873), pp. 313ff.

81 M. Daunou (ed.), 'Gesta Sancti Ludovici noni Francorum regis auctore monacho Sancti Dionysii anonymo', *Recueil des Historiens des Gaules et de la France*, 20, pp. 51–2.

82 Repeated by Ivo: 'Omni etiam anno in prefato festo aut intererat vel si tunc occupatus interesse non poterat, quam citius postea accendens ad altare sancti Dionysii cum maxima devotione, nudo capite, flexis genibus, oratione praemissa vocato ad hoc presente filio suo domino Philippo, ponens quatuor auri bisantios primo super caput suum tenens cum manu postmodum cum multa reverencia eosdem bisantios, osculans altare, super illud devotissime offerebat.' BN MS. lat. 5286, fol. 207 r. On the question of the hereditary implications of the act see Paul R. Hyam's 'The form of manumission charters and ideas about freedom' (unpublished paper). I would like to thank Hyams for sending me a copy of his paper.

83 M. Daunou (ed.), 'Vie de Saint Louis par le confesseur de la Reine Marguerite', *Recueil des Historiens des Gaules et de la France*, 20, p. 76.

84 Delaborde, 'Pourquoi Saint Louis faisait acte de servage à Saint Denis', p. 255.

85 Vatican, Ottoboni lat. 2796. Register A, fol. 12 v. John Baldwin discovered this entry while studying Philip's Register A at the Vatican. I would like to thank him for sharing it with me and for his advice concerning its date.

86 Bossuat, 'Traditions populaires', p. 483.

87 K. Gorski, 'La Naissance des états et le Roi-Saint, problème de l'idéologie féodale', in *L'Europe aux IXe–XIe siècles*, Colloque international sur les origines des Etats Européens aux IXe–IXe siècles (Warsaw, 1968), pp. 425–32.

88 Gorski points out that one of the benefits of this ideal model of the 'holy king' was its freedom from influences of the Roman Empire. It could, thus, serve as an instrument of national claims against the theoretical hegemony of the Empire.

89 J. Strayer, 'France, the Holy Land, the Chosen People, the Most Christian King', in *Action and Conviction in Early Modern France*, ed. by T. E. Rabb and J. E. Siegel (Princeton, 1969), p. 5.

90 Schramm, *Der König von Frankreich*, p. 77.

91 Strayer, 'France, the Holy Land, the Chosen People', p. 5.

92 Guenée, 'L'Histoire de l'état en France à la fin du moyen âge vue par les historiens francais depuis cent ans', *Revue Historique*, 232 (1964). p. 346.

93 E. Kantorowicz, 'Kingship under the impact of scientific jurisprudence', in *Twelfth-century Europe and the Foundations of Modern Society*, ed. by M. Clagett *et al.* (Madison, 1966), p. 101; and Kantorowicz, *The King's Two Bodies: A Study in Mediaeval Political Theology* (Princeton, 1966).

94 G. Langmuir, 'Community and legal change in Capetian France', *French Historical Studies*, 6 (1970), p. 286.

95 Strayer speaks of the cult of the kingdom of France as early as 1300. See his *On the Medieval Origins of the Modern State* (Princeton, 1970), p. 54.

96 In P. Viollet, *Histoire des institutions politiques et administratives de France* (Paris, 1898), 2, p. 20.

❖◆❖◆❖◆❖◆❖◆❖◆❖◆❖◆❖◆❖◆❖◆❖◆❖◆❖◆❖◆❖◆❖◆❖◆❖

5

*The politics of canonization in the thirteenth century: lay and Mendicant saints**

MICHAEL GOODICH

In the thirteenth century the Roman papacy, despite an outward appearance of strength, faced a severe struggle for survival. Within Catholic Europe itself, the Hohenstaufen and their allies questioned clerical prerogatives and, as a result, often suffered excommunication and anathema. In southern France and northern Italy the alarming growth of heresy threatened to detach a significant area of Europe from allegiance to Rome. Simultaneously, a Mongol army menaced Europe's eastern flank, while the Crusader states were soon to fall again into Muslim hands. In Italy papal involvement in communal politics fanned suspicion and distrust of clerical motives. Within the Church itself, debate raged between conservatives and radicals, contemplative and active orders, concerning the best means of combating these threats while fulfilling the Christian Gospel.

In the face of these mounting difficulties, the papal see, under the leadership of such capable men as Innocent III, Gregory IX and Innocent IV, launched a major offensive aimed at both spiritual renewal and organizational efficiency. A whole new arsenal of weapons was forged to strengthen the Church against its alleged foes: these tools included the newly founded schools and universities; the Mendicant orders and their associated lay confraternities; the collection and publication of the Canon Law; the reduction of episcopal power and the periodic summoning of local synods; and the centralization of the church bureaucracy in papal hands. One of the most effective means of harnessing popular energy to the papal cause was a vast proliferation of saints' cults, dedicated to men and women sympathetic to the Roman viewpoint. With the aid of such cults, and the organizations which supported them, the church hierarchy could control and oversee a form of religious enthusiasm which might otherwise find more destructive channels. Through the trials, processions and

*Reprinted with permission from *Church History*, 44 (1975), pp. 294–307.

pilgrimages involved in the agitation for canonization of a local hero, Rome was able to widen its popular base and draw potential opponents into its circle of influence. This ability to unify a particular region or class around the banner of one or another charismatic figure was a potent force through which the papacy successfully maintained the unity and universality of a beleaguered faith.[1]

The propaganda campaign and agitation whch preceded papal consideration of a putative saint's claim to canonization is a valuable indicator of this base of support enjoyed by Rome; for the general lines of papal policy and the classes and regions which Rome sought to reward are reflected in the canonization procedures and the trials which they produced. In this paper we will examine two genres of thirteenth-century saint: the Mendicants and lay royalty. The two other major 'saintly' groups, that is, members of religious orders and bishops, are not survived by such complete dossiers, and clearly appealed to a much narrower, and largely clerical constituency. While the Cistercian saints, for example, spent much of their lives within a cloister, and the canonized bishops were often members of the papal diplomatic corps, the Mendicant and lay saints had more contact with the greater body of Christians. The result is that at the canonization trial of Gilbert of Sempringham, for example, of the eighty-three reported witnesses, the majority were *conversi*, nuns, clergy or laity of the priories of Sempringham, along with some residents of the surrounding Lincolnshire countryside; the virtues and miracles of a king's daughter like Margaret of Hungary, on the other hand, were attested to by lay and clergy, male and female, rich and poor, urban and rural folk.[2]

From 1200 to 1334, that is, from Innocent III to John XXII, despite the enormous number of persons who became the objects of purely local cults, only twenty-six were officially canonized.[3] In selecting these individuals out of the many who could claim virtuous and miraculous lives, Rome was often guided as much by political as by religious considerations. Each town, village, diocese or religious order had its own favourite cult-object; but, in addition to a candidate's pious attributes, the degree of success in achieving papal support might well depend upon conformity to Rome's immediate needs: the anti-Hohenstaufen alliance, the fight against heresy, secular encroachments on clerical liberty, or the Crusades. Every royal family of Europe was credited with at least one such saint, and more if its policies adhered more closely to those of Rome. The Andechs of Central Europe could boast no fewer than twenty-one saints and *beati* between 1150 and 1500.[4] The Castilian royal family numbered four local saints in the thirteenth century alone.[5]

While the accepted secular régime naturally might have its cult-heroes confirmed by the pope, so did its political opponents. Most of the British saints, for example, were drawn from the episcopate which opposed the pretensions of the ruling Plantagenets: for example, Edmund of Canterbury, Richard of Chichester and Thomas of Hereford.[6] In Italy likewise, all of the leading communal families were so honoured with at least a local hero: the Patrizi, Piccolomini, Pucci-Franceschi, Buonaccorsi, and so forth.[7] In all of these 'political' cases, the directing hand of the secular authorities was apparent in the agitation which preceded consideration by Rome of an individual's saintly merits.

In order to determine the base of support enjoyed by the successful canonization cases, one must determine the sources of the campaigns which preceded papal action. Such campaigns characteristically involved the receipt of letters describing the putative saint's miracles and the composition of a tentative *Vita et Miracula*. It will become apparent that while these letters of postulation and *Vitae* were produced with the assistance of the governing authorities, all of the saints in addition possessed a wider popular following. The wider occupational, sex and age groups, as well as the geographical regions to which the saint appealed, may be reconstructed, albeit only imperfectly, through a census of those persons who testified at canonization hearings, or who were touched by the putative saint's miracles. Some clear distinctions may thereby be drawn between the constituencies of monastic, Mendicant, episcopal and lay saints.

I LAY AND DYNASTIC SAINTS

The first stage of the process aimed at papal consideration of a putative saint's case was the receipt by Rome of petitions from leading lay and ecclesiastical figures. This was soon followed by the composition of a *Vita et Miracula* based upon an informal hearing, aimed at bolstering the candidate's case. Clearly, petitions drawn up by the Hohenstaufen or Plantagenets were less likely to succeed than those emanating from Andechs or Angevin chanceries. The earliest cause of the thirteenth century concerned Empress Cunegunda, whose case began under Celestine III and was completed by Innocent III. Rome had been deluged with letters from various lay and ecclesiastical officials of the Empire, particularly from the diocese of Bamberg, some of whom visited Rome to sue for her case.[8] The canonization of Landgravine Elizabeth of Thuringia, who had ruled under the stern guidance of the papal legate Conrad of Marburg, was likewise preceded by letters from the most prominent princes, archbishops and abbots of the Empire. This literature suggests an organized campaign, perhaps directed by the local episcopate.[9] Hedwig of Silesia's case was promoted by letters from the King of Bohemia and the Archbishop of Gnesen and his suffragans, the recipients of so many ducal benefactions.[10] Margaret of Hungary's trial was likewise aided by a request from her brother King Stephen of Hungary.[11]

The cults which arose around the memories of the two Angevin saints, Louis IX of France and Louis of Toulouse [or Anjou], were both clearly under royal patronage. In the case of Louis IX the people of Paris hardly needed the sanction of pope or bishop to dub their beloved monarch a saint. As his bones were being carried to Saint-Denis for burial, the spectators already spoke of the curative powers of 'saint' Louis, and the transportation of his relics to France from the Holy Land was accompanied by numerous miracles.[12] Even prior to the canonization proceedings, Louis's nephew Louis of Toulouse was also the object of a popular cult. Despite his contact with the Spiritual Franciscans, Louis's family connections ensured recognition. Immediately following burial at Marseille, omens of his sanctity had appeared, and at Aix a feast was held yearly and a confraternity dedicated to his memory was formed. His father, Charles II of Anjou, who had at first opposed his son's religious vocation, now addressed a letter to Boniface VIII urging an investigation into Louis's sanctity. His request was supported by three Provençal archbishops, their suffragans and cathedral chapters; a certain John of Rocca Guglielma was dispatched to the papal curia as a spokesman for his cause.[13]

While all of the letters of postulation received by the curia contained descriptions of miracles allegedly performed by the putative saint, such brief evidence would not be sufficient to ensure papal action. In recognition of the new, more rigorous judicial standards now demanded at Rome, the interested bishop often conducted his own inquiry, either in the form of notarized statements or a fully-fledged *Vita et Miracula*. The papally-ordered trial of Elizabeth of Thuringia was preceded by several such reports of her miracles which may have found their way into her 'file'.[14] The two Lives of Louis IX by Geoffrey of Beaulieu (1272/1273) and William of Chartres (1276/1282) seem to have been a product of this pre-canonization propaganda, as was the Life of Elzéar of Sabran by the Franciscan scholar Francis of Meyronnes.[15] In 1327 King Edward III likewise established a commission to inquire into the life and miracles of his uncle Thomas of Lancaster; this case did not succeed.[16]

These dynastic saints represent an old tradition within Western Christianity, most common in the Early Middle Ages in frontier areas, when the acts of a local ruler were decisive in the spread of the new faith. These 'national' saints apparently drew support from all classes, urban and rural, lay and clerical. Of course the 'Life' of the saint was largely reported by intimates, friends, servants and family. But the miracles were reported by a cross-section of the population; while the pious life of Elizabeth of Thuringia was largely attested to by her four maidservants, over six hundred persons testified about her miracles. Of these, nearly one-third were women; most of them came from small villages in the dioceses of Mainz and Trier, with several from Wurzburg, Halberstadt, Paderborn,

Liège, and Cologne. Most were probably of peasant backgrounds. Of the eighty whose occupations are identifiable, twenty-eight were clergy and sixteen either *nobiles* or *miles*. Also included were six servants, two judges, five hospital officials and a scattering of artisans; nine were described as citizens (*cives*), mostly from Marburg.[17]

Although the canonization trial of Elizabeth's niece, Duchess Hedwig of Poland, does not survive, her *Vita majora* (*c.* 1300) is derived from it, and names those assisted by her miraculous intercession, rather than the witnesses at her trial. Most were drawn from Gnesen, Bratislava and nearby. Forty-nine were women, compared with twenty-seven men, and many of these were youngsters. Twenty-one of the recipients were religious; three were members of the duke's or duchess's household; eight were noblemen or members of noble families; while nine were styled citizens (*cives*); also mentioned were two *pauperes*, a servant, miller, judge and smith.[18] The extant documents concerning another member of the Andechs clan, Margaret of Hungary, who was placed in a convent at the age of two, names thirty-seven women from the convent at Veszprem, her confessor Marcel, and several Dominicans connected with the convent, along with witnesses from all classes drawn from Buda and its environs.[19]

The surviving documents dealing with Louis IX of France suggest a similarly wide-ranging constituency, centred however in the royal lands around Paris. The *Vie* of St Louis by Queen Margaret's confessor William of St Pathus, based upon the 1282 hearings at Saint-Denis, names thirty-seven witnesses who spoke of Louis's life and behaviour.[20] These all came from the royal court, including his sons King Philip and Count Peter of Alençon, and his brother King Charles of Sicily; also heard from were two bishops, three abbots, a dozen leading peers of the realm, several court clerics and a smattering of wealthy citizens of Saint-Denis attached to the court. Of the several hundred witnesses who described Louis's miracles, the reports of only twenty survive; all come from the vicinity of Paris and Saint-Denis. The list includes seven women and thirteen men; seven artisans and/or their wives, three clergy, one bourgeois and a count.[21] Louis's nephew Bishop Louis of Toulouse is survived by a complete transcript of his canonization hearing.[22] The witnesses included some of the leading noblemen and clergy of southern France. As in the case of Elizabeth of Thuringia, ten members of Louis's household spoke about his life; twenty-two of the speakers were clergy, including such notables as James Duèze, Bishop of Fréjus and later Pope John XXII, the bishops of Rapolla, Gaeta, Vence and Troia, the Franciscan Minister General Raymond Gauffridi, and the Benedictine Abbot of Saint-Victor of Marseille, William of Sabran; the testimony of his brother Duke Robert of Calabria was transmitted through one Adam, a Franciscan master of theology. The lay spokesmen were drawn largely from the citizenry of Marseille, the major site of Louis's cult.

In marked contrast to these nobles, laymen without ties to the curia stood little chance of achieving papal canonization. The papal process favoured two groups: clergymen and powerful noblemen. From 1198 to 1334 among non-noble laity, only the Cremonese merchant Homobonus (can. 1199) was so favoured by Innocent III; but the Life by his confessor Osbert of Saint-Gilles does not survive.[23] We do possess a notarized collection of miracles brought together between 10 June and 5 July 1315 concerning the impoverished notary Henry of Bolzano (d. 1315); but this hearing was ordered by the local bishop and did not achieve papal adjudication;[24] the Lives of Seraphina of San Gimignano and Peter Cresci by John of San Gimignano likewise suggest a similar notarial process, but were equally abortive.[25] The failure of these 'popular' heroes to achieve papal recognition appears to have been based upon political grounds. The ardently anti-Ghibelline historian Salimbene de Adam refers to two popular lay saints whose cults did not achieve papal favour because of the Ghibelline orientation of their partisans.[26] The historian roundly debunks the miracles attributed to Albert of Val d'Ogna at Parma, Reggio and Cremona in 1279.[27] This wine and grain porter is described as a drinker and sinner, hardly the fit object of veneration. The *Annales Placentini Gibellini* and the *Annales Parmenses Majores*, on the other hand, describe Albert as a 'good man' (*bonus homo*), while the historian Albert Milioli calls him *beatus*.[28] As a result of the miracles performed by Albert, many porters of the region, along with noblemen and women, flocked to his tomb. They organized a cult in his honour, replete with processions, singing, and so forth. Tents were even set up in the town square of Parma, masses were celebrated, and pictures of Albert were drawn at the church of St Peter in the piazza, before which miracles reportedly occurred.[29] According to Salimbene, in order to curry the people's favour, priests had images of the dead man painted in their churches; although communal regulations prohibited this, the more zealous devotees even defaced the walls of the city with images of Albert. Those who did not attend the ceremonies were regarded as envious, or heretics; the Franciscans and Dominicans who stayed were chastised for believing that only their saints could perform miracles. Devotees went about the communes collecting money in Albert's memory. Salimbene suggests that these funds were used by the collectors themselves.[30] Other historians report that the over three hundred imperial pounds collected were used to establish a hospital in Albert's memory beside the house of the Malebranchi. The lavishness of these activities is partially explained by the great grain harvest of 1279. Many of Albert's fellow porters were presumably celebrating their new prosperity.

Salimbene suggested that the priesthood was cowed into accepting the honours accorded this new saint. In fact, he continued, when the dead porter's toe was brought to Parma and carried in procession, Canon

Anselm of San Vitale reported that it reeked of an odour which proved Albert's fraudulence; a true saint's relic remains incorrupt. A clove of garlic was subsequently found embedded in the relic. Salimbene's and Anselm's Guelfism also probably influenced their scepticism in this instance.[31] Nevertheless, Albert's cult remained vigorous, especially at Cremona, where most of his relics lay.

Salimbene further cast aspersions on the cult of Anthony Peregrinus of Padua. The fifteenth-century hagiographer Sicco Polentino, chancellor of Padua in 1413, described Anthony as a scion of the noble Manzoni, and an opponent of Ezzelino the Tyrant.[32] Anthony devoted his entire life to religious pursuits, and refused to take part in commercial affairs. When his father died and left Anthony all of his wealth, he piously distributed it to the poor, an act which greatly incensed his two sisters, both of whom were nuns. In order to serve God more fully, Anthony castigated his flesh and became a wandering Mendicant. After leaving Padua, he settled at the village of Bassano, outside Bologna; there he cared for an old and sickly priest. Following years of wandering to the pilgrimage sites of Europe and the Holy Land, Anthony finally returned to Padua and became an oblate at S. Maria de Porciula, where he died on 10 January 1267. Between 2 February and 31 March 1267, thirty-eight miracles were attested to in the presence of the notary Thealdo de Soligio. Despite Salimbene's earlier displeasure, public honours were accorded Anthony by the commune of Padua in 1324. This coincided with the great triumph of the Ghibelline faction in that city and throughout northern Italy; Anthony's opposition to Ezzelino may therefore have been a later invention.

Salimbene suggested a number of grounds upon which the veneration of saints like Albert of Val d'Ogna and Anthony Peregrinus rested.[33] The infirm were attracted to such cults because of the cures which they experienced; while the curious enjoyed the sight of novelties. The clergy felt envious towards the new orders and put forth rival saints. The bishops and canons were greedy for wealth; for this reason, he argued, the clergy of Ferrara supported the cult of Ermanno Pungilupo, whose body was exhumed and burned as heretical in 1301 despite the miracles which had occurred before his tomb.[34] The clergy had nevertheless profited from their native town's hope that peace would come through the miraculous deeds of those 'saints,' permitting them to return to their homeland and regain their possessions. The chronicler suggested that the Ghibellines were most likely to profit from this general amnesty, and were the chief partisans of these popular saints. This suggested a tacit alliance between the devotees of these apparently 'working class' *beati*, and the older nobility.

The *political* character of sainthood was merely suggested by the cult of Anthony and Albert, both of whom appear to have stood for the anti-clerical city population; consequently those like Salimbene, who opposed the emperors and their vicars, questioned the efficacy of saints venerated by their supporters. The power of a saint rested upon his conformity to a tradition of sainthood accepted by the community he served. If that group, for the moment, stood outside the papal sphere, he might still have been regarded as holy, despite the displeasure of the authorities. Thus, many were viewed as saints by the 'outgroup' to which they belonged, but as heretics by their opponents. Most of the contemporary saints in England belonged to a particular anti-royal faction; as supporters of Rome they eventually found an acceptable constituency for their cults.[35] The Ghibelline saints, on the other hand, did not always find acceptance so readily, even after the local victory of their party.

II FRANCISCAN SAINTS

If we are searching for saints whose cults enjoyed the most local, concentrated, but popular enthusiasm, they are to be found among the founders of the new, largely Mendicant orders which blossomed in the thirteenth century. Unlike their dynastic counterparts, such cults were largely restricted to a small geographical area: the vicinity of Sulmona, in the case of Peter Celestine, or Barcelona, in the case of Raymund of Penyafort. But their success was no less a product of local patriotism and a means whereby Rome accorded favour to local political factions. In the early part of the century, during the pontificates of Gregory IX, Innocent IV and Alexander IV, the Franciscans and Dominicans were the major beneficiaries of this papal favour. After 1260, with the recrudescence of episcopal power and retrenchment at Rome, the Mendicants encountered greater opposition and difficulty in achieving canonization. They were then replaced by the Augustinians as recipients of sainthood.

In the case of Francis himself, the Seraphic Father was already addressed as 'il santo' in his lifetime. Immediately following Francis's death, on 3 October 1226, the Franciscan Minister General Elias addressed a letter to Gregory of Naples and the Mendicants of France announcing the saint's death and the stigmata borne by him.[36] These wounds were to represent the most visible sign of Francis's sainthood. After the general chapter of 1227 Elias requested Pope Gregory IX, former cardinal-protector of the order, to canonize the Seraphic Father. He then secured a plot of land in Assisi on which a shrine was to be erected. By April 1228, the pope issued the bull *Recolentes qualiter*, announcing the construction of a church and soliciting contributions. Thus, even prior to a canonization hearing, the decision had been made. A similar case of prejudgement was to mark the canonization of Clare of Assisi, foundress of the companion order of Poor Clares.[37] While the trial of Francis is not extant, the case of Clare survives in a fragmentary Umbro-Italian translation of the testimony of twenty inhabitants of Clare's home convent of San Damiano, including her closest companions; they did testify to the general awe in which the public of Assisi held her.[38] The *Vita* by Thomas of Celano, which was a product of the 1254 hearing, does not name the witnesses, but describes thirteen miracles, the majority experienced by male children drawn from the leading cities of Umbria.[39]

The successful case of Francis of Assisi was followed in the 1230s and 1240s by similar attempts by communal authorities aimed at the re-cognition of local Franciscan heroes. Anthony of Padua's canonization in 1233 was preceded by repeated requests from the podestà and commune of Padua. Ambrose of Massana was supported by the council and 'people' of Orvieto; Benvenuto of Gubbio by letters from the clergy and 'people', that is, council, of Cornetto, the site of his relics; while the trial of Simon of Collazzone was requested by the commune and podestà of Spoleto, and that of Rose of Viterbo by the bishop-elect, clergy, council and 'people' of Viterbo.[40]

The fragmentary extant trials of the Franciscans suggest the primarily urban Italian character of the friars' constituency. Furthermore, while episcopal saints were represented by largely clerical testimony, the Fran-ciscans betrayed a marked popularity within the artisan class, with higher female participation. The case of Ambrose of Massana was supported by 67 male and 144 female witnesses at Orvieto in 1240/41.[41] Those whose origins are cited include fifteen religious, largely Franciscans, including the Bishop of Sessa. Thirty-eight were identified by their own occupation or that of a husband or brother; eight were smiths or their spouses, two notaries, two equerries; others a saddlemaker, comb-maker, merchant, miller, three carters, a servant, the city executioner, a hatter, bowmaker, ploughman, locksmith, the city chamberlain; seven were labelled simply *cives*, and two were relatives of the Bishop of Orvieto. A similarly wide-ranging constituency spoke at the abortive trial of the Franciscan Gerard Cagnoli (1267–1342), held at Pisa in 1347.[42]

The 1232 *Vita prima* of Anthony of Padua, probably composed shortly after his trial, reports sixty-three miracles, in which female recipients slightly outnumbered males.[43] Most came from the vicinity of Padua, with a scattering from other northern Italian towns such as Ferrara, Piacenza and Venice. Only four were identified by occupation; two were religious, one a *cives*, one a knight (*miles*). The trial of Simon of Collazzone (held 2–19 July 1252) lists seventy-eight local witnesses reporting on twenty-five miracles.[44] The vast majority were drawn from the Spoleto area. While a bare majority of the miracles were performed on men, two-thirds of the witnesses were women; all of the witnesses who spoke about his virtues were Franciscans from Simon's convent.

III DOMINICAN AND AUGUSTINIAN SAINTS

The second Mendicant order, the Dominicans, particularly involved in scholarly and anti-heretical activities, fared equally well in the early part of the century, although apparently lacking the ties to communal authorities which the Franciscans possessed. Among the Friars Preachers, the movement to have the founder Dominic canonized apparently orginated at Bologna under the patronage of John of Vicenza, Stephen of Lombardy, Ventura of Bologna and other Dominicans attached to the university; it was materially aided by the intense religious excitement of the Alleluia of 1233.[45] That very year was to witness the canonization of Anthony of Padua, Virgil of Salzburg and Dominic, as well as activity on behalf of Elizabeth of Thuringia and Hildegard of Bingen. Dominic's canonization would clearly serve as an outstanding symbol of the social reform and evangelization which accompanied the preaching friars in central Italy. As in the case of Francis and Clare, the pope's letter initiating proceedings again suggested that Dominic would necessarily be canonized. His case was further supported by the eloquent *Libellus* of Jordan of Saxony, an account of the first years of the order. This document was apparently circulated privately among the Friars Preachers as documentary evidence to support their case.[46]

The case of the second Dominican saint, Peter of Verona, another staunch opponent of Catharism, received equally rapid attention as a result of petitions from the government of Milan following his assassination in 1252. Despite this canonization, the Dominicans appear, by and large, to have been more closely associated with the Ghibellines. Just as the Franciscan Salimbene had displayed scepticism concerning the accomplishments of the lay saints, so he likewise doubted the efficacy of miracles performed by the Dominicans. The Franciscans were described with due reverence and respect. The leading Dominican preacher, John Schio of Vicenza, was treated as a scoundrel and charlatan. Salimbene reported that although John lacked education (he had in fact attended the University of Bologna), he was popularly regarded as a saint, and even believed himself capable of performing miracles without the aid of God.[47] When he was reproved by his fellow-Dominicans for such rashness, John replied that, just as he had exalted St Dominic, whose bones had lain forgotten at Bologna for twelve years after his death until the canonization in 1233, so he could just as easily vilify the saint and the deeds of the Dominicans. Such was Salimbene's report. Thomas of Cantimpré, on the other hand, speaking from a Dominican perspective, accepted John's ability to rout heretics and raise the dead from their graves.[48] In 1233, among other deeds, John served as mediator between the warring Guelph and Ghibelline factions and wrote a treaty which provided for the repatriation of exiles and the return of their property.[49] Thus, opinion might differ over his sanctity, depending upon one's orientation.

But despite their early successes the Dominicans, like the Franciscans, fared poorly after 1260. The case of Ambrose Sansedonius of Siena was supported by notarized statements from nineteen women and nine men of Siena in 1287, but the case never reached Rome;[50] Pope Benedict XI became the subject of an inquiry, but again to no avail.[51] Only Thomas Aquinas, who was supported by petitions from King Charles II and Queen Maria of Sicily, several Italian nobles and the University of Naples, was successfully canonized by Pope John XXII in 1323.[52] The persistent failure encountered by the Preachers in the latter part of the century is illustrated by the case of the great canonist Raymund of Penyafort.[53] The estrangement between the Aragonese crown and the papacy after the Sicilian Vespers led to a postponement of Raymund's case; and once the principals had died, interest waned. Immediately after Raymund's death in 1275, an inquiry into his miracles was held at the Dominican church in Barcelona at the order of Bishop Arnaldo de Gurb. In 1279 Nicholas IV was asked to act by the council of Tarragona and King Peter of Aragon, who named a special proctor in 1282 to promote the case before the curia. Although Martin IV apparently named a commission of inquiry, the process was frustrated by the break in papal–Aragonese relations. Under Boniface VIII the case was vainly pursued by the Dominicans of Aragon and the municipal authorities at Barcelona and other Catalan cities. As a result of letters sent by James II of Aragon in 1317 to John XXII, a commission was re-established, which examined the 1279 'procés-verbal' brought by the proctor Arnald Burguet. A diocesan hearing was held at Barcelona in 1318. A subsequent request was sent in 1349 by Peter IV of Aragon, and a new *Vita* was commissioned by the Dominicans of Barcelona. Canonization was nevertheless delayed until the sixteenth century.

The constituency of these Dominican saints may again be determined from an examination of the fragmentary canonization trials. Because of his unique international connections, the trial of Dominic had been held in two places, Bologna and Provence. Portions of the Bolognese testimony, given between 6 August and 15 August 1233, survive in a fragmentary fifteenth-century manuscript, and contain the remarks of nine preachers connected with the university.[54] The hearings in Languedoc involved over three hundred persons; depositions were taken throughout the region, at Toulouse, Fanjeaux and elsewhere. Of the few witnesses whose names survive, the majority were clergy, including Bishop Fulk of Toulouse. The extant Life of Peter Martyr of Verona, by Thomas Agni of Lentini, probably based on the canonization hearing, names over fifty persons who received Peter's miracles, with a bare male majority.[55] While the majority occurred in such Lombard towns as Milan, Brescia and Parma, a sizeable number came from Spain and southern France. Thus, the Dominicans were marked by both an Italian and a trans-Alpine constituency. Eight were identified as religious, three as noble, three as *cives*, two as merchants; one one was a *pauper*, one an arms-bearer (*scutifer*), one a member of the household of the bishop of Como.

In the abortive case of Raymund of Penyafort, reports of thirteen miracles survive, presented in 1318 before the bishop of Barcelona.[56] A total of seventeen male and twenty-one female witnesses spoke, all from Barcelona and its environs. Here again, as in the case of Ambrose of Massana, a markedly 'popular' constituency was apparent. The class or occupation of twenty-one witnesses or their husbands was given; only one was a priest; fourteen were styled *cives* or members of their families. Many occupations were represented: candlemaker, merchant, woodworker, physician, silver-smith, bottlemaker, weaver, launderer. By the fourteenth century, however, the popular character of the Dominican constituency seems to have diminished. While Raymund had been deeply involved in international and local politics, Thomas Aquinas largely confined his activities to scholarly and ecclesiastical circles. Consequently, the extant canonization trial, held between 2 July and 18 September 1319 before Archbishop Humbert of Naples, is restricted to thirty-two male witnesses, all identifiably either ecclesiastics or local nobility of southern Italy.[57] Among the witnesses were three members of the household of the king and queen of Sicily, and Thomas's biographer, William of Tocco.

Because of their more traditional, contemplative approach, and consistent espousal of Roman causes, the Augustinian hermits replaced the older Mendicant orders in papal favour after 1260, particularly in Italy. The factionalism and heretical leanings of the Franciscans in this period were a marked contrast to the theological orthodoxy of the Augustinians, all of whose saints were portrayed as staunch opponents of the Ghibellines, Spiritual Franciscans or other papal foes. Even Clare of Montefalco reportedly held theological discussions with errant Franciscans like Bentivenga of Gubbio, and assisted in the campaign against the Brethren of the Free Spirit in the Spoleto diocese.[58] The importance which Rome attributed to the canonization process is highlighted by the case of the first Augustinian saint, John Buoni of Mantua, whose canonization coincided with the unification of four eremitical orders under the Augustinian rule.[59] In addition to his personal merits, John's canonization may also represent a reward for the role which this new order was to play in tackling the doctrinal and political problems which beset the older Mendicant orders; further, it was a reward to those hermits who, unlike the Brethren of the Sack, submitted to clerical and canonical discipline. The witnesses who appeared at John's trial frequently reiterated his opposition to heretics and the excommunicated partisans of Frederick II. John's case had been supported by letters from Bishop Jacobus da Porta of Mantua and two Mantuan noblemen, Bartholomew and Nicholas, sent to Rome on behalf of the commune. John's constituency betrays a clearly 'popular', urban-dwelling character. During the hearings held at Mantua and Cesena in 1251 and 1253/54, a total of 114 males and 115 females testified; these included thirty-two Augustinians of all ranks, four members of the order of penitence, one 'humiliatus' and the bishop of Cesena himself. The secular occupations represented included merchants, notaries, judges, barbers, tool-makers, glass-blowers, tailors, porters, a town-crier's wife, stewards, physicians, carpenters, servants and a baker; five were described as simply *nobiles*, or *miles*.

The case of the eremitical Pope Celestine V, who spent most of his life in the mountainous regions near Sulmona in the Marche, called forth a veritable avalanche of popular feeling among the rural folk of the area.[60] A total of 322 witnesses testified at the trial held in 1307. Every local occupation was represented – goldsmith, notary, knight, physician, priest, judge, canon, barber. And despite Peter's strenuous efforts to avoid the sight of women, at least a third of the witnesses were female. This canonization represented a victory for the party opposed to Boniface VIII and allied to Charles of Anjou. An equally widespread cult was devoted to the Augustinian hermit Nicholas of Tolentino.[61] In the course of his trial, which lasted from 7 July to 28 September 1325, and was promoted by letters of postulation from both French and Italian bishops, 371 witnesses of all classes testified. Among these were 150 friends, relatives and associates who had first-hand knowledge of the saint. Again, many small villages of the Marche were represented.

IV THE FUNCTION OF CANONIZATION

The basis of this marked rise in papal canonization was undoubtedly the alarming reappearance of heresy and its effect on the wavering faith of Christians. Through the enthusiasm generated by such cases, Rome was able to reward its allies and maintain popular support. Those families, religious orders or localities which had served the papacy in its conflict with Saracen, heretic or Hohenstaufen were duly accorded recognition through the institution of sainthood. Beginning with Innocent III, all canonization bulls were prefaced by an explanation of the grounds upon which an individual had achieved sainthood. In his bull of 12 January 1199 canonizing Homobonus of Cremona, Innocent argued that the merchant's virtuous behaviour and miraculous deeds assisted in the refutation of heretics, since they were signs of God's favour towards the Catholic faith.[62] This same argument was reiterated in the case of Cunegunda, canonized on

3 April 1200, whose miraculous deeds were described as the surest bulwarks against heresy.[63] In his bull concerning Gilbert of Sempringham, Innocent further noted that even Satan, Pharaoh's magicians, the Pharisees and the Antichrist were capable of befuddling good Christians by performing miracles or good deeds.[64] Consequently, canonization required incontrovertible proof of a virtuous life and miraculous deeds, attested to by sworn, reliable witnesses testifying at a trial, presenting first-hand evidence. After this, Rome often rejected episcopal hearings on the grounds of inadequate or conflicting evidence, or imperfect judicial procedure. Such caution was to frustrate the cases of Wulfstan of Worcester, Maurice of Carnoet, and Hildegard of Bingen, among many others.[65]

During Innocent's reign, this anti-heretical theme remained paramount. The martyrdom of the papal legate Peter of Castelnau in 1208 in fact became the excuse for the launching of the Albigensian Crusade. And while Innocent's successor, Honorius III, canonized only bishops and Cistercians, his justification remained unchanged. In the case of Abbot William of Eskill (can. 1224), the pope noted that 'Satan may often transform himself into an angel of light', necessitating a reliable trial before canonization.[66] In the case of William of York (can. 1227), Honorius noted that the function of saints is to 'confound the Jews and heretics, to shame pagans, and lead sinners to repentance'.[67]

This defensive anti-heretical theme continued to characterize the papal approach to canonization cases throughout the century. All of the lay saints had shown themselves firm allies of Rome. Elizabeth of Thuringia had governed with the aid of the papal inquisitor Conrad of Marburg, sent to uproot the Stedingers in the Empire. Louis IX's major virtues, as described in his canonization bull, were his two Crusades in the East and his uprooting of heretics.[68] In Margaret of Hungary's abortive case Pope Innocent V specifically instructed his inquisitors to search for 'signs and prodigies which confound heretics and strengthen the faith',[69] and Hedwig of Silesia is described as a Jael and Judith whose numerous benefactions assisted the Church in its hour of need.[70]

The Dominican Order had been established with the express aim of opposing heresy through word and deed. It is therefore not surprising that the corner-stone of every successful Dominican canonization case was the service of the Preaching Friars in the pursuit of heretics. Dominic's canonization bull was nothing less than an extended metaphor in which the timely deeds of the Old Testament prophets in saving the Jews from idolatry were compared to the anti-heretical activities of the Dominicans.[71] For Dominic had allegedly decided to found his order following contact with Albigensians; the first half of the semi-official *Vita* of Jordan of Saxony was devoted to his encounters with heresy.[72] The second Dominican saint, Peter of Verona, had been martyred at the hands of Milanese heretics. And finally, the official *Vita* of Thomas Aquinas by William of Tocco (1323) dwelt at some length on Thomas's refutation of Jews, schismatics and heretics, including Averroists, Siger of Brabant, William of St Amour, the Fraticelli and the Brethren of the Free Spirit.[73]

While the Franciscan and Augustinian orders were less aggressively involved in the anti-heretical struggle, their saints were no less rewarded for active combat on the side of Rome. 'The signs and prodigies [of the saints] confound heretics and confirm the Catholic faith', repeated all of the popes from Innocent III to John XXII.[74] The examples they set were sufficient to convert Jews and pagans.[75] But while the Dominicans largely served in the war against the Albigensians, the other Mendicant orders were praised for their service against the Hohenstaufen foe. Thus, Clare of Assisi was credited with saving Assisi from Frederick II's ally, Vitalis of Aversa; Rose of Viterbo was allegedly expelled from Viterbo for opposing Ezzelino the Tyrant; and John Buoni's trial was replete with testimony concerning his refutation of the Hohenstaufen 'schismatics'.[76]

These canonization cases have thus told us something about the direction of official church policy and the social groups which supported those programmes. In northern Europe, the dynastic families which opposed the Hohenstaufen predominated. Their canonization trials, while carefully orchestrated, demonstrated a wide popular following; this represented an old tradition of royal identification with Rome, and consequent veneration of dynastic saints. The marked female participation in these trials was a contrast to the humble position otherwise accorded women by both the church and secular society, and paralleled the growth of the 'women's movement'. The Mendicant saints were more specifically urban in character, with the exception of such hermits as Peter Celestine and John Buoni, who flourished in rural, mountainous regions. The Dominicans exhibited a more trans-Alpine appeal, in addition to the primarily Italian orientation of Mendicancy. Again, more frequent female participation was evident. The function of these trials and the publicity they engendered has been shown to be a product of Rome's need to counteract the resurgent heretical threat; service against the Saracens and Hohenstaufen were subsidiary goals. While the Christian idealism and *imitatio Christi* embodied in the life of the saint of course remained paramount, the immediate aims behind papally confirmed sainthood were specific, and limited by the political interests of Rome.

NOTES

1 Augustin Fliche *et al.*, *La Chrétienté romaine (1198–1274)* (Paris, 1950) covers the period admirably. On canonization procedures, see Ludwig Hertling,

'Materiali per la storia del processo di canonizzazione', *Gregorianum*, 16 (1935), pp. 170–95; Stephan Kuttner, 'La réserve papale du droit de canonisation', *Revue Historique du Droit Français et Étranger*, 4th series, 17 (1938), pp. 172–228; Eric W. Kemp, *Canonization and Authority in the Western Church* (London, 1948); Margaret R. Toynbee, *S. Louis of Toulouse and the Process of Canonisation in the Fourteenth Century* (Manchester, 1929). The main source for the Lives of the saints is Socii Bollandiani, *Acta Sanctorum ...*, new edition, 66 vols. (Paris, 1863–1940), hereafter referred to as *AS*, followed by the saint's day, with volume number and pages in parentheses.

2 Raymonde Foreville (ed.), *Un Procès de canonisation à l'aube du xiiiᵉ siècle (1201–1202), Le livre de saint Gilbert de Sempringham* (Paris, 1943), pp. 43–79; William Franknoi (ed.), *Monumenta romana episcopatus Vesprimiensis*, 6 vols. (Budapest, 1896–1950), 1, pp. 163–384.

3 Theodor Klauser, 'Die Liturgie der Heiligsprechung', in Odo Casel (ed.), *Heilige Überlieferung, Festschrift Ildefons Herewegen...* (Münster, 1938), pp. 213–33. For canonization bulls, see Giusto Fontanini (ed.), *Codex constitutionum quos summi pontifices ediderunt in solemni canonizatione sanctorum* (Rome, 1729). Such bulls will be cited by their number in August Potthast, *Regesta pontificium romanorum unde ab anno post Christum natum MCXCVIII*, 2 vols. (Berlin, 1874–5), hereafter referred to as *RPR*.

4 Joseph Gottschalk, *St Hedwig Herzogin von Schlesien* (Cologne, 1964); *AS*, 17 October (8, 265–7) for *Genealogia*.

5 *AS*, 30 May (7, 280–414); 8 March (1, 748); 2 May (1, App., 763).

6 Josiah C. Russell, 'The Canonization of Opposition to the King in Angevin England', in Charles H. Taylor (ed.), *Anniversary Essays in Mediaeval History by students of Charles Homer Haskins* (Boston, 1929), pp. 279–90.

7 Vittorio Spreti (ed.), *Enciclopedia storico-nobiliare italiana*, 7 vols. (Milan, 1928–35), *passim*, is filled with such examples from every leading Italian family.

8 *RPR*, 1000; *AS*, 3 March (1, 279–80); *Patrologia Latina*, 140, pp. 219–22, (hereafter *PL*).

9 Albert Huyskens, *Quellenstudien zur Geschichte der hl. Elisabeth* (Marburg, 1908).

10 Gottschalk, *St Hedwig*, p. 5; *AS*, 17 October (8, 220–3).

11 Franknoi, *Monumenta Romana*, 1, p. 160.

12 H.-François Delaborde (ed.), 'Fragments de l'enquête faite à Saint-Denis en 1282 en vue de la canonisation de Saint Louis', *Mémoires de la Société de l'Histoire de Paris et de l'Ile de France*, 23 (1896), p. 62.

13 'Processus canonizationis et Legendae variae sancti Ludovici O.F.M.', in *Analecta Franciscana*, 7 (Quaracchi, 1921), pp. 93, 455.

14 Huyskens, *Quellenstudien*, *passim*.

15 *AS*, 27 September (8, 528–94); C. V. Langlois, 'François de Meyronnes, frère mineur', *Histoire Littéraire de la France*, 36 (1927), pp. 305–42; *AS*, 25 August (5, 541–70) for Lives of Louis IX.

16 Thomas Rymer (ed.), *Foedera...*, 20 vols. (London, 1704–17), 4, pp. 268–9, 421–2, 478–80.

17 Huyskens, *Quellenstudien*, pp. 161 ff.

18 *AS*, 17 October (8, 224–64).

19 Franknoi, *Monumenta Romana*, 1, pp. 163–383.

20 H.-François Delaborde (ed.), *Vie de saint Louis par Guillaume de Saint-Pathus confesseur de la reine Marguerite* (Paris, 1899), pp. 7ff.

21 Delaborde, 'Fragments'.

22 *Processus*; see also Toynbee, *S. Louis*, pp. 174–86.

23 *RPR*, 573; *PL*, 214, pp. 483–5.

24 *AS*, 10 June (2, 376–91).

25 *AS*, 12 March (2, 241–2); John Gori of S. Gimignano, 'Legenda Beati Petri de Fulginco confessoris', ed. by M. Faloci Pulignani, *Analecta Bollandiana*, 8 (1889), pp. 358–69; *AS*, 19 July (4, 663–8).

26 Salimbene de Adam, 'Cronica', ed. by Oswald Holder-Egger, *Monumenta Historica Germanica SS.* (hereafter *MGH*), 32 (Hanover, 1913), pp. 63–5, 68, 228–36, 295–312, 322–9, 418, 554, 556–9, 595 describes miracle-working activities in this period.

27 *Ibid.*, 32, pp. 500–3.

28 Philippe Jaffé (ed.), 'Annales Placentini Gibellini', in *MGH SS.*, 18 (Hanover, 1863), pp. 571–2; *idem.*, 'Annales Parmenses Majores', *MGH SS.*, 18 (Hanover, 1863), p. 687; Albert Milioli, 'Liber de temporibus', ed. by O. Holder-Egger, *MGH SS.*, 18 (Hanover, 1863), pp. 369, 553.

29 Jaffé, *Annales Parmenses*, p. 687; Salimbene, '*Cronica*', pp. 502–3.

30 Salimbene, 'Cronica', p. 503; Giuliano Bonazzi (ed.), 'Chronicon Parmense', in *Rerum Italicarum Scriptores* (hereafter *RIS*), 9, Pt 9 (Città di Castello, 1902), pp. 34–45; Jaffé, *Annales Parmenses*, p. 687.

31 Anselm was a nephew of Pope Innocent IV (Fieschi) and brother of Opizzo of San Vitale, Bishop of Parma. Opizzo was the only bishop at the Council of Ravenna (1261) to defend the papal privileges received by the Mendicants. See Raoul Manselli, 'I vescovi italiani, gli ordini religiosi e i moviment popolari religiosi nel secolo XIII', *Italia Sacra*, 5 (Padua, 1965), pp. 329–30; Salimbene, 'Cronica,' pp. 265, 403, 650; Ireneo Affò, *Storia della città di Parma*, 4 vols. (Parma, 1957), 4, *passim*, on the Fieschi of Parma.

32 'Vita Antonii Peregrini', *Analecta Bollandiana*, 13 (1894), pp. 417–25; 'Miracula beati Antonii Peregrini', *Analecta Bollandiana*, 14 (1895), pp. 108–14; Salimbene, 'Cronica', p. 503.

33 Salimbene, 'Cronica', pp. 503–4.

34 *Ibid.*, p. 504; Affò, *Storia*, 4; L. A. Muratori (ed.), 'Excerpta ex Chronica Jordani', in *Antiquitates italicae medii aevi*, 4 (Milan, 1741), p. 1022.

35 Russell, 'Canonization'.

36 M. Bihl, 'De canonizatione S. Francisci', *Archivum Franciscanum Historicum*, 21 (1928), pp. 468–511; *Analecta Franciscana*, 10 (Quaracchi, 1941), pp. 525–8; J. H. Sbaralea (ed.), *Bullarium Franciscanum*, 3 vols. (Rome, 1759–65), 1, p. 40.

37 *RPR*, 15158.

38 Zefferino Lazzeri (ed.), 'Il processo di S. Chiari d'Assisi', *Archivum Franciscanum Historicum*, 13 (1920), pp. 302–507.

39 *AS*, 12 August (2, 765–8).

40 *RPR*, 8937, 8938, 8941; *AS*, 10 November (4, 571–2); *RPR*, 10129, 14568, 14782.

41 *AS*, 10 November (4, 566–608).
42 Filippo Rotolo, 'La Leggenda del B. Gerarde Cagnoli...', *Miscellanea Franciscana*, 57 (1957), pp. 267–446; *idem.*, 'Il trattato dei miracoli del B. Gerardo Cagnoli...', *Miscellanea Franciscana*, 66 (1966), pp. 128–92.
43 Leon de Kerval (ed.), *Sancti Antonii de Padua Vitae duae...* (Paris, 1904), pp. 83ff.; see Joseph M. Pou y Marti, 'De fontibus vitae S. Antonii Patavini', *Antonianum*, 6 (1931), pp. 225–52.
44 Michele Faloci Pulignani, 'Il B. Simone da Collazzone e il suo processo nel 1252', *Miscellanea Franciscana*, 12 (1910), pp. 97–132.
45 André Vauchez, 'Une Campagne de pacification en Lombardie autour de 1233', *Mélanges d'Archéologie et d'Histoire*, 78 (1966), pp. 503–49 discusses the ramifications of this movement.
46 Jordan of Saxony, 'Libellus de principiis ordinis praedicatorum', ed. by H. Chr. Scheeben, *Monumenta ordinis praedicatorum historica*, 16 (Rome, 1935).
47 Salimbene, 'Cronica', p. 78, '... erederet etiam sine Deo se veraciter miracula posse facere'.
48 *AS*, 2 July (1, 481).
49 John of Vicenza, 'Instrumentum pacis inter Guilfos et Guibellinos', in Muratori, *Antiquitates*, 4, pp. 1172–4; see also Jacques Quétif and Jacques Echard, *Scriptores ordines praedicatorum...*, 2 vols. (Paris, 1719–23), 1, pp. 150–3. For other favourable remarks about John, see the 'Historia' of Gerard Maurisio (pp. 37–9), the 'Chronicon' of Rolandinus of Padua (pp. 203–5, 306ff.), the 'Chronicon' of a monk of Padua (p. 674), the 'Chronicon Veronese' of Parisio de Cereta (pp. 626ff.), and the 'Chronica' of Antonio Godi (p. 80), all edited in *RIS*, 8 (Milan, 1726).
50 *AS*, 2 March (3, 179–250).
51 'De vita prima et miraculis B. Benedicti papae XI auctore Bernardo Guidonis', *Analecta Bollandiana*, 19 (1900), pp. 14–36.
52 *AS*, 7 March (1, 657ff.).
53 Jose Rius-Sierra (ed.), *Sancti Raymundi de Penyaforte opera omnia* (Barcelona, 1949–54), 3, pp. 182ff.
54 V. J. Koudelka, 'Procès de canonisation de S. Dominique', *Archivum Fratrum Praedicatorum*, 42 (1972), pp. 46–67; Quétif and Echard, 1, 44–56; A. Walz (ed.), 'Processus canonizationis S. Dominici', in *Monumenta ordinis praedicatorum historica* (Rome, 1935), 16, pp. 123–67.
55 *AS*, 29 April (3, 686–727).
56 Rius-Serra, *Sancti Raymundi*, 3, pp. 207ff.
57 *AS*, 7 March (1, 688ff.).
58 Livario Oliger, *De Secta spiritus libertatis in Umbria saec. XIV* (Rome, 1943), p. 103 for testimony concerning Clare's involvement with heretics.
59 *AS*, 22 October (9, 732–4) for Innocent IV's bull *Admonet nos*, which summarized the history of the Augustinian Order. The trial testimony follows.
60 Franz Xaver Seppelt, *Monumenta Coelestiniana. Quellen zur Geschichte des Papstes Coelestin V* (Paderborn, 1921), pp. 211–331 for trial. *AS*, 4 May (1, 419ff.) lists witnesses.
61 *AS*, 10 September (3, 636–743).
62 *RPR*, 574; *PL*, 214, pp. 483–5.

63 *AS*, 3 March (1, 279–80); *RPR*, 1000.
64 *RPR*, 1612; C. R. Cheney and W. H. Semple (eds.), *Selected Letters of Pope Innocent III Concerning England (1198–1216)* (London, 1953), pp. 26–32.
65 *RPR*, 1900, 7469, 10329, 11182.
66 *RPR*, 3323, 3324, 3353, 5822, 7154.
67 *RPR*, 7551.
68 *AS*, 25 August (5, 528ff.).
69 Franknoi, *Monumenta Romana*, pp. 160ff.
70 *AS*, 17 October (8, 220).
71 *RPR*, 9529, 9485, 9489.
72 *AS*, 4 August (1, 542ff.)
73 *AS*, 29 April (3, 624ff.) on Peter Verona; 1 March (1, 656–84) on Thomas.
74 *RPR*, 12891, 8938.
75 *RPR*, 8937, 8938, 8941; *AS*, 13 June (2, 215–16).
76 Lazzeri, 'Il Processo', pp. 456, 472, 483; *AS*, 4 September (2, 435); 22 October (9, 716, 818, 821, 844, 832).

6

Towards a sociological study of canonized sainthood in the Catholic Church

PIERRE DELOOZ

Some years ago, P. A. Sorokin[1] remarked that, while more and more books on criminology were produced, no one studied social success. The delinquent child, youth or adult was subjected to intensive research, but virtuous people did not seem to be worthy of scholarly attention. Sorokin aimed, for his part, to fill the gap with a study of what he called *good neighbours*, and of Catholic saints. His explorations in the wide field of canonized sainthood opened up an important chapter in the sociology of religion, extending over two millennia of history. However, despite the fact that he tried to apply to saints his historical scheme concerning the evolution of civilizations, he did not seem to perceive the full implications of his investigation. In any case, since his basic data were defective, he was bound to fall short of his aims.

THE POINT OF DEPARTURE

We may begin with an observation: for nearly two thousand years, a social group, the Roman Catholic Church, has been recognizing certain persons as saints. The study of these persons is likely to teach us something about the group which selected them. It is likely, in particular, that certain aspects of its structural evolution will be made apparent. Since saints were the witnesses of the group, considered by the group to be ideal models, they will doubtless reveal its successive changes and structures.

Listing the saints

Sorokin does not seem to have realized that the validity of research on this topic depends primarily and essentially on making sure that one knows who is a saint or who is recognized as such. Even if a definition of a Catholic saint can be easily agreed upon – a person whose cult is officially sanctioned by the Church – it is impossible to draw up an exact list of those to whom this definition may be applied. Sorokin seems oblivious of this, and he states quite calmly that the Church has 'sanctified', as he puts it, 3,069 people.

How did he arrive at this figure? By going through the twelve volumes of the *Lives of the Saints* by Butler and Thurston in the edition published from 1926 onwards, ignoring incidentally Attwater's thirteenth volume.[2] And yet the authors of this collection never claimed to have drawn up a complete catalogue of Catholic saints. Their work was one of edification and aimed to give Christians a few brief biographical details about the saints that interested them. They followed the order of the calendar, listing saints taken from the *Roman Martyrology*, and adding a few others, especially those honoured in Great Britain, Nor did the authors claim to have written a critical work. The 1926 edition is of course more critical than Alban Butler's which dates from the eighteenth century; but it still refers without batting an eyelid (or almost) not only to legends but also to figures known never to have existed. Sorokin ought to have suspected this. One only has to consult the volumes edited by the Benedictines of Paris to double the number of saints (or nearly) in one go.[3] Thus Butler and Thurston's January volume contains 258 entries, while the Benedictines of Paris have 509 for the same month (322 long and 177 short articles).

With nothing but a work of edification as a basis, Sorokin has to admit to enormous gaps in information concerning most of the subjects whom he is studying. For example, to analyse the geographical distribution of the saints, he bases himself mainly on their place of death. Unfortunately, he says, 74.3 per cent of these places of death are unknown.[4] Unknown that is to anyone who remains content to consult Butler and nothing else; but for hagiographers, on the contrary, information here is particularly full. Nearly all uncertainty has been eliminated as far as the last thousand years are concerned and we are left, in my estimation, with less than 0.3 per cent of uncertain cases.

More serious still, Sorokin does not seem to have grasped that the mode of designating saints has changed over time, and that there might be different sociological meanings involved, say, in the cult of the dead, which was spontaneous at the time of the Roman Empire and led to the cult of martyrs, and in twentieth-century canonization procedure. Is he not, perhaps, one of those 'sociologists in a hurry' referred to by Gabriel Le Bras, 'who jump from the pontificate of Siricius to that of Pius XII, who pick out types ignoring the series to which they belong, and who speculate on examples with whose context they are unfamiliar'?[5] In a word, the seam was rich, but it has been badly worked. It would have been better to begin by drawing up a critical list of Catholic saints.

The way in which saints are designated

One only needs an elementary idea of how saints are designated in order to realize that a complete list of saints will never be established. The cult of saints was born in Antiquity from the cult of martyrs, itself a form of the cult of the dead. Local churches honoured certain of their members who had fallen victim to persecution. As to how many martyrs were honoured in this way with a public cult, who would be bold enough to guess? Some of them are well-known, since their 'Acts' have come down to us; others are less so, with only traces of them preserved by traditions or in monumental remains; others have been forgotten completely.

For several centuries, saints were chosen by small groups, who started new cults without holding an inquiry or a tribunal. The bishop, at his people's insistence, would raise or transfer the relics, thus marking his official approval. It was only a thousand years later that the pope began occasionally to intervene in the official consecration of saints. In 1234, however, he reserved for himself the right to canonize. From them on, the pressure of a small group of the faithful became insufficient. The case had to be taken before a tribunal, and a whole judicial machine had to be set in motion, its rules growing more detailed and complex until the Constitution of Urban VIII in 1634, which drew up the rules of procedure which are still, in the main, operative today.

It can therefore be seen that a list of saints from the first thousand years AD can only be drawn up in piecemeal fashion from sources of very unequal value. It is possible to draw up a list of the saints designated by the Holy See from 993 onwards, the date of the first papal canonization, but this list is not complete either. Quite lengthy periods are not documented at all, and it is really only from the beginning of the sixteenth century that we can be sure that the list has no gaps. Even then, not all saints will have been included. Between 993 and 1234 bishops continued to ratify 'popular' canonizations. And later, many public cults still came into existence independently of papal approval, which had been solicited only – if at all – several centuries after the cult had become established. From 1634 onwards, the list of saints and of the beatified (a distinction sanctioned in Urban VIII's legislation) is relatively easy to draw up, although one has never been published. It is sufficient to name all those who were solemnly proclaimed saints following an official examination of their case by the Congregation of Rites.

This survey indicates that at least the following eight categories among the saints should be distinguished:
— those designated in the first thousand years AD by a local church;
— those designated by the pope between 993 and 1234;

— those who were designated by a local church between 993 and 1234 without papal intervention;

— those who between 1234 and 1634 were designated and canonized by the Holy See according to the old procedure;

— those who between 1234 and 1634 were designated by local churches in spite of the papal reservation;

— those who were canonized after 1634 according to the new procedure;

— those who were only beatified after 1634;

— those who were designated by local churches between 1159 and 1634 but whose cult was ratified by the Holy See according to the new procedure.[6]

This involves making many distinctions, but they are all important. The sociological significance of a local canonization originating in a small rural community is not the same as that of pontifical canonization taking place after a fifty-year procedure and through the pressure of an international religious order. These categories contain statistical groups of varying sizes. For example, between 993 and 1234 there were only seventy-three papal canonizations at most, but about 500 persons became the objects of local public cult. The first group requires further examination. It covers a thousand years of Christian history, and thus needs to be more finely differentiated.

Sainthood and cultural area

Here the first distinctions to be made are those based not on modes of designating sanctity, but on different cultures, different civilizations, in Arnold Toynbee's sense of the word. The saints of the first five centuries or so belonged on the whole to Ancient Greco-Roman civilization. They were the contemporaries of Seneca, Tacitus and Marcus Aurelius, and lived in the same cultural environment. We must, however, distinguish sub-groups among them, and first the original nucleus of founders who belonged to the Jewish people and lived in what Toynbee called the Syriac civilization. Next came a group of martyrs whose cult was expressed very generally according to the cultural models of classical, 'Hellenic', civilization. These were the contemporaries of Tacitus and Marcus Aurelius and lived in the first three centuries AD. After the third century, the saints belonged either to the dying Hellenic civilization of the West – the civilization of Ambrose and Augustine – or to Byzantine civilization. Among the latter, those exemplifying learned religion such as Chrysostom or Gregory of Nyssa, the direct heirs of Hellenic culture, stand out from saints reflecting 'popular' religion among whom monks were especially important, and who were the forerunners of that form of Eastern Christianity which after 1054 became the Orthodox Church.

Though all too brief, these indications at least invite caution and qualification. They also explain why, within the compass of this article, we will only be able to pose questions or at the most sketch out a programme for a sociology of canonized sainthood which has still to be undertaken and which remains a gigantic task.[7]

SANCTITY

In confining ourselves to the official notion of a Catholic saint – a person whom the Church honours with an official cult – we have not forgotten that sanctity is a value which goes far beyond this particular application. There are the official saints, but sanctity extends to a multitude of other persons: to God first of all, to superhuman beings (angels), to material objects (holy relics), to institutions (the tribunal of the Holy Office), and so on. In this wider sense, sanctity is regarded as a value. For the sociologist, then, like all other values it is situated in collective representations and must be expressed in systems of associated conduct or behaviour within a given network of social relations. What is the content of these collective representations; what is the behaviour through which they are expressed; and what networks of social relations are involved? Contemporary sociology is clearly incapable of providing a global answer to such questions; rather a specific area of observation has to be defined, which brings us back to the saints who are officially recognized by the Catholic Church.

But, one may ask, why that area rather than any other? The reason is that it has important advantages. Primarily, because it is, as we shall see, clearly definable by objective criteria, the first of which has already been discussed: the existence of a public cult. It has an impressive continuity over nearly two thousand years. Its origins are rooted in another religion: Judaism; and in two distinct civilizations (in Arnold Toynbee's sense of the word): the 'Syriac' and the Ancient Greek; and fruitful comparisons should, therefore, be possible. It also covers portions of at least three different cultures: Hellenic, Byzantine and Western. Finally, it offers the scholar exceptionally rich documents, probably among the richest sociology will ever have at its disposal for the comprehension of the past and particularly for the last few centuries. Sociologists sometimes dream of going back in time to conduct inquiries based on interviews. This area of investigation is doubtless one of the only ones in which this is possible, for the beatification procedures contain records of interviews held several centuries ago. Thus we have questions and answers from thousands of witnesses concerning the same subject. The evolution of collective mentalities can be followed here at first hand, as it can be nowhere else.

Sanctity in recollection

Sociology has access to sanctity only *as recollected by others*. It is never concerned with sanctity as lived by someone inside a community, but only with a community's recollection of such a person's behaviour. Our point of departure must be that, although the Church does not limit sanctity to its official declarations, it never declares a living person to be a saint, in the sense of being 'the object of an official cult'. Only the dead can be saints. And so sainthood is automatically situated in recollection. If someone is the object of an official cult today, it is because he is a saint; but he is a saint now, because it is believed that he was during his lifetime, in the past, and because one is assured that he was indeed so. Sainthood therefore depends on a community's recollection of a dead person's past existence. The whole process of beatification and canonization, throughout its historical evolution, has depended on memories that people have retained of the past.

Sanctity in the opinion of others

The immediate consequence of this sanctity through recollection is that it also depends on the opinion of others, that is on value judgments made by others. One is never a saint except *for other people*. But for exactly which other people?

First of all saints are, broadly speaking, saints in the eyes of the whole community of the Church, but this reference to the whole Church is usually tenuous and inexplicit. In effect, saints are first and foremost local saints. Originally, moreover, they were exclusively local. A martyr who was killed in a particular place was honoured by those who had witnessed his martyrdom and then by their descendants. A few especially famous names passed from one community to another, but this was always exceptional. And then – it is difficult to pinpoint when – the cult of certain saints was imposed throughout the whole Church. These persons are now certainly saints for all Catholics, but alongside them locally honoured saints partake of the same universality, even if they are mainly completely unknown; and both make up the undifferentiated body of the saints.

Though most saints are the saints of a local community, it should be noted that a community does not always have a purely geographical definition. Some saints are honoured, for example, by a religious order and only by that religious order. But being a saint *for other people* means essentially being a saint for those who initiated the cult. One might think at first sight that it would only be contemporaries, struck by someone's saintly qualities, who would consecrate them after his death. There are, however, several cases in which sainthood has been attributed to someone by people who have never known the person. A celebrated instance here is that of St Philomena, a fourth-century Christian who only became the object of a public cult in the nineteenth century. The case is particularly interesting for it clearly illustrates how sainthood is born in the opinion of others. On 25 May 1802, a body was discovered in the Priscillian catacomb on the Via Salaria. On the basis of a few indications, it was declared to be the body of a martyred virgin. Miracles took place, and the new saint became popular. Though this case is particularly striking because of the gap of fifteen centuries, it is by no means unique. Several people have been considered to be saints in a similar way, without anything being known about them beyond a few scraps of legend: in the last resort saints do not need to have existed at all, and this is true of more than one.

We must therefore clearly distinguish *real* saints from *constructed* saints. Most saints were once real people, about whom objective facts may be established: their sex; their place of birth, and, particularly, of death; the manner of their death; sometimes their age at death; the time at which died; their civil status; and whether they belonged to a religious community. In many cases, particularly the more recent, much more is historically certain. These facts must be studied to see what these people, selected according to a given mode of canonization, can tell us about the social group in which they lived and about the social group which chose them, which were not always the same. But beside the real saints are what we may call the *constructed* saints. All saints are more or less *constructed* in that, being necessarily saints *for other people*, they are remodelled in the collective representation which is made of them. It often happens, even, that they are so remodelled that nothing of the real original is left, and, ultimately, some saints are solely *constructed* saints simply because nothing is known about them historically: everything, including their existence, is a product of collective representation.

Anthony of Padua is a historical figure about whom one has a fair amount of definite information. He is a *real* saint, many of whose traits may be defined, but he is also a *constructed* saint. At different times, he has been perceived according to models far removed from reality. For example, the popular preacher became in collective representations the saint carrying the Child Jesus in his arms, at a time precisely, from the Later Middle Ages (and this long after his death), when family feeling and concern for children were becoming increasingly important in Europe. St Anthony's iconography, moreover, shows him playing a range of very different roles: for Sebastian del Piombo, at the Carrara Academy in Bergamo, he is a sage; for Tiepolo in Venice, he is a healer; for Van Dyck, at the Brera in Milan, he is caressed by the Child Jesus on his mother's knees; while in the Franciscan museum at Assisi, he is wearing a Spanish admiral's insignia and driving the Moors from Oran.[8]

In the fourth century, there was a bishop of Myra, in Asia Minor, called

Nicholas. That is all that is known of the *real* saint. But the *constructed* saint has probably been one of the most popular characters in the world, at least since 9 May 1087, the date of the translation of his body to Bari. Thousands of churches are dedicated to him, and huge numbers of Christians bear his name. He is the patron saint of sailors on the Aegean Sea, and of children of today.

St Anne is an even more *constructed* figure. Nothing is known about her, except that somebody must have existed who filled the role of mother to Mary, the mother of Jesus. The *real* saint is Jesus' anonymous maternal grandmother. Everything else has been constructed. But what a gigantic construction! It began in the second century, with the account, probably of Egyptian origin, now known as the *Protoevangelium of James*. This alone did not lead to a cult until the sixth century, when Justinian had a church in her honour erected in Constantinople. This provided the necessary impetus. By the sixteenth century, she had become a very popular saint; Luther swore an oath by St Anne that he would become a monk. But it was Luther, too, who caused the sudden collapse of her cult throughout northern Europe, and then nearly everywhere else. And yet she had fulfilled so many roles over the centuries: the role of mother and grandmother linked to the increasing importance of the family from the fifteenth century onwards; the role of teacher – as in the picture by Rubens in Antwerp cathedral; the role of helper at difficult confinements; the role of witness to the dogma of the Immaculate Conception. Why is she also the patron saint of carpenters, and why are so many cemetery chapels dedicated to her? The vast iconography related to her is some indication of how very important the constructed personality of this saint has been.[9]

One step further on, and we find Catherine of Alexandria, who never was a *real* person. In her case, everything has been *constructed*. Again, the construction has been enormous, and has spanned the centuries, ultimately making her the patron saint both of philosophers and of spinsters.

These constructions are cause for reflection, for they are not totally arbitrary. They tell us something about the social groups who were responsible for them. We have already stressed the influence of family sentiment, which lent new features, from the middle of the fifteenth century, to much older figures such as Anne, Nicholas or Anthony of Padua. But this is only one of thousands of examples, and explains nothing by itself, since it is only a correlation. We need to know more exactly just what this family sentiment was, and why it appeared in Europe around 1450.[10]

A close study of the iconography of saints would be relevant here. It should reveal the rules which lay behind the construction of saints by social groups, though only if it were possible to distinguish what was inspired by learned religion and what by popular devotion. A picture commissioned by a bishop of the Counter-Reformation period as a model destined to edify his flock must not be interpreted in the same way as a rough wooden statue born of rustic piety. Such a study should be possible now that the University of Princeton has drawn up an index of Christian art which is intended to be exhaustive. But there are nearly one hundred thousand photographs and half a million index cards to sort through for the period up to 1400 alone.[11]

If it is true that saints are saints *for other people*, in the sense defined above, let us look more closely at who these other people are. They are, obviously, not all contemporaries, nor even all those who knew the person in question. Joan of Arc, for example, was condemned to death as a heretic by an ecclesiastical tribunal. Her sainthood, one may say, was contested by some of her contemporaries, and, indeed, she was canonized only some four centuries later. Similarly, a man like the ambitious and brutal Engelbert of Berg, Archbishop of Cologne, ambushed and killed in 1225, must certainly have made many enemies. It took centuries for his misdeeds, his excommunication, his shameless disobedience of the pope's orders to be forgotten. Finally, in 1617, another pope granted him the public cult that his inclusion in Baronius's *Roman Martyrology* at the end of the sixteenth century warranted. Although the phenomenon is not generally so flagrant, one must recognize that there are always people for whom a person is not a saint.

Even for those who believe someone to be a saint, there is a whole range of intensity in their attitudes. We do not yet have the tools to measure this intensity or to define its nature. Why does Thérèse Martin have an image in most Catholic churches in preference to hundreds of other saints? Why do pilgrims flock in their thousands to her tomb in Lisieux, while the tombs of other saints are neglected? Why did Martin of Tours, who died at the end of the fourth century, have innumerable devotees over the following millennium and why did his cult then decline?

This is all part of the still obscure problem of social 'energetics'. And to answer such questions, we would doubtless have to start by charting the development of the cult of certain saints on the ground. For, though some saints remained local, the saintly reputation of others expanded: maps would show the paths along which devotion to them spread and the geographical distribution of those for whom they were saints.[12] We would also have to distinguish between saints of 'popular' and of 'learned' religion, and we might find that each had its distinct field of communication. An analysis of sainthood in the opinion of others would also require elucidation of the roles which people attribute to saints. Here, at least five kinds of quite distinct role may be discerned: that of intercessor; of ideal pattern, as defined by Linton;[13] of community witness; of beneficial power; and of figure promoted to the highest position of moral and religious success. Each of these deserves analysis in depth, to throw light on the Catholic community and perhaps to reveal something of the nature of the energies involved in the exercise of these roles.

The procedure of canonization could also be studied to see how the opinion of others is expressed during the investigations which gather the information on which the religious authorities can base their decision. The process is clearly similar to that of an opinion poll on *fama sanctitatis*. Those pursuing the inquiry do not ask: 'Do you think X is a saint?' but: 'Do you think that people think he is a saint?' And to whom do they put their questions? If possible, to eyewitnesses. If not, to people who have formed an opinion on the matter, sometimes centuries later. Concerning Joan of Arc (who died in 1431 and was canonized in 1920), a historian, Godefroid Kurth, was questioned: there were no other witnesses after four centuries. Nearly all the accounts of these interviews over the last three centuries have been preserved. In them we can trace the content of collective representations concerning sainthood, for the people who were questioned quite frequently explained the basis on which they arrived at their opinion. Some of these accounts, moreover, date back five hundred years or more; and they constitute sociological documents of prime value. These inquiries also allow one to determine fairly clearly for whom a person was judged to be a saint, whether the view was strictly local or more widely held, whether it was held by professionals (the clergy) or by laymen, and so on.

They usually show that only a relatively limited number of people were questioned. These were privileged witnesses, as we would now say. Questions were put to those who were presumed to have something to say. Up to now, statistically valid sampling has not been used to sound out general opinion in a given population. But we must beware of anachronism. The notion of sampling is a recent one, and, in any case, the procedure has followed exceptionally rigid rules laid down in great detail, although changes have been made from time to time; for example, at no stage of the proceedings may a typewriter be used. And yet it would be quite in the order of things for the Congregation of Rites itself to use the modern opinion poll method some day.

Finally, we might try to discover why unfavourable opinions regarding sainthood are sometimes not powerful enough to prevent the final decision, and why in other cases they are. This would be one of the problems to be solved by a study of abortive beatification procedures over the last few centuries. But the question is a complex one because proceedings can be blocked for centuries and then finally succeed none the less. Thus, the cause of Robert Bellarmine, who played a major role in the condemnation of Galileo, was blocked for a long time, not because of this but because one of his works had been put on the Index in 1590. In his *Controversiae de Summo Pontifice*, he had condemned the direct temporal power of the papacy at a time when the reigning pope, Sixtus V, upheld it. He had to wait for doctrine to evolve, and, in 1930, Pius XI canonized him, and even declared him a Doctor of the Church in the following year. Another example is provided by Juan de Ribera who died in 1611. He was canonized in 1960. The inquiry concerning his cause must have begun in the eighteenth century. Why was it eventually favourable to him? As an archbishop, his political role had been highly contested, while, as Viceroy, he had been one of the promoters of the dramatic expulsion of the Moriscos.

Sanctity through the pressure of others

Saints are saints *for other people* but they are also made saints *by other people*. The opinion of others is not sufficient in itself to create a saint. Opinion must be strong enough to provoke a public cult. In the first millennium AD, 'popular' pressure or pressure from a small community, such as a monastery, was sufficient. Episcopal sanction, which could have been an obstacle, was usually implicit. Gregory of Tours relates how the cult of Crescentia began in Paris.[14] Following a miracle and a dream, a group of adherents built a chapel and initiated a pilgrimage to the tomb of an unknown woman who had died a century or so before. There is no mention of any episcopal intervention. Even when such controls became more explicit, unorganized popular pressure was usually still the main impetus behind the official consecration of a saint. However, it would be worth taking a closer look at the conflicts which occasionally – though rarely in the West – set popular pressure against a reluctant bishop. As early as 348, the second Council of Carthage warned against the honours that some communities were paying to false martyrs. But it was only after the first millennium that bishops and popes began to resist automatic recognition of informally established cults. For example, Anselm of Canterbury ordered a community of nuns to cease their cult of a person whose sainthood he judged to be ill-founded. A few years later, in 1190, Pope Alexander III forbade the cult of a drunkard. In 1234 the text of this ban was inserted in the decretals and established that canonization was legally reserved to the Holy See.

As soon as a judicial procedure before a bishop or the Holy See became obligatory or at least general practice, pressure from an unorganized community became insufficient. And so we see groups being formed to take up causes and press them towards a successful conclusion.[15] Moral reputation and financial credit, competence in canon law and perseverance well beyond a single human life-span became essential elements here. Religious, whose orders could play the necessary role of pressure groups, thus came to have a considerable advantage over lay candidates for canonization.

From the Middle Ages onwards we can nearly always distinguish the group which prepared the way for a pontifical canonization. This makes possible a historical study of the mechanisms which were actually at work and which were set in motion by the pressure of one group to be eventually slowed down either by legal and bureaucratic inertia or by the opposition of another group. Again we encounter a problem of social energetics.[16]

This action by organized groups developed fairly rapidly into a characteristic of the social structure of the Catholic Church. It is in this context, it seems, that one should interpret the decision by the Lateran Council in 1215 to forbid the creation of any new religious orders. The bishops obviously feared the intervention of groups which they could no longer control. However, as we know, the decision had no practical effect. It was circumvented in numerous ways, and most of the religious orders were in fact created after 1215, which represents a triumph for the very groups which the episcopacy had sought to eliminate. It is not surprising therefore that the men and women who founded religious orders and congregations are among the main beneficiaries of canonizations which took place after 1215. Between 1662 and 1960, sixty-seven of them were made saints.

One might think that when organized groups became necessary in order to obtain canonizations, the emergence of spontaneous cults of obscure or non-existent figures would cease. This is not, however, the case. We have already come across the example of St Philomena, whose cult sprang up at the beginning of the nineteenth century in exactly the same way as that of Crescentia had done in the sixth century. An unorganized 'popular' movement was still able to impose a saint, although this was by then quite exceptional. There is, however, an even more curious case which deserves a detailed study, since it concerns a non-existent person, Felix of Valois, who, through the power of persuasion of an organized group, was eventually canonized in spite of all the doubts that might have been raised.[17] This extraordinary case must not lead us to conclude that a well-organized group is omnipotent and can obtain all the canonizations that it wants. There are several examples of candidates who were supported by groups which had had numerous other successes but who did not gain canonization. For example, Claude de La Colombière seemed at first sight to have had everything necessary for success. He was a Jesuit and a devotee of the Sacred Heart, who had helped to introduce this cult into the Church following the visions of Marguerite-Marie Alacoque, one of his penitents. Since he was both a Jesuit – that is a member of one of the Church's most powerful groups – and one of the originators of a form of devotion which has spread throughout the Church, his qualifications ought in theory to have assured his canonization. But they did not. He died in 1682 and was only beatified in 1929. He requires a second miracle for his canonization to be considered, while his penitent, who died in 1690, was canonized in 1920, again through Jesuit sponsorship. We have here a case where the action of one particular group has been blocked by the inertia of a wider social group. From the sociological point of view, the missing miracle means that 'popular' pressure has not been strong enough. It is as if Claude de La Colombière was not popular enough to awaken the faith required to effect a miracle.

Alongside conscious pressure, there is room for unconscious pressure, which is more or less outside the control of its agents. Thus, in the twentieth century the increase in canonizations of women results from the pressure of social forces, which the groups supporting these canonizations will not necessarily have perceived. In the same way, there are grounds for believing that some canonizations are the result of latent conflict within the Christian community; in particular, they may be a form of social protest. The canonization of rebels like Thomas Becket or Hugh of Avalon was a way of successfully expressing resistance to royal power.

Juridical sanctity

The memory, opinion and pressure of others do not make a saint, or have not done so in the last few centuries, unless they are expressed via official juridical channels. The influence of *legal rules and procedure* on memory, opinion and pressure must therefore be studied. Juridical norms – need we refer to Durkheim? – provide one of the firmest bases for sociological explanation.

At this stage, it must be noted that the final decision concerning sainthood is not taken by the judicial bodies which have examined the causes but by the executive power in the person of the pope. There is thus room for a further study to see how power is distributed in the Catholic Church. This would probably show that the centralization of the executive and of the judiciary has followed the same curve of evolution through the centuries and that the separation of the two powers has never been realized in practice. It would therefore follow that the judicial procedure of canonization would always have to be completed by an extra-judicial decision of a political nature. In which case there would have to be a canonization policy,[18] which would, given its absolute predominance over the judiciary, actually determine the shape and nature of the judicial procedures, though to what degree remains uncertain. This lack of independence in the judiciary could lead – if the analogy with secular society is valid – to the two extreme possibilities of obstructive behaviour in the case of conflict, on the one hand, or of servile behaviour where the supremacy of the executive power is effectively exercised at all levels, on the other; but a whole range of situations between these extremes may be envisaged, including criticism of them.

The juridical aspect of sainthood brings us to a closer examination of the principal criteria used to determine sainthood in canonization procedure. Here, we are no longer dealing with general sociological factors relating to sanctity, but with special criteria.

THE SPECIAL CRITERIA OF JURIDICAL SANCTITY

Here we shall examine four criteria: writings; heroic virtue; martyrdom; and miracles.

Writings

Anything a candidate for sainthood may have written is closely scrutinized by the Congregation of Rites. Great importance is attached to this, and a suspect text can end the whole procedure. The assumption behind this attitude is that a person is revealed in his writings, and that any one piece of writing can reveal that an otherwise saintly person does not deserve juridical sainthood. Imagine a religious who dies with a reputation for saintliness; social pressure plays its part, and his cause is presented. Among his papers, an examiner from the Congregation of Rites finds a will, just one page. In theory, his cause would then be stopped definitively. A religious is not supposed to have possessions; if he makes a will – let us suppose that we are in the Ancien Régime – this means that he has property and thus that he has not fully observed his vow of poverty. The example is not imaginary. The cause of Nicholas Molinari, a Capuchin friar and Bishop of Bovino at his death on 18 January 1792, seems to have been stopped for this reason.

Here then is sainthood that will never be recognized, because on one legal point something that was written reveals an infringement of a juridical norm. Among other things, we need to define the sociological bases of such decisions, and to discover why the procedure is so strict – if indeed it always is – as far as writings are concerned. Underlying such investigations and practices is a whole theory of cultural models and of what constitutes information. It is disturbing, too, to think how easily relevant documents may disappear. Imagine that an unscrupulous admirer of our candidate had found and pocketed the will. What then? We should note, too, that writings are used only in so far as they provide evidence to counter claims to sanctity. Favourable elements are not taken into account.

Moreover, here as elsewhere, martyrdom excuses everything. One of the Gorcum martyrs, a priest who for a while became an apostate, wrote a book against the cult of the saints – very appropriately – but this was not held against him, since he returned to the Catholic faith and died as a martyr for it. He is now the object of a cult himself.[19] Nevertheless for reasons that are unclear, writings of martyrs are also examined.

One further question: since when have writings of candidates been checked in this way? And in what social context was the practice initiated?

Heroic virtue

When a candidate for beatification is presented who has no claim to martyrdom, he is judged on the *heroic nature of his virtues*.[20] The question is whether he has practised better than ordinary men the three theological virtues of faith, hope and charity, and the four moral or 'cardinal' virtues of fortitude, justice, prudence and temperance, to which are added, for religious, the observance of the three vows of poverty, chastity and obedience and of the rules of their community. A long tradition, the details of which are to be found in the *Summa Theologica* of Thomas Aquinas, allows any number of other virtues to be included in the list. Thus, to justice were added the virtues of piety and obedience; to fortitude, magnanimity, patience, constancy; to temperance, humility, chastity, and so on. Each candidate had to prove that he practised these virtues. Thus the records of the procedure provide a summary of his conduct, virtue by virtue.

From a sociological point of view, there are at least two very interesting domains for research here. First, there is the question why these particular virtues were selected as ones which revealed saintliness. Here, one would need to start not with the particular virtue but with social structures, so as to see how the structures explain the choice of those virtues as models. Then it would be necessary to see whether the content generally corresponded to the models, i.e. whether the conduct which is supposed to express and illustrate a certain virtue has always been interpreted in the same way. For it is obvious that, for a sociologist, it is not virtue itself which is important, but the way in which people interpret behaviour in terms of virtue (first the people who behave in a certain way and then the people who find a certain meaning in their behaviour).

The first field of research – the classification of virtues in terms of social structures – would require vast historical erudition and, doubtless, years of work by a whole team of researchers, in order to reach valid results. Lucien Febvre in *Le Problème de l'incroyance au XVIe siècle* (Paris, 1942) gives an idea of what the study of virtue through social structures might be like.

The second study – the interpretation of behaviour in terms of virtue – could use the mass of documents from the *positiones* of the canonical procedures. They contain hundreds of actions listed according to specific virtues. They make up an almost year-to-year picture of mental representations on the subject. Let us take a specific example. The virtue of fortitude, says Thomas Aquinas in the *Summa Theologica*, implies the virtue of constancy.[21] In theory, a saint should practise it to a heroic degree, which is to say better than ordinary mortals. But the lives of the saints and the beatified show that quite frequently they do not stay in the congregation which they first enter. Magdalena di Canossa, for example, entered the Carmelite Order, left it, re-entered it, and then left it yet again to found a congregation of her own, which suited her better. Maria Magdalena Martinengo entered the Order of Poor Clares, in which several saints had persevered, but left it to become a Capuchin. John Southworth became a diocesan priest, then entered the Benedictine Order; he failed in this course and became a diocesan priest again. Thomas Tzugi entered the Society of Jesus, left it, and re-entered it. We have already come across Jacques Lacops; he was a Catholic priest, he apostatized, and became a Protestant minister; then he changed his mind again and became a Catholic priest once more. Anthony Mary Claret entered a seminary, but did not feel at ease there, so he left it to become a Carthusian. He had not even reached the monastery before he turned back to the seminary, where he was ordained a diocesan priest. He left that position, however, to become a Jesuit novice, but this did not suit him, so he became a diocesan priest again. He went to Latin America, where he became an archbishop; a series of attempts were made on his life. He went back to Spain as the queen's confessor and followed her into exile in Paris. Wanted by the French police, at the instance of the Spanish government, he took refuge in a Cistercian monastery, where he took up the monastic life, and where he died. He had himself founded a religious congregation which still exists and it was this congregation, naturally, which brought about his canonization.[22]

Examples such as these show how unwise it would be to imagine that saints must be 'a model of every virtue'. It is clear that constancy, when it is considered as a virtue, is given a very special interpretation. It would be interesting to see also if certain virtues, which seem essential to us today, were used as criteria in canonization procedures. Sincerity, for example, does not seem to have been examined by the Congregation of Rites.

This is where the problem of the relationship between sainthood and moral perfection arises. Sociology is obviously not a normative discipline like ethics, but an empirical one; however, as such, it can none the less study moral conduct in action and assess the relationship between types of sanctity and types of moral perfection. Here it is, of course, important to guard against slipping from the empirical to the normative and thus distorting any eventual conclusions. It should be possible to differentiate very clearly between sanctity and morality, which only partly overlap.[23]

Finally, the relationship between sanctity and mental health must also be studied. Must saints be 'normal'? Here, the sociologist's description of mental health cannot be the same as the psychiatrist's, which generally refers only to contemporary Western culture. The lives of saints over the last two thousand years in a variety of cultures provide exceptionally interesting material for the assessment of what constitutes psychological equilibrium. The behaviour of 'stylites' or recluses, which today seems abnormal, could be taken in certain milieux as a sign of sanctity. But besides behaviour which determines a whole way of life, there are actions, which may seem incidental, but which are symptomatic of underlying mental states. How are these to be interpreted by the individual himself, by contemporaries, by those conducting the canonization procedure, or by the sociologist? How is one to interpret, for example, the gesture of Francis Xavier, who once swallowed the pus running from a patient's abscess in a hospital? Or of John of God, who ran away from home at the age of eight and never returned? Or of Pompilio Pirotti, who ran away at the age of sixteen? One only has to read the Lives of Benedict Joseph Labre or of Salvator of Horta to be convinced that the question of mental health is related to that of sanctity. More exactly, it seems clear that a sociological study of the mental health of saints would make necessary a reconsideration of the notion of social integration, which is still used as the criterion of mental health by many psychiatrists. The last two saints mentioned were certainly poorly integrated, at least at the most obvious level. In the same way, the famous St Jerome was, to say the least, an eccentric figure; he was extremely aggressive, and his social integration mainly expressed itself via interminable conflicts.

The relationship between the structure of certain social groups, sanctity and mysticism must also be studied. It would seem that the full meaning of certain mystical phenomena in the domain of sanctity can only be explained by reference to their social context. But to what extent is this the case?

Mention of these selected sociological aspects of heroic virtues shows that there is room for further investigations of the greatest interest. Many already published studies could, moreover, be used within a more strictly sociological framework.

Let us mention finally a point which is widely taken for granted and yet which seems essential and deserves more attention. Catholics often say that a minimum of material well-being is necessary for the practice of virtue. Is this really so? Do the lives of the saints demonstrate such economic conditioning? The question has not hitherto been seriously studied. Or is it that this conditioning affects, not the saints, but only the rest of us, as the distinction made on this point by St Thomas Aquinas between ordinary and heroic virtue suggests?

Martyrdom

Only those who died as martyrs may be beatified or canonized without being recognized as heroically virtuous. The notion of martyrdom and the meaning of the word 'martyr' have changed several times during the two thousand years of Christian history. Collective representations have been linked to the situation of Christian society, and have been modified as it evolved. The first saints were all martyrs in the sense that they were victims of a bloody repression. However, some saints seem to have been called martyrs without having died a violent death: for example, several popes. Possibly 'martyr' was synonymous with 'saint'. When the Barbarians attacked the Roman Empire, they naturally killed many Christians, and particularly bishops. In 407, for example, Nicasius and all his clergy were killed in Reims. They were martyrs. After the great invasions, when the Barbarians had been more or less converted, respected figures could still die violent deaths. Thus, Edmund, King of East Anglia, died fighting the Viking invaders; Olaf, King of Norway, died while opposing the conquests of Canute the Great. They were martyrs. And the meaning of the term shifted still further: King Edward, assassinated on the orders of his mother-in-law, was considered a martyr, and so was Helen of Skvöde, who was killed under the pretext of blood-vengeance. It became sufficient to have died a violent death to be regarded as a martyr, so long as a cult developed. For example, Margaret of Roskilde, hanged by her husband, was a martyr; so was William of Rochester, a baker killed by his apprentice. The religious context, probably never wholly absent from such cases, becomes more apparent in the deaths of numerous inquisitors, who were killed to avenge their victims.[24] They were considered to be martyrs, although all assassinated inquisitors were not automatically regarded as saints. The famous Conrad of Marburg, inquisitor in Germany, was certainly killed in 1233, but he has not been made a saint. During the Reformation and the Wars of Religion, Catholics who fell victim to the Protestants became martyrs. Their ranks were noticeably increased in this period. Further recruits at the same time were the victims of missionary expansion in the Far East and in the East and West Indies. The religious element in the death of a martyr was now taken more seriously. In this perspective, the victims of the French Revolution and of the missionary movement of the nineteenth and twentieth centuries were considered to be martyrs. Violent death by itself was no longer sufficient. Juvenal Ancina, who was poisoned by a monk, and Joan of Arc were not declared martyrs. However, Maria Goretti, who was killed at the age of twelve by a boy whose advances she resisted, was a martyr.

The only thing which these people seem to have in common is the fact that the Church considers them to be martyrs.[25] As a saint is a saint for and by others, that is in the mind of others, so a martyr is a martyr for others. This explains how it is that many martyrs have certainly not freely accepted their fate. The victim's intentions are not an essential element. Thus Pedro Arbués was only killed because he was unable to escape the attack of some

Jews who had ambushed him as a reprisal. But there are clearer examples. Several two- or three-year-old children have been declared martyrs; and here one cannot refer to their motives, but only to those of the Christian community which made martyrs of them, without their having anything to do with the matter.

In the eyes of the Catholic community, martyrdom by itself is sufficient to ensure sainthood, even if it has sometimes been preceded by a scandalous life.[26] However, not every heroic death is the gateway to sainthood. We must look more closely here, and particularly at those cases of persons who have not been beatified, while others in exactly analogous circumstances have been. Thus in 1628, Louis Nihachi, and his two sons, Francis, aged five, and Dominic, aged two, were executed in Nagasaki. All three were beatified in 1867. In 1900, Teresa Chang-Huey-Chu and her two children, Joseph, aged eight, and Mary, aged two, were executed in Chang-Kia-Tsi. The mother was beatified in 1955, but her two children were not. Why this difference?

The social contexts which produce martyrs according to different models have not yet been elucidated. It would doubtless be interesting to study them further.[27] For in so far as martyrdom stems from ideological conflict, it would be of the greatest value to unravel the reasons – the collective situations – which lead men to kill each other and to exalt certain victims.

Miracles

The Catholic Church has nearly always considered miracles to be an obligatory criterion of sainthood. Today, this means miracles which have been juridically established as such. The juridical rules concerning miracles should be studied. It would be necessary to establish the history of these rules, and then a history of miracles associated with sanctity could be undertaken, which in turn would only be possible as part of a more general history of miracles. The significance of the exceptions to the general pattern would then require analysis. Some saints never performed miracles, whereas others have a long list to their names. Why is there this difference? As will be seen, the problems are enormous, and their various aspects cannot even be touched on here, let alone exhaustively treated. For example, we would have to determine the presuppositions which lead a social group to make miracles part of a juridical procedure. These would include the following: (a) the social group believes miracles are possible; (b) it believes that miracles do actually take place; (c) it thinks that there are means by which miraculous events may be distinguished from others; (d) it thinks that there is a link between miracles and the sanctity of a dead person (only miracles occurring after the death of a candidate for sainthood are taken into account). The Catholic Church thus sees miracles as *revealers* of sainthood; this means that an *event* can signify *to others* that a given person intervened in it precisely as a saint. The miracle is thus, from our sociological point of view, a *social event*, since it can only exist as a miracle if someone sees it as such; but it is also an event which expresses the saintly quality of the person who is presumed to intervene in this way.

These few statements require considerable elaboration. To start with, *real* and *constructed* miracles need to be distinguished. We can be sure that certain miraculous events actually took place at a certain time, in a certain place and in a certain social context. Their exceptional nature does not mean *a priori* that they are not verifiable historical events.[28] Consider this example from the Middle Ages. One day in December 1387, a boy named Richard was walking with a priest on the bridge at Avignon. A boat laden with stones was passing beneath. The boy leant over the parapet at a point near the chapel of St Nicholas. The workers guiding the boat with a cable from on top of the bridge shouted to the boy to get out of the way; but he stayed where he was. A sudden movement of the cable pitched him into the water. The priest in a panic made a vow to Cardinal Peter of Luxembourg – who had recently died and was reputed to be a saint – to offer ten pounds of wax at his tomb, if he would save the child. The child in the churning water below was waving his arms, but did not sink. People in a boat two arches along spotted him and hoisted him out of the water with a boat-hook. The child was crying, because he had lost his hood. The priest took him back into the town. We have all the details that we could wish for: the boy's statement – that he could not swim, he had tried to at the washing-place, he had not swallowed much water, and he had been in the river for half an hour; the priest's statement – that the scene had lasted long enough for him to say two *Miserere* psalms; the statement of the boatman who pulled the child out with the hook; of the worker, who was handling the cable from up on the bridge and who shouted to the boy to get out of the way; and lastly, that of another boatman, who threw the cable to the people in the boat, which was laden with stones – he had seen the child fall and the priest kneeling on the bridge. We have their names, ages, professions, addresses. We know that the child was wearing short breeches, which came to just below his knees. Can we seriously deny that an event like this *really* happened?[29]

We can clearly see the *social* aspect of the miracle, too. The priest was the first to perceive the event as miraculous, believing that the child did not drown because of his vow; then the witnesses, including the child, having heard the priest's version and perhaps having been influenced by it, connected the unexpected rescue with the saint's supernatural intervention.

When Pope Benedict XIV announced the canonization of Elizabeth of

Portugal in the *Bullarium* of 1742, he described her five miracles: (a) a carpenter fell from the roof which he was building, he invoked the saint and found that he and the beams that had fallen with him were back in position; (b) a crippled nun was able to walk again; (c) a wet-nurse, who was unable to suckle, drank some wine prepared according to the saint's prescription, and, having been completely dry, was then able to nurse two children again; (d) a woman developed angina and could not suckle; her husband prayed to the saint, and, though she did not know that he had prayed for her, his wife was suddenly cured; (e) a woman, who had a mouth ulcer, kissed the bier on which the saint's body had been carried and soon afterwards noticed that the ulcer had disappeared.[30] It will be noted that the cure in the fourth miracle only became miraculous from the moment that the husband asked his wife when she had felt better, and realized that it was exactly at the time when he had prayed. Social relations are essential for an event to take on a miraculous character. It is also noteworthy that four of the five miracles happened to women. Is this a general rule? On the evidence of a fair number of canonization procedures, it seems that miracles do in fact happen more often to women than to men. But this would have to be verified, and then explained.

It would be necessary to examine all the miracles considered by the Congregation of Rites to see whether there are recurring factors in this mass of events, and particularly whether over the centuries there has been an evolution in the type of miracle put forward and considered. The *positiones* of the canonization procedures contain the documents necessary for such a study. They are an exceptional mine of information, containing reports and statements by the beneficiaries, the witnesses, the experts, the promoters of the faith playing devil's advocate, and so on. One could easily follow here the historical itinerary of miracles and their interpretation over the last few centuries. One could also work out which events are never miraculous, and in what circumstances miracles never take place. Possibly, too, some regions, at certain times at least, are not conducive to miracles.

It would also be very interesting to try to unravel the intentions of the ecclesiastical authorities, who sometimes require miracles and sometimes dispense with them. Here, it should be clearly understood that the sociologist's job is not to probe into hearts and minds, but only to interpret behaviour by trying to discover the reasons which lend it coherence. In the seventh century, a man named Birinus came to Great Britain from Italy to preach the Gospel. He died a saintly death at Dorchester in Wessex where he was buried. His body was later taken to Winchester. Years passed, and then, in the thirteenth century, the canons of Dorchester near Oxford, another Dorchester, claimed that they were in possession of the saint's body. The matter could not be settled and finally an appeal was made to the pope, who decided in 1216 that the affair was to be resolved by the number of miracles which had occurred. Let us pause to consider the fact that the pope was convinced that miracles were obtained by the veneration which took place at two tombs, which were both supposed to contain the same saint's body. He decided that the saint's body must actually be in the tomb where the most miracles occurred. Why? If we continue with the story, we learn that the canons of Dorchester near Oxford triumphed because they produced more miracles than the canons of Winchester, which was in fact the real place of burial.[31] In this way, social pressure produced miracles on a false basis, if we assume that they should have happened only in so far as the invoked saint's remains were authentic.

The canonization procedure of John of Nepomuk contains an even more enigmatic case. A miracle occurred, which appears to confirm a legend which critical history cannot accept as well-founded.[32]

The non-decomposition of a body a long time after death is quite frequently cited as miraculous. It was for this reason that the cause of Germaine Cousin was considered: her body, when it was found several years after her death, had not decayed. Again, in 1375 in Munich, the Poor Clares found the incorrupt body of a little girl, who had died a quarter of a century before, and from this they deduced that she must have been a saint. The girl was Agnes, the daughter of Ludwig IV, Duke of Bavaria, and she died on 11 November 1352 at the age of seven.[33] Andrew Bobola was killed by the Cossacks in 1657, but his body did not decompose; after the 1917 Revolution, the Bolsheviks placed it in a museum and from there it was transferred to Rome with a view to his canonization.

A typology of miracles could also be established. They do in fact correspond to certain models, whose chronological and spatial evolution can sometimes be charted. For example, at the *Abaton* of Epidaurus, miraculous healings took place according to the cultural model of incubation. The same cultural model is to be found in the Hellenistic period in Egypt, used by another religion, for example at the Serapeum in Memphis. It also appears well into the Middle Ages at certain Christian shrines in southern Italy, and even further afield and later in time. Very probably a typology of miracles would reveal a link between certain models and certain geographical regions. For example, the miraculous liquefaction of clots of blood is found only in the Naples region.

We would also have to study other relationships between miracles and the tombs of saints or between miracles and relics. They each have their different histories and have passed through phases of varying intensity. Very important also is the link between miracles and prayer, or miracles and pilgrimage, which is a special form of prayer. One could also perhaps investigate possible links between miracles and collective preoccupations of a political nature. For example, in the Middle Ages, resistance to royal power in England took the unexpected form of the canonization of saints.

The canonization of Thomas Becket, notably, consecrated a person who had opposed the monarch. Several other causes were presented under the same aegis,[34] and each one, including those of known excommunicates, produced its crop of miracles.

In all these cases it is possible, with caution and insight, to study the sociological co-ordinates of *real* miracles. But *constructed* miracles must also be studied. On the basis of a real event, a social group very frequently builds up an account which is more or less imaginary; it would be interesting to know the rules according to which such accounts are elaborated. It seems, for example, that in some cases a saint's corpse gives off a sweet smell, which is noticed by many of those present. One could, at a pinch, in one or two instances, regard this as a real miracle. But hagiographical accounts report hundreds of such examples, in such a way that we can be sure that here we have a sort of convention, which is not concerned with historical reality. And why should a sweet smell be proof of a dead person's sanctity?

Besides constructed miracles which derive from real miracles, there is a mass of entirely *constructed* miracles which exist only in collective mental representations. A register of these should be compiled, and the most common types identified; classified according to time and place, they should yield precious information about the social groups which selected, elaborated and transmitted them. This would be a formidable task since it would require that real and constructed miracles be distinguished, and in most cases the distinction is not obvious. It would then require that constructed miracles based on real ones be distinguished from wholly constructed ones, which would similarly be difficult in most cases, perhaps so difficult that both categories would have to be taken together. It would be a formidable task, too, because of the enormous mass of evidence that would have to be studied; for there must be at least a hundred thousand testimonies. There are tens of thousands of cases of healing alone. How are the real and the constructed miracles to be distinguished here? For modern cases, one can trust the papal investigations, but for the rest? There are thousands of resurrections of babies. It is certainly possible to identify some cases that are definitely real and others that are definitely constructed, but how many fall in between? There are numerous cases of saints putting out fires, miraculously lighting lamps, making springs gush forth, going through fire without being burnt, causing rain to fall during a drought, changing water into wine, multiplying bread and wine, freeing prisoners from gaol or from irons at a distance or after their deaths, walking on water or making others walk on water. How can we make sense of it all? And yet we ought to try,[35] for it must be possible to distinguish constant factors. We noted in passing that in the mass of resurrections, those of children were the most numerous. Why should children and tiny babies be the beneficiaries, above all, of a miraculous return to life? Miracles would throw light on so many aspects of human societies, and not only on those aspects dubbed 'folkloric'. A comparison of miracles in different religions would extend this knowledge further, and would also give depth to our knowledge of the Catholic Church.[36]

CONCLUSION

Sainthood seems to be an important road to the understanding of religious societies and of the sociability and energetics which provide social groups with cohesion and dynamism. In particular, the analysis of criteria for sainthood – as we have defined it – seems to open up new perspectives for explanation in sociology. Data furnished by positive observation and spread over several centuries make possible here a type of analysis which remains problematical in many other domains. The road which opens up would certainly lead to the confines of sociology and theology, and also to the border between sociology and history, and would doubtless oblige these disciplines to define their relations one with another. It would allow them to assess the nature and extent of these relationships in a more radical way than has hitherto been attempted.

NOTES

1 In *Altruistic Love* (Boston, 1950).
2 Butler, Thurston and Attwater, *The Lives of the Saints* (London, 1926–49), 13 vols.
3 The Benedictine Fathers of Paris, *Vie des Saints et Bienheureux selon l'ordre du calendrier avec l'historique des fêtes* (Paris, 1934–59), 13 vols.
4 Sorokin, *Altruistic Love*, p. 109.
5 G. Le Bras in *Actes de la IVe Conférence Internationale de Sociologie Religieuse* (Paris, 1955), p. 187.
6 These were candidates dealt with under a special procedure by virtue of Canon 2125 of the *Code of Canon Law*. By 'new procedure' here, we mean the provisions established by Urban VIII in 1634.
7 The project has been in preparation for some years: it is the subject of a doctoral thesis to be submitted to the University of Liège. [This thesis has since been completed and published as *Sociologie et Canonisations* (Liège and The Hague, 1969). S.W.]
8 Many other examples may be found in B. Kleinschmidt, *Antoninus von Padua in Leben und Kunst, Kult und Volkstum* (Düsseldorf, 1930).
9 B. Kleinschmidt, *Die Heilige Anna, Ihre Verehrung in Geschichte, Kunst und Volkstum* (Düsseldorf, 1930).
10 P. Ariès proposes this date in *L'Enfant et la vie familiale sous l'Ancien Régime* (Paris, 1960); published in English translation as *Centuries of Childhood*

(London, 1962). He provides some very suggestive and tentative answers to these questions, but his study hardly touches on Mediterranean Europe, where family sentiment probably appeared earlier. There are images in Genoa cathedral of St Anne, Mary and Jesus (grandmother, mother and child), dating from 1320; also a picture painted in 1367 by Luca di Tommè, now in the Pinacoteca Nazionale in Siena.

11 When completed, H. Aurenhammer *et al.*, *Lexikon der christlichen Ikonographie* (Vienna, 1959–) will be a valuable tool. It covers the period down to the end of the nineteenth century, but has not yet finished the letter A. [One complete volume of this reference work has now appeared, ending at the entry *Christus*. S. W.]

12 A start, and a successful one, has already been made by M. Zender, *Räume und Schichten mittelalterlicher Heiligenverehrung in ihrer Bedeutung für die Volkskunde* (Düsseldorf, 1959).

13 [Ralph Linton, *The Study of Man, An Introduction* (New York, 1936), Ch. XXVI; and Linton, *The Cultural Background of Personality* (London, 1947), esp. pp. 34–5. S.W.]

14 'Liber de Gloria Beatorum Confessorum', *PL*, 71, Ch. CV. This also illustrates the creation of sainthood after a long time-lag, which we have already discussed. No one had actually known Crescentia, and her sainthood was created out of nothing by the opinion of Christians of the Merovingian period.

15 These groups sometimes have all the characteristics of what are called *pressure groups* in the technical sense.

16 In a canonization like that of Osmund, who died in 1099 but who was not canonized until 1457, one can clearly see the inertia of the competent jurisdictions being regularly stimulated by money sent by the Salisbury Chapter. One can also see the intervention of imponderables of a collective kind: when Eugenius IV was urged even by the king of England to proceed with the canonization, he asked if people wanted him to die immediately. Tradition has it that a pope dies shortly after celebrating a canonization, a notion that may exercise some kind of counter-pressure. Under Nicholas V, whose health was fragile, the Salisbury Chapter debated whether it would be worth incurring expenses which risked being wasted if the pope should die: here the canonization process was slowed down as a result of financial considerations. Cardinal Borgia, a supporter of Osmund's cause, admitted that if he had belonged to a Mendicant order, he would have been canonized much earlier; but the fact that he was a secular cleric had been a reason for the endless delays, and a reason which the Cardinal found insulting. Why? Fortunately, Cardinal Borgia was then elected Pope under the name of Calixtus III. The Chapter made one last payment, and Osmund was canonized. See A. R. Malden, *The Canonization of Saint Osmund* (Salisbury, 1901).

17 The Trinitarian Order, dedicated to buying back captives, was founded in 1198 by John of Matha. That Innocent III approved the Order on 17 December 1198 is beyond doubt. However, John of Matha was not honoured by the Trinitarians in the Middle Ages; and he does not figure in any calendar. Moreover, the papal bulls approving the Order mention no associate of his. But in the seventeenth century, the Trinitarians thought that they had two

founders, John of Matha and Felix of Valois, and they wanted glory for both of them. And, thanks to the intervention of the French king (was not Felix of the royal blood?), on 14 August 1666, the Congregation of Rites approved their cult as immemorial. The Congregation cannot have looked too closely at the case, for all the testimony was worthless, including a supposed canonization by Urban IV for which the Trinitarians were unable to provide documents and of which Roman Archives bear no trace. It seems quite certain that the Congregation knew that there was no documentary proof of this canonization. A closer look would have shown that Felix of Valois had never existed. He was created by Trinitarian writers, who were attempting to endow their Order with lustre. No serious document lends support to the fact that he even existed. In spite of all this, Innocent XI, who was later himself beatified by Pius XII, appointed 20 November as his feast-day, and on 19 May 1694, Innocent XII ordered that this feast be celebrated by the whole Catholic Church, which implied equipollent canonization. The *Vie des Saints* by the Benedictine Fathers of Paris (Paris, 1954), XI, pp. 669–70, talks of mystification; but in vol. II (1936), p. 191, it is assumed that Felix of Valois did exist.

18 See Hermelink, *Die Katholische Kirche unter den Pius-Päpsten des 20. Jahrhunderts* (Zurich, 1949), pp. 113ff., which mentions this policy. However, when the author attempts to outline it, he makes certain statements, which cannot withstand criticism. He claims, for example, that recent popes have tried to give our contemporaries new patron saints, replacing the agrarian saints with saints of the tarmac and the telephone, who could be models for modern ways of life. But this is unfounded. No mother of a family has ever been canonized, no factory worker, no chemist or physicist, nor anyone born in the United States, and so on. It may happen one day, but for now – and these are the author's examples – when a patron for motorists was required St Christopher was chosen, a half-legendary figure to say the least. When a patron for scientists was needed, Albert the Great was chosen, a scholar who lived in the thirteenth century; while when they were looking for a patron for aviators, the Holy House of Loreto was suggested, since it had been transported by angels from Palestine to Italy.

19 This is Jacques Lacops, born in 1538 at Oudenarde, a Premonstratensian priest, then a Calvinist minister, and then again a Premonstratensian priest, who was hanged at Brielle in 1572.

20 The history of this notion, from a theological point of view, is outlined by R. Hoffman, *Die heroische Tugend, Geschichte und Inhalt eines theologischen Begriffes* (Munich, 1933), pp. 133–69. The doctrine, in its explicit form, was first applied juridically in beatification procedures under Benedict XIV. Its theoretical elaboration was the work of the great Scholastics, who borrowed it from the *Nicomachean Ethics* of Aristotle. Before this, the notion was implicit and covered a variety of patterns of behaviour.

21 IIa, IIae, q.137.

22 The record for instability must go to Jean-Martin Moyë. In 1754, he was a diocesan priest. He served as curate in several parishes, and founded the Congregation of the Sisters of Providence, who ran primary schools in the Metz region. He became the spiritual director at the diocesan seminary, but

was dismissed after he had published a pamphlet in which he lamented the fate of the many children who died without baptism, as a result of the negligence of those responsible (in other words of the *curés*). A curate once more, he was suspended because of a distorted report about him which reached the bishop. He was unable to find employment. He founded some more schools, then went to Saint-Dié to be the head of the seminary of another diocese, but it closed after a year. He left for Paris, where he entered the Société des Missions Etrangères. But he did not stay long there, returning to the East to re-launch the schools run by his Sisters of Providence. In September 1771, he left for China; he came across some Madagascans when his ship called at Mauritius, and had to be dissuaded from going on a mission to Madagascar. He reached China in September 1772 and settled in Szechwan. His colleagues found his austerity and zeal hard to bear. After ten years, the situation had become untenable, so he re-embarked for France in July 1783. It took him a year to reach Paris, where his superiors gave him a very cold welcome; he was virtually retired, and returned to his native region to concern himself with the congregation which he had founded and to preach missions. In 1789 he emigrated to Trier, and he died of typhus there on 4 May 1793.

23 The relations between sanctity and moral perfection have been discussed by Ludwig von Hertling, 'Kanonisationsprozess und Vollkommenheit', *Zeitschrift für Aszese und Mystik* (1930), pp. 257–66; but he is primarily concerned with moral theology.

24 In 1242, eleven inquisitors were murdered near Toulouse. On 6 April 1252, Peter of Verona, a Dominician inquisitor, was killed by the Cathars outside Como. In 1277, Pagano di Lecco was killed, together with two notaries. In 1365, at Susa in Piedmont, the Dominican, Pietro Cambiani di Ruffia, was stabbed while carrying out his inquisitorial duties. Other victims include Antonio Pavoni in 1374, Bartolomeo Cerveri di Savigliano in 1466, and Pedro Arbués in 1485.

25 As with canonization in general, the respective influence of 'popular' collective attitudes, of certain organized groups, of episcopal authority and of the bureaucracy in Rome varied considerably from one period to another.

26 In 1929, Edward Coleman was beatified – an ambiguous figure to say the least. He was the political agent of Louis XIV in England, and, as such, he secretly plotted the subversion of his country. He solicited, obtained and distributed French money for ends which may have had some religious intention, but in a context which was extremely dubious. He was finally arrested and executed in London in 1678. In 1955, Mark Ki-T'ien-Siang was beatified. The doctor was a notorious sinner to whom the sacrament had been refused for over thirty years, because he was an inveterate opium-smoker and a cause for scandal in his milieu. But he died well, encouraging his family to stand fast when they were arrested by the Boxers, and asking to be the last to die so as to be sure that none of the family would weaken. Obviously neither Edward Coleman nor Mark Ki was considered to be a saint because of the life which he had led; it was rather the nature of their death which led to the official verdict making them saints. In the view of others, heroic death can be enough in certain conditions to guarantee sainthood.

27 A sociological study of the early martyrs exists: D. W. Riddle, *The Martyrs, A Study of Social Control* (Chicago, 1931). Unfortunately, the book is not of much use. The author fails to draw the distinction, which is necessary here, between real martyrdom and constructed martyrdom, and attributes to the Christian communities regular collective attitudes, without asking whether this regularity may not, rather, be a construction proper to the literary genre of a certain type of *passion*.

28 The example of Thomas Becket is relevant here. At the level of collective mental representations, his character has been constructed on the basis of well-documented real events. In his book, *The Development of the Legend of Thomas Becket* (Philadelphia, 1930), P. A. Brown follows the development and various expressions of this construction, but he places all miraculous elements in the domain of the *constructed*, which is a methodological mistake.

29 See the account of the canonization procedure in *Acta Sanctorum*, 1 July, pp. 565ff.: the names and addresses of witnesses, p. 566; the account of the miracle, p. 570; the statement of the priest, p. 591; of the boy, p. 592; of the workers, p. 593.

30 Pope Benedict XIV, *Bullarium* (Rome, 1746), I, pp. 157.

31 An account of these various developments and of the strong arguments in favour of Winchester may be read in *Les Vies des Saints* (Paris, Claude Hérissant, 1739), VIII, pp. 341–2.

32 One may of course shrug one's shoulders and claim that the miracle did not take place. But this attitude is scientifically untenable. The doctors' reports are quite categorical: an undecayed tongue was found in a tomb which otherwise contained nothing but bones; when this was discovered, everyone was convinced that John of Nepomuk had been killed for refusing to betray the seal of the confessional. The coincidence was striking, except that later it was discovered that Jean of Nepomuk had not been killed for that reason. Yet the miracle had nevertheless occurred. How can this be explained?

33 The Benedictine Fathers of Paris, *Vie des Saints*, XI, p. 327.

34 J. C. Russell, 'The Canonization of Opposition to the King in Angevin England', in *Haskins Anniversary Essays in Mediaeval History* (Boston and New York, 1929), pp. 279–90. One can read of the two hundred or more miracles attributed to Simon de Montfort in J. O. Halliwell (ed.), *The Chronicle of William de Rishinger of the Baron's Wars* (London, Camden Society, 1840), pp. 67ff.; yet Simon de Montfort had been excommunicated.

35 C. G. Loomis tried in *White Magic, An Introduction to the Folklore of Christian Legend* (Cambridge, Mass., 1948). He lists some ten thousand miracles performed by saints, grouped according to folkloric themes. But what is to be done with this gigantic mass? The author does not seem to have noticed the distinction to be made between real and constructed miracles; or rather, for him, they are all constructions. Moreover, he makes no distinctions by period or by cultural area; he engages in no criticism of the sources; and he makes no use of the canonization procedures, except for those reproduced in the *Acta Sanctorum*. The whole enterprise must, therefore, be started all over again.

36 A first step in this direction is G. Mensching, *Das Wunder im Glauben und Aberglauben der Volker* (Leiden, 1957).

7

Religious feeling and popular cults during the French Revolution: 'patriot saints' and martyrs for liberty

ALBERT SOBOUL

For a long time historians of the French Revolution have seen the revolutionary cults as nothing more than political expedients. In reaction against this tendency, Albert Mathiez emphasized the specifically religious nature of these cults.[1] Just what constitutes the religious must be agreed on however: on this question Mathiez closely follows Durkheim who asserts that religious phenomena are essentially recognizable by their form. Like his predecessors, Mathiez does not seem to have attempted to study the religious feeling expressed by those who took part in the ceremonies of the revolutionary cults; it is from that standpoint, however, that it might be possible to determine whether they were political expedients or truly religious phenomena.

The task is undeniably difficult. Available documents bear witness to the creation of new sets of ceremonies. But to what extent do they throw light on the precise beliefs of those who took part in the new rituals? Herein lies the difficulty of studying historical psychology. The relative abundance of documents of popular origin, particularly relating to the cult of the martyrs for liberty, seems to us nevertheless to justify this preliminary attempt.

I

Naturally, Catholic writers have denied revolutionary cults any religious character at all, seeing them as no more than a weapon against the Church. In his *Histoire des sectes*, Grégoire particularly emphasized the element of persecution.[2] More recently, abbé Sicard has attempted to analyse the dogmas of the *civic religion* which the revolutionaries, according to him, were trying to establish;[3] but though he described its symbols, rites and ceremonies, he, too, considered it to be a political creation without any real religious character.

Michelet was the first to sense the religious character of the great manifestations of the Revolution, and particularly of the Federations,

217

which he rightly saw as paving the way for the creation of the revolutionary cults.[4] But he concluded that these various initiatives were simply political structures empty of dogma: 'Fertile in laws, sterile in beliefs [the Revolution] could not satisfy the eternal hunger of the human soul, always hungering and thirsting after God... The two parties of Reason, the Girondins and the Jacobins, barely took this into account. The Gironde entirely ignored the matter, the Jacobins eluded it. They thought that they could buy God off with words.'[5]

Aulard thought the revolutionary cults sufficiently important to make a special study of the cult of Reason and of the cult of the Supreme Being. But he emptied them of all religious content, seeing them as 'the necessary and essentially political consequence of the war which was forced on the Revolution by the opposition of the Ancien Régime to the new spirit'. The men who in the year II 'enthroned the goddess of Reason in Notre-Dame or glorified the God of Rousseau on the Champ de Mars had above all a political end in view and generally used their struggles against the established religion as they did their other acts of actual or verbal violence, as instruments in the defence of the nation'.[6]

Mathiez agrees with Aulard that these religious endeavours were part not only of a struggle against the Church but also of the defence of the new France; but he goes further: the revolutionary cults constituted a real religion.[7] To pin down their religious nature, Mathiez takes Durkheim as his methodological guide,[8] for whom, as we have seen, a religion is defined above all by its form; obligatory faith and worship and obligatory external practices were for Durkheim the two essential characteristics, and so they are for Mathiez. Following from these premisses, Mathiez studied not so much the revolutionaries' common creed as the manifestations of the new faith, its practices and ceremonies, and its revolutionary symbolism. 'If I can show all this, will I not be able to conclude that there was a revolutionary religion analogous in essence to all other religions?'[9] And Mathiez asserts at the end of his study: 'There was a revolutionary religion whose object was the institution of society itself. It had its obligatory dogmas (the Declaration of Rights, the Constitution), its symbols which inspired a mystical veneration (the Tricolour, the Trees of Liberty, the Altar of the Patrie, etc.), its ceremonies (the civic festivals), its prayers and its hymns.'[10]

Mathiez only studied the surface of things. Not that one should reproach him for keeping on a purely historical plane, for that is what even the historian of religions must do. Rather, Mathiez incorrectly characterizes the religious phenomenon when he assimilates the religious and the collective. He applies to the eighteenth century an assimilation that was justifiable in Durkheim's context of study. The latter described archaic societies in which everything was impregnated with a diffuse religiosity;

the social and the religious were largely identical. Can one say the same of the end of the eighteenth century? Rationalism had been spreading since the previous century, and the function of religion had become specialized and now only involved one part of collective life. It must therefore be defined in and by itself, and both religious beliefs and specifically religious ceremonies must be considered in isolation from civic or secular ceremonies. It is very probably correct to argue, as Mathiez does, that religious facts are to be distinguished by their form, but the form in question must be specified and religious facts must be considered in their entirety, rites, symbolism, dogmas and beliefs, the latter like all mental phenomena being approachable only by indirect means.

It would seem that the problem of the revolutionary cults was incorrectly posed by its two most important historians, each of them missing what was specifically religious, with Aulard's political preoccupations and Mathiez's sociological bias distorting their respective viewpoints. They were both more interested in the official institutions created by the ruling bourgeoisie than in popular cults: not that any particular cult was at the time the exclusive property of any particular class; but the popular cults enable us to capture the most direct expressions of the religious spontaneity of the revolutionary masses. Both Aulard and Mathiez emphasize the break between the traditional and the new religion, thus agreeing, though for different reasons, with the Catholic historians of the revolutionary cults. The break can hardly be denied, and it is precisely this innovation which is interesting; the question again is how to characterize it and what factors are involved in it.

Whatever the importance of the political upheaval between 1789 and 1794, the Revolution did not destroy traditional religion in the hearts of the populace. Rather, it set its own imprint on it and gave rise to a kind of evolution from Catholicism towards a new popular religion. Without doubt, once the revolutionary crisis was over, the men and women who had embraced the new cult through spiritual need turned back to the traditional religion. But, although the momentary abandonment of Catholicism did constitute a break, it is still necessary to study the revolutionary cults by placing oneself in the perspective of the traditional religion.

The study of the new rituals, on which Mathiez bases his whole argument, is doubtless important; but their syncretism with the old forms and the way in which the new ceremonies borrowed from Catholic ritual must also be elucidated. What were the new beliefs, moreover, and to what extent were they linked to the traditional ones? A religious cult implies (particularly in the context of eighteenth-century Catholicism) that the believer should venerate its object, and that this object which is both transcendent and supernatural should appear to him to be endowed with effective power both here below and in the after-life. The believer has access to this power through the cult which is in a sense an exchange of prestations between men and the supernatural. Religion also has important implications for the life of the individual. These features characterize traditional religion: to what extent are they applicable to the revolutionary cults?

II

The cult of the 'patriot saints' illustrates one aspect of the transition from the Catholic religion to the revolutionary cults: it brings together the old religious context and new political elements which are fitted into traditional forms of worship.

Perrine Dugué came from a family of small farmers in Thorigné, a village in the department of the Mayenne, bordering on the Sarthe. The whole family (Perrine had five brothers) was strongly in favour of the Revolution and was actively opposed to the Chouans; two of the brothers were in the mobile units defending Sainte-Suzanne, a town to the north of Thorigné, against the 'brigands'. On 22 March 1796, Perrine, who was then nearly nineteen, ignoring the threats she had received, set off for the fair in Sainte-Suzanne where she also hoped to see her brothers whom she was accused of supplying with information. Half-way there she was killed by three Chouans; she was found next day and buried three days later in a nearby field. Both sides accused each other of murdering her, and it may be that these mutual accusations reunited all sections of the local population in a common commiseration, for the murder had struck a vivid chord in the popular imagination. Three contemporary ballads make no allusion to Perrine's Republican ideas and portray her simply as a good Christian girl who preferred death to being raped. However, her political sentiments were well-known and Perrine was generally regarded as a Republican 'saint'. Abbé Coutard reports that she had been seen 'ascending to heaven on tricolour wings', and crowds quickly gathered at her tomb where cures were effected. The story of these miracles spread and pilgrims came from the neighbouring departments of the Orne, the Sarthe and the Maine-et-Loire. A chapel was built in 1797. Though the restoration of Catholicism put an end to the cult of Perrine, the Republican saint, since the Church did not recognize her miracles, it did not blot out her memory, which lingered on for a long time.[11]

The example of Perrine Dugué is not unique. In the forest of Taillay, on the borders of the Loire-Inférieure and the Ille-et-Vilaine, is a famous tomb called 'the girl's tomb'. The girl in question was Marie Martin, from Tresboeuf. Either for having told the Republican army of a Royalist band's refuge or for having refused to reveal her masters' hiding place, she was attacked and killed by the Chouans. She was buried at the place of her death. An account dated 1950 tells of two crosses at her head; little niches containing small statues were nailed to nearby oak trees; money offerings were placed in one of these niches and, until the Great War, these were collected by a woman every Sunday and on days of pilgrimage. Even now there are pilgrimages to the tomb from all the neighbouring parishes, particularly on the Feast of St John at midsummer and on Easter and Whit Mondays. St Pataude (as she is known locally, Pataud being the Chouan name for a Republican) is said to grant all the favours that she is asked. Mothers bring their young children in order to get them to learn to walk early, and make them go round the tomb three times taking normal steps. The tomb is still cared for by the local people who leave ex-voto offerings. Wood-cutters say that no axe could penetrate the trunk of the tree where the saint was bound and martyred.[12]

These two examples show how there was amalgamation with the old forms. The traditional cult was enlarged to include Republican and patriot saints but the old religious forms were still much stronger than the new political additions. There was definitely an underlying religious belief, although the Church condemned it. The patriot saints were believed to be endowed with special power, and they worked miracles. The revolutionary cult remains very close to Catholicism.[13]

III

The cult of the martyrs for liberty seems to be the culmination of the evolution of revolutionary religious feeling from the basis of the traditional cult. Here the new forms and political aspects which were still secondary in the patriot saint cult are much more important than the old religious context.

The historians of the revolutionary cults were more interested in the cult of Reason and of the Supreme Being which were artificial creations of the ruling elements of the Revolution than they were in the spontaneous development of the 'popular' cult of the martyrs for liberty and of Marat in particular, despite the fact that the latter would have enabled them to chart the evolution of religious feeling during the Terror. This popular cult developed from July 1793 onwards in the Parisian *sections*, the 'grass-root' organizations of the *sans-culottes*. Its objects of veneration were three famous victims of the Counter-Revolution: first Marat, assassinated on 13 July 1793; then Lepeletier de Saint-Fargeau, assassinated on 20 January 1793 by the bodyguard, Paris; and finally Chalier, condemned by reactionaries and guillotined at Lyon on 17 July 1793.

The part which Marat had played from the start of the Revolution had given him immense prestige in the eyes of the Parisian *sans-culottes*. His

assassination (setting aside its political consequences) led to the development of a form of popular veneration that was one of the most original
traits of the *sans-culotte* mentality. The new cult began in the days immediately following his assassination with the real competition for the body
of 'the People's Friend'. Who was to have these 'precious remains'? Marat's
section (that of the Théâtre-Français, which soon took his name) claimed
them. The Jacobins and the Cordeliers were in conflict for the possession of
his heart, the Cordeliers eventually prevailing. The women of the society of
Républicains-Révolutionnaires solemnly swore, on 17 July, to bring up
their children in the 'cult' of Marat and never to give them any other
'gospels' but his collected works.[14] On 26 July, the Cordeliers decided to
'erect an altar to the heart of Marat the Incorruptible'.[15] The ceremony
took place at the beginning of August; Marat's heart was placed in a vase
and these 'precious remains of a god', to quote a patriot's invocation, were
hung from the vault of the meeting-room:[16] was this the imitation of an old
rite or the creation of a new one? A few days beforehand, a popular
brochure had at some length compared Marat to Jesus, who had also fallen
'under the blows of fanaticism, while working with all his strength for the
salvation of mankind'.[17] The aim was doubtless to make Jesus a
revolutionary; but concomitantly Marat participated in the divine nature
of Jesus.

Here we must emphasize the equivocal character of many words which
were directly transposed from religious vocabulary and which induced
psychological confusion.[18] When the leaders declared that Marat was
immortal, they meant that he lived on in their memories; but for the *sans-
culottes*, brought up as Catholics, the word 'immortal' was inseparable from
the immortality of the soul, and the word 'saint' applied to Marat could not
be separated from the 'sacred'. Martyrs were eminent among the saints
usually invoked, so for the *sans-culotte*, to call Marat a martyr was assuredly
to promote him to the ranks of the saints. Whereas the militant sought
some stimulus for his revolutionary activity from 'the People's Friend' who
lived on in his memory, the *sans-culotte* hoped that Marat, having become a
saint, would ensure the success of the Revolution, which was seen very
much in terms of 'good tidings', as a 'gospel' bringing salvation to all
mankind. For the *sans-culotte*, reared on Catholic practice, salvation had a
temporal as well as an ultimate meaning, as the ex-votos in the churches
witnessed. We have not found ex-votos dedicated to 'the People's Friend',
but in the 'popular' mind to invoke Marat, a martyr for liberty who had
given his life for the Revolution and thus for the salvation of humanity,
must have had the same implications.

During August, several sections and popular societies held funeral
ceremonies in honour of Marat or proceeded to instal busts of him and of

Lepeletier. In these ceremonies the characteristics of the new cult began to take shape.

On 4 August, the Société Fraternelle des Patriotes des Deux Sexes unveiled busts of the martyrs in its meeting-room.[19] On 8 August, the Contrat-Social section exhibited in the church of Saint-Eustache, its meeting-place, 'an effigy of the people's representative on his death bed'.[20] This spectacle which borrowed the traditional religious framework was calculated to strike the popular imagination. Again, the Hommes-du-Dix-Août society heard a funeral oration for Marat on 15 August at the Filles-Dieu where it had its headquarters.[21]

How should we characterize these ceremonies? A speech at the unveiling of a bust does not in itself, of course, constitute a religious ritual. The *sans-culottes* derived new energy from these ceremonies which usually ended with a civic oath; but what was involved here was recourse not to supernatural aid, but to the comfort naturally drawn from belonging to a group. We may nevertheless assume that for many of those present these funeral ceremonies in Marat's honour, which often took place in churches, were like masses said for the peace of his soul.

At the same time, the external features of the new cult became clearer. Here is a description of the funeral service held for Marat on 18 August 1793 in the church of Bonne-Nouvelle:

The effigy of Marat was laid in state in the nave on a sarcophagus draped with a starred blue cloth; at either end were two candelabra in the antique style; in front, on another stepped sarcophagus was the bust of Lepeletier; the two sarcophagi were decorated with wreaths of cypress with inscriptions celebrating the virtues of the two great men. Behind Marat was a reproduction of the bath... On the church's main altar was enthroned the figure of Liberty. All round the church were great draperies in the national colours and festooned candelabra. Over the main entrance to the church was a transparent tricolour panel, on which was written 'Entrance to the Temple of Liberty'.[22]

Here we have the creation of a new set of ceremonies and the beginnings of an amalgamation with the old forms of the Catholic cult. Draperies, candelabra, sarcophagi are taken from the traditional religious ceremonial; but the national colours replace funereal black, and cypress wreaths and inscriptions evoke memories of Antiquity. The plastic arts, painting and sculpture, are used to strike the imagination of the faithful. The representation of Marat's bath recalls that of the instruments of the Passion; the statue of Liberty replaces that of the Virgin. Thus, elements taken from Catholicism or from Antiquity and revolutionary elements contribute to the gradual creation of a new ceremonial and a new system of symbols. But the new cult remains essentially revolutionary: the documents show us what the new ceremonies took from the Catholic service, but nothing is said of the influence of Catholic beliefs as such. The new ritual serves above all to exalt the civic sentiment of the *sans-culottes*: the oral element in the rituals – sermons, invocations and prayers – is essentially political in content.

Towards the end of August 1793, the popular impetus gained strength. During September the *sans-culottes* definitively triumphed in the sections which they had not previously controlled. The cult of the martyrs for liberty then became generalized and at the same time took clearer shape. Henceforth, Lepeletier was always associated with Marat. The ceremonial expanded: choirs (but patriotic choirs) and then processions came to lend the new cult a truly religious pomp.

On 1 September 1793, the Fontaine-de-Grenelle section unveiled busts of Marat and Lepeletier.[23] On 15 September, the Molière et Lafontaine section, now called Brutus, held a ceremony in their honour in the church of Saint-Joseph, rue Montmartre.[24] On the same day, the 're-generated' (i.e. 'sans-culottized') Montagne section staged an 'apotheosis' of Lepeletier and Marat.[25] These ceremonies were generally celebrated on Sundays in the churches where the general assemblies took place; in this way the new cult gradually replaced the old one, assuming many of its external characteristics in the process. On 22 September the Panthéon-Français section added celebration of Brutus to that of Marat and Lepeletier, an innovation which created a real Republican trinity.[26] On the following Sundays, 29 September and 6 October, these ceremonies proliferated; their public was probably in part a church-going one. On 6 October the Halle-au-Blé and Guillaume-Tell sections added to the now usual speeches and choirs a procession through the streets of their districts; here again Brutus preceded Lepeletier and Marat. The addition of Brutus and the consecration of a stone from the Bastille on which the Declaration of Human Rights was engraved emphasized the civic character of the ceremony.[27] On 9 October in the district of the Piques section, there was a real procession.[28] All of this confirms that this new element was becoming established as part of the cult of the martyrs.

There had been Catholic processions in the various *quartiers* of Paris up to the spring of 1793, and notably that for the Fête-Dieu which had, however, been marred here and there by incidents, and which was the last Catholic procession to take place. The processions of the cult of martyrs gradually took their place. Since religious processions were an important part of traditional popular life, militants in the sections and clubs adapted them to their own ends. But to what extent did the faithful transfer their Catholic beliefs to the new ceremonies? Historical documents either do not mention this important point or are difficult to interpret. To the traditional procession with its songs and its halts at altars along the route and before the images of saints, the *sans-culottes* added not only Republican themes and symbols but also elements taken from the national festivals, instituted in 1790 to celebrate the great Revolutionary anniversaries, and in particular the element of military display. There developed in this way in honour of the martyrs for liberty a popular processional art of both religious and patriotic inspiration, which contributed to the upsurge of civic sentiment in the autumn of 1793. But how can we determine the part played by specifically religious feeling among the adherents of the new cult?

The first processions, still short, were organized by the Halle-au-Blé and the Guillaume-Tell sections on 6 October and by the Piques section on the 9th. On Sunday the 13th, the Révolutionnaire section (previously called Pont-Neuf) walked in long procession through the streets of the district with banners and effigies of the martyrs, patriotic choirs and military bands.[29] In the afternoon of 16 October, the Museum section (David's section) processed through the streets round the Louvre, and then went through the colonnade into the Cour Carrée.[30] In the lead were two lines of drummers and gunners; then came the popular societies with their emblems, the Parisian sections preceded by their banners, and the various corporate bodies; an armed detachment followed, led by a flag and drums, and then the rest of the section. A 'musical corps' then preceded a deputation from the Convention which was followed by some of the first conscripts carrying oak branches in their hands; in their midst were the women citizens of the section, dressed in white, holding their children by the hand and carrying flowers. A detachment of troops brought up the rear. In the courtyard of the Louvre were sarcophagi on which stood original paintings by David of the assassinated Lepeletier and Marat. A funeral service was held with hymns and civic speeches which were vaguely religious in tone. As in Catholic ceremonies, all the arts lent their prestige to the exaltation of the faithful. The *sans-culottes* partook of some kind of communion by thus commemorating their martyrs. But to what extent did these ceremonies imply real veneration of their object? To what extent, that is, did religious sentiment inspire civic feeling? The documents seem to suggest the presence of religious fervour; but it is impossible to pin down its precise manifestations.

Little by little, the new cult reached all sections, at the same time developing its final shape. On 9 Brumaire, the Bonne-Nouvelle section started up new forges for the manufacture of arms, and when this was done, busts of Marat and Lepeletier were then consecrated.[31] Patriotic effort and civic enthusiasm thus went together. On the same day the Temple section celebrated 'this feast-day created by patriotism'. 'The people's benefactors must have their altars ... Paris is erecting temples to the martyrs for liberty... Priests and all the enemies of the Republic dare to degrade our solemn worship of them – let the people's representatives wreak vengeance on them for their calumny.'[32] Here, for the first time, opposition to Catholicism and the role played by the new cult in dechristianization are clearly expressed. Although the new ceremonies, taken as a whole, borrowed certain features from Catholicism, it would seem that for their instigators at any rate there was no question of deliberate syncretism with the old beliefs. There is no reference here to Catholic saints (although Marat and Lepeletier are dubbed 'apostles'), only to the deified heroes of Antiquity: 'the inventor of the plough, the courageous mortal who dared to avenge the tyrants' ill-treatment of humanity'. In the same way, the syncretism appears to have been purely formal, when on 10 Brumaire, the Champs-Elysées section asked the Convention 'if the first two days of the Republican era should not bear the names of its first two martyrs?'[33]

The cult of the martyrs for liberty took on its final shape when to Lepeletier and Marat was added Chalier, who was guillotined on 17 June 1793, in Lyon by the Counter-Revolutionaries: the Revolutionary triad or trinity – depending on whether reference was made to Antiquity or to Catholicism – was complete. But this move stemmed from a political initiative rather than from any popular spontaneity and never seems to have attracted any feeling of religious veneration. The addition of Chalier was another step towards the non-religious and, though he was associated with the two other martyrs, represents a third stage in the evolution of the cults, beyond the cult of the patriot saints and that of Marat, towards complete unbelief.

It was Chaumette, the public prosecutor of the Commune of Paris, who instigated the cult of Chalier, and in doing so he was certainly engaged in political manoeuvring. The cult of the martyrs had developed spontaneously in the sections without any intervention from the municipal authorities; the revolutionary fervour of the sans-culottes was here expressed in religious terms and received new stimulus from the ceremonies. It is significant that during the summer of 1793, while the new cult was taking shape, the Commune did not itself organize a single ceremony. It was only towards the middle of Brumaire, when the cult of the martyrs had become general without the authorities having in any way approved it, that Chaumette intervened, but he did so to add to Marat and Lepeletier a martyr who fitted in better with his own brand of politics. On 11 Brumaire (1 November 1793), Chaumette delivered a funeral oration for Chalier at the Conseil Général of the Commune: he portrayed the Lyon Jacobin in the guise of a hero of Antiquity rather than of a saint of the new religion.[34] Praise of Chalier's Republican virtues, a 'simple factual account' of his final moments, his last words, Socratic in tone, all contributed to make of him a figure well suited to strike the popular imagination, and to render him worthy of belonging to the Republican Pantheon; but there was nothing to incite veneration or to inspire religious feeling.

Here we can see a difference in behaviour between the *sans-culottes* as such and the militants from the petty or middling bourgeoisie: the latter, having a certain classical education, tend to refer to Antiquity when constituting the new cults, while the former draw on their Catholic upbringing. But again, to what extent did this syncretism reach beyond the ceremonial aspect to belief itself? There is no document which testifies to the worship of Marat as a saint. His tomb never became a place imbued with effective power where miracles occurred; this points to an important difference between the cult of the patriot saints and beliefs as they later evolved.

It seems, however, that the ceremonies held in Marat's honour must be considered as more than mere demonstrations of esteem for a politician, despite the fact that the section militants in charge of the new cult emphasized its civic dimension. Although they maintained the external forms of traditional litany, invocation and prayer, the new content informing these was essentially political.[35] However, it must be noted that those attending the ceremonies of the traditional and then the revolutionary cults were often the same people: did this element of continuity mean that there was also in people's minds a transfer of the old beliefs concerning the saints to the new martyrs? Reports by police observers frequently emphasize that large crowds attended the decadal services into which the cult of the martyrs was integrated. On 10 Ventôse, for example (28 February 1794), in the Bonne-Nouvelle section, 'there were a lot of people, mainly women' in the Temple of Reason, previously the church of Bonne-Nouvelle. On the same day in the Gravilliers section, 'the whole of the *ci-devant* church of Saint-Nicolas-des-Champs was nearly full and there were many young people'. On 30 Ventôse (20 March 1794), a police observer remarked in his report that 'there always used to be many more women than men in churches: the same can be said of the temples of Reason. Few men and a lot of women'.[36] Did these women see the martyrs of the new trinity as saints enthroned in heaven? One may suppose that they did, although no document can confirm it. The religious setting had not changed; the ritual of the new cult was comparable to that of the old. It is not unlikely that these women of the people who formed the bulk of the faithful had simply transferred their adoration of Catholic saints to the Republican martyrs.

The dechristianization movement which developed in Brumaire Year II (Autumn 1793), and whose origins were far from 'popular', gave new impetus to the cult of the martyrs. Sections which had dragged their feet hurried to institute it. It now appeared to be one of the elements of the Republican cult which section militants sought to build on the ruins of traditional religion. Devotion to the Republican Trinity was combined with the cult of Reason, which was too abstract a divinity by itself, even when it was given the features of a young lady from the Opera.

The persistence of religious feelings in new forms did however provoke opposition. Catholic believers accused the new cult of being idolatrous. On 26 Brumaire (16 November 1793), the Arcis revolutionary committee arrested a candle-maker's assistant for fanaticism: he had refused to attend a ceremony in the honour of Marat saying 'that he would prefer to die a thousand deaths rather than be present at such a carnival'.[37] This man, moreover, was a good *sans-culotte* who had taken up arms on all the great 'days' of the Revolution: his case was not an isolated one.

At the other extreme, the cult of the martyrs was attacked by atheists, political reasons mingling here with ideological motives. On 8 Frimaire (28 November 1793), at a meeting of the Jacobins, Hébert condemned the cult of Marat: 'It has already been said that the Parisians have substituted Marat for Jesus.'[38] And the 315th issue of his *Père Duchesne* claimed that 'the Parisians now acknowledge no other god but Marat'. On 12 Frimaire, Danton snubbed a petitioner at the bar of the Convention who began to read a litany in praise of Marat.[39] Was this reaction the result of political or personal hostility, or did it stem from a conviction that, because the new cult was religious, it was still too close to traditional religion? Probably a combination of all these reasons explains the halt that was called.

The cult of the martyrs, incorporated into the cult of Reason, persisted nevertheless up to the spring of 1794, with the decadal ceremonies drawing big crowds composed mainly of women and children. However, the general movement of reaction which began with the trial and execution of Hébert (24 March 1794) proved fatal to it. Marat was to a certain extent implicated in the discredit that was thrown on *Père Duchesne* and its editor, and the moderates managed effectively to confuse the people. As early as 27 Ventôse (17 March 1794), a police observer heard it said that 'if Marat were still alive, he would now be charged and perhaps guillotined'. On 5 Germinal (25 March 1794) it was rumoured that the Marat section in a complete volte-face had covered over their portrait of 'the People's Friend'. A police observer reported, on 8 Germinal, that the inhabitants of villages near Paris were disconcerted by the rumours circulating about Marat: 'If they think that even Marat may have deceived them, they will no longer trust anyone.'[40]

This campaign was abruptly halted by the authorities of the Commune of Paris who threatened on 9 Germinal (29 March 1794) to declare 'suspect' all those who tried to belittle the esteem that was 'rightly owed' to the martyrs for liberty.[41] But esteem was very different from veneration, and the Robespierrist authorities of the Commune thereby indicated the narrow margins within which they were prepared to allow the cult of Marat to continue. There was no longer to be religious fervour, but only civic sentiment. The month of Germinal Year II heralded the reaction of the Year III; the Counter-Revolutionaries and Catholics were then given free rein to get rid of the statues of the martyrs for liberty. By 30 Thermidor Year III (17 August 1795), in the Nord section 'the statues installed by the Terror in the choir of the church of Saint-Laurent' had been destroyed,[42] and the same was true of all sections.

At the end of our study, leaving to one side the political aspect of the popular cults, we can see that in 1793 the social and political crisis had a profound impact on the religious feelings of the revolutionary masses. But how should we interpret the resulting popular cults within the general evolution of religious feeling at the end of the eighteenth century? Are we to think that in the ten years of the Revolution there was a general dechristianization and that the popular cults that we have studied represent the different stages of this movement? Or should we consider the cults as new forms of sects through which traditional religion was regenerated? This raises a much wider problem: when the Christian faith is losing ground, is complete unbelief arrived at via the intermediary stage of sectarianism? We can do no more than pose these questions. We would, moreover, have to investigate the different social categories which created or which simply took part in these cults, in order to obtain a fuller and more realistic picture of them; the petty or middling bourgeoisie, in the former category, seem to have been mainly unbelievers, while the *sans-culottes* proper, in the latter, probably remained attached to the traditional religious context.

This highlights the fatal obstacle in the way of the popular cults. If one can sense in them the factors which have always contributed to the germination of religions, the latter have had theologians whereas the cults could not have. The militants who organized the cults were rationalists; but the people transposed their way of thinking into the framework of their own religious upbringing. Did the orators at the ceremonies in honour of the martyrs for liberty suspect that this transposition was taking place? If so, they would surely have opposed this survival of the very clerical education that they were trying to eradicate through dechristianization. The people were obviously quite incapable of formulating a theology for the new cults, but their leaders were no more capable of doing so.

The ephemeral nature of the revolutionary cults explains why no critical, independent thinker was able to perceive the popular transposition and to leave us with written traces of it. Without adequate documents, we can only point to the problems involved and set down a few markers.[43]

NOTES

1 Albert Mathiez, *Les Origines des cultes révolutionnaires (1789–92)* (Paris, 1904). For the development of Mathiez's position and commentary on it, see below.

2 Henri-Baptiste Grégoire, *Histoire des sectes religieuses ... depuis le commencement du siècle dernier jusqu'à l'époque actuelle* (Paris, 1810).

3 Augustin Sicard, *A la recherche d'une religion civile* (Paris, 1895).

4 See chapters XI and XII in Book III of Jules Michelet, *Histoire de la Révolution française*, 'De la religion nouvelle'.

5 *Histoire de la Révolution française*, Book XIV, chapter I. This chapter has the significant title, 'La Révolution n'était rien sans la Révolution religieuse' (The Revolution was nothing without the religious Revolution).

6 Alphonse Aulard, *Le culte de la Raison et le culte de l'Etre suprême* (Paris, 1892), pp. vii-viii.

7 Mathiez, *Cultes révolutionnaires*.

8 Relying particularly on his article, 'De la définition des phénomènes religieux', *Année Sociologique* (1899).

9 Mathiez, *Cultes révolutionnaires*, p. 13.

10 *Ibid.*, p. 62.

11 Abbé Augustin Ceuneau, *Un Culte étrange pendant la Révolution, Perrine Dugué, la sainte aux ailes tricolores, 1777–96* (Laval, 1947). See also G. Lefebvre, 'Perrine Dugué, la sainte patriote', *Annales Historiques de la Révolution Française* (1949), p. 337.

12 Roger Joxe, 'Encore une sainte patriote : Sainte Pataude', *Annales Historiques de la Révolution Française* (1952), p. 91. According to *Le Journal de Chateaubriant*, 4 (May–July 1950), entitled 'La fosse à la fille', St Pataude means St Republican. It is an interesting fact that St Pataude and St Tricolore both appeared in the west of France. It would seem from this that the people of the region, even when they supported the Revolution, remained as attached to the traditional religion as the Royalists. Possibly even more so, for there is no known case of a Chouan having been spontaneously promoted to sainthood by popular feeling.

13 This analysis is obviously insufficient. But one can only pose questions to which the documents permit no reply. Concerning Perrine Dugué : does some commentary exist which explains the significance of her ascension? What did people do at her chapel? Were there occasional or regular ceremonies there? On what dates? What did they consist of? How was Perrine's memory preserved? Concerning Marie Martin: are there any sources prior to that of 1950? When did her cult begin? What is known about the history of ceremonies at her tomb? What is done there now at Easter, at Whitsun and on the Feast of St John? Why do people go there on Mondays? Is there syncretism here, with Sundays being reserved for traditional religion and Mondays for the new cult? Generally : in these cults, what elements are there – ceremonies, rituals, prayers, symbols? Who takes part in the rituals? What categories of the population? What age-groups? How many? Were the adherents good Catholics or only luke-warm? What was the attitude of the Church? Exactly what share did politics have in the content of the beliefs and dogmas involved?

14 A(rchives) N(ationales) C. 262, d. 580, p. 2.

15 AN C. 259, d. 540; *Moniteur*, XVII, 243.

16 *Journal de la Montagne*, 3 August 1793.

17 B(ibliothèque) N(ationale) Lb 40 1994; Tourneux [Maurice Tourneux, *Bibliographie de l'Histoire de Paris pendant la Révolution française* (Paris, 1890–1913), 5 vols. S. W.], 8417.

18 See Ferdinand Brunot, *Histoire de la langue française*, IX: 'La Révolution et l'Empire' (Paris, 1937), p. 625, on the transposition of religious words.

19 *Affiches de la Commune*, 3 and 6 August 1793; *Journal de la Montagne*, 4 August 1793; *Moniteur*, XVII, 300.

20 AN C. 266, pl. 629, p. 17; *Affiches de la Commune*, 6 August 1793; *Journal de la Montagne*, 7 August 1793; *Moniteur*, XVII, 323, 331. See also Marat's funeral oration delivered by Guirant in the same section, Contrat-Social, on 9 August 1793 (printed, 8°, 15 pp., mentioned in Tourneux, 8751).

21 *Affiches de la Commune*, 15 August 1793; *Journal de la Montagne*, 16 August 1793.

22 Bibliothèque Victor Cousin MS 177.

23 *Affiches de la Commune*, 1 September 1793; *Moniteur*, XVII, 545. On 2 September, a deputation from Fontaine-de-Grenelle announced at the Jacobin club that the next child to be born in their section would be given the first name 'Marat'; and on 4 September, a child was named Marat (Bibliothèque Victor Cousin MS 120).

24 BN Lb 40 1752 and 1979; *Tourneux*, 8131 and 8132; *Moniteur*, XVII, 659.

25 AN C. 275, pl. 710, p. 29; *Journal de la Montagne*, 16 September 1793. During this ceremony the speeches were punctuated by choirs, apparently for the first time.

26 BN Lb 40 2036; Tourneux, 8872; *Journal de la Montagne*, 23 September 1793; *Moniteur*, XVII, 721.

27 Archives de la Préfecture de Police AA/266; BN Lb 40 1879; Tourneux, 8242; *Journal de la Montagne*, 5 October 1793; *Moniteur*, XVIII, 34.

28 BN Lb 40 2053 and Lb 40 489 bis; Tourneux, 8695 and 8696; *Moniteur*, XVIII, 76.

29 Archives de la Préfecture de Police AA/266; BN Lb 40 2102; Tourneux, 8268; *Journal de la Montagne*, 23rd of the first month of Year II; *Moniteur*, XVIII, 114. 'A ceremony remarkable both for its orderliness and for the eager participation of all the citizens', declared the Commissioners of the Conseil Général of the Commune.

30 BN Lb 40 1996; Tourneux, 8420. Concerning this procession in honour of Marat, see David's request at the Convention on 14 October 1793 (AN C. 276, pl. 714, p. 17; *Moniteur*, XVIII, 125). David announced that he had just finished a picture of 'Marat à son dernier soupir'; he requested permission to lend it and his painting of the assassinated Lepeletier to his fellow citizens of the Museum section (David's section). Art was no longer the preserve of a privileged minority.

31 AN C. 280, pl. 761, p. 9; BN MSS Nouv. acq. fr. 2173, fol. 52.

32 AN C. 279, pl. 760, p. 20; *Journal de la Montagne*, 7 Brumaire Year II.

33 Archives Départementales de la Seine, D 976; Tourneux, 7996; *Journal de la Montagne*, 10 Brumaire Year II.

34 BN Lb 40 1154m; *Affiches de la Commune*, 10, 11 and 12 Brumaire Year II.

A funeral service in honour of Chalier was held on 30 Frimaire Year II (20 December 1793). The organizers took care not only to recall the great actions of Chalier, but also to make known 'his prophecies': a procedure borrowed from hagiography. In the procession three groups carried banners on which the 'prophecies' of Chalier were proclaimed. The third banner, referring to the repression which followed the capture of Lyon by the troops of the Convention, read as follows: 'Aristocrats, *Feuillants, Rollandins*, egotists, moderates and all misguided people; tremble! At the first blow struck against liberty, the waters of the Saône and of the Rhône will flow with blood, and will carry your bodies out to the terrified sea.' BN Lb 40 1337, Tourneux, 6452. If the tone is apocalyptic, the allusion remains purely political.

35 See, for example, *Pratique du bon français*, read in the Temple of Reason, in the Tuileries section on 10 Brumaire Year II (31 October 1793) (BN Lb 40 2181; Tourneux, 9028). This pamphlet comprises: a Republican Invocation, a Republican Salutation, a Republican Creed, and Republican Commandments. See also *Prières républicaines du matin et du soir*, read at the Tuileries section (BN Lb 40 2199; Tourneux, 9029). For example, here are the first two of the Republican Ten Commandments, published by the popular society of the Friends of Liberty, Bonnet-Rouge section:

> I. Frenchman, thou shalt defend thy country
>   In order to live freely.
> II. Thou shalt pursue all tyrants
>   To Hindustan and beyond.

36 AN W. 112.

37 AN F. 7 4474 83, André Prieur dossier.

38 *Journal de la Montagne*, 10 Frimaire Year II; *Moniteur*, XVIII, 549.

39 *Moniteur*, XVIII, 575.

40 AN W. 112, Report by Prévost; W. 174, Report by Monie.

41 BN Lb 40 1154; *Moniteur*, XX, 88.

42 Archives de la Préfecture de Police A A/266.

43 Since this article was written, Monsieur Deschamps, a bookseller, of the Cour de Rohan, Paris 6ᵉ, has been kind enough to bring to my attention an anonymous manuscript dating probably from the time of the Empire and entitled: 'Observations et réflexions critiques sur les *Pensées théologiques*.' 'The story of Perrine Dugué which has created such a stir in the department of the Sarthe' is mentioned, and also her miracles 'attested by thousands of people who claim to have been eye-witnesses of these marvellous occurrences and to have seen sick people immediately healed simply by touching St Dugué's relics' (Chapter XVI, 'Des miracles', p. 183). This manuscript was a refutation of Dom Gamin's work, *Pensées théologiques relatives aux erreurs du temps* (Paris, 1770).

8

Cults of saints in the churches of central Paris

STEPHEN WILSON

Cults of saints in traditional rural society or in European societies of the past have been studied by scholars in various disciplines;[1] but less attention has been paid to such cults in modern urban settings, where they are also an important part of 'popular' Catholicism, and an example of the continuing vigour of 'popular' or 'folk' culture in industrial society.[2] This paper is a modest contribution in this comparatively neglected area of study and sets out to describe and analyse the cults of saints (including cults of the Virgin Mary and other devotions) in the churches and chapels of the ten central *arrondissements* of Paris. This limited zone was chosen since it includes a good variety of economic and other activities, and of residential areas of different classes, while remaining fully metropolitan in character. It could, moreover, be suitably encompassed in the time available for field-work. Of a possible total of forty-four churches (excluding Notre-Dame-de-Paris, Saint-Louis-des-Invalides, and churches which are no longer Roman Catholic), thirty-three were visited; and, in addition, seven chapels were visited, of a possible total of sixteen (excluding the Sainte-Chapelle and the Chapelle-Expiatoire, both of which are now public monuments). Field-work was done in August and September 1978, and churches or chapels were usually visited in the late afternoon or on Saturday morning, though a selection was also visited on other occasions.[3]

Table 1 lists the most popular saints (those with a cult in more than one church or chapel), together with the material aspects of their cults. It will be seen that a small number are particularly popular, six having more than ten statues, and two (Ste Thérèse and St Antoine) more than thirty. Certain characteristics of the nineteen saints in Table 1 may be pointed out.[4] Thirteen (including St Michel) are male, and six are female, a male predominance that is more than counterbalanced by the cults of the Virgin, as we shall see. Ten saints are of French nationality, including the joint patron saints of France, Ste Jeanne d'Arc and Ste Thérèse,[5] and the patron saint of Paris, Ste Geneviève. The date of canonization (or beatification) is

Table 1   Paris: Cults of saints found in more than one church or chapel

Name of saint	Date of canoni-zation	Statues	Candles	Ex-votos	Chapels or altars	Tronc	Position R	Position L
Ste Thérèse de l'Enfant Jésus	1925	32	31	15	5	5	19	8
St Antoine de Padoue	1232	32	29	17	4	9	18	10
St Joseph	Early Church	21	16	16	19	4	12	10
Ste Jeanne d'Arc	1920	19	7	6	3	—	9	9
Ste Rita	1900	11	11	7	0	4	6	6
Ste Anne	Early Church	10	7	9	4†	—	9	3
St Vincent de Paul	1737	7	4	2	5*	—	5	4
Le Curé d'Ars (St Jean-Baptiste Vianney)	1925	6	5	—	1	—	2	2
St Michel	Early Church	5	3	—	1†	—	2	3
St Pierre	Early Church	4	2	—	?	—	2	1
Ste Geneviève	Medieval	3	2	8	9*†	—	8	2
Ste Louise de Marillac	1934	3	0	—	1*	—	1	4†
St Nicolas	Early Church	2	2	2	1*†	—	1	1
St François Xavier	1622	2	1	2	?	—	2	0
Blessed Martyrs of September 1792	Modern beatification	0	1	0	2	—	5	2†
St Benoît Labre	1883	1	0	1	1	—	3	0
St Martin	Early Church	1	1	2	?*	—	1	1
St Roch	Medieval	1	1	2	1†	—	2	—
St François de Sales	1655	1	1	—	1	—	0	2

† Denotes including commemorative plaques to these saints; 2 for Ste Louise and 6 for the Blessed Martyrs of 1792.

*Denotes including relics.

also of some significance: six are saints of the Early or pre-medieval Church; three are medieval; two are from the seventeenth century; one from the eighteenth century; and seven were canonized or beatified in the late nineteenth or early twentieth centuries. Of the thirteen medieval or post-medieval saints, eight are religious, and two are members of the secular clergy (the Curé d'Ars and St François de Sales, a bishop). The relatively modern emphasis of the cults is also marked by the fact that most of the statues of the saints appear to date from this century or late in the last century, though there are a few exceptions.[6] It is striking, indeed, how little of the artistic wealth of the churches of Paris is incorporated in existing popular cults. In only six cases (including both the body and the heart of St Vincent-de-Paul, which are kept in the Chapelle-des-Lazaristes, rue de Sèvres, and in the Chapelle-de-la-Médaille-Miraculeuse respectively), are relics of the saint involved in the cult, and in only three of these (St Vincent de Paul, Ste Louise de Marillac, and Ste Geneviève) are the relics of the saint a prominent part of the cult.[7] The popularity of most of these cults can begin to be explained by reference to the traditional importance, the French nationality, or the recent canonization, of the saint concerned. The two most difficult cults to explain along such lines are those of St Antoine and Ste Rita. St Antoine is a medieval saint whose cult, at the popular level, seems to have been continuous since the Middle Ages, though it seems also to have changed considerably in character over the centuries. It is certain that the modern image of the saint as a friar carrying the Child Jesus differs from the more youthful figure of Italian primitive painting, for example in the Louvre. The other explicit modern association of the saint is with the 'pain des pauvres', and not with lost objects, though this may be implicit. It is probably fair to assume also that the proclamation of St Antoine as a Doctor of the Church in 1946 was the recognition, but also acted as the reinforcement, of a popular cult. The cult of Ste Rita, 'the saint of desperate cases', is the most recent in Paris, and seems to have been imported from the Iberian Peninsula after the Second World War. In general, attention may be drawn to the contrast between this list of popular saints and more traditional preferences.[8]

In addition to these nineteen saints who are the object of cult or devotion in more than one church or chapel (high-incidence cults), a further twenty-one are the object of cult in only one place (low-incidence cults). Of the twenty-one saints involved in low-incidence cults, ten are male and eleven are female; the same balance of the sexes is found here as with the high-incidence cults, including those to the Virgin. Eight are of French nationality, including two (Ste Clotilde and Ste Catherine Labouré) who have a special association with Paris. Nine are saints of the Early Church (St Philippe, Ste Marie-Madeleine, Ste Elisabeth, Ste Cécile, Ste Monique, Ste Hélène, St Christophe, Ste Espérance and perhaps St Expédit; four are medieval (Ste Clotilde, St Merri, St Louis and St Eugène); and six were canonized or beatified in the late-nineteenth or twentieth century (Ste Catherine Labouré, 1947; the Blessed François-Régis Clet, 1900; the Blessed Jean-Gabriel Perboyre, 1889; St Jean-Baptiste de La Salle, 1900; Ste Marguerite-Marie, 1920; St Pie X, 1954). To this last group should be added St Raphaël, whose cult in the West dates from this century, and Ste Philomène, whose cult was authorized in 1837.[9] Five of the low-incidence saints are religious; and one is a secular cleric and pope. The low-incidence cults are thus similar to the high-incidence ones in a number of ways: the sexes are balanced; French nationality is important; there is a relative emphasis on new saints. However, lay people predominate among the low-incidence saints unlike those of high incidence, although there is the same emphasis among the clergy on religious.

The low-incidence cults are also different in other ways. Here they can be divided into two groups. In the first group are twelve which have a special connection with the church or chapel where they occur, either because it is dedicated to them or because it contains their relics. These are the cults of St Philippe, Ste Clotilde, Ste Marie-Madeleine, St Merri, Ste Elisabeth, St Louis, Ste Cécile and St Eugène; and to these may be added Ste Monique, who has two statues, one with candles, a chapel and ex-votos in the church of Saint-Augustin, dedicated to her son. In the same category also are St Vincent de Paul, St Nicolas, St François Xavier, St Martin and St Roch, from the saints in Table 1, in one or two instances each. St Nicolas is the object of cult in both Saint-Nicolas-des-Champs and Saint-Nicolas-du-Chardonnet; St François Xavier in the church dedicated to him and in the church of Saint-Ignace. Such connections are likely *a priori* to be most important among the low-incidence cults, where there is a one-to-one relationship between church and cult. Any such connection is usually missing from the high-incidence cults, and indeed generally, for 'dedicatees' are by no means necessarily the object of cult in their churches. St Laurent, for example, has an old chapel in the church dedicated to him, but no statue, candles or ex-votos; St Leu and St Gilles have no cult in the church dedicated to them. Three saints form a second category within this first group: Ste Hélène, whose relics were presented to the church of Saint-Leu–Saint-Gilles in 1820, and where two ex-votos exist by the reliquary; Ste Catherine Labouré, whose body lies to the right of the altar of the Chapelle-de-la-Médaille-Miraculeuse, where she had her visions of the Virgin Mary in 1830; and the Blessed F. R. Clet, whose tomb lies in a special side-chapel in the Chapelle-des-Lazaristes, rue de Sèvres, with lights and ex-votos. Despite the importance of the second of these cults in particular, we find here confirmed the relative insignificance of relics in the cults of saints in Paris.

The second group of low-incidence cults comprises nine saints: St

Table 2 *Paris: Cults devoted to Christ*

Form of devotion	Statues	Candles	Ex-votos	Chapels or altars	Troncs	Position R	L
Sacred Heart	18	19	15	19+	1+	13	12
Holy Face	8 (pictures)	3	2	—	—	4	3
Crucifix (as object of cult)	4	2	—	—	—	1	3
Child Jesus (of Prague)	3	3	1	—	—	2	1

Christophe, Ste Espérance, St Expédit, St Jean-Baptiste de La Salle, Ste Marguerite-Marie, Ste Philomène, St Pie X, St Raphaël and the Blessed Jean-Gabriel Perboyre. These are mainly recently canonized or saints of doubtful authenticity; they probably represent, therefore, both new cults, possibly in the ascendant, and old ones (notably that of Ste Philomène), now in decline and official disfavour.

We may conclude that low-incidence cults include purely localized cults and both potential and declining high-incidence ones. However, the relative absence of localized cults among those of high-incidence suggests that there is little likelihood or history of localized Parisian cults becoming general within the city, and we have seen that the most generalized high-incidence cults have been imported.

Before taking the discussion further, we must now include in the cults of the 'saints' those devoted to Christ and to the Virgin Mary, in their various forms, for, although theologically distinct, they are similar in most material aspects, as Tables 2 and 3 illustrate. The predominance of the cult of the Sacred Heart is not surprising, and it is reinforced by the fact that in three cases the Holy Face is in the chapel or by the altar of the Sacred Heart (at Sainte-Clotilde, where there are two pictures of the Holy Face; at ND-de-Bonne-Nouvelle; and at Saint-Eugène–Sainte-Cécile). It should perhaps be pointed out, however, that though the importance of the cult dates from the seventeenth century, the feast was not extended to the whole Church until 1856.[10] It is thus, like many of the cults previously discussed, an essentially modern one. The same is probably true of the cult of the Child Jesus, to which we will return below. In addition to the devotions to Christ listed in Table 2, a few others are found: for example, at Saint-François-Xavier there are ex-votos by a marble statue of Christ (2nd chapel, left); and at the Chapelle-des-Lazaristes a tableau of Gethsemane has lights and is the object of a cult sponsored particularly by the Archiconfrérie de la Sainte

Table 3   *Paris: Cults of the Virgin*

Form of cult	Statues	Candles	Ex-votos	Chapels or altars	Tronc	Position R	L
'Vierge' or 'Marie' unqualified	37 +	34	20	29 +	?	7	19
ND de Lourdes	13	11	6	1 +	3	4	12
(Ste Bernadette)	(3?)	(2)	(1)	(—)	(—)	(1)	(2)
ND des Sept Douleurs	4	—	5	1	—	2	4
ND des Victoires	3	2	2	2	?	1	1
ND du Perpétuel Secours	1 (picture)	—	3	2	—	1	3
Immaculate Conception	2	2	2	?	—	1	1
ND du Sacré Coeur or Coeur de Marie	1 (picture)	1	2	1	—	1	1
ND de Pellevoisin	1	1	2	1	—	1	—
ND Consolatrice	—	—	2	—	—	1	1
Others*	8 (inc. pictures)	7	8	8	?	2	4
Total	70 + (inc. pictures)	58	52	45 +	3 +	21	46

* These are cults which occur in only one place, namely: ND de la Paix, Mater Misericordia, ND des Servites, Mater Dei Benedicta. ND de Bonne Garde, ND de Saint-Leu, ND de Lorette, ND d'Ostrobrama of Vilna, ND de Bonne Nouvelle, ND du Suffrage and ND de Carmel.

Agonie. One ex-voto to the Trinité was noted in the church of that dedication.

The cult of the Virgin is therefore more important than any single cult of the saints, but it does not outdistance the most popular of the latter to a disproportionate degree, although, as we shall see, it is more institutionalized. Of the fifteen or so sub-cults of the Virgin, that of ND de Lourdes is by far the most popular; and seven, including this one, are cults which have a general feast in the church calendar. Three of these are modern (Mater Dei, ND de Lourdes and the Coeur de Marie). Four sub-cults are related to the church in which they are found, but in all these cases but one (ND de Saint-Leu), the church is named after the cult, and not vice-versa, as seems to be the case with the localized cults of saints discussed above. In addition to ND de Lourdes and ND de Lorette, which is to some extent comparable, two other sub-cults are local cults that have been imported to Paris from rather unlikely places, Pellevoisin and Vilna, possibly by immigrants. The cults of the Virgin are similar in this respect to the high-incidence cults of the saints.

The cults in general have various material forms of expression, as Tables 1–3 indicate, and these are frequently combined, so that a particular saint may have a chapel or altar dedicated to him or her, a statue representing the saint, one or more candleholders with many, few or no candles burning, flowers on or by the statue or altar, a collection-box (*tronc*), and ex-votos to express thanks for requests granted. Again, as the Tables show, few saints enjoy all these forms of devotion at once, and some forms are more common than others. Most common is a statue with candles. Statues are usually life-size and of uncoloured stone (or simulated stone). A few are polychrome, for example, three of St Joseph, four of Ste Thérèse, five of St Antoine, and nine of ND de Lourdes. A few are made of metal or of wood; for example, there is a silver St Joseph in Saint-Vincent-de-Paul, and a gold-coloured Ste Jeanne d'Arc in Saint-Eugène–Sainte-Cécile. Statues of Ste Rita are usually small and often wooden. Fashions in statuary are visible here, and the wealthier churches have been most able and willing to keep up with the fashion, which proceeds chronologically from polychrome through uncoloured stone to pseudo-primitive (usually in wood) or reproduction medieval. Polychrome statues, therefore, are found predominantly in certain churches, and notably in Saint-Eugène–Sainte-Cécile and in ND-de-Bonne-Nouvelle, both in relatively poor *quartiers*. In the former, they are part of the splendid, if now slightly tatty, neo-Gothic interior; in the latter, they have no aesthetic *raison-d'être* in the neo-classical décor and are tokens rather of the church's neglect. The statue, rather than the dedicated altar or chapel, is most characteristic of the cult of the most popular saints, as opposed to those of the Sacred Heart and the Virgin. Ste Thérèse, for example, has five chapels or altars as against thirty-two statues; and St Antoine has four chapels or altars as against thirty-two statues. This is an indication of the popular nature and origin of these cults, we would suggest, as against the officially sponsored cults expressed in the dedication of chapels, most of which do not house active cults.

The same distinction, moreover, is manifested in other ways. Two nineteenth-century churches, for example, Sainte-Clotilde and Saint-Vincent-de-Paul, have series of stained-glass windows in the aisles representing the saints, but very few of these are saints who enjoy popular cults. Again, some cults which we have listed are very clearly officially sponsored ones which have little or no popular following, for example those of the Martyrs of September 1792 and of Ste Louise de Marillac, whose main form of expression is an official plaque. Relevant also here is the relative lack of popular interest in some privileged altars and authorized shrines. Of the ten which were noted, those of ND des Victoires, the Chapelle-de-la-Médaille-Miraculeuse, St François Xavier, Ste Geneviève (Saint-Etienne-du-Mont), and of St Vincent de Paul and the Blessed J.-G. Perboyre, both in the Chapelle-des-Lazaristes, are or have been popular, though in varying degrees as indicated by the order of listing. But four other privileged altars, those of St Joseph in ND-de-Lorette and Saint-Leu–Saint-Gilles, and of the Virgin at Saint-Thomas-d'Aquin and Saint-Augustin, are either neglected or the site of no particularly important cult.

Disparities between the number of statues of a particular saint and of chapels or altars dedicated to him or her also point to the way the cults have developed and changed over time. The cult of Ste Thérèse, for example, is comparatively recent, and thus has few altars or chapels, but that of St Joseph, though popular, is older, and thus has achieved a further degree of official institutionalization, having nineteen chapels or altars, a number nearly equalling its twenty-one statues. The same is true, of course, of the cults of the Virgin and of the Sacred Heart. The case of St Joseph, a still thriving cult, moreover, may be compared with that of Ste Geneviève. She has at least nine altars or chapels, but only three statues, which indicates a declining cult. Again, in contrast to both these, is the newest cult, that of Ste Rita, who has no chapels or altars, but eleven statues, all with candles.

Another phenomenon to note in this context is that of displacement. A new saint displaces an old one in time and becomes the real object of devotion or attention in a chapel that may still be officially dedicated to the old saint. For example, in ND-des-Victoires, statues of Ste Bernadette, Ste Jeanne d'Arc and Ste Rita are the actual objects of cult in the chapel of St Augustin; in Saint-Germain-des-Prés, St Antoine and St Benoît Labre are the objects of cult in the adjoining chapels of Ste Marguerite and St Maur; in Saint-Sulpice, Ste Thérèse is the object of cult in the chapel of St Louis; while in Saint-Eugène–Sainte-Cécile, Ste Jeanne d'Arc is the object of cult in the chapel of Ste Geneviève. Ultimately the chapel may be rededicated to the new saint; for example, at Saint-Gervais–Saint-Protais, the old chapel of Ste Philomène, formerly that of the Souls in Purgatory, is now the chapel of St Benoît Labre.[11]

Most chapels, altars or statues have candles burning in or in front of them, and this has been taken as an essential sign of an active cult. The most popular and active cults, such as those of Ste Thérèse, St Antoine and Ste Rita, are those where nearly every statue has its candles. The greatest number of saints by far have one candleholder with candles, but some have two; and in a small number of instances more than two candleholders are found. Three candleholders with candles occurred in a single location for St Expédit, Ste Geneviève, Ste Anne, Ste Rita and St Antoine; in two places for Ste Thérèse and ND de Lourdes; and in three for the Virgin (undifferentiated). Five candleholders occurred in one instance each for Ste Geneviève and for Ste Jeanne d'Arc, and in two instances for ND de Lourdes. These cases indicate a special importance and local intensity in the cult concerned, and, save for one, concern the most popular cults. They may be contrasted with those cases, discussed below, in which a saint shares a candleholder with one or more other saints. Further variations that may be significant are in the size and the shape of the candleholder and in the type of candles. Candleholders may have one, three or five tiers and may be round or oblong. In a few cases candleholders are an integral part of the statue, forming a surround to it, and in some cases candles are stuck in sand-boxes rather than in metal candleholders. While nearly all candles are long white *cierges*, a few are squat *veilleuses* in red glass containers; these are more expensive to buy and seem to be reserved for very special occasions and purposes, though their rarity, like that of sand-boxes, is also an indication of their novelty.[12]

The significance of the burning candles seems not to be in doubt: to offer and light a candle is a private act of devotion and a gift whose object is to obtain the granting of a wish or to render thanks for one that has been granted. Here there is only a divergence between the current ecclesiastical view and the implicit one of practitioners of the cult in the interpretation of what is involved. The former seeks to transpose the cult to the symbolic level, referring, for example, to the candle's burning as symbolizing the consuming of pride and egoism in the individual soul and the rekindling there of the love of God and of others. Another official notice, by the 'tronc des cierges' in the church of La Trinité, makes more concessions to the mechanism of the cult, but ignores the role of the saints in it: 'Les cierges que vous allumez symbolisent l'offrande de votre esprit à Dieu. Faites donc une prière et la cire en se consumant sera vraiment l'hommage de votre dévotion et Dieu vous exaucera!'[13] From observation of their behaviour and from the evidence of the material aspects of the cults (statues, ex-votos), it seems that practitioners are less, or less directly, engaged in acts involving God and acts of self-sacrifice, and more exclusively engaged in acts involving the saints and the gratification of wishes. The official notice refers rightly to the wish to be granted, and to the magical connection between the burning of the candle wax and the granting of the wish, but it transposes the agency invoked from the statue and the saint to an impersonal deity. Closer to the reality of the cult, we would suggest, and more characteristic of it, are those occasional statues which are made with dual collection-boxes in their bases, one for 'demandes' and the other for 'offrandes' (for example, Ste Thérèse in Sainte-Elisabeth; St Antoine in Sainte-Clotilde). It is probably fair to guess that the other collection-boxes, sometimes found in saints' chapels or by their statues, attract less those offerings that the official motto invites 'for the upkeep of the chapel', etc., than gifts of money destined to engage the patronage of the saint, or to express gratitude for its successful deployment. Indeed, examples are found where this intention is explicit; for instance, a collection-box in ND-des-Blancs-Manteaux has the motto: 'Remerciements à Ste Thérèse'.

Before pursuing this theme further via an analysis of ex-votos, we must note another characteristic offering found on or by altars and statues: flowers and plants. These are less common than candles as well as less conspicuous. Three forms of offering are found: cut flowers, pot-plants and artificial flowers. Though not exclusive to female saints, they are most frequently associated with them, and particularly with Ste Rita, Ste Thérèse and the Virgin. Flowers and plants were noted, for example, by statues of St Antoine in seven cases out of thirty-two, but by statues of Ste Rita in six cases out of eleven, and by statues of Ste Thérèse in twelve cases out of thirty-two. Offerings ranged from a single rose laid at the base of the statue of Ste Rita in La Trinité, to the five large artificial bouquets and array of cut flowers and pot-plants which surround that of ND de Lourdes in La Madeleine. Such differences obviously reflect the comparative wealth of the clientèle, and the policy of parish clergy; some churches have no flowers – for example, Saint-Thomas-d'Aquin. But this form of offering and its variations have further meanings. If the bunch of cut flowers with its short life resembles the candle that burns away, the potted plant and even more so the artificial bouquet are semi-permanent gifts, and ones which, in the former case, renew themselves. Again, like the flame of the candles, the plant symbolizes life that is offered and sacrificed to the saint;[14] and here perhaps the emphasis on female and thus maternal recipients finds its explanation.

The variety and colour of the flowers and plants can also be significant. Most obvious, in the first case, is the association of Ste Rita and Ste Thérèse with roses. In two instances, reference is made in a motto on the statue of Ste Thérèse to the promise: 'Après ma mort je ferai tomber une pluie de roses', and in a third instance (in La Trinité), the statue has a built-in surround of glass roses that can be lit electrically by inserting a 1 franc piece. In at least seven other instances, real roses are found by a statue of Ste Thérèse. The symbolism of the colour of the flowers and plants generally seems not to be too explicit or consistent, though it does correspond, to some degree, with other aspects of colour symbolism. The Virgin (and particularly ND de Lourdes, whose statue is usually blue and white) is generally given flowers and plants that are white, green, and occasionally blue, while red and yellow flowers are more common offerings to other saints, whose statues are more often of earth colours. Statues of Ste Thérèse, the Carmelite, for example, are brown and white, when they are coloured. In the general context of colour symbolism, there is a contrast here between sky and earth colours, between cold and warm colours, which has perhaps other implicit meanings, as one striking parallel example suggests – the contrast in La Madeleine between the many white candles burning in front of ND de Lourdes and the equally large number of red ones in front of Ste Marie-Madeleine herself.

Candles, flowers and plants are gifts to the saints, in return for which the saints grant, or intercede to obtain the granting of, wishes. Maintaining the reciprocal relationship, some recipients of favours express their gratitude by placing an ex-voto in the chapel or by the statue of the saint concerned, just as they do in a more ephemeral way by giving money and/or a candle. Most ex-votos are small engraved plaques of a uniform size and design, which are fixed to the walls and columns of the church or chapel, and sometimes to the altar or even to the statue of the saint. A few of the older plaques are larger. In only two cases were ex-votos of a different, more traditional, kind noted (a large number of gold-coloured hearts in Saint-Thomas-d'Aquin, and two military medals in Saint-Augustin), though such representational ex-votos are found in other modern settings in France, for example in the nineteenth-century basilica of ND-de-la-Garde in Marseille.[15] A few of the Parisian ex-votos are not permanently attached but are simply placed by statues, and at least two of them are handwritten. The erection of ex-votos, of all but the last kind, clearly involved more expense and effort than the other expressions of gratitude or devotion, and is thus less characteristic of the cults, as Tables 1–3 indicate; it also depends more closely on the good-will and co-operation of the ecclesiastical authorities. Thus it will be seen from Tables 1–3 that instances of ex-votos are well exceeded by instances of candles. Moreover, correlations between the two are by no means uniform. In the cults of Ste Anne and St Joseph, for example, instances of the two kinds of devotion are fairly evenly balanced, which they are not in the cults of St Antoine and Ste Thérèse, a phenomenon partly to be explained by the longer standing of the first two cults. There is no doubt, however, that ex-votos are an authentic popular expression. They provide, moreover, precious indications about the development, content and intensity of the cults. Many of the ex-votos are dated, and they can therefore be used to trace the history of particular cults, though here account must be taken of the fact that it takes time for ex-votos to be placed in position and then to accumulate, and they thus usually reflect the heyday of a cult, though one can sometimes see earlier and later stages. One must also be aware of the possibility that ex-votos have been removed, though this can usually be detected, for example at Saint-Thomas-d'Aquin.

Tables 1–3 indicate how many times a saint has ex-votos, but not the number of ex-votos involved in each case. These vary from one or two to the thousands that cover every available space, including under steps and inside confessionals, in ND-des-Victoires. Tables 4 and 5 list the instances

Table 4   *Paris: Accumulations of ex-votos to the Virgin*

Church or chapel	Form of cult	Number	Dates
ND-des-Victoires	ND des Victoires	1000s	1850–present
Chapelle-de-la-Médaille-Miraculeuse	Implicitly Virgin of the Miraculous Medal or Virgin undifferentiated	1000s	1900s–1960s; mainly 1940s–1960s
ND-de-Bonne-Nouvelle	ND de Bonne Nouvelle	*c.* 250	Mainly 1860s
Saint-Augustin	ND de Lourdes; ND des-Sept Douleurs; and undiff.	*c.* 250	1890s–1960s; mainly 1900s–1940s
Saint-Leu–Saint-Gilles	Mainly undiff.	*c.* 200	1860–1943; mainly later 19th century
Saint-Nicolas-du-Chardonnet	ND de Secours Perpétuel; and undiff.	*c.* 200	?
Saint-François-Xavier	ND de Lourdes; ND de Secours P.; Marie Immaculée; and undiff.	*c.* 160	1885–1950
Sainte-Clotilde	Undiff.	*c.* 150	1880–1890s; some 1920s
Saint-Germain-l'Auxerrois	ND de Bonne Garde	*c.* 150	Mainly 1900s–1930s
ND-des-Blancs-Manteaux	ND de Perpétuel S.; and undiff.	*c.* 120	1860s–1950s; mainly 1860s
Saint-Eugène–Sainte-Cécile	ND de Lourdes; ND de Secours P.; and undiff.	*c.* 100	1872–1951; mainly 1900–1920
Saint-Nicolas-des-Champs	Undiff.	*c.* 100	1878–1945; mainly 1880s–1900s
Sainte-Elisabeth	ND des Victoires; ND de Lourdes; and undiff.	*c.* 100	1890s–1900s; 1920s–1930s
Saint-Vincent-de-Paul	Undiff.	*c.* 100	1890s–1900s
ND-de-Lorette	ND de Lorette; and undiff.	*c.* 100	Many 1920s
Saint-Laurent	Undiff.	*c.* 100	1860s onwards
Saint-Etienne-de-Mont	ND de Lourdes; and undiff.	*c.* 40	1914–1945
Saint-Germain-des-Prés	Mainly undiff.	*c.* 40	Mainly 1880s
La Trinité	Undiff.	*c.* 20	Mainly 1920s
Chapelle-des-Lazaristes	ND de Lourdes	*c.* 20	1940–1952

Table 5   *Paris: Accumulations of ex-votos to saints (including the Sacred Heart)*

Saint	Church or chapel	Number	Dates
St Antoine	Saint-Augustin	*c.* 200	Late 1890s–1960s
St Antoine	Saint-Nicolas-des-Champs	*c.* 80	1900–1930
St Antoine	Saint-François-Xavier	*c.* 50	*c.* 1900–1910
St Antoine	Saint-Martin-des-Champs	*c.* 50	1899–1950
St Antoine	Saint-Eugène–Sainte Cécile	*c.* 50	1900s; and 1920s–1944
St Antoine	ND-des-Blancs-Manteaux	*c.* 50	1900–1957
Ste Anne	Saint-Sulpice	*c.* 250	1890s–1930s
Ste Anne	Saint-Augustin	*c.* 100	1898–1962; mainly 1930s–1940s
Ste Anne	ND-de-Lorette	*c.* 100	Mainly 1920s; up to 1942
Ste Thérèse de l'Enfant Jésus	Saint-Sulpice	*c.* 200	1926–1950s
Ste Thérèse de l'Enfant Jésus	Saint-Augustin	*c.* 100	1925 onwards; mainly 1930s–1940s
Ste Thérèse de l'Enfant Jésus	Saint-Martin-des-Champs	*c.* 80	1929–1941
St Joseph	Saint-Sulpice	over 200	Mainly 1880s–1900s; but up to 1950s
St Joseph	Saint-Augustin	*c.* 60	1890s–1942
Ste Geneviève	Saint-Etienne-du-Mont	*c.* 100	Up to 1918; mainly 1850s–1860s
Ste Geneviève	ND-de-Lorette	*c.* 100	Mainly 1920s; up to 1942
Ste Rita	Saint-Augustin	*c.* 150	1954–1977
Sacred Heart	Saint-Thomas-d'Aquin	*c.* 150	Later nineteenth century?
The Blessed J.-G. Perboyre	Chapelle-des-Lazaristes	*c.* 120	1880s–1900
Ste Clotilde	Sainte-Clotilde	*c.* 50	Mainly 1880s–1900s

where twenty or more ex-votos are found, in the case of the Virgin, and fifty or more in other cases, thus establishing a new measurement of the importance of cults that differs from those used previously.

It will be noted that accumulations of ex-votos to the Virgin are by far the most numerous, and that these are the largest accumulations. Instances of over one hundred ex-votos to the Virgin are found in a total of sixteen churches or chapels (40 per cent of the sample). It will also be noticed that certain churches seem to be particularly encouraging towards the accumulation of large numbers of ex-votos, most notably, as far as the saints are concerned, Saint-Augustin and Saint-Sulpice. Only a few of these accumulations can be explained by special sacred circumstances; for example, that for the Virgin in the passage to the Chapelle-de-la-Médaille-Miraculeuse by the visions of 1830; that for Ste Geneviève in Saint-Etienne-du-Mont by the presence of the saint's shrine in the church; that for the Blessed J.-G. Perboyre in the Chapelle-des-Lazaristes by the fact that he is a Lazarist martyr. General explanation must be sought therefore in the areas of clerical policy and the social complexion of a church's clientèle, though it is not possible to determine the precise weight of each related factor without further historical research. It is relevant to allude here to the small number of churches that have no ex-votos, and to point out that two of these at least, Saint-Louis-d'Antin and ND-des-Champs, seem to be mainly 'bourgeois' churches.

Table 4 illustrates the development and intensity of accumulations of ex-votos to the Virgin. It will be seen that large numbers tend to group around the 1860s, around the last two decades of the nineteenth century and the early 1900s, and around the 1920s: trends to some extent typified by the largest accumulations. That of ND-des-Victoires spans the longest period of time of all the cults, from the 1850s to the present, and, although by no means in serious decline after that period, its largest accumulations date from the second half of the nineteenth century, with an important emphasis in the 1850s and 1860s. The accumulations in ND-de-Bonne-Nouvelle and ND-des-Blancs-Manteaux also date from this first period, which was of course one of great significance in the development of devotion to the Virgin both in France and in the Church as a whole. However, more instances of large accumulations fall into the second period. In some cases this emphasis coincides with the first years of the building's history (for example, Saint-François-Xavier), and this might explain the sharp decline which often follows it. The second very large accumulation, that of the Chapelle-de-la-Médaille-Miraculeuse, has a smaller time-span than that of ND-des-Victoires, from 1900 to the present, with the highest concentration in the 1940s, 1950s and 1960s. It also seems to be less representative, for the other accumulations in this century, as we have seen, centre on the 1920s. These later accumulations should probably be associated with the cult of ND de Lourdes, although the association is not always explicit. The two largest accumulations of ex-votos explicitly addressed to ND de Lourdes are those in Saint-Eugène–Sainte-Cécile and in the Chapelle-des-Lazaristes. No ex-voto to ND de Lourdes was noted earlier than the second decade of this century, when her feast was extended to the whole Church. The other sub-cults listed in Table 4 are those found already in Table 3, and they are relatively unimportant. Here the general point should be made that the preferred form of address in ex-votos to the Virgin is the familiar 'Marie' rather than any of the more formal titles attached to the sub-cults.

After that of the Virgin, the most popular cult in terms of ex-votos is undoubtedly that of St Antoine, with six large accumulations and eleven others. If one assumes that gratitude is expressed at a constant rate for all saints, then, after the Virgin, he is the most effective saint in the granting of wishes, and the numbers of ex-votos advertise this fact to the faithful. The dates of the large accumulations indicate that the cult became important from the 1890s, and has continued to be so up to the 1960s. The dates of eight smaller accumulations (at La Trinité, Saint-Germain-l'Auxerrois, Sainte-Clotilde, Saint-Merri, Saint-Germain-des-Prés, Saint-Joseph-des-Carmes, Sainte-Elisabeth, and the Chapelle-des-Lazaristes) in general confirm this chronology, though ex-votos to St Antoine start from the 1880s in Saint-Merri, and a falling-off from 1930 or 1940, already evident in some larger accumulations, is also discernible in the smaller ones. Here the general point should be made that a decline in the number of ex-votos does not necessarily mean a decline in the cult, as it does not in the case of St Antoine. We have already referred to the puzzle which the cult of St Antoine presents – a medieval saint whose cult revived in the nineteenth century, or survived into it, though with a new image – and the history of his ex-votos adds to the puzzle, since there is no obvious reason why they should begin in the 1880s and 1890s, save that this was a period when the modern form of ex-voto became very popular generally.

For Ste Anne, the mother of the Virgin, the time-span is roughly the same as for St Antoine, though there are significant differences in detail. If one includes four smaller accumulations (at Saint-Germain-l'Auxerrois, Saint-Séverin, Saint-François-Xavier and Saint-Leu–Saint-Gilles), the earliest date is 1874 and the latest 1962; in addition to having an earlier starting date, the ex-votos to St Anne are also less evenly spread than those to St Antoine, with a greater concentration in the 1900s and 1930s, and a more marked falling-off after then. The cult of Ste Anne is older, which is also indicated by the existence of pre-nineteenth-century statues, for example the sixteenth-century alabaster one in Saint-Leu–Saint-Gilles; and the serious decline in ex-votos after the Second World War almost certainly represents a real decline in the cult, which, we have noted, has as many instances of ex-votos from the past as of statues that are now honoured with candles.

A comparatively new saint, Ste Thérèse (like Ste Rita) has had less time to attract ex-votos than the others in Table 5, and her accumulations are therefore the more indicative of the importance of her cult. In addition to the three large accumulations shown in the Table, five smaller ones exist (at

Saint-Eugène–Sainte-Cécile, ND-des-Blancs-Manteaux, Saint-Nicolas-du-Chardonnet, the Chapelle-de-l'Hôpital-Laennec and the Chapelle-des-Lazaristes). The ex-votos start in the year of her canonization, 1925; become numerous in the 1930s, remaining so through the 1940s and 1950s; and then decline, though an odd one is still found for the 1970s (for example, in ND-des-Victoires). There is some reason to think that perhaps Ste Rita has to some extent replaced Ste Thérèse here, a point to which we will return, but it should be made clear that in other respects, unlike the cult of Ste Anne, that of Ste Thérèse is widespread and flourishing. What is indicated in this case therefore most strongly perhaps, and more so than with St Antoine, is the decline of the ex-voto as such as an expression of the popular cults of saints in Paris.

The case of St Joseph in some ways parallels that of Ste Anne, though he is a more popular saint, particularly in terms of ex-votos. In addition to the large accumulations in Table 5, eleven small accumulations exist (at La Trinité, Saint-Martin-des-Champs, Saint-Vincent-de-Paul, Saint-François-Xavier, Saint-Louis-en-l'Ile, Saint-Eugène–Sainte-Cécile, ND-des-Blancs-Manteaux, Saint-Gervais–Saint Protais, Saint-Nicolas-du-Chardonnet, Saint-Merri and the Chapelle-des-Lazaristes). Ex-votos start here in the 1860s, but do not become very numerous until the 1880s, a trend shared by the large and small accumulations. Taking both together, there is an emphasis on the last decades of the nineteenth century and the first decade of this century, with a marked decline after 1930, though a few ex-votos are found in the 1950s. The cult of St Joseph, like that of Ste Anne but to a lesser extent, is represented by past ex-votos as much as by statues with candles, an indication of the long standing of the cult and of the prestige of the saint, but also of the comparative decline of both.

Such a decline is more evident in the peculiar case of Ste Geneviève. Of the two large accumulations, one dates mainly from the 1850s and 1860s and does not extend beyond 1918; while the other dates mainly from the 1920s. Two smaller accumulations exist (at Saint-Séverin and Saint-Augustin) mainly from the early 1900s. The latest ex-votos for the saint are from the mid-1940s. the time-span involved therefore is long, but the accumulations are discontinuous, and the cult goes into an absolute decline after the Second World War if not earlier. As we saw in Table 1, it is now represented overwhelmingly by chapels and ex-votos and not by statues with candles.

We have already referred to Ste Rita, whose cult shares some of the characteristics of those of both St Antoine and Ste Thérèse. Although she lived in the fourteenth century, Ste Rita's is the most recent cult to develop or to be accepted in the churches of Paris, and although she was canonized in 1900, the ex-votos dedicated to her indicate that her cult became important only in the 1950s. She has one very large accumulation, and three smaller ones (at La Trinité, Saint-Martin-des-Champs and Saint-Eugène–Sainte-Cécile). In terms of ex-votos, moreover, Ste Rita's is the most active cult today; indeed it is the only cult in which ex-votos still play an important part. The earliest dated ex-voto to her at La Trinité is from 1968, and a number of ex-votos, there and elsewhere, are dated 1977. More telling perhaps of the impetus behind this aspect of her cult, a number of ex-votos to Ste Rita in particular are not yet permanently installed but are simply placed on or by her statues, and, something found in no other case, she has two hand-written ex-votos (at La Trinité and Saint-Philippe-du-Roule). The language of some ex-votos as well as observation of participants in the cult confirm the suggestion made earlier that the cult of Ste Rita is particularly supported by immigrants from Spain and Portugal.

The two large accumulations for the Blessed J.-G. Perboyre and for Ste Clotilde are unique, and require no further discussion. Ex-votos to the Sacred Heart are also included in Table 5. The large accumulation in Saint-Thomas-d'Aquin is atypical in form, as we have noted, and cannot be certainly dated, though it seems to be late-nineteenth-century. Five smaller accumulations exist (at La Trinité, Saint-François-Xavier, Saint-Augustin, Saint-Eugène–Sainte-Cécile, and ND-des-Blancs-Manteaux). Here the earliest date is in the 1870s (date of the commencement of the Basilique-du-Sacré-Coeur) and the latest 1962, but the emphasis is on the later nineteenth century, with very few after the First World War. This confirms the view, obtained from consideration of Table 2, that this cult, though still important, has been in decline for several decades; and one may add that a number of chapels dedicated to the Sacred Heart (for example at Sainte-Clotilde, ND-de-Lorette and Saint-Leu–Saint-Gilles) are either disused or used to store old furniture.

Most of the ex-votos are simply expressions of thanks, and bear only the words 'Merci' or 'Reconnaissance', but a number do indicate the favour for which thanks are rendered. These include the traditional cures of disease (one's own or that of a relative), for example, 'pour une guérison obtenue' (to St Vincent de Paul, Chapelle-de-la-Médaille-Miraculeuse), or 'd'avoir guéri notre papa' (to Marie, same place); and the birth of children, for example, 'une naissance inespérée' (to Marie, same place). But more exclusively modern concerns also find expression. Among these may be noted: 'pour une conversion' (to Marie, same place); and, more frequent, 'succès dans un examen', found, for example, addressed to the Sacred Heart in Saint-Louis-en-l'Ile, to St Antoine in Saint-François-Xavier, to Ste Geneviève in Saint-Séverin, and to Ste Clotilde – testimony to the importance of examinations in the French educational system from the later nineteenth century and to the anxieties which they created. Finally, there are thanks for having spared the life of the donor or his or her relative in the First World War, though these are often not explicit, but must be inferred from the dates carefully specified in the ex-votos. Examples in this category are one to Ste Geneviève in La Trinité dated '1914–1919', and another to Ste Jeanne d'Arc in Saint-Eugène–Sainte-Cécile, which is dated in the same way. Also to be included in this category are the two military medals, to which we have already referred in another context, and which are found among the plaque ex-votos to the Virgin in Saint-Augustin. Although such specific ex-votos are few in number, it is reasonable to guess that they do not give a misleading picture of the wishes of most participants in the cults.

The ex-votos do not, in general, indicate any special connection between particular saints and particular kinds of request or protection, for example, in connection with particular diseases, such as one finds in 'traditional' societies,[16] although there does seem to be one exception, linked significantly to the modern cult of patriotism. Ste Jeanne d'Arc and Ste Geneviève are thanked more often than others for sparing lives in the First World War, and plaques in at least two churches (Sainte-Elisabeth and Saint-Louis-en-l'Ile) refer to the protection of the Sacred Heart to explain why they were not bombed in 1918. The general absence of specialities could be simply a reflection of the fact that the ex-votos are, on the whole, uninformative; but it seems likely that it also reflects the generalized nature of the modern cults and their distance from 'traditional' ones, indicative of wider changes in mentality, including perhaps increasing theological sophistication. It is thus of wider significance that, as we have seen, Ste Marguerite, whose statue dates from 1705, has been displaced from her chapel in Saint-Germain-des-Prés by St Antoine and St Benoît Labre. She was invoked in the past by women in labour, and, as Boinet notes, Saint-Germain was the centre of an important local cult into the eighteenth century.[17]

The material aspect of the cults can be considered from another point of view, that of the position in the church or chapel of the statue or altar of the saint. It is noted in Tables 1–3 whether these are found on the right or the left of the building, and it can be seen that the popular saints in Table 1 are found more often on the right than on the left; in the case of St Antoine and Ste Thérèse, this preference is very marked. Where a preference for the right is not evident, placings are generally equally balanced between left and right, for example, in the case of Ste Jeanne d'Arc and that of Ste Rita. This same balance is found among the saints whose cult is found in only one church, nine of these being on the right and eight on the left. There is no saint whose cult is markedly left-oriented. Moreover, there seems to be no distinction on other grounds between right-oriented saints and those oriented in both directions. St Antoine and Ste Thérèse, an old and a new cult, are strongly right-oriented; while St Joseph and Ste Rita, also an old and a new cult, are balanced between right and left. It seems, however, that for the most popular female saints a stronger bias to the right exists than for

Table 6 *Paris: the position of cults along the east—west continuum**

Cult	West	Middle	East	Pattern		
				W	M	E
Virgin Mary (undiff.)	12	17	24	1	2	3
ND de Lourdes	2	9	6	1	3	2
Sacred Heart	1	14	11	1	3	2
Ste Thérèse	9	6	14	2	1	3
St Antoine	6	12	10	1	3	2
St Joseph	4	14	9	1	3	2
Ste Jeanne d'Arc	2	7	11	1	2	3
Ste Rita	3	6	3	1	2	1
Ste Anne	2	5	5	1	2	2
St Vincent de Paul	1	3	4	1	2	3
Curé d'Ars	0	3	3		1	1
St Michel	0	1	4		1	2
Ste Geneviève	1	3	7	1	2	3

* For the purpose of this table, all churches have been supposed to point east, though some, of course, do not.

the most popular male saints. Of the former, the placings for Ste Thérèse, Ste Anne and Ste Geneviève are strongly biased to the right, while those of Ste Jeanne d'Arc and Ste Rita are balanced. Of the latter, only the cult of St Antoine has a strong bias to the right. This pattern continues for the position of the various cults devoted to Christ and particularly for that of the Sacred Heart (see Table 2). This association of the right with the female rather than the male is something of a surprise,[18] but the pattern of Table 3 helps to explain the anomaly. Cults of the Virgin, if they are not centrally situated in 'chapelles de la Vierge' behind the main altar, are found preponderantly on the left of churches, thus complementing the cults of the saints, male and female together, which are mainly on the right; and female saints, in particular, are kept off the Virgin's territory. Why this should be on the left is a question that we are not in a position to answer, though it deserves an answer.

Remembering that a certain element of chance may enter into such things and allowing for the exigencies of existing and often ancient church architecture, let us now consider the position of the cults of the saints along the east—west continuum. Information about the most important cults in this respect is given in Table 6.

First, it is clear that the west end of the church is the least favoured position, presumably because it is furthest from the sacred east where the mass is usually performed. On this basis one would expect that the east end would be the most favoured, and that the most popular and active cults would occupy this most sacred space. This is true for the cult of the Virgin, but not for the other popular cults. If one represents schematically the frequency with which each cult is found in each of the three spaces (west, middle and east) and places them in order (see the last column of Table 6), the cults of St Antoine, St Joseph, the Sacred Heart and ND de Lourdes have the pattern 1, 3, 2; while those of Ste Rita and Ste Anne have 1, 2, 1 and 1, 2, 2 respectively. This phenomenon must be explained in part, of course, by the fact that the most sacred space cannot be occupied by all the cults at once, although the system of radiating chapels off ambulatories would go a long way towards satisfying such a demand. Here, it should be noted that many such chapels are not used for the popular cults, and are sometimes not in use at all. The custom of having saints' chapels in the aisles of churches is also very well established. There must therefore be other reasons for the preponderance of the popular cults in the middle ground of the churches.

It might also be supposed that cults would progress from west to east as they gained support and that the older cults would thus be more likely to have the 1, 2, 3 pattern than the newer ones. There is some evidence that this is so; the older cults of Ste Geneviève and St Vincent de Paul do fall into the 1, 2, 3 pattern, while none of the newer cults do, except that of Ste Jeanne d'Arc; but the older cults of St Joseph and St Antoine do not fall into the 1, 2, 3 pattern. We suggest that there is a significant distinction to be made between authentically popular cults and those which are officially sponsored, though the distinction cannot be sharply drawn. The authentically popular cult may enter by the door quite literally (the most popular saints, Ste Thérèse, St Antoine and Ste Rita are found with some frequency at the west end and statues of Ste Rita are found in four cases by an entrance door); it may then progress into the body of the church, where it tends to remain in the middle area, the people's space, rather than move into the clergy's eastward space.[19]

As already noted, the most popular cults are, on the whole, cults of statues and not of officially consecrated altars and chapels. Cults which do progress, or are taken at once, into the east end tend to be those which are taken up officially by the clergy, though not always via the consecration of a chapel. It is significant that Ste Jeanne d'Arc is the only new saint with the 1, 2, 3 pattern, for she is an official saint, the patron of France. Ste Thérèse, though a peculiar case, would fit into this interpretation. As a popular saint, her cult is quite often situated in the west of the church, though it is more often situated in the east, and rarely in the middle. This suggests a cult that is still authentically popular, as we have put it, but which has forced its way into the space of the clergy, receiving, of course, official sanction in the same way as Ste Jeanne d'Arc, as national patron saint.

So far the cults have been generally discussed as if each one were separate from the other, but, as the problems of position make clear, the cults are related to each other spatially and in other ways. For example, in the first chapel on the left in the church of ND-des-Champs, there are three statues, a Pietà flanked by Ste Thérèse and St Antoine, with three separate and one common candleholder in front of them; in addition, there is a single collection-box with the motto: 'Offrandes pour la Sainte Vierge, St Antoine, Ste Thérèse et les âmes du Purgatoire'. Similarly, at the west end of the church of Sainte-Elisabeth, there is a grouping of a statue of ND de la Paix with plaques commemorating the Dead in the First World War, statues of Ste Thérèse and St Antoine on either side of the aisle, with collection-boxes in their bases, ex-votos on the walls to the Virgin and the two saints, two candleholders, and three further collection-boxes for ND de la Paix, 'les âmes en Purgatoire' and Ste Rita. In addition to such large clusters, instances of which could be multiplied, pairings are also common. What significance, if any, do these arrangements have?

If we take the examples of three popular saints, we find the following spatial associations. Ste Thérèse is associated three times with St Antoine, with Ste Jeanne d'Arc, and with the Virgin (in two of these cases with ND de Lourdes); and she is associated in a single instance each with St Joseph, St Louis, Ste Geneviève, St Michel, the Curé d'Ars and the Holy Face. In addition to his link with Ste Thérèse, St Antoine is associated in a single instance each with St Benoît Labre, St Joseph, Ste Rita, Ste Cécile, the Virgin, the Sacred Heart, St Vincent de Paul and the Curé d'Ars. Ste Jeanne d'Arc is associated three times with Ste Thérèse, as we have seen, twice with ND de Lourdes, and in a single instance each with Ste Clotilde, St Louis, Ste Geneviève and St Michel. The explanation for such varied associations seems to be simply that saints can be associated in a large number of ways. There is a rich network of associations that is fully used and few or no incompatibilities. Ste Thérèse and Ste Jeanne, for example, as we have seen, are co-patrons of France, and are of the same sex; Ste Thérèse and St Antoine are not only the most popular saints, but fellow religious, complementing each other by sex. This complementarity is explicitly represented in Saint-Philippe-du-Roule, where the two saints are found on the left and the right of the entrance to the chapelle de la Vierge. Ste Jeanne d'Arc is similarly paired with two male warrior saints, St Michel (in Sainte-Elisabeth), by complementarity, and St Louis (in ND-des-Blancs-Manteaux), by proximity. Saints of the same vintage may also be associated, for example, the Curé d'Ars and Ste Thérèse, both canonized in 1925; or the association may be via a cult especially linked with the saint:

for example, in Saint-Joseph-des-Carmes there is a stained-glass image of the Holy Face in the chapel of Ste Thérèse;[20] while in Saint-Augustin, a statue of Ste Bernadette is found beside those of Ste Anne and ND des Lourdes;[21] and one of Ste Marguerite-Marie beside those of ND de Pellevoisin and the Sacred Heart.[22]

From the point of view of participants in the cults, one can see a dual rationale in such flexible associations. They leave a great deal of room for local and even personal variations and choices, which are the mark of paraliturgical cults in contrast to the uniformity of the liturgy proper. Moreover, they allow participants to seek combined and strengthened patronage, and this consideration, in particular, would seem to explain the combination of cults of saints with that of the Virgin, the ultimate interceder, as well as of cults of other saints with those of the patron saints of the church in which the cult is situated (for example, Ste Jeanne d'Arc with Ste Clotilde, or Ste Thérèse with St Louis).

Such combined devotions are also expressed in the placing and sometimes the wording of ex-votos. For example, in the first chapel on the left in Sainte-Elisabeth, there are ex-votos to 'Marie', St Joseph, Ste Elisabeth, ND de Lourdes, ND des Victoires, 'Marie et St Antoine' and 'Jésus et Marie'; and in the chapelle de la Vierge in Saint-Vincent-de-Paul, there are ex-votos to 'Marie', St Anne, St Joseph, Ste Thérèse, the Sacred Heart and the 'Sainte Famille'; and many other similar clusters could be cited. Particularly evident in these ex-votos is the family link that is made, often explicitly, between the Virgin, St Joseph and Christ (and also Ste Anne). This relationship can be stressed in other ways. For example, in ND-des-Victoires, where many ex-votos link Marie and Joseph, the chapels on the right side of the church are dedicated, in order, to St Joseph, the Sacred Heart, St Anne and ND des Victoires herself (right transept). This theme of the Holy Family is, of course, an old one, and earlier iconographical expression of the Holy Family as another Trinity is found from the seventeenth century in the churches of Paris.[23] Most significant here perhaps are its perenniality and relative lack of development, which raise questions about attitudes towards the family over the centuries, both generally and on the part of the Church.

A recent wooden sculpture of the Holy Family is the object of a cult in Saint-Louis-d'Antin, and this represents the only explicit up-dating of the theme which we encountered. However, the related theme of childhood, and particularly the childhood of Christ, is very well represented in the cults. Not only are there, as we have noted in Table 2, a few instances of cults specifically devoted to the Child Jesus, and the odd *tronc* or chapel dedicated to 'la Sainte Enfance', but three of the popular cults of saints, those of Ste Thérèse, St Antoine and St Vincent de Paul, are associated with the Child Jesus or with children. The two latter saints are often represented carrying a child; and to them should be added St Jean-Baptiste de La Salle, the founder of the Frères des Ecoles Chrétiennes. The Virgin is most often represented, too, with the Child Jesus; but it is significant that the most characteristic modern cults of the Virgin, those of ND de Lourdes and of ND de la Médaille Miraculeuse, represent her as a young girl and alone. It seems fair to conclude that the resistance of the Church to family-oriented religion, noted for earlier centuries,[24] though much weakened, has not disappeared; and that the childhood of which the 'Sainte Enfance' is a paradigm is less that of the modern child-oriented family and more that of the catechism, the First Communion and the school. But it is hard to determine whether the popular cults themselves reflect such attitudes, or different ones over which the latter are superimposed.

Before presenting any general conclusions, we must briefly discuss one further cult – that devoted to the Dead. The main modern manifestation of this is in the plaques commemorating those killed in the First World War, which are found in twenty-one churches. Compared with victims of the First World War, those of other wars receive little attention, which probably rightly reflects the numbers concerned. In Saint-Joseph-des-Carmes, there are plaques to pupils of the Ecole Préparatoire des Carmes killed in the Franco-Prussian War, and additions have usually been made to the First World War plaques to accommodate the names of victims of the Second; but the special chapel in Saint-Roch for the victims, military and civilian, of the Second World War, with special emphasis on those who died in concentration camps, is unusual. In six cases the First World War plaques have candleholders by them, and in two cases cut flowers. They are most often found at the west end of churches, and are associated with saints and the Virgin in fifteen cases (the Virgin six; Ste Thérèse three; Ste Jeanne d'Arc two). The absence of St Michel, traditionally associated with the Dead and with war,[25] is perhaps surprising. However, older cults of the Dead are present in the churches of Paris: nine have 'chapelles des âmes en Purgatoire',[26] and two (Saint-Germain-l'Auxerrois and Saint-Séverin) have 'chapelles de la Bonne Mort'. Collection-boxes 'pour les âmes en Purgatoire' exist in a further six cases; and three churches contain old pictures of saints interceding for souls in Purgatory, though only two of these are in chapels which still have the corresponding dedication.[27] In addition, another three churches have collection-boxes for masses for the dead, without any explicit association with Purgatory; and one ex-voto to 'les âmes en Purgatoire' was noted (in Saint-Augustin). While neither very active nor widespread, the traditional cult of souls in Purgatory does manifest in various ways a notable persistence into the modern period. The cult of the Dead in the First World War has sometimes been associated with it, lending it new life; in six cases (Saint-Roch, ND-de-Bonne-Nouvelle, Sainte-Elisabeth, Saint-Nicolas-des-Champs, Saint-Louis-en-l'Ile and Sainte-

Eugène–Sainte-Cécile), the plaque commemorating the Dead in the war is placed either in the old 'chapelle des morts' or 'chapelle des âmes en Purgatoire', or has a collection-box for the souls in Purgatory by it.[28] But, in a further six cases (Saint-Thomas-d'Aquin, Saint-François-Xavier, Saint-Augustin, Saint-Etienne-du-Mont, Saint-Sulpice and Saint-Nicolas-du-Chardonnet), the plaques to the Dead in the First World War and a chapel or collection-box for the souls in Purgatory co-exist in the same church, but in different locations. In these cases it seems that the older cult has, or had, more vitality of its own and thus continued a separate existence. The chapel in Saint-Sulpice has a nineteenth-century altar; that in Saint-Nicolas-du-Chardonnet has, together with the old painting already referred to, a framed list of members of the Association pour le soulagement des Ames en Purgatoire, that seems to date from the late nineteenth century; and we have referred to the 'indulgence plénière' for the profit of souls in Purgatory attached to Saint-François-Xavier in 1897; the old chapel in Saint-Etienne-du-Mont, moreover, still has a candleholder.

A number of general conclusions may be drawn from our study, some of which are more tentative than others. First, one remains struck by the large number of cults and the complexity of their inter-relationships. One can see here a variety of incarnations of the divine, which allows complementary or even contradictory aspects to be worshipped or invoked successively or at once, as in the Hindu or Greek pantheons. The clearest example of this is that of the different cults of the Virgin and particularly the co-existence of cults of Mary the mother and Mary the girl. This complexity can also be related to perhaps the essential function of the cults, their invocation of supernatural patronage, which can thereby be reinforced. However, secondly, despite the wide variety of networks of associations, certain structural lines are evident. Though they follow the same general pattern, the cults each have their individuality, even if this is not always explicit. They also fall into groups according to different criteria. Of particular interest here is the grouping of saints' cults into pairs, not only spatially but thematically: so Ste Thérèse and St Antoine go together, Ste Jeanne d'Arc and St Michel, St Vincent de Paul and Ste Louise de Marillac.

Thirdly, the cults are authentically popular in two senses. They are cults of the laity, though obviously accepted by the clergy and doubtless also promoted by some of them. The cults' main expression is via statues and candles, and to a lesser extent ex-votos, and not via altars and chapels that have been officially dedicated; they are thus only partly institutionalized, only partly or provisionally incorporated into the architecture of churches; here it is significant that they tend to occupy the middle ground of churches, and to avoid the space that is, or was, more specially reserved for the clergy. Also very important in this context is the fact that the cult of the saints is essentially one of individual, private and spontaneous acts of devotion, albeit within a set framework of recommended prayers, stereotyped statues and so on. It is therefore, in a sense, contra-rather than merely para-liturgical. Characteristic here also is the fact that although many, if not most, statues are unnamed, they are at once recognizable to the faithful,[29] which again emphasizes the grounding of the cults in popular as much as, if not rather than, clerical culture. This brings us to the second sense of popular. No analysis of the social complexion of participants in the cults is here possible, but it is noteworthy that the cults are found in churches and chapels in every *quartier* of central Paris. Moreover, there are some indications that the cults are and have been supported with particular intensity in the less fashionable *quartiers*.

Fourthly, attention should be drawn to the role of the religious orders in the maintenance and propagation of the cults. In a few instances, this is clearly a predominant factor, particularly in the case of cults situated in chapels of religious orders, though the paucity of cults in Saint-Ignace and the Chapelle-des-Missions-Etrangères should not be forgotten. Of even more significance is the fact that so many of the popular cults are devoted to saints who were religious; this suggests another possible divergence between the cults and the clergy of the parishes. Fifthly, and related to this, in so far as the saints of the cults are exemplars of particular virtues, which they are only indirectly, they exemplify the virtues of the religious: humility, voluntary poverty, charity, obedience, chastity, and not the more heroic and 'worldly' virtues. The cults could therefore be said to reflect a marginal attitude to the social world that is more generally characteristic of the modern Church and its adherents, and which is perhaps in contrast with the attitudes of earlier centuries.

Finally, we should stress once more the importance of the cults of the saints in modern urban Catholicism. The modern cults differ from the traditional and historical ones in a number of ways; often different saints are invoked; the urban cult is private and individualistic compared with the rural traditional one with its communal feasts and confraternities; specialisms are less obvious; relics have become relatively unimportant; but the same underlying mechanism of seeking help and protection through the saints as patrons and intermediaries, if not directly, is always present. And it is clear that the cults fulfil an important function in a modern city, as they do in less developed rural areas in Europe, and as they did more generally in the past.

NOTES

1 See, for example, for France in particular, Arnold van Gennep, *Culte populaire des saints en Savoie* (Paris, 1973), a collection of older articles; and Hertz, Ch. 1 above; Anatole Le Braz, *Les Saints Bretons d'après la tradition populaire en*

Cornouaille (Paris, 1937); Roger Lecotté, *Recherches sur les cultes populaires dans l'actuel diocèse de Meaux (Département de Seine-et-Marne)*, *Mémoires de la Fédération Folklorique de l'Ile-de-France*, IV (Paris, 1953); and the bibliography and comments by Claude Langlois in J. Bauberot *et al.*, *L'Histoire Religieuse de la France, 19ᵉ–20ᵉ siècle, problèmes et méthodes* (Paris, 1975, pp. 65–9). Mention should also be made of the work of Emile Mâle; and of Pierre Delooz in Ch. 6 above.

2 The latter point is made by Marcelle Bouteiller, Françoise Loux, and Martine Segalen, *Croyances et coutumes*, Musée National des Arts et Traditions Populaires, Guides ethnologiques, 12 (Paris, 1973), p. 5.

3 An invaluable aid in any study of Parisian churches is Amédée Boinet, *Les Eglises parisiennes* (Paris, 1958–64), 3 vols. Also useful was Marquis de Rochegude et Maurice Dumolin, *Guide pratique à travers le vieux Paris* (Paris, 1923). Most of the churches and chapels which were not visited were closed on more than one occasion (including one in September). The Parisian churches are not excluded from the annual August shut-down. In subsequent references, the conventional abbreviation ND will be used for Notre-Dame, and saints are given their local French names.

4 The following reference books were used here and elsewhere; William E. Addis and Thomas Arnold, *A Catholic Dictionary* (London, 1960); John T. Delaney and James Edward Tobin, *Dictionary of Catholic Biography* (London, 1962); and Donald Attwater, *The Penguin Dictionary of Saints* (Harmondsworth, 1965).

5 Ste Thérèse was declared co-patron of France in 1944.

6 See here Claude Savart, ' A la Recherche de l' "art" dit de Saint-Sulpice', *Revue de l'Histoire de la Spiritualité*, 52 (1976), pp. 265–82, which was not seen, however, until after this article was written. In addition to considering the phenomenon of Saint-Sulpice art generally, Savart studied eighteen churches in the rural Haute-Marne, where he found that the most popular saints were St Joseph, St Antoine, Ste Thérèse de Lisieux, and Ste Jeanne d'Arc.

7 This makes an important contrast, of course, with cults of saints in the past in Europe, and particularly in the Middle Ages; see, for example, Achille Luchaire, *Social France at the Time of Philip Augustus* (1909) (New York, 1967), pp. 28–36; J. Huizinga, *The Waning of the Middle Ages* (1924) (Harmondsworth, 1955), pp. 166–78 and *passim*; J. A. MacCulloch, *Mediaeval Faith and Fable* (London, 1932), Ch. IX; Nicole Herrmann-Mascard, *Les Reliques des Saints: Formation contumière d'un droit* (Paris, 1975); Pierre Riche, 'Translations de reliques à l'époque carolingienne: Histoire des reliques de Saint Malo', *Moyen Age*, 82 (1976), pp. 201–18; and Ronald C. Finucane, *Miracles and Pilgrims, Popular Beliefs in Medieval England* (London, 1977).

8 The most popular saints in the diocese of Meaux, according to Lecotté (*Recherches*, pp. 212–28), were St Fiacre, Ste Geneviève, St Jean, St Loup, St Martin, St Roch, St Sebastien and St Vincent, only three of whom figure in our Table 1. However, as we have seen, Savart's findings from another rural area are very different, which suggests that Lecotté may have been looking for specifically 'folkloric' cults and may have ignored more modern ones.

9 The cult of Ste Philomène was particularly sponsored in France by the Curé

d'Ars; see Alfred Monnin, *Life of the Blessed Curé d'Ars* (London, no date), pp. 180–3 and *passim*; and Francis Trochu, *La 'petite Sainte' du Curé d'Ars, Sainte Philomène, Vierge et Martyre* (Lyon and Paris, 1929). An 'archiconfrérie' devoted to the saint was founded in the church of Saint-Gervais – Saint-Protais in 1836. She was removed from the Calendar of Saints in 1961 since 'she has been revered because of popular fervour rather than liturgical fact', in the obscure words of Delaney and Tobin. The cult of St Expédit is also essentially a nineteenth-century one; see Dom Théophile Bérengier, 'Un nouveau thaumaturge, Saint Expédit, martyr en Arménie et patron des causes urgentes', *Les Missions Catholiques*, XXVIII (Jan. 1896), pp. 128–31.

10 The cult of Ste Marguerite-Marie is also, of course, associated with that of the Sacred Heart; see n. 22 below. The first chapel dedicated to the Sacred Heart in Paris was that in Saint-Sulpice in 1748.

11 On this saint, see J. Gadille, 'Autour de Saint Benoît-Joseph Labre: Hagiographie et critique au XIXᵉ siècle', *Revue d'Histoire de l'Eglise de France*, 52 (1966) pp. 113–26.

12 Of the nine instances of the use of red lights noted, three are for the Virgin (including ND de Lourdes), and one each for St Antoine, Ste Thérèse, St Joseph, Ste Rita, Ste Marie-Madeleine, St Philippe, and St Raphaël. Red lights are found mostly in a few churches only and notably La Madeleine and Saint-Eugène–Sainte-Cécile, where they probably reflect local clerical policy. The related novelties of red lights and sand-boxes are probably in general inspired as much by clerical concern for tidiness and the reduction of fire risk as by any popular devotional preference.

13 The same tendency to play down the significance of the invocation and intercession of the saints, in themselves, is found in the two Catholic dictionaries cited in n. 4.

14 For a general discussion of the mechanisms of sacrifice, see Henri Hubert and Marcel Mauss, *Sacrifice: Its Nature and Function* (1898) (London, 1964).

15 The practice was traditional and was transferred to the new basilica, built in 1864, from an older chapel on the site; see, for example, Thomas Forester, *Rambles in the Islands of Corsica and Sardinia with Notices of their History, Antiquities and Present Condition* (London, 1858), p. 13, who refers to 'the chapel of *Notre-Dame-de-la-Garde*, held in great reverence, and much resorted to, by mariners and fishermen; the walls and roof being hung with votive offerings, commemorating deliverances from shipwreck and other ills'. On traditional ex-votos elsewhere in provincial France, see, for example, *Le Monde Alpin et Rhodanien* (1977), articles by Bernard Cousin and Christian Loubet, with illustrations; and ex-votos from Sainte-Anne-d'Auray (Morbihan) in *L'Homme et son corps dans la société traditionelle*, Exhibition, Musée National des Arts et Traditions Populaires (Paris, 1978), Items 409–23.

16 See, for example, Pedro Ciruelo, *A Treatise Reproving All Superstitions and Forms of Witchcraft* (1530) (Rutherford, Madison, Teaneck and London, 1977), p. 255; MacCulloch, *Mediaeval Faith*, Ch. VIII; Lecotté, *Recherches*, esp. pp. 254–77; and M. Leproux, *Dévotions et saints guérisseurs* (Paris, 1957).

17 Boinet, *Les Eglises parisiennes*, I, pp. 54–5.

18 In this context, see Robert Hertz, 'La Prééminence de la main droite, Etude sur

la polarité religieuse' (1909), in Hertz, *Sociologie religieuse*, pp. 84–109; and R. Needham (ed.), *Right and Left: Essays on Dual Symbolic Classification* (Chicago, 1973).

19 This schema has been altered in theory by the recent repositioning of main altars, but in practice this change seems yet to have had little effect.

20 For Ste Thérèse's sponsorship of the cult of the Holy Face, see, for example, 'Prayers of Saint Thérèse', in Thomas N. Taylor, *Saint Thérèse of Lisieux, The Little Flower of Jesus* (London, 1944), pp. 450–2.

21 A perusal of the monumental work by René Laurentin and Bernard Billet, *Lourdes, Dossier des documents authentiques* (Paris, 1957–64), 7 vols., reveals no special connection of Ste Anne with the Lourdes cult, though there may be one. On the general development of the Lourdes cult in France, see R. P. Lecanuet, *La Vie de l'Eglise sous Léon XIII* (Paris, 1930), pp. 140–7.

22 See, for example, Mgr Demimuid, *Saint Margaret Mary (1647–1690)* (London, 1927). The cult of ND de Pellevoisin derives from a series of visions experienced by Estelle Faguette, servant in the Rochefoucauld household at Pellevoisin (Indre) in 1876; see John Beevers, *The Sun her Mantle* (Dublin, 1953), pp. 129–40 (where, however, Pellevoisin seems to be wrongly located near Châlons-sur-Marne). I am grateful for this reference, and for other helpful comments, to an anonymous reader.

23 See particularly four pictures illustrating this theme in the Chapelle-de-l'Hôpital-Laennec, ND-des-Blancs-Manteaux, Saint-Louis-en-l'Ile and Saint-Médard (not one of the churches visited). Boinet, *Les Eglises parisiennes*, II, p. 203; and III, pp. 217–18.

24 See John Bossy, 'The Counter-Reformation and the People of Catholic Europe', *Past and Present*, 47 (1970), pp. 51–70.

25 For examples of the former, see Geoffrey Rowell, *The Liturgy of Christian Burial, An Introductory Survey of the Historical Development of Christian Burial Rites* (London, 1977), pp. 45 and 62.

26 This includes the church of Saint-François-Xavier, which does not have a chapel, but to which the Pope granted in 1897 an 'indulgence plénière applicable aux âmes en Purgatoire' for attendance at certain offices, as a plaque records.

27 These are a picture by Sebastiano Ricci (1662–1734) of St Grégoire and St Vital interceding for the souls in Purgatory in Saint-Gervais–Saint-Protais; a reduced copy of the same picture in Saint-Nicolas-des-Champs; and a seventeenth-century picture of St Ignace and St François Xavier interceding in Saint-Nicolas-du-Chardonnet; see Boinet, *Les Eglises parisiennes*, I, pp. 334 and 385–6; and III, p. 60. As we have noted, the 'chapelle des âmes en Purgatoire' in Saint-Gervais–Saint-Protais was rededicated in the nineteenth century to Ste Philomène, and later to St Benoît Labre.

28 For the same phenomenon in Provence, see Gaby and Michel Vovelle, *Vision de la mort et de l'au-delà en Provence d'après les autels des âmes du purgatoire, XVe–XXe siècles* (Paris, 1970), pp. 56–7. This work has also been of general guidance in our study.

29 But not always to the ethnographer; and doubtless some errors of attribution have entered into our analysis as a result.

9

The Portuguese 'romarias'

PIERRE SANCHIS

I INTRODUCTION

Although some Portuguese *romarias* are urban, most are rural. Either they are centred on a hermitage, or they constitute, if not the patronal festival, then at least one of the main festivals of a village. Of those which take place in towns, or council or district capitals, there are very few which do not betray their para- or peri-urban origins by their location outside or on the outskirts of the agglomeration.

At all events, their essential feature is that they are organized around the 'memory' of a 'saint', who is represented by relics or by an image. A *romaria* is a popular pilgrimage to a place made sacred by the special presence of such a 'saint'. Sometimes other activities, organized by the local or regional authorities, have been added to the religious core. Some important *romarias* have thus become 'council holidays'.[1] By their size and nature, these events cannot be fitted into the traditional model, although the core of the latter survives, albeit almost entirely obscured by official excrescences, as for example in the case of the festival of St John at Braga. Our description will ignore these supplementary elements and concentrate on the 'elementary forms' of the *romaria*. Some of the festivals which we shall be discussing, moreover, are called *romarias* only by extension of the term. The *Rainha Santa* [the festival of the Holy Queen Isabel, S.W.] at Tinalhas, for example, is a village festival; but there are other festivals at Tinalhas in the course of the year which are simpler, less frequented by non-villagers and totally intra-mural. For the *Rainha Santa*, however, the whole population leaves the village to go to the chapel of the shrine, crowds come from round about, and the whole pattern of the event generally fits the classic model of the *romaria*.

So, we have two main types of *romaria*: one which directly concerns a single village, but which other people may attend as guests of the village community, which thus plays host to its neighbours; and another which serves as an epicentre for a wider region. The latter also takes place on the

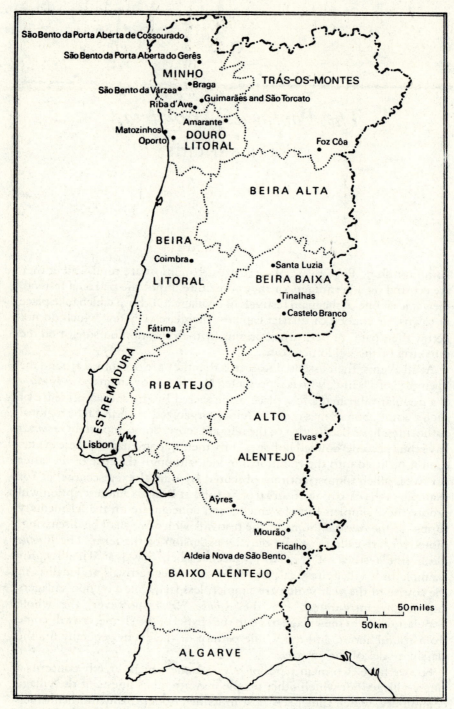

Map 2 Portugal: *romarias*, towns and festivals most frequently mentioned

territory of one parish, but all the inhabitants of the region regard themselves as equally at home at it. The regional *romaria* is everyone's festival, and all the participants consider the patron saint to which it is dedicated as 'their' saint. These are types, of course, and any number of intermediate forms are possible.

The essential point is that every *romaria* is a gathering, an encounter, a time of life in common, comprising either recurrent exchanges of visits, or a 'multiconvergence' expressive of regional unity or even, all along the frontier from north to south, a setting-aside of political barriers[2] and a fleeting manifestation of fraternization. At all levels, these 'reunions' are an opportunity for all kinds of exchange: cultural, commercial and agonistic.

II THE SAINT

Leaving aside certain interesting exceptions, *romarias* are centred on country shrines, usually situated on the outskirts of villages, but sometimes several kilometres away from one or even in a completely isolated site. It is only very rarely that the shrines are still to be found in their primitive form. An example exists, however, in the modest hermitage of Nossa Senhora das Pazes at Ficalho, which retains its sixteenth-century appearance[3] with its white 'Alentejano Gothic', a plain Gothic style with horizontal lines and rounded arches, still close to its Romanesque origins and which, here at least, softens angles and straight lines under successive layers of whitewash, as does the local secular architecture. Usually, however, the shrines are built in a variety of the Baroque style, blended occasionally with the neo-Classical when they have been enlarged or rebuilt in the seventeenth, eighteenth or even nineteenth centuries. But there are also other forms, including the Romano-Byzantine São Torcato, and such modern examples as the unpretentious – and unattractive – *Rainha Santa* chapel at Tinalhas, built when a new festival was deliberately instituted there fifty years ago, eclipsing those attached to older and more beautiful buildings; or the great 'modern' church of São Bento da Várzea, the third of the same name to be built on the site in the space of a few centuries. Tradition is not fixed here either; it is a living thing in a state of continual renewal and with no attachment to any particular form.

Sometimes natural elements take on a characteristic religious significance. These included water, in the form of sacred bathing-places,[4] or miraculous springs,[5] trees or plants (*medronheiro* and *alfâdega* at São Bento da Porta Aberta, *cizirão* and rosemary at Aldeia Nova de São Bento, leeks and basil at the festival of St John at Braga,[6] and also the holm oak at Fátima),[7] and rocks.[8] But, today at least, the depositary and historical[9] representative of the sacred is the 'saint' associated always with the main object of devotion. Whether this is an image of Christ, or of the Virgin, or the image or remains of a canonized person, the term 'saint' is always used in connection with it, often in an affectionate diminutive form: the 'little saint' or 'our little saint'; and it is often referred to with real tenderness: 'our little St Benedict!...Ah! Jesus!'

The saint's presence, whether in the form of relics or 'effigy', symbolizes the community, encapsulating its history and acting as the focus of its energies. If it is a guardian presence and a permanent guarantee of continuity, life and abundance at all times, it is because, like a deified ancestor, it allows the group to be conscious of its own being, intensifies its self-awareness, creates a sense of being socially 'rooted', and provides a sure identity. For the community, to lose its 'saint' would mean the abandonment of this identity and would present it with the prospect of being reduced to anonymity and merged into that wider social whole which already to a large extent dominates it.

When King Manuel I (1495–1521) tried to remove relics from the villages, allegedly in the interests of religious decorum, and to collect them together in the bigger urban agglomerations, the Chapter of Guimarães, together with the municipal council, the leading citizens and the people of the town, set out for São Torcato 'with much dancing, festivity and music'. But their way was barred by a wall of people from the parish and from neighbouring villages who would not let them come near the church, shouting: 'We would rather die than let the saint leave our hands.'[10] In 1637, the same thing happened on the occasion of a false alarm,[11] which only underlines the suspicion which rural communities had of townspeople and of the central or episcopal authorities. Similarly, at Foz Côa, people living in a hamlet on whose territory the chapel of Nossa Senhora da Veiga was situated were ready to use force against the priest one morning, when he attempted to take the venerated statue away with him to the town. He had taken the precaution of making this attempt before dawn, but men and women came armed with sticks to stop 'their' saint from leaving the chapel, shouting: 'Victory to Nossa Senhora da Veiga! She shall not leave us!' The priest had to have recourse to the police authorities, in order to protect himself and to command obedience.[12]

We could cite examples, all of which demonstrate the same resistance to such centralizing tendencies on the part of a local community or a network of groups attached to having 'their own' saint.

Among the 216 *romarias*, of all sizes, that we have identified in the course of our research, nearly half – 99 to be exact – are devoted to the cult of the Virgin Mary, 83 to that of a saint, and 20 to that of Christ. Apart from the last, God is only the object of a *romaria* cult in the form of a divine 'person', the Holy Spirit, whose cult was introduced in the fourteenth century by Isabel of Aragon, the *Rainha Santa*. This cult is still celebrated at fourteen Portuguese shrines at least, as well as in Brazil, the Azores and Madeira.

One of these, at Tomar, has become very important.[13] It is famous for its *tabuleiros*, baskets in which thirty loaves of bread, decorated with artificial flowers and ears of corn, are piled up to a height at least equal to that of the white-robed girls who carry them on their heads. At the very top are placed a crown and a dove, symbol of the Holy Spirit.[14] With this one exception, it is always an actual but deceased human being who crystallizes the presence of the sacred.[15]

Invocation of Christ is usually addressed to the Crucified; here Calvary figures twice, the Cross itself six times, the 'Good Jesus' on the Cross four times, the Lord of Pity once, the Lord of the Afflicted once, and the Lord of Navigators once.[16]

The Virgin is invoked under 68 different titles, which we can divide into two main categories. In one category are names which are, one may say, emotionally neutral: either these are toponymic, being related to the location of the shrine or to some characteristic local feature, for example, the Virgin 'of the Castle', 'of the Rock', 'of the Abbey', 'of the Olive Tree', 'of Aŷres', 'of Sameiro' (occurring on sixteen occasions); or they are historical or legendary, for example, 'of the Snows', 'of Victory' (occurring on five occasions); or they recall some famous Marian shrine, for example, Fátima, Lourdes, La Salette, Montserrat (occurring on six occasions).

In the second category are names which, on the contrary, are expressive of devotional sentiment, giving it some special affective charge either in an oblative and purely devotional sense, or in a more manipulative way and with reference to human needs. Among these names three groups may be distinguished. The first refer to one of Mary's 'mysteries', to one of her titles to glory, or they express admiration for her or at least draw attention to Mary as a person to whom a cult is addressed: 'St Mary', 'St Mary the Great', 'Our Lady of the Whole World', 'Our Lady of the Rosary', 'of Mount Carmel', 'of Hope', 'of the Conception', 'of the Visitation', 'of the Assumption', and so on. The second group of names honour her through reference to events in her life, which have their equivalent in the existence of the ordinary man or woman. Through these names devotion is specialized, and local Virgins are invoked as patrons of the basic human conditions (particularly of birth and death) which correspond to them: 'Our Lady of Milk', 'of the Hour' or 'of Deliverance', 'of the Nativity', 'of the Sorrows', 'of Agony', 'of Peaceful Death', and so on.[17] Names in the last group are directly anthropocentric and the Virgin is called on here for protection, either in the course of occupational activities (usually linked with fishing: 'Our Lady of the Safe Voyage', 'of Good Weather'), or in the general course of life ('Our Lady of Peace', 'of Succour', 'of Mercy', 'of Poverty),[18] or against ill-health ('Our Lady of Health', 'Our Lady of Healing').

We would not, of course, claim that pilgrims today display markedly different religious attitudes depending on the category of shrine which they are visiting, but it is probably not by pure chance that in certain regions one or other of our categories of invocation should be traditionally dominant. Thus, in the north (essentially in Douro Litoral and Minho, but also in Trás-os-Montes), the Virgin is mainly invoked in connection with the protection which she affords to human existence and activities: of her titles there from the 'affective' category, 87 per cent are from the second and third groups (37 per cent and 50 per cent respectively); and we found no fewer than seven shrines dedicated to 'Our Lady of Health' and two to 'Our Lady of Healing'. In the south, on the other hand (Alentejo and, to a lesser extent, Algarve), 64 per cent are from the first group (the more 'objective' titles), and only 36 per cent from the last (concerning concrete human needs),[19] while the middle group is not present at all. Moreover, we did not come across a single Marian shrine whose name evoked curing or healing.[20] This points, we believe, to a difference in religious sentiment between the two regions and, more fundamentally, in the personality of the two populations concerned. What is more, it is to be expected that the *romaria*, which is an expression of an eminently practical religion[21] and of a familiar bartering with the supernatural, should be much more characteristic of northern religion. It is in fact relatively rare and discreet in Alentejo, and attains its maximum density and intensity in Minho.

The saints, too, vary from region to region. Leaving aside the three 'popular saints', St John, St Peter and St Anthony, who are revered all over Portugal but whose cult does not always take the form of a *romaria*,[22] one other saint seems to be the object of a particularly large number of pilgrimages. This is St Benedict (or Bento), the importance of whose cult reflects the powerful monastic presence which existed in Portugal before the religious orders were suppressed in 1834. He has eight *romaria* shrines in the north, which are among the most important, and one in the south.[23] His cult is usually linked with that of St Maurus – who, in addition, has at least two shrines in his own name – and with that of St Scholastica.[24] Following these in importance in the north are St Martha (with four shrines) and St Bartholomew (with three). The cult of St Sebastian is found in all three regions (three in the north, one in the centre, and two in the south), while that of the *Rainha Santa* is more characteristic of the centre, where she lived and where her tomb is located (three shrines), and of the south where she died (one shrine). St Lawrence, St Michael, St Gonçalo, St Roch, St Barbara, St Mark, St Lucy and St Christopher all have at least one shrine each, while seventeen further saints are also the object of *romarias*.[25]

One feature, above all, characterizes the devotion paid to these saints, as well as to the Virgin Mary and to the Good Lord Jesus, and it is also a distinguishing feature not only of the festival but of popular religion generally, and that is the vow.

III THE VOW

The vow is a means of contact between the actual human condition and the environment of 'sanctity' which everywhere surrounds it. It forms part of a certain conception of the world, and is an essential mode of communication within that conception. Here, it is allied to the notion of sacrifice, while it also belongs within the framework of an economy based on exchange.

A 'vow' is made to a 'saint' when an essential element of individual, family or social existence or security is in danger. Examination of the ex-votos which fill the chapels of both modest and famous shrines[26] and which sometimes specify the 'miracle' for which thanks are rendered, together with direct contact with grateful pilgrims themselves, allow one to gauge the great variety of situations which give rise to vows: accidents, journeys, problems in love or marriage, examinations, the loss or theft of objects, fires, natural disasters, business affairs, harvests, and so on. There are two categories which are clearly predominant, however: vows relating to health – one's own, that of relatives or that of farm animals; and, particularly nowadays, vows relating to the safety of young men called up for active military service overseas. However, the habit of making vows goes far beyond the framework of these critical situations; for many people, they constitute routine investments and are a part of normal life and of the way that the universe functions. Between the two societies, the human and the 'divine', that of vulnerability to the destructive forces of the cosmos and of the passions and that represented by 'sanctity', a solidarity is established and maintained through these repeated exchanges. On the one side are offered homage in the form of suffering, long journeys on foot to the shrine or walking on bleeding knees around the church or the statue, or semi-ritual offerings and the sacrifice of one's most precious possessions, often replaced today by their equivalent in money. In return, one obtains an increased sense of security, certainty that one is protected and a contact with the sacred which will thereafter accompany the routine of daily life. All this constitutes a commerce by means of which the world goes round and the normal train of existence is upheld.

An old man whom we met at São Bento da Porta Aberta de Gerês had been coming for fifty years without interruption to 'pay' his vow; another, aged 74, had come for the thirty-eighth time, walking for eight hours across the mountains on foot, despite his children's objections. He had had something wrong with his leg, which the doctors had been unable to cure, but he had 'done a deal with St Benedict, and *pronto*!' So now every year he had to fulfil what he had promised 'until he was no longer able to do so'. He had brought 580 escudos (compared with 430 the previous year), which represented a huge sum for him,[27] though, smilingly, he declared that it was 'gladly given'. After two hours' rest, he was ready to make the journey back.

When what is involved is not the co-existence of the two worlds – the one of immediate experience and the 'other' which surrounds and transcends it – but rather, in an individual and diachronic perspective, the relationship between and the passage from life and existence after death, then again the connection is dependent on vows. By building bridges, in effect, it is vows which make an easy passage possible. When we asked a group of men, *festeiros* gathered in readiness for their *romaria*, what they thought about life after death, they were perplexed, but stronger than this was their conviction that there was a survival, which had the character of a sanction ('something more than for animals'). And this conviction rested on the existence and value of vows. They are what enable a man, who is a creature destined for death ('like a dog'), to transcend the limits of his earthly life and to communicate with the cosmic mystery which surrounds and awaits him. And this communication can be regarded very much as a deferred payment, since if there is anyone for whom death will indeed be the opening-up of a void, an absolute end, it is 'among others, the person who never makes vows'.

This sense of an obligation inherent in the structure of the universe and in the nature of things is sometimes hidden behind psychological reactions attributed to the saint. St Benedict, for example, is said to be particularly 'vindictive', not only at Gerês but also at most of his other shrines. There are many stories in oral circulation of agreements broken when vows were not accomplished, and of the catastrophes which might ensue in such circumstances:[28] warts which have been cured but which grow again, wounds which re-open, and harvests which are ruined. It is very necessary, therefore, to weigh up one's strength before entering into a vow, particularly when the patron saint chosen, however familiar he may have become to his devotees, likes to maintain an aura of mystery about himself. 'Our little St Torcato has come back to us', we were told by a *romeiro*, standing by his tomb.[29] 'Little St Benedict hasn't. [And whispering:] He can't as long as his family is alive [he repeats this].[30] And then, among ourselves [he lowers his voice, and looks for agreement from his companions], in confidence, and without saying anything – God forbid! – against our little St Benedict, he is rather, how can I put it? Just a little . . . I'm not saying anything against him, mind, I'm just telling the truth [again he seeks the approval of the others, who are following the conversation in silence and who nod], a little vindictive. He's strict. Little St Torcato's different. For example, you make a mistake (*um erro*) or I make a mistake – it can happen to anyone [a neighbour adds: 'There is only one who is pure!']. I would forgive you, wouldn't I? Little St Torcato would forgive you, too. But little St Benedict doesn't. You see: St Torcato has come back to us, but St Benedict hasn't yet. And he won't ... [there are knowing smiles].' Then, with a sweeping gesture, he indicated the 100 kilometre return journey to the shrine of São Bento da Porta Aberta, and added: 'My wife has been there several times. But I have never vowed that I would walk there, because may be I wouldn't be able to make it. [The others agree emphatically.]'

A vow thus sets in motion a mechanism, which is no less ineluctable for being purely social, and no incapacity of the person making the vow can halt that mechanism. Nor can the intervention of a human authority, for the social relationship involved is between the society of men and that of the world beyond. In 1910, at Elvas (Alentejo), in the heart of the most anticlerical region of Portugal and not far from a diocese from which the bishop once had to flee for his life, the Republican authorities came up against a crowd armed with sticks when they tried to close a chapel and thus deprive devotees of access to it. Only the priest is qualified to intervene in such matters, but his voice is not always heeded. The chaplain at São Bento da Porta Aberta spends all his time in the 'house of miracles', where he is mainly occupied in reassuring anxious consciences, but his authority is often insufficient to overcome the feeling of having contracted a debt which must at all costs be repaid. This stems not from fear of 'punishment', but from a conviction that the balance (of health, for example) achieved thanks to a vow would be immediately upset were the vow not to be 'paid';[31] or from a sense that the order of the world would be reduced to absurdity, if a favour already granted and which could not be undone (such as the safe accomplishment of military service overseas) were not matched by the fulfilment of the vow which had obtained the favour in the first place.

A young woman had promised to go on her knees over the four kilometres of stony track at São Bento da Porta Aberta, which separate the two bridges in the valley of the shrine. She got to within sight of the church and then collapsed; but she declared that she would fully accomplish her vow the following year despite the intervention of the chaplain who wanted to give her dispensation from it. In 1961, a man was walking the forty kilometres from Fafe to São Bento da Porta Aberta, his feet bare and bleeding, when he, too, collapsed. A priest, in a passing car, stopped and offered him a lift, but was told: 'You are a man of God! And yet you sin against the Fifth Commandment of God's law! Be off with you!'[32] In 1971, a member of a commando unit, who had returned safely from the war in Africa, undertook to crawl twenty-five times round the church. In front of a crowd excited by his heroism, bleeding and a long way from his goal, he answered a bishop who tried to dissuade him from continuing: 'I will stop, but on one condition: that you finish in my place.' For in one way or another, this return gift had to be paid into St Benedict's treasury.

But 'in one way or another' is not to put it strongly enough. The response given to the official representative of ecclesiastical authority in the presence of a group of pilgrims points to another dimension of vows. For it establishes the existence of a clear opposition between 'us' and 'them', that is, between the devotees' direct relationship with 'their' saint and the same relationship mediated through and socially regulated by the Church as an institution and an authority. Involved in the whole practice of vows, and particularly of painful and, in a certain sense, scandalous vows, there is a 'popular' movement of independence, of resistance to the clergy's religious monopoly, and a demand for autonomy so far as relations with the sacred are concerned. Autonomy at the individual level, first and foremost,[33] but this leads to the creation, through the intersection of multiple initiatives, of a network of solidarity in which symbolic prestations circulate continuously, from one family to another, from one year to another, in that system of deferred reciprocity which constitutes the multiform exchange economy of the *romaria*. For vows are not made only for oneself. Relations, neighbours or friends in need can benefit from a spontaneous gesture of intercession, on the implicit understanding, however, that they will one day pay one back.[34] There are, moreover, many other ways in which others may participate in one's vow,[35] and there are cases where a vow is made not only 'in favour of', but even 'in the name of', another person, pledging that person's will vis-à-vis the saint when it cannot pledge itself, and thus treating it as an extension of that of the individual making the vow.[36]

Of course, these prestations and counter-prestations in times of trial and trouble bring individuals and families together into a community linked to its celestial protector. Such communities are built up gradually and selectively (vows are not made for just anyone, nor to just any saint for anyone indiscriminately), and they come into play both on the journey to the shrine (groups accompany those who have made a major vow, and the status of the latter, already marked by a flower in the mouth or a sack of salt on the head, for example, is thereby further emphasized all along the way), and in the presence of the saint when the essence of the promised prestation is accomplished (here it is not infrequent for the pilgrim struggling painfully on his knees to be surrounded and supported by members of his family or by friends, or, in the case of a young person, by his peers, all wearing the serious expressions appropriate to the carrying-out of official functions). And there are always spectators at these scenes, a crowd eager to participate in the strong emotions which will link it both to the main privileged officiants and to the sacred world which lies behind them.

Moreover, the clergy has nothing to do with the organization of this dual interaction. First, because its members are rarely consulted on the subject except in exceptional cases of doubt and even then their advice is often ignored. Secondly, because they very rarely participate in this painful type of prestation and, indeed, try to restrict it in favour of other kinds of vow, which are either much less dramatic (and are thus less likely to arouse the emotions and possibly lead to uncontrollable excesses)[37] or more directly linked to sacramental ritual in which their own sovereign intervention is necessary; or, finally, of more immediate economic profit to the shrine or to the clerical body.[38] A peasant selling refreshments at the shrine of Gerês told us: 'What really seems to me to prove that all these penances are useless is that you never see a priest going in for them, and they are the ones who know. If they don't go in for it ...' He thus ironically criticized an established religion through its institutional representatives, precisely by acknowledging their legitimate authority and the reliability of their opinions about what constituted 'efficacious' religious behaviour.

Sometimes the order of the two prestations, that of men and that of the saints, is reversed. Here we no longer have vows, but an antecedent ritual gesture either of preventive prophylaxy or of propitiatory prayer. For example, pig farmers drive their herds nine times round the Santo das Taburnelas rock near Arnoia (Bastos), in order to protect them from epidemic disease.[39] Girls looking for a husband used to pull at the belt of St Gonçalo's robe at Amarante or embrace a mysterious statue near the chapel of São Braz at Matozinhos. At Gondomar, sterile women used to scrape limestone from the hill of St Simon – and today they gather dust from the floor of his chapel – in both cases placing the debris in small bags to make talismans which will aid them to have children.[40] In all these cases, and in many others, the relationship with the sacred is established in inverse order: by means of a symbolic gesture, man tries to gain a hold over forces which go beyond him and in the face of which he is normally powerless.

It is here that a magical colouring appears most directly: the propitiatory rite is more rigidly codified, and the elements of traditional magic are often present in it (odd numbers; black cocks, as at São Bartolomeu do Mar;[41] talismans). These also include those aggressively indecent or scatological actions that have today almost disappeared,[42] but which used to feature prominently in the cult of saints especially connected with sexual matters or with fertility (for example, St Gonçalo, St John and St Anthony).[43] Nevertheless, it is difficult, even in this context, to talk of pure magic. For, although the initiative is taken by man who makes a gesture which is supposed to give him access to forces which he does not naturally control, it is not hard to detect a prayer behind the gesture, that is to say, the mediation of a being conceived of as a supernatural model of the human will. For, although the saint is part of the world of the sacred and of power, he has not left behind all traces of human psychology. Sometimes, he is considered to be wholly concerned with providing protection and wholly beneficent. For example, at Riba d'Ave, our informants described for us a propitiatory rite in terms which quite excluded any questioning of its efficacity: to overcome 'fear', children are passed under the *andor* of St

Bartholomew and touch his knife, and, having accomplished this ritual, 'they can walk'.[44] In other cases, a saint may take part, sometimes with a certain amount of humour, in a game of psychological exchange. We have already mentioned St Benedict and his 'vindictive' personality. Between him and St Torcato there is often a certain rivalry – St Torcato is powerful but St Benedict can outwit him.[45] St Anthony and St John, who are 'marrying saints', also enjoy the homage which pretty girls pay them;[46] when their wishes have not been granted or when they have not found a husband, however, the latter may take their revenge by lowering the saints down a well, turning them against the wall and breaking a bottle of wine on their backs. St Paio of Torreira, the saint of seasonal fevers, and 'the man with the club' near St Blaise's shrine at Matozinhos can also be the victims of similar actions expressing either importunity or resentment.[47] The fact that a ritual employs magical elements is not sufficient reason to classify it as magic. The reference to a 'magical milieu', which Marcel Mauss considers to be essential,[48] is absent here, and the traditional magical elements, albeit probably deriving from older cults which were entirely magical in nature, are now incorporated in a new structure, whose obviously two-way modality seems to us to rule out their being generally characterized in this way.

There are, however, other examples to which we have already alluded and which are less ambiguous. The *romaria* – vow complex is sometimes inserted as such into a fully 'magical milieu': this is when a witch (*bruxa*) intervenes in that capacity at a *romaria*, or orders those who consult her to carry out a given vow at a particular *romaria*. We were not able to verify this personally, but references, drawn from the confessional and mentioned in the shrine magazines edited by priests, leave no room for doubt as to the existence of such practices.[49]

IV THE GIFT

Before the festival itself, the confraternities organize door-to-door collections. More and more frequently, people give money, or objects and food-stuffs bought in shops, and assessments of gifts, which we heard, were made in terms of their monetary value. In certain villages around Castelo Branco, which is itself a wine-producing district, good bottles of rosé or port from local shops have for some time been the standard offering made to the festival collectors, and members of the committee gauge each other's influence by the number of bottles which they manage to accumulate. Some obtain several hundred. It is a sure sign of a movement towards a monetary economy when such commercial products have greater prestige than local produce.

Elsewhere, the impact of a subsistence economy is still considerable. For example, H. Marçal gives a detailed account of the *peditório* or collection made among the farmers at Perafita (Douro Litoral) around 1960.[50] It was announced by the priest and took place after Michaelmas, when the harvest was in. The *mordomos* were received in each house by the head of the family, according to an unchanging ceremony: wine and a light meal in the 'best room' (a special room used only on this occasion and for the 'Lord's visit' at Easter); a stereotyped conversation about the harvest, and then a 'tour' round the house and outbuildings; finally, in the storeroom, the householder and his visitors discussed how much grain he should contribute to the festival. The former would be reluctant, the latter insistent. They would try to obtain an extra 'measure' (20 litres) of maize, and would refuse to allow the 'scraper' to be used on the measure, so that the 20 litres would in practice become 22 or 24. Sacks were filled with potatoes, beans and onions, and, while everyone else went back to the 'best room', the daughters of the household would mischievously add large stones to the sacks which the *mordomos* would later have to carry to their cart. The produce would then be stored in a reliable house – and in only one so that it could be more easily guarded – until the auction which ended the festival.

These varied gifts are still only partially linked to vows, but, during the course of the *romaria* itself, many others will be added to them. Money, for example, is put in the collection-plate on the table round which the members of the committee stand, either inside the chapel, or in the 'miracle room', or in the 'hall of the confraternity'. A pilgrim who gives money receives an image of the saint, called a *registo*; sometimes the size of the *registo* varies in accordance with the value of the offering.[51] The old custom of attaching it to one's hat as a sign that one is on pilgrimage is still to be found here and there. In any event, the *registo* is later taken home where it acts as a protective presence, and it may be used the following year on the journey to the shrine. Since it has today almost lost this function of being a mark of the *romeiro*, people quite often decline the offer of one 'this year', saying that they 'already have one at home'.[52]

Others prefer, where the clergy are not opposed to the practice, to pin their bank-notes to the saint's cloak, if it is made of cloth, or to attach them to his hands or to the decoration of the *andor*. These offerings – in Portuguese currency, or sometimes, near the frontier, in Spanish, or, more recently, in French money – will then be solemnly carried in procession. If someone donates a very large sum, the whole village will thus know who it is and why it is given.[53] The donor's family may even take part in the procession as a distinct, compact group surrounding the beneficiary of the vow. Sometimes a particular form of dress will emphasize that a person is taking part in a particular capacity (military uniform, for example, or a child dressed as an angel or a saint).

Monetary gifts are usually destined 'for the saint', which means that they are put at the disposal of the organizers (the priest, the members of the confraternity, the committee), in order to be used for the festival and for the upkeep of the shrine. The donor does not mind exactly what his gift is used for. Even, and perhaps especially, if he is very poor, if he has gone through painful self-imposed hardship in order to accomplish his vow, he does not feel that he has any right to say how his money should be spent; for this abdication in a sense doubles the value of his 'blood money'. Deep down – or so at least he tells himself – he has no particular preference for a 'lasting' investment, for example, in works destined to maintain or improve the shrine, or in the purchase of religious ornaments or other objects. On the contrary, such donors are often heard to say that they prefer the transient show, the ephemeral display, provided by fireworks, rockets, squibs or music. They are happy to see the fruit of all their fervour and suffering 'burn up' in a moment, while the whole community looks on in ecstasy. That the Church or 'reasonable people' should be scandalized at the spectacle of such thoughtless waste does not affect them in the slightest. Thanksgiving must be both spectacular and gratuitous; and it is of no consequence whether it is useful or whether it leaves any trace behind – other than in the memories of those who will tell their families all about it when they get home and who will continue to talk about it for years to come. 'It comes to the same thing. It's all for the *Rainha Santa*. Don't people let off rockets to welcome the President? Why shouldn't we do the same for God and his saints?'[54] We shall see, moreover, that this attachment to a 'quaternary' economy[55] and to an ethic of spending is at the heart of a dispute over the *romarias* between 'popular' religious fervour, on the one side, and the religious and economic rationality of the official representatives of authority, on the other.

Sometimes, however, gifts are ear-marked for specific purposes, such as financing a sermon or a mass in the saint's honour. The practice of giving money for a sermon fits quite naturally into the collective mentality which we have evoked, and in the past used even to figure as a provision in wills: is not a eulogy of him the best gift that one can give a saint? Today the sermon is still one of the most important elements in the *romaria*. However, the introduction of modern technology – in the form of sound equipment, microphones and loudspeakers – has again enabled the Church to transform what used to be part of the dispersed, multicentred and differentiating play of multiple vows into a uniform collective event, relatively easily programmed and controlled. The sermon is now confined to the mass, to the 'Holy Hour', or sometimes to the return of the procession, and it is given by an officially invited speaker. But this was not always the case. As late as 1918, at the *romaria* of Senhor da Serra, a shrine situated in a deserted and inaccessible mountain region (Semede in the diocese of Coimbra), 246 'votive sermons' were preached during the festival (15–22 August), and so many sermons had been paid for that 199 had to be postponed to the following year.[56] One can imagine the mountain wilderness, invaded by thousands of pilgrims and becoming for a week a 'desert assembly', with congregations succeeding one another, not only in the chapel but also perhaps under the trees, by the rocks, in clearings, in order to listen enthusiastically, day and night,[57] to the accounts which they had ordered of the glorious exploits of the 'Lord' of the shrine.

Such a practice, even in its present attenuated form, figures like 'demand' in a market economy, contributing to preform and characterize the product: the homiletics of the *romaria*.[58] Here official religion and popular custom reinforce each other. What the pilgrims want to hear is the saint's Life, repeated to saturation point, and particularly accounts of the miraculous episodes which demonstrate his power. Any departure from this pattern is always badly received. For example, if a sermon for the *Rainha Santa* at Tinalhas should involve consideration of the 'situation of Christian women in Portugal today in a time of war and of male emigration', people will hardly bother to listen and will not be satisfied, saying: 'He didn't tell the story of the saint!' Or, at Elvas, in a more socially select setting, if the preacher applies to the present situation in Portugal the lesson of St Matthew's vocation as seen through the categories of the last Council, he will 'not have been a great success this year'. By contrast, as at Riba d'Ave, the saint may even be promised a few coins more, for 'every time that the preacher pronounces the name of St Peter'.

The preacher (always announced on the programme as 'a well-known sacred orator') must adopt a tone which corresponds to the same expectation of a eulogy which is serious but as enthusiastic as possible. The simplicity of an ordinary Sunday sermon is not likely to be appreciated. Thus, it was in the purely rural and 'popular' *romarias* and sometimes from the mouths of young priests from Minho, who invited one another for deliberate practice, that we heard the real collectors' pieces as far as oratory is concerned, characterized by an academic fullness, carefully polished phrasing, purist vocabulary, sweeping gestures and dramatic intonation.

Sometimes, private devotions may be centred on a particular shrine but may not have its principal patron as their object: thus, for example, one may find a sermon in honour of Our Lady of Fátima at one of the masses at the *romaria* of St Benedict.[59] More frequently, the date of the pilgrimage[60] may exclude the possibility of celebrating the saint's mass. When this happens, the preacher is hard put to it to bring the saint into the discussion of the prescribed Bible reading for the day; this becomes 'like putting Pilate in the Creed', as the popular saying has it. And, since the number of masses, and therefore of sermons, that can be completed during a *romaria* is limited, sermons are 'offered' to the saint throughout the year, though at a different rate: at the shrine of St Rita at Ermesinde (Oporto), for example, where votive sermons are particularly numerous, a sermon during the festival costs 1,200 escudos, but at any other time the price is only 300.

Paying for a mass is not, of course, a phenomenon peculiar to *romarias*. The huge economic circulation brought about in the Christian world, particularly in the Middle Ages and the Early Modern period, by testamentary provision for 'perpetual masses' is well-known.[61] In certain cases, pilgrimage shrines were founded, directly or indirectly, as a result of provisions of this kind.[62] It seems also that the offering of masses was in the past linked to *romarias*. After the secularization of 1830 and 1834, by which all ecclesiastical property was placed in the hands of the *Juntas de Freguesia* or municipal councils, the *Junta* of Rio Caldo wanted to close the screen around the high altar at São Bento da Porta Aberta, but the chaplain objected. His main argument was that the many priests, called on to celebrate mass at the shrine throughout the year, would be inconvenienced by such a measure. And the *Junta* acknowledged in its reply that at least during the three main festivals, many votive masses were celebrated, sometimes as many as several dozen a day during the August festival.[63] According to the former chaplain, now the priest at Rio Caldo, before the last war only one mass was celebrated at the shrine during the 'great festival' between 10 and 15 August.[64] So the custom had disappeared in the course of a century. The *romarias*, in effect, had in great part escaped the official control of the Church. By contrast, the regaining of control over the last few decades has been marked by an increase in the number of official acts of solemn worship and by a revival of the offering of masses.[65]

This observation is of special significance. We have seen how vows were associated with solutions to immediate problems of everyday life; they were part of a practical religion related to a fragmented existence and geared to its rhythms. Offerings 'to the saint' were destined to be used up at once in the explosive outburst of the festival. Offering masses, by contrast, usually for the dead or with one's own life after death in view, constitutes a long-term investment, a prevision springing from quite different considerations and denoting a new kind of economic mentality. It is not irrelevant that the latter practically disappears when ecclesiastical control is relaxed and popular religious spontaneity can function more freely.[66] The conflict of interests, economic or political, is here mediated via a clash of two opposed economic mentalities, just as money is offered to fulfil vows. This is not to say that calculation is absent from the mentality of the faithful who attend the *romarias*: on the contrary, nearly all of them belong to a confraternity in their village which guarantees to provide them with a certain 'capital' of prayers after their death;[67] and the shrines of the *romarias* are themselves the headquarters of these confraternities. However, the ecclesiastical authorities have fought unceasingly, where this is the case, to get the confraternity to respect the wishes of testators, among other things, and not to 'dissipate' all available funds in ephemeral apotheoses of music and fireworks. And, very recently, now that the Church authorities have again gained almost entire control over the *romarias*, they have tried to revive the old custom of offering masses. 'Why have gifts and pious bequests to the shrines come to an end?', asked the magazine *São Torcato* in 1955; and suggested that it was probably because the confraternities, swayed by political passions, were not at all keen to respect the conditions attached to this form of transferring property, preferring almsgiving and vows without any legal obligations attached to them. But now makers of wills need have no fear: the confraternities were entirely controlled by the ecclesiastical authorities, and the state itself saw to it that testamentary dispositions were respected. Leaving a bequest to the shrines, even on condition that so many prayers should be said, was to make an investment 'in the bank which pays dividends after death'. In former days, the message was understood by the people who gave property (*prédios*, or immovable property in general) not only to finance masses for the peace of their souls but also to pay for the building and upkeep of shrines and to meet the expenses of the cult celebrated in them. 'These testaments must be revived... St Torcato, himself, is telling his devotees: "My friends, you can do yourselves good by placing your goods at my service"... Who will be the first to hear his voice?'[68]

These observations make us realize that, from a certain point of view, the *romarias* have tended involuntarily to become sociological museums, reliquaries in which former collective attitudes are preserved, the refuge and outlet not only of a 'popular religion', which can be in opposition to that of the clergy, but also of certain aspects of a civilization of direct exchange and of an economic mentality far removed from the calculation of long-term profit. But this civilization and this mentality are now being submerged in the sphere of religion as well as in other fields of activity, even in the case of the social groups which still maintain some attachment to them.[69]

There are, finally, other characteristic types of gift. Though gifts in kind are less systematically given than before, they still play an important part. Some are ritual gifts and correspond to the recognized miraculous qualities of the saint concerned. For example, carnations (usually white) are given to St Benedict, St John of Arga and St Roch; black chickens to St Bartholomew; white chickens, salt[70] and eggs to St Benedict; 'living eyes' (pigeons and rabbits) to St Lucy; tiles to St John,[71] St Lawrence[72] and St Saturninus.[73] These tiles, like the maize offered to St Roch at Albergaria a Velha, have a further peculiarity: they are linked with ritual transgression, since they have to have been stolen.[74]

Other cases do not seem to have any particular significance, being simply an accumulation of local produce: potatoes or maize in the north, oil and wheat in the south, poultry, pigs or cattle throughout the country. If an important offering is being made, such as a cow, the bells are sometimes rung to greet it and it is included in the procession. Except for oil, which is often kept and used for religious purposes at the shrine, all such produce or livestock is auctioned at the end of the festival.[75] It is thus transformed into abstract value, but in an agonistic atmosphere favouring extravagant spending.[76] One detail, mentioned in connection with several *romarias*, indicates that auctions do not eliminate the original meaning of the offering as something produced by the work of a family and subtracted from its means of subsistence. It frequently happens that a man who has given a beast will bid up the auction price himself until he regains possession of his offering. He gives a certain sum of money to the shrine in this way, which he could easily have calculated without going through this apparently useless rigmarole. But he would then have deprived the community, and himself, of the joyful, symbolic staging of an act of sacrifice.

V CONCLUSION

It would be quite wrong to imagine that the *romaria* is a gathering of 'believers', or that it is exclusively devoted to formally religious activities. The *romaria* is experienced as a festival, that is, as a total event, which constitutes a break with daily life and represents the irruption into it of an 'other world'.

Should we describe this festival as a utopian event? Certainly, in so far as it does essentially stand back from the actual and concrete functioning of society and, in so doing, implicitly presents an alternative general model, which reactivates hidden potentialities. But, within the concept of utopia, festivals have their own specificity; they are neither written utopias, nor utopias put into practice, which would imply the realization of a programme; rather they approach the category of the dream. The festival is a dream which is lived through, where fantasies become gestures, and each of whose elements can be considered as a dream fragment brought to life. In this perspective, we may relate gestures to festivals in the same way that ritual has been related to ideology.[77] For ideology tends to be tied up in the rituals of everyday life even more obviously than it is in formal discourse.[78] In the same way, utopia reveals itself in festivals through a series of evanescent and open gestures, which take on the fluidity, the lack of clear outlines and the moving forms of the dream. Meanings circulate among these gestures, and it follows from this ambiguity that they are far removed from any conceptual model but are rich in multiple symbolic suggestions. Taken as a whole, finally, they designate a 'non-real' configuration of social life, in which all the cards in the social pack (status, roles, functions and 'fields') have not only been redistributed, but redistributed in a fashion which leaves them mixed up, indistinct, overlapping and out of focus. It is here that we perceive the sense and the limits of the notion of a 'return to primitive chaos', which a certain school of sociological phenomenology has seen as an essential ingredient of festivals, but which, it must be acknowledged, does not always manifest itself in the kind of unstructured commotion which such an image generally evokes.

NOTES

1 The administrative divisions of the district and the council roughly correspond to French departments and cantons [or British counties and districts. S.W.]. A council is a more important administrative division than the French canton, however; parishes are headed by a *Junta de Freguesia* which has only three members and minimal functions, and the councils, based in small towns or larger villages, are effectively the basic units of local government. A 'council holiday' is thus a festival both for the town itself and for the surrounding rural area. Two further practical remarks: first, following common Portuguese practice, the name of a village is sometimes followed in the text by the name, in brackets, of the borough or town to whose council it is attached; secondly, the names of the old provinces, which have only recently disappeared from official terminology, are still in common use, and further variations in the names of provinces are found as the result of successive changes in official terminology. The region between the Douro and the Minho rivers, for example, is roughly equivalent to 'Minho', while the 'Douro Litoral' is the Oporto region.

  This article is based on a thesis (3ᵉ cycle) presented by the author at the Ecole des Hautes Etudes in 1976 with the title: 'Arraial, la fête d'un peuple: Les pèlerinages populaires au Portugal'.

2 The frontier is officially 'thrown open' on these occasions, and this long-awaited event is announced in advance. Sometimes, however, it is only announced at the very last moment, which gives rise to much anxious or disappointed comment. The opening may even be used as a means of pressure by either one of the national governments, as we were able to observe in 1973 at São Bento da Porta Aberta (near the Portela do Homem frontier post), to draw attention either to the urgent need for road repairs or to the slow progress being made in the organization of official frontier services. Examples of important border-region *romarias* are: Seixas, Sra da Peneda, São Bento da Porta Aberta, Sra do Almurtão at Idanha a Nova, the Campo Maior festival, Sta Maria da Barrancos, Senhor Jesus da Piedade at Elvas, and Sra das Pazes at Ficalho. Ribeiro has studied the small *romaria* of N. Sra da Luz at Trás-os-Montes. The chapel is situated at the actual frontier between the two countries, near the boundary stone itself, on which the customs officers of each side symbolically place their coats. The two processions converge there and exchanges take place in the traditional manner. See M. Ribeiro, 'Nossa Senhora da Luz, Notas etnográficas da raia mirandesa', *Revista de Etnografia*, 16 (Oporto, no date).

3 See F. Valente Machado, *Ermida da Sra das Pazes* (Beja, 1973)

4 See J. Dias, 'Banhos Santos', in Dr J. Leite de Vasconcellos (ed.), *A. do Colóquio de Estudos Etnográficos* (Oporto, 1960), III, pp. 1–6.

5 At São Torcato, São Bartolomeu do Mar, Terena, Bencatel, Mondim da Beira, Cabeceiras de Bastos, Guimarães, etc.

6 Basil and garlic (the word for 'leek' in Portuguese means literally 'leek garlic') have prophylactic qualities in the traditional magic of various peoples, and still do today in the Mediterranean region: they ward off spells, evil spirits and evil influences; see *Dictionnaire des symboles* (Laffont, Paris, 1969), articles on 'ail' and 'basilic'.

7 The powerful imagery of the sacred tree and the implicit model of Fátima would seem to explain a strange but significant mistake in the 1972 programme for the Senhor Bom Jesus festival at Elvas. The foreword by the *Juiz* of the confraternity contains the phrase: 'The simple image of Jesus crucified which appeared more than two hundred years ago on the ancient trunk of an olive tree', whereas nothing in the history of the cult justifies such an allusion, there being no legend about an apparition of any kind.

8 See B. E. Pereira, 'Vestígios do culto das pedras no Norte de Portugal', *Publicações de XXVI Congresso Luso-Espanhol* (Oporto, 1962), Section 7.

9 We mean 'historical' here as opposed to 'natural' and not to 'legendary'.

10 *Vida preciosa e glorioso martírio de S. Torcato*, 16th edition (no place or date), pp. 19–20.

11 *Vida preciosa*, p. 20.

12 C. J. A. Marrana, *História do culto de Na Sra da Veiga em V. N. de Foz Côa* (Oporto, 1959).

13 This *romaria* is urban like most of those, at least in mainland Portugal, which preserve this tradition of directly courtly origin.

14 In 1972, the procession still included nearly 500 *tabuleiros*, most of which came from surrounding villages – in addition to over 1,000 'official' participants.

15 J. Le Goff notes quite rightly that the saints are less successors to the gods, as the title of P. Saintyves's famous book suggests, than to demi-gods and heroes; see 'Culture cléricale et tradition folklorique dans la civilisation mérovingienne', in L. Bergeron (ed.), *Niveaux de culture et groupes sociaux* (Paris and The Hague, 1967), p. 28, n. 3. [Also published in *Annales*, 22 (1967), pp. 780–91; and, in English translation, in *Social Historians in Contemporary France, Essays from Annales* (New York, 1972), pp. 131–40 and 299–306, esp. n. 28. S.W.] Similarly and even more appositely, C. Jullian in *Histoire de la Gaule*, VIII (1926) (reprinted Brussels, 1964), refers to 'guardian spirits and tutelary divinities' (p. 312, n. 4), to 'guardian spirits of places and regions, and tutelary divinities of towns and villages' (p. 320), to 'little deities . . . mother goddesses and innumerable spirits peopling earth and air' (p. 329). These expressed 'the sense of nature as a presence, as an eternal being', which was transmitted through them to the new religion: 'Through them, millennia of ancestral beliefs were linked with Christianity' (pp. 316–17). For, in spite of successive acculturations, these intermediaries take us back to the most ancient cultural layer, which is both perpetually present and in continual process of transformation.

A second theme must, however, be added to the last in order to account for the personality of the 'saints'. The analysis in the previous pages has led us to consider the saints also as the tutelary dead, ancestors whose *return* is beneficial and life-giving; see A. Varagnac, *Civilisations traditionnelles et genres de vie* (Paris, 1948), p. 84. It is this *return* which is realized in the festival, especially during the procession, and which contrasts with the dreaded *return* of the dead who have no resting-place. Fear of the latter *return* is well attested in Portuguese ethnography; see, among others, J. de Vasconcellos, 'Tradições populares', *Revista Lusitana*, XXV (Lisbon, 1923–5), pp. 49–56. It is still widespread in the mentality of rural people, and is sometimes directly related to the *romarias*.

16 Including a festival of the Sacred Heart and one of the Blessed Sacrament, the one recently introduced and the other a continuation (now broken) of the old 'popular' and civic ceremonies, which used to be patronized by the Church and the Court.

17 Even more curious names are found, presumably deriving from some peculiar feature of the statue, but whose function is the same: a specialization of the Virgin as the protector of a certain part of the body or of one of the senses, for example, 'Our Lady of Sight', 'of the Nose', 'of the Head'.

18 Or 'Mother of the Poor', a name which the Church has recently tried to substitute.

19 Moreover, the name of the shrine at Ficalho on the Spanish frontier, 'das Pazes' (of the Peace Treaties) refers to historical events.

20 They are found (for example, at Serpa, Brinches, Messejana, and São Romão), but, as far as we know, either they do not have a *romaria* attached to them, or it can be shown that they were originally imported by the central authorities. We must emphasize, however, that we are not engaged in drawing up an exhaustive or even a systematic list, but can only refer to instances which we happen to have come across, in either written or oral form, in the course of our researches which have been mainly concerned with Minho and Alentejo.

21 See F. Ortiz, *Los negros brujos*, p. 34, cited by Roger Bastide, *Les Religions africaines au Brésil* (Paris, 1960), p. 196: 'Their theanthropic economy is not one of long-term credit, of wealth accumulation, or of profits invested in a Heaven which will pay out eternal interest after death; it is a religion for immediate use and its rituals are ones of exchange without credit or accumulation of interest.'

22 Our list nevertheless includes six *romarias* for St John (all in the north), four for St Peter (three in the north and one in the centre), and six for St Anthony (three in the north, one in the centre and two in the south). We are of course discounting St John's Day at Oporto, the big festival of the *nortenha* capital, which has not, for a long while, had any notion of pilgrimage attached to it – and may never have had.

23 There are others, too, which are mentioned in works on the subject; see G. Felgueiras, 'O culto popular a S. Bento', *Conselho de Santo Tirso, Boletim cultural*, V (1956), pp. 85–92; and G. de Souza, 'S. Bento na história e na tradição popular', *ibid.*, IV (1956), pp. 239–57.

24 'Three children of the same family', as people sometimes say, although St Scholastica is also taken to be an 'Our Lady'.

25 Some of which are among the more important. The saints concerned are: St

Blaise, St Gualtar [Walter, S.W.], St Torcato, St Matthew, St Rita, St Gens [Genesius? S.W.], St Tirso, St Anthony the Hermit, St Marina, St Leocadia, St Agnes, St Sylvester, St Simon, St Andrew, St Paio, St Mamas and the Blessed Vincent of St Anthony. There are finally two *romarias* which are attached to local relics: 'the Relics' and 'the Martyrs'.

26 The Portuguese shrines which are richest in ex-votos seem to be, in the north, Bom Jesus at Matozinhos, Bom Jesus do Monte (Braga), São Gonçalo at Amarante and São Torcato; in Lisbon, N. Sra da Penha de Franca; and, in the south, N. Sra of Aŷres and Senhor Jesus da Piedade at Elvas. At this last, there are nearly five thousand ex-votos including one thousand paintings, some of which date back as far as the year in which the Hermitage was founded (1737). They have been studied in detail by E. Gama, *Os ex-votos da igreja do Senhor Jesus da Piedade de Elvas*, I (Braga, 1972) – a second volume which will contain colour reproductions has not yet been published. On Portuguese ex-votos in general and their historical continuity, see Rocha Peixoto, 'Etnografia portuguesa, *Tabulae votivae*', *Portugalia*, II (1905–8), pp. 187–212; J. Leite de Vasconcellos, *Religões da Lusitânia* (Lisbon, 1913), III, pp. 395ff.; L. Chaves, 'A colleção de "Milagres" do Museu Etnológico Português', *O arqueólogo Português*, XIX (1914), pp. 152–76 and 245–8; Dra C. e Silva, in Dr de C. P. de Lima(ed.), *A arte popular em Portugal*, II, pp. 85ff.; and R. Smith, *Pinturas de ex-votos existentes em Matozinhos e outros santuários portugueses* (Matozinhos, 1966).

27 Approximately £14 and £8 [in values of 1977. S.W.]

28 We heard such stories at the hospital chapel at Braga, at São Bento da Porta Aberta do Gerês, and at São Bento de Cossourado. Dr Molho de Faria discusses this belief at some length in his book *São Bento da Porta Aberta* (Gerês, 1947), pp. 47–60, and he notes that the *romeiros* do not thereby intend to run down St Benedict, but on the contrary to do him honour. On the vengeance taken by another saint, see J. Tavares, 'Tradições de Aveiro, A festa de S. Gonçalinho', *Arquivo do Distrito de Aveiro*, I (1935), p. 130.

29 That is, his body has been discovered. However, the resonance of the expression, with its allusion to the 'return' of the dead saint, evidently reaches far beyond this purely material meaning.

30 This reference to the saint's 'family' is by no means out of the ordinary. It is part of the complex of familiarity surrounding the saint, whose function it is to render the sacred immediate by making the saint an 'ancestor' belonging to one of the community's genealogies. For example, for other pilgrims the portraits of benefactors hanging in the room where the offerings are made are portraits of 'São Torcato's family' (the term 'the brothers of São Torcato' used to designate members of the confraternity helps to encourage such confusion). To return to São Bento, at the shrine of Cossourado, people say that 'this St Benedict is the brother of the one at Gerês, and a cousin of the one at Santo Tirso'; see J. Correia, *Paredes de Coura*, p. 22); while at São Bento da Porta Aberta do Gerês, when we asked a devotee if he had known the saint personally, he replied: 'No, he was before my time', as if he were referring to a contemporary of his grandfather.

31 On the subject of a girl who had 'made an arrangement with little St Benedict' to get rid of an abscess, but who had not kept her vow which meant that the

abscess had come back in the same place, a woman at Cossourado told us: 'The little saints like to help us, but we have to keep our vows, or else...' The reference to 'paying' a vow should not be misunderstood. It is a traditional expression, and, although today the 'price' of many vows is valued in money, the expression itself dates back to a time when the monetary economy was still very secondary in these areas, and it still bears the mark of this situation. As witness to this, we may adduce the following dialogue (heard in 1973) between a woman who had vowed to give her gold 'string' (or necklace) to St Benedict and the priest in charge of the offerings:

'I vowed to give this string, but I wonder if I couldn't just leave the money it's worth?'

'Of course! In any case, the string wouldn't be kept; in a year or two, it would be sold. Just have it valued by the goldsmith.' [There is always a travelling goldsmith at a *romaria*.]

'I have already. He said it was worth four *contos* [about £70 in values of 1977. S.W.]. But I promised the string. I vowed never to wear it again.'

'Then keep it for your children, as a family heirloom.'

The woman hesitated, went away, then came back and gave up the necklace. 'I vowed to give this', she said, 'and not the money.'

32 *São Bento da Porta Aberta* (December 1961).

33 Sometimes, however, the vow is directly collective, either when all the families in a village are involved, as in the case of the *romaria* of the Quinta de Roque Amador at Baraçal, studied by D. Nabais, *Baraçal, Um caso de mudança social* (Lisbon, 1970), pp. 278–82, or when it binds the community as a whole. Thus, in the latter category, the village of Santo Antonio das Areias (Mourão) promised St Mark a bullock at the *romaria* of Na Sra da Luz at Castelo de Vide, to be paid at the feast of the saint (25 April), if the agricultural year proved to be a good one; see A. Gordo, *No Alto-Alentejo, Crônicas narrativas* (Lisbon, 1954), pp. 45–50; and M. Ribeiro, 'Nossa Senhora da Luz', p. 17.

34 For, example, at São Bento do Gerês, we spoke to a family who had arrived there during the night after a journey of nine hours on foot, in part across the mountains, and who were ready to return after two hours' rest. They said that they had come to fulfil a number of vows. The son had fallen from a ladder, breaking several ribs, and had vowed to make the journey on foot if he recovered; his mother had made the same vow in his favour. She had also vowed to give the saint a wax ex-voto figure of a cow, if her neighbour's cow would stop refusing to eat, which it had – a vow made without telling the neighbour. Lastly, she had vowed to give a candle as long as the injured limb, if her cousin, who had broken his arm, recovered the use of it. In addition to his personal vow, the son had vowed, on behalf of a sick aunt, to offer the shrine the honorarium for a mass (30 escudos). The money had been collected from door to door in small change, which meant that at least 300 people had a share in his gesture.

35 We have seen an example of this in the previous note. But the custom can take diverse forms: sometimes, the alms (in coins, salt, etc.) must be collected in towns and villages along the way to the shrine, sometimes only from those who have the same Christian name as the beneficiary of the vow, etc.; see *São Bento*

da Porta Aberta, (August 1961). This custom also exists in the south; at Elvas, for example, 200 escudos were once put in the collection-plate, all in coins of the lowest value.

36 This phenomenon is associated fairly directly with patriarchal ties, as one might have guessed. For example a man from Tinalhas vowed that if one of his sons finished his military service without having to take part in the colonial war, he and his family would all go to the shrine at Fátima with the son, who was not, however, consulted and who had in the meanwhile and without his father's knowledge given up all forms of religious practice. Another son, who was married and had children, was also committed by the vow without being asked, as was their mother. Conversely, some vows involving painful procedures are fulfilled through the agency of other people in return for payment (cases of this are cited at Matozinhos). In the Middle Ages, this practice was, of course, quite common, for both penances and pilgrimages.

37 The first issue of *São Bento da Porta Aberta* (1961) includes accounts of former festivals in order to illustrate how things have changed; it relates that in 1948 (or 1956) the Republican Guard had to intervene to restore order, in circumstances obviously relating to the accomplishment of vows, since the editor exclaims: 'How very odd that it should be necessary to intervene to keep the peace when all that is involved is giving and fulfilling what one has promised!'

38 Compare the concordant analyses of the fourteenth-century movement of Flagellants, made respectively by E. Delaruelle, 'Dévotion populaire et hérésie au Moyen Age', and G. Szekcly, 'Le Mouvement des flagellants au XIVe siècle, Son caractère et ses causes', in J. Le Goff (ed.), *Hérésie et société dans l' Europe préindustrielle* (Paris and The Hague, 1968), pp. 147–55 and 229–41. The movement was persecuted 'because it threatened to render the Church superfluous' (p. 235), and made absolution independent of clerical intervention (p. 152). Moreover, through rejecting the sacraments and the social life of the Church, the movement was also a threat to it 'from a financial point of view' (p. 236).

39 B. E. Pereira, 'Vestígios do culto das pedras', p. 6.

40 Information supplied by Canon A. Ribeiro (Braga). The scattering of dust scraped from sacred stones and the homologous dispersal of the down in which participants cover themselves form part of the fertility rites of Australian tribes where the fertility both of the totem species and humans is involved; see W. B. Spencer and F. J. Gillen, *The Native Tribes of Central Australia* (London, 1899), p. 170; and G. Roheim, *The Riddle of the Sphinx* (London, 1934), pp. 111ff. But, whereas the symbolism of these gestures connotes an explosion of power which spreads over the whole social space (see Emile Durkheim, *Les Formes élémentaires de la vie religieuse* (Paris, 1912) (Eng. trans. London, 1915), esp. Book III, Chs. II and III; and J. Cazeneuve, *Les Rites et la condition humaine* (Paris, 1958), pp. 321–2), in the Gondomar pilgrimage each individual appropriates the sacred power for himself and *takes home* its embodiment. The ideological representation of society here figures at the level of the family.

41 See E. V. de Oliveira, 'A *Romaria* de São Bartolomeu do Mar', *Geographica, 26*, pp. 42–9; and C. Callier-Boisvert, 'Survivances d'un bain sacré au

Portugal: *São Bartolomeu do Mar'*, *Bulletin des Etudes Portugaises*, New series **XXX** (1969).

42 Notably the breaking of wind in front of a saint's statue, a practice which the clergy has had difficulty in suppressing. C. Gaignebet, *Le Folklore obscène des enfants* (Paris, 1974) has recently put forward the hypothesis that, in certain children's games, deliberately breaking wind, 'an offering that is anal in origin and spiritual in nature' (p. 134), is a decadent form of a pre-Christian rite (p. 318). Associated with the sacred in an anxiogenic context, it was originally neither a form of magic nor a manifestation of the sacred transgression. Related to the feasts of fools and to the abbeys of misrule, of which it represented an essential element, it gradually came to be given a demonic interpretation and finds a place in descriptions of the witches' Sabbath (p. 160ff.). Hence its character as a disapproved and repressed obscenity; for the obscene is what 'offends modesty and decency', but only 'as defined by the disapproval and repression of adults' (p. 318).

43 E. V. de Oliveira, 'Manifestations de la vie spirituelle, des traditions et de l'allégresse du peuple portugais', *Diário Popular* (Lisbon, special issue), pp. 136–43. At Amarante, on the saint's day, phallic cakes are still sold, popularly known as 'St Gonçalo's c—s'; they are stylized versions of biscuits that used to be more realistic. Their sale is in theory forbidden, and where they are displayed on mobile stalls, some of the women stall-holders go through a curious procedure when the procession passes by, covering the cakes discreetly with a white cloth so that the saint may not see them: an indication of how their sacred nature has been effectively repressed.

44 In accordance with his legend, St Bartholomew is represented holding the knife which was used to flay him alive, and dominating the figure of a vanquished devil. He is invoked in Portugal against demonic possession, both in its major manifestations (epilepsy) and in its minor ('fear', difficulties in walking or talking experienced by children, stammering, etc.). 'Fear' is, moreover, one of the popular names for the devil. At Riba d'Ave and at St Bartholomew's other *romarias* (at Cerzedela, for example), it seems that the consequences of 'fear' are envisaged exclusively in terms of a child's difficulty in walking. [The *andor* is the wooden litter on which the statue of the saint is carried in procession. S.W.]

45 'São Bento lhe passa a perna', in the words of a youth of eighteen at São Bento da Porta Aberta.

46 For St Anthony, see, for example, the *quadras* cited by T. Bastos, 'Santo António', *Revista do Minho*, I (Barcelos, 1886), pp. 25–70. For St John, we may cite a *quadra* presented in 1973 at the forty-fifth *quadras* competition organized by the *Jornal de Notícias* in Oporto: 'You dance so charmingly/That St John's head spins./Being a saint, he says,/Has disadvantages.'

47 E. V. de Oliveira, 'Manifestations de la vie spirituelle'. Colouring or dyeing statues may well represent a stage in the 'civilizing' of customs that may be found in their crude form elsewhere: we refer to the reddening with various substances of the penis of statues of gods or of phallic protuberances on sacred stones, in magical fertility rites; see J. Finne, *Erotisme et sorcellerie* (Brussels, 1973). As for rituals whose rude familiarity seems to show a lack of respect for

the saint concerned, they are not, as Cocchiara claims, the result of a Christian humanization of religious feeling, but seem rather to be a survival of ancient gestures and the reflection of an archaic mentality; see G. Cocchiara, 'Paganitas, Sopravvivenze folkloriche del paganesimo siciliano', *Atti del Primero Congresso Internazionale di Studi sulla Sicilia Antica* (Palermo, 1964), pp. 401–16; and Le Goff, 'Culture cléricale et tradition folklorique', p. 28, n. 3.

48 Marcel Mauss, *Sociologie et Anthropologie* (Paris, 1950), p. 93.

49 For example, from *São Bento da Porta Aberta* (October 1961) and *ibid.* (August 1962): a *bruxa* orders a *romeiro* to light seven or thirteen candles, to offer silver coins and bottles of oil, to crawl round the shrine, and to wash the saint's statue until the paint comes off it... ; or from *São Torcato*, 8–13 (15 August 1948): 'The shame of it! A *bruxa* was called to São Torcato, and no one asked the police to arrest her!; or 75–6 (March 1956): the fulfilment of a vow imposed by a *bruxa* is a sin.

50 H. Marçal, 'A missão dos mordomos na Festa de S. Mamede de Perafita', *Boletim da Biblioteca Municipal de Matozinhos*, 8 (no date).

51 On the subject of *registos*, see, among others, the studies by L. Chaves in *O Arqueólogo Português*, XXI–XXV (1916–21); and, by the same author, *Registos de santos* (Lisbon, 1925).

52 At Amarante, for example, six thousand *registos* were distributed in 1973, but far more than six thousand pilgrims made offerings. According to the chaplain and the sacristan, ten to twelve thousand people came to worship at the saint's 'tomb', and experienced observers estimated that pilgrims accounted for about half of the thirty thousand people in town for the *romaria*, which has become the municipal festival.

53 Anonymous donations are made, however, and these are greatly admired: 'We found some 1,000 escudo notes, and we don't know who gave them!' At Aldeia Nova de São Bento, in 1971, the money needed to acquire bulls for the bullfight was given by a benefactor who remained anonymous, despite all efforts to discover who he was. At Elvas, the biggest offerings are always placed anonymously in the collection-plate.

54 This remark was noted at Tinalhas, but the argument based on the analogy of the reception given to a political figure or of the birthday celebrations for a relative or distinguished person is common everywhere.

55 Poirier contrasts this type of economy with that of classical rational economic theory; see J. Poirier, 'L'économie quaternaire et l'oblation', *Economie et Société*, II (April 1948), pp. 867–96. According to him, it has four characteristics: lavish circulation of wealth (gift and counter-gift), ceremonial or sacralized prestations, prestige spending, and functional waste; see, by the same author, 'Les fonctions sociales de l'ostentation économique', *Tiers-Monde*, IX (1968), p. 4.

56 *Boletim da Diocese de Coimbra*, IV, 12 (1918), p. 196.

57 This may not have happened at the *romaria* of Senhor da Serra, which was particularly strictly regulated owing to the massive presence of the clergy and the attendance of the bishop, accompanied by representatives of the administrative authorities; but elsewhere, and even later, cases of midnight sermons

have been noted; see *Boletim da Diocese de Coimbra*, XIII, 23–4 (1928), p. 165.

58 We have collected some thirty *romaria* sermons. We shall not attempt a full sociological analysis of them here, but will merely indicate that they may be placed on a continuum which features four main types. The first is characterized by glorification of the 'saint' and of his or her powers, by narrative form, and by great emotional fervour and the exaltation of popular faith. This type corresponds fairly exactly to the kind of 'popular religion' which is expressed generally in the *romarias*. The second type is characterized by a more conventional piety, by special devotions and by sacramental practice, always in an individual perspective (for example, St Benedict's devotion to the Blessed Sacrament may be emphasized). In the third type, moral exhortation is linked to the Life of the saint, and there is some emphasis on sin, and particularly on the sins of the flesh. Appeal is also made to the traditions of ecclesiastical discipline. Patriotic glorification of the historic religion of Portugal and the Christian mission of the nation are important themes. These last two types correspond in different ways to the official religion of recent years and to the political situation under Salazar, in which the Church collaborated with the new State. In the fourth type, attempts are made to open up a humanist perspective. Emphasis is placed on the responsibility of Christians to act for social change, in an international context. This type corresponds to the 'new Church', and is politically out on a limb or even in virtual opposition to official policy. It is in an obviously minority situation, and takes the greatest precautions in its language, seeking refuge especially in a high level of abstraction.

These types reflect simultaneously the four types of saints, coupled in pairs of opposites, which succeeded one another in medieval homiletics: the inimitable saint who can only be admired, and the saint as a direct moral example; the saint who has fled the world in order to sanctify himself, and the saint who remains in the world in order to transform it from within (see J.-Cl. Poulin, 'Les Saints dans la vie religieuse populaire au Moyen Age', in *Les Religions populaires*, Colloque International, 1970 (Laval, 1972), p. 71. Popular sensibility tends to prefer the first of each pair, while the official Church prefers the second (of the first pair in the past, and of the second today).

59 At Cossourado in 1973.

60 There is, in fact, a tendency to transfer *romarias*, which liturgically speaking ought to take place at other times of the year, to the summer months which are more suitable for making journeys and for open-air events. 'Reforming' bishops call for the liturgical calendar to be respected, but usually in vain.

61 Masses and offerings 'for the departed' are much older and date back to the earliest Christian times, especially in Africa (see the article by Dom H. Leclercq, 'Défunts', in *Dictionnaire d'Archéologie Chrétienne et de Liturgie*, IV, cols. 427–45); but it was in the seventh century that requests for annual commemoration appeared in wills, in addition to offerings *pro remedio animae*, and from these stem endowments for masses. The immense accumulation of landed property by the Church owes a great deal to both; see L. Bréhier and R. Aigrain, *Grégoire le Grand, les états barbares et la conquête arabe* (Paris, 1938), A. Fliche and V. Martin (eds.), *Histoire de l'Eglise*, V, pp. 556–7.

62 Indirectly in the case of the Senhor Jesus da Piedade at Elvas; directly in that of N. Sra dos Remedios at Romão.

63 Molho de Faria, *São Bento da Porta Aberta*, p. 83.

64 'One high mass, at least. There may have been others, but people always said: "Just one mass".'

65 At Fátima, where the traditional *romaria* has been remodelled in line with official religious conceptions, 'vows' and 'offerings of masses' have been implicitly combined under the same heading.

66 The importance of foundations for masses as indicators in the study of changes in religious mentality has recently been emphasized (in the context of 'dechristianization') by M. Vovelle, *Piété baroque et déchristianisation en Provence au XVIIIe siècle* (Paris, 1973); see also the discussion in P. Ariès, *Essais sur l'histoire de la mort en Occident du Moyen Age à nos jours* (Paris, 1975).

67 Sometimes, when there are two, people 'belong to both so as to have the right to double the number of masses' (Tinalhas).

68 'Doações e legados pios', *São Torcato*, 69–70 (September–October 1955).

69 A further indication: while the village confraternities, which are mutual benefit societies with a view to the hereafter, usually recruit the entire population, we may observe that, curiously, the confraternities of the big *romaria* shrines, even the most prestigious which could guarantee their members a host of spiritual benefits, have relatively few members. (The Confraternity of São Torcato, for example, has hardly more than two hundred effective members, and two hundred *irmãos de peditório*, whose role is to collect offerings.) This suggests that it is a different type of relationship with the treasury of sacred power, which pilgrims look for in the *romaria*.

70 Salt is offered to many other saints besides St Benedict. What is its symbolic meaning? As is well known, E. Jones argues in *Essays in Applied Psycho-analysis* (London, 1923), pp. 112–203, that in the unconscious it is the symbolic equivalent of human semen and urine. Carnations, salt and eggs are certainly often found together as offerings in rituals which consecrate sexuality or in propitiatory fertility rites. Canon A. Ribeiro, however, has put forward a historical hypothesis to explain the huge quantity of salt that is offered at São Bento da Porta Aberta. The monks of the neighbouring shrine of Abadia were the concessionnaires by royal favour of numerous salt-works on the coast. The salt carriers, who had to pass through São Bento to reach Abadia, must have timed their journey to coincide with the great festival of 15 August at the latter shrine, and, since São Bento was their last stopping-place, the semi-feudal delivery came gradually to be seen as a *romaria* offering; see *São Bento da Porta Aberta*, (November 1961), an article included in his book *Senhora da Abadia*. However, this thesis hardly explains the presence of salt at many other *romarias*, and, even so far as this case is concerned, it is not clear why salt should be offered at São Bento rather than at Abadia.

71 St John of Arga, or at Vairão, Vila do Conde, etc.

72 Vila Chao (Esposende).

73 Meneches (Serra das Areias).

74 J. Leite de Vasconcellos, 'Excursão pela Estremadura cistagana et Norte de Portugal', *O Arqueólogo Português*, XXII (1917), p. 153; J. R. dos Santos jr, 'As

telhas do teu telhado, Nota etnográfica', *Arquivos do Seminário de Estudos Galegos*, VI (Compostela, 1933–4), pp. 105–24; E. V. de Oliveira, 'Roubo ritual', *Boletín de la Comisión Provincial de Monumentos Históricos y Artísticos de Orense*, XX, 1–4 (1959–60), pp. 99–101; and Oliveira, 'Manifestations de la vie spirituelle', p. 140. The same ritual of stolen tiles occurs at the festival of St Ovídio, the patron of deceived wives, in the Serra de Arga, and at the festival of St Dominic, in the Beira Baixa; see J. R. Araújo, 'Os santos da Serra de Arga', *Diário Popular*, p. 96; and J. L. Dias, 'Distrito Etnográfico, S. Domingos de entre Zebreira e Rosmaninhal', *Acção Regional*, II (Castelo Branco, 1926), p. 79.

75 Auctions are not always held on the day of the pilgrimage. Some (like the offerings) are spread over several Sundays; others are reserved for the most favourable time of year. In São Bento da Porta Aberta, the salt is sold in November when the pigs are slaughtered and salted. Local families thus become the special clients of the saint. Sometimes, when offerings amount in all to a considerable quantity, the whole lot may be bought by a retailer. At Cossourado in 1973 (a quiet year), 'because the war in Angola has quietened down; there are hardly any more casualties; people are less frightened', there were only twenty or so chickens by the late afternoon; but there were nearly 200 dozen eggs (compared with the usual 250–300 dozen). At Aÿres, it is now rare for the amount of corn to exceed two hundredweight, but in the past many landowners used to reserve a special 'field for Our Lady of Aÿres', or a pig or a mule 'for Our Lady of Aÿres'. However, at São Torcato 300 kilos of potatoes were offered one Sunday in 1955, outside the festival season, *São Torcato*, 67–8 (July–August 1955).

76 This is perceived in a great variety of ways. Nowadays, sudden, spectacular bidding seems to have become rare, though sometimes still, with the help of a good deal of wine, a man, often from among the very poor, will risk a dramatic gesture. We observed a negative reaction to such behaviour, particularly among emigrants or local shopkeepers who are upwardly mobile: 'He obviously doesn't know what it is to work for his money.'

77 We established a parallel between the ideal-type *gesture* and the ideal-type *ritual* in *Liturgie en conserve et liturgie vivante, Le cas de la Masse du Morro* (Paris, 1971), pp. 210–18 (Mémoire E.P.H.E).

78 See H. Lefebvre, *Critique de la vie quotidienne*, I (Paris, 1961).

10

The cult of saints among the Muslims of Nepal and northern India

MARC GABORIEAU

The cult of saints in Indian Islam had its hour of glory under the Emperor Akbar (1542–1605). The Emperor was a great devotee of Mu ʿin-ud-dīn Cishtī (1141–1236), who established the Cishtī order, one of the oldest in India, and who is regarded as one of the great spiritual ancestors of the Muslim community in India. Over a long period during his reign, the Emperor made annual pilgrimages to the saint's tomb at Ajmer in Rajasthan, and it was thanks to the intercession of Salīm Cishtī (d. 1568), an influential member of the order, that he was blessed with a son.

As this well-known example illustrates, the cult of saints has links with Sufism, but did it remain confined, in its forms and aims, within the limits of this great codified tradition, or did it overflow this framework, as happened elsewhere in Islam, to link up with the multisecular traditions of the region in which it was found? Such are the problems I have discussed elsewhere, either in passing or in connection with a particular example,[1] and which I wish to discuss here in a more general and systematic way. I shall attempt to list the different forms of the cult of saints and to define its functions in relation to the Muslim community of the Indian subcontinent and also in relation to the Hindu community, in so far as it, too, participated in the cult.

The term most frequently used to designate saints in the Indian context is *pīr* (P),[2] which means both a living member of an order and any person considered to be a saint after his death. The word *walī* (plural *ʾawliyā*) (A), so common in the central Islamic lands, is rarely used.[3] Some well-known saints such as Madār are called *shāh* (P), which means king.

I have drawn on two types of material: on the one hand, field-work observations made mainly in Nepal, and, on the other, literary descriptions written either by Muslims themselves or by administrators of the British period and dating principally from the end of the nineteenth or the beginning of the twentieth century. The general climate of opinion throughout most of the twentieth century has not been favourable to this

291

kind of study. Reform movements inside the Muslim community of India, similar in inspiration to the Wahhabite movement in the Arab world, threw discredit on to these forms of popular religion which had been gradually built up during the Middle Ages. The best-educated Muslims were ashamed of them, and very little was written on the subject, save to condemn recourse to the intercession of saints in the name of a disdainful orthodoxy. It is only very recently that anthropologists or historians have again drawn attention to these forms of piety which still persist widely today in traditionalist milieux.

In such studies it is usual to begin with the biographies of the saints, examining their cults only in conclusion. This procedure derives from a centuries-old literary convention. The orders compiled and preserved collections of saints' Lives; and the writing of whole works devoted to famous saints became an established literary genre. At a more popular level, there were ballads orally transmitted by travelling bards or popular printed compilations in Urdu. But the disadvantage of starting with these narratives, which their authors' imagination can prolong interminably, is that one loses sight of what is important for the faithful, of what is done for the saints, and of what is expected from them in return. The best approach therefore is to analyse the cults which are rendered to the saints, and we shall start here by analysing the institutions related to the cults; we shall then go on to classify the functions fulfilled by the saints, and we shall only draw on biographies in order to illustrate certain aspects of the rites or functions.

I THE ORGANIZATION OF THE CULT

There is no doubt that the cult of saints begins during their lifetime. Akbar venerated Salīm Cishtī; and any *pīr* or member of an order who demonstrates his supernatural powers becomes in a sense the object of a cult well before his death. However, we shall confine ourselves to those saints who have been, as it were, definitively 'canonized' by the establishment after their deaths of a regular cult, with certain well-defined institutions. Saints may, of course, be venerated privately in the hearts or homes of the faithful; but a cult is marked by a high degree of institutionalization, having well-established and often highly organized shrines. These are served by specialized officiants who constitute well-defined classes or even castes, and the forms of the cult are by tradition elaborately codified.

(i) The shrines

The shrines display different degrees of complexity,[4] but they all have one element in common: the tomb of the saint, which in the simplest cases is itself the whole shrine and which even in the most complex constitutes the central element.

The word for a tomb is *qabr* (A). Most tombs in cemeteries, those of the ordinary dead, are never described in any other way. But once a dead person begins to be venerated as a saint, his tomb is given a nobler name, that of *mazār* (A), the 'place that is visited', or sometimes *ziyāra* (A), 'visit', in allusion to the ritual which is central to all saints' cults (see (iii) below). This term strictly refers to the tomb in which the saint is actually buried, and, by extension, to a cenotaph or to any copy of the original tomb, where shrines of a well-known saint have multiplied within a region or across several provinces. Thus, Shāh G̲h̲iyāṣ-ud-dīn, founder of the Kashmiri Muslim community of Katmandu, has only one *mazār*, his real tomb which lies in the cemetery beside the Kashmiri mosque of the city. But Madār Shāh, a saint of northern India, who lived in the fourteenth and fifteenth centuries, has hundreds or even thousands of *mazār*; his actual tomb is in Makanpur, north of Kanpur in Uttar Pradesh, but his cenotaphs are dispersed all over northern India, Bangladesh and Nepal. Similarly, the actual tomb of G̲h̲azī Mīyā is in Bahraich in Uttar Pradesh, while his cenotaphs are scattered over almost as wide an area as those of Madār Shāh.

A tomb may be very simply indicated: a stone slab; a stone parallelepiped covered with a layer of stucco or cement, sometimes with an inscription, sometimes not; or even, in villages, a plain cube of masonry, rendered with clay; in short, just a symbol providing the basis for a cult.

If the local community has the means, the shrine may be enlarged; the tomb or cenotaph may be isolated and protected within a walled enclosure, and then covered over with a stone canopy resting on columns. The result is a building with the *mazār* in the centre and a space around it where the faithful can walk. In rich urban shrines, the building may be of marble and crowned with one or more domes; in humble villages it may be a simple thatched hut. The essential element of the shrine, therefore, is the tomb, with an optional building to house it; and this simple type of shrine is always called a *mazār*.

For more complex types the still nobler term, *dargāh* (P), is used, meaning palace or royal court. A typical example is Niẓām-ud-dīn 'Awliyā, in the outlying district of Delhi called precisely Nizamuddin. Walls, in which several monumental gates are set, enclose numerous buildings around a series of inner courtyards. The essential, central element is the saint's tomb itself, which is always covered with rich fabric and is housed in a white marble building. To the left of it is a mosque built by a Muslim sovereign, and, close by, the pool in which the faithful bathe and whose water is believed to have miraculous powers. The other buildings nearby accommodate the guardians of the shrine, both members of the Cishtī order to which the saint belonged and other officiants of more modest rank, and also the *dargāh* library and archives. Tombstones are scattered all around, for many noble or royal persons have chosen to be buried near the saint whom they venerated. Every day crowds gather both inside and outside the enclosure: the faithful bringing offerings and musicians and singers paid to extol the saint, but also beggars, cripples, idiots and lunatics, the usual motley company of those who live off the alms of the faithful. Some *dargāh*, like that of Muʿin-ud-dīn Cishtī in Ajmer, have a music house, the *naubat khānah* (P), where the passing of the hours is marked with drums, long trumpets and oboes, this is also found in royal palaces and is, indeed, a sign of royalty.

Finally, if the saint was a member of an order his tomb may be part of his monastery, *khānqah* (P); in this case the tomb and the building around it form part of a much larger monastic complex.

The basic resources of these shrines are provided by the regular offerings of the faithful, to which may be added occasional more substantial gifts from generous donors. Once a shrine becomes important, it is established as a foundation, a legal entity having its own possessions and being recognized by the civil authorities. Where Muslim law is applied, as in India or Pakistan, the foundation is recognized as *waqf* (A). In Nepal, foundations are called *guṭhī* (N), like the analogous Hindu institutions. Administrators, who are accountable to the civil authorities, manage the foundation's movable and immovable property, together with the income deriving from it and from the offerings of the faithful. They share out the income among the various headings of expenditure: the upkeep of the shrine, the organization of festivals and the remuneration of officiants.[5]

(ii) The officiants

Except for minor tombs which only come to life for annual or occasional acts of worship, the shrines have regular officiants, who fall into various categories.

In the big shrines, there are several categories of person attached to the saint's tomb who perform a whole range of services, and these are arranged in a hierarchy. At the top, there are those who participate in the ritual, and who themselves fall into two categories. First are the higher specialists, who are, strictly speaking, the technicians of the ritual; they welcome the faithful, help them to present their offerings and to accomplish the proper rites, and later they provide them with counsel and advice. They are usually descendants of the saint, as their name indicates, *pīr-zādah* (P), sons of *pīr*, or they may simply be members of the same order called *pīr*; otherwise, they are educated men, *mullah* (A *maulā*), having no particular link with the saint's spiritual lineage.[6]

At a lower level are the 'servants', permanently attached to the shrine, who bear the slightly derogatory name of *mujāwir* (A), literally 'those who live near' (the saint);[7] they carry out all the humbler tasks, and particularly the cleaning of the shrine – hence the common translation of their name as 'sweepers'. However, they should not be confused with members of the untouchable caste who normally exercise this profession; they are in fact people of higher status who have a vocation for religious service. As far as we know, they are recruited either among the orders of lower standing, such as that of the Madārī,[8] or among the faithful hereditarily devoted to the saints. Both are guaranteed a regular wage by the shrine which employs them.

In addition to these specialists with specifically religious functions, there are others whose role is closer to profane activities. First, there are the musicians; where there is a *naubat khānah*, they sound the hours, but they also perform at religious ceremonies and provide processions with instrumental music; where music is permitted, other musicians, or the same ones, execute the devotional songs, the *qawwālī* (H),[9] as an aid to mystical exercises. This classic Islamic framework seems to have been rapidly extended to include purely Indian characteristics: at least until the last century, processions comprised not only instrumental bands but also dancing girls, who were more or less prostitutes and who figure in festivals throughout India.[10] Some shrines, for example, in Lucknow,[11] or in southern India,[12] even used to employ sacred prostitutes, like those in Hindu temples, on a permanent basis. All this utterly scandalized the puritan *ʿulamāʾ* who throughout the centuries unceasingly protested against the immoderate use of music and the presence of dancing girls; but these customs have survived even if they are no longer mentioned now that reformers outweigh traditionalists.

At the village level, in the smaller shrines there is usually only one regular officiant who undertakes all the religious functions: such as the rites and the upkeep of the shrine. The recruitment of these guardians is interesting. Recent anthropological monographs show that they usually belong to one of the lower orders, such as the Madārī, the Dafalī, and had been subordinates, *mujāwir*, in a big shrine before taking sole charge of a small one.[13] Where no member of an order is available, any householder with a minimum of competence in ritual matters may run the shrine. He may be called *mullah*, but in practice there is a tendency for Hindu terminology to be adopted, and he is usually called *pujārī*, like the officiants at Hindu temples. For music, castes of untouchable musicians are called on, some of which, such as the Dafalī, actually specialize in the cult of saints. Some devotional chants are sung by the men and others by the women of the community.

The situation is thus much simpler than in the bigger shrines; but there is one complication at the village level, in the form of a figure far removed from the classical traditions of Islam: this is the medium, a man or a woman who is able to go into trances in the shrine, and through whom the saint is supposed to talk, providing answers like an oracle to questions posed by the faithful.[14]

To summarize: there are three specific officiating roles each of which may be absent or may be divided between several people according to the complexity of the shrine: specialist in ritual, musician and medium.

(iii) The Cult

Ceremonies honouring the saints can be classified according to their periodicity: weekly, monthly, or annual. This first classification cuts across another one made in terms of which section of the community participates in them, which we shall examine below. We shall start with the elements common to all ceremonies of whatever category, and return to the problems involved in their interpretation at the end of the article.

Generally speaking, the cult of saints comprises at least four common elements. The first is a personal visit to the shrine, which means travelling to it, walking round the tomb and touching it. Secondly, the worshipper must bring offerings: money, food in the form of fruit or rice, etc., and sacrificial victims (chickens, goats, sheep). Thirdly, he must recite or have the officiant recite a prayer called either *fātiḥa* (A), after the first *sūra* of the Koran, which it includes, or simply *duʿāʾ* (A). This is a prayer of entreaty, not to be confused with the canonical prayer, *ṣalāt* (A), and takes the following form: 'O God Almighty, we bring you these offerings in the name of such and such a saint! May the merit of our action fall on the saint and his faithful!' Fourthly, and lastly, the offerings are partly appropriated by the guardians of the shrine (the money and some of the food), while the rest is consumed by the faithful who thus participate in the sacrifice.[15]

The cult can be occasional: here the faithful go individually to the tomb, to pray and to bring offerings, following a vow or in order to seek a favour. There is no periodicity, and no particular day is fixed for these activities. There are also periodical ceremonies. The most frequently held, but which attract the fewest people, for they are a matter of individual devotion, take place every week on Thursday evenings or on Fridays during the day. Friday is the Muslim holy day, on which community prayer takes place in the afternoon. Muslims count days in the same way as Jews and Hindus: a day begins and ends at sunset, so that their Friday begins on our Thursday evening and ends on our Friday evening. The faithful therefore go to the shrine either on our Thursday evening or on Friday before sunset – either individually or in small processions.[16]

The occasion which attracts all the devotees of a saint from within the general sphere of influence of his shrine is the annual festival, commemorating the anniversary of the saint's death; this is called ʿ*urs*, an Arabic term meaning 'wedding', and which is here used in a mystical sense to refer to the saint's union to his God through death.[17] The date is usually fixed according to the Muslim lunar calendar, but in certain cases of old and very popular saints, such as Ghazī Mīyā, a date in the Indian solar calendar has been adopted.[18]

The ritual carried out on such occasions includes all the essential elements defined above, to which others are added, giving the festival an extra dimension. The most general of these are the processions. The day before the festival, or several days before in the case of the very big shrines, the faithful arrive in highly coloured processions, more like our wedding than our religious processions; for they are led by bands and sometimes by dancing girls and by fakirs of the different orders. The faithful carry poles with strips of fabric attached to them like banners: these are called *charī* (H) 'sticks', *neza* (P) 'lances', or *phaṇḍa* (H) 'banners'. The processions are usually called *charī* after the poles, or sometimes *mednī* (H). When they reach the shrine, the pilgrims stick their poles into the ground near the tomb, and these are recovered at the end of the festival. When the pilgrims leave, they again form very colourful processions. Those who were unable to take part in the festival give the pilgrims a warm welcome, claiming from them souvenirs and consecrated objects brought back from the shrine.[19]

Between the two sets of processions is the festival itself, which has two aspects, one sacred, the other profane. The rituals involved are both individual and collective. As in the occasional rites, the faithful go around the tomb, touch it and leave offerings individually. But the annual festivals also involve a collective cult, which always includes recitation from the Koran and canonical prayers.[20] Where music is allowed, there is also devotional and mystical chanting. Lastly, animals, usually goats, are sacrificed to God in the name of the saint and are offered up to him symbolically together with the food prepared for the faithful. The latter then consume both in a banquet which, though it may seem like a picnic, is in the context of the festival a sort of sacrificial meal: the faithful eat the remainder of the food which has been blessed and offered up in the name of the saint.[21]

After this, the rest of the festival becomes entirely profane: a sort of fair lasting all night (the ceremonies having begun at sunset) and the rest of the following day.[22] This is called *melā* (H), the name given to the same type of gathering at the shrines of Hindu gods. One also finds there the same mixture of commercial activity and entertainment. It is a great occasion for traders and restaurateurs who set out their wares by the shrines and do brisk business. There are all kinds of entertainments: Muslim fakirs do turns, such as walking through fire. There are large numbers of jugglers, tumblers and exhibitors of animals, all of whom are often members of Sufi orders. There are also musicians, dancing girls and prostitutes. The faithful sing and dance too. The fair quickly becomes a carnival, one of whose functions is to allow a certain licence. Such then are the general lines along which the cult of saints is organized.

II   FUNCTIONS OF THE CULT OF SAINTS

What functions does this cult of saints fulfil? This question is linked to several others. Who are the devotees of the cults? How do they conceive of the saints and their powers? What roles do the saints play for individual devotees and for the community as a whole?

(i) Interpretation of the cult

The rituals briefly described above raise a number of problems of interpretation. Should we take the prayers quite literally or should we look for a wider interpretation of the rituals as a whole?

As we have seen, the prayers recited at the tombs are called *du ʿāʾ* or invocations (not to be confused with the *ṣalāt*, the canonical prayers said five times a day at fixed times), or *fātiḥa*. Are they such as to offend purists? Nearly a century and a half ago, Garcin de Tassy emphasized: 'These *fātiḥa* are not addressed to the saints exactly; the best comparison would be with the collects which are said during Catholic masses in honour of the saints, but which do not involve direct prayer to them. Thus, although Indian Muslims are very devoted to their saints, it cannot be said that they pray directly to them' (p. 26). Invocations observed in the field between 1964 and 1975 absolutely confirm this judgment. They all follow the same model: 'O God, we present these offerings to you! May you recompense such and such a saint and the faithful here present!' Even the most orthodox could find no fault with these prayers, for overtly there is no trace of idolatry in them; they are addressed to God and to God alone, and the saints are not directly venerated.

Yet, as early as the eighteenth century, reformers had caught a whiff of something else, for they openly accused the saints' devotees of idolatry. And, indeed, if we put aside the texts of their prayers and the orthodox interpretation of them, and question ordinary devotees and study the rites which they celebrate, we can see that they actually perceive the saints quite differently.[23]

First of all, what they say about the saints is unequivocal: they believe that the saint is in some way present in the tomb; they go there to pray not to God but to the saint himself; they take offerings to the saint, not to God; the gifts which they make to the shrines are for the saints. The representations underlying the rites confirm this clear language: there is probably little to say about the ordinary offerings of produce or money, but the object of sacrifices is more evident. For example, at the annual festivals, the rites often have a specific aim. The devotees offer the first corn to Ghazī Mīyā so as to obtain a good crop the following year; for rain, they sacrifice goats at the foot of a pole which is thought to link heaven and earth;[24] and, as they openly say, these offerings are destined for the saint who controls natural forces. This interpretation is made even more obviously applicable in the case of the exceptional rites which follow a vow; if the devotee requires a favour from the saint, he makes him the following promise: 'If you grant me this favour, I will make you a certain offering.' It is a kind of bargain struck between devotee and saint.[25] Finally, other rites with a distinctly pagan character place devotees in direct communication with the saint; for example, the exceptional sacrifices offered up to Ghazī Mīyā to obtain rain during a drought,[26] or, even more telling, the rites of possession linked to the cult of saints: the latter are thought to take possession of mediums and to talk through them directly to the faithful. I was able to study this institution in the shrines of Ghazī Mīyā in Nepal and it is widely attested in northern India and Pakistan, for example in the cult of Shaikh Saddu.[27]

All these indications gathered by direct observation or from interviews with informants amply demonstrate that ordinary devotees commonly address the saints themselves. This attitude is doubtless strongly disapproved of today by the more orthodox, but medieval thought gave a large place to it, by constructing a whole intellectual scheme according to which it was the saints who governed the universe. It was therefore quite legitimate to address the saints directly. The doctrine was widely adopted in the Muslim world, as witness an author who lived nine centuries ago in Lahore, in what is now Pakistan: '[God] has made the saints the governors of the universe; they have become entirely devoted to His business, and have ceased to follow their sensual affections. Through the blessing of their advent the rain falls from heaven, and through the purity of their lives the plants spring up from the earth, and through their spiritual influence the Muslims gain victories over the unbelievers.'[28]

(ii) Functions of the cult of saints

Having made this point, we must now ask ourselves what functions the saints fulfil for their devotees. The question has barely been investigated, though two types of classification have been made. The first is inherited from medieval thought and presents a complex hierarchy of the saints according to their functions in the ordering of the universe;[29] although literature concerning India testifies to its existence there,[30] I have never come across it at the popular level with which we are concerned here. The

faithful themselves are not concerned with making any reasoned classification of their saints. We are left with two classifications drawn up by
Western observers at the end of the nineteenth and the beginning of the
twentieth centuries.[31] These are not entirely rational in that they use a
variety of criteria which are sometimes incompatible, such as questions of
origin, function, and so on. We will attempt to introduce some order into
the classifications by concentrating on the functions of the cults from the
point of view of the faithful. Our first distinction is between saints who
have a universal function and those whose function is specialized in some
way.

The first category consists of saints who are invoked in all circumstances
to obtain all kinds of favours; they can best be described by quoting this
song that women sing at a shrine of Ghazi Mīyā in western Nepal:[32]

> [Prayer of the faithful]:
> Bees, what juice shall we get?
> We would like honey.
>
> [Reply of the saint]:
> I will give you sons to hold in your lap:
> Touch my tomb.
> I will give a son and milk:
> Touch my tomb.
> I will give grain and money:
> Touch my tomb.
>
> We will get a palace;
> We will get the object of our desires.
>
> You have given sons to those who had none.
> You have given riches to the disinherited.
> You have given clothes to those who were naked.
> You have given bodies to lepers.

These universal saints can be further classified according to the size of
the section of the population which venerates them. Apart from the
Prophet Muḥammad himself (the anniversary of whose birth is in many
ways celebrated like the festival of a saint), only his two grandsons, Ḥasan
and Ḥusayn, it seems, have festivals which are traditionally observed
throughout the Indian subcontinent. In fact, the first ten days of the month
of Muḥarram (the first month of the lunar calendar) are consecrated to
them, though purists like the Kashmiri Muslims of the Katmandu valley
devote only the tenth day to them with a modest celebration of the ʿāshūrāʾ
(A).[33] However, most Muslims, Sunnites as well as Shīʿites, celebrate the
first ten days in a big way (and are joined in this by many Hindus). In each
town, in each district, there is a place (an enclosure or a building) which is
especially reserved for this celebration. In the centre of it is a platform, on

which a cenotaph, *ta῾zīya* (A), of wood and paper is built on the first day. Every day, thereafter, the cenotaph is carried in a procession through the streets to the sound of music; and the faithful gather to listen to songs of lament evoking the births, marriages and deaths of Ḥasan and Ḥusayn and their companions. On the evening of the tenth day, the cenotaph is thrown into a river.[34]

Other saints, without being so widely venerated, nevertheless have a very large following over the whole subcontinent. These include the Pañch Pīr,[35] a group of five saints particularly venerated among the lower classes. Their identity varies from region to region; only their number, five, is important. Sometimes there are five saints as such; elsewhere the Prophet Muḥammad and his two grandsons are included in the set; and sometimes, even, a goddess of Hindu origin is introduced. In one example which I studied in the mountains of Nepal, the five Pīr were: the Prophet, his two grandsons, the saint Madār Shāh, founder of the Madārī order, and the goddess Sahajā Māī.[36] Finally a legendary saint, belonging to the widest Islamic tradition, is almost universally venerated; Khwājā Khiẓr. A mythical figure, the companion of the Prophet Elijah, he is immortal and reigns over the source of life, over water and over vegetation; he is represented as an old man dressed in green and riding on a fish. We shall come across him again in more specialized roles; but let us mention here that he has an annual festival, either on the last Thursday of the year, if computed by the lunar calendar, or on the last Thursday in the month of Bhadon (August–September by the solar calendar). On that evening, offerings to him are placed, together with a lighted lamp, on a tiny clay boat which is then floated down a river or on the sea.[37]

The cults of other saints who grant all sorts of favours are supported only by certain sections of the population, determined by locality or by social group. Local saints have audiences of varying sizes. Mu῾in-ud-dīn Cishtī, who is considered to be the first great propagator of Islam in India, is venerated by nearly all the inhabitants of the subcontinent; and his annual festival, between the 6th and the 14th of the month of Rajab, is celebrated nearly everywhere; pilgrims come from all directions to his tomb in Ajmer.[38] The audience of other local saints is much more limited, being confined to a region, a province or a town. Thus Qādir Walī Ṣāhib is known only in southern India, while the cult of Ghazī Mīyā is confined to the north. Then there are saints who are even more localized. The Kashmiri Muslims of Katmandu venerate Shāh Ghiyāṣ-ud-dīn, who is said to have founded their community at the end of the sixteenth century. According to oral tradition, it was he who obtained from the king the land and funds required to set up a mosque and a cemetery; and when the community is in difficulties, he is prayed to and will intervene.[39] So, when a prime minister, at the beginning of this century, ordered that the mosque should be moved so that he could enlarge the gardens of his palace, an old man appeared to him in a dream the following night and threatened him with dreadful misfortunes if he did not reverse his decision; and the next day he annulled the order. The Kashmiri see this as an intervention by Ghiyāṣ-ud-dīn.

Some saints are more local still:

In Lucknow, in the quarter known as Golanganj, there is the tomb of a saint of little-known reputation, who is specially worshipped by the people of the locality, over whose welfare he is supposed to preside. On one occasion, when new buildings of the Lucknow Christian College were being erected, some very heavy steel girders had to be raised, which placed many lives in jeopardy. After they had all been safely raised, the Muslim workers proceeded to procure some sweetmeats, and forthwith went to the tomb to make the offering and express their gratitude.[40]

In certain regions, there are also saints who protect the smallest spatial unit, the house:

Muhammadan domestic worship is largely concerned with the propitiation of the household Pīr. In almost every house is a dreaded spot where ... is the abode or corner of the Pīr, and the owner erects a little shelf, lights a lamp every Thursday night, and hangs up garlands of flowers.[41]

The faithful can also become devotees of a particular saint by virtue of the social groups to which they belong. Two quite distinct types of social group are involved here, orders and castes, although they may overlap. Despite having been in decline for several centuries, the orders have nevertheless preserved the essential features of their organization.[42] The dervishes or fakirs who are, as it were, full-time members of the orders must, of course, venerate the founders and other saints of their own order and particularly those who are buried in the monasteries to which they are attached. In addition to these 'monks', there are innumerable laymen who are affiliated to the orders, constituting a sort of 'third order'; they, too, venerate the founding saints of their spiritual association. Thus in Katmandu, the Kashmiri observe the annual festivals of the founders of whichever of the three great orders they may be attached to: ʿAbd-ul-Qādir Al-jilānī, founder of the Qādirīya, Muʿin-ud-dīn Cishtī, founder of the Cishtīya, or Khwājā Muḥammad Naqshaband, founder of the Naqshbandīya.[43]

The faithful may also venerate certain saints by virtue of belonging to a professional group. In other parts of the Muslim world we would speak of corporations,[44] but here we must talk rather of castes. Some of them, the lowest in the hierarchy with strictly defined professional specializations, have a patron saint. Several lists of these have been published,[45] and may be briefly summarized. Khwājā Khiẓr protects all castes associated with water: washermen, watercarriers, boatmen; the last also have two other patron saints: Qādir Walī Ṣāhib in southern India, and

Ma ʿlūm-i-yār in northern India. The blacksmiths invoke Ḥazrat Da ʿūd, or King David. Athletes and wrestlers invoke Sakhi Sarwar, also known as Lākhdāta; and turners, Firoz Shāh Jilānī. Oilmen (Telī) and dyers (Rangrez) have patron saints whose family names refer to their professions: Ḥasan Telī and Pīr Alī Rangrez. The sweepers and cesspool clearers honour Lāl Beg, and so on.

However, it should not be thought that there is a very elaborate system covering all the professions: in fact, the range of saints honoured by any given group is generally determined by the three factors listed above: locality, professional specialization and the influence of the orders. Thus each case will form a specific constellation, as I was able to see when I was working on the Muslim minorities of Nepal. The Kashmiri of Katmandu, urban merchants of high status, honour saints from the local community and the founders of the three great orthodox orders. By contrast, the bracelet-makers, dispersed in the mountains, venerate the saints who are generally preferred in the lower castes. Their professional specialization is brought to bear only in this wider sense, since they do not have a specific patron saint. The operative factors here are locality and the influence of the orders. Bracelet-makers are divided into two groups: those of central Nepal who are under the heterodox influence of the Madārī order, and who venerate its founder Madār Shāh whose tomb in Makanpur near Kanpur in India is very close to their place of residence; and those of western Nepal who are influenced by another order, that of the Dafalī, priests of Ghazī Mīyā, whose tomb is closer to their place of residence and whom they venerate.[46]

Besides these saints of universal vocation, who are selected for the reasons we have seen, there are others who specialize in certain types of favour. To be more exact (for the two categories sometimes overlap), there are saints who are especially venerated for particular types of favour, even if they are also venerated in a general way. This specialization of saints is known to exist throughout Islam: 'Popular belief...has...inclined to specialize [the power of the saints], each of them having in the eyes of the multitude the power of performing a special miracle, like curing a particular disease, bringing success in a particular kind of business, guiding travellers, discovering secrets, etc.'[47] In India and Nepal, this specialization, which is far from systematic, covers two main areas: disease and the agricultural cycle.

We have lists of saints who specialize in certain diseases.[48] Those reputed to cure sterility are legion; Sakhi Sarwar in the Punjab relieves eye complaints; he and Makhdūm Ṣāhib exorcize the possessed; Shaikh Saddu cures melancholy; Guga Pīr and Madār Shāh cure people who have been bitten by snakes; Pīr Jahāniyā cures leprosy, and so on.

It is noteworthy that, at least in the north of the Indian subcontinent (including Nepal and Pakistan), certain saints used to specialize in the protection of the harvest. This is clearly the case for G͟hazī Mīyā whom I have studied in detail.[49] His festival is fixed by the solar calendar on the first Sunday in the month of Jeṭh (May–June), and is thus in harmony with the agricultural calendar, coinciding with the corn harvests which would not be the case if it had a lunar date. Literary accounts emphasize events in the saint's life: his marriage and his martyrdom.[50] In strictly ethnographic descriptions, however, the saint's link with the harvest has pride of place. His festival is first and foremost a kind of harvest festival. In Islam generally, the first fruits of the harvest are simply offered to Allah; but here, G͟hazī Mīyā is an essential intermediary. Muslims are absolutely forbidden to consume the new corn before the festival; and it has to be the whole community which offers up the first fruits. Each family brings a plateful of flour; flat cakes are made and fried in oil, and then some of them are placed on the saint's tomb and are offered up to God in his name, although in the eyes of the ordinary believers it is to the saint that they are being offered. It is only after this that the faithful may themselves eat the other cakes and then begin to make use of the rest of the harvest. The saint thus appears to be the master of the corn harvest. More generally, he also controls all crops since it is he who governs the rain. On his festival, a kid is sacrificed at the foot of a pole flanking his tomb in order to obtain the rainfall necessary for the other crops and for the following year's corn. In general, a single sacrifice is sufficient. However, in bad years when the rains do not come, the officiant performs two rites at the shrine. The first involves a kind of symbolic magic, and consists of pouring water over the foot of the pole. The second is an offering: one or more kids have their throats cut in such a way that their blood soaks into the wood of the pole. Thus the saint has a double link with the agricultural cycle: he protects the corn harvest and he ensures rain. G͟hazī Mīyā is not the only saint to fulfil these functions. In north-west India, the first fruits of the sugar cane crop are offered up to Baba Farīd-ud-dīn Shak͟harganj, whose last name means 'sugar mountain'.[51] Elsewhere, other saints, such as Guru Mastan Shāh, protect the harvest from hail.[52]

The specialization of saints in relation to disease is better known than their specialization in relation to the agricultural cycle. Much research remains to be done on the latter, which would certainly throw new light on the close interconnection between the cult of saints and rural life generally.

These, then, are the functions of the cult of saints, ranging from the general to the particular. The following of saints who dispense all types of favour may be narrowed down by locality, caste or social group. The specialization of the others goes in two directions: the curing of disease and guaranteeing the harvest.

What conclusions may we draw from this brief account? That the faithful prefer to address saints rather than Allah and that usually they do not have to go far to find a saint who can grant their wishes.

If we review our procedure, we see that in the second part we have considered the available information on the functions of the saints, and have drawn up a provisional classification. At every stage, it proved impossible to be systematic here; since each case leaves a great deal of room for individual choice and for historical contingencies. One might object that this was a question of gaps in our knowledge, and that further detailed research would reveal a more systematic pattern. This is certainly true but only up to a point, for there are certain built-in limitations in the Islamic context.

First, only the canonical ritual (profession of faith, prayers, fasting, etc.) is entirely systematic, since it is totally codified, and is identical for all the faithful. The cult of saints, on the contrary – like Sufism to which it is linked – forms part of those non-obligatory devotions in which a great freedom of choice is left to individuals or groups. Each individual may choose the saints whom he venerates. Social groups (ethnic and professional groups or castes) have been free to make divergent choices in the course of their history, to attach themselves to saints of certain orders, or to venerate their own saints from within their midst; so much so, that in historical research, the cult of saints is one of the surest indicators that groups, which are now geographically separated, shared a common origin.[53]

Secondly, it is impossible to be completely systematic because the cult of saints is not the only means by which the faithful may achieve their ends; they may also choose from the ancient stock of indigenous Hindu cults. Thus the cult of saints among the central Nepalese bracelet-makers is minimal and, in order to obtain important favours, the faithful turn instead to the spirits of those of their community who have died a violent death or to local divinities.[54]

If these alternatives are available, it is because there is an affinity between the cult of saints on the one hand, and the cult of the dead and of divinities on the other. They are all popularly given the same name, *deutā* (H), meaning 'god'.[55] This observation is not new. The first Western author to have studied the subject, Garcin de Tassy, remarked on it,[56] and he in turn was following an analysis made the previous century by reformers such as Shāh Walī Ullāh,[57] whose ideas, together with those of his successors, have now filtered through to large sections of the population.[58]

This affinity between the cult of saints and the cult of gods is indubitable. It fills the vast gap which separates Muslim monotheism from Hindu polytheism; and it explains the two-way syncretism present at the popular level. As many observations confirm, Hindus visit the tombs of Muslim saints and Muslims do not hesitate to venerate Hindu gods; the violent doctrinal opposition is tempered in day-to-day practice. But affinity does not mean identity; the cult of saints retains specifically Islamic characteristics – the tomb seen as a symbol, and the prayer of invocation.[59]

NOTES

For details of works mentioned here, see pp. 307–8 below.

1 See Gaborieau, 1977, pp. 33 and 51–2; and Gaborieau, 1975.
2 The transliteration system used here is taken from Platts's dictionary; the origin of words in italics is indicated by the following letters, placed in brackets: A = Arabic; P = Persian; H = Hindi; N = Nepalese.
3 Garcin de Tassy, pp. 15 and 23; *Shorter Encyclopaedia of Islam*, pp. 629–31 (art. *walī*).
4 On the shrines, see Garcin de Tassy, pp. 24–5; Subhan, pp. 106–7; Herklots, pp. 144–5.
5 See Schwerin.
6 Garcin de Tassy, pp. 26 and 59.
7 Platts, p. 1002.
8 Siddiqui, pp. 52 and 71.
9 Platts, p. 795.
10 Garcin de Tassy, pp. 28–9 and 48.
11 Chanana, p. 169.
12 Herklots, p. 145.
13 Mayer, 1960, pp. 40 and 72; Aggarwal, *passim*; Gaborieau, 1977, pp. 122–7.
14 Gaborieau, 1975, pp. 312–13; Rose, I, p. 644; Herklots, p. 139.
15 Garcin de Tassy, pp. 25–6; Herklots, pp. 134–6; Gaborieau, 1975, pp. 303 and 307–9; Titus, pp. 141–2.
16 Garcin de Tassy, p. 25; Subhan, p. 106.
17 Titus, pp. 142–4; Gaborieau, 1975, pp. 296–7.
18 Garcin de Tassy, pp. 72–84.
19 Garcin de Tassy, pp. 25 and 56–7; Gaborieau, 1975, pp. 300 and 309.
20 Titus, p. 143.
21 Gaborieau, 1975, pp. 306–9.
22 Garcin de Tassy, pp. 27–9 and *passim*; Titus, pp. 142–3; Gaborieau, 1975, pp. 303–4.
23 Gaborieau, 1975, p. 314.
24 Gaborieau, 1975, pp. 310–11.
25 Herklots, pp. 134–40; Titus, p. 142.
26 Gaborieau, 1975, p. 310.
27 See n. 14.
28 Al-Hudjwiri, Ali, *Kashf al-Maḥjūb*, cited by Subhan, p. 103; see also *Shorter Encyclopaedia of Islam*, p. 629.
29 For references, see *Shorter Encyclopaedia of Islam*, p. 629.

30 Herklots, p. 287; Subhan, pp. 104–6.
31 Crooke, I, pp. 183–229; Titus, pp. 145–52.
32 Gaborieau, 1975, p. 311.
33 Gaborieau, 1977, p. 51.
34 Garcin de Tassy, pp. 30–41; Herklots, pp. 151–85; Meer Hassan Ali, pp. 1–55; Gaborieau, 1977, pp. 121–2.
35 Garcin de Tassy, p. 16; Greeven; Crooke, I, pp. 202–6; *Shorter Encyclopaedia of Islam*, p. 457 (art. *pandj pīr*).
36 Gaborieau, 1977, p. 123.
37 Garcin de Tassy, pp. 80–3; Herklots, pp. 135–7; Titus, p. 146; Subhan, pp. 115–17; *Shorter Encyclopaedia of Islam*, p. 235.
38 Garcin de Tassy, p. 60; Subhan, pp. 192–208; *Encyclopaedia of Islam*, II, pp. 49–50.
39 Gaborieau, 1977, pp. 31–7 and 51.
40 Titus, p. 143.
41 Crooke, I, p. 204.
42 Herklots, pp. 283–300; Subhan, pp. 118–377.
43 Gaborieau, 1977, p. 51.
44 *Shorter Encyclopaedia of Islam*, p. 630.
45 Herklots, pp. 197–200; Crooke, I, pp. 202–3 and 210; Titus, pp. 149–50.
46 Gaborieau, 1977, pp. 120–9.
47 *Shorter Encyclopaedia of Islam*, p. 629.
48 Crooke, I, pp. 209–16 and 221; Herklots, *passim*.
49 Gaborieau, 1975.
50 Garcin de Tassy, pp. 72–9.
51 Crooke, I, p. 216; Briggs, pp. 483–5.
52 Gaborieau, 1975, p. 311.
53 Gaborieau, 1977, pp. 120–30.
54 Gaborieau, 1977, pp. 183–5; see also Garcin de Tassy, p. 21.
55 Gaborieau, 1975, p. 132; Gaborieau, 1977, p. 123.
56 Garcin de Tassy, pp. 10–11 and 15.
57 See for example, his work *Balāgh-ul-mubīn* (Delhi, Kitab Khanah Mas ʿūdīya, no date), Urdu translation.
58 Gaborieau, 1977, pp. 178–83.
59 Gaborieau, 1975, pp. 313–16.

BIBLIOGRAPHY

Aggarwal, Partap C., *Caste, Religion and Power, An Indian Case Study* (New Delhi, 1960).
Ahmad, Imtiaz (ed.), *Ritual and Religion among Muslims in India* (Delhi, 1981).
Briggs, G. W., *The Doms and their Near Relations* (Mysore, no date – after 1953).
Chanana, Dev Raj, *Slavery in Ancient India* (Delhi, 1960).
Crooke, William, *The Popular Religion and Folklore of Northern India*, 3rd edn (Delhi, 1968), 2 vols.
Encyclopaedia of Islam (Leiden and London, 1960).

Gaborieau, Marc, 'Légende et culte du saint musulman Ghazi Miya au Népal occidental et en Inde', *Objets et Mondes*, XV (1975), pp. 289–318.

Minorités musulmanes dans le royaume hindou du Népal (Paris, 1977).

Garcin de Tassy, M., *Mémoire sur les particularités de la religion musulmane dans l'Inde d'après les ouvrages hindoustanis*, 2nd edition (Paris, 1869).

Greeven, R., *The Heroes Five* (Allahabad, 1898).

Herklots, G. A., *Islam in India*, ed. W. Crooke (Oxford, 1921; Delhi, 1972).

Jeffery, Patricia, *Frogs in a Well, Indian Women in Purdah* (London, 1979).

'Creating a Scene: The disruption of ceremonial in a Sufi shrine', in Imtiaz Ahmad (ed.), *Ritual and Religion* (1981), pp. 163–94.

'The Wages of Death: Some aspects of the political economy of a Sufi shrine', unpublished paper.

Mayer, Adrian C., *Caste and Kinship in Central India* (London, 1960).

'*Pīr* and *murshid*: An Aspect of Religious Leadership in West Pakistan', *Middle Eastern Studies*, III (1967).

Meer Hassan Ali, Mrs, *Observations on the Mussulmauns of India* (1832), edited by W. Crooke (London, 1917), reprinted (Karachi, 1974).

Platts, J. T., *Urdu, Classical Hindi and English Dictionary* (London, 1884).

Rose, H. A., *A Glossary of Tribes and Castes of the Punjab and North-West Frontier Province* (Lahore, 1911–16), 3 vols.

Schimmel, Annemarie, *Islam in the Indian Subcontinent* (Leiden, 1980), particularly pp. 126–38.

Schwerin, Karin, 'Functions and Sources of Income of Muslim Dargahs in India', in M. Gaborieau and A. Thorner (eds.), *Asie du Sud: tradition et changements. Vth European Conference in Modern South Asian Studies* (Paris, 1979), pp. 279–81.

Shorter Encyclopaedia of Islam (Leiden and London, 1961).

Siddiqui, M. K. A., *Muslims of Calcutta, A Study in Aspects of Their Social Organization* (Anthropological Survey of India) (Calcutta, 1974).

Subhan, John A., *Sufism, Its Saints and Shrines* 2nd edn (New York, 1970).

Titus, Murray T., *Islam in India and Pakistan*, 2nd edn (Calcutta, 1959).

Annotated bibliography

STEPHEN WILSON

While this Bibliography aims to be fairly comprehensive, it is inevitably constrained within limits set by the Christianocentric bias of the literature, by the languages and disciplines with which the compiler is more or less acquainted, and by the current availability of items in British libraries. Biographies of saints, which are not primarily concerned with their contemporary or subsequent cults, have been generally excluded, as have books and articles providing 'background', for example, in religious sociology.

The bibliography is grouped under the following headings:

ABBREVIATIONS

AA	*American Anthropologist*
AB	*Analecta Bollandiana*
ABr.	*Annales de Bretagne*

ACNSS	*Actes du... Congrès National des Sociétés Savantes*
AFLNW	*Arbeitsgemeinschaft für Forschung des Landes Nordrhein-Westfalen*
AK	*Archiv für Kulturgeschichte*
AM	*Annales du Midi*
AN	*Annales de Normandie*
ANLP	*Accademia Nazionale dei Lincei*, Problemi attuali di Scienza e di Cultura, Atti del Convegno Internazionale sul tema: *L'Oriente Cristiano nella storia nella civiltà*
ANLR	*Accademia Nazionale dei Lincei, Rendiconti*, Classe di scienze morali, storiche e filologiche
Ann.	*Annales*
AOC	*Archives de l'Orient Chrétien*
ASR	*Archives de Sociologie des Religions*, later *Archives de Sciences Sociales des Religions*
ATP	*Arts et Traditions Populaires*
BEC	*Bibliothèque de l'Ecole des Chartes*
BKMR	*Beiträge zur Kulturgeschichte des Mittelalters und der Renaissance*
BSAO	*Bulletin de la Société des Antiquaires de l'Ouest*
Byz.	*Byzantion*
BZ	*Byzantinische Zeitschrift*
CCM	*Cahiers de Civilisation Médiévale*
CF	*Cahiers de Fanjeaux*
CFMA	Classiques Français du Moyen Age
CH	*Church History*
CSSH	*Comparative Studies in Society and History*
CSSM	*(Convegni del) Centro di Studi sulla Spiritualità medievale*
CUASCA	Catholic University of America, Studies in Christian Antiquity
DOP	*Dumbarton Oaks Papers*
EETS	Early English Text Society
EF	*Ethnologie Française*
EHR	*English Historical Review*
FL	*Folk-Lore*
HJ	*Historisches Jahrbuch*
HR	*History of Religions*
JEH	*Journal of Ecclesiastical History*
JTS	*Journal of Theological Studies*
LJ	*Liturgisches Jahrbuch*
MA	*Moyen Age*
MAR	*Monde Alpin et Rhodanien*
Med. A	*Medium Aevum*
MEFR	*Mélanges de l'Ecole Française de Rome*, Moyen Age – Temps Modernes
MF	*Miscellanea Francescana*
MIOG	*Mitteilungen der Instituts für Österreichische Geschichtsforschung*
MS	*Mediaeval Studies*
MSAF	*Mémoires de la Société (Nationale) des Antiquaires de France*
MSHPI	*Mémoires de la Société de l'Histoire de Paris et de l'Ile-de-France*

NA	*Norfolk Archaeology*
OZV	*Österreichische Zeitschrift für Volkskunde*
PH	*Provence Historique*
PIMS	Pontifical Institute of Medieval Studies
PP	*Past and Present*
RAM	*Revue d'Ascétique et de Mystique*
RB	*Revue Bénédictine*
RBPH	*Revue Belge de Philologie et d'Histoire*
RC	*Revue Celtique*
RHE	*Revue d'Histoire Ecclésiastique*
RHEF	*Revue d'Histoire de l'Eglise de France*
RHLR	*Revue d'Histoire et de Littérature Religieuses*
RHMC	*Revue d'Histoire Moderne et Contemporaine*
RHR	*Revue de l'Histoire des Religions*
RHS	*Revue d'Histoire de la Spiritualité*
RJV	*Rheinisches Jahrbuch für Volkskunde*
RQ	*Römische Quartalschrift für Christliche Altertumskunde und für Kirchengeschichte*
RQH	*Revue des Questions Historiques*
RSB	*Rivista Storica Benedettina*
RSCI	*Rivista di Storia della Chiesa in Italia*
RSR	*Revue des Sciences Religieuses*
RTP	*Revue des Traditions Populaires*
SAV	*Schweizerisches Archiv für Volkskunde*
SC	*Social Compass*
SCh.	Sources Chrétiennes
SCH	Studies in Church History
SG	*Studi Gregoriani*
SH	Subsidia Hagiographica
SM	*Studi Medievali*
Sp.	*Speculum*
TAASDN	*Transactions of the Architectural and Archaeological Society of Durham and Northumberland*
Tr.	*Traditio*
VR	Variorum Reprints
ZK	*Zeitschrift für Kirchengeschichte*
ZSS	*Zeitschrift der Savigny-Stiftung für Rechtsgeschichte*, Kanonistische Abteilung
ZV	*Zeitschrift für Volkskunde*

I DICTIONARIES AND REFERENCE WORKS

(A) GENERAL

1. Alban Butler, *The Lives of the Fathers, Martyrs and other Principal Saints: Compiled from Original Monuments and other authentick records: Illustrated with the Remarks of judicious modern cricks and historians* (London, 1756–9), 4/5 vols.; 2nd edition (Dublin, 1779), 12 vols.; and many subsequent editions. Scholarly dictionary by English Catholic priest, arranged by calendar; first edition published anonymously. A version 'edited, revised and supplemented' by Herbert Thurston and Donald Attwater appeared in 4 vols. (London, 1956); while more accurate and updated, this loses the Gibbonian flavour of the original.

2. Agnes B. C. Dunbar, *A Dictionary of Saintly Women* (London, 1904–5), 2 vols. Although female saints are in a distinct minority, they have received a disproportionate amount of scholarly attention.

3. *The Catholic Encyclopedia* (New York, 1907–14), 15 vols. See entries on Beatification, Canonization, Martyrs, Relics, Saints, etc.

4. James Hastings (ed.), *Encyclopaedia of Religion and Ethics* (Edinburgh and New York, 1908–26), 13 vols. Important articles on Beatification, Canonization, Mary, Pilgrimage, Relics, and Saints and Martyrs.

5. *Encyclopaedia Britannica* (New York, 1910–11), 11th edition, 29 vols. Valuable articles by Albert Hauck and H. Delehaye on Canonization, Martyrology, Pilgrimage, Relics, and Saints.

6. Alfred Baudrillart *et al.* (eds.), *Dictionnaire d'histoire et de géographie ecclésiastique* (Paris, 1912–   ). In progress; latest fascicule 112 (1981) ends at 'García'. A very scholarly reference work.

7. S. Baring-Gould, *The Lives of the Saints* (Edinburgh, 1914). Revised edition, 16 vols., with index. Arranged by calendar.

8. A. Vacant and E. Mangenot (eds.), *Dictionnaire de théologie catholique* (Paris, 1923–50), 15 vols., esp. 14, pp. 870–978, 'Saints (Culte des).' With good index.

9. F. G. Holweck, *A Biographical Dictionary of the Saints* (New York and London, 1924). Arranged alphabetically; essential.

10. Fernand Cabrol and Henri Leclercq (eds.), *Dictionnaire d'archéologie chrétienne et de liturgie* (Paris, 1924–53), 15 vols. Scholarly encyclopedia of great value.

11. R. Naz *et al.* (eds.), *Dictionnaire de droit canonique* (Paris, 1924–   ). In progress.

12. Dom Baudot, *Dictionnaire d'hagiographie* (Paris, 1925). One-volume French dictionary; still very useful.

13. *Enciclopedia Cattolica* (Vatican City, 1948–54), 12 vols.

14. Theodor Klauser *et al.* (eds.), *Reallexicon, Sachwörterbuch zur Auseinandersetzung des Christentums mit der antiken Welt* (Stuttgart, 1950–   ). In progress; has reached H.

15. John Coulson (ed.), *The Saints, A Concise Biographical Dictionary* (London, 1958). Brief entries on a large number of saints by team of scholarly contributors; well-illustrated.

16. *Bibliotheca Sanctorum* (Rome, 1961–70), Istituta Giovanni XXIII della Pontificia Università Lateranense, 13 vols. with index. Full alphabetical biographical dictionary; best of its kind.

17. Donald Attwater, *The Penguin Dictionary of Saints* (Harmondsworth, 1965). Useful and learned compendium.

18. *New Catholic Encyclopedia* (New York, 1967–78), 17 vols. with Supplements.

19. David Hugh Farmer, *The Oxford Dictionary of Saints* (Oxford, 1978). Emphasis on English saints.

See also **416, 418, 428, 430, 431, 432, 434, 435, 505, 1171, 1259, 1300**.

(B) PARTICULAR COUNTRIES OR REGIONS

(i) England and Wales

20. (Bishop Challoner), *A Memorial of Ancient British Piety or, A British Martyrology...* (London, 1761). Arranged by calendar.
21. Richard Stanton, *A Menology of England and Wales, or Brief Memorials of the Ancient British and English Saints* (London, 1887). Arranged by calendar.
22. S. Baring-Gould and John Fisher, *The Lives of the British Saints* (London, 1907–13), 4 vols.
23. R. L. P. Milburn, *Saints and their Emblems in English Churches* (London, 1949). Small alphabetical dictionary.

(ii) Germany

24. Jakob Torsy, *Lexikon der deutschen Heiligen, Seligen, Ehrwürdigen und Gottseligen* (Cologne, 1959). Comprehensive alphabetical dictionary; not exclusively German.

(iii) Greece

25. Otto F. A. Meinardus, *The Saints of Greece* (Athens, 1970). Brief alphabetical dictionary.

(iv) Ireland

26. Daphne D. C. Pochin Mould, *The Irish Saints* (Dublin, 1964). Brief lives with bibliographies.

(v) Poland

27. O. Romualda Gustawa (ed.), *Hagiografia Polska* (Poznań, Warsaw and Lublin, 1971–2), 2 vols. Fundamental reference work, in Polish.

II GENERAL STUDIES

(A) SOCIOLOGICAL AND STATISTICAL

28. John M. Mecklin, *The Passing of the Saint: A Study of a Cultural Type* (Chicago, 1941). Study centred on Sts Bernard and Francis, rightly emphasizing that the saint must be seen in social context, but lacking historical knowledge to follow the precept; suggests that saints and modern capitalistic society are largely incompatible, a thesis which fails to take account of importance of modern cults.

29. Pitirim A. Sorokin, *Altruistic Love: A Study of American 'Good Neighbours' and Christian Saints* (Boston, 1950 and New York, 1969). Pioneering sociological analysis, based on Butler's Lives as revised by Thurston; unfortunately the data provided from this source is incomplete and is not critically examined; the juxtaposition with a study of 'good neighbours' is not very successful either; a valuable appendix on 'Russian Orthodox saints'.

30. Katherine and Charles H. George, 'Roman Catholic Sainthood and Social Status, A Statistical and Analytical Study', *Journal of Religion*, XXXV (1955), pp. 85–98. Good short study, also based on revised version of Butler; stresses superior social status of saints.

31. John F. Broderick, 'A Census of the Saints (993–1955)', *American Ecclesiastical Review*, 135 (1966), pp. 87–115. Analysis by Jesuit of papally canonized saints, with tables; critical of Sorokin but acknowledges convergence of their findings.

32. Jacques Maître, 'La Sociologie de catholicisme chez Czarnowski, Halbwachs, Hertz et Van Gennep', *ASR*, 21 (1966), pp. 55–68. Important re-evaluation of work that has been neglected.

33. Pierre Delooz, *Sociologie et canonisations* (Liège and The Hague, 1969). An amplification of Delooz (Ch. 6); a thorough and comprehensive analysis of saints venerated in the West from 1000 to the present with valuable section on canonization procedure; supersedes all previous attempts.

34. R. Mols, 'Une Approche sociographique de la "sainteté"', *Nouvelle Revue Théologique*, 95 (1973), pp. 748–63. Review and summary of above.

35. François-A. Isambert, 'Religion populaire, sociologie, histoire et folklore, II – De Saint Besse à Saint Rouin', *ASR*, 46 (1978), pp. 111–33. Survey of studies of popular religion by French scholars, including Saintyves, Czarnowski and Hertz; a rare appreciation of the value of the last in particular.

(B) THEOLOGY OF THE CULT: ROMAN CATHOLIC

36. J. C. Trombelli, *De Cultu Sanctorum, Dissertationes decem* (Bologna, 1740–3), 4 vols. Exposition in Latin of the official theology of saints, following Pope Benedict XIV (see 43); with indexes.

37. H. Delehaye, 'Les Lettres d'Indulgences collectives', *AB*, 44 (1926), pp. 342–79; 45 (1927), pp. 97–123 and 323–44; and 46 (1928), pp. 149–57 and 287–343. Detailed documentary study.

38. Aléxis H. M. Lépicier, *Indulgences, Their Origin, Nature and Development* (London, 1928). 3rd revised edition of important study by French cardinal.

39. Jacques Douillet, *What is a Saint?* (London, 1958). Translated from the French; brief introduction to the Roman Catholic position, with a historical section.

40. Paoli Molinari, *I Santi e il loro culto* (Rome, 1962), Collecteana Spiritualia, 9. Modern theological statement by Jesuit; important.

(C) CANONIZATION

(i) Orthodox and Russian

41. P. Peeters, 'La Canonisation des saints dans l'Eglise russe', *AB*, 33 (1914), pp. 380–420; and 38 (1920), pp. 172–6. Important well-documented study, not superseded; the ecclesiastical authorities originally simply approved popular cults and introduced them into the formal liturgy; a trend towards centralized control is evident in the seventeeth century with canonization via the Holy Synod, culminating in the eighteenth and nineteenth centuries in virtual state canonization; very few saints canonized.

42. 'The Canonization of Saints in the Orthodox Church', *The Christian East*, XII (1931), pp. 85–9. Valuable.

(ii) Western

43. Benedicti XIV olim Prosperi de Lambertinis (Pope Benedict XIV), *Opera Omnia* (Venice, 1767), 7 vols. I–V, *De servorum Dei beatificatione et beatorum canonizatione*. Massive scholarly work in Latin on canonization and its history (originally published 1734–8), with index; an English translation of part of it was published as *Heroic Virtue* (London, 1850–3), 3 vols.

44. *Ibid.*, VI, *Acta et Decreta in causis beatificationum et canonizationum*. Codification of acts and decretals, with index.

45. Thomas F. Macken *The Canonization of Saints* (Dublin, 1910). Probably still the best general account in English of Roman procedure.

46. Emile Valvekens, 'La "Canonisation" de Saint Norbert en 1582', *Analecta Praemonstratensia*, X (1934), pp. 10–47. Discussion of later canonization of an already recognized founder saint.

47. L. Hertling, 'Materiali per la storia del processo di Canonizzazione', *Gregorianum*, 16 (1935), pp. 170–95. Still valuable.

48. Stephan Kuttner, 'La Réserve papale du droit de canonisation', *Revue Historique du Droit Français et Etranger*, 17 (1938), pp. 172–228; and in Kuttner, *The History of Ideas and Doctrines of Canon Law in the Middle Ages* (VR, London, 1980), Ch. VI. Careful argument on precise legal issue by eminent student of Canon Law, suggesting that papal reserve was established by Gregory IX rather than by Alexander III.

49. Eric Waldram Kemp, *Canonization and Authority in the Western Church* (London, 1948). Standard account of the history of formal canonization from legal and institutional point of view; essential.

50. Damian Joseph Blaher, *The Ordinary Processes in Causes of Beatification and Canonization, A Historical Synopsis and a Commentary* (Washington D.C., 1949). Catholic University of America Canon Law Studies, 268. Thorough legal-historical study.

51. Renate Klauser, 'Zur Entwicklung des Heiligsprechungsverfahrens bis zum 13. Jahrhundert', *ZSS*, 71/3 (Kan. Abt. 40), pp. 85–101. On canonization procedures.

52. Marcel Emérit, 'Une Manœuvre antijanséniste: La canonisation de Vincent de Paul', *ACNSS*, 99 (1976), Histoire Moderne, I, *La Piété populaire*, pp. 139–50. Makes the damaging suggestion that the saint was canonized for political reasons and may in fact have been a heretic.

See also **265**.

(D) CANONIZATION PROCEDURES AND THEIR
SOCIO-HISTORICAL VALUE

53. H. François Delaborde, 'Fragments de l'enquête faite à Saint-Denis en 1282 en vue de la canonisation de Saint Louis', *MSHPI*, 23 (1896), pp. 1–71. Details of three miracles from canonization procedure; Latin text, with introduction and résumé in French.

54. A. R. Malden, *The Canonization of Saint Osmund from the Manuscript Records in the Muniment Room of Salisbury Cathedral* (Salisbury, 1901), Wiltshire Record Society. Latin text with introduction; testimony on *c.* 40 miracles.

55. Raymonde Foreville, *Un Procès de canonisation à l'aube du XIIIe siècle (1201–1202), Le livre de saint Gilbert de Sempringham* (Paris, 1943). Introduction and critical edition of earliest extant canonization procedure, with accounts of miracles.

56. Romeo De Maio, 'L'Ideale eroico nei processi di canonizzazione della Controriforma', *Richerche di Storia Sociale e Religiosa*, I/2 (1972), pp. 139–60. Important study on Early Modern period.

57. Jacques Paul, 'Témoignage historique et hagiographie dans le procès de canonisation de Louis d'Anjou', *PH*, XXIII (1973), pp. 305–17. Valuable study.

58. Gabriele De Rosa, 'Sainteté, clergé et peuple dans le Mezzogiorno italien au milieu du XVIIIe siècle', *RHS*, 52 (1976), pp. 245–64. French version of paper given in 1975 and included in De Rosa, *Chiesa e religione popolare nel Mezzogiorno* (Rome and Bari, 1978). Study based on canonization procedure of St Gerard Majella.

59. J. Paul, 'Miracles et mentalité religieuse populaire à Marseille au début du XIVe siècle', *CF*, XI (1966), *La Religion populaire en Languedoc du XIIIe siècle à la moitié du XIVe siècle*, pp. 61–90. Study of miracles accomplished at tomb of St Louis of Anjou; important finding that most occurred in response to a vow rather than through initial contact with the shrine, though the vow was regarded in a contractual or magical light.

60. André Vauchez, 'La Religion populaire dans la France méridionale au XIVe siècle, d'après les procès de canonisation', *CF*, XI (1966), pp. 91–107. Study of cult of St Dauphine, already regarded in her lifetime as a saint with miraculous powers, by people from all social levels.

61. Jean-Michel Sallmann, 'Image et fonction du saint dans la région de

Naples à la fin du XVIIe siècle et au début du XVIIIe siècle', *MEFR*, 91 (1979), pp. 827–74. Important study based on two canonization procedures.

See also **288, 981**.

(E) HISTORICAL AND GEOGRAPHICAL

(i) General

62. Donald Attwater, *Martyrs from St Stephen to John Tung* (London, 1958).

(ii) England and Wales

63. Rice Rees, *An Essay on the Welsh Saints or the Primitive Christians usually considered to have been the Founders of Churches in Wales* (London, 1836). Important work of scholarship.

64. Rotha Mary Clay, *The Hermits and Anchorites of England* (London, 1914). Scholarly; still useful.

See also **554–60, 650, 1195**.

(iii) France and regions

65. Dom François Chamard, *Les Vies des Saints personnages de l'Anjou* (Paris and Angers, 1863), 3 vols. Detailed and systematic study of local cults, from Dark Ages to eighteenth century.

66. Abbé S. -M. Mosnier, *Les Saints d'Auvergne, Histoire de tous les personnages de cette province honorés par l'Eglise d'un culte public* (Paris, 1900), 2 vols. Detailed entries by calendar; Lives and legends retailed with little criticism but based on old sources.

67. J. Loth, *Les Noms de saints bretons* (Paris, 1910). Valuable list, with short conclusion.

68. Chanoine J. Burlet, *Le Culte de Dieu, de la Sainte Vierge et des saints en Savoie avant la Révolution, Essai de géographie hagiologique* (Chambéry, 1922), Documents de l'Académie des Sciences, Belles-Lettres et Arts de Savoie, IX. Extensive list of dedications, confraternities, etc., with bibliography; valuable. See also **1240**.

69. L. Christiani, 'Liste chronologique des Saints de France, des origines à l'avènement des Carolingiens (Essai critique)', *RHEF*, XXXI (1945), pp. 5–96. See also G. Bardy's critique in *ibid.*, pp. 219–36.

See also **546–8, 565, 569, 931**.

(iv) Germany

70. *Achthundert Jahre Verehrung der Heiligen Drei Könige in Köln 1614–1964*

(Cologne, 1964). Collected anniversary studies on all aspects of cult by Torsy and others; illustrated.

See also **421, 549–53, 689.**

(v) Greece

71. Mary Hamilton, *Greek Saints and their Festivals* (Edinburgh and London, 1910). Important.
72. H. Delehaye, 'Greek Neomartyrs', *Constructive Quarterly*, 9 (1921), pp. 701–12; and in Delehaye, *Mélanges d'hagiographie grecque et latine* (Brussels, 1966), SH 42, Ch. 12. Short study of victims of Turkish repression.
73. Stella Georgoudi, 'Sant' Elia in Grecia', *Studi e Materiali di Storia delle Religioni*, XXXIX (1968), pp. 293–319. Study of popular cult of Old Testament saint associated with mountains.
74. J. W. Nesbitt, 'A Geographical and Chronological Guide to Greek Saint [*sic*] Lives', *Orientalia Christiana Periodica*, XXXV (1969), pp. 443ff. Useful guide to complement Halkin's *BHG* (**861**).

See also **25, 323, 861** and **1057.**

(vi) North Africa

75. Victor Dejardins, *Les Saints d'Afrique dans le martyrologe romain* (Oran, 1952).

See also **221.**

(vii) Russia

76. Augustin Arndt, 'Demetrius in Russland', *Stimmen aus Maria-Laach*, 39 (1890), pp. 479–508. See also **1162.**
77. E. Behr-Sigel, 'Notes sur l'idée russe de sainteté d'après les saints canonisés de l'Eglise russe', *Revue de l'Histoire et de la Philosophie Religieuses*, XIII (1933), pp. 537–54.
78. E. Behr-Sigel, 'Etudes d'hagiographie russe', *Irénikon*, XII (1935), pp. 241–54.
79. G. P. Fedotov, *The Russian Religious Mind* (Cambridge, Mass., 1946–66), 2 vols. Valuable study of religious life, paying considerable attention to the Lives and cults of saints.
80. E. Behr-Sigel, *Prière et sainteté dans l'Eglise russe suivi d'un essai sur le role du monachisme dans la vie spirituelle du peuple russe* (Paris, 1950). Good short essay on types of Russian saint, with section on canonization; resumes two articles.
81. Nadejda Gorodetzky, *Saint Tikhon Zadonsky, Inspirer of Dostoevsky* (SPCK,

London, 1951). Biography of eighteenth-century saint, with chapter on cult.

82. Ivan Kologrivof, *Essai sur la sainteté en Russie* (Bruges, 1953). General historical and biographical account.

83. Constantin de Grunwald, *Saints of Russia* (London, 1960). General book.

84. Pierre Kovalevsky, *Saint Serge et la spiritualité russe* (Paris, 1969). Small illustrated study of life and influence.

85. Dmitri Obolensky, 'Popular Religion in Medieval Russia', in Andrew Blane (ed.), *The Religious World of Russian Culture (Russia and Orthodoxy, II): Essays in Honor of Georges Florovsky* (The Hague and Paris, 1975), pp. 43–54; and in Obolensky, *The Byzantine Inheritance of Eastern Europe* (VR, London, 1982), VII. Discusses popular cults of Sts Boris and Gleb and pilgrimage songs of the *kaliki*.

86. Valentine Zander, *St Seraphim of Sarov* (London, 1975). Life of nineteenth-century saint in full hagiographical tradition.

See also **29, 1149, 1150**.

(viii) Scandinavia

87. Ellen Jørgensen, *Helgendyrkelse i Danmark, Studier over Kirkekultur og Kirkeligt liv fra det 11te Aarhundredes midt til Reformationen* (Copenhagen, 1909). Cults in medieval Denmark, with résumé in French.

88. Sigrid Undset, *Saga of Saints* (London, 1934). General study of Norwegian saints; translated.

89. John Mooney, *St Magnus – Earl of Orkney* (Kirkwall, 1935). Biographical study based on sagas, with important section on cult of the Norse saint.

90. Adolphe B. Benson, 'Scandinavian Saints and Legends: A Résumé', *Germanic Review*, XXXI (1956), pp. 9–22. Introductory account.

91. Ole Widding *et al.*, 'The Lives of the Saints in Old Norse Prose, A Handlist', *MS*, 25 (1963), pp. 294–337. Valuable reference work.

(F) CULTS OF PARTICULAR SAINTS

See also III (C) (ii) and (D) (ii).

(i) St Michael

92. Siméon Luce, *Jeanne d' Arc à Domrémy, recherches critiques sur les origines de la mission de la Pucelle* (Paris, 1886). Ch. IV, 'Le culte de Saint Michel au XVe siècle et la victore du Mont-Saint-Michel'. Still valuable.

93. E. A. Wallis Budge (ed.), *Saint Michael the Archangel: Three Encomiums by Theodosius, Archbishop of Alexandria, Severus, Patriarch of Antioch, and Eustathius, Bishop of Trake* (London, 1894). Seventh-century encomiums delivered on the saint's festival: Coptic and Arabic bilingual texts, with introduction and English translation; a valuable primary source.

94. Olga Rojdestvensky, *Le Culte de Saint Michel et le Moyen Age latin* (Paris, 1922). Short but important study.

95. E. Delaruelle, 'L'Archange Saint Michel dans la spiritualité de Jeanne d'Arc', *Millénaire monastique du Mont-Saint-Michel* (Paris, 1967), II, pp. 363–74; and in Delaruelle, *La Piété populaire* (**249**), pp. 389–400. Valuable study, revealing an internalized and spiritual cult at the popular level rather than one of a warrior or of the angel of the Apocalypse.

96. Wolfgang von Rintelen, *Kultgeographische Studien in der Italia byzantina, Untersuchungen über die Kulte des Erzengels Michael und der Madonna di Constantinopoli in Süditalia* (Meisenheim am Glan, 1968), Archiv für Vergleichende Kulturwissenschaft, Herausgegeben von Anton Hikkman, 3. Pt II studies the cult of St Michael in southern Italy.

See also **497, 600, 659, 1177.**

(ii) St George

97. A. Parisotti, 'Nota sulla legenda e sul culto di S. Giorgi', *Bessarione*, VIII (1903), pp. 92–110, 236–45 and 328–43. Still of value.

98. H. Delehaye, *Les Légendes grecques des saints militaires* (Paris, 1909). Critical studies with Greek texts, including study of St George.

99. J. B. Aufhauser, *Das Drachenwunder des Heiligen Georg in der grieschischen und lateinischen Überlieferung* (Leipzig, 1911), Byzantinisches Archiv, 5. Study of the classic myth associated with the saint.

100. Paolo Toschi, *La Leggenda di San Giorgio nei canti popolari italiani* (Florence, 1964), Biblioteca di *Lares*, XVIII. Short study of Italian popular songs by leading folklorist; texts with long introduction and illustrations.

101. David Howell, 'St George as Intercessor', *Byz.*, XXXIX (1969), pp. 121–36. Important study of early Byzantine cult.

102. Joseph Fontenrose, *Python, A Study of Delphic Myth and its Origins* (New York, 1974). Appendix 4, 'Saint George and the Dragon'. A short discussion in the context of Greek and other combat myths.

See also **745, 809, 1119.**

(iii) St Nicholas

103. Gustav Anrich, *Hagios Nikolaus, Der Heilige Nikolaus in der griechischen Kirche, Texte und Untersuchungen* (Leipzig and Berlin, 1913–17), 2 vols. Detailed study with texts.

104. *Nikolauslegenden, Leben und Legenden des Heiligen Bischofs von Myra* (Munich, 1964), Slawisches Institut. Short illustrated study.

105. Karlheinz Blaschke, 'Nikolaipatrozinien und städtische Frühgeschichte', *ZSS*, 84 (Kan. Abt. 53) (1967), pp. 273–337. Comprehensive discussion of dedications to the saint in Middle Ages.

106. E. Wilbur Bock, 'The Transformation of Religious Symbols: A Case Study of St Nicholas', *SC*, XIX (1972), pp. 531–48. Changing avatars of the saint from fourth-century martyr to Santa Claus.

107. Charles W. Jones, *Saint Nicholas of Myra, Bari and Manhattan* (Chicago and London, 1978). A much fuller study of the changing avatars of the saint, and of the translations of his relics.

See also **437, 511, 600, 793.**

(iv) St Martin

108. A. Lecoy de La Marche, *Saint Martin* (Tours, 1881). Large study by a local Catholic historian; the second, and most interesting, part of the book deals with the cult, and is still valuable.

109. E. C. Babut, *Saint Martin de Tours* (Paris, 1912). Critical study, which aroused much scholarly controversy when it appeared; still of some interest.

110. Marc Bloch, 'Saint Martin de Tours, à propos d'une polémique', *RHLR*, VII (1921), pp. 44–57; and in Bloch, *Mélanges historiques*, II (Paris, 1963), pp. 939–47. A propos the controversy between Babut and Delehaye.

111. *RHEF*, XLVII (1961), No. 144, Special issue 'Mémorial de l'année martinienne'. Contributions include: E. Ewig, 'Le culte de Saint Martin à l'époque franque'; Pierre Ganshof, 'Le tombeau de Saint Martin et les invasions normandes dans l'histoire et dans la légende'; André Stegman, 'Le Tombeau de Saint Martin et les Guerres de Religion'; and May Vieillard-Troiekouroff, 'Le Tombeau de Saint Martin retrouvé en 1860'.

112. J. Fontaine, 'Sulpice Sévère a-t-il travesti Saint Martin de Tours en martyr militaire?', *AB*, 81 (1963), pp. 31–58. Further discussion of the classic hagiography by leading Martinian scholar.

113. Jean Fournée, *Enquête sur le culte populaire de saint Martin en Normandie* (Paris, 1963), Société Parisienne d'Histoire et d'Archéologie Normandes, *Cahiers Léopold Delisle*, Numéro spécial. A detailed local study with 56 pages of photographs and a gazetteer, as well as pages of general analysis.

See also **344, 437, 453, 656, 757, 768, 853, 854, 996, 1009, 1020.**

(v) St Patrick

114. S. Czarnowski, *Le Culte des héros et ses conditions sociales, Saint Patrick héros national de l'Irlande* (Paris, 1919). A sociological study by a Polish pupil of Durkheim, with a preface by Hubert; provides an interesting discussion of the relationship between the cults of Irish saints and clan structure, and of St Patrick as a national or supra-clan saint; but Frazerian conjecture about festivals and sacrifice has dated.

115. Paul Grosjean, 'Notes sur les documents anciens concernant St Patrice', *AB*, 62 (1944), pp. 42–73. Scholarly.

116. R. P. C. Hanson, *Saint Patrick, His Origins and Career* (Oxford, 1968). A serious study against which to test Czarnowski.

See also **661, 663, 786.**

(vi) St Joan of Arc

117. Siméon Luce, *Jeanne d' Arc à Domrémy, Recherches critiques sur les origines de la mission de la Pucelle* (Paris, 1886). Scholarly study of piety and then of the cult of Joan; half text and half documents.

118. E. Delaruelle 'La Spiritualité de Jeanne d'Arc', *Bulletin de Littérature Ecclésiastique* (Toulouse), LXV (1964), pp. 17–33 and 81–98; and in Delaruelle, *La Piéte populaire* (**249**), pp. 355–88. A sophisticated study of Joan's own traditional piety, and of her unusual variety of sanctity.

119. Georges and Andrée Duby (eds.), *Les Procès de Jeanne d' Arc* (Paris, 1973). Documentary extracts with good commentary; most accessible version of one of the archetypal unjust trials.

120. Marina Warner, *Joan of Arc, The Image of Female Heroism* (London, 1981). Most recent discussion of an enduring and complex saint's legend, from a loosely 'feminist' angle.

See also **1086.**

(vii) Miscellaneous

121. P. Beda Kleinschmidt, *Die Heilige Anna, Ihre Verehrung in Geschichte, Kunst und Volkstum* (Düsseldorf, 1930), Forschungen zur Volkskunde, 103. Good study by Franciscan with iconographical emphasis. See also **479, 805, 1036, 1177, 1178.**

122. Romuald Bauerreiss, *Stefanskult und frühe Bishofsstadt* (Munich 1963), Veröffentlichungen der Bayerischen Benediktinerakademie, III. Short study of cult in France, Germany and Italy. See also **318, 1025.**

(G) PROTESTANTISM AND THE SAINTS

(i) Opposition

123. Joseph Priestley, *A History of the Corruptions of Christianity* (1782); and many later editions, e.g. (London, 1871). Pt IV 'The History of Opinions relating to Saints and Angels'. A late-eighteenth-century liberal Protestant view.

124. J. F. Davis, 'Lollards, Reformers and St Thomas of Canterbury', *University of Birmingham Historical Journal*, 9 (1963–4), pp. 1–15. Detailed study of opposition to and attacks on this popular cult by Protestant militants and by the government of Henry VIII.

(ii) Protestant notions of sainthood

125. Edmund S. Morgan, *Visible Saints, The History of a Puritan Idea* (New York, 1963 and 1965). On the radical Protestant notion.

126. Carl C. Rasmussen, 'Saint and Saints', in Julius Bodensieck (ed.), *The Encyclopedia of the Lutheran Church* (Minneapolis, 1965), 3 vols., II, pp. 2093–4.

(iii) Protestant martyrs and hagiography

127. George Townsend (ed.), *The Acts and Monuments of John Foxe* (London, 1841 and New York, 1969), 8 vols. Probably the best of many editions of classic English Protestant Acts of Martyrs.
128. J. F. Mozley, *John Foxe and His Book* (SPCK, London, 1940), Good study of most famous Protestant hagiographer.
129. Léon-E. Halkin, 'Hagiographie protestant', *AB*, 68 (1950), pp. 453–63. Important general introduction.
130. C. Moreau, 'Contributions à l'histoire du Livre des Martyrs', *Bulletin de la Société de l'Histoire du Protestantisme Français*, CIII (1957), pp. 173–99. Study of *Martyrologe* of Crespin.
131. William Haller, *Foxe's Book of Martyrs and the Elect Nation* (London, 1963). Important.
132. J. F. Gilmont, 'La Genèse du Martyrologe d'Adrien van Haemstede (1559)', *RHE*, LXIII (1968), pp. 379–414. Study of first Dutch Protestant martyrology.
133. J. F. Gilmont, 'Un instrument de propagande religieuse: les martyrologes du XVIᵉ siècle' in *Sources de l'histoire religieuse de la Belgique, Moyen Age et Temps modernes, Actes du Colloque de Bruxelles, 30 nov. – 2 déc. 1967* (Louvain, 1968), pp. 376–88.
134. A. J. Jelsma, *Adriaan van Haemstede en zijn martelaarsboek.* (The Hague, 1970). Important study of Dutch martyr account and its author.
135. John T. McNeill, 'John Foxe: Historiographer, Disciplinarian, Tolerationist', *CH*, 43 (1974), pp. 216–29.

III HISTORY OF THE CULT

(A) ANTIQUITY AND EARLY CHURCH

(i) General

136. Edward Gibbon, *The History of the Decline and Fall of the Roman Empire* (London, 1776–88; and many subsequent editions), Ch. XXVIII, 'Introduction of the Worship of Saints, and Relics, among the Christians'. The superior tone should not allow Gibbon's real insights into the nature and functions of the cults to be missed.
137. Albert Dufourcq, *La Christianisation des foules: Etude sur la fin du paganisme populaire et sur les origines du culte des saints* (Paris, 1906), 3rd edition. Still of interest, not least for its adumbration of the theme of patronage taken up by more recent writers on the subject.
138. Max von Wulf, *Ueber Heilige und Heiligenverehrung in den ersten christlichen*

Jahrhunderten (Leipzig, 1910). Comprehensive account, from the time of Christ to the Early Middle Ages.

139. Salomon Reinach, *Cultes, mythes et religions IV* (Paris, 1912), Ch. XVII, 'Thekla'. Study of popular Eastern cult by historian of religions.

140. E. Vacandard, 'Les origines du culte des saints', in Vacandard, *Etudes de critique et d'histoire religieuse*, 3rd series (Paris, 1912), pp. 57–212. Probably still the best historical account, by a liberal Catholic historian.

141. H. Delehaye, *Les Saints stylites* (Brussels and Paris, 1923 and 1964), SH, 14. Still the definitive work on the subject by the great Bollandist scholar.

142. H. Delehaye, *Sanctus, Essai sur le culte des saints dans l'antiquité* (Brussels, 1927 and 1970), SH, 17. A masterly survey.

143. J. R. Palanque *et al.*, *The Church in the Christian Roman Empire. II. The Life of the Church in the Fourth Century* (London, 1952). English translation of Fliche and Martin (eds.), *Histoire de l'Eglise*, III, Pt III. Ch. I, Sections I, II and IV, and Ch. II, Section III, by Pierre de Labriolle, deal with the Desert Fathers, Eastern pilgrimages and the worship of relics.

144. Peter Brown, 'The Rise and Function of the Holy Man in Late Antiquity', *Journal of Roman Studies*, LXI (1971), pp. 80–101. An influential article on the Syrian saint as local patron and mediator.

145. Karl Baus, Hans-Georg Beck *et al.*, *The Imperial Church from Constantine to the Early Middle Ages* (New York, 1980), Herbert Jedin and John Dolan (eds.), *History of the Church*, II, English translation of *Handbuch der Kirchengeschichte*, II/2. Pt III, Ch. 18 by Baus deals with the 'cult of martyrs and saints' and with early Christian pilgrimage; Pt IV, Ch. 30 by Beck with the early Byzantine cult.

146. Peter Brown, *The Cult of Saints, Its Rise and Function in Latin Christianity* (Chigaco, 1981). An expanded version of the Haskell Lectures, 1978. Stresses the importance of the idiom of late Roman patronage in the cult of the martyrs in the West; the translation of relics is presented as the expression of a network of solidarity within a new Christian élite, and the spread of the cult of the saints generally as an instrument of the forward march of structured power; written with the author's accustomed flair, this important and suggestive study does not ultimately escape the two-tier model (popular and élite) of religion which it sets off by attacking.

(ii) The communion of saints

147. J. P. Kirsch, *Die Lehre von der Gemeinschaft der Heiligen im christliche Alterthum, Eine dogmengeschichtliche Studie* (Mainz, 1900), Forschungen zur Christliche Literatur- und Dogmengeschichte, I. English translation as *The Doctrine of the Communion of Saints in the Ancient Church* (Edinburgh and London, 1910). Still the basic Catholic work on the subject.

148. Stephen Benko, *The Meaning of Sanctorum Communio* (Naperville, Ill., 1964), Studies in Historical Theology, 3. A short but dense account of the credal article, putting forward the Protestant sacramental interpretation of its original meaning.

(iii) Pagan origins and precedents

149. Hermann Usener, *Legenden der heilige Pelagia*. Introduction to texts published in *Festschrift für die XXXIV Versammlung deutscher Philologen und Schulmänner zu Trier* (Bonn, 1879); republished in Usener, *Vorträge und Aufsätze* (Leipzig, and Berlin, 1907), pp. 189–215. Argues that the cult of St Pelagia (of Tarsus) is a direct christianization of the cult of Aphrodite Pelagia.

150. E. Vacandard, 'L'Idolâtrie en Gaule au VIe et au VIIe siècle', *RQH*, LXV (1899), pp. 424–54. On the struggle between Christianity and paganism, by a Catholic historian.

151. Ernst Lucius, *Die Anfänge des Heiligenkults in der christlichen Kirche* (Tübingen, 1904) (French translation – Paris, 1908). Large (posthumous) scholarly work by Protestant, which stresses the analogies between pagan and early Christian saints' cults.

152. P. Saintyves (Emile Nourry), *Essais de mythologie chrétienne, Les Saints successeurs des dieux* (Paris, 1907). Main French version of the thesis that the cult of saints was a Christian assimilation of, or substitute for, pagan equivalents, by a scholarly folklorist.

153. Johannes Geffcken, *Der Ausgang des griechisch-römischen Heidentums* (Heidelberg, 1920). English translation by Sabine MacCormack, *The Last Days of Greco-Roman Paganism* (Amsterdam, 1978). A classic, which sets the relationship between the cult of saints and late pagan beliefs and rituals well in context; see Ch. 5 especially.

154. Alwyn D. Rees, 'The Divine Hero in Celtic Hagiology', *FL*, XLVII (1936), pp. 30–41. Interpretation of Celtic saints' Lives using the structural features of hero legends proposed by Lord Raglan.

155. Theodor Klauser, 'Vom Heroon zur Märtyrbasilika, Neue archäologische Balkanfunde und ihre Deutung', *Kriegsvorträge der Rheinischen Friedrich-Wilhelms Universität, Bonn*, 62 (1942), pp. 275–91; and in Klauser, *Gesammelte Arbeiten zur Liturgiegeschichte, Kirchengeschichte und christlichen Archäologie* (Münster, Westphalia, 1974). On early martyria and hero shrines.

156. M. Simon, 'Saint Barnabé au Puy-de-Dôme', *Revue d'Auvergne*, 57 (1943), pp. 1–11; and in Simon, *Le Christianisme antique et son contexte religieux, Scripta Varia* (Tübingen, 1981), 2 vols., Wissenschaftliche Untersuchungen zum neuen Testamentum, 23, I, pp. 131–41. Suggests that the cult of the apostolic saint was substituted by the Church during the Dark Ages to replace a pre-existing pagan cult associated with the mountain and with the solstice.

157. A.-J. Festugière, *La Sainteté* (Paris, 1949). Short essay on Christian saints and Greek heroes by Dominican.

158. M. Simon, 'Les Dieux antiques dans la pensée chrétienne', *Zeitschrift für Religions- und Geistesgeschichte*, VI (1954), pp. 97–114; and in Simon, *Le Christianisme antique*, I, pp. 187–204. A wide-ranging discussion.

159. Stephen McKenna, *Paganism and Pagan Survivals in Spain up to the Fall of the Visigothic Kingdom* (Washington, D.C., 1958), Catholic University of

America Studies in Mediaeval History, NS, 1. Of interest for the conflict between paganism and early Christianity.

160. M. Simon, 'Bellérophon chrétien', *Mélanges offerts à Jérôme Carcopino* (Paris, 1966), pp. 890–904; and in Simon, *Le Christianisme antique*, I, pp. 297–311. On the Christianization of a pagan hero.

161. Michel Meslin, *La Fête des kalendes de janvier dans l' Empire romain: Etude d'un rituel de nouvel an* (Brussels, 1970), Collection Latomus, 115. Short study, of interest for the persistence of a pagan festival in the face of the disapproval of the Early Church.

For parallels, see **1270** and **1282**; see also **856–7**.

(iv) Shrines and cults of antiquity

162. Alphonse Defrasse and Henri Lechat, *Epidaure, Restauration et description des principaux monuments du sanctuaire d'Asclépios* (Paris, 1895). Well-illustrated volume with suggested reconstruction following excavation of site; Ch. 5 on the *abaton* and miracles.

163. J. G. Frazer (ed.), *Pausanias's Description of Greece* (London, 1898), 6 vols. Vol. III, pp. 236–51; and vol. V, pp. 570–81, for Frazer's commentary on the shrine of Asclepius at Epidaurus.

164. Charles Michel, 'Le culte d'Esculape dans la religion populaire de la Grèce ancienne', *RHLR* 5, NS, 1 (1910). Good account.

165. R. Pfister, 'Kultus', *Paulus Real-Encylopädie der Classischen Altertumswissenschaft* (Stuttgart, 1922), XI, cols. 2106–92. On cults in Antiquity.

166. Marie Delcourt, *Les Grands Sanctuaires de la Grèce* (Paris, 1947). Sections on Dodona, Olympus, the shrines of Apollo, Epidaurus and Eleusis, plus bibliography.

167. R. A. Tomlinson, *Greek Sanctuaries* (London, 1976). Short but comprehensive account of buildings and sites.

(v) Oracles

168. Marie Delcourt, *L'Oracle de Delphes* (Paris, 1955). Important study of the classic oracle.

169. Robert Flacelière, *Greek Oracles* (London, 1965). Translation of French edition of 1961. Good short study.

170. Paul J. Alexander, *The Oracle of Baalbek, The Tiburtine Sibyl in Greek Dress* (Washington, D.C., 1967). By Byzantinist.

171. Joseph Fontenrose, *The Delphic Oracle, Its Responses and Operations with a Catalogue of Responses* (Berkeley, 1978). Valuable study of classic oracle.

See also **102**.

(vi) Miracles in the ancient world

172. Otto Weinrich, *Antike Heilungswunder, Untersuchungen zum Wunderglauben der Griechen und Römer* (Giessen, 1909; and reprint), Versuche und Vorarbeiten, VIII. Still of interest.

173. Lellia Gracco Ruggini, 'The Ecclesiastical Histories and the Pagan Historiography: Providence and Miracles', *Athenaeum, Studi Periodici di Letteratura e Storia dell' Antichità*, NS, 55 (1977), pp. 107–26.

(vii) The early cult of martyrs: primary sources

174. J. B. Lightfoot (ed.), *The Apostolic Fathers* (London, 1890–1), 7 vols. Texts of St Clement, St Ignatius, Polycarp, etc., with introduction, notes and translations.

175. F. C. Conybeare (ed.), *The Armenian Apology and Acts of Apollonius and other Monuments of Early Christianity* (London and New York, 1896). English translations of the Acts of Paul and Thecla, Phocas, Polyeuctus and other early martyrs.

176. R. P. Dom H. Leclercq (ed.), *Les Martyrs* (Paris, 1902–23), 15 vols. French translations of accounts of Christian martyrdom from the earliest times to the First World War, with valuable introductions; vols. I–III cover the period to the end of the fifth century.

177. W. H. Shewring (ed.), *The Passion of SS Perpetua and Felicity MM, A New Edition and Translation of the Latin text* (London, 1931). With sermons by St Augustine on their feast.

178. Edgar Goodspeed (ed.), *The Apostolic Fathers* (New York, 1950). Another translation into English.

179. Maxwell Staniforth (ed.), *Early Christian Writings, The Apostolic Fathers* (Harmondsworth, 1968), Penguin Classics. The latest and current English translation.

180. Herbert Musurillo (ed.), *The Acts of the Christian Martyrs* (Oxford, 1972). Modern critical edition with translations into English.

181. P. G. Walsh (ed.), *The Poems of St Paulinus of Nola* (New York, 1975), Ancient Christian Writers, 40. English translation with introduction and notes of late fourth- early fifth-century source; includes fourteen poems addressed to St Felix.

(viii) The early cult of martyrs: secondary works

182. Karl Künstle, *Hagiographische Studien über die Passio Felicitatis cum XII Filiis* (Paderborn, 1894). Ultra-critical.

183. Albert Dufourcq, *Etude sur les Gesta Martyrum romains* (Paris, 1900–10), 4 vols., Bibliothèque des Ecoles Françaises d'Athènes et de Rome, 83. Thorough and scholarly analysis of accounts, traditions and legends of first Roman martyrs, with texts; two further vols. were projected, but never published.

184. Paul Allard, *Dix leçons sur le martyre* (Paris, 1906). English translation as *Ten Lectures on the Martyrs* (London 1907). Lectures originally given at Institut Catholique in Paris; still of value as a general account; Lecture X on the cult of the martyrs.

185. Albert Ehrhard, *Die Griechischen Martyren* (Strasbourg, 1907), Schriften der Wissenschaftlichen Gesellschaft in Strassburg, 4. Short study by the distinguished Byzantinist; to some extent superseded by Halkin (**201**).

186. H. Delehaye, *Les Origines du culte des martyrs* (Brussels, 1912 and 1930), SH, 20. Standard work by the great modern Bollandist, refuting the Usener thesis; a marvellous and enduring piece of scholarship.

187. Ethel Ross Barker, *Rome of the Pilgrims and Martyrs, A Study in the Martyrologies, Itineraries, Syllogae, and other contemporary documents* (London, 1913). A clear and scholarly guide to the historiography of the cult of martyrs in Rome; still very valuable; of interest also for its translated citations from documents.

188. Peter Dörfler, *Die Anfänge der Heiligenverehrung nach den römischen Inschriften und Bildwerken* (Munich, 1913), Veröffentlichen aus dem Kirchenhistorischen Seminar, München, IV, 2. Study of inscriptions and iconography.

189. P. Monceaux, 'Les Martyrs Donatistes, Culte et relations', *RHR*, 68 (1913), pp. 146–92 and 310–44. Important study.

190. F. Grossi-Gondi, *Principi e problemi di critica agiografica, Atti e spoglie dei martiri* (Rome, 1919). Critical study of Acts and cult of martyrs by Jesuit.

191. H. Delehaye, *Les Passions des martyrs et les genres littéraires* (Brussels, 1921), SH, 13B. Still the standard work on the hagiography of the early Christian martyrs.

192. H. Delehaye, 'Martyr et Confesseur', *AB*, 39 (1921), pp. 20–49. Study of terminology, later incorporated into (**142**).

193. Georg Graf, 'Das Martyrium des heilige Pappus und seiner 24,000 Gefährten', in A. M. Koeniger (ed.), *Beiträge zur Geschichte des christlichen Altertums und der byzantinischen Literatur, Festgabe Albert Ehrhard zum 60. Geburtstag* (Bonn and Leipzig, 1922), pp. 200–17. Study of the Eastern equivalent of the Theban Legion.

194. M. Viller, 'Martyre et perfection', *RAM*, VI (1925), pp. 3–25. Analysis of meaning of martyrdom in the Early Church.

195. Donald W. Riddle, *The Martyrs, A Study in Social Control* (Chicago, 1931). Chicago school sociological study.

196. Hans Freiherr von Campenhausen, *Die Idee des Martyriums in der alten Kirche* (Göttingen, 1936 and 1964). Scholarly study.

197. H. Delehaye, *Etude sur le légendier romain, Les Saints de novembre et de décembre* (Brussels, 1936), SH, 23. Texts of legends of Roman martyrs with discussion of them.

198. André Grabar, *Martyrium, Recherches sur le culte des reliques et l'art chrétien antique* (Paris, 1946 and London, 1972), 2 vols. A comprehensive study of both architecture and iconography, relating trends in art history and in religious feeling; of particular interest for its examination of contrasting developments in East and West and for the development of icon worship in the East.

199. Edelhard L. Hummel, *The Concept of Martyrdom according to St Cyprian of Carthage* (Washington, D.C., 1946), CUASCA, 9. On third-century notions of martyrdom.

200. Jean Lassus, *Sanctuaires chrétiens de Syrie, Essai sur la genèse, la forme et l'usage liturgique des édifices du culte chrétien, en Syrie, du IIIᵉ siècle à la conquète musulmane* (Paris, 1947), Institut Français d'Archéologie de Beyrouth, Bibliothèque Archéologique et Historique, XLII. Chapters on martyria, liturgical manifestations of the cult of martyrs, and on images and asceticism; a mainly archaeological study, well illustrated.

201. François Halkin, *Etudes d'épigraphie grecque et d'hagiographie byzantine* (VR London, 1973). Part I, 'Inscriptions grecques relatives à l'hagiographie' (with indices), comprises six studies which appeared in *AB* between 1949 and 1953, and were conceived as a supplement to Delehaye (**186**).

202. Manlio Simonetti, *Studi agiografici* (Rome, 1955). Short study of Acts of martyrs.

203. Denis van Berchem, *Le Martyre de la Légion Thébaine, Essai sur la formation d'une légende* (Basel, 1956), Schweizerische Beitrage zur Altertumswissenschaft, 8. Important short study of legend behind cult discussed by Hertz.

204. Baudouin de Gaiffier d'Hestroy, 'Réflexions sur les origines du culte des martyrs', *Maison-Dieu*, 52 (1957), pp. 19–43; and in Baudouin de Gaiffier, (**843**) Pt I, pp. 7–30. Study by Bollandist, to be read in conjunction with Delehaye (**186**).

205. Theodor Klauser, 'Christlicher Märtyrerkult, heidnischer Heroenkult und spätjüdische Heiligenverehrung', *AFLNW*, 91 (1960), pp. 27–38; and in Klauser, *Gesammelte Arbeiten* (**155**), pp. 221–32.

206. Louis Dupraz, *Les Passions de S. Maurice d'Agaune, Essai sur l'historicité de la tradition et contribution à l'étude de l'armée pre-Dioclétienne (260–286) et des canonisations tardives de la fin du IVe siècle* (Fribourg, 1961), Studia Friburgensia, NS, 27. Thorough study of the Theban Legion and the legends associated with it.

207. H. Hoppenbrouwers, *Recherches sur la terminologie du martyre de Tertullien à Lactance* (Nijmegen, 1961), Latinitas Christianorum Primaeva, 14. Important study by Benedictine scholar.

208. Charles Pietri, 'Concordia Apostolorum et Renovatio Urbis (Culte des Martyrs et propagande pontificale)', *Mélanges d'Archéologie et d'Histoire de l'Ecole Française de Rome*, LXXIII (1961), pp. 275–322. On ecclesiopolitical uses of martyr cult.

209. W. H. C. Frend, *Martyrdom and Persecution in the Early Church, A Study of a Conflict from the Maccabees to Donatus* (Oxford, 1965). Large book with bibliography, setting early martyrdom in context.

210. J. B. Ward-Perkins, 'Memoria, Martyr's Tomb and Martyr's Church', *Studi di Antichità Cristiana*, XXVII (1965), *Akten des VII. Internationalen Kongresses für christliche Archäologie, Trier*, I, pp. 3–25. Discussion of martyria, with some criticism of Grabar (**198**).

211. Sandro Carletti, 'Santuari di martiri romani negli "Itineraria" del VII secolo', *Studi Romani*, XVIII (1970), pp. 51–67. On the pilgrimage cult of Roman martyrs in the seventh century.

See also **845, 846, 848, 852.**

(ix) Apostolicity and early cults of apostles

212. L. Duchesne, 'Saint Martial de Limoges', *AM*, IV (1892), pp. 289–330. Critical study of legend of 'apostolic' saint.

213. L. Duchesne, 'Saint Barnabé', *Mélanges G. B. De Rossi, Recueil de travaux publiés par l'Ecole Française de Rome en l'honneur de M. le Commandeur Giovanni Battista De Rossi, Mélanges d'Archéologie de d'Histoire*, XII (1892), Supplement, pp. 41–71. On legend and cult of companion of St Paul; read in conjunction with **156**.

214. L. Duchesne, 'Saint Jacques en Galicie', *AM*, XII (1900), pp. 145–79. Study of legend of St James related to the Compostela pilgrimage; still of value.

215. J. Loth, 'Le texte original de la légende de la translation des reliques de Saint Mathieu en Bretagne', *AB*, 18 (1902–3), pp. 603–6.

216. Francis Dvornik, *The Idea of Apostolicity in Byzantium and the Legend of the Apostle Andrew* (Cambridge, Mass., 1958), Dumbarton Oaks Studies, IV. Important monograph.

217. Eugen Ewig, 'Der Petrus- und Apostelkult in spätrömischen und frankischen Gallien', *ZK*, LXXI, 4th series, IX (1960), pp. 215–51. Important article.

218. Francesco Susman, 'Il Culto Di S. Pietro a Roma dalla morte di Leone Magno a Vitaliano (461–672), *Archivio della Società Romana di Storia Patria*, LXXXIV, 3rd series, XV (1961), pp. 1–93. Detailed study with full bibliography.

See also **253–6, 353, 354, 356, 515**.

(x) Ascetic saints and the Desert Fathers: secondary works

(For primary works see X Hagiography (B).)

219. L. Duchesne, *Histoire ancienne de l'Eglise* (Paris, 1908), II, Ch. XIV, 'Les Moines d'orient'. English translation as *Early History of the Christian Church* (London, 1914–24). Still useful.

220. M. Viller, 'Le Martyre et l'ascèse', *RAM*, VI (1925), pp. 105–42. On the assimilation of asceticism to martyrdom, down to the fifth century.

221. De Lacy O'Leary, *The Saints of Egypt* (SPCK, London, 1937). An alphabetical catalogue of Coptic saints with calendar, and essays on the Egyptian martyrs and ascetics.

222. Edward E. Malone, *The Monk and the Martyr, The Monk as the Successor of the Martyr* (Washington, D.C., 1950), CUASCA, 12. Scholarly study by Benedictine of early ideals of sanctity and of the conception of monastic life as a spiritual martyrdom, in Late Antiquity and the Early Middle Ages.

223. Louis Bouyer, *La Vie de S. Antoine, Essai sur la spiritualité du monachisme primitif* (Saint-Wandrille, 1950). Analytical account of early Christian asceticism.

224. Basil Steidl (ed.), *Antonius Magnus Eremitica 356–1956, Studia ad antiquam monachismum spectantia* (Rome, 1956), Studia Anselmiana, XXXVIII. Collection of scholarly studies of Lives of St Anthony, and of their significance.

225. Arthur Vööbus, *History of Asceticism in the Syrian Orient, A Contribution to*

the History of Culture in the Near East (Louvain, 1958 and 1960), 2 vols., Corpus Scriptorum Christianorum Orientalium, Subsidia 14 and 17. Standard work.

226. A. -J. Festugière. *Les Moines d'Orient, I, Culture et sainteté, Introduction au monachisme oriental* (Paris, 1961). A critical analysis of the ascetic 'way' of the Desert Fathers by a Dominican.

227. Derwas J. Chitty, *The Desert A City, An Introduction to the Study of Egyptian and Palestinian Monasticism under the Christian Empire* (London and Oxford, 1977). The best account.

(B) BYZANTINE

(See also XI (c).)

228. Gilbert Dagron, 'Le Christianisme dans la ville byzantine', *DOP*, 31 (1977), pp. 1–25. Some remarks on saints as urban patrons and on the cult of relics.

229. Averil Cameron, 'Images of Authority: Elites and Icons in Late Sixth-Century Byzantium', *PP*, 84 (1979), pp. 3–35. Argues that the cult of the Virgin and of icons generally was used to strengthen the Christian view of the Empire and hence the authority of the emperor; the evidence is thin, especially where icons are concerned.

230. Angeliki E. Laiou-Thomadakis, 'Saints and Society in the Late Byzantine Empire', in Laiou-Thomadakis (ed.), *Charanis Studies, Essays in Honor of Peter Charanis* (New Brunswick, N. J., 1980), Ch. 7, pp. 84–114. Use of hagiography as source for social history and ideology, revealing the aristocratic bias of saints' Lives and their compilers; 'positivist' approach.

231. Sergei Hackel (ed.), *The Byzantine Saint* (London, 1981), University of Birmingham Fourteenth Spring Symposium of Byzantine Studies, Supplement to *Sorbornost*, 5. The main theme in the collection is the changing role of the saint or holy man in Byzantine society, with emphasis on his political role, on the process of canonization, and on the problem, for the authorities, ecclesiastical and secular, of controlling the potentially subversive power of the saint. The most significant contributions, by Patlagean, Rydén and Vryonis, are listed separately below.

See also **1214.**

(C) THE WEST IN THE MIDDLE AGES

(i) General

232. William Copeland Borlase, *The Age of the Saints, A Monograph of Early Christianity in Cornwall* (Truro, 1878). Still of interest.

233. Abbé M. Renet, *Saint Lucien et les autres saints du Beauvaisis, Etudes historiques, liturgiques, chronologiques* (Beauvais, 1892–5), 3 vols. Lengthy and erudite study by local Catholic historian.

234. A. Marignan, *Etudes sur la civilisation française, II, Le culte des saints sous les Mérovingiens* (Paris, 1899). A subtle and comprehensive study of the cult of saints in Merovingian Gaul; 'structuralist' approach, unusual for its time.

235. Carl Albrecht Bernoulli, *Die Heiligen der Merowinger* (Tübingen, 1900). An important study.

236. Hermann Siebert, *Beiträge zur vorreformatischen Heiligen- und Reliquienverehrung* (Freiburg im Breisgau, 1907), Erläuterungen und Ergänzungen zu Janssens Geschichte des deutschen Volkes, VI, Vol. 1, Pt 1. Short study of cult in Later Middle Ages.

237. J. Huizinga, *The Waning of the Middle Ages, A Study of the Forms of Life, Thought and Art in France and the Netherlands in the Fourteenth and Fifteenth Centuries* (London, 1924, and subsequent editions). Revised translation of book which first appeared in Dutch in 1919. Sections in Ch. XII on the cult of saints, and in Ch. XIII on ideals of sanctity; brief but illuminating discussion by a great humanist historian.

238. J. A. MacCulloch, *Medieval Faith and Fable* (London, 1932). Foreword by Frazer; chapters on 'The Virgin: Cult and Legends', 'The Saints' and 'Relics'; well-documented general account.

239. J. Lestocquoy, 'Les Saints et les églises de l'abbaye de Saint-Vaast d'Arras au VIIIe siècle', *Revue du Nord*, XXVI (1943), pp. 197–208. Local cults.

240. Bernhard Töpfer, *Volk und Kirche zur Zeit der Beginnenden Gottesfriedensbewegung in Frankreich* (Berlin, 1957), Neue Beiträge zur Geschichtswissenschaft, I. See for relics and miracles.

241. Eleanor Duckett, *The Wandering Saints* (London, 1959). On Celtic and other peripatetics, fifth–ninth centuries.

242. Nora K. Chadwick, *The Age of the Saints in the Early Celtic Church* (London, 1961). Riddell Memorial lectures.

243. Matthias Zender, *Räume und Schichten, Mittelalterliche Heiligenverehrung in ihrer Bedeutung für die Volkskunde, Die Heiligen des mittleren Maaslandes und der Rheinlande in Kultgeschichte und Kultverbreitung* (Düsseldorf, 1959). Local historical and geographical study, with maps and illustrations.

244. Etienne Delaruelle *et al., L'Eglise au temps du Grand Schisme et de la crise conciliaire (1378–1449)*, II (Paris, 1964), Fliche and Martin (eds.), *Histoire de l'Eglise*, XIV. Pt 5, 'La vie religieuse du peuple chrétien', by Delaruelle, has sections on confraternities, devotion to the Virgin Mary, saints and relics, pilgrimages and indulgences; a good introduction.

245. Carmen García Rodríguez, *El Culto de los Santos en la España romana y visigoda* (Madrid, 1966). Comprehensive study.

246. Gregorio Penco, 'L'Imitazione di Cristo nell' agiografia monastica', *Collectanea Cisterciensia*, 28 (1966), pp. 17–34. On an important element in late medieval notions of sanctity.

247. Derek Baker, '*Vir Dei*: Secular Sanctity in the Early Tenth Century', in G. J. Cuming and Derek Baker (eds.), *Popular Belief and Practice* (Cambridge, 1972), SCH, 8, pp. 41–53. A study based on Odo's Life of Gerald of Aurillac. See also **760**.

248. Joseph-Claude Poulin, 'Les Saints dans la vie religieuse au Moyen-Age', in Benoît Lacroix and Pietro Boglioni (eds.), *Les Religions populaires* (Quebec,

1972), Collection Histoire et Sociologie de la Culture, 3, pp. 65–74. Brief introductory study.

249. Etienne Delaruelle, *La Piété populaire au Moyen Age* (Turin, 1975). 24 collected studies by a pioneer in the field, many of which deal with the cult of the saints and pilgrimage. Some of these are listed separately.

250. Teresa Dunin-Wasowicz, 'Le Culte des saints en Pologne au Xe siècle', *CCM*, XVIII (1975), pp. 229–38. Examines the political motives for the promotion of particular cults.

251. H. Mayr-Harting, 'Functions of a Twelfth-Century Recluse', *History*, 60 (1975), pp. 337–52. Study of Wulfric of Haselburg.

252. Michael Goodich, 'A Profile of Thirteenth-Century Sainthood', *CSSH*, 18 (1976), pp. 429–37. A valuable quantitative analysis of over 500 saints venerated in the period, indicating that the majority were male, of noble origin, and members of religious, and especially Mendicant, orders.

252a. André Vauchez, *La Sainteté en Occident aux derniers siècles du Moyen Age d'après les procès de canonisation et les documents hagiographiques* (Rome, 1981), Bibliothèque des Ecoles Françaises d'Athènes et de Rome, 1st Series, 242. Essential.

See also **1212, 1213**.

(ii) Cults of particular saints

(See also II (F).)

(a) ST MARY MAGDALENE

253. L. Duchesne, 'La Légende de Sainte Marie-Madeleine' *AM*, V (1893), pp. 1–33. Study of important 'apostolic' cult centred in Provence and later attached to the abbey of Vézelay; still of value.

254. Victor Saxer, 'L'Origine des reliques de Sainte Marie Madeleine à Vézelay, dans la tradition historiographique du Moyen Age', *RSR*, 29 (1955), pp. 1–18. Incorporated in **255**.

255. V. Saxer, *Le Culte de Marie Madeleine en Occident des origines à la fin du moyen âge* (Auxerre and Paris, 1959), 2 vols. A comprehensive account by a Catholic scholar of a cult which reached its apogee in the twelfth century with lists of shrines, maps and full critical apparatus.

256. V. Saxer, *Le Dossier vézelien de Marie Madeleine, Invention et translation des reliques en 1265–1267, Contribution à l'histoire du culte de la Sainte à Vézelay à l'apogée du Moyen Age* (Brussels, 1975), SH, 57. Brief text with long introduction.

See also **819, 906**.

(b) ST DENIS

257. François Delaborde, 'Le Procès du chef de Saint Denis en 1410', *MSHPI*, XI (1884), pp. 297–409. Study with texts, relating to dispute over this relic between the monks of Saint-Denis and the canons of Notre-Dame-de-Paris.

258. Henry Martin, *Légende de Saint Denis, Reproduction des miniatures du manuscrit*

original présenté en 1317 au roi Philippe le Long (Paris, 1908). See for the cult and its iconography; the miniatures have also been used as a source of general social history.

259. Robert Bossuat, 'Traditions populaires relatives au martyre et à la sépulture de saint Denis', *MA*, 11 (1956), pp. 479–509. Useful complement to Spiegel.

(c) ST FRANCIS

260. Beda Kleinschmidt, *Sankt Franziskus von Assisi in Kunst und Legende* (Mönchen-Gladbach, 1911), Monographien zur Geschichte der christlichen Kunst, II. Short study, mainly iconographical.

261. Gerhart B. Ladner, 'Das Älteste Bild des Hl. Franziskus von Assisi, Ein Beitrag zur mittelalterlichen Porträtikonographie', in *Festschrift Percy Ernst Schramm zu seinen siebzigsten Geburstung von Schülern und Freunden Zugeeignet* (Wiesbaden, 1964), 2 vols., I, pp. 449–60. Iconographical study.

262. André Vauchez, 'Les Stigmates de Saint Francois et leurs détracteurs dans les derniers siècles du Moyen Age', *Mélanges d'Archéologie et d'Histoire de l'Ecole Française de Rome*, LXXX (1968), pp. 595–625. Study of hostility evoked by this central aspect of the cult of St Francis.

263. *Convegni CSSM*, IX (1971), *San Francesco nella ricerca storica degli ultimi ottanta anni*. Contributions by Delaruelle, Manselli and others.

See also **442, 750, 755, 770, 882**.

(d) ST LOUIS OF ANJOU OR TOULOUSE

264. Emile Bertaux, 'Les Saint Louis dans l'art italien', *Revue des Deux Mondes*, LXX (1900), 4ᵉ période, pp. 616–44. A still valuable discussion of the propagation of the cults of both St Louis of France and St Louis of Anjou in Italy, by the Franciscans and by the House of Anjou.

265. Margaret R. Toynbee, *S. Louis of Toulouse and the Process of Canonization in the Fourteenth Century* (Manchester, 1929), Publications of the University of Manchester, CXCIX, Historical Series, LV. The account of canonization procedure should be supplemented by later studies (see esp. **48** and **49**); includes an interesting chapter on the cult and its promotion, and remains an important study.

266. M.-H. Laurent, *Le Culte de S. Louis d'Anjou à Marseille au XIVᵉ siècle, Les documents de Louis Antoine de Ruffi* (Rome, 1954), Temi e Testi, 2. Documents.

267. Jacques Paul, 'Saint Louis d'Anjou, franciscain et évêque de Toulouse (1274–1297)', *CF*, VII (1972), pp. 59–90. Good historical study.

See also **57** and **59**.

(e) ST THOMAS OF CANTERBURY

268. James Craigie Robertson, *Materials for the History of Thomas Becket, Archbishop of Canterbury* (London, 1875–83), 7 vols., Rolls Series.

Important primary source; includes Lives and Miracles.

269. Abbé M. Renet, *Saint Thomas Becket, ses historiens, son culte, sa naissance, son passage, ses parents dans le Beauvaisis, Mémoires de la Société Académique d'Archéologie, Sciences et Arts du Département de l'Oise*, XIII (1886). Interesting local study of important medieval cult; read with **274**.

270. Paul Alonzo Brown, *The Development of the Legend of Thomas Becket* (Philadelphia, 1930). A valuable study.

271. J. Charles Wall, *The Four Shrines of St Thomas at Canterbury* (London, 1932). Pamphlet published by the Antiquarian Association, with illustrations; valuable for the topography of this important pilgrimage site, with its four sacred places: the place of martyrdom; the crypt which contained the first tomb; the 'chef' or head shrine; and the great shrine.

272. Raymonde Foreville, *Le Jubilé de Saint Thomas Becket du XIIIe au XVe siècle (1220–1470), Etudes et documents* (Paris, 1958), Bibliothèque Générale de l'Ecole Pratique des Hautes Etudes. Important study of the pilgrimage and official cult; see also for notion of jubilee and for indulgences.

273. R. Foreville, 'Mort et survie de saint Thomas Becket', *CCM*, 14 (1971), pp. 21–38. A brief account of the many aspects of the cult.

274. R. Foreville, 'Les origines normandes de la famille Becket et le culte de saint Thomas en Normandie', *Mélanges Pierre-Andrieu-Guitrancourt, L'Année Canonique*, XVII (1973), pp. 433–78.

275. R. Foreville (ed.), *Thomas Becket, Actes du colloque international de Sedières, 19–24 août 1973* (Paris, 1975). A number of contributions on the cult of St Thomas in France.

276. R. Foreville, *Thomas Becket dans la tradition historique et hagiographique* (VR, London, 1981). Sixteen collected studies by leading Becket scholar, including **273**, **274** and **1163**.

See also **124, 439, 647, 790, 1038, 1100**.

(f) MISCELLANEOUS

277. L. V. E. Bougaud, *Etude historique et critique sur la mission, les actes et le culte de Saint Bénigne Apôtre de la Bourgogne, et sur l'origine des églises de Dijon, d'Autun et de Langres* (Paris, 1859). Still of value; by Bishop of Laval.

278. Stephan Beissel, *Der heilige Bernward von Hildesheim als Künstler und Förderer der deutschen Kunst* (Hildesheim, 1895). Short study by Jesuit of saint honoured as an artist and patron of the arts.

279. A. Bouillet and L. Servières, *Sainte Foy, Vierge et martyre* (Rodez, 1900). Large and thorough study by Catholic scholars of the life and legend of the saint, of the history of the abbey of Conques which possessed her relics, and of the cult in France generally and elsewhere; includes a critical study of the Acts of the Martyrdom of the saint and of the translation and liturgies, together with a French version of the Miracle Accounts. See also **792**.

280. Francesco Lanzoni, *San Petronio, Vescovo di Bologna, nella Storia e nella leggenda* (Rome, 1907). Study of legend of local saint. See also **1080**.

281. Robert Fawtier, *Sainte Catherine de Sienne, Essai de critique des sources, Sources*

hagiographiques (Paris, 1921), Bibliothèque des Ecoles Françaises d'Athènes et de Rome, 121. Important study, with emphasis on the 'critical'. On cult of this saint, see also **441** and **761**.

282. Reginald Maxwell Woolley, *St Hugh of Lincoln* (SPCK, London, 1927). Biography of St Hugh the Great, with chapters on miracles and on canonization and translation.

283. Corrado Ricci, *Umbria Santa* (London, 1927), translated from the Italian. Ch. IV on St Rita and her cult.

284. Fr. Dvornik, *The Life of Saint Wenceslas* (Prague, 1929). Short study of the life and cult by professor of theology.

285. Paul de Vooght, *Hussiana* (Louvain, 1960), Pt 5, Ch. III, pp. 400–41, 'Jean de Pomuk'. Thorough study by Benedictine scholar of case of saint who died in 1393, supposedly as a martyr in defence of the secrecy of the confessional, and which establishes that his death was not a martyrdom at all; with the Latin text of the *Acta*.

286. Iris Origo, *The World of San Bernardino* (London, 1963). A charming study of the Tuscan Franciscan saint and preacher, which discusses his cult both before and after his death.

287. M.-H. Vicaire, *Saint Dominic and His Times* (London, 1964). Translation of the 'official' biography; Ch. XX on the canonization.

288. *Convegni CSSM*, XIV (1974), *S. Bonaventura Francescana*. Studies by various hands, including Stanislao da Campagnola, 'Le vicende della canonizzazione di S. Bonaventura'.

See also **440, 443, 444**.

(D) THE WEST IN THE EARLY MODERN PERIOD

(i) General

289. Robert Ricard, *The Spiritual Conquest of Mexico, An Essay on the Apostolate and the Evangelizing Methods of the Mendicant Orders in New Spain: 1523–1572* (Berkeley, 1966). Translated from French edition of 1933; see esp. Ch. 11 on processions and festivals.

290. Leopold Willaert, *Après la Concile de Trente, La Restauration catholique (1563–1648)*, II (Paris, 1960), Fliche and Martin (eds.), *Histoire de l'Eglise*, XVIII. Section on 'La Sainteté dans l'Eglise'.

291. Jean Delumeau, *Catholicism between Luther and Voltaire, A New View of the Counter-Reformation* (London and Philadelphia, 1977), English translation of French book, which appeared in 1971; see for general context and pp. 166–70 on the popular cult of saints.

292. Julio Caro Baroja, *Las formas complejas de la vida religiosa, Religión, sociedad y carácter en la España de los siglos XVI y XVII* (Madrid, 1978). Pt I, Chs. III and IV discuss hagiography, saints and society, miracles and images; by Spain's leading historian of 'popular' culture.

293. W. A. Christian, *Local Religion in Sixteenth-Century Spain* (Princeton, 1981). Based on royal enquiries into local religious observance, paying special attention to collective vows and local shrines and pilgrimages.

294. W. A. Christian, *Apparitions in Late Medieval and Renaissance Spain* (Princeton, 1981). Fascinating, mainly descriptive, account of apparitions of the Virgin Mary, but also of the saints, a phenomenon which became characteristic of modern Catholicism.

See also **1241, 1242, 1245, 1247, 1249.**

(ii) Cults of particular saints

295. Pierre Coste, *Monsieur Vincent, Le Grand Saint du Grand Siècle* (Paris, 1931–2), 3 vols. Standard work on St Vincent de Paul. Vol. II, Chs. LXVI–LXVIII deal with the beatification and canonization (in the face of strong Jansenist opposition), with the relics and the cult. See also **53.**

(E) THE WEST IN THE NINETEENTH AND TWENTIETH CENTURIES

(i) General

296. Raoul Plus, *Holiness in the Church* (London, Edinburgh and St Louis, Mo., 1929). Study by Jesuit, translated from French; a good example of modern notions of sanctity.

297. *Saints d'hier et sainteté d'aujourd'hui* (Paris, 1966), Centre Catholique des Intellectuels Français, Recherches et débats, 56. Essays by André Vauchez, Pierre Delooz, Philippe Rouillard, Alain Guillermon and Jean-François Six, together with an analysis of replies to a questionnaire on saints and sanctity, and an article by Paul Cochois on the teaching of Vatican II on sanctity.

298. Philippe Boutry, 'Les Saints des Catacombes, Itinéraires français d'une piété ultramontaine (1800–1881)', *MEFR*, 91 (1979), pp. 875–930. Important study of the Ultramontane cult of martyrs exhumed from the Catacombs in Rome in the nineteenth century.

See also **1248.**

(ii) Cults of particular saints

299. Jacques Gadille, 'Autour de Saint Benoît-Joseph Labre, Hagiographie et critique au XIXe siècle', *RHEF*, 52 (1966), pp. 113–26. Of interest for late-nineteenth-century notions of sanctity.

300. Giacomo Lercaro and Gabriele De Rosa, *John XXIII, Simpleton or Saint?* (London, 1967). Translated from the Italian. Two essays on a saint in the making.

301. Pierre Mabille, *Thérèse de Lisieux* (Paris, 1937 and 1975). A critical examination of one of the most popular of modern saints.

302. Jean-François Six, *Thérèse de Lisieux au Carmel* (Paris, 1973). An attempt to situate St Thérèse and her religious style in historical context; by a Catholic priest. See also **827–9, 969.**

303. Philippe Boutry, 'Un sanctuaire et son saint au XIXe siècle, Jean-Marie-Baptiste Vianney, Curé d'Ars', *Ann.*, 35 (1980), pp. 353–75. Study of pilgrimage associated with a country priest in his lifetime; it had become the most important in France when he died in 1859.

304. Philippe Boutry and Michel Cinquin, *Deux pèlerinages au XIXe siècle, Ars et Paray-le-Monial* (Paris, 1980). Two separate studies, based on *mémoires de maitrise*, and devoted to two of the most important and characteristic pilgrimages of nineteenth-century France: to the living saint who was *curé* of Ars (an expanded version of Boutry (303)); and to the site where St Margaret-Mary Alacoque received her visitation from Christ and her message relating to the Sacred Heart in the seventeenth century; the latter cult was reanimated in the 1860s and particularly the 1870s, a period of national crisis.

IV MANIFESTATIONS OF THE CULT: RELICS

(A) GENERAL

305. Dominici Anfossii, *De Sacrarum Reliquiarum Cultu, Veneratione, Translatione atque Identitate Brevis* (Brescia, 1610). Early Modern official text, in Latin.

306. Jean-Baptiste Thiers, *Traité des superstitions qui regardent tous les sacremens, selon l'écriture sainte, les décrets des conciles, et les sentimens des Saints Pères et des théologiens* (Paris, 1704), 4 vols. Vol. I. Book 2, Ch. I, discusses false relics; and Book 4, Ch. IV, superstitious uses.

307. Gustave Julliot and Maurice Prou (eds.), Geoffrey de Courlon, *Le Livre des reliques de l'abbaye de Saint-Pierre-le-Vif de Sens* (Sens, 1887), Société Archéologique de Sens. Primary source; list of relics and other documents in the original Latin.

307a. Stephan Beissel, *Die Verehrung der Heiligen und ihrer Reliquien in Deutschland während der zweiten Hälfte des Mittelalters* (Freiburg im Breisgau, 1892), Ergänzungshefte zu den 'Stimmen aus Maria-Laach', 54. Brief but still important.

308. Maria Paolina Kuefstein, 'Reliquie e tradizioni domestiche interno a Santa Francesca Romana', *RSB*, 3 (1908), pp. 265–75. Cult of late medieval saint, canonized in 1608.

309. H. Moretus, 'Les Reliques de la cathédrale d'Osnabruck en 1343', *AB*, 28 (1909), pp. 281–98. On relic collection.

310. Friedrich Pfister, *Der Reliquienkult im Altertum* (Giessen, 1909–12; and reprint), Religionsgeschichtliche Versuche und Vorarbeiten, V. On the cult of relics in Antiquity; Ch. XIV deals with the relationship between this and early Christian practice.

311. P. Saintyves, *Les Reliques et les images légendaires* (Paris, 1912). Important study by folklorist; of special interest for chapters on the phenomenon of liquefying blood, and on talismans, relics and statues falling from the sky.

312. Joseph Braun, *Der christliche Altar in seiner geschichtlichen Entwicklung*

(Munich, 1924), 2 vols. Huge scholarly history of the Christian altar, by Jesuit; see esp. I, pp. 525–662; and II, pp. 545–73 (on reliquary altars), with plates.

312a. Eugene A. Dooley, *Church Law on Sacred Relics* (Washington, D.C., 1931), Catholic University of America Canon Law Studies, 70. Pt I historical; Pt II 'a canonical guide to the right observance'.

313. Giuseppe Gagov, 'Uso e significato del termine "corpus" nell'antica agiografica cristiana', *MF*, 48 (1948), pp. 51–73. Important study of terminology; see in conjunction with **316, 317** and **328**.

314. Heinrich Fichtenau, 'Zum Reliquien wesen in früheren Mittelalter', *MIOG*, LX (1952), pp. 60–89. Important study by eminent medievalist.

315. Dom Joseph Thiron, 'Les Reliques de Jumièges', in *Jumièges, Congrès Scientifique du XIIIᵉ Centenaire, Rouen, juin 1954* (Rouen, 1955), II, pp. 889–99. On relics of important Norman abbey.

316. Giuseppe Gagov, 'Il termino "nomina" sinonimo di "reliquiae" nell' antica epigrafia cristiana', *MF*, 55 (1955), pp. 3–13. Further valuable study of terminology.

317. G. Gagov, 'Il culto delle reliquie nell' antichità riflesso nei due termini "patrocina" e "pignora"', *MF*, 58 (1958), pp. 484–512. See **313** and **316**.

318. Hans Hochenegg, 'Die St-Stephanus-Reliquie in Ischyl', *Schlern-Schriften*, 167 (1962), pp. 17–25. Brief account of local cult.

319. Wilfrid Bonser, 'The Cult of Relics in the Middle Ages', *FL*, 73–4 (1962–3), pp. 234–56. Descriptive.

320. Bernhard Kötting, *Der frühchristliche Reliquienkult und die Bestattung im Kirchengebäude* (Cologne, 1964), *AFLNW*, 123. Important short study with illustrations; discusses relationship between cult of relics and practice of burial in churches.

321. Friedrich Prinz, 'Stadtrömisch-italische Märtyrerreliquien und fränkischer Reichsadel im Maas-Moselraum', *HJ*, 87 (1967), pp. 1–25. On relics and spread of Roman influence in the Early Middle Ages; a local study.

322. Hans K. Schulze, 'Heiligenverehrung und Reliquienkult in Mitteldeutschlands', in Walter Schlesinger (ed.), *Festschrift für Friedrich von Zahn, I, Zur Geschichte und Volkskunde mitteldeutschlands* (Cologne and Graz, 1968), pp. 294–312. Useful local medieval study.

323. Otto Meinardus, 'A Study of the Relics of Saints of the Greek Orthodox Church', *Oriens Christianus*, 54 (1970), pp. 130–278. Comprehensive list with short introduction.

324. Patrice Boussel, *Des Reliques et de leur bon usage* (Paris, 1971). General and historical account by the Conservateur à la Bibliothèque Historique de la Ville de Paris, with detailed chapters on relics of Christ and the Virgin; a curious mixture of erudition, vulgarization and tongue-in-cheek.

325. Denis Bethell, 'The Making of a Twelfth-Century Relic Collection', in *Popular Belief and Practice* (**247**), pp. 61–72. Interesting study of the collection of Reading abbey, which also raises general methodological questions.

326. George P. Majeska, 'St Sophia in the Fourteenth and Fifteenth Centuries:

The Russian Travelers on the Relics', *DOP*, 27 (1973), pp. 69–87. Evidence of abundance of miraculous icons, and primary and secondary relics in the cathedral.

327. Nicole Herrmann-Mascard, *Les Reliques des Saints, Formation coutumière d'un droit* (Paris, 1975). Much more than a legal history; essential.

328. John M. McCulloh, 'The Cult of Relics in the Letters and "Dialogues" of Pope Gregory the Great: A Lexicographical Study', *Tr.*, 32 (1976), pp. 145–84. A careful examination of the writings of Gregory, establishing that Rome and the West had not accepted the translation or dismemberment of sacred bodies at the time, and also pointing to the crucial distinction made between different kinds of secondary relic, the *brandea*, deriving from cloths dipped in the blood of the martyrs having special significance; an important scholarly contribution; read in conjunction with Gagov (**313, 316** and **317**).

329. P. R. L. Brown, *Relics and Social Status in the Age of Gregory of Tours* (Reading, 1977). The 1976 Stenton Lecture; links cults of saints and of relics in particular with the need to focus community sentiment around the bishop, stressing the complexity of the sentiment involved; allusive.

(B) RELICS OF THE PASSION

330. F. de Mély, *Exuviae Sacrae Constantinopolitanae*, III (Paris, 1904). Includes sections on the Holy Lance and the Crown of Thorns, with full citations from contemporary documents.

331. J. Charles Wall, *Relics of the Passion* (London, 1910). Short factual account with illustrations; not too critical.

332. H. M. Gillett, *The Story of the Relics of the Passion* (Oxford, 1935). Scholarly in parts.

333. Walther Holtzmann, *König Heinrich I und die heilige Lanze, Kritische Untersuchungen zur Aussenpolitik in den Anfängen des deutschen Reiches* (Bonn, 1947). Short study of imperial cult of Holy Lance.

334. Steven Runciman, 'The Holy Lance Found at Antioch', *AB*, 68 (1950), pp. 197–205.

335. Martin Lintzel, 'Zur Erwerbung der heiligen Lanze durch Heinrich I', *Historische Zeitschrift*, 171 (1951), pp. 303–10.

336. A. Frolow, *La Relique de la Vraie Croix, Recherches sur le développement d'un culte* (Paris, 1961), Archives de l'Orient Chrétien, 7. Brief essay with much longer catalogue of documents.

337. Howard L. Adelson, 'The Holy Lance and the Hereditary German Monarchy', *Art Bulletin*, 48 (1966), pp. 177–92. Illustrated.

(C) RELIQUARIES

338. A. de Waal, 'Die antiken Reliquiare der Peterskirche', *RQ*, VII (1893), pp. 245–62. With three plates.

339. Joseph Braun, *Die Reliquiare des christlichen Kultes und ihre Entwicklung* (Freiburg im Breisgau, 1940). Comprehensive illustrated study by Jesuit.

340. André Grabar, 'Quelques reliquaires de Saint Démétrios et le martyrium du Saint à Salonique', *DOP*, 5 (1950), pp. 2–28. Illustrated.

341. A. Frolow, *Les Reliquaires de la Vraie Croix* (Paris, 1965). Archives de l'Orient Chrétien, 8. Important study.

342. Victor H. Elbern, 'Der fränkische Reliquienkasten und Tragaltar von Werden', in V. H. Elbern (ed.), *Das Erste Jahrtausend, Kultur und Kunst im Werdenden Abendland am Rheim und Ruhr* (Düsseldorf, 1962), 3 vols., I, pp. 436–70.

343. Irmingard Achten, 'Die Kölner Petrusreliquien und die Bautätigkeit Erzbischof Brunus (953–965) am Kölner Dom', in *ibid.*, II, pp. 948–91. Two detailed local studies.

See also **439**.

(D) TRANSLATIONS

344. Emile Mabille, 'Les Invasions normandes dans la Loire et les pérégrinations du corps de Saint Martin', *BEC*, XXX, 6th series, 5 (1869), pp. 149–94 and 425–60. Valuable study.

345. Comte P. Riant, 'Des Depouilles religieuses enlevées à Constantinople au XIIIe siècle par les Latins et des documents historiques nés de leur transport en Occident', *MSAF*, 36, 4th series, VI (1875), pp. 1–214. Important study of important phase in the history of relic veneration in the West.

346. C. Kohler, 'Translation de reliques de Jerusalem à Oviedo', *Revue de l'Orient Latin*, V (1897), pp. 1–21. Latin text with introduction.

347. Ferdinand Lot, 'Date de l'exode des corps saints hors de Bretagne', *ABr.*, XV (1899–1900), pp. 60–76. Translations to escape Normans.

348. F. Lot, 'Sur la date de la translation des reliques de Sainte Foi d'Agen à Conques', *AM*, 16 (1904), pp. 502–8. On important translation for subsequent history of Conques.

349. L. Levillain, 'La Translation des reliques de Saint Austremoine à Mozac et le diplôme de Pépin II d'Aquitaine (863)', *MA*, 2nd series, VIII (1904), pp. 281–337.

350. L. Duchesne, 'Sur la translation de S. Austremoine', *AB*, 24 (1905), pp. 105–14. Discussions of ninth-century translation.

351. Marguerite Bondois, *La Translation des Saints Marcellin et Pierre, Etude sur Einhard et sa vie politique de 827 à 834* (Paris, 1907), Bibliothèque de l'Ecole des Hautes Etudes, 160. Valuable study of use of translation for political reasons.

352. Wilhelm Hotzelt, 'Translationen von Martyrerreliquien aus Rom nach Bayern im 8. Jahrhundert', *Studien und Mitteilungen zur Geschichte des Benediktiner-Ordens und seiner Zweige* 53 (1935), pp. 286–343. On translations and spread of Roman influence.

353. Ugo Monneret de Villard, 'La fiera di Batnae e la traslazione di S. Tomaso a Edessa', *ANLR*, Classe di Scienci morali, storiche e filologiche, CCCXLVIII, 8th series, VI (1951), pp. 77–104. On early translation in Syria.

354. Leona C. Gabel (ed.), *Memoirs of a Renaissance Pope, The Commentaries of Pius II* (London, 1960). Book VII on the translation of the head of St Andrew to Rome from Narni in 1462; English translation of primary source.

355. A. J. M. Edwards, 'An Early Twelfth Century Account of the Translation of St Milburga of Much Wenlock', *Transactions of the Shropshire Archaeological Society*, LVII (1961–4), pp. 134–42. Rare English contribution.

356. Baudouin de Gaiffier, 'Hagiographie Salernitaine, La Translation de S. Mathieu', *AB*, 80 (1962), pp. 82–110. Apostolic translation.

357. Klemens Honselmann, 'Reliquientranslationen nach Sachsen', in V. H. Elbern (ed.), *Das Erste Jahrtausend* (**342**), I, pp. 159–93. On Saxony.

358. Eugenio Duprè Theseider, 'La "Grande rapine dei corpi santi" dall' Italia al tempo di Ottone I', *Festschrift Percy Ernst Schramm* (**261**), I, pp. 420–32. Important.

359. Louis Carolus-Barre, 'Saint Louis et la translation des corps saints', in *Etudes d'Histoire de droit canonique dédiées à Gabriel Le Bras* (Paris, 1965), 2 vols., II, pp. 1087–112. Important.

360. Franco Strazzullo, 'La politica di Ferrante I nei riflessi della traslazione delle ossa di S. Gennaro', *Atti della Accademia Pontaniana*, NS, XV (1965–6), pp. 73–89, and Plates 1–8. Political aspects of translation.

361. Dom Guy Oury, 'Les Pérégrinations de reliques: Saint Révérend de Nouâtre', *Bulletin Trimestriel de la Société Archéologique de Touraine*, XXXV (1968), pp. 279–93. Important study of local cult, translation of relics and hagiography.

362. Gerd Tellenbach, 'Zur Translation einer Reliquie des heiligen Laurentius von Rom nach Lüttich im Elften Jahrhundert', *Storiografia e Storia, Studi in onore di Eugenio Duprè Theseider* (Rome, 1974), 2 vols, II, pp. 601–15. Important study by leading German medieval historian.

363. Pierre Riché, 'Translations de reliques à l'époque carolingienne, Histoire des reliques de Saint Malo', *MA*, 82 (1976), pp. 201–18. Important study of acquisition by stealth of the relics of St Malo in the ninth century by the Breton church of Alet as a means of boosting its prestige.

See also **255–6, 279, 282, 298, 642, 1109, 1110, 1144.**

(E) RELIC THEFT AND RELIC TRADE

364. Edmond Le Blant, 'Le Vol des reliques', *Revue Archéologique*, 3rd series, IX (1887), pp. 317–28. Pioneering study.

365. Jean Guiraud, 'Le Commerce des reliques au commencement du IXe siècle', in *Mélanges G. B. De Rossi* (**213**), pp. 73–95. Still of value.

366. G. H. Doble, 'The Relics of Saint Petroc', *Antiquity*, 13 (1939), pp. 403–15. Twelfth-century account of relic theft, with English version and photographs of reliquaries; valuable text.

367. Hubert Silvestre, 'Commerce et vol de reliques au Moyen Age', *RBPH*, 30/2 (1952), pp. 721–39. Important.

368. Pierre Héliot and Marie-Laure Chastang, 'Quêtes et voyages de reliques au profit des églises françaises du Moyen Age,' *RHE*, LIX (1964), pp. 789–822; and LX (1965), pp. 5–32. Valuable.

369. David M. Knipe, 'The Heroic Theft: Myths from Ryveda IV and the Ancient Near East', *HR*, VI (1967), pp. 328–60. Study of sacred theft; provides a new angle on medieval relic theft for students of the subject to explore.

370. P. J. Geary, *Furta Sacra, Thefts of Relics in the Central Middle Ages* (Princeton, 1978). Short but authoritative study.

371. P. J. Geary, 'The Ninth-Century Relic Trade, A Response to Popular Piety?', in James Obelkevich (ed.), *Religion and the People 800–1700* (Chapel Hill, 1979), pp. 8–19. The introduction of the relics of Roman saints into the Frankish Empire is seen as part of a policy of religious control.

See also **363**.

(F) OPPOSITION OR DOUBTS

372. Jean Calvin, *Traité des reliques* (1543) (Paris, 1921), Collection des Chefs d'oeuvre méconnus. With introduction by Albert Autin. The classic Protestant critique.

373. J. A. S. Collin de Plancy, *Dictionnaire critique des reliques et des images miraculeuses* (Paris, 1821–2), 3 vols. A general introduction, followed by alphabetical entries; Voltairean in tone, but contains useful material; vol. III includes Calvin's *Traité des reliques* (pp. 251–329); and abbé L. de Cordemoy's *Traité des saintes reliques* of 1719 (pp. 331–61).

374. Abel Lefranc, 'Le Traité des reliques de Guibert de Nogent et les commencements de la critique historique au Moyen Age', in *Etudes d'Histoire du Moyen Age dédiées à Gabriel Monod* (Paris, 1896), pp. 285–306. Useful; see also **376** and **377**.

375. L. T. Lefort, 'La Chasse aux reliques des martyrs en Egypte au IVe siècle', *La Nouvelle Clio*, VI (1954), pp. 225–30. Brief discussion and translation of Coptic catechism condemning practices associated with the cult of relics.

376. Klaus Guth, *Guibert von Nogent und die hochmittelalterliche Kritik an der Reliquienverehrung* (Ottobeuren, 1970), *Studien und Mitteilungen zur Geschichte des Benediktiner-Ordens und seiner Zweige*, Suppl. 21. Short, but important study.

377. Colin Morris, 'A Critique of Popular Religion: Guibert of Nogent on *The Relics of the Saints*', in *Popular Belief and Practice* (**247**), pp. 55–60. An examination of the attitude of a twelfth-century intellectual towards relic veneration.

(G) AUTHENTICATION

378. Maurice Prou and abbé E. Chartraine, 'Authentiques de reliques conservées au trésor de la cathedrale de Sens', *MSAF*, 6th series, IX (1890), pp. 129–72. Catalogue of authenticated relics, with reproduction of texts.

379. P. Louis Batiffol, 'La Science des reliques et l'archéologie biblique', *Revue Biblique*, I (1892), pp. 186–202. Suggests a classificatory scheme.

380. Fedele Savio, 'Il monasterio di San Giusto di Susa', *RSB*, II (1907), pp. 205–20.

381. Ph. Kieffer, 'Saint Just de Suse', *RSB*, III (1908), pp. 374–405 and 495–503. Controversy between Savio and Kieffer over the authenticity of the relics of St Just at Susa; a characteristic example of problems that preoccupied Catholic and other scholars of an earlier generation.

382. Klaus Schreiner, 'Zum Wahrheitsverständnis im Heiligen- und Reliquienwesen des Mittelalters', *Saeculum*, 17 (1966), pp. 131–69. Comprehensive study with bibliographical notes; returns to the subject of authentication as a historical problem.

383. K. Schreiner, '"Discrimen veri ac falsi", Ansätze und Formen der Kritik in der Heiligen- und Reliquienverehrung des Mittelalters', *AK*, 48 (1966), pp. 1–53. Substantial study on same theme.

V MANIFESTATIONS OF THE CULT: IMAGES AND ICONOGRAPHY

(A) GENERAL

384. Edwyn Bevan, *Holy Images, An Inquiry into Idolatry and Image-Worship in Ancient Paganism and in Christianity* (London, 1940 and New York, 1979). Part of 1933 Gifford Lectures; a short and comprehensive account, with more emphasis on theory than practice.

385. Jaroslav Pelikan, *The Christian Tradition, A History of the Development of Doctrine*, 2, *The Spirit of Eastern Christendom (600–1700)* (Chicago and London, 1974). Ch. 3 on images.

(B) THE BYZANTINE ICONOCLASTIC CONTROVERSY

386. Edward James Martin, *A History of the Iconoclastic Controversy* (SPCK, London, 1930). Still probably the best general account in English.

387. Louis Bréhier and René Aigrain, *Grégoire le Grand, les états barbares et la conquête arabe (590–757)* (Paris, 1938), Fliche and Martin (eds.), *Histoire de l'Eglise*, V. Ch. XIII, 'La querelle des images jusqu'au concile iconoclaste de 754', by Bréhier.

388. Gerhart B. Ladner, 'Origin and Significance of the Byzantine Iconoclastic Controversy', *MS*, II (1940), pp. 127–49.

389. Emile Amann (ed.), *L'Epoque carolingienne* (Paris, 1941), Fliche and Martin (eds.), *Histoire de l'Eglise*, VI, Chs. III and VII. General account.

390. Norman H. Baynes, 'The Icons before Iconoclasm', *Harvard Theological Review*, XLIV (1951), pp. 93–106; and in N. H. Baynes, *Byzantine Studies and Other Essays* (London, 1955), pp. 226–39. Discussion of pagan and Jewish critiques of Christian image worship in the sixth and seventh centuries, and of Christian replies to them.

391. G. B. Ladner, 'The Concept of the Image in the Greek Fathers and the Byzantine Iconoclastic Controversy', *DOP*, 7 (1953), pp. 1–34. A careful examination of the way in which the notion of the image was used to conceptualize the Trinity, the Creation and the Incarnation, thus indicating the very wide dimensions of the controversy.

392. Ernst Kitzinger, 'The Cult of Images in the Age before Iconoclasm', *DOP*, 8 (1954), pp. 83–150. Major study by art historian.

393. N. H. Baynes, 'Idolatry and the Early Church', in Baynes, *Byzantine Studies* (**390**), pp. 116–43. Good study of the changing attitude of the Church towards images from the earliest times.

394. André Grabar, *L'Iconoclasme byzantin, Dossier archéologique* (Paris, 1957). More general than the sub-title implies.

395. P. J. Alexander, *The Patriarch Nicephorus of Constantinople, Ecclesiastical Policy and Image Worship in the Byzantine Empire* (Oxford, 1958). Study of the controversy in historical context.

396. G. E. von Grunebaum, 'Byzantine Iconoclasm and the Influence of the Islamic Environment', *HR*, II (1962), pp. 1–10. Discounts specific Islamic influence on iconoclasm.

397. Peter Brown, 'A Dark-Age Crisis: Aspects of the Iconoclastic Controversy', *EHR*, CCCXLVI (1973), pp. 1–34. An imaginative reassessment which relates icon-worship to centrifugal civic religion, and iconoclasm to centralizing trends in Byzantine politics and society, the latter achieving the upperhand when a reason was sought for the success of the Arab incursions of the seventh century and found in iconodule 'idolatry'; for criticisms, see **398** and **399**.

398. Stephen Gero, 'Notes on Byzantine Iconoclasm in the Eighth Century', *Byz.*, XLIV (1974), pp. 23–42. Contains a critique of Brown (**397**).

399. Patrick Henry, 'What was the Iconoclastic Controversy About?', *CH*, 45 (1978), pp. 16–31. A criticism of Brown (**397**), particularly on the grounds that he ignores the theological and practical distinctions between images of Christ and images of saints, and thus over-emphasizes the relationship between icons and intercession.

400. Anthony Bryer and Judith Herrin (eds.), *Iconoclasm* (Birmingham, 1977). Papers given at the Ninth Spring Symposium of Byzantine Studies, 1975; with contributions by Leslie Barnard on 'The Theology of Icons', by Oleg Grabar on 'Islam and Iconoclasm', and by David Freedberg on 'The Structure of Byzantine and European Iconoclasm', a useful comparative study.

See also **1077**.

(C) ICONS

401. Nikodim Pavlovich Kondakov, *The Russian Icon* (Oxford, 1927). Translated from the Russian; a well-illustrated history by eminent art historian, with a chapter on the use of icons; still of value.

402. A. J. Anisimov, *Our Lady of Vladimir* (Prague, 1928). Brief history of this famous icon, with analysis of its composition and style.

403. G. and M. Sotiriou, *Icones du Mont Sinai* (Athens, 1956–8), 2 vols. Illustrated volume with text, relating to probably the best and most extensive series of icons. See also **408**.

404. H. P. Gerhard, *Welt der Ikonen* (Recklinghausen, 1957). English translation as *The World of Icons* (London, 1971). Illustrated, mainly art historical, but sets icons in religious context; good general study.

405. L. Ouspensky, *Essai sur la théologie de l'icone dans l'Eglise orthodoxe* (Paris, 1960). Good scholarly study.

406. Konard Onasch, *Icons* (London, 1961). Large illustrated volume on Russian icons.

407. Chalva Amiranachvili, *Les Emaux de Georgie* (Paris, 1962). Illustrated book; includes some icons of saints.

408. Kurt Weitzmann *et al.*, *Icons from South-Eastern Europe and Sinai* (London, 1968). Richly illustrated volume.

409. Athanasius Papageorgiou, *Icons of Cyprus* (London, 1969). Illustrated volume.

410. John Stuart, *Ikons* (London, 1975). Like most books on the subject, this is concerned primarily with icons as art objects.

411. *Icones bulgares IX*ᵉ*–XIX*ᵉ *siècle, Musée du Petit-Palais, March–June 1976* (Paris, 1976). Well-illustrated exhibition catalogue.

412. K. Weitzmann, *The Icon, Holy Images Sixth to Fourteenth Century* (London, 1978). 48 plates in colour with commentary by leading art historian in the field; the best general introduction.

413. *Novgorod Icons, 12th–17th Centuries* (Oxford, 1980). Book of sumptuous reproductions, with iconographical index.

414. Svetozar Radojčič, *Icones de Serbie et de Macedoine* (Belgrade, 1961). Book of plates, mainly black and white, with short introduction.

415. George Galavaris, *The Icon in the Life of the Church, Doctrine, Liturgy, Devotion* (Leiden, 1981), Iconographies of Religions, XXIV, fasc. 8. An interpretative essay and 48 black and white plates; important.

(D) SAINTS IN WESTERN ART

(i) General and reference

416. C. Cahier, *Caractéristiques des saints dans l'art populaire* (Paris, 1867 and Brussels, 1966), 2 vols. Thorough iconographical dictionary, arranged by theme, by Jesuit.

417. Adolphe Napoléon Didron, *Christian Iconography, or The History of Christian Art in the Middle Ages* (London, 1891–6 and New York, 1965), 2 vols. First appeared in French in 1851; vol. I includes useful section on the nimbus or halo.

418. Lucy Menzies, *The Saints in Italy, A Book of Reference to the Saints in Italian Art and Dedication* (London, 1924). Useful.

419. Karl Künstle, *Ikonographie der christlichen Kunst, II, Ikonographie der Heiligen* (Freiburg im Breisgau, 1926). Alphabetical iconographical dictionary by Catholic scholar; superseded to some extent by Réau (**430**) and Kirschbaum (**434**).

420. H. Delehaye, 'Les Caractéristiques des saints dans l'art', *Le Correspondent*, 313 (25 November 1928), pp. 481–500. Still a valuable introduction.

421. Joseph Braun, *Tracht und Attribute der Heiligen in der deutschen Kunst* (Stuttgart, 1943). Alphabetical iconographical dictionary of German art, by the indefatigable Jesuit scholar; illustrated.

422. Martin Davies (ed.), *A Few Saints from the Pictures in the National Gallery* (London, 1946). Interesting collection of plates; mainly details in monochrome.

423. E. Mâle, *L'Art religieux de la fin du Moyen Age en France, Etude sur l'iconographie du Moyen Age et sur ses sources d'inspiration* (Paris, 1949), 5th edition (original edn 1908). Ch. V on 'Les aspects nouveaux du culte des saints'. Part of a huge survey; essential reading.

424. E. Mâle, *L'Art religieux de la fin du XVIe siècle, du XVIIe siècle et du XVIIIe siècle, Etude sur l'iconographie après le Concile de Trente, Italie – France – Espagne – Flandres* (Paris, 1951), 2nd edition (original edn 1932). Chapters or sections on Art and Protestantism, the cults of saints, relics, martyrs and St Joseph; essential.

425. Roger Aubenas and Robert Richard, *L'Eglise et la Renaissance (1449–1517)* (Paris, 1951), Fliche and Martin (eds.), *Histoire de l'Eglise*, XV. Book II, Ch. VI has relevant section on art and piety.

426. George Kaftal, *Iconography of the Saints in Tuscan Painting* (Florence, 1952). Alphabetical iconographical dictionary, with introduction, calendar, index of attributes and signs, and bibliography; illustrations in black and white; first volume of extremely useful reference work on saints in 'fine' Italian painting. See also **433** and **436**.

427. E. Mâle, *L'Art religieux du XIIe siècle en France, Etude sur les origines de l'iconographie du Moyen Age* (Paris, 1953), 6th revised edition (original edn 1922). Chapters on saints and pilgrimages; a basic work.

428. Helen Roeder, *Saints and their Attributes, with a Guide to Localities and Patronage* (London, 1955). Useful dictionary, probably the best on this topic.

429. E. Mâle *L'Art religieux du XIIIe siècle en France, Etude sur l'iconographie du Moyen Age et sur ses sources d'inspiration* (Paris, 1958), 9th edition (original edn 1898). English translation as *Religious Art in France, XIII century* (London, 1913); and *The Gothic Image* (London, 1961). Ch. IV on the saints and the Golden Legend.

430. Louis Réau, *Iconographie de l'art chrétien, III, Iconographie des saints* (Paris, 1958 and Nendeln, Lichtenstein, 1974), 3 vols. Comprehensive alphabetical dictionary with details of history, legend, geography of cult, specialisms, patronages, as well as of iconography; essential.

431. Hans Aurenhammer, *Lexikon der christlichen Ikonographie* (Vienna, 1959–67). Alphabetical dictionary without illustrations; one volume only has appeared.

432. George Ferguson, *Signs and Symbols in Christian Art* (New York, 1961). Section X of this relatively short dictionary is devoted to the saints; useful.

433. George Kaftal, *Iconography of the Saints in Central and South Italian Schools of Painting* (Florence, 1965). Sequel to **426**.

434. Engelbert Kirschbaum *et al.* (eds.), *Lexikon der christlichen Ikonographie, 5–8, Ikonographie der Heiligen* (Rome, Freiburg, Basel and Vienna, 1973–6). Comprehensive alphabetical iconographical dictionary in four large volumes; an alternative or complement to Réau (**430**).

435. Gertrude Grace Sill, *A Handbook of Symbols in Christian Art* (New York, 1975). Short guide with section on saints.

436. George Kaftal and Fabio Bisogni, *Iconography of the Saints in the Paintings of North East Italy* (Florence, 1978). Sequel to **426** and **433**.

(ii) Particular saints

437. *L'Art et les saints*, Collection published by Henri Laurens (Paris, 1917–37). 42 small volumes devoted to individual saints, with illustrations and bibliographies; contributions include Henry Martin on St Martin, St Hubert, St Mark and St Andrew; Georges Goyau on St. Genevieve; Auguste Marguillier on St Nicholas.

438. E. Mâle, *Art et artistes du Moyen Age* (Paris, 1927), Ch. XI, 'La vie de Saint Louis racontée par les peintres du XIVe siècle'.

439. Tancred Borenius, *St Thomas Becket in Art* (London, 1932). Short but comprehensive; well illustrated; includes reliquaries.

440. George Kaftal, *St Dominic in Early Tuscan Painting* (Oxford, 1948). Valuable study with scenes from the Life and accompanying texts; 41 plates.

441. G. Kaftal, *St Catherine in Tuscan Painting* (Oxford, 1949). Same format as above, but a much richer iconography in terms of religious psychology.

442. G. Kaftal, *St Francis in Italian Painting* (London, 1950). Reproductions of paintings of scenes from the Life and posthumous miracles accompanied by extracts from the hagiography; a most successful combination.

443. Elisabeth Dubler, *Das Bild des heiligen Benedikt bis zum Ausgang des Mittelalters* (St Ottilien, 1953). Short study with 150 small plates.

444. Alexandre Masseron, *Saint Jean Baptiste dans l'art* (Paris, 1957). Important short study, well illustrated.

444a. *Vita Sanctae Coletae (1381–1447), The Pictures of the Manuscript belonging to the Convent of the Colettine Poor Clares in Ghent* (Tielt and Leiden, 1982). Facsimile reproduction of illustrations from fifteenth-century French Life, with essays by Cazaux and others.

See also **104, 121, 260, 261, 264, 640, 991, 1176.**

(E) POPULAR ICONOGRAPHY, WESTERN

(i) General

445. Paolo Toschi, *Arte Popolare Italiana* (London, 1959). Good comprehensive account, profusely illustrated; pp. 325–72, section on religious art: pictures, ex-votos, amulets, etc.

446. Antonino Buttitta, *Folk Art in Sicily* (Palermo, 1961). Chapters on popular religious art and on cart-paintings; also discusses emblems of confraternities; well illustrated, with bibliography.

447. Lenz Kriss-Rettenbeck, *Bilder und Zeichen religiösen Volksglauben* (Munich, 1963). Study of south German religious art, with sections on saints' cults and ex-votos; many remarkable photographs and full bibliography; important.

448. Paule and Roger Lerou, 'Objets de culte et pratiques populaires, Pour une méthode d'enquête', in Bernard Plongeron (ed.), *La Religion populaire dans l'Occident chrétien, Approches historiques* (Paris, 1976), pp. 195–237. Methodological.

449. Caroline Williams, *Saints, Their Cults and Origins* (London, 1980). Short study of interest for the reproductions of modern popular imagery.

450. John Salmon, *Saints in Suffolk Churches* (Ipswich, 1981). Pamphlet on local iconography.

See also **1249.**

(ii) Statues

451. Paul Gruyer, *Les Saints bretons* (Paris, 1926), Collection Les Visites d'Art. Short study of 'popular' statues, with 45 photographs.

452. C. Duprat, 'Trésors d'art populaire: Statuaire religieuse', *ATP*, IV (1956), pp. 243–8 and 344–8, with photographs. Valuable descriptive study of French examples.

453. *Charité de Saint Martin, 21 groupes sculptés d'églises du département de l'Oise et diocèse de Beauvais, accompagnés d'oeuvres d'art et de documents illustrant la vie et la légende de Saint Martin de Tours*, Exposition, Musée des Arts et Traditions Populaires, mars–mai 1961. Catalogue, with introduction by Clémence Duprat and 12 photographs.

454. Claude Savart, 'A la recherche de l'"art" dit de Saint-Sulpice', *RHS*, 52 (1976), pp. 265–82. Important exploratory essay on what was the dominant mode of sacred statuary in France and elsewhere from the 1850s until recently.

455. Sylvie Forestier, 'Art industriel et industrialisation de l'art: L'exemple de la statuaire religieuse de Vendeuvre-sur-Barse', *EF*, 8 (1978), pp. 191–200. Valuable study of nineteenth-century French pottery specializing in production of statues of saints.

(iii) Prints and pictures

456. Maurice Jusselin, *Imagiers et cartiers à Chartres* (Paris, 1957). Important study of popular religious prints of the eighteenth century; with illustrations.

457. W. W. Williamson, 'Saints on Norfolk Rood-Screens and Pulpits', *NA*, 31 (1957), pp. 299–346. A classified list.

458. Robert Wildhaber, 'Der "Deserteur" ein Walliser Maler religiöser Volkskunst', *RJV*, 12 (1961), pp. 211–26. Study of popular religious painter. See also **459.**

459. *Folklore Suisse*, 54, Nos. 3/4 (1964), pp. 29–70. Number devoted to Ch. F. Le Brun 'dit le "Déserteur"'; various studies of nineteenth-century painter of saints in 'Epinal' style, with 21 plates.

460. Alberto Vecchi, *Il Culto delle immagini nelle stampe popolari* (Florence, 1968). Study of mainly eighteenth-century Italian popular devotional prints, with 33 illustrations; an important aspect of popular religion; also considers the ambiguous attitude of the clergy towards the devotions associated with them: popular religiosity to be encouraged and directed? or superstition to be curbed?

461. M.-H. Froeschlé-Chopard, 'Univers sacré et iconographie au XVIIIᵉ siècle: Eglises et chapelles des diocèses de Vence et de Grasse', *Ann.*, 31 (1976), pp. 489–519. Valuable study of pictures in churches and chapels, paying special attention to the relationship between saints, the Virgin and God, and noting important distinctions between 'popular' cults and those promoted by the clergy. For an expanded version, with illustrations, see **1249**.

(iv) Ex-votos

462. Richard Andrée, *Votive und Weihegaben des katholischen Volks in Süddeutschland, Ein Beitrag zur Volkskunde* (Braunschweig, 1904). Pioneering study of ex-votos and pilgrimage in south Germany, with illustrations; representational ex-votos of parts of the body and of animals in metal, of special interest.

463. Paul Sébillot, 'Les Ex-voto', *RTP*, 21 (1906), pp. 161–4. Brief essay by the eminent French folklorist.

464. Rudolf Kriss, 'Votive unde Weihegaben des italienischen Volkes', *ZV*, NS, II (1931), pp. 249–71. Important study of Italian ex-votos.

465. Adalberto Pazzini, 'Il significato degl' "ex-voto" ed il concetto della divinità guaritrice', *ANLR*, 6th series, XI (1935), pp. 42–79. Mainly on the Ancient World.

466. Joan Amades, *Els Ex-Vots, Art Popular* (Barcelona, 1942). General and historical work by curator of the Museum of Popular Art in Barcelona, with emphasis on Catalonia; good colour illustrations.

467. Paolo Toschi, *Saggi sull'arte popolare* (Rome, 1944). Includes chapter on ex-voto paintings; by eminent folklorist.

468. U. M. Radford, 'The Wax Images Found in Exeter Cathedral', *Antiquaries Journal*, 29 (1949), pp. 162–8. Study of wax ex-votos from tomb of Bishop Edmund Lacey (1420–55); with photographs.

469. Fernand Benoît and Sylvain Gagnière, 'Pour une histoire de l'ex-voto, Ex-voto en métal découpé de la région de Saint-Rémy-de-Provence', *ATP*, II (1954), pp. 23–34. Important study of a type.

470. Arnaldo Ciarrocchi and Ermanno Mori, *Le Tavolette votive italiane* (Udine, 1960). Book of colour plates, with short introduction and bibliography; examples of ex-voto paintings from the fifteenth century onwards, mainly to the Virgin Mary.

471. Rudolf Kriss and Hubert Kriss-Heinrich, 'Beiträge zum religiösen

Volksleben auf der Insel Cypern mit besonderer Berücksichtigung des Wallfahrtswesens', *RJV*, 12 (1961), pp. 135–210. Valuable study of local shrines in an Orthodox milieu, with photographs of ex-votos of human forms and parts of the body as well as of the shrines themselves.

472. Mario Tabanelli, *Gli Ex-voto poliviscerali Etruschi et Romani* (Florence, 1962). Study of antique ex-votos of internal organs; important.

473. Wolfgang Brückner, 'Volkstümliche Denkstrukturen und hochschichtlichen Weltbild im Votivwesen, Zur Forschungssituation und Theorie des bildlichen Opferkultes', *SAV*, 59 (1963), pp. 186–203. Study of figurative ex-votos.

474. Paul Cassar, 'Medical Votive Offerings in the Maltese Islands', *Journal of the Royal Anthropological Institute*, 94 (1964), pp. 23–9. Illustrated study.

475. Paolo Toschi, *Bibliografia degli Ex-voto italiani* (Florence, 1970), Biblioteca di Bibliografia Italiana, LX. Important catalogue by artist and place.

476. Paolo Toschi and Renato Penna, *Le Tavolette votive della Madonna dell' Arco* (Naples, 1971). Large book of plates, mainly in colour, with scholarly introduction, devoted to one of the most important accumulations of ex-votos in existence: 4,500 pictures dating from the fifteenth century onwards, precious objects, models of parts of the body, guns, swords, medals, etc.; essential.

477. G. M. Cambiè, 'Mestieri e vita popolare nelle figurazioni delle tavolette votive', *Economia e Storia*, XVIII (1971). pp. 439–56, including 9 plates. Use of ex-voto paintings as source for study of social and economic life.

478. Lenz Kriss-Rettenbeck, *Ex Voto, Zeichen Bild und Abbild im christlichen Votivbrauchtum* (Zurich and Freiburg im Breisgau, 1972). Comprehensive account of all kinds of ex-votos – objects of all sorts, paintings, sculptured figures – from Europe and Latin America; German lands well represented; over 200 illustrations; essential.

479. J. Danigo, 'Les Anciens ex-votos de Sainte-Anne d'Auray', *Bulletin de la Société Polymathique du Morbihan* (1973), pp. 63–89. Description of ex-votos from important Breton shrine, dating from seventeenth century onwards.

480. Klaus Beitl, 'Votivbildstudien', *OZV*, NS, XXIX (OS, 78) (1975), pp. 104–18. Studies of ex-votos of shrines in Tyrol and Graz region, dating from seventeenth and eighteenth centuries.

481. Dominique-Marie Lavedrine, 'Les "Ex-voto" marins du Roussillon', *RHMC*, 23 (1976), pp. 408–17. Good local study of a particular type of ex-voto painting.

482. Bernard Cousin, 'Dévotion et société en Provence, Les ex-voto de Notre-Dame-de-Lumières' *EF*, VII (1977), pp. 121–42. Quantitative and iconographical analysis of ex-voto paintings from this shrine over long period 1660–1900, with illustrations, tables and charts; methodologically innovative and important.

483. B. Cousin, 'Ex-voto provençaux et histoire des mentalités', *MAR* (1977), *Religion populaire*, pp. 183–212. Short general and methodological account, with 16 plates.

484. Christian Loubet, 'Ex-voto de Notre-Dame d'Oropa en Piémont

(XVIe–XXe siècle), Images d'une dévotion populaire', *ibid.*, pp. 213–45. Quantitative analysis, with illustrations.

485. *Ex-voto du terroir marseillais* (Marseille, 1978). Illustrated catalogue of exhibition, with essays by Michel Vovelle and Bernard Cousin, and valuable notes.

486. B. Cousin, 'L'Ex-voto, document d'histoire, expression d'une société', *ASR*, 48 (1979), pp. 107–24. Important introductory study of ex-voto painting, mainly in France; illustrated.

487. Jean Arrouge, 'Un ex-voto martégal, Essai d'interprétation sémiologique', *EF*, 9 (1979), pp. 179–85. Methodologically interesting discussion of an atypical painted ex-voto.

488. Giovanni Battista Bronzini, '"Ex-voto" e cultura religiosa popolare, Problemi d'interpretazione', *Rivista de Storia e Letteratura Religiosa*, I (1979), pp. 3–27. Important study, with bibliographical references.

See also **1023**.

(v) Secular equivalents or extensions

489. Maurice Agulhon, 'La "statuomanie" et l'histoire', *EF*, 8 (1978), pp. 145–72. Introductory study of the vogue for secular statues in nineteenth-century France by eminent social historian; illustrated.

490. M. Agulhon, *Marianne into Battle, Republican Imagery and Symbolism in France 1789–1880* (Cambridge, 1981). Study of secular political iconography.

VI MANIFESTATIONS OF THE CULT: THE LITURGY

(A) GENERAL, WESTERN

491. J. Loth, 'Les Anciennes Litanies des saints en Bretagne', *RC*, XI (1890), pp. 135–51.

492. L. Duchesne, *Origines du culte chrétien, Etude sur la liturgie latine avant Charlemagne* (Paris, 1909), 5th revised edition. English translation of 4th edition as *Christian Worship: Its Origin and Evolution, A Study of the Latin Liturgy up to the time of Charlemagne* (SPCK, London, 1912). Ch. VIII deals with the festivals of saints; a classic.

493. A. Poncelet, 'Le Légendier de Pierre Calo', *AB*, 29 (1910), pp. 5–116. Especially valuable for introduction on the general development of legendaries.

494. Edmund Bishop, *Liturgica Historica. Papers on the Liturgy and Religious Life of the Western Church* (Oxford, 1918). Includes paper on 'The Litany of the Saints in the Stowe Missal', pp. 137–64, which first appeared in 1905.

495. R. Delamare, *Le Calendier de l'église d'Evreux, Etude liturgique et hagiographique* (Paris, 1919), Bibliothèque Liturgique, XXI. Local study with special emphasis on saints.

496. F. Duine, *Inventaire liturgique de l'hagiographie bretonne* (Paris, 1922), Collection La Bretagne et les Pays Celtiques, 16. Reference work.

497. Charles Plummer, *Irish Litanies* (London, 1925), Henry Bradshaw Society, LXII. Latin and Irish texts with English translation; includes two litanies of the saints, who are designated by numbers and place rather than individually, a reflection of Celtic notions of sanctity: also litanies of the Virgin and St Michael.

498. Maurice Coens, 'Anciennes litanies des saints', *AB*, 54 (1936), pp. 5–37; 55 (1937), pp. 49–69; 59 (1941), pp. 272–98; and 62 (1944), pp. 126–68; and in Coens, *Recueil d'Etudes Bollandiennes* (Brussels, 1963), SH, 37, Pt II. Important study of litanies from Germany, France and the Netherlands.

499. V. L. Kennedy, *The Saints of the Canon of the Mass* (Vatican City, 1938), Studi di Antichità Cristiana, XIV. Important historical and liturgical study.

500. Theodor Klauser, 'Die Liturgie der Heiligsprechung', in *Heilige Uberlieferung, Ausschnitte aus der Geschichte des Mönchtums und des heiligen Kultes*, I (Münster, 1938), pp. 212–33; and in Klauser, *Gesammelte Arbeiten* (**155**), pp. 161–76.

501. Silas M. Harris, *St David in the Liturgy* (Cardiff, 1940). Brief study of Welsh patron.

502. Dom Gregory Dix, *The Shape of the Liturgy* (London, 1945), Classic liturgical history, with full references to cult of saints.

503. F. Wormald, 'The English Saints in the Litany in Arundel MS 60', *AB*, 64 (1946), pp. 72–86.

504. Stephen A. Van Dijk, 'The Litany of the Saints on Holy Saturday', *JEH*, I (1950), pp. 51–62. Study by Franciscan.

505. Robert Lesage (ed.), *Dictionnaire pratique de Liturgie romaine* (Paris, 1952). Approved reference work.

506. Baudouin de Gaiffier, 'La Lecture des Actes des Martyrs dans la prière liturgique en Occident à propos du passionnaire hispanique', *AB*, 72 (1954), pp. 134–66.

507. Kathleen Hughes, 'The Offices of S. Finnian of Clonard and S. Cíanán of Duleek', *AB*, 73 (1955), pp. 342–72. Irish examples.

508. D. R. Dendy, *The Use of Lights in Christian Worship* (London, 1959), Alcuin Club Collections, XLI. Ch. VII, on the history of lighting candles for saints; important.

509. Baudouin de Gaiffier, 'De l'usage et de la lecture du martyrologe, Témoignages antérieures au XIe siècle', *AB*, 74 (1961), pp. 40–59. Valuable.

510. Ludwig Eisenhofer and Joseph Lechner, *The Liturgy of the Roman Rite* (Freiburg, Edinburgh and London, 1961). A good general account, with section on saints.

511. Charles W. Jones, *The Saint Nicholas Liturgy and Its Literary Relationships* (*Ninth to Twelfth Century*) (Berkeley and Los Angeles, 1963). Text and discussion; important.

512. Theodor Klauser, *A Short History of the Western Liturgy, An Account and*

Some Reflections (London, 1969). Translated from German edition of 1965. General account with references to cult of saints.

See also **933, 1145**.

(B) GENERAL, EASTERN

513. H. Delehaye, *Synaxarium Ecclesiae Constantinopolitanae, Propylaem ad Acta Sanctorum Novembris* (Brussels, 1902). Greek text with introduction and commentary in Latin.

514. Léon Clugnet, *Vie et office de Sainte Marine* (Paris, 1905), Bibliothèque Hagiographique Orientale. Latin, Greek, Coptic, Arabic, Syriac, Ethiopian, German and French texts; unusual primary source.

515. John Bannerman Wainewright, *The Office for the Commemoration of the Holy, Glorious and All-Praiseworthy Apostles and Chief Primates Peter and Paul . . . according to the Byzantine Rite* (London, 1909). English translation of primary source.

516. C. Osieczkewska, 'La Mosaïque de la Porte Royale à Sainte-Sophie de Constantinople et la Litanie de tous les saints', *Byz.*, IX (1934), pp. 41–83. On the relationship between iconography and the liturgy.

517. Sophie Antoniadis, *Place de la Liturgie dans la tradition des lettres grecques* (Leiden, 1939), Pt III. Ch. II has section on 'La Vie des saints'.

518. Nicholas Cabasilas, *A Commentary on the Divine Liturgy* (SPCK, London, 1960 and 1971). Fourteenth-century Byzantine text; Chs. 33, 49 and 50 discuss the place of the commemoration of the saints in the Eastern liturgy.

519. Jacques Noret, 'Ménologes, synaxaires, ménées, Essai de clarification d'une terminologie', *AB*, 86 (1968), pp. 21–4. Very brief, but helpful.

520. Casimir Kucharek, *The Byzantine–Slav Liturgy of St John Chrysostom, Its Origin and Evolution* (Combermere, Ontario, 1971). Ch. LXIII on 'The Commemoration of the Church Triumphant'.

See also **858**.

(C) CALENDARS

521. Dom Prosper Guéranger, *The Liturgical Year* (Dublin, 1867–83), 8 vols. Translated from the French; still important for pre-Vatican II Roman calendar and place of the saints in the liturgy.

522. Alexander Penrose Forbes, *Kalendars of Scottish Saints with Personal notices of those of Alba, Laudonia and Strathclyde* (Edinburgh, 1872). Texts of medieval calendars and martyrologies, with a valuable alphabetical list of Scottish saints.

523. J. B. De Rossi and L. Duchesne, *Martyrologium Hieronymianum ad fidem codicum adiectis prolegomenis* (Paris, 1894), Acta Sanctorum, 65. Critical study of crucial source.

524. H. Delehaye, 'Les Ménologes grecs', *AB*, 16 (1897), pp. 311–29. One of earliest studies by the great Bollandist.

525. George Herzfeld, *An Old English Martyrology* (London, 1900), EETS, OS, 116. Ninth-century Mercian text, with translation into modern English.

526. H. Achelis, *Die Martyrologien, ihre Geschichte und ihr Wert* (Göttingen, 1900), Adhandlungen der Königliche Gesellschaft der Wissenschaften zu Göttingen, Philologisch-historische Klasse, NS, III. Comprehensive.

527. F. Duine, 'Le Calendrier breton de Rennes au XIIe siècle', *ABr.*, XVIII (1902–3).

528. H. Delehaye, 'Le Témoignage des Martyrologes', *AB*, 26 (1907), pp. 78–99.

529. Dom Henri Quentin, *Les Martyrologes historiques du moyen âge, Etude sur la formation du martyrologe romain* (Paris, 1908). Long and detailed historical study by Catholic scholar; still basic.

530. Jules Baudot, *Le Martyrologe* (Paris, 1911). Good short account.

531. H. Delehaye, *Commentarium Perpetuus in Martyrologium Hieronymianum* (Brussels, 1931), Acta Sanctorum, 66. Perhaps the last great work of European scholarship to be written in Latin.

532. Paul Perdrizet, *Le Calendrier parisien à la fin du Moyen Age d'après le Bréviaire et les Livres d'Heures* (Gap, 1933), Publications de la Faculté des Lettres de l'Université de Strasbourg, 63. Compares the two sources; a mine of fascinating information in notes.

533. *The Roman Martyrology in accordance with the Reforms of Pope Pius X* (London, 1937). English text.

534. Fernand Cabrol, *The Year's Liturgy, The Sundays, Feriae and Feasts of the Liturgical Year*, II, *The Sanctoral* (London, 1940). Brief and probably the best guide to the saints celebrated in the Roman Calendar, by Benedictine liturgical scholar.

535. John Hennig, 'Kalendar und Martyrologium als Literaturformen', *Archiv für Liturgiewissenschaft*, VII (1961), pp. 1–44. Literary study.

536. J. B. Connell (ed.), *The Roman Martyrology, in which are to be found the Eulogies of the Saints and Blessed approved by the Sacred Congregation of Rites up to 1961* (London, 1962). Official English text.

537. Jacques Dubois, *Le Martyrologe d'Usuard, Texte et commentaire* (Brussels, 1965), SH, 40. Important study of ninth-century martyrology.

(D) SERMONS

538. Theodor Erbe (ed.), *Mirk's Festial: A Collection of Homilies by Johannes Mirkus*, I (London, 1905), EETS, Extra series, XCVI. Primary source; sermons for saints' days and other festivals.

539. G. R. Owst, *Literature and Pulpit in Medieval England, A Neglected Chapter in the History of English Letters and of the English People* (Cambridge, 1933). Ch. III on the place of saints in English sermons, and on discussion of the cult of the saints and of images in the Later Middle Ages.

540. Cyrille Lambot, 'Les Sermons de S. Augustin pour les fêtes de martyrs',

AB, 67 (1949), pp. 249–66. Discussion of important early examples of genre.

541. Baudouin de Gaiffier, 'Sermons latins en l'honneur de S. Vincent antérieurs au Xe siècle', *ibid.*, pp. 267–86.

See also **93, 798**.

VII MANIFESTATIONS OF THE CULT: DEDICATIONS AND NAMES

(A) CHURCH DEDICATIONS

(i) General

542. Charles Browne, 'The Dedications of Churches', *Transactions of the St Paul's Ecclesiological Society*, I (1881–5), pp. 267–94. An attempt at a general approach to the topic, with a list of English cathedral dedications.

543. Edgar Hennecke, 'Patrozinienforschung', *ZK*, XXXVIII (1920), pp. 337–55.

544. H. Delehaye, 'Loca Sanctorum', *AB*, 48 (1930), pp. 5–64. Important study of church dedications and place-names associated with saints in the West; footnotes contain valuable bibliography to date.

545. Josef A. Jungmann, 'Vom Patrozinium zum Weiheakt', *LJ*, 4 (1954), pp. 130–48. On dedication ritual.

See also **105**.

(ii) France

546. Eugen Ewig, 'Die Kathedralpatrozinien im Römischen und im Fränkischen Gallien', *HJ*, 79 (1960), pp. 1–61. On cathedral dedications in Gaul.

547. J. de Font-Reaulx, 'Les Saints honorés dans l'ancien diocèse d'Aix', *PH*, XXII (1972), pp. 186–92. Short study of church and chapel dedications.

548. J. -B. Marquette, 'Paroisses dédiées à Notre-Dame et occupation du sol en Bordelais et en Bazadais au Moyen Age (V^e–Xe siècle)', *AM*, 90 (1978), pp. 3–23. Detailed local study indicating that parishes in the region were being dedicated to the Virgin in the Dark Ages.

(iii) Germany

549. M. Fastlinger, 'Die Kirchenpatrozinien in ihrer Bedeutung für Altbayerns ältestes Kirchenwesen', *Oberbayerisches Archiv für vaterländische Geschichte*, 50 (1897), pp. 339–440. Catalogue, with maps.

550. Johann Dorn, 'Beiträge zur Patrozinienforschung', *AK*, 13 (1917), pp. 9–49 and 220–55. Important study, with bibliographical references to date, and lists of dedications.

551. Herbert Helbig, *Untersuchungen über die Kirchenpatrozinien in Sachsen auf siedlungsgeschichtlicher Grundlage* (Berlin, 1940), Historische Studien, 361. Study of church dedications, cults and patterns of settlement in medieval Saxony; thorough.

552. Hans-Walter Krumwiede (ed.), *Die mittelalterlichen Kirchen- und Altarpatrozinien Niedersachsens* (Göttingen, 1960). Catalogue of church and altar dedications by various hands.

553. Eugen Ewig, 'Die ältesten Mainzer Patrozinien und die Frühgeschichte des Bistums Mainz', in W. H. Elbern (ed.), *Das Erste Jahrtausend* (**342**), I, pp. 114–27. Good local study.

(iv) Great Britain

554. Frances Arnold-Forster, *Studies in Church Dedications or England's Patron Saints* (London, 1899), 3 vols. With tables and statistical summary; still useful.

555. John Fisher, 'Welsh Church Dedications', *Transactions of the Honourable Society of Cymmrodorion* (1906–7), pp. 76–108. Introductory.

556. James Murray Mackinlay, *Ancient Church Dedications in Scotland* (Edinburgh, 1910–14), 2 vols. Vol. I on Scriptural, Vol. II on non-Scriptural dedications; still the standard work.

557. Francis Bond, *Dedications and Patron Saints of English Churches, Ecclesiastical Symbolism, Saints and their Emblems* (London, 1914). Important compendium.

558. W. Levison, 'Medieval Church-Dedications in England: Some Problems', *TAASDN*, X (1946), pp. 57–79. Important.

559. K. E. Kirk, *Church Dedications of the Oxford Diocese* (Oxford, 1946). Valuable compilation by a bishop of the diocese.

560. C. L. S. Linnell, *Norfolk Church Dedications* (York, 1962), St Anthony's Hall Publications, 21. Pamphlet, with list and introduction; exemplary local study.

(v) Italy

561. Gian Piero Bognetti, 'I "Loca Sanctorum" e la storia delle Chiesa nel regno dei Longobardi', *RSCI*, VI (1952), pp. 165–204; and in Gajano, *Agiografia altomedievale* (**920**), pp. 105–43. Good study.

(B) PLACE-NAMES AND PATTERNS OF SETTLEMENT

562. P. W. Joyce, *The Origin and History of Irish Names of Places* (Dublin, 1870–1913), 3 vols. Vol. I, Ch. III, pp. 135–52 on early Irish saints and place-names; pioneering, and still basic, work on the subject.

563. Constantin Jireček, 'Das christliche Element in der topographischen Nomenclatur der Balkanländer', *Sitzungsberichte der Philosophisch-historischen Classe der Kaiserlichen Akademie der Wissenschaften*, 136, IX

(Vienna, 1897). Substantial study of saints' names and place-names in the Balkans.

564. James Murray Mackinlay, *Influence of the Pre-Reformation Church on Scottish Place-Names* (Edinburgh and London, 1904). Chapters on saints and on church founders; still valuable.

565. René Largillière, *Les Saints et l'organisation chrétienne primitive dans l'armorique bretonne* (Rennes, 1925). Important local topographical study.

566. Jacques Soyer, 'Etude sur l'origine des toponymes "Martroi" et "Martres"', *Revue des Etudes Anciennes*, XXVII (1925), pp. 213–27. On place-names supposedly relating to martyrdom.

567. Clovis Brunel, 'Saint-Chély, Etude de toponymie', *Mélanges d'histoire du Moyen Age offerts à M. Ferdinand Lot par ses amis et ses élèves* (Paris, 1925), pp. 83–101. An exemplary critical study in a now unfashionable field.

568. William J. Watson, *The History of the Celtic Place-Names of Scotland* (Edinburgh and London, 1926). Ch. X discusses saints' names.

569. Albert Dauzat, *Les Noms de lieux, Origine et évolution* (Paris, 1926), pp. 150–1 and 160–5, with 2 maps. Good short section for medieval France.

570. Paul Aebischer, 'Sur les martyria et les martyreta en général et les "martereys" fribourgeoises en particulier, Contribution à l'étude de la christianisation de la Suisse romande', *Zeitschrift für Schweizerische Geschichte*, 8 (1928), pp. 149–224. Relating names associated with martyrs to patterns of settlement and christianization.

571. Gérard Lavergne, 'Les Noms de lieux d'origine ecclésiastique', *RHEF*, 15 (1929), pp. 31–49, 177–202 and 319–32. 2nd part deals specifically with 'le souvenir des saints', in French context only.

572. E. G. Bowen, *The Settlements of the Celtic Saints in Wales* (Cardiff, 1954 and 1977). Short study of the siting of Celtic churches and of the cults associated with them; points out that Celtic dedications related to founders and secular patrons, and notes the reflection of Norman penetration in Wales in dedications to non-Celtic saints.

(C) CHRISTIAN NAMES

573. H. Duffaut, 'Recherches historiques sur les prénoms en Languedoc', *AM*, XII (1900), pp. 180–93 and 329–54. With lists; an important study.

574. Karl Michaëlsson, *Etudes sur les noms de personne français d'après les rôles de taille parisiens (Rôles de 1292, 1296–1300, 1313)*, Uppsala Universitets Årsckrift (1927). Provides lists of most used baptismal names; all but one are saints' names.

575. Harry Jacobsson, *Etudes d'anthroponymie Lorraine, Les bans de tréfonds de Metz (1267–98)* (Göteborg, 1955). Short section, pp. 21–4 on the influence of the cult of saints on naming.

576. O. Leys, 'La Substitution de noms chrétiens aux noms préchrétiens en Flandre occidentale avant 1225', *Fifth International Congress of Toponymy*

and Anthroponymy, Salamanca, April, 1955, Proceedings and Transactions, Acta Salmanticensia, Filosofiá y Letras, XI, 1 (1958). Valuable study, suggesting that the change occurred around 1200 and was a cultural rather than a religious phenomenon.

577. Benjamin Z. Kedar, 'Noms de saints et mentalité populaire à Gênes au XIVe siècle', *MA*, 73 (1967), pp. 431–46. The switch to saints' names as given names among Genoese citizens between the twelfth and the fourteenth centuries is related to the advent of the *popolo* to citizenship and to the effects of the Black Death in stimulating a need for religious protection.

(D) SHIPS' NAMES

578. Geneviève and Henri Bresc, 'Les Saints protecteurs de bateaux 1200–1460', *EF*, IX (1979), pp. 161–77. Quantitative survey for western Europe, with maps.

579. Jean Lepage, 'Les Saints protectures de navires dans la Normandie des XVIIIe et XIXe siècles', *AN*, 30 (1980), pp. 35–53. Socio-historical study of ships' names.

VIII PILGRIMAGE

(A) GENERAL AND NON-CHRISTIAN

580. Pierre Deffontaines, *Géographie et Religions* (Paris, 1948), Collection, Géographie humaine, 21. Pt IV, Ch. III, a long chapter on the geography of pilgrimages; Ch. IV on religious festivals and fairs; a pioneering work of synthesis, interdisciplinary and cross-cultural.

581. *Les Pèlerinages, Egypte ancienne – Israel – Islam – Perse – Inde – Tibet – Indonésie – Madagascar – Chine – Japon* (Paris, 1960). Valuable collection of essays by various hands.

582. Rudolf Kriss and Hubert Kriss-Heinrich, *Volksglaube im Bereich des Islam, I, Wallfahrtswesens und Heiligenverehrung* (Wiesbaden, 1960). Important study of Egypt; Jordan, Syria and the Lebanon; and Turkey and Yugoslavia.

583. Agehananda Bharati, 'Pilgrimage in the Indian Tradition', *HR*, III (1964), pp. 135–67. Important.

584. Surinder Mohan Bhardwaj, *Hindu Places of Pilgrimage in India (A Study in Cultural Geography)* (Berkeley, Los Angeles and London, 1973). Good historical and contemporary study, with maps, photographs and tables.

585. Victor Turner, 'The Centre Out There: Pilgrim's Goal', *HR*, XII (1973), pp. 191–230. General discussion by social anthropologist.

586. Charles F. Keyes, 'Buddhist Pilgrimage Centers and the Twelve-Year Cycle: Northern Thai Moral Orders in Space and Time', *HR*, XV (1975), pp. 71–89. Study by social anthropologist.

See also **1265, 1273, 1287, 1290.**

(B) CHRISTIAN, GENERAL

587. J. Charles Wall, *Pilgrimage* (London, 1926). Anecdotal, but contains interesting information; illustrated.

588. Georg Schreiber (ed.), *Wallfahrt und Volkstum im Geschichte und Leben* (Düsseldorf, 1934), Forschungen zur Volkskunde, 16–17. Interesting collection of studies; long essay by Schreiber.

589. Rudolf Kriss and Lenz Rettenbeck, *Wallfahrtsorte Europas* (Munich, 1950). An encyclopaedic survey of Europe's main pilgrimages, with brief accounts of each and excellent photographs of shrines, statues and ex-votos.

590. Hans Dünninger, 'Was ist Wallfahrt?', *ZV*, 58 (1962), pp. 221–32. General discussion.

591. Rudolf Kriss, 'Zur Begriffsbestimmung des Ausdruckes "Wallfahrt"', *OZV*, NS, XVII, 66 (1963), pp. 101–7. Discussion of terminology.

592. Alphonse Dupront, 'Pèlerinage et lieux sacrés', in *Mélanges en l'honneur de Fernand Braudel, Méthodologie de l'histoire et des sciences humaines*, II (Toulouse, 1973), pp. 189–206. Stimulating general discussion by director of a long-term research project on pilgrimages being conducted by the VI\u1d49 section of the Ecole des Hautes Etudes.

593. A Dupront, 'Anthropologie du sacré et cultes populaires, Histoire et vie du pèlerinage en Europe occidentale', *Miscellanea Historiae Ecclesiasticae*, V (Louvain, 1974), Colloque de Varsovie, Octobre 1971, sur la cartographie et l'histoire socio-religieuse de l'Europe jusqu'à la fin du XVII\u1d49 siècle, pp. 235–58. A most suggestive and wide-ranging essay, mainly on France.

594. Victor and Edith Turner, *Image and Pilgrimage in Christian Culture, Anthropological Perspectives* (Oxford, 1978). Discusses medieval and modern European as well as Mexican examples, stressing the element of 'liminality'.

595. L. S. B. Mac Coull, 'Child Donations and Child Saints in Coptic Egypt', *East European Quarterly*, XIII (1979), pp. 409–15. Discussion of eighth- and ninth-century practice of giving children to monasteries at whose shrines they had been cured.

(C) CHRISTIAN, LATE ANTIQUITY

596. Bernhard Kötting, *Peregrinatio Religiosa, Wallfahrten in der Antike und das Pilgerwesen in der alten Kirche* (Regensburg and Münster, Westphalia, 1950), Forschung zur Volkskunde, 33–5. Standard work on all aspects of pilgrimage in Antiquity and the Early Church to the fifth century.

597. Marcel Simon, 'Les Pèlerinages dans l'antiquité chrétienne', in *Pèlerinages, Etudes d'histoire des religions*, I (Paris, 1974), pp. 95–115; and in Simon, *Le Christianisme antique* (**156**), II, pp. 562–80.

See also **740** and **1017**.

(D) CHRISTIAN, MEDIEVAL

(i) General

598. Edmond-René Labande, 'Recherches sur les pèlerins dans l'Europe des XIe et XIIe siècles', *CCM*, I (1958), pp. 159–69 and 339–47; and in E.-R. Labande, *Sprirualité et vie littéraire de l'Occident, X^e–XIVe s.* (VR, London, 1974), Ch. XII. Socio-historical study of material aspects of pilgrimage in particular.

599. Raymond Oursel, *Les Pèlerins du Moyen Age, Les hommes, les chemins, les sanctuaires* (Paris, 1963). General historical account, with illustrations.

600. *Pellegrinaggi e culto dei santi in Europa fina alla Prima Crociata, Convegni CSSM*, 4 (1963). Important studies by Baudouin de Gaiffier, E. Delaruelle, A. Dupront, E.-R. Labande and others, including: Cyrille Vogel, 'Le pèlerinage pénitentiel', pp. 37–94; Armando Petrucci, 'Aspetti del culto e del pellegrinaggio di S. Michele Arcangelo sul monte Gargano', pp. 145–80; Adriano Prandi, 'La Tomba di S. Pietro nei pellegrinaggi dell'età medievale', pp. 283–448, with illustrations; and Antonio Gambacorta, 'Culto e pellegrinaggi a San Nicolo di Bari fino alla prima Crociata', pp. 485–523.

601. F. Garrisson, 'A propos des pèlerins et de leur condition juridique', in *Etudes d'histoire du droit canonique dédiées à Gabriel Le Bras* (Paris, 1965), II, pp. 1165–89. Legal study.

602. E.-R. Labande, '"Ad limina": le pèlerin médiéval au terme de sa démarche', in Pierre Gallais and Yves-Jean Riou (eds.), *Mélanges offerts à René Crozet... à l'occasion de son soixante-dixième anniversaire* (Poitiers, 1966), pp. 283–91; and in Labande, *Spiritualité et vie littéraire* (**598**), Ch. XIV. Brief but illuminating study of the final stage of medieval pilgrimages.

603. Arnold Angenendt. *Monachi peregrini, Studien zu Pirmin und den monastischen Vorstellungen des frühen Mittelalters* (Munich, 1972), Münsterische Mittelalter-Schriften, 6. Solid study.

604. Pierre-André Sigal, *Les Marcheurs de Dieu, Pèlerinages et pèlerins au Moyen Age* (Paris, 1974). Good short account based on recent research.

605. Jonathan Sumption, *Pilgrimage, An Image of Mediaeval Religion* (London, 1975). General account of saints' cults as well as of pilgrimage proper.

(ii) The major international pilgrimages

(a) JERUSALEM AND THE HOLY LAND

Primary sources

606. B. de Khitrow (ed.), *Itinéraires Russes en Orient* (Geneva, 1889). French translations of Russian and other accounts of pilgrimages to the Holy Land and elsewhere, including that of Daniel the Higumene from the twelfth century.

607. Stephen Graham, *With the Russian Pilgrims to Jerusalem* (London, 1913). A fascinating modern account, with photographs.

608. Malcolm Letts (ed.), *The Pilgrimage of Arnold Von Harff, Knight* (London, 1946), Hakluyt Society 2nd Series, XCIV. Interesting late-fifteenth-century account of pilgrimage to Rome, Alexandria, Sinai and the Holy Land.

609. Hélène Pétré (ed.), *Ethérie, Journal de voyage* (Paris, 1948), SCh., 21. Now classic fourth-century account of pilgrimage to the Holy Land; Latin text, French translation and Introduction.

610. George E. Gingros (ed.), *Egeria: Diary of a Pilgrimage* (New York and Paramus, 1970). Ancient Christian Writers Series, 38. Another good edition of the same text in English translation.

611. John Wilkinson, *Egeria's Travels* (London, 1971). Another good edition, in English.

612. John Wilkinson, *Jerusalem Pilgrims before the Crusades* (Warminster, 1977). English translation of texts, with good maps and plans.

Secondary sources

613. Ludovic Lalanne, 'Des Pèlerinages en Terre Sainte avant les Croisades', *BEC*, 2nd series, II (or VII), 1845–6, pp. 1–31. Good general study, with list of individual pilgrimages and of sources.

614. Paul Riant, *Expéditions et pèlerinages des Scandinaves en Terre Sainte au temps des croisades* (Paris, 1865), 2 vols. Important work.

615. Einar Joranson 'The Great German Pilgrimage of 1064–5', in Louis J. Paetow, *The Crusades and Other Historical Essays presented to Dana C. Munro by his former students* (New York, 1928), pp. 3–43. On collective pilgrimage to Jerusalem; important for process of pilgrimage becoming crusade.

616. Maurice Halbwachs, *La Topographie légendaire des évangiles en Terre Sainte, Etude de mémoire collective* (Paris, 1941). Historical study of the elaboration of the complex system of Christian holy sites in Jerusalem and elsewhere by one of Durkheim's most distinguished pupils.

617. Paul Alphandéry, *La Chrétienté et l'idée de croisade* (Paris, 1954–9), 2 vols. Edited by Alphonse Dupront from lectures; vol. I, Pt I, Ch. I, pp. 9–42 on 'Pèlerinages et croisades'; important study, with bibliography.

618. H. F. M. Prescott, *Jerusalem Journey, Pilgrimage to the Holy Land in the Fifteenth Century* (London, 1954). Attractive and straightforward account based closely on contemporary memoirs and descriptions.

619. H. F. M. Prescott, *Once to Sinai, The Further Pilgrimage of Friar Felix Fabri* (London, 1957). Sequel to above; late-fifteenth-century pilgrimage to Sinai, based closely on first-hand account.

620. E. Delaruelle, 'Deux guides de Terre Sainte aux XIVᵉ et XVᵉ siècles', *Eleona* (Toulouse), XI (April 1960), pp. 7–13; and in Delaruelle, *La Piété populaire* (**249**), pp. 547–53. Guides to pilgrimage which still retained its appeal in the Later Middle Ages.

621. Georg Schnath, 'Drei niedersächsische Sinaipilger im 1330...', in *Festschrift P. E. Schramm* (**261**), I, pp. 461–78.

622. J. M. Fiey, 'Le Pèlerinage des Nestoriens et jacobites à Jérusalem', *CCM*, 12 (1969), pp. 113–26. Early medieval pilgrimage to Jerusalem of Christians from what is now Iraq.

623. Giovanni Miccoli, 'Dal Pellegrinaggio alla Conquista: Povertà a ricchezza nelle prima crociata', *Convegni CSSM*, VIII (1969), *Povertà e Richezza nella spiritualità dei secoli XI e XII*, pp. 43–80. On relationship between pilgrimage and crusade.

624. Kurt Weitzmann, '*Loca Sancta* and the Representational Arts of Palestine', *DOP*, 28 (1974), pp. 31–55. On the iconography of holy places.

See also **674, 1292**.

(b) ROME

625. C. A. Mills (ed.), John Capgrave, *Ye Solace of Pilgrimes, A Description of Rome circa AD 1450* (Oxford, 1911). Late medieval description of pilgrimage sites.

626. L. Gougaud, 'Sur les routes de Rome et sur le Rhin avec les "Peregrini" insulaires', *RHE*, XXIX (1933), pp. 253–71.

627. Mario Romani, *Pellegrini e viaggiatori nell' economia di Roma del XIV al XVII secolo* (Milan, 1948). Comprehensive study of economy of the Rome pilgrimage for the city.

628. Gustave Bardy, 'Pèlerinages à Rome vers la fin du IVᵉ siècle', *AB*, 67 (1949), pp. 224–35. Competent study.

See also **187, 208, 211, 218, 600**.

(c) SANTIAGO DE COMPOSTELA

629. Eugenio López-Aydillo, *Os Miragros de Santiago* (no place, 1918). Gallegan version of twelfth-century codex attributed to Pope Callixtus II; text and careful study.

630. Jeanne Vieillard (ed.), *Le Guide du pèlerin de Saint-Jacques de Compostelle* (Mâcon, Bordeaux and Paris, 1938), Bibliothèque de l'Ecole des Hautes Etudes Hispaniques, XXIV. Latin text, with French translation, of twelfth-century guide, probably by Aimery Picard.

631. Luis Vázquez de Parga *et al.*, *Las Peregrinaciones a Santiago de Compostela* (Madrid, 1948–49), 3 vols. Large-scale study of major pilgrimage; vol. III comprises documents, bibliography and 148 plates.

632. Y. Renouard, 'Le Pèlerinage à Saint-Jacques-de-Compostelle et son importance dans le monde médiéval (d'après quelques ouvrages récents)', *Revue Historique* 206 (1951), pp. 254–61. Useful introduction.

633. Elie Lambert, *Le Pèlerinage de Compostelle, Etudes d'histoire médiévale* (Toulouse and Paris, 1959). Extracts from *Etudes Médiévales* (1957–8); valuable studies on many aspects of the pilgrimage: history, orders and confraternities, routes, architecture of pilgrimage routes, etc., with maps and plates.

634. T. D. Kendrick, *St James in Spain* (London, 1960). Historical study of the legend of Santiago, and of objections raised to it and claims rested upon it – down to modern times.

635. Vera and Hellmut Hell, *The Great Pilgrimage of the Middle Ages, The Road of St James of Compostela* (London, 1966). Translated from German edition of 1964, with historical introduction by Kendrick; most of book is made up of beautiful photographs of places, buildings and sculpture along the pilgrimage route.

636. M. L. Fracard, 'Gîtes d'étapes pour pèlerins sur quelques chemins du Poitou central (Deux-Sèvres) en direction de Compostelle vers la fin du XIVe siècle', *BSAO*, 4th series, VIII (1965), pp. 45–60. With map.

637. René de La Coste-Messelière and Jeannine Warcullier, 'Hôpitaux à l'usage des pèlerins, Chapelles et confréries de Saint Jacques', *ACNSS*, 94 (1969), Section d'Archéologie et d'Histoire d'Art, pp. 351–65. Good local study.

638. Osmin Ricau, 'Pour débrousailler les chemins de Saint-Jacques', *ibid*, pp. 367–74. On pilgrimage routes.

639. Jole Scudieri Ruggieri, 'Il Pellegrinaggio compostellano e l'Italia, *Cultura Neolatina*, XXX (1970), pp. 185–98. On importance of pilgrimage in Italy.

640. André Georges, *Le Pèlerinage à Compostelle en Belgique et dans le nord de la France, suivi d'une étude sur l'iconographie de saint Jacques en Belgique* (Brussels, 1971), Mémoires de l'Académie Royale de Belgique, Classe des Beaux Arts, XIII. Comprehensive study of pilgrims, shrines and confraternities with map; iconographical part has 214 photographic plates; an important work.

641. Elias Valiña Sampedru, *El Camino de Santiago, Estudio histórico-jurídico* (Madrid, 1971). Chapters on the juridical status of pilgrims, expiatory pilgrimage and pilgrimage routes in Spain; important.

642. Baudouin de Gaiffier, 'Notes sur quelques documents relatifs à la translation de Saint Jacques en Espagne', *AB*, 89 (1971), pp. 47–66. Detailed.

643. Mario Damonte, 'Da Firenze a Santiago di Compostella: Itinerario di un anonimo pellegrino nell' anno 1477', *Studi Medievali*, 3rd series, XIII,2 (1972), pp. 1043–71. Short Italian text with introduction; interesting primary source.

644. Edwin Mullins, *The Pilgrimage to Santiago* (London, 1974). A general historical account and modern travelogue, not too happily combined, but makes an agreeable introduction.

See also **214, 657, 705, 950, 1153**.

(iii) England

645. Richard Hart, 'The Shrines and Pilgrimages of the County of Norfolk', *NA*, VI (1864), pp. 277–94. Interesting local study.

646. W. Sparrow Simpson, 'On the Pilgrimage to Bromholm in Norfolk', *Journal of the British Archaeological Association*, 30 (1874), pp. 52–9. Pilgrimage to cross allegedly made of the True Cross.

647. J. G. Nichols (ed.), *Desiderius Erasmus, Pilgrimages to Saint Mary of*

Walsingham and Saint Thomas of Canterbury (London, 1875). Primary source; contemporary sceptical account by the great humanist.

648. J. Charles Wall, *Shrines of British Saints* (London, 1905). Comprehensive and well illustrated.

649. H. M. Gillett, *Walsingham, The History of a Famous Shrine* (London, 1946). Brief historical account, with bibliography, of important Marian shrine.

650. Christina Hole, *English Shrines and Sanctuaries* (London, 1954). A popular account by erudite folklorist.

651. J. C. Dickinson, *The Shrine of Our Lady of Walsingham* (Cambridge, 1956). Historical and archaeological account of shrine and pilgrimage; the best book on Walsingham.

652. D. J. Hall, *English Mediaeval Pilgrimage* (London, 1966). General account of eight shrines and their history: little about pilgrimage as such.

653. Colin Stephenson, *Walsingham Way* (London, 1970). General account of the medieval and the modern cult.

See also items on St Thomas of Canterbury **268–276**.

(iv) France

654. Dom Henri Leclercq, *Saint-Benoît-sur-Loire, Les reliques, le monastère, l'église* (Paris, 1925). Collection Les Grands Pèlerinages de France. Short historical account.

655. Lucien Musset, 'Recherches sur les pèlerins et les pèlerinages en Normandie jusqu'à la Première Croisade', *AN*, 12 (1962), pp. 127–50. Thorough study both of local pilgrimage centres and of centres elsewhere frequented by Normans; notes the interesting phenomenon of the local reproduction of foreign shrines.

656. E. Delaruelle, 'La Spiritualité des pèlerinages à Saint-Martin de Tours du Ve au Xe siècle', in *Pellegrinaggi e culto dei santi* (**600**), pp. 201–43; and in Delaruelle, *La Pieté populaire* (**249**), pp. 477–519. Socio-historical study of one of the most important pilgrimage centres of the period.

657. Georges Gaillard, 'Une Abbaye de pèlerinage: Sainte-Foy de Conques et ses rapports avec Saint-Jacques', *Compostellanum, Revista Trimestriel de la Archidiocesis de Santiago de Compostela*, Sección de Estudios Jacobeos, Número extraordinario, X (1965), pp. 335–55, with 9 plates. Useful. See also **279**.

658. E. Delaruelle, 'La Spiritualité du Pèlerinage de Rocamadour au Moyen Age', *Bulletin de la Société des Etudes Littéraires, Scientifiques et Artistiques du Lot*, 87 (1966), pp. 68–85; and in Delaruelle, *La Pieté populaire* (**249**), pp. 529–45. Study of important international shrine associated particularly with expiation.

659. E.-R. Labande, 'Les Pèlerinages au Mont-Saint-Michel pendant le Moyen Age', in *Millénaire monastique du Mont-Saint-Michel* (Paris, 1971), II, pp. 237–50; and in Labande, *Spiritualité et vie littéraire* (**598**), Ch. XV. Important.

660. E. -R. Labande, 'Saint Louis pèlerin', *RHEF*, LVII (1971), pp. 5–18; and in Labande, *Spiritualité et vie littéraire* (**598**), Ch. XVI.

(v) Ireland

661. H. Delehaye, 'Le Pèlerinage de Laurent de Pászthó au purgatoire de S. Patrice', *AB*, 27 (1908), pp. 35–60. Early-fourteenth-century text on penitential pilgrimage of Lough Dergh.
662. Kathleen Hughes, 'The Changing Theory and Practice of Irish Pilgrimage', *JEH*, 11 (1960), pp. 143–51. On pilgrimages of exile, penance and wandering in the Early Middle Ages.
663. Robert Easting, 'Peter of Cornwall's Account of St Patrick's Purgatory', *AB*, 97 (1979), pp. 397–416. Early-thirteenth-century text with commentary.

(vi) Penal and expiatory pilgrimage

664. D. U. B.(erlière), 'Les Pèlerinages judiciaires au Moyen Age', *RB*, 7 (1890), pp. 520–6. Still useful.
665. Etienne Van Cauwenbergh, *Les Pèlerinages expiatoires et judiciaires dans le droit communal de Belgique au moyen âge* (Louvain, 1922), *Recueil de Travaux*, Université de Louvain, 48. Important work.
666. L. de Valon, 'Les Pèlerinages expiatoires et judiciaires de la Belgique au sanctuaires de la Provence au Moyen-Age', *Provincia, Revue Trimestrielle d'Histoire et d'Archéologie Provençales*, XV (1935), pp. 30–53; and *Bulletin Trimestriel de la Société des Etudes Littéraires, Scientifiques et Artistiques du Lot*, 58 (1937), pp. 6–37. Good study.
667. F. L. Ganshof, 'Pèlerinages expiatoires flamands à Saint-Gilles pendant le XIVᵉ siècle', *AM*, 78 (1966), pp. 391–407. Another important study of the use of pilgrimage as a sanction.

See also **594, 600, 641, 658, 661–3, 960**.

(vii) Pilgrims' badges, medals, etc.

668. Etienne Michon, 'La Collection d'ampoules à eulogies du Musée du Louvre', *Mélanges G. B. de Rossi* (**213**), pp. 183–200. On ampullae used to keep oil from shrines.
669. André Grabar, *Ampoules de Terre Sainte (Monza-Bobbio)* (Paris, 1958). Detailed study of early pilgrims' souvenirs.
670. Kurt Köster, 'Religiöse Medaillon- und Wallfahrtsdevotionalien in der flämischen Buchmalerei des 15. und frühen 16. Jahrhunderts', in *Buch und Welt, Festschrift für Gustav Hofmann zum 65. Geburtstag dargebracht* (Wiesbaden, 1965), pp. 459–504, with 12 plates. Study of pilgrims' badges as depicted in book illustrations.

671. Esther Cohen, '*In haec signa*: Pilgrim-badge trade in Southern France', *Journal of Medieval History*, 2 (1976), pp. 193–214. Study of an increasingly important commercial aspect of late medieval pilgrimages.

(viii) Notions of pilgrimage and pilgrimage as metaphor

672. Jean Leclercq, 'Mönchtum und Peregrinatio im Frühmittelalter', *RQ*, 55 (1960), pp. 212–25. On early wandering saints and monks and notion of pilgrimage.
673. Jean Leclercq, 'Monachisme et pérégrination du IXe au XIIe siècle', *Studia Monastica*, III (1961), pp. 33–52. Pilgrimage as form and metaphor of monastic life.
674. Adriaan H. Bredero, 'Jérusalem dans l'Occident médiéval', in *Mélanges...René Crozet* (**602**), pp. 259–71. Idea of Jerusalem in medieval literature.
675. A. Guillaumont, 'Le Dépaysement comme forme d'ascèse dans le monachisme ancien', *Annuaire de l'Ecole Pratique des Hautes-Etudes*, LXXVI (1968–9), pp. 29–58. Important.
676. F. C. Gardiner, *The Pilgrimage of Desire, A Study of Theme and Genre in Medieval Literature* (Leiden, 1971). Study of theme of life as a pilgrimage in medieval commentary on Scripture, letters and pilgrim plays.
677. Christian K. Zacher, *Curiosity and Pilgrimage, The Literature of Discovery in Fourteenth-century England* (Baltimore and London, 1976). On Chaucer and Mandeville; from theme of pilgrimage to that of travel and escape.

See also **241**, **603**, **662**.

(ix) Opposition and criticism

678. Léon-E. Halkin, 'Le Thème du pèlerinage dans les Colloques d'Erasme', *Actes du Congrès Erasme (Rotterdam, Octobre 1969)* (Amsterdam and London, 1971), pp. 88–98. Careful study with texts of Erasmus's critique of the cult of saints and pilgrimages, or certain aspects of and excesses associated with them. See also **647**.
679. Giles Constable, 'Opposition to Pilgrimage in the Middle Ages', *Studia Gratiana*, XIX (1976), pp. 123–46. Interesting study.

(E) CHRISTIAN, EARLY MODERN PERIOD

680. Abbé A. Sachet, *Le Pardon annuel de la Saint-Jean et de la Saint-Pierre à Saint-Jean de Lyon 1392–1790* (Lyon, 1914). Detailed local history; study of popular and clerical manifestations of pilgrimage.
681. Robert Sauzat, 'Pèlerinage panique et pèlerinage de dévotion: Notre-Dame de Rochefort au XVIIe siècle', *AM*, 77 (1965), pp. 375–97. Important study of regional pilgrimage centre in context of the Counter-Reformation.
682. Hervé Barbin and Jean-Pierre Duteil, 'Miracle et pèlerinage au XVIIe

siècle', *RHEF*, LXI (1975), pp. 246–56. Good discussion of three French shrines, their functions and clientèle.

(F) CHRISTIAN, MODERN: LOCAL

(See also XVI (A) (*v*).)

683. Denys Shyne Lawlor, *Pilgrimages in the Pyrenees and Landes* (London, 1870). Mainly on Marian shrines; of special interest for early history of the Lourdes pilgrimage.

684. Anatole Le Braz, *Au pays des pardons* (Paris, 1900). English translation as *The Land of Pardons* (London, 1906) – with very interesting photographs. Study of five Breton pilgrimages, known locally as 'pardons', by local amateur folklorist. See also **1217**.

685. Léon Coutil, 'La Chapelle Saint-Eloi de Nassandres, Etude sur le culte des pierres, des sources et des arbres dans les départements de l'Eure, la Seine-Inférieure et la Normandie', *Recueil des Travaux de la Société Libre d'Agriculture, Sciences, Arts et Belles-Lettres de l'Eure*, 7th series, V (1917), pp. 159–276. Comprehensive survey of local shrines and pilgrimages, most of which are associated with a 'curing' saint; some interesting photographs of ex-votos.

686. Abbé J. Raison-du-Cleuziou, 'Contribution à l'histoire du pardon de Saint-Servais', *ACNSS*, 77 (1952), pp. 287–95. Valuable description of important local Breton pilgrimage, characterized by inter-village conflict.

687. Francis Beauchesne Thornton, *Catholic Shrines in the United States and Canada* (New York, 1954). Encyclopaedia of shrines to saints and the Virgin Mary; illustrated.

688. Daphne D. C. Pochin Mould, *Irish Pilgrimage* (Dublin, 1955). Good folkloric study, approved by the Catholic hierarchy.

689. W. Bruckner, 'Wallfahrtsforschung im deutschen Sprachgebiet seit 1945', *ZV*, 54 (1958), pp. 115–29. Bibliographical survey of work on pilgrimages in German-speaking lands.

690. Georg R. Schroubek, *Wallfahrt und Heimatsverlust, Ein Beitrag zur religiösen Volkskunde der Gegenwart* (Marburg, 1968). Comprehensive contemporary study.

691. Daniel R. Gross, 'Ritual and Conformity: A Religious Pilgrimage to North-eastern Brazil', *Ethnology*, 10 (1971), pp. 129–48. Good specific study of general interest, particularly for its suggestion of a connection between the vow and debt relations in the social milieu of pilgrims.

692. Régis Bertrand, 'Un Sanctuaire de la fécondité en Haute-Provence: Notre-Dame des Oeufs', *MAR*, 1977, pp. 173–81. Historical and contemporary study.

693. Yves-Marie Hilaire, *Une Chrétienté au XIXe siècle? La vie religieuse des populations du diocèse d'Arras (1840–1914)* (Villeneuve-d'Ascq, 1977?), 2 vols. A thesis completed in 1976; vol. I has short section on pilgrimages, old and new, pp. 392–416.

See also **303–4, 1220, 1228, 1232, 1234, 1242**.

IX CONFRATERNITIES

(A) GENERAL

694. Joseph Duhr, 'La Confrérie dans la vie de l'Eglise', *RHE*, 35/I (1939), pp. 437–78. General historical account of an institution frequently associated with the cult of saints.

695. G. Meersseman, 'Etude sur les anciennes confréries dominicaines', *Archivum Fratrum Praedicatorum*, XX (1950), pp. 5–113; and XXI (1951), pp. 51–96. Detailed studies of confraternities of St Dominic and St Peter Martyr, with documents; thirteenth–seventeenth centuries.

696. Gabriel Le Bras, *Etudes de sociologie religieuse*, II (Paris, 1955), pp. 418–62. Two studies: 'Esquisse d'une histoire des confréries (1941)', and 'Les Confréries chrétiennes', by one of France's leading ecclesiastical historians.

697. G. G. Meersseman, 'Per la storiografia delle confraternite laicali nell' alto medio evo', in *Storiografia e Storia, Studi in onore di Eugenio Duprè Theseider* (**362**), I, pp. 39–62. Useful for literature on very early confraternities.

See also **637, 640, 1242, 1247, 1249, 1267, 1285, 1286, 1288**.

(B) FRANCE

698. E. Levasseur, *Histoire des classes ouvrières et de l'industrie en France avant 1789* (1900–1), 2 vols., 2nd edition. See chapters on confraternities and 'corps de métiers'.

699. Eugène Martin, 'Essai sur les confréries de dévotion dans le diocèse de Toul', *Mémoires de l'Académie de Stanislas*, 6th series, X (1912–13), pp. 219–38. Study of religious as opposed to professional or sociable groups.

700. Jean Mellot, 'Les Confréries de métiers dans le département du Cher à l'époque contemporaine', *ATP*, III (1955), pp. 193–207. Contemporary local study.

701. Michel Veissière, 'La Confrérie de Saint-Fiacre à Provins, Notes sur la confrérie et sur la culture maraîchère ... (1784–1962)', *Bulletin de la Société d'Histoire et d'Archéologie de l'Arrondissement de Provins (Seine-et-Marne)*, 117 (1963), pp. 64–81. On a professional confraternity, which survived into the modern period.

702. Marguerite Corvaisier, 'Les Anciennes confréries de la paroisse Saint-Léonard-de-Fougères, *ACNSS*, 91 (1966), *Bulletin philologique et historique*, pp. 687–97. Good local study.

703. M. Veissière, 'Les Confréries à Provins au XVIIIe et XIXe siècles', *ACNSS*, 91 (1966), Section d'Histoire Moderne et Contemporaine, II, pp. 343–63. Thorough factual account.

704. Maurice Agulhon, *Pénitents et francs-maçons de l'ancienne Provence* (Paris, 1968). Now classic study of 'Southern sociability'; includes some account of confraternities of saints.

705. Marie-Louise Fracard, 'La Confrérie des pèlerins de Saint-Jacques à Niort et sa réorganisation au XVIIe siècle', *ACNSS*, 94 (1969), *Bulletin*

Philologique et Historique, pp. 471–83. Interesting study of confraternity, originally of pilgrims.

706. L. Stouff, 'Une Confrérie arlésienne de la première moitié du XVe siècle: La confrérie de Saint Pierre de Luxembourg', *PH*, XXIII (1973), pp. 339–60. Good local study.

707. André Dubuc, 'Les Charités du diocèse de Rouen au XVIIIe siècle', *ACNSS*, 99, I (1974), pp. 211–36. With maps and lists.

708. Michel Bée, 'La Piété des confréries de charité normandes, Solidarité de la prière et honneur de la célébration', *ibid.*, pp. 97–106. Seventeenth–twentieth centuries.

709. Marius Hudry, 'Les Confréries religieuses dans l'archidiocèse du Tarentaise aux XVIIe et XVIIIe siècles', *ACNSS*, 100 (1975), Section d'Histoire Moderne et Contemporaine, pp. 347–60. Factual account.

710. Martine Segalen, *Les Confréries dans la France contemporaine, Les charités* (Paris, 1975). A contemporary and historical study, mainly of confraternities in Normandy; emphasizes the importance of the patron saints of the confraternities; but is more concerned with their organization and secular functions.

711. Jacques Chiffoleau, 'Les Confréries, la mort et la religion en Comtat Venaissin à la fin du moyen âge', *MEFR*, 91 (1979), pp. 785–825. Good study.

(c) GREAT BRITAIN

712. Joshua Toulmin Smith, *English Gilds, The Original Ordinances of more than one hundred early English Gilds* (London, 1870), EETS, OS, 40. Preliminary essay by L. Brentano includes a section on religious guilds; primary and secondary source.

713. H. F. Westlake, *The Parish Gilds of Medieval England* (London, 1919). Short study, with list of guilds or confraternities and their patron saints; still useful.

(d) ITALY

713a. G. M. Monti, *Le Confraternité medievali dell' alta e media Italia* (Venice, 1927). Standard work.

714. Charles M. de La Roncière, 'La Place des confréries dans l'encadrement religieux du Contado Florentin: L'exemple de la Val d'Elsa', *MEFR*, 85 (1973), pp. 31–77 and 633–71. Good study.

X HAGIOGRAPHY: PRIMARY SOURCES

(With a few exceptions only editions providing translation into English or French have been included.)

(A) GENERAL

715. Joannes Bollandus *et al.*, *Acta Sanctorum*... (1643–   ). Three editions exist: the original begun in Antwerp in 1643 and continued in Brussels,

the latest being the *Propylaeum ad Acta Sanctorum Decembris* (1940); the Venice edition (1734–70), which is incomplete; and the Paris edition (1863–87), 64 vols., which includes a valuable index by L. M. Rigollet (1875). A vast collection of saints' Lives, critically edited, with commentary in Latin, and arranged by calendar; one of the greatest scholarly enterprises of all time; Lives in Greek, in Oriental and in European vernacular languages were introduced only in the later nineteenth century; for further bibliographical details, see Delehaye (**833**), pp. 246–57.

(B) DESERT FATHERS

716. W. K. Lowther Clarke, *The Lausiac History of Palladius* (SPCK, London, 1918). Introduction and English Translation.

717. E. A. W. Budge, *Stories of the Holy Fathers* (Oxford, 1934). English Translations of Syriac versions of Athanasius' Life of St Anthony, the Lausiac History of Palladius, the Rule of Pachomius and the History of the Monks by St Jerome.

718. E. A. W. Budge, *The Wit and Wisdom of the Christian Fathers of Egypt. The Syriac Version of the Apophthegmata Patrum by ʿAnān Ishōʿ of Bēth ʿAbhē* (Oxford, 1934). English translation.

719. Helen Waddell (ed.), *The Desert Fathers* (London, 1936). English translation of St Jerome's Life of St Paul the Hermit, the History of the Monks by Rufinus, *The Verba Seniorum*, The Life of St Pelagia the Harlot by James the Deacon, and the Life of St Mary the Harlot by St Ephraim of Edessa.

720. Robert T. Meyer (ed.), St Athanasius, *The Life of St Anthony* (Westminster, Maryland and London, 1950), Ancient Christian Writers Series, 10. English translation of early hagiographical classic.

721. H. Hoppenbrouwers, *La Plus Ancienne Version latine de la Vie de S. Antoine par S. Athanase, Etude de critique textuelle* (Nijmegen, 1960), Latinitas Christianiorum Primaeva, 14. Critical edition and study by Benedictine scholar.

722. A.-J. Festugière, *Les Moines d'Orient*, IV/1, *Enquête sur les moines d'Egypte (Historia Monachorum in Aegypto)* (Paris, 1964). French translation.

723. A.-J. Festugière, *Les Moines d'Orient*, IV/2, *La Première Vie grecque de S. Pachôme* (Paris, 1965). French translation, with very full introduction.

724. Birger A. Pearson (ed.), *The Life of Pachomius* (*Vita Prima Graeca*) (Missoula, Montana, 1975), Early Christian Literature Series 2, Texts and Translations 7. Greek text and English translation by Apostolos A. Athanassakis.

725. Benedicta Ward (ed.), *The Sayings of the Desert Fathers, The Alphabetical Collection* (London and Oxford, 1975). English translation of the *Apophthegmata Patrum*.

726. Norman Russell and Benedicta Ward (eds.), *The Lives of the Desert Fathers, The Historia Monachorum in Aegypto* (London, Oxford and Kalamazoo, Mich., 1981). Translation into English of classic fourth-century text, with approving introduction.

(C) BYZANTINE

727. W. K. Lowther Clarke (ed.), St Gregory of Nyssa, *The Life of St Macrina* (SPCK, London, 1916), Early Christian Classics. English translation of early Life of female saint; and see **737.**

728. Elisabeth Dawes and Norman H. Baynes (eds.), *Three Byzantine Saints, Contemporary Biographies translated from the Greek* (London, 1948). The Lives of St Daniel the Stylite, St Theodore of Sykeon and St John the Almsgiver, with introduction and notes.

729. Vitalien Laurent (ed.), *La Vie merveilleuse de Saint Pierre d' Atron* (Brussels, 1956), SH, 29. Critical edition of Greek text from ninth century with introduction and French translation.

730. A. -J. Festugière, *Les Moines d'Orient*, II, *Les Moines de la région de Constantinople* (Paris, 1961). French translations of Callinicus' Life of Hypatius and of anonymous Life of Daniel the Stylite.

731. D. Gorce (ed.), *Vie de Sainte Mélanie* (Paris, 1962), SCh., 90. Greek text of fifth century, with full introduction and French translation.

732. A. -J. Festugière, *Les Moines d'Orient*, III/1, *Les Moines de Palestine* (Paris, 1962). French translation of Cyril of Scythopolis' Life of St Euthymius.

733. A. -J. Festugière, *Les Moines d'Orient*, III/2, *Les Moines de Palestine* (Paris, 1962). French translation of Cyril of Scythopolis' Life of St Sabas.

734. Paul van den Ven, *La Vie ancienne de S. Syméon Stylite le Jeune (521–592)*. (Brussels, 1962–70), 2 vols., SH, 32. Greek text with full commentary and French translation; also includes Greek Life of St Martha, the Stylite's mother.

735. A. -J. Festugière, *Les Moines d'Orient*, III/3, *Les Moines de Palestine* (Paris, 1963). French translations of Cyril of Scythopolis' Lives of Sts John the Hesechyst, Kyriakus, Theodosius, Theognius and Abramius; and of Theodore of Petra's Life of St Theodosius.

736. A. -J. Festugière, *Vie de Théodore de Sykéon* (Brussels, 1970), 2 vols., SH, 48. Greek text with French translation and commentary.

737. Pierre Maraval (ed.), Grégoire de Nysse, *Vie de Sainte Macrine* (Paris, 1971), SCh., 178. Introduction, Greek text and French translation.

738. A. -J. Festugière and Lennart Rydén (eds.), Leontinus de Neapolis, *Vie de Syméon le Fou et Vie de Jean de Chypre* (Paris, 1974), Institut Français d'Archéologie de Beyrouth, Bibliothèque Archéologique et Historique, XCV. Greek texts with French translations and full critical apparatus.

(D) ORIENTAL

739. Agnes Smith Lewis, *Select Narratives of Holy Women from the Syro-Antiochene or Sinai Palimpsest* (London, 1900), Studia Sinaitica IX and X. Lives of eleven female saints, including Eugenia, Barbara and Sophia, dating from the seventh and eighth centuries; Syriac text and English translation.

740. E. A. W. Budge, *Texts Relating to Saint Mêna of Egypt and Canons of Nicaea in a Nubian Dialect* (London, 1909). Introduction, Ethiopian and Nubian texts. Important primary source for one of the most important cults of Late Antiquity in the Middle East. See also **1017** and **1024**.

741. A. J. Wensinck (ed.), *Legends of Eastern Saints Chiefly from Syriac Sources* (Leiden, 1911), 2 vols. Vol. I, 'The Story of Archelides'; vol. II, 'The Legend of Hilaria'; Arabic and Syriac texts with English translations.

742. Agnes Smith Lewis (ed.), *The Forty Martyrs of the Sinai Desert and the Story of Eulogios from a Palestinian Syriac and Arabic Palimpsest* (Cambridge, 1912), Horae Semiticae, IX. Early medieval texts with introduction and English translation.

743. Voyeslav Yanich and C. Patrick Hankey, *Lives of Serbian Saints* (SPCK, London, 1921). Translations of Christian Literature Series, VII. English translations of selected Lives from Serbian martyrologies.

744. E. W. Brooks (ed.), John of Ephesus, *Lives of the Eastern Saints* (Paris, 1923–6), Patrologia Orientalis, 17–19. Syriac text with English translation.

745. E. W. Brooks, *Acts of St George, Le Muséon* (1925?), pp. 67–115. Syriac text with English translation.

746. James Drescher, *Three Coptic Legends, Hilaria – Archellites – The Seven Sleepers* (Cairo, 1947), Annales du Service des Antiquités d'Egypte, Supplement, vol. 4. Greek and Coptic texts with introduction and English translations.

747. David Marshall Lang, *Lives and Legends of the Georgian Saints* (London, 1956). English translation of selected texts.

748. D. M. Lang, *The Balavariani (Barlaam and Josaphat), A Tale of the Christian East* (London, 1966). English translation of Old Georgian version, with introduction by Ilia V. Abuladze; an adaptation of the legendary biography of the Buddha, for long accepted by both Eastern and Western Churches as an authentic account of 'saints' Barlaam and Josaphat and their efforts to propagate Christianity in India.

See also **93, 717, 718**.

(E) MEDIEVAL LATIN

749. Bernard Ward (ed.), *St Edmund, Archbishop of Canterbury, His Life as told by Old English Writers* (London, 1903). Valuable compilation; Ch. VIII on miracles, translation and cult.

750. T. Okey *et al.* (ed.), *'The Little Flowers of St Francis' with the 'Mirror of Perfection'* (London, 1910). Everyman edition of Franciscan classics, with the Life by St Bonaventure, in English (from Latin and Italian). See also **755** and **770**.

751. M. R. James, 'Lives of St Walstan', *NA*, XIX (1917), pp. 238–67. Short Latin and English metrical Lives of 'an obscure Norfolk saint', with introduction; Lives refer to miracles and ex-votos.

752. Teodor de Wyzewa (ed.), Jacques de Voragine (Jacobus de Voragine), *La Légende dorée* (Paris, 1935); and another French edition edited by J. -B. M. Roze and Hervé Savon (Paris, 1967), 2 vols. Translations of most popular

collection of saints' Lives of the Later Middle Ages. See also **769, 802, 891–3, 914.**

753. Bertram Colgrave, *Two Lives of Saint Cuthbert* (Cambridge, 1940). Lives by Bede and by the Monk of Lindisfarne; Latin texts and translations.

754. Charles W. Jones, *Saints' Lives and Chronicles in Early England, Together with the first English translations of the Oldest Life of St Gregory the Great by a monk of Whitby and The Life of St Guthlac of Crowland by Felix* (Ithaca, N.Y., 1947). Literary study, valuable for its translated Lives.

755. Otto Karrer (ed.), *St Francis of Assisi, The Legends and Lauds* (London, 1947). Edited texts in English translation of the Legend of the Three Companions, the Writings of Brother Leo and his companions, the Lives by Thomas of Celano and Bonaventure, the *Fioretti*, and St Francis's own writings, with introduction and notes. See also **770.**

756. R. J. Deferrari *et al., Early Christian Biographies* (New York, 1952), Fathers of the Church Collection, 15. English translations of Pontius' Life of St Cyprian, Paulinus' Life of St Ambrose, Possidius' Life of St Augustine, St Athanasius' Life of St Anthony, St Jerome's Lives of St Paul the Hermit, St Hilarion and Malchus, Ennodius' Life of St Ephiphanius, and St Hilary's Sermon on the Life of St Honoratius; an important primary source.

757. F. H. Hoare (ed.), *The Western Fathers* (London and New York, 1954). English translations of Sulpicius Severus' Life of St Martin, together with the Letters and Dialogues, of Paulinus' Life of St Ambrose, Possidius' Life of St Augustine, St Hilary's Sermon on the Life of St Honoratius, and Constantius of Lyon's Life of St Germanus; a valuable collection, and an alternative to Deferrari.

758. C. H. Talbot (ed.), *The Anglo-Saxon Missionaries in Germany* (New York, 1954). English translations of the Lives of St Willibrord, St Boniface, St Sturm, St Leoba and St Lebuin, with other documents and introduction.

759. B. Colgrave (ed.), *Felix's Life of St Guthlac* (Cambridge, 1956). Historical and critical introduction; Latin text with English translation.

760. Dom Gerard Sitwell, *St Odo of Cluny, Being the Life of St Odo of Cluny by John of Salerno and the Life of St Gerald of Aurillac by St Odo* (London and New York, 1958). English translation of two tenth-century Lives, with introduction; the second has received some attention as a rare example of lay sanctity. For discussion, see **247.**

761. George Laws (ed.), Blessed Raymond of Capua, *The Life of St Catherine of Siena* (London, 1960). English translation of Life of important female saint.

762. Geoffrey Webb and Adrian Walker (eds.), *St Bernard, The Story of his Life as recorded in the Vita Prima Bernardi by certain of his contemporaries* (London, 1960). English translation.

763. Decima L. Douie and Dom Hugh Farmer, *The Life of St Hugh of Lincoln* (London, 1961–2), 2 vols., Nelson Medieval Texts. Latin text, introduction and English translation; Life of twelfth-century bishop, by Adam of Eynsham.

764. R. W. Southern (ed.), *The Life of St Anselm, Archbishop of Canterbury by*

Eadmer (London, 1962), Nelson Medieval Texts. Latin text with English translation and introduction; the Life is a mixture of model hagiography and biography; to it is appended an additional 'description of the miracles' of Anselm, which is of particular interest.

765. René Borius (ed.), Constance de Lyon (Constantius of Lyon), *Vie de Saint Germain d'Auxerre* (Paris, 1965), SCh., 112. Long introduction, text and French translation.

766. J. F. Webb (ed.), *Lives of the Saints* (Harmondsworth, 1965), Penguin Classics. English versions of The Voyage of St Brendan, Bede's Life of St Cuthbert, and Eddius Stephanus' Life of St Wilfrid.

767. Clinton Albertson, *Anglo-Saxon Saints and Heroes* (Fordham?, 1967). English translation of Lives of Sts Cuthbert, Wilfrid, Guthlac, Willibrord, Boniface etc.

768. Jacques Fontaine (ed.), Sulpice Sévère (Sulpicius Severus), *Vie de Saint Martin* (Paris, 1967), 2 vols., SCh., 133–5. Best modern critical edition, with lengthy and valuable introduction and French translation.

769. Granger Ryan and Helmut Ripperger (eds.), Jacobus de Voragine, *The Golden Legend* (New York, 1969), English translation. See also **752, 802, 891–3, 914.**

770. Marion A. Habig, *St Francis of Assisi, Writings and Early Biographies, English Omnibus of the Sources for the Life of St Francis* (Chicago, 1972), 3rd edition. Franciscan publication with introduction and bibliography; most complete source in English.

771. Michael Winterbottom (ed.), *Three Lives of English Saints* (Toronto, 1972), PIMS, Medieval Latin Texts Series. Critical editions of Aelfric's Life of St Ethelwold, Wulfstan's Life of St Ethelwold; and Abbo's Life of St Edmund; the last of interest for royal saints.

772. Edward Peters (ed.), *Monks, Bishops and Pagans, Christian Culture in Gaul and Italy 500–700* (Philadelphia, 1975), University of Pennsylvania Sources of Medieval History. English translations of various hagiographic sources, including Paul the Deacon's Poems in honour of St Benedict, extracts from Jonas's Life of St Colombanus, from the Life of St Gall, and from Gregory of Tours's Lives of the Fathers, and Gregory's version of 'The Seven Sleepers of Ephesus'.

773. Marie-Denise Valentin (ed.), Hilaire d'Arles (Hilary of Arles), *Vie de S. Honorat* (Paris, 1977), SCh., 235. Introduction, Latin text and French translation.

(F) MEDIEVAL CELTIC (MAINLY LATIN)

774. Alexander Penrose Forbes (ed.), *Lives of S. Ninian and S. Kentigern* (Edinburgh, 1874), The Historians of Scotland, V. Texts of twelfth-century Lives in Latin with introduction and English translation.

775. A. P. Forbes (ed.), *Life of Saint Columba* (Edinburgh, 1874), The Historians of Scotland, VI. Ninth-century Life by Adamnan; Latin text, introduction and English translation.

776. Robert Fawtier, *La Vie de Saint Samson, Essai de critique hagiographique* (Paris

1912), Bibliothèque de l'Ecole des Hautes Etudes, 1977. Critical edition of Latin text. See also **781, 930, 932, 942.**

777. H. J. Lawlor (ed.), St Bernard of Clairvaux, *Life of St Malachy of Armagh* (SPCK, London, 1920). Translations of Christian Literature. Introduction and English translation of Life and Sermons.

778. Charles Plummer, *Bethada Náem nErenn, Lives of Irish Saints* (Oxford, 1922), 2 vols. Vol. I, introduction and Irish texts; vol. II, English translations.

779. A. W. Wade-Evans, *Life of St David* (SPCK, London, 1923). Introduction and English translation of twelfth-century Latin text.

780. C. Plummer, *Miscellanea Hagiographica Hibernica* (Brussels, 1925 and 1964), SH, 15. Lives of Sts Mac Creiche, Naile and Cranat in Irish with English translations, together with a valuable 'tentative catalogue of Irish Hagiography'.

781. Thomas Taylor, *The Life of St Samson of Dol* (SPCK, London, 1925). Introduction and English translation of seventh-century Life. See also **776.**

782. A. W. Wade-Evans, 'Beuno Sant', *Archaeologia Cambrensis*, LXXXV (1930), pp. 315–41. English translation of medieval Life, with notes.

783. A. W. Wade-Evans, *Vitae Sanctorum Britanniae et Genealogiae* (Cardiff, 1944). Lives of Welsh saints; Latin texts and English translations.

784. Carl Selmer (ed.), *Sancti Brendani Abbatis from Early Latin Manuscripts* (Notre Dame, Ill., 1959), University of Notre Dame Publications in Mediaeval Studies, XVI. Full critical edition of Latin text. See also **766.**

785. W. W. Heist (ed.), *Vitae Sanctorum Hiberniae* (Brussels, 1965), SH, 28. Latin texts from the Codex Salmanticensis.

786. A. B. E. Hood (ed.), *St Patrick, His Writings and Muirchu's Life* (London and Chichester, 1978). Latin texts with English translations.

(G) MEDIEVAL VERNACULAR – FRENCH, PROVENÇAL AND CATALAN

787. A. T. Baker, 'An Anglo-French Life of St Osith', *Modern Language Review*, VI (1911), pp. 476–502. Text in verse with commentary.

788. Clovis Brunel (ed.), Bertran de Marseille, *La Vie de Sainte Enimie* (Paris, 1917), CFMA, 17. Critical edition of short thirteenth-century Provençal Life.

789. Raymond Thompson Hill, *Two Old French Poems on Saint Thibaut* (New Haven, 1936), Yale Romance Studies, XI.

790. Emmanuel Walberg (ed.), Guernes de Pont-Sainte-Maxence, *La Vie de Saint Thomas Becket* (Paris, 1936), CFMA, 77. Critical edition of oldest French Life of St Thomas.

791. Alexander Joseph Denomy, 'An Old French Life of Saint Barbara', *MS*, I (1939), pp. 148–80. Text with introduction.

792. A. T. Baker, 'Vie anglo-normande de Sainte-Foy par Simon de Walsingham', *Romania*, LXVI (1940–1). pp. 49–84. Text in verse with introduction.

793. Einar Ronsjö (ed.), *La Vie de Saint Nicolas par Wace* (Lund and Copenhagen, 1942), Etudes Romanes de Lund, V. Critical edition of twelfth-century verse Life.

794. Ingegärd Sume (ed.), *La Vida de Sant Honorat, Poème provençal de Raimond Feraud* (Uppsala, 1943). Critical edition.

795. A. J. Denomy, 'An Old French Version of the Julian Episode in the Life of St Basil', *MS*, 18 (1956), pp. 105–24.

796. Carl J. Odenkirchen, *The Life of St Alexius in the Old French Version of the Hildesheim Manuscript* (Brookline, Mass., and Leiden, 1978). Early twelfth-century text with English translation of one of most popular saints' Lives.

797. Charlotte S. Maneikis Kniazzeh and Edward J. Neugaard, *Vides de Sants Rosselloneses* (Barcelona, 1977), 3 vols. Critical edition of thirteenth-century Catalan Lives.

(H) MEDIEVAL VERNACULAR, ENGLISH

798. Walter W. Skeat (ed.), *Aelfric's Lives of Saints, being a Set of Sermons on Saints' Days formerly observed by the English Church* (Oxford, 1881–90 and 1966), 2 vols., EETS, OS, 76, 82, 94 and 114. Homilies on Lives of selected saints; Anglo-Saxon text with translation into modern English.

799. Eugen Einenkel (ed.), *The Life of Saint Katherine* (London, 1884), EETS, OS, 80. Latin and Old English texts relating to St Catherine of Alexandria.

800. Carl Horstmann (ed.), *The Early South-English Legendary or Lives of the Saints* (London, 1887), EETS, OS, 87. Golden Legend type compilation in verse.

801. C. Horstmann (ed.), John Capgrave, *The Life of St Katharine of Alexandria* (London, 1893), EETS, OS, 100. In verse.

802. F. S. Ellis (ed.), William Caxton, *The Golden Legend or Lives of the Saints* (London, 1900), 7 vols., Temple Classics. Classic translation of Voragine.

803. J. J. Munro (ed.), *John Capgrave's Lives of St Augustine and St Gilbert of Sempringham* (London, 1910), EETS, OS, 140. Early fifteenth-century text.

804. Henry L. Savage (ed.), *St Erkenwald, A Middle English Poem* (New Haven, 1926 and Hamden, Conn., 1972). Fourteenth-century text with introduction of puzzling story about discovery of intact corpse of pagan judge. A modern English translation exists: Brian Stone (ed.), *The Owl and the Nightingale: Cleanness: St Erkenwald* (Harmondsworth, 1971).

805. Roscoe E. Parker (ed.), *The Middle English Stanzaic Version of the Life of St Anne* (London, 1928), EETS, OS, 174. Important text.

806. Frances M. Mack (ed.), *Seinte Marherete the Meiden ant Martyr* (London, 1934), EETS, OS, 193. Early thirteenth-century text.

807. S. T. R. O. d'Ardenne, *An Edition of the Liflade ant te Passiun of Seinte Iuliene* (Paris and Liège, 1936, Bibliothèque de la Faculté de Philosophie et Lettres de l'Université de Liège, LXIV, and London, 1961, EETS, OS, 248). Full critical edition of two Middle English versions.

808. Mary S. Serjeantson (ed.), Osbern Bokenham, *Legendes of Hooly Wummen* (London, 1938), EETS, OS, 206. Early fifteenth-century compilation, including Lives of Sts Margaret, Anne, Faith, Catherine, Mary Magdalene, Lucy and Elizabeth.

809. William Nelson (ed.), *The Life of St George* (London, 1955), EETS, OS, 230. Early Tudor verse Life.

810. Charlotte d'Evelyn and Anna J. Mill, *The South English Legendary* (London, 1956–9), 3 vols., EETS, OS, 235–6 and 244. Two vols. of text and one of commentary.

811. Joyce Bazire (ed.), *The Metrical Life of St Robert of Knaresborough together with other Middle English Poems* (Oxford, 1958 and 1968), EETS, OS, 228. Very interesting text for the punishments administered by the saint and for his encounters with the devil.

812. J. E. Van der Westhuizen (ed.), John Lydgate, *The Life of Saint Alban and Saint Amphibal* (Leiden, 1974). Critical edition of late medieval Life.

813. Cyril Lawrence Smetana (ed.), *The Life of St Norbert by John Capgrave, OFAA (1393–1464)* (Toronto, 1977), PIMS. Interesting English vernacular Life, full of demonic manifestations.

(I) WESTERN, EARLY MODERN

814. *Eloge historique ou Vie abrégée de Sainte Frémont de Chantal, Fondatrice, et Première Supérieure de l'Ordre de la Visitation de Sainte Marie* (Paris, 1768). Life of St Jane Chantal, produced on occasion of her canonization, with Canonization Brief.

815. John Peter Giussano, *The Life of St Charles Borromeo, Cardinal Archbishop of Milan* (London and New York, 1884), 2 vols. English translation of important example of early-seventeenth-century hagiography.

816. P. Bouhours, *Vie de St Francois Xavier de la Compagnie de Jésus, Apôtre des Indes et du Japon* (Paris and Braine-le-Comte, 1872). Lengthy late-seventeenth-century Life by fellow-Jesuit.

817. C. Horstmann (ed.), *The Lives of Women Saints of our Contrie of England, also Some other Lives of Holie Women written by some of the Auncient Fathers* (London, 1886), EETS, OS, 86. Early-seventeenth-century prose Lives of female saints.

818. C. Horstmann (ed.), Henry Bradshaw, *The Life of Saint Werburghe of Chester* (London, 1887), EETS, OS, 88. Early-sixteenth-century Life.

819. Oskar Sommer (ed.), Thomas Robinson, *The Life and Death of Mary Magdalene* (London, 1899), EETS, Extra series, LXXVIII. Important early-seventeenth-century text.

820. Benedict Zimmermann (ed.), *The Life of St Teresa of Jesus of the Order of Our Lady of Carmel, written by Herself* (London, 1916). Sixteenth-century classic autobiography in English translation, together with *The Relations or Manifestations of Her Spiritual State*.

821. Elsie Vaughan Hitchcock (ed.), William Roper, *The Lyfe of Sr Thomas Moore, Knight* (London, 1935), EETS, OS, 197. Critical edition of classic Life.

822. Leonard Perotti (ed.), St Charles of Sezze, *Autobiography* (London, 1963). Edited version in English of Life of seventeenth-century south Italian

Franciscan mystic, canonized in 1959; a historical and religious document of the first importance.

823. John Wilson, *The English Martyrologe*... (London, 1975), English Recusant Literature 1558–1640, 232. Compendium of saints' Lives arranged by calendar, first published in 1608.

(J) MODERN

824. Dom Prosper Guéranger, *Life of Saint Cecilia, Martyr* (Philadelphia, 1866). Translated from the French; good example of mid-nineteenth-century hagiography by liturgical scholar.

825. F. Trochu, *La 'petite Sainte' du Curé d'Ars, Sainte Philomène, Vierge et Martyre* (Lyon and Paris, 1929). Modern hagiographical work; primary source on cult of early martyr 'invented' in nineteenth century.

826. Father Amadeo, *Blessed Gemma Galgani (1878–1903)* (London, 1935). Translated from the Italian; Life of modern visionary.

827. Thomas N. Taylor (ed.), *Saint Thérèse of Lisieux, The Little Flower of Jesus, A Revised Translation of the Definitive Edition of Her Autobiography and Letters* (London, 1944). No longer 'definitive'; see **829**.

828. Abbé Combes (ed.), *Collected Letters of Saint Thérèse of Lisieux* (New York, 1949). Further writings by one of the most popular modern saints.

829. Sainte Thérèse de l'Enfant Jésus, *Manuscrits autobiographiques* (Lisieux, 1957). The definitive text of a religious and psychological classic. For discussion, see **301, 302,** and **969**.

XI HAGIOGRAPHY: SECONDARY WORKS

(See also II (G) (iii).)

(A) GENERAL

830. Hugues Vaganay, 'Essai de bibliographie des Sonnets relatifs aux saints', *AB*, 19 (1900), pp. 377–438. Valuable catalogue of a neglected type of hagiographical literature; down to the nineteenth century.

831. H. Delehaye, *Les Légendes hagiographiques* (Brussels, 1905, 1955 and 1973), SH, 18A. English translation by V. M. Crawford under title: *The Legends of the Saints, An Introduction to Hagiography* (London, 1907). Still valuable discussion of types, functions, modes of analysis, etc., though some of the book's concerns have dated; read in conjunction with Aigrain (**839**).

832. Arnold van Gennep, 'Vie des Saints et roman-feuilleton', in Gennep, *Religions, moeurs et légendes, Essais d'ethnographie et de linguistique (Troisième série)* (Paris, 1911), pp. 149–59. Brief indication of the importance of hagiography as popular literature.

833. H. Delehaye, *L'Oeuvre des Bollandistes 1615–1915, A travers trois siècles* (Brussels, 1920 and 1959), SH, 13A^2. English translation under title: *The Work of the Bollandists through Three Centuries 1615–1915* (Princeton, 1922). A history of one of the greatest scholarly enterprises in Western culture by

an eminent participant in it, with bibliography. See also **836** and **840**.

834. Rudolf Günther, 'Über die abendländische Heiligenlegende', *Theologische Rundschau*, NS, 3 (1931), pp. 18–48. On Western hagiography.

835. H. Delehaye, *Cinq leçons sur la méthode hagiographique* (Brussels, 1934 and 1968), SH, 21. Chapters on Lives, martyrologies, relics and iconography; still an incomparable introduction to the subject.

836. Paul Peeters, *L'Oeuvre des Bollandistes, Mémoires de l'Académie Royale de Belgique*, Classes des Letters, XIX (1942); and SH, 24 (Brussels, 1942). Good general account, updating Delehaye (**833**).

837. C. Grant Loomis, *White Magic, An Introduction to the Folklore of Christian Legend* (Cambridge, Mass., 1948). Short pioneering study of saints' legends.

838. Heinrich Günter, *Psychologie der Legende, Studien zu einer wissenschaftlichen Heiligen-Geschichte* (Freiburg, 1949). French edition, 1954. Important study of saints' legends.

839. René Aigrain, *L'Hagiographie, Ses sources, ses méthodes, son histoire* (Paris, 1953). Encyclopedic historical and analytical account by professor at Université Catholique de l'Ouest, with bibliographies; essential.

840. David Knowles, *Great Historical Enterprises: Problems in Monastic History* (London, 1963). Essays on the Bollandists and the Maurists by English monastic historian.

841. M. Coens, 'Geneviève de Brabant, une Saint? Le terrior de sa légende', in Coens, *Recueil d'Etudes Bollandiennes* (**498**), pp. 101–18. Study of local popular legend; collection also includes various studies on the Bollandists.

842. H. Delehaye, *Mélanges d'hagiographie grecque et latine* (Brussels, 1966), SH, 42. Posthumous collection of minor studies, including **72, 880, 885, 1134**.

843. Baudouin de Gaiffier, *Etudes critiques d'hagiographie et d'iconologie* (Brussels, 1967), SH, 43. Collection of a lifetime's work by modern Bollandist; of special interest for studies of Spanish and Flemish hagiography and cults, and of folkloric themes, for example, 'le diable voleur d'enfants' and 'le pendu miraculeusement sauvé'; also includes essay on the work of the Bollandists in the seventeenth century.

844. Baudouin de Gaiffier, *Recueil d'hagiographie* (Brussels, 1977), SH, 61. Eightieth birthday collection, mainly of minor pieces previously published elsewhere; includes 'Le Patronage de Saint Antoine pour les "res perditas"', Ch. V.

See also **1272, 1275, 1278**.

(B) EARLY CHURCH AND LATE ANTIQUITY

(See also III (A) (viii).)

845. Otto Bardenhewer, *Patrology, The Lives and Works of the Fathers of the Church* (Freiburg im Breisgau and St Louis, Mo., 1908). Translated from 2nd German edition. Still useful for reference.

846. Manlio Simonetti, 'Nuovi studi agiografici', *Rivista di Archeología Cristiana*, 31 (1955), pp. 223–52. Studies of early martyrs.

847. P. Van den Ven, 'La Patristique et l'hagiographie au Concile de Nicée de 787', *Byz.*, XXV–XXVII (1955–7), pp. 325–62. See for uses of hagiography; with lists.

848. Berthold Altaner, *Patrology* (Freiburg and London, 1960). From 5th German edition; Ch. 6 on hagiography, Acts of martyrs and pilgrimage accounts.

849. E. Hendrikx, 'Saint Jerôme en tant qu'hagiographe', *Ciudad de Dios*, 181 (1968), pp. 661–7. Brief study of early and influential practitioner.

850. Jacques Fontaine, *La Littérature latine chrétienne* (Paris, 1970). Good short survey up to seventh century, with bibliography.

851. Bernd Reiner Voss, 'Berührungen von Hagiographie und Historiographie in der Spätantike', *Frühmittelalterliche Studien, Jahrbuch des Instituts für Frühmittelalterforschung der Universität Münster*, 4 (1970), pp. 53–69. On influence of classical biography on early hagiography, esp. Sulpicius Severus and St Athanasius.

852. Marie-Louise Guillaumin, 'Une jeune fille qui s'appelait Blandine, Aux origines d'une tradition hagiographique', in Jacques Fontaine and Charles Kannengiesser (eds.), *Epektasis, Mélanges patristiques offerts au Cardinal Jean Daniélou* (Paris, 1972), pp. 93–8. On cult of early female martyr.

853. A. Loyen, 'Les Miracles de Saint Martin et les débuts de l'hagiographie en Occident', *Bulletin de Littérature Ecclésiastique*, LXXIII (1972), pp. 147–57. Study in Martinian hagiography. See also **109, 110, 112, 757, 768**.

854. Jacques Fontaine, 'Hagiographie et politique de Sulpice Sévère à Vénance Fortunat', *RHEF*, 62 (1976), pp. 113–40. Study of the successive lives of St Martin and St Radegund.

855. Martin Heinzelmann, 'Neue Aspekte der biographischen und hagiographischen Literatur in der lateinischen Welt (1.–6. Jahrhundert)', *Francia*, I (1973), pp. 27–44. Bibliographical references in notes.

(c) BYZANTINE

(See also III (b).)

856. Ludwig Radermacher, 'St Phokas', *Archiv für Religionswissenschaft*, VII (1904), pp. 445–52.

857. R. Lübeck, 'Der heilige Phokas von Sinope', *HJ*, XXX (1909), pp. 743–61. Two studies of legendary marine patron.

858. Albert Ehrhard, *Überlieferung und Bestand der hagiographischen und homiletischen Literatur der griechischen Kirche* (Leipzig, 1937–52), Texte und Untersuchungen zur Geschichte der Altchristlichen Literatur, 4th series, 5–7. Three large volumes; an essential reference work; also deals with liturgy.

859. Paul Van den Ven, 'A propos de la Vie de Saint Syméon Stylite le Jeune', *AB*, 67 (1949), pp. 425–43. Critical study of important text.

860. Paul Peeters, *Le Tréfonds oriental de l'hagiographie byzantine* (Brussels, 1950), SH, 26. Posthumously published work by modern Bollandist; important.

861. François Halkin, *Bibliotheca Hagiographica Graeca* (Brussels, 1957), 3rd edition, 3 vols., SH, 8a. Catalogue of editions of Saints' Lives in Greek, with supplement, index and tables; essential reference work.

862. Hans-Georg Beck, *Kirche und theologische Literatur im byzantinischen Reich* (Munich, 1959 and 1977), Handbuch der Altertumswissenschaft, 12th series, Vol. 2, Pt I, esp. Section II. Indispensable reference work; updates Ehrhard (**858**).

863. Donald Attwater, *Saints of the East* (London, 1963). Selected Lives.

864. F. Halkin, 'L'Hagiographie byzantine au service de l'histoire', *Thirteenth International Congress of Byzantine Studies, Oxford 1966, Main Papers,* XI (Oxford, 1966), pp. 1–10. Valuable introduction to hagiographical sources and their potential value to the historian.

865. F. Halkin, *Recherches et documents d'hagiographie byzantine* (Brussels, 1971), SH, 51. Collected studies by leading scholar in the field, including **864**.

866. F. Halkin, *Saints moines d'Orient* (VR, London, 1973). Studies from *AB*.

867. Evelyne Patlagean, 'Sainteté et pouvoir', in Hackel (ed.), *The Byzantine Saint* (**231**), pp. 88–105. Analysis of ninth- and tenth-century Lives.

(D) ORIENTAL

868. *Bibliotheca Hagiographica Orientalis* (Brussels, 1910), SH, 10. Catalogue compiled by Bollandists; essential reference work.

869. Irénée Hausherr, 'Contemplation et sainteté, Une remarquable mise au point par Philoxène de Mabboug (†523)', *RAM*, XIV (1933), pp. 171–95. For notions of sanctity.

870. Antoine Poidebard and René Mouterde, 'A propos de Saint Serge', *AB*, 67 (1949), pp. 109–16. On Syrian cult.

871. Paul Peeters, *Recherches d'histoire et de philologie orientales* (Brussels, 1951), 2 vols., SH, 27. Collected studies dealing with Armenian, Coptic and Syriac examples.

(E) MEDIEVAL, WESTERN

(i) General

872. Emmanuel Cosquin, 'La Légende des Saints Barlaam and Josaphat', *RQH*, XXVIII (1880), pp. 579–600. On one of the strangest hagiographical 'kidnappings'. See also **748**.

873. Alfred Maury, *Croyances et légendes du Moyen Age* (Paris, 1896). Second part on religious legends is still valuable; has index.

874. *Bibliotheca Hagiographica Latina, Antiquae et Mediae Aetatis* (Brussels, 1898–1911), 3 vols., SH, 6 and 12. Catalogue of Saints' Lives in Latin and their provenance, with supplementary volume and index of authors; in Latin, essential reference work.

875. L. van der Essen, *Etude critique et littéraire sur les Vitae des saints mérovingiens* *de l'ancienne Belgique* (Louvain and Paris, 1907), *Recueil de Travaux d'Histoire et de Philologie*, Université de Louvain, 17. Comprehensive.

876. Ludwig Zoepf, *Das Heiligen-Leben im 10. Jahrhundert* (Leipzig and Berlin, 1908), *BKMR*, I. Still valuable.

877. Max Manitius, *Geschichte der lateinischen Literatur des Mittelalters* (Munich 1911–31), 3 vols., *Handbuch der klassischen Altertumswissenschaft*, IX, 2. Standard reference work; deals with hagiography.

878. E. C. Jones, *Saint Gilles, Essai d'histoire littéraire* (Paris, 1914). Discussion of literary legends of popular Provençal saint.

879. Manfred Stimming, 'Die heilige Bilnildis, Ein Beitrag zur Forschung über Urkundenfalschung und Heiligenlegende', *MICG*, XXXVII (1917), pp. 234–55. Critical study of local legend and its manufacture.

880. H. Delehaye, 'La Légende de saint Eustache', *Bulletin de l'Académie Royale de Belgique, Classe des Lettres* (1919), pp. 175–210; and in Delehaye, *Mélanges d'hagiographie* (**842**), Ch. 10. On important legend.

881. Renier Podevyn, 'Etude critique sur la *Vita Gudulae*', *RBPH*, II (1923), pp. 619–41.

882. *St Francis of Assisi: 1226–1926: Essays in Commemoration* (London, 1926). Includes essays by E. G. Gardiner on the 'Little Flowers', and by H. E. Good on 'The Dilemma of St Francis and the Two Traditions'.

883. Benjamin P. Kurtz, *From St Antony to St Guthlac, A Study in Biography* (Berkeley, 1926), University of California Publications in Modern Philology, 12/2. Comparative study.

884. J. -Th. Welter, *L'Exemplum dans la littérature religieuse et didactique du Moyen Age* (Paris and Toulouse, 1927). Important study for context of didactic hagiography.

885. H. Delehaye, 'La Légende de la bienheureuse Ida de Toggenburg', *Nova et Vetera*, 4 (1929), pp. 359–65; and in Delehaye, *Mélanges d'hagiographie* (**842**), Ch. 24.

886. P. Saintyves, *En marge de la Légende Dorée, songes, miracles et survivances, Essai sur la formation de quelques thèmes hagiographiques* (Paris, 1930). Study of hagiography by eminent folklorist.

887. Hilde Vogt, *Die literatische Personenschilderung des frühen Mittelalters* (Leipzig and Berlin, 1934), *BKMR*, 53. Short study of biographies and particularly saints' Lives.

888. Oskar Köhler, *Das Bild des geistlichen Fürsten in den Viten des 10., 11. und 12. Jahrhunderts* (Berlin, 1935), Abhandlungen zur mittleren und neueren Geschichte, 77. Short study.

889. Baudouin de Gaiffier, 'Le Martyrologie et le Légendier d'Hermann Greven', *AB*, 54 (1936), pp. 316–58. On work of fifteenth-century hagiographer.

890. H. Delehaye, 'Hagiographie napolitaine', *AB*, 57 (1939), pp. 5–64; and 59 (1941), pp. 1–33. Detailed study of calendar and early saints; does not deal with more recent cults.

891. Sister Mary Jeremy, 'Caxton's *Golden Legend* and Voragine's *Legenda Aurea*', *Sp.*, 21 (1946), pp. 212–21. On the relationship between the two collections. See **752, 769, 802, 914, 957**.

892. R. F. Seybolt, 'Fifteenth-century Editions of the *Legenda Aurea*', *ibid.*, pp. 327–38. List indicating the popularity of the collection in Latin and vernacular versions.

893. R. F. Seybolt, 'The *Legenda Aurea*, Bible and *Historia Scholastica*', *ibid.*, pp. 339–42. Confirms popularity of the first.

894. Baudouin de Gaiffier, 'L'Hagiographie et son public au XIe siècle', in *Miscellanea Historica in Honorem Leonis van der Essen* (Louvain, 1947), *Recueil de Travaux*, Université de Louvain, 3rd series, 28, I, pp. 135–66; and in Gaiffier, *Etudes critiques* (**843**), pp. 475–506.

895. Simone Roisin, *L'Hagiographie cistercienne dans le diocèse de Liège au XIIIe siècle* (Louvain and Brussels, 1947), *Recueil de Travaux d'Histoire et de Philologie*, Université de Louvain, 3rd series, 27. An important detailed study of hagiography of a particular religious order.

896. *Etudes méroviengiennes, I (Actes des Journées de Poitiers 1– 3 Mai 1952)* (Paris, 1953). Hagiographical studies by Aigrain, Delaruelle and others, esp. on St Radegund.

897. Hubert Silvestre, 'Le Problème des faux au Moyen Age (A propos d'un livre récent de M. Saxer)', *MA*, 4th series, 15 (1960), pp. 351–70. On important methodological and technical problems; relates to **255**.

898. František Graus, 'Die Gewalt bei den Anfängen des Feudalismus und die "Gefangenbefreiungen" der merowingischen Hagiographie', *Jahrbuch für Wirtschaftsgeschichte* (1961), 1, pp. 61–156. Important study, see also **902**.

899. Jean Györy, 'Hagiographie hétérodoxe', *Acta Ethnographica, Academiae Scientiarium Hungaricae*, XI (1962), pp. 375–90. Discussion of the *Vie de Saint Alexis* and the *Chanson de Sainte Foy*, seen as dualist and pantheist, respectively.

900. Theodor Wolpers, *Die englische Heiligenlegende des Mittelalters, Eine Formgeschichte des Legendenerzählens von der spätantiken Lateinischen Tradition bis zur Mitte des 16, Jahrhunderts* (Tübingen, 1964), Buchreihe der Anglia, Zeitschrift für Englische Philologie, 10. Comprehensive study.

901. Karl Bosl, 'Der Adelsheilige, Idealtypus und Wirklichkeit, Gesellschaft und Kultur im merowingerzeitlichen Iargen des 7. und 8. Jahrhunderts', in Clemens Bauer *et al.* (eds.), *Speculum Historiale, Festschrift für Johannes Spörl* (Freiburg and Munich, 1965), pp. 167–87; and in Italian as 'Il santo nobile' in Boesch Gajano, (**920**), pp. 161–90. Important socio-historical study.

902. František Graus, *Volk, Herrscher und Heiliger im Reich der Merowinger, Studien zur Hagiographie der Merowingerzeit* (Prague, 1965). Important socio-historical study by Czech scholar.

903. Gregorio Penco, 'Significato e funzione dei prologhi nell' agiografia Benedettina', *Aevum*, 40 (1966), pp. 468–76. Brief discussion of monastic hagiography.

904. Gérard Viard, 'Les Sept Saints dormants d'Ephèse', *AB*, 73 (1966), pp. 599–606. On important legend. See also **746, 772, 1142, 1272, 1275**.

905. Emil H. Walter, 'Hagiographisches in Gregors Frankengeschichte', *AK*, 48 (1966), pp. 291–310. On Gregory of Tours.

906. Erhard Dorn, *Der sündige Heilige in der Legende des Mittelalters* (Munich, 1967), *Med. A*, 10. Study of saints who were sinners.

907. Friedrich Prinz, 'Heiligenkult und Adelsherrschaft im Spiegel merowingischer Hagiographie', *Historische Zeitschrift*, 204 (1967), pp. 529–44. Important study exploring relationship between aristocracy and hagiography.

908. Wolfram von den Steinen, *Menschen im Mittelalter, Gesammelte Forschungen, Betrachtungen, Bilder* (Berne and Munich, 1967). Collected studies, including 'Heilige als Hagiographen' (1930), and 'Franz von Assisi' (1958).

909. Gisbert Kranz, *Europas christliche Literatur von 500 bis 1500* (Munich, Paderborn and Vienna, 1968). Book II, Ch. VI on hagiography.

910. Baudouin de Gaiffier, 'Mentalité de l'hagiographie médiévale d'après quelques travaux récents, *AB*, (1968), pp. 391–9. Valuable.

911. G. Penco, 'Le Figure bibliche del *Vir Dei* nell' agiografia monastica', *Benedictina*, XV (1968), pp. 1–13. On monastic ideals of sanctity as reflected in hagiography.

912. Gerhard Strunk, *Kunst und Glaube in der lateinischen Heiligenlegende, Zu ihrem Selbstverständnis in den Prologen* (Munich, 1970), Med. A., 12.

913. Baudouin de Gaiffier, *Recherches d'hagiographie latine* (Brussels, 1971), SH, 52. Collection of previously unpublished minor studies.

914. Maria von Nagy and N. Christoph de Nagy, *Die Legenda aurea und ihr Verfasser Jacobus de Voragine* (Munich, 1971). Short descriptive and analytical study of popular late medieval collection of saints' Lives. See also **769, 802, 891–3**.

915. Louise Gnädinger, *Eremitica, Studien zur altfranzösischen Heiligenvita des 12. und 13. Jahrhunderts* (Tübingen, 1972), Beihefte zur Zeitschrift für romanische Philologie, 130. Studies of Lives of Sts Alexis, Giles and Jehan Bouche d'Or; detailed literary work with full bibliography; study of St Alexis discusses the literary tradition down to modern times.

916. André Vauchez, 'Sainteté laïque au XIIIᵉ siècle: La vie du bienheureux Facio de Cremone (v. 1196–1272)', *MEFR*, 84 (1972), pp. 13–53. Interesting study, with text.

917. F. Prinz, 'Gesellschaftsgeschichtliche Aspekte frühmittelalterlicher Hagiographie', *Zeitschrift für Literatur-Wissenschaft und Linguistik*, 3, II (1973), pp. 17–36. Important for early medieval hagiography and its socio-political function.

918. C. E. Stebbins, 'Les Origines de la légende de saint Alexis', *RBPH*, LI (1973), pp. 497–507. Study of important literary legend. See also **915, 924, 958, 959, 965**.

919. F. Graus, 'Sozialgeschichtliche Aspekte der Hagiographie der Merowinger-und Karolingerzeit, Die Viten der Heiligen des südalemannischen Raumes und die sogenannten Adelsheiligen', in Arno Borst (ed.), *Mönchtum, Episkopat und Adel zur Gründungszeit des Klösters Reichenau* (Sigmaringen, 1974), Vorträge und Forschungen, XX. Important study of local hagiography in socio-historical perspective.

920. Sofia Boesch Gajano (ed.), *Agiografia altomedievale* (Bologna, 1976).

Collection of essays, including translations into Italian of Patlagean (see Ch. 2 above) and Delooz (see Ch. 6 above), and of Bosl (**901**) and extracts from Graus (**902**); with introduction and valuable bibliography of works in French, Italian and German.

921. Hugues Dedieu, 'Quelques traces de religion populaire autour des Frères Mineurs de la province d'Aquitaine', *CF*, XI, pp. 227–49. Cult of two Franciscan saints as depicted in the hagiography of the Order.

922. Lucien Musset, 'De Saint Victrice à Saint Ouen, La christianisation de la province de Rouen d'après l'hagiographie', *RHEF*, 62 (1976), pp. 141–52.

923. K. F. Morrisson, 'The Structure of Holiness in Othloh's *Vita Bonifatii* and Ebo's *Vita Ottonis*', in Kenneth Pennington and Robert Sommerville (eds.), *Law, Church and Society, Essays in Honor of Stephen Kuttner* (Philadelphia, 1977), pp. 131–56.

924. Ulrich Mölk, 'La *Chanson de Saint Alexis* et le culte du saint en France aux XIe et XIIe siècles', *CCM*, XXI (1978), pp. 339–55. Traces cult in literary and liturgical sources, which were its main vehicle.

925. Joseph Claude Poulin, *L'Idéal de sainteté dans l'Aquitaine carolingienne d'après les sources hagiographiques (750–950)* (Quebec, 1979), Travaux du Laboratoire d'Histoire Religieux de l'Université Laval, I. Important study with useful bibliogrphy.

925a. *Hagiographie, Culture et Sociétés, IV–XIIe siècles, Actes du Colloque organisé à Nanterre et à Paris (2–5 mai 1979)* (Paris, 1981), Université de Paris, Centre de Recherches sur l'Antiquité tardive et le haut Moyen Age. Interesting collection of thirty-two papers by scholars from many countries, including studies of miracles, miracle accounts and royal saints.

(ii) Celtic

926. Fr. Albert Le Grand, *Les Vies des saints de la Bretagne armorique* (Brest and Paris, 1837, ed. Daniel-Louis Miorcec de Kerdanet; and Quimper, Paris, Brest and Rennes, 1901, ed. Guy Autret *et al.*). Seventeenth-century compendium of Lives of Breton saints arranged by calendar; scholarly, with generous quotation from older sources, but uncritical; valuable as an example of pre-Bollandist hagiography, and contains some references to popular practices and piety; and see **938**.

927. L. Duchesne, 'La Vie de Saint Malo, Etude critique', *RC*, XI (1890), pp. 1–22.

928. Ferdinand Lot, *Mélanges d'histoire bretonne (VI–XIe siècles)* (Paris, 1907). Collection of papers and texts; a 'positivist' critique, which concludes that the Breton Lives of the saints are historically valueless.

929. Robert Latouche, *Mélanges d'histoire de Cornouaille V^e–XIe siècle* (Paris, 1911), Bibliothèque de l'Ecole des Hautes Etudes, 192. Another 'positivist' and ultra-critical approach to Breton saints' Lives; with Latin text of Life of St Guénolé or Winwaloe.

930. F. Duine, *Questions d'hagiographie et Vie de S. Samson* (Paris, 1914). Collection La Bretagne et les Pays Celtiques, 8. Two detailed studies.

931. F. Duine, *Memento des sources hagiographiques de l'histoire de Bretagne, Les* *fondateurs et les primitifs (du Ve au Xe siècle)* (Rennes, 1918). Dictionary of local saints and their Lives, with full references.

932. R. Fawtier, 'Saint Samson Abbé de Dol, Réponse à quelques objections', *ABr.*, 35 (1921–3), pp. 137–86. Contribution to controversy on historicity of the saint and authenticity of his Life. See also **776, 781, 930, 942.**

933. F. Duine, *Inventaire liturgique de l'hagiographie Bretonne* (Paris, 1922), Collection La Bretagne et les Pays Celtiques, 16. Detailed reference work.

934. F. Duine, *Catalogue des sources hagiographiques, Pour l'histoire de la Bretagne jusqua'à la fin du XIIe siècle* (Paris, 1922), ibid., 17. Reference work.

935. W. J. Watson, 'Saint Cadoc', *Scottish Gaelic Studies*, 2 (1927), pp. 1–12.

936. Paul Grosjean, 'Notes d'hagiographie celtique', *AB*, 61 (1943), pp. 91–107; and 63 (1945), pp. 65–130. On topic (relatively) neglected by the Bollandists previously.

937. Robin Flower, *The Irish Tradition* (Oxford, 1947). Ch. II on early Irish saints in literature.

938. Dominique Conduché, 'Méthode de travail d'Albert Le Grand, Hagiographe breton', *ACNSS* (1966), *Bulletin Philologique et Historique*, pp. 661–71. On seventeenth-century hagiographer; see **926.**

939. Pierre Riché, 'Les Hagiographes bretons et la Renaissance carolingienne', *ibid.*, pp. 651–9. On scholarly interest in Breton hagiography *c*. 1900.

940. Valerie M. Lagorio, 'Pan-Brittonic Hagiography and the Arthurian Grail Cycle', *Tr.*, 26 (1970), pp. 29–61. Literary study. See also **951.**

941. G. H. Doble, *Lives of Welsh Saints* (Cardiff, 1971). Studies of Lives of five saints; edited with introduction by D. Simon Evans.

942. J.-C. Poulin, 'Hagiographie et politique, La première vie de saint Samson de Dol', *Francia*, 5 (1977), pp. 1–26. Hagiography used to boost metropolitan claims.

(iii) Vernacular

943. Gaston Paris, *La Littérature française au Moyen Age (XIe–XIVe siècle)* (Paris, 1909), 4th edition, ed. Paul Meyer. Chapters on legends of the Virgin and the saints; slight, but still a valuable introduction.

944. J. D. M. Ford, 'The Saint's Life in Vernacular Literature in the Middle Ages', *Catholic Historical Review*, XVII (1932), pp. 268–77. Brief discussion of French Lives and analysis of types; over 200 Old French Lives in verse have survived, together with a large number in prose.

945. Willis H. Bowen, 'Present Status of Studies in Saints' Lives in Old French Verse', *Symposium*, I, No. 2 (1947), pp. 82–6. Dry.

946. Z. W. B. Zaal, '*A Lei Francesca*' *(Sainte Foy v. 20)*. *Etude sur les Chansons de saints gallo-romains du XIe siècle* (Leiden, 1962). Brief scholarly study; also discusses relationship between *chansons de geste* and hagiography.

947. W. F. Manning, 'Les Vies médiévales de Saint Dominique en langue vulgaire', *CF*, I, *Saint Dominique en Languedoc* (1966), pp. 48–69. Together with another brief study by same author: 'Les Manuscripts et miniatures des Vies en langue vulgaire', pp. 69–73.

948. S. C. Aston, 'The Saint in Medieval Literature', *Modern Language Review*,

65 (1970), pp. xxv–xliii. Valuable survey of French and English vernacular Lives, calling for a more systematic study of a genre, which is more edited than used and analysed.

See also **91**.

(iv) Hagiography and epics

949. G. Paris, 'La Chanson de pèlerinage de Charlemagne', *Romania*, 9 (1880), pp. 1–50.

950. Joseph Bédier, *Les Légendes épiques, Recherches sur la formation des Chansons de geste* (Paris, 1908–13), 4 vols. Vol. I, Ch. IV discusses links between early French epics and saints' cults; Vol. III, pp. 39–182 'Les Chansons de geste et le pèlerinage de Compostelle'; Bédier sees a positive connection between the epics and pilgrimages.

951. C. Grant Loomis, 'King Arthur and the Saints', *Sp.*, 8 (1933), pp. 478–82. Brief account of Arthurian legend in hagiographical literature. See also **940**.

952. René Louis, *De l'histoire à la légende, Girart de Vienne* (Auxerre, 1947–8), 2 vols. Opposing Bédier's thesis.

953. V. Saxer, 'Légende épique et légende hagiographique, Problèmes d'origine et d'évolution des Chansons de geste', *RSR*, 33 (1959), pp. 372–95. Discussion of Bédier–Louis controversy.

954. Stephen G. Nichols, Jr, 'The Interaction of Life and Literature in the *Peregrinationes ad Loca Sancta* and the *Chansons de Geste*', *Sp.*, 44 (1969), pp. 51–77. Literary study of pilgrimage accounts and epics.

955. *Medievalia et Humanistica, Studies in Medieval and Renaissance Culture*, NS, 6 (1975). Special issue on 'Medieval Hagiography and Romance'.

See also **946, 1124**.

(F) EARLY MODERN

956. Rudolf Kapp, *Heilige und Heiligenlegenden in England, Studien zum 16, und 17. Jahrhundert* (Halle and Saale, 1934). Good book; did second volume ever appear?

957. Helen C. White, *Tudor Books of Saints and Martyrs* (Madison, Wis., 1963). Comprehensive study from Caxton's *Golden Legend* to Foxe's *Book of Martyrs* and accounts of contemporary Catholic martyrs.

(G) SOCIOLOGICAL AND SOCIOHISTORICAL APPROACHES

958. Baudouin de Gaiffier, 'Source d'un texte relatif au mariage dans la Vie de S. Alexis, BHL 289', *AB*, 63 (1945), pp. 48–55. Use of hagiographical text to explore attitude towards marriage.

959. Baudouin de Gaiffier, 'Intactam Sponsam Relinquens, A propos de la vie de S. Alexis', *AB*, 65 (1947), pp. 157–95. On theme of forced marriage followed by celibacy.

960. C. Vogel, 'La Discipline pénitentielle en Gaule des origines au IXe siècle, Le dossier hagiographique', *RSR*, 30 (1956), pp. 1–26 and 157–86. Use of hagiography as historical source on penitential practices.

961. H. J. Magoulias, 'The Lives of the Saints as sources of data for the History of Byzantine Medicine in the Sixth and Seventh Centuries', *BZ*, LVII (1964), pp. 127–50. Much more to be said in this particular area.

962. Léopold Génicot, 'Sur l'intérêt des textes hagiographiques', *Académie Royale de Belgique, Bulletin de la Classe des Lettres et de Sciences Morales et Politiques*, 5th series, LI (1965), pp. 65–75. On value of hagiography for study of mentalities.

963. François Kerlouegan, 'Essai sur la mise en nourriture et l'éducation dans les pays celtiques d'après le témoignage des textes hagiographiques latins', *Etudes Celtiques*, XII (1968–71), pp. 101–46. Interesting socio-historical study.

964. J. Rougé, 'Topos et Realia: La tempête apaisée de la Vie de saint Germain d'Auxerre', *Latomus*, 27 (1968), pp. 197–202. Episode of calming storm is seen as 'precious evidence of maritime practice'.

965. Michel Mollat (ed.), *Etudes sur l'histoire de la pauvreté (Moyen Age – XVIe siècle)* (Paris, 1974), 2 vols., Publications de la Sorbonne, Série Etudes, 8. Vol. I, Pt I, Ch. III, 'La pauvreté dans les textes hagiographiques'; valuable studies by A. Gieysztov on St Alexis, by P.-A. Sigal on various texts, and by A. Vauchez on St Elizabeth of Thuringia.

966. Jean-Louis Derouet, 'Les Possibilités d'interprétation sémiologique des textes hagiographiques', *RHEF*, 62 (1976), pp. 153–62. Novel approach.

967. Marc Van Uytfanghe, 'Les Avatars contemporains de l'"hagiologie": A propos d'un ouvrage récent sur Saint Séverin du Norique', *Francia*, 5 (1977), pp. 639–71. Uses review of book by Lotter to discuss general renewal of hagiographical studies; especially valuable on German work.

See also **898, 901, 902, 907, 910, 917, 919, 921.**

(H) PSYCHOLOGICAL AND PSYCHOANALYTICAL APPROACHES

968. William' James, *The Varieties of Religious Experience, A Study in Human Nature* (London and Cambridge, Mass., 1902, and many subsequent editions), The Gifford Lectures, 1901–2. Lectures XI–XV discuss 'saintliness'; important contribution by the eminent American philosopher.

969. I. F. Grant-Duff, 'A Psycho-Analytical Study of a Phantasy of St Thérèse de l'Enfant Jésus', *British Journal of Medical Psychology*, 5 (1925), pp. 345–53. A classic Freudian hypothesis based on the Autobiography. A revised version appeared in German as 'Die Geschichte der Phantasie einer Heiligen', *Imago*, 16 (1930), pp. 486–501; and French translations of both with a critical introduction by Jacques Maître: 'Recherches

psychoanalytiques sur un cas de sainteté canonisé, Thérèse Martin (1873–1897)', *ASR*, 41 (1976), pp. 109–36. See also **301**.

970. Thomas Verner Moore, *Heroic Sanctity and Insanity, An Introduction to the Spiritual Life and Mental Hygiene* (New York and London, 1959). A theological and psychological work on relationship between 'sanctity' and 'abnormality' by a Carthusian; includes chapters on St Teresa of Lisieux.

XII SPECIALISMS, CURES AND MIRACLES

(A) SAINTS, DISEASE AND CURING

971. J. -B. Thiers, *Traité des superstitions* (**306**), I, Book 6, Ch. IV on notion of folk-healers as descendants of saints.

972. Henri Gaidoz, *La Rage et St Hubert* (Paris, 1887). Good historical and folkloric study of local curing cult with several peculiar features. See also **980, 989**.

973. L. Deubner, *De Incubatione, Capita Quattuor* (Leipzig, 1900). Short work in Latin on practice of incubation at antique pagan and Christian shrines. See also **977, 978, 986**.

974. Félix Chapiseau, *Le Folk-Lore de la Beauce et du Perche* (Paris, 1902), 2 vols. Vol. I, Pt II, Ch. II, 'La médecine religieuse: Saints protecteurs et guérisseurs', pp. 109–58; also contains chapter on holy wells and springs.

975. C. Fraysse, 'Les Saints guérisseurs au pays de Bauge', *RTP*, XX (1905), pp. 238–47. Brief folkloric study.

976. H. Folet, 'Rabelais et les saints préposés aux maladies', *Revue des Etudes Rabelaisiennes*, IV (1906), pp. 199–216. Of interest especially for its examination of the notion that saints produce as well as cure the diseases associated with them.

977. Mary Hamilton, *Incubation or the Cure of Disease in Pagan Temples and Christian Churches* (London, 1906). Important study.

978. Marian C. Harrison, 'A Survival of Incubation? (In the Abruzzi)', *FL*, XIX (1908), pp. 313–15, with photographs. On festival of the Virgin near Sulmona.

979. P. Saintyves, 'Les Saints protecteurs des nourrices et les guérisseurs des maladies des seins', *RTP*, XXI (1916), pp. 77–84. Still valuable on this common aspect of popular cults.

980. Henry M. R. Martin, *Saint Hubert* (Paris, 1921), Collection L'Art et les Saints. Good little book.

981. Ernest Wickersheimer, 'Les Guérisons miraculeuses du Cardinal Pierre de Luxembourg (1387–1390)', *Comptes-Rendus du Deuxième Congrès International de l'Histoire de Médecine* (Evreux, 1922), II, pp. 373–89. Account based on canonization procedure and paying attention to all circumstances of cures (mode of cure, vows, punishment by saint, etc.), although main emphasis is on the medical aspect.

982. C. Grant Loomis, 'Hagiological Healing', *Bulletin of the History of Medicine*, VIII (1940), pp. 636–42. Brief account of types of cure found in saints' Lives.

983. Henry Chaumartin, *Le Mal des ardents et le feu Saint-Antoine, Etude historique, médicale, hagiographique et légendaire* (no place, 1946). Important study by medical historian of the association of St Anthony the Great with ergotism, centred on the relics of the saint at the shrine of Saint-Antoine-du-Viennois; also discusses the exploitation of the cult by the local religious order of Hospitallers of St Anthony.

984. A. A. Barb, 'St Zacharias the Prophet and Martyr, A Study of Charms and Incantations', *Journal of the Warburg and Courtauld Institutes*, XI (1948), pp. 35–67. Interesting study of Old Testament saint.

985. Adalberto Pazzini, *La Medicina popolare in Italia (Storia – tradizioni – leggende)* (Trieste, 1948). Has short section on curing saints.

986. Domenico Mallardo, 'L'incubazione nella cristianità medievale napoletana', *AB*, 67 (1949), pp. 465–98. Important.

987. Erik V. Kraemer, *Les Maladies désignées par le nom d'un saint, Societas Scientiarum Fennica, Commentationes Humanorum Litterarum*, XV/2 (1950). Valuable study of diseases associated specifically with a saint in France, with bibliography.

988. M. Coens, 'L'Etole de Saint Forannan, abbé de Waulsort et la rage, Un cas de concurrence déloyale', in *Etudes d'histoire et d'archéologie namuroises dédiées à Ferdinand Courtoy* (Gembloux, 1952), pp. 257–63; and in Coens, *Recueil* (**498**), pp. 94–100. On rival to St Hubert as curer of rabies.

989. André Dubuc, 'Le Culte de Saint Hubert en Normandie', *AN*, IV (1954), pp. 67–70. Brief complement to Gaidoz (**972**).

990. Marc Leproux, *Dévotions et saints guérisseurs* (Paris, 1957). Essential study of folklore of the Charente.

991. Heinz Skrobucha, *Kosmas und Damian* (Recklinghausen, 1965). Short iconographical study of pair of healing saints.

992. M. Bouteiller, *Médecine populaire d'hier et d'aujourd'hui* (Paris, 1966). Good general study with valuable chapters on recourse to curing saints in France.

993. Dietlinde Goltz, 'Über die Rolle des Arzneimittels in antiken und christlichen Wunderheilingen', *Archiv für Geschichte der Medizin*, 50 (1966), pp. 392–410. On the use of drugs in miracle cures.

994. Madeleine Saint-Eloy, 'Quand la peste régnait à Nevers, 1399–1628', *ACNSS* (1966), *Bulletin Philologique et Historique*, pp. 335–66. On the invocation of St Anthony and others against the plague; also for vows and processions.

995. A. Adnès and P. Canivet, 'Guérisons miraculeuses et exorcismes dans l'"Histoire philothée" de Théodoret de Cyr', *RHR*, 167 (1967), pp. 53–82 and 149–79. Important study of fifth-century Syrian Christian source.

996. Aline Rousselle, 'Du sanctuaire au thaumaturge: La guérison en Gaule au IVᵉ siècle', *Ann.*, 31 (1976), pp. 1085–107. Discussion of the healing of St Martin in the context of prevailing pagan practice.

997. Alban Bensa, *Les Saints guérisseurs du Perche-Gouët, Espace symbolique du*

Bocage (Paris, 1978). Important local research with valuable interpretative essay; illustrated.

See also **595, 685**.

(B) SPECIALISMS, RESUSCITATION OF BABIES

998.　Pierre Saintyves, 'Les Résurrections d'enfants morts-nés et les sanctuaires à "rèpit"', *Revue d'Ethnographie et de Sociologie*, 2nd series, II (1911), pp. 65–79. Pioneering study of a particular type of shrine specializing in the revival of babies, usually still-born, so that they could be baptized legitimately.

999.　Maurice Vloberg, 'Les Réanimations d'enfants mort-nés dans les sanctuaires, dits "à répite", de la Vierge', *Sanctuaires et Pèlerinages*, 18 (1960), pp. 17–32. French examples.

1000.　Marguerite Rebouillet, 'Les Sanctuaires de Bourgogne dits "à répit"', *ACNSS*, 99 (1976), I, pp. 173–92. Detailed local study, mainly of Marian shrines.

1001.　Jacques Gélis, 'De la Mort à la vie, Les "sanctuaires à répit"', *EF*, XI (1981), pp. 211–24. With illustrations and bibliography.

(C) MISCELLANEOUS SPECIALISMS

1002.　Louis Du Broc de Segange and Louis-François Morel, *Les Saints patrons des corporations et protecteurs spécialement invoqués dans les maladies et dans les circonstances critiques de la vie* (Paris and Moulins, 1887), 2 vols. Lives of saints, arranged by calendar, approved by bishops; patronages and special invocations less central than title suggests.

1003.　H. Delehaye, 'Saint Expédit et le martyrologie hiernonymien', *AB*, 25 (1906), pp. 90–8. On saint whose popularity derives from pun on his name; supposed to 'expedite' requests.

1004.　Septime Gorceix, 'Saint Léonard accoucheur, Les vertus de ses reliques et leur rôle dans la naissance de Louis XIV', *Aesculape*, 3 (1913), pp. 7–11. With illustrations.

1005.　Arnold van Gennep, 'Le Culte populaire de sainte Agathe en Savoie', *Revue d'Ethnographie*, 17 (1924), pp. 28–36; and in Gennep, *Culte populaire des saints en Savoie* (**1240**). Study of local cult associated with protection against fires as well as with breast-feeding, by leading folklorist.

1006.　J. Stany-Gauthier, 'Les Saints bretons protecteurs des récoltes et des jardins', *ATP*, I (1953–4), pp. 307–21. Interesting.

1007.　Jean Mellot, 'Un "complexe" original de cultes berrichons: Saint Posen et les "vendredis blancs" au XIXe et au début du XXe siècle', *ACNSS*, 99 (1976), I, pp. 347–61. Factual and folkloric account of cults related to the protection of livestock.

See also **1235, 1237**.

(D) MIRACLE ACCOUNTS

(i) Primary sources

1007a. J. O. Halliwell (ed.), *The Chronicles of William de Rishanger of the Barons' Wars: The Miracles of Simon de Montfort* (London, 1840), Camden Society. Latin text.

1008. J. Stevenson (ed.), *Libellus de Vita et Miraculis S. Godrici, Heremitae de Finchale auctore Reginaldo Monacho Dunelmensi* (London and Edinburgh, 1847), Surtees Society, 20. Critical edition of Latin text.

1009. Henri-Léonard Bordier (ed.), Gregory of Tours, *Les Livres de Miracles et autres opuscules* (Paris, 1857–64), 4 vols., Société de l'Histoire de France, 75–8. Revised texts and French translations of De Gloria Martyrium, the Miracles of St Julian, the Miracles of St Martin (Vol. II), the Vitae Patrum, the Miracles of St Andrew, and other works.

1010. E. de Certain (ed.), *Les Miracles de Saint Benoît écrits par Adrevald, Aimon, André Raoul Tortaire et Hugues de Sainte-Marie, moines de Fleury* (Paris, 1858), Société de l'Histoire de France, 79. Introduction and critical edition of Latin text.

1011. Augustus Jessopp and Montague Rhodes James, *The Life and Miracles of St William of Norwich by Thomas of Monmouth* (Cambridge, 1896). Original text and English translation. See also **1104.**

1012. Alfred Largeault and H. Bodenstaff, 'Miracles de Sainte Radegonde (XIIIe et XIVe siècle)', *AB*, 23 (1904), pp. 433–47. Introduction and Latin text.

1013. Edmond Albe (ed.), *Les Miracles de Notre-Dame de Roc-Amadour au XIIe siècle, Texte et tradition* (Paris, 1907). Important text and discussion.

1014. Ludwig Deubner, *Kosmas und Damian, Texte und Einleitung* (Leipzig and Berlin, 1907). Important text and introduction.

1015. Ronald Knox and Shane Leslie, *The Miracles of King Henry VI* (Cambridge, 1923). Text and English translation of account relating to 'unofficial' royal saint. See also Grosjean (**1016**).

1016. P. Grosjean, *Henrici VI Angliae Regis Miracula Postuma* (Brussels, 1935), SH, 22. Latin text with long introductory study, also in Latin.

1017. James Drescher, *Apa Mena, A Selection of Coptic Texts relating to St Menas* (Cairo, 1946). Publications de la Société d'Archéologie Copte. Coptic texts of account of martyrdom and miracles, with English translation and an important introductory essay on the cult. See also **740** and **1024.**

1018. Henri Platelle, *Les Chrétiens face au miracle, Lille au XVIIe siècle* (Paris, 1968). Study of miracles occurring at shrines in Lille between 1590 and 1663; introduction and texts from private and episcopal inquiries; valuable Early Modern source.

1019. Denis Bethell, 'The Miracles of St Ithamar', *AB*, 89 (1971), pp. 421–37. Twelfth-century Latin text and commentary.

1020. Edward Peters (ed.), *Monks, Bishops and Pagans* (**772**), Ch. 8. English translation of the First Book of Gregory of Tours's Miracles of St Martin.

1021. Yves Chauvin (ed.), *Livre des Miracles de Sainte-Catherine-de-Fierbois*

1375–1470) (Poitiers, 1976), Archives Historiques du Poitou, LX. Critical edition of account in French, including 237 miracles; the vow is characteristic, and many beneficiaries are escaped or released prisoners of war; supersedes earlier edition by abbé Bourassé (Tours, 1858), which was translated into English by Andrew Lang as *The Miracles of Madame Sainte Katherine of Fierbois* (1897). For discussion, See **1034**.

1022. Geneviève Renaud, 'Les Miracles de S. Aignan d'Orléans (XIᵉ siècle)', *AB*, 94 (1976), pp. 245–74. Latin text with commentary.

1022a. Gilbert Dagron, *Vie et miracles de Sainte Thècle* (Brussels, 1978), SH, 62. Greek text with French translation and commentary.

See also **268, 279, 764, 1191.**

(ii) Secondary works

1023. James Fowler, 'On a Window representing the Life and Miracles of S. William of York, at the North End of the Eastern Transept, York Minster', *Yorkshire Archaeological and Topographical Journal*, III (1875), pp. 198–348. Detailed iconographical study of representations of miracles in glass, parallel to ex-voto pictures.

1024. H. Delehaye, 'L'Invention des reliques de Saint Menas à Constantinople', *AB*, 29 (1910), pp. 112–50. Article with short Greek texts; of particular interest for miracle accounts.

1025. H. Delehaye, 'Les Premiers "Libelli Miraculorum"', *AB*, 29 (1910), pp. 427–34. Discussion of St Augustine's accounts of miracles of St Stephen. See also **1043–5.**

1026. H. Delehaye, 'Les Recueils antiques de Miracles des Saints', *AB*, 43 (1925), pp. 5–85 and 305–25. Comprehensive and pioneering study of accounts of miracles at Eastern and Western Christian shrines to the end of the seventh century; essential.

1027. Georg Schreiber (ed.), *Deutsche Mirakelbücher, zur Quellenkunde und Sinngebung* (Düsseldorf, 1938), Forschungen zur Volkskunde, 31–2. General study by Schreiber, and particular studies by E. Friess and G. Gugitz, K. H. Schäfer and F. Zoepf on accounts from Austrian, Swabian, and Bavarian shrines of the Early Modern period.

1028. C. Grant Loomis, 'The Miracle Traditions of the Venerable Bede', *Sp.*, 21 (1946), pp. 404–18.

1029. Alexandre Vidier, *L'Historiographie à Saint-Benoît-sur-Loire et les Miracles de Saint Benoît* (Paris, 1965). Critical study of Miracle Accounts in Pt II of a thesis written in 1898.

1030. A. Stacpoole, 'Hugh of Cluny and the Hildebrandine Miracle Traditions', *RB*, 77 (1967), pp. 341–63. Useful.

1031. Peter Assion, 'Die mittelalterliche Mirakel-Literatur als Forschungsgegenstand', *AK*, 50 (1968), pp. 172–80. Important short study by folklorist.

1032. P. -A. Sigal, 'Maladie, pèlerinage et guérison au XIIᵉ siècle, Les miracles de Saint Gibrien à Reims', *Ann.*, 24 (1969), pp. 1522–39. An important and influential socio-historical study.

1033. Dominique Gonthier and Claire Le Bas, 'Analyse socio-économique de quelques recueils de miracles dans la Normandie du XIe au XIIIe siècle', *AN*, 24 (1974), pp. 3–36. Admirable quantitative study with maps and tables.

1034. Y. Chauvin, 'Le Livre des Miracles de Sainte-Catherine-de-Fierbois', *BSAO*, 4th series, XIII (1975), pp. 281–311. Important study of regional shrine *c.* 1400, with quantification of data. See also **1021**.

1035. Bernard Cousin, 'Deux cents miracles en Provence sous Louis XIV', *RHS*, 52 (1976), pp. 225–43. Study of miracle accounts of shrine of Notre-Dame-des-Lumières near Goult; with tables and maps.

1036. Stéphanie Peigné-Janssen, 'Les Miracles de Sainte Anne d'Auray', in Jean Delumeau (ed.), *La Mort des pays de Cocagne, Comportements collectifs de la Renaissance à l'âge classique* (Paris, 1976), pp. 170–83. Short description and analysis of accounts from seventeenth-century Breton shrine, based on *mémoire de maîtrise*; read in conjunction with **479**.

1037. Ronald C. Finucane, *Miracles and Pilgrims, Popular Beliefs in Medieval England* (London, 1977). Important study of English shrines, based mainly on miracle accounts, with good illustrations.

1038. R. Foreville, 'Les "Miracula S. Thomae Cantuarensis"', *ACNSS*, 97 (1972), Section de philologie et d'histoire jusqu'à 1610 (Paris, 1979), pp. 443–68; and in Foreville, *Thomas Becket dans la tradition historique et hagiographique* (**276**), VII. Important study, with tables.

See also **53–61, 853, 981, 1108**.

(E) MIRACLES AND THEIR INTERPRETATION

1039. (Baron d'Holbach), *Recherches sur les Miracles* (London, 1773). Short book, published anonymously; a classic rationalist critique.

1040. Cobham Brewer, *A Dictionary of Miracles, Imitative, Realistic and Dogmatic* (London, 1884). Useful compilation; see especially Pt I, 'Miracles of Saints in Imitation of Scripture Miracles'.

1041. Paul Rousset, 'Le Sens du merveilleux à l'époque féodale', *MA*, 62 (1956), pp. 25–37. Good general discussion.

1042. Peter Browe, *Die eucharistischen Wunder des Mittelalters* (Breslau, 1938), Breslauer Studien zur Historischen Theologie, NS, IV. Study by Jesuit of important genre of eucharistic miracles, to compare with saints' miracles.

1043. D. P. De Vooght, 'La Notion philosophique du miracle chez Saint Augustin, Dans le "De Trinitate" et le "De genesi ad litteram"', *Recherches de Théologie Ancienne et Médiévale*, 10 (1938), pp. 317–43.

1044. De Vooght, 'Les Miracles dans la vie de Saint Augustin', *ibid.*, 11 (1939), pp. 5–16.

1045. De Vooght, 'La Théologie de miracle selon Saint Augustin', *ibid.*, pp. 197–222. Three important studies of a most influential view and its formation.

1046. J. A. Hardon, 'The Concept of Miracle from St Augustine to Modern Apologetics', *Theological Studies*, XV (1954), pp. 229–57. Useful survey.

1047. Gustav Mensching, *Das Wunder im Glauben und Aberglauben der Völker* (Leiden, 1957). Important short study; cross-cultural.

1048. Uda Ebel, *Das altromanische Mirakel, Ursprung und Geschichte einer literarischen Gattung* (Heidelberg, 1965), Studia Romanica, 8. Short study of a particular genre of miracle in hagiography.

1049. Marcel Bernos, 'Réflexions sur un miracle à l'Annunciade d'Aix-en-Provence', *AM*, 83 (1970), pp. 5–20. Interesting study.

1050. *Revue d'Histoire de la Spiritualité*, 48/2 (1972), Special issue *La Fonction du miracle dans la spiritualité chrétienne*. Important.

1051. Marcel Bernos, 'Miracles chez les Servites en Provence à l'époque moderne', *RHS*, 49 (1973), pp. 243–56. Important.

1052. Claude Langlois, 'La Conjoncture miraculaire à la fin de la Restauration, Migné, miracle oublié', *ibid.*, pp. 227–41. Important study of modern apparition of cross.

1053. R. C. Finucane, 'The Use and Abuse of Medieval Miracles', *History*, 60 (1975), pp. 1–10. Short discussion of English miracles with some remarks on their historiography.

See also **172, 173, 294, 1276**.

XIII SAINTS AND PATRONAGE

(A) LOCAL PATRONS AND THEIR FESTIVALS

(See also XVII.)

(i) General

1054. Giuseppe Pitrè, *Spettacoli e feste popolari Siciliane* (Palermo, 1880), Biblioteca delle tradizioni popolari Siciliane, XII. Pt II is a detailed account of the religious festivals of the year, including saints' festivals; standard work.

1055. Estella Canziani, *Through the Apennines and the Lands of the Abruzzi, Landscape and Peasant Life* (Cambridge, 1928). Various accounts of cults and festivals with illustrations by the author; see esp. Ch. XVII, 'San Domenico of Cocullo', on local festival in which statue is processed with live snakes.

1056. Arnold van Gennep, *Le Folklore du Dauphiné (Isère), Etude comparée de psychologie populaire*, I (Paris, 1932). Pt II, on 'les cérémonies périodiques', including saints' festivals.

1057. Lawrence Durrell, *Prospero's Cell, A Guide to the landscape and manners of the island of Corcyra (Corfu)* (London, 1945 and 1962). Ch. II on 'The Island Saint'; perceptive page on St Spiridion, island patron or 'influence'.

1058. Louis Dumont, *La Tarasque, Essai de description d'un fait local d'un point de vue ethnographieque* (Paris, 1951). On festival of dragon associated with St Martha; historical and ethnographical study of major importance; early work by leading French anthropologist.

1059. Michael Kenny, 'Patterns of Patronage in Spain', *Anthropological Quarterly*, 33 (1960), pp. 14–23. Draws the analogy between secular and supernatural patronage.

1060. Paul-Albert Février, 'Fêtes religieuses de l'ancien diocèse de Fréjus', *PH*, XI (1961), pp. 163–89. Good historical study of three saints' festivals.

1061. Clara Alcini Tartaglini, 'Le feste dei santi patroni nel territorio di Civitell de' Pazzi', *Lares*, 29 (1963), pp. 191–200. Succinct folkloric description, with photographs.

1062. Susan Tax Freeman, 'Religious Aspects of the Social Organization of a Castilian Village', *AA*, 70 (1968), pp. 34–49. Study by social anthropologist, stressing importance and integrative functions of saints' festivals.

1063. José Cutileiro, *A Portuguese Rural Society* (Oxford, 1971), Chs. XXVIII and XXX. Discussion of the cult of saints in a village community in terms of a search for 'divine patronage'.

1064. Clara Gallini, *Il consumo del sacro, Feste lunghe di Sardegna* (Bari, 1971). Important study of festivals in Sardinia.

1065. Joyce F. Riegelhaupt, 'Festas and Padros: The Organization of Religious Action in a Portuguese Parish', *AA*, 75 (1973), pp. 835–52. Important historical and contemporary study by social anthropologist.

1066. Michel Vovelle, *Les Métamorphoses de la fête en Provence de 1750 à 1820* (Paris, 1976). Changes and permanence in festivals in Provence through the Revolutionary period.

1067. Speros Vryonis Jr, 'The Panēgyris of the Byzantine Saint: A Study in the nature of a medieval institution, its origins and fate', in Hackel (ed.), *The Byzantine Saint* (**231**), pp. 196–227. Major study of the regional and international festivals and fairs associated with saints' shrines, which were important occasions for commercial and cultural exchange.

See also **1273, 1289, 1292, 1293, 1303**.

(ii) Processions

1068. R. Janin, 'Les processions religieuses à Byzance', *Revue des Etudes Byzantines*, XXIV (1966), pp. 69–88. On important and relatively neglected topic.

1069. Marie-France Gueusquin-Barbichon, 'Organisation sociale de trois trajets rituels (les Rogations, la Fête-Dieu et la Saint-Roch) à Bazoches, Morvan', *EF*, VII (1977), pp. 29–44. Contemporary study.

1070. Marc Venard, 'Itinéraires de processions dans la ville d'Avignon', *ibid.*, pp. 55–62. Historical.

1071. Paule and Roger Lerou, 'Les itinéraires cérémoniels des fêtes de saint Fiacre', *ibid.*, pp. 83–94. Contemporary French study, with photographs.

See also **1058**.

(B) SAINTS AND LOCAL FACTIONALISM

1072. Giovanni Verga, 'Guerra di santi', in *Vita dei Campi, Nuove novelle* (Milan, 1880), pp. 173–93; and in *Tutte le Novelle*, I (Verona, 1970), pp. 205–13. English translation in Verga, *Cavalleria Rusticana and Other Tales of Sicilian Peasant Life*, translated by Alma Strettell (London, 1893), pp. 165–89; and Giovanni Cecchetti (ed.), Verga, *The She-Wolf and other stories* (Berkeley, Los Angeles and London, 1973), pp. 95–107. Fictionalized account of factionalism within village projected via 'war of the saints'.

1073. Alan R. Beals, 'Conflict and Interlocal Festivals in a South Indian Village', *Journal of Asian Studies*, XXIII (June 1964), 'Aspects of Religion in South Asia', pp. 99–113. For comparison.

1074. Jeremy Boissevain, *Saints and Fireworks, Religion and Politics in Rural Malta* (London and New York, 1965). Important social anthropological study; of special interest for its discussion of the expression of factionalism via competing saints' festivals.

(C) URBAN PATRONS AND DEFENDERS

1075. Norman H. Baynes, 'The Supernatural Defenders of Constantinople', *AB*, 67 (1949), pp. 165–77; and in Baynes, *Byzantine Studies* (**390**), pp. 248–60. Important study of protection of city militarily and otherwise by the Virgin and the saints, and on the acquisition of their relics.

1076. Hans Conrad Peyer, *Stadt und Stadtpatron im mittelalterlichen Italien* (Zurich, 1955), Wirtschaft, Gesellschaft, Staat, 13. Important study of city patrons, including St Mark of Venice and St Ambrose of Milan.

1077. Cyril Mango (ed.), *The Homilies of Photius, of Constantinople* (Cambridge, Mass., 1958). English translation, introduction and commentary relating to ninth-century source; Homilies III and IV illustrate belief in protection of city by Mother of God and its escape from Russian attack through procession of the Virgin's robe; Homily XVIII relates to the restoration of the images of St Sophia after the iconoclastic purge was over.

1078. Alba Maria Orselli, *L'Idea e il culto del santo patrono cittadino nella letteratura latina cristiana* (Bologna, 1965), Studi e ricerche, NS, XII. Important.

1079. Richard C. Trexler, 'Florentine Religious Experience: The Sacred Image', *Studies in the Renaissance*, XIX (1972), pp. 7–41. Valuable study of the cult of the Virgin of Impruneta, one of Florence's patron 'saints' resorted to in times of crisis – in the context of some tilting at academic windmills.

1080. A. M. Orselli, 'Spirito cittadino a temi politico-culturali nel culto di San Petronio', *Convegni CSSM*, XI (1972), *La Coscienza cittadina nei comuni italiani del duecento*, pp. 283–343. Further important study by this author. See also **280**.

1081. Antonio Carile, 'La coscienza civica di Venezia nella sua prima storiografia', in *ibid.*, pp. 95–136. Discusses cult of St Mark, etc.

1082. Averil Cameron, 'The Theotokos in Sixth-Century Constantinople, A City Finds its Symbol, *JTS*, NS, XXIX (1978), pp. 79–108. Read with **1075**.

1083. A. M. Orselli, 'La Città altomedievale e il suo santo patrono: (ancora una volta), Il "campione" Paveso', *RSCI*, 32 (1978), pp. 1–69. Another valuable contribution.

1084. A. Cameron, 'The Virgin's Robe: An Episode in the History of Early Seventh-Century Constantinople', *Byz.*, XLIX (1979), pp. 42–56. Introduction to text relating to this important relic of the city's main patron.

See also **70**.

(D) NATIONAL PATRONS

1085. David B. Miller, 'Legends of the Icon of Our Lady of Vladimir: A Study of the Development of Muscovite National Consciousness', *Sp.*, 43 (1968), pp. 657–70. Factual.

1086. Rosemonde Sanson, 'La "fête de Jeanne d'Arc" en 1894', *RHMC*, XX (1973), pp. 44–63. On politico-religious controversy aroused by the proposal to make the feast of Joan of Arc a national holiday in France.

See also **114–16, 257–9,** and **1196**.

(E) CULTS OF LIVING SAINTS

(i) General

1087. Ennemond Boniface, *Padre Pio de Pietrelcina – Vie – Oeuvres – Passion, Essai historique* (Paris, 1966). Good factual book by an adherent.

1088. Barbara June Mecklin and N. Ross Crumrine, 'Three North Mexican Folk Saint Movements', *CSSH*, 15 (1973), pp. 89–105.

1089. W. A. Christian, 'Holy People in Peasant Europe', *ibid.*, pp. 106–14. Discussion of mid-twentieth-century cults, including that of Padre Pio, and of the sceptical or hostile attitude of the Church.

1090. Claude Carozzi, 'L'Estamen de sainte Douceline', *PH*, XXIII (1973), pp. 270–9. On minor 'popular' cult of holy woman in thirteenth-century Marseille.

1091. C. Carozzi, 'Douceline et les autres', *CF*, XI (1976), pp. 251–67. Further study, paying special attention to the saint's entourage and attitudes towards her body.

1092. George Gruzinski and J. -M. Sallmann, 'Une Source d'ethnohistoire: Les vies de "vénérables" dans l'Italie méridionale et la Mexique baroques', *MEFR*, 88 (1976), pp. 789–822. Interesting comparative study.

See also **60, 144, 303,** and **304**.

(ii) Holy Fools

1093. G. P. Fedotov, *The Russian Religious Mind* (**79**), II, Ch. XII. Valuable account.

1094. Ewa M. Thompson, 'The Archetype of the Fool in Russian Literature', *Canadian Slavonic Papers*, 15 (1973), pp. 245–73. Study of the theme of holy fool in later literature.

1095. Natalie Challis and Horace W. Dewey, 'Divine Folly in Old Kievan Literature: The Tale of Isaac the Cave Dweller', *Slavic and East European Journal*, NS, 22 (1978), pp. 255–64. Example from popular literature.

1096. John Saward, *Perfect Fools, Folly for Christ's Sake in Catholic and Orthodox Spirituality* (Oxford, 1980). The most complete study to date.

1097. Lennart Rydén, 'The Holy Fool', in Hackel (ed.), *The Byzantine Saint* (**231**), pp. 106–13. Brief but cogent.

See also **738**.

(F) SANCTUARY

1098. J. Charles Fox, *The Sanctuaries and Sanctuary Seekers of Mediaeval England* (London, 1911). Still of value.

1099. T. A. McGoldrick, 'The Mediaeval Right of Sanctuary', *TAASDN*, X (1948), pp. 165–78.

XIV POLITICAL USES OF CULTS: ECCLESIASTICAL

(A) MONASTIC PROMOTION OF CULTS

(i) General

1100. C. Eveleigh Woodruff, 'The Financial Aspect of the Cult of St Thomas of Canterbury', *Archaeologia Cantiana, Transactions of the Kent Archaeological Society*, XLIV (1932), pp. 13–32. Study of monastic accounts suggests that the financial advantages of the cult to the monastery were less than might have been expected; post-1174 rebuilding was not paid for from pilgrims' offerings, though rebuilding of nave in last quarter of fourteenth century was; jubilees, and hospitality, especially for royal visitors, were a great expense.

1101. C. R. Cheney, 'Church-building in the Middle Ages', *Bulletin of John Rylands Library*, XXXIV (1951–2), pp. 20–36; and in Cheney, *Medieval Texts and Studies* (Oxford, 1973), pp. 346–63. Brief discussion of influence of cult of relics on church-building, and on the role of the cult of saints in providing funds.

1102. *Jumièges* (**315**), I, Chs. 40–6. On 'Rayonnement de Jumièges' and the role of the cult of St Philibert in the influence exercised by the monastery.

1103. G. De Poerck, 'Les Reliques des Saints Maixent et Léger aux IXe et Xe siècles et les origines de l'abbaye d'Ebrueil en Bourbonnais', *RB*, LXXII (1962), pp. 61–95. Example of the importance of translation and miracles in the history of a monastery.

1104. M. D. Anderson, *A Saint at Stake, The Strange Death of William of Norwich 1144* (London, 1964). Popular account of an ultimately unsuccessful promotion, with strong antisemitic connotations; read in conjunction with **1011**.

See also **279, 348, 792**.

(ii) Self-defence

1105. Léon Van der Essen, 'Jean d'Ypres ou de Saint-Bertin (1383), Contribution à l'histoire de l'hagiographie médiévale en Belgique', *RBPH*, I (1922), pp. 475–94. Discusses use of hagiography to defend 'ecclesiastical possessions, immunities and privileges', in context of fourteenth-century Life, which is of a different kind.

1106. Baudouin de Gaiffier, 'Les Revendications de biens dans quelques documents hagiographiques du XIe siècle', *AB*, 50 (1932), pp. 123–38. Important study of use of hagiography and cults to lay claim to and defend church property.

1107. H. Platelle, 'La violence et ses remèdes en Flandre au XIe siècle', *Sacris Erudiri*, XX (1971), pp. 101–73. General discussion of ways of containing violence in the period; for 'background'.

1108. H. Platelle, 'Crime et châtiment à Marchiennes, Etude sur la conception et le fonctionnement de la justice d'après les Miracles de Sainte Rictrude (XIIe s.)', *ibid.*, XXIV (1980), pp. 155–202. Important study of way in which monasteries, in conflict with lay seigneurs or agents in times of weak central authority, sought supernatural protection via the saints, their relics and miracles; also a significant example of what Miracle Accounts can yield to the imaginative social historian.

See also **1111**.

(iii) Monastic rivalries

1109. François Baix, *Etude sur l'abbaye et principauté de Stavelot-Malmédy, I, L'abbaye royale et bénédictine (Des origines à l'avènement de S. Poppon, 1021)* (Paris and Charleroi, 1924). Interesting details on monastic promotion of cults, and on role of hagiography and translation in rivalries of monastic houses.

1110. Maurice Coens, 'Translations et Miracles de Saint Bavon au XIe siècle', *AB*, 86 (1968), pp. 39–52. Important study of propaganda use of translations; also discusses 'punishment' of usurpers by saint and has reference to 'clamour'.

1111. M. Coens, 'A propos d'un miracle de S. Bavon, Le *Clamor* de vant les corps saints', *AB*, 87 (1969), p. 416. Important addition to above, and to Geary (See Ch. 3 above).

(iv) Punishment by saints

1112. P. Rousset, 'La Croyance en la justice immanente à l'époque féodale', *MA*, 54 (1948), pp. 225–48. Valuable general study; discusses punishment by saints.

1113. P. -A. Sigal, 'Un aspect du culte des saints: Le châtiment divin aux XIe et XIIe siècles d'après la littérature hagiographique du Midi de la France', *CF*, XI (1976), pp. 39–59. Punishment by the saint as an expression of a belief in immanent justice and as a means of protecting church property and interests in a time of disorder; important.

See also **811**.

(B) IDENTIFICATION OF SAINT WITH DIOCESE

1114. Edmund Craster, 'The Patrimony of St Cuthbert', *EHR*, CCLXXI (1954), pp. 177–99. Good study of Durham.

See also **942**.

(C) CULTS OF SAINTS AND THE PAPACY

1115. Theodor Schnitzler, 'Der heilige Pius X, Eine Skizze zum Verständnis seiner Persönlichkeit', *LJ*, 4 (1954), pp. 73–84. Biographical study of modern canonized Pope.

1116. Walter Ullmann, 'Romanus Pontifex Indubitanter Efficitur Sanctus: Dictatus Papae 23 in Retrospect and Prospect', *SG*, VI (1959–61), pp. 229–64. On use of the term *'sanctus'* to designate the Pope *qua* successor to Peter and vicar of Christ, with implications for papal claims to exclusive canonization rights as well as to general sovereignty; important study by leading Cambridge scholar who has made the field of papal ideology his own.

1117. Dominikus Lindner, 'Die sogenannte Erbheiligkeit des Papstes in der Kanonistik des Mittelalters', *ZSS*, 84 (Kan. Abt. 53) (1967), pp. 15–26. Another view of papal sanctity.

1118. Cyriakus Hienrich Brakel, 'Die vom Reformpapsttum geförderten Heiligenkulte', *SG*, IX (1972), pp. 239–311. On cults promoted by eleventh-century reforming popes.

See also **208, 217, 218, 300, 321, 338, 343, 352**.

XV POLITICAL USES OF CULTS: SECULAR

(See also XIII.)

(A) SAINTS AND MONARCHIES

(i) Sacred kingship

1119. James G. Frazer, *The Golden Bough, A Study in Magic and Religion* (London, 1911–36), 3rd revised edition, 13 vols. with *Aftermath*, esp. Pts I and III. Starting point for much discussion of the topic; vastly influential on an earlier generation of writers; vol. II, Ch. XIX on St George.

1120. Marc Bloch, *Les Rois thaumaturges, Etude sur le caractère surnaturel attribué à la puissance royale particulièrement en France et en Angleterre* (Strasbourg and Paris, 1924); English translation as *The Royal Touch, Sacred Monarchy and Scrofula in England and France* (London, 1973). Classic study of curing powers of English and French monarchs; see also Book II, Ch. IV, on cult of St Marcoul.

1121. Percy Ernst Schramm, *A History of the English Coronation* (Oxford, 1937 and Ann Arbor, 1980). Important general account by German medievalist.

1122. A. M. Hocart, *Kingship* (London, 1941). Short brilliant study by off-beat English social anthropologist.

1123. E. E. Evans-Pritchard, 'The Divine Kingship of the Nilotic Sudan' (1948), in Evans-Pritchard, *Essays in Social Anthropology* (London, 1962 and 1969), Ch. 4. Frazer Lecture; essential.

1124. Karl-Heinz Bender, 'La Genèse de l'image littéraire de Charlemagne, Elu de Dieu, au XIe siècle', *Boletín de la Real Academia de Buenas Letras de Barcelona*, XXXI (1965–6), pp. 35–49.

1125. William A. Chaney, *The Cult of Kingship in Anglo-Saxon England, The Transition from Paganism to Christianity* (Manchester, 1970). Important.

1126. Manabu Waida, 'Sacred Kingship in Early Japan, A Historical Introduction', *HR*, XV (1975), pp. 319–42.

1127. J. L. Nelson, 'Symbols in Context: Rulers' Inauguration Rituals in Byzantium and the West in the Early Middle Ages', in Derek Baker (ed.), *The Orthodox Churches and the West*, SCH, 13 (1976), pp. 97–119.

1128. Benjamin Ray, 'Sacred Space and Royal Shrines in Buganda', *HR*, 16 (1976–7), pp. 363–73. Study of African dynastic shrines.

1129. J. L. Nelson, 'Inauguration Rituals', in P. H. Sawyer and I. N. Wood (eds.), *Early Medieval Kingship* (Leeds, 1977), Ch. 3. Further study of crucial ritual element.

1130. Eva Catafygiotu Topping, 'On Earthquakes and Fires: Romanus' Encomium to Justinian', *BZ*, 71 (1978), pp. 22–35. See for link between sanctification of Christian rulers and the Roman imperial ruler cult.

1131. K. J. Leyser, *Rule and Conflict in an Early Medieval Society, Ottonian Saxony* (London, 1979). Pt III on 'Sacral Kingship'.

(ii) Royal saints and royal patrons

1132. Lord Francis Hervey (ed.), *Corolla Sancti Eadmundi, The Garland of Saint Edmund King and Martyr* (London, 1907). Texts of various medieval Lives, including that by Abbo, and other documents, with English translations.

1133. Leonard Smith, 'The Canonization of King Henry VI', *Dublin Review*, 168 (1921), pp. 41–53. Good short study of abortive attempt at royal canonization. See also **1015** and **1016**.

1134. H. Delehaye, 'La Légende de Saint Napoléon' in *Mélanges d'histoire offerts à Henri Pirenne par ses anciens élèves à l'occasion de sa quarantième année d'enseignement à l'Université de Gand, 1886–1926* (Brussels, 1926), I, 8 pp. (no consecutive pagination); and in Delehaye, *Mélanges* (**842**), 20. Cult created for political reasons at start of the First Empire in France.

1135. Lord Francis Hervey (ed.), *The History of King Eadmund the Martyr and of the Early Years of his Abbey* (Oxford, 1929). Latin text with translation and brief commentary.

1136. Joan Evans (ed.), Jean Sire de Joinville, *The History of St Louis* (London, 1938). Introduction and English translation; mixture of biographical memoir and hagiography.

1137. Georg Schreiber, *Stephan I der Heilige, König von Ungarn (997–1038), Eine hagiographische Studie* (Paderborn, 1938). Valuable short study.

1138. Robert Folz, *Etudes sur le culte liturgique de Charlemagne dans les églises de l'Empire* (Paris, 1951), Publications de la Faculté des Lettres de l'Université de Strasbourg, 115. Important study of cult, which in many places dated only from the Later Middle Ages, and which was promoted for political reasons; with map.

1139. Bernhard W. Scholz, 'The Canonization of Edward the Confessor', *Sp.*, 36 (1961), pp. 38–60. Study of first papal canonization of an English saint and of the political motives for its promotion by the abbey of Westminster and by Henry II. See also **1140, 1142,** and **1144.**

1140. Frank Barlow (ed.), *The Life of King Edward who rests at Westminster* (London, 1962). Introduction, text and English translation of the *Vitae Aedmundi Regis* attributed to the Monk of Saint-Bertin, a late-eleventh-century Life in Latin verse and prose; Book II is perhaps later and has been linked with the campaign to have the king canonized; Appendix D, pp. 112–33 on 'The development of the cult of King Edward', which was never very extensive.

1141. R. Folz, 'Vie posthume et culte de Saint Sigisbert, Roi d'Austrasie', in *Festschrift P. E. Schramm* (**261**), I, pp. 7–26.

1142. F. Barlow, 'The *Vita Aedwardi* (Book II); The Seven Sleepers: Some Further Evidence and Reflections', *Sp.*, XL (1965), pp. 385–97. On composition of Life of royal saint, paying special attention to prophecies and miracles.

1143. Karol Gorski, 'Le Roi-Saint: Un problème d'idéologie féodale', *Ann.*, 24 (1969), pp. 370–6. Discusses different types of royal saint in north and east Europe in the eleventh and twelfth centuries.

1144. F. Barlow, *Edward the Confessor* (London, 1970). Ch. 12 discusses Edward's cult and canonization; Appendix E his first translation.

1145. R. Folz, 'La Sainteté de Louis IX d'après les textes liturgiques de sa fête', *RHEF*, 57 (1971), pp. 31–45. Notion of royal sanctity as manifested in liturgical texts was in some conflict with more secular notions of kingship.

1146. J. L. Nelson, 'Royal Saints and Early Medieval Kingship', *Sanctity and Secularity: The Church and the World*, SCH, 10 (Oxford, 1973), pp. 39–44. Brief but cogent.

1147. David O'Connell, *Les Propos de Saint-Louis* (Paris, 1974). Texts in French with commentary.

1148. Erich Hoffmann, *Die heiligen Könige bei den Angelsachsen und den skandinavischen Völkern, Königheiliger und Könighaus* (Neumünster, 1975), Quellen und Forschungen zur Geschichte Schleswig-Holsteins, 69. Study of English and Scandinavian royal saints.

1149. Stephen Maczko, 'Boris and Gleb: Saintly Princes or Princely Saints?', *Russian History*, II (1975), pp. 68–80. Interesting political interpretation of cult of suffering saints as a sacralization of their princely family.

1150. Michael Cherniavsky, 'Ivan the Terrible and the Iconography of the Kremlin Cathedral of Archangel Michael', *ibid.*, pp. 3–28, including 61 plates. Iconographical study of use of cult of saints to boost dynasty.

See also **53, 257–9, 333, 335, 337, 656, 660, 771, 1015, 1016**.

(iii) Opposition cults

1151. Josiah C. Russell, 'The Canonization of Opposition to the King in Angevin England', in C. H. Taylor (ed.), *Anniversary Essays in Mediaeval History by Students of Charles Homer Haskins* (Boston, 1929 and New York, 1978), pp. 279–90; and in Russell, *Twelfth Century Studies* (New York, 1978), Ch. 12. Pioneering piece.

1152. J. W. McKenna, 'Popular Canonization as Political Propaganda: The Cult of Archbishop Scrope', *Sp.*, 45 (1970), pp. 608–23. Factual.

(B) SAINTS' CULTS AND THE SPREAD OF POLITICAL AND CULTURAL INFLUENCE

1153. Abbé A. Bouillet, 'Sainte-Foy de Conques, Saint-Sernin de Toulouse, Saint-Jacques de Compostelle', *MSAF*, 53 (1892), pp. 117–28. On relationship between diffusion of cult of St Faith and architectural history.

1154. E. Ewig, 'Die Verehrung orientalischer Heiliger im spätrömischen Gallien und im Merowingerreich', *Festschrift P. E. Schramm* (**261**), I, pp. 385–400. On cult of Eastern saints in Gaul.

1155. Enrica Follieri, 'Santi occidentali nell' innografia byzantina', *ANLP*, 62 (1964), pp. 251–72. Cult of Western saints in Byzantium; iconographical study.

1156. Pier Maria Conti, 'Residui di culti Milanesi ai margini della Provincia metropolitica papale', *Rivista di Storia e Letteratura Religiosa*, II (1966), pp. 48–68. On survival of old cults.

1157. T. Dunin-Wasowicz, 'Saint-Gilles et la Pologne aux XIe et XIIe siècles', *AM*, LXXXIII (1970), pp. 123–35. On links between Provençal shrine and Poland via princes.

1158. Baudouin de Gaiffier, 'Relations religieuses de l'Espagne avec le nord de la France, Transferts de reliques (VIII–XIIe siècles)', in *Recherches d'hagiographie latine* (**913**), I, pp. 7–29. On function of relics and their transfer in forging social and cultural ties.

1159. W. von Rintelen, 'Kult- und Legendenwanderung von Ost nach West im frühen Mittelalter', *Saeculum*, 22 (1971), pp. 71–100.

1160. *ACNSS*, 94 (1969), *Bulletin philologique et historique (jusqu'à 1610) du Comité des Travaux Historiques et Scientifiques* (Paris, 1972), I, 'Les relations franco-espagnoles jusqu'au XVIIe siècle'. Articles by P. Lefrancq, A. Moreau-Néret and R. de La Coste-Messelière on cults of saints and pilgrimage.

1161. T. Dunin-Wasowicz, 'Tradition hagiographique romaine en Pologne médiévale: Saint Maurice et la Légion Thébaine', *Archaeologia Polna*, XIV (1973), pp. 405–20. On the circumstances of the spread of this cult to Poland.

1162. Dimitri Obolensky, 'The Cult of St Demetrius of Thessaloniki in the History of Byzantine–Slav Relations', *Balkan Studies*, 15 (1974), pp. 3–20; and in Obolensky, *The Byzantine Inheritance of Eastern Europe* (**85**), IV. On spread of cult of patron of Greek city into the Slavonic lands; political and cultural implications.

1163. R. Foreville, 'La Diffusion du culte de Thomas Becket dans la France de l'ouest avant la fin du XIIᵉ siècle', *CCM*, XIX (1976), pp. 347–69; and in Foreville (**276**), IX. Major study of diffusion of a cult, via pilgrimage, Miracle Accounts, relics, church dedications, etc., and of wider significance of same.

See also **146, 217, 298, 321, 329, 345, 351, 352, 362, 368, 600, 626, 632, 633, 639, 640, 1067.**

XVI FEMALE SANCTITY

(A) THE CULT OF THE VIRGIN MARY

(i) General

1164. F. G. Holweck, *Calendarium Liturgicum Festorum Dei et Dei Matris Mariae* (Philadelphia, 1925). Important for liturgical cult; in Latin.

1165. Martin Jugie, *La Mort et l'Assomption de la Sainte Vierge, Etude historico-doctrinale* (Vatican City, 1944), Studi e Testi, 114. Exhaustive study.

1166. Hubert du Manoir (ed.), *Maria, Etudes sur la Sainte Vierge* (Paris, 1949–71), 8 vols. Comprehensive collection of studies on all aspects of the Marian cult, world-wide.

1167. M. Jugie, *L'Immaculée Conception dans l'ecriture sainte et dans la tradition orientale* (Rome, 1952), Biblioteca Immaculatae Conceptionis, 3. Detailed official theological history of early stages of development of this important doctrine.

1168. Paul F. Palmer, 'Mary in Protestant Theology and Worship', *Theological Studies*, XV (1954), pp. 519–40. Useful.

1169. Giovanni Miegge, *The Virgin Mary, The Roman Catholic Marian Doctrine* (London and Toronto, 1955). An Italian Protestant account.

1170. René Laurentin, *Court traité de théologie mariale* (Paris, 1959), 4th edition. Good short account of official Catholic view – historical and theological.

1171. Donald Attwater, *A Dictionary of Mary* (London and New York, 1956–7). Useful.

1172. Walter Delius, *Geschichte der Marienverehrung* (Munich and Basel, 1963). Good general introduction.

1173. Hilda Graef, *Mary, A History of Doctrine and Devotion* (London and New York, 1963 and 1965), 2 vols. Definitive study by Catholic , as far as doctrine and learned opinion are concerned; less thorough on popular devotions; the main modern apparitions in Europe are briefly described, but the cult elsewhere is ignored.

1174. K. Algermissen *et al.*, *Lexikon der Marienkunde* (Regensburg, 1967–) First vol. of projected series which promises to be a basic reference work on the subject.

1175. Marina Warner, *Alone of All Her Sex, The Myth and the Cult of the Virgin Mary* (London, 1976). General interpretative study by lapsed Catholic; well illustrated.

1176. Gertrud Schiller, *Ikonographie der christlichen Kunst*, 4/2 (Gütersloh, 1980). Important iconographical study.

See also **402, 470, 476, 478, 482, 484, 653, 692, 999, 1000, 1075, 1082, 1084.**

(ii) Ethiopian

1177. E. A. W. Budge (ed.), *The Miracles of the Blessed Virgin Mary and the Life of Hannâ (Saint Anne), and The Magical Prayers of 'Aheta Mîkâêl* (London, 1900), Lady Meux Manuscripts, 2–5. English translation of Ethiopian texts of fourteenth–seventeenth centuries, with reproductions of Illustrations.

1178. E. A. W. Budge (ed.), *Legends of Our Lady Mary the Perpetual Virgin and her mother Hannâ* (London, Liverpool and Boston, 1922). English translation of early Ethiopian texts, with Introduction on cult of Virgin in Egypt and Ethiopia and comparison with Isis cult.

See also **1182.**

(iii) Western, medieval

1179. Stephan Beissel, *Geschichte der Verehrung Marias in Deutschland während des Mittelalters, Ein Beitrag zur Religionswissenschaft und Kunstgeschichte* (Freiburg im Breisgau, 1909). Huge work; still standard.

1180. G. E. Phillips, *Loreto and the Holy House, Its History Drawn from Authentic Sources* (London, 1917). Historical account of cult of 'relic' of the Virgin and its legend, by Catholic priest.

1181. H. von E. Scott and C. C. Swinton Bland (eds.), Caesarius of Heisterbach, *The Dialogue on Miracles* (London, 1929), 2 vols. English translation of medieval text; Vol. I, Book VII, on miracles of the Virgin.

1182. Enrico Cerulli, *Il Libro etiopico dei miracoli di Maria e le sue fonti nelle letteratura del Medio Evo Latino* (Rome, 1943), Reale Università di Roma, Studi Orientali, I. Important study of source of Western collections, with Oriental texts.

1183. R. W. Southern, *The Making of the Middle Ages* (London, 1953), Ch. 5. Pioneering and imaginative pages.

1184. Peter Bloch, *Kölner Madonna, Die Muttergottes in der Kölner Bildnerei des Mittelalters* (Mönchen-Gladbach, 1961). Small illustrated book.

1185. Beverly Boyd, *The Middle English Miracles of the Virgin* (San Marino, Calif., 1964), Huntington Library. Texts in modern English translation, with notes.

1186. Reinhold Lange, *Das Marienbild der frühen Jahrhunderte* (Recklinghausen, 1969). Short illustrated iconographical study.

See also **497, 548, 647, 649, 651, 943, 1013.**

(iv) Western, Early Modern

1187. S. Beissel, *Geschichte der Verehrung Marias im 16. und 17. Jahrhundert, Ein Beitrag zur Religionswissenschaft und Kunstgeschichte* (Freiburg im Breisgau, 1910). Sequel to **1179.**

1188. Paul Hoffer, *La Dévotion à Marie au déclin du XVII*^e *siècle, Autour du Jansénisme et des 'Avis Salutaires de la B. V. Marie à ses Dévots indiscrets'* (Paris, 1938). Important monograph.

See also **681, 682, 1035, 1079, 1085.**

(v) Modern shrines and cults

(a) GENERAL

1189. Auguste de Reaume, *Les Vierges miraculeuses de la Belgique, Histoire des sanctuaires où elles sont vénérées ; légendes, pèlerinages, confréries* (Brussels, 1856). Detailed study.

1190. J. Spencer Northcote, *Celebrated Sanctuaries of the Madonna* (London, 1868). By Catholic priest.

1191. Liam Ua Cadhain (W. D. Coyne), *Cnoc Mhuire, or The Irish Shrine of the Holy Rosary with accounts of some Remarkable Cures 1879–1937 (Knock, Co. Mayo)* (Dublin, 1937). Small booklet on shrine associated with a modern Marian apparition; primary source.

1192. Ruban Vargas Ugarte, *Historia del Culto de María en Iberoamérica y de sus imágenes y santuarios más celebrados* (Buenos Aires, 1947). Encyclopaedic but largely uncritical survey of Latin American shrines by Jesuit; with some illustrations of images.

1193. Z. Aradi, *Shrines to Our Lady around the World* (New York, 1954). General illustrated study.

1194. John Bushnell, 'La Virgen de Guadalupe as Surrogate Mother in San Juan Atzingo', *AA*, 60 (1958), pp. 261–5. Short but interesting attempt to relate emotional ties with the Virgin to early weaning practices and lack of trusting relationships after this within or outside the family.

1195. H. M. Gillett, *Shrines of Our Lady in England and Wales* (London, 1957). Comprehensive account of old and new shrines.

1196. Eric R. Wolf, 'The Virgin of Guadalupe: A Mexican National Symbol', *Journal of American Folklore*, 71 (1958), pp. 34–9. Good short piece. See also **594, 1196a.**

1196a. Simone Watson, *The Cult of Our Lady of Guadalupe* (Collegeville, Minn., 1964). Short historical study of Mexican cult by Benedictine.

1197. C. Savart, 'Pour une sociologie de la ferveur religieuse: L'Archiconfrérie de Notre-Dame-des-Victoires', *RHE*, LIX (1964), pp. 823–44. On modern French cult.

1198. Raoul Auclair, *Kerizinen, Apparitions en Bretagne?* (Paris, 1968). On a series of Marian apparitions in Brittany which began in 1938 and became more frequent in the 1950s and 1960s; with full text of messages imparted.

1199. Jean Gabriel, *Présence de la Très Sainte Vierge à San Damiano* (Paris, 1968). Account of apparitions at village near Piacenza in 1960s to Mamma Rosa; with photographs.

1200. C. Savart, 'Cent ans après: Les apparitions mariales en France au XIXe siècle, un ensemble?', *RHS*, 48 (1972), pp. 205–20. General socio-historical interpretation.

1201. Giuseppe De Lutiis, *L'Industria del santino* (Rimini, 1973). Study of post-war 'boom' in Marian and other pilgrimages and apparitions, particularly in Italy; indicts the Church for exploiting popular credulity for political and financial ends.

1202. Iso Baumer, 'Apparizioni e messaggi della Madonna – Un capitolo di religiosità popolare', in *Demologia e folklore, Studi in memoria di Giuseppe Cocchiara* (Palermo, 1974), pp. 231–75. Study of recent Marian apparitions in perspective of 'popular religion'.

1203. Pierre Lacroix, 'Un centre Jurassien de piété populaire: Notre-Dame de Mièges', *ACNSS*, 99 (1976), II, pp. 215–35. Important historical study.

1204. Gérard Cholvy, 'Piété ultramontane et sentiment religieux dans le peuple de l'Hérault au XIXe siècle, *ACNSS*, 99 (1976), I, pp. 273–88. Stresses importance of local Marian pilgrimages; with map.

See also **683, 687, 692, 978**.

(b) LOURDES

1205. L.-J.-M. Cros, *Histoire de Notre-Dame de Lourdes d'après les documents et les témoins* (Paris, 1925–6), 3 vols. Detailed historical study by Jesuit.

1206. René Laurentin and Bernard Billet, *Lourdes, Dossier des documents authentiques* (Paris, 1957–64), 7 vols. Definitive documentary study of characteristic modern cult which the authorities, ecclesiastical and secular, at first tried to suppress.

1207. Patrick Marnham, *Lourdes, A Modern Pilgrimage* (London, 1980). Good general account of the modern shrine.

(B) OTHER FEMALE SAINTS AND FEMALE SANCTITY

1208. Ludovico Frati (ed.), Vespasiano da Bisticci, *Vite di Uomoni illustri del secolo XV* (Bologna, 1892–3), 3 vols., Collezione di Opere inedite o rare dei primi dei tre secoli della lingua, III, pp. 245–306 on 'Donne illustri'. English edition under title *The Vespasiano Memoirs* (London, 1926) has translation of the 'Life of Alessandra de' Bardi', pp. 439–62. Fifteenth-century Life of a holy woman.

1209. Lucy Menzies, *Mirrors of the Holy, Ten Studies in Sanctity* (London, 1928). Studies of female sanctity.

1210. William Patterson Cumming (ed.), *The Revelations of Saint Birgitta* (London, 1929), EETS, OS, 178. Fifteenth-century version of classic prophetic text.

1211. Marie Delcourt, 'Le Complexe de Diane dans l'hagiographie chrétienne', *RHR*, 153 (1958), pp. 1–33; and revised version in English in Delcourt, *Hermaphrodite, Myths and Rites of the Bisexual Figure in Classical Antiquity* (London, 1961), Appendix, pp. 84–102, 'Female Saints in Masculine Clothes'. Important study of denial of femininity in legends of female saints.

1212. Ortrud Reber, *Die Gestaltung des Kultes weiblicher Heiliger im Spätmittelalter, Die Verehrung der Heiligen Elisabeth, Klara, Hedwig und Birgitta* (Hersbruck, 1963). Good short study of late medieval female saints' cults.

1213. Hermann Holzbauer, *Mittelalterliche Heiligenverehrung – Heilige Walpurgis* (Kevelaer, 1972). Introductory essay followed by full catalogue of manifestations of mainly German cult; some illustrations and map.

1214. E. Patlagean, 'L'Histoire de la femme déguisée en moine et l'évolution de la sainteté féminine à Byzance', *SM*, 3rd series, XVII (Spoleto, 1976), pp. 597–623; and in Patlagean, *Structure sociale, famille, chrétienté à Byzance, IVe–XIe siècles* (VR, London, 1981), XI. Important study of changing models of female sanctity in Byzantine hagiography, which raises more general problems of notions of male and female, and attitudes towards procreation, marriage and the family.

See also **2, 117–120, 121, 149, 177, 253–6, 279, 281, 283, 301, 302, 304, 308, 348, 355, 441, 727, 731, 734, 737, 739, 741, 746, 761, 791, 792, 799, 801, 805, 806, 808, 814, 817–19, 852, 885, 896, 1012, 1021, 1034.**

XVII SAINTS, POPULAR RELIGION AND FOLKLORE

(See also XIII (A).)

(A) GENERAL

1215. Raymond de Bertrand, 'Dévotions populaires chez les Flamands de France de l'arrondissement de Dunkerque', *Annales du Comité Flamand de France* (1853–4) pp. 191–235. Local folkloric account, with valuable information.

1216. *Revue des Traditions Populaires* (1886–1917), 32 vols. Regular cumulative features on miraculous imprints, automobile or resistant statues, pilgrimages, etc.

1217. Anatole Le Braz, 'Les Saints bretons d'après la tradition populaire', *ABr.*, VIII (1892–3) – XI (1895–6) and XIII (1897–8), many instalments; later revised and collected as *Les Saints bretons d'après la tradition populaire en Cornouaille* (Paris, 1937). Based on research undertaken on behalf of the

Ministry of Public Instruction; engaging studies of popular cults and legends by local schoolmaster–folklorist with considerable literary talent. See also **684**.

1218. P. Odilo Ringholz, 'Die Ausbreitung der Verehrung des heilige Meinrad', *SAV*, IV (1900), pp. 85–130. On distribution of cult in Germany and Switzerland; with map.

1219. E. A. Stückelberg, 'San Lucio (S. Uguzo), der Sennenpatron', *ibid.*, 14 (1910), pp. 36–70. Important study of north Italian cult associated with pastoralism; with illustrations and map.

1220. Gabriel Jeanton, *Le Mâconnais traditionaliste et populaire* (Mâcon, 1920–3), 4 vols. Vol. II on 'Pèlerinages et légendes sacrées', with illustrations; Vol. III on festivals; good studies by folklorist.

1221. Jost Trier, *Der heilige Jodocus, Sein Leben und seine Verehrung* (Breslau, 1924), Germanistische Abhandlungen, 56. Detailed study of saint venerated particularly in northwest France and Brittany; historical and contemporary.

1222. Giovanni Pansa, *Miti, leggende e superstizioni dell' Abruzzo (Studi comparati)* (Sulmona, 1924–7), 2 vols. Studies of cults of stones, phallic rituals and saints' legends; of great interest.

1223. C. Leroy, 'Le Culte de Saint Eloi en Artois et dans le nord de la France', *Revue de Folklore Français et Colonial*, V (1934), pp. 217–52. Comprehensive and descriptive.

1224. A. van Gennep, *Le Folklore de la Flandre et du Hainaut français (Département du Nord)*, I (Paris, 1935), Pt III. Lengthy section on the cult of saints; important.

1225. A. van Gennep, *Manuel de folklore français et contemporain*, III (Paris, 1937). Bibliography, pp. 435–506, 'Les Cérémonies calendaires, Le culte de la Vierge et des Saints'; sections on 'patronages', patronal festivals, rural chapels, popular iconography, as well as entries by province and by saint; unequalled wealth of bibliographical information on local saints and their cults in France.

1226. Joseph Sautel, *Les Chapelles de campagne de l'archidiocèse d'Avignon et de ses anciens diocèses* (Avignon and Lyon, 1938). Valuable historical and architectural study of 17 chapels; with photographs and maps.

1227. E. P. Baker, 'The Cult of St Oswald in Northern Italy', *Archeologia*, XCIV (1951), pp. 167–94. On cult of Anglo-Saxon saint in south Tyrol and the Veneto; mainly archaeological and iconographical, but some folkloric details; illustrated.

1228. J.-A. Durbec, 'Notes historiques sur quelques pèlerinages, processions, fêtes et jeux de Provence', *ACNSS*, 77 (1952), Section d'Histoire Moderne et Contemporaine, pp. 247–86. Descriptive.

1229. Alfons A. Barb, 'Der Heilige und die Schlangen', *Mitteilungen der Anthropologischen Gesellschaft im Wien*, LXXXIII (1953), pp. 1–21. On protection against snakes. See also **1055**.

1230. Roger Lecotté, *Recherches sur les cultes populaires dans l'actuel diocèse de Meaux (Département de Seine-et-Marne)* (Paris, 1953), Mémoires de la Fédération Folklorique de l'Ile-de-France, 4. Comprehensive.

1231. Georg Schreiber, 'Privilegia sanctorum, Volkstümliche Kanonistik und Hagiographie', *ZSS*, 74 (Kan. Abt. 43) (1957), pp. 327–42.

1232. Georg Schreiber *et al.*, *Die Vierzehn Nothelfer in Volksfrömmigkeit und Sakralkultur, Symbolkraft und Herrschaftsbereich der Wallfahrtskapelle, vorab in Franken und Tirol* (Innsbruck, 1959), Schlern-Schriften Veröffentlichungen zur Landeskunde von Südtirol, 168. Collection of studies, historical and folkloric, on the fourteen 'needhelpers' or saints of special efficacy.

1233. Saverio La Sorsa, 'Religiosità popolare Pugliese', *Lares*, 28 (1962), pp. 134–42. Short descriptive study of typical situation.

1233a. Christina Hole, *Saints in Folklore* (London, 1966).

1234. Seán O' Suilleabhain, *Irish Folk Customs and Belief* (Dublin, 1967). Little book; Ch. VII on festivals and pilgrimage.

1235. Jean Mellot, 'Le Culte de Saint Vincent en Berry depuis la fin de la période révolutionnaire', *ACNSS*, 94 (1969), Section d'Histoire Moderne et Contemporaine, II, pp. 289–300. Study devoted to local patron of viticulture.

1236. Ralph Della Cava, *Miracle at Joaseiro* (New York and London, 1970). Important study of modern schismatic cult in northeast Brazil.

1237. Dietmar Assmann, 'Volksetymologie und Heiligenverehrung', in *Studien zur Namenkunde und Sprachgeographie, Festschrift für Karl Finsterwalder zum 70. Gerburtstag* (Innsbruck, 1971), pp. 405–13. Study of folk etymology; of particular relevance for specialisms.

1238. W. A. Christian, *Person and God in a Spanish Valley* (New York and London, 1972). Study of religious practices and belief in region in north Spain; good description of shrines, and discussion of their functions and of the idioms in which relationship of individuals with the divine is cast, including the mediation of the saints.

1239. Jean Fournée, *Le Culte populaire des saints en Normandie, Etude générale* (Paris, 1973). Admirable local study; comprehensive.

1240. A. van Gennep, *Culte populaire des saints en Savoie* (Paris, 1973). Valuable collection of older articles by the great folklorist.

1241. Marie-Hélène Froeschlé-Chopard, 'Les Dévotions populaires d'après les visites pastorales: Un exemple, le diocèse de Vence au début du XVIIIe siècle', *RHEF*, 60 (1974), pp. 85–100. Emphasizes the importance of rural saints' chapels in village religious life, and clerical disapproval of these and other 'popular' elements.

1242. Jean-François Soulet, *Traditions et réformes religieuses dans les Pyrénées Centrales au XVIIe siècle* (Pau, 1974). Ch. IX on cults of saints, confraternities, pilgrimages, processions and miracles.

1243. Franco Manganelli, 'Religione e tradizioni nell' Agro Nolano, La Manna di San Felice', *Sociologia*, NS, 9 (1975), pp. 111ff. Important study of folkloric aspects of one of most ancient Christian cults.

1244. Serge Bonnet, *Prières secrètes des Français d'aujourd'hui, Epiphane* (Paris, 1976). Selection of 'prayers' from registers provided for the purpose at eleven contemporary French shrines, giving a unique insight into the mentality of supplicants; a human and religious document of prime importance.

1245. Joannès Chetail, 'Deux saints populaires: Saint Concord et Saint Anthelme', *ACNSS*, 99 (1976) I, pp. 193–9. Brief study of popular cults in south-eastern France in seventeenth and eighteenth centuries.

1246. Louis Pérouas, 'La Piété populaire au travail sur la mémoire d'un saint, Grignion de Montfort', *ibid.*, pp. 259–72. On the making of a popular cult.

1247. Arlette Playoust-Chaussis, *La Vie religieuse dans le diocèse de Boulogne au XVIIIe siècle (1725–1790)* (Arras, 1976). Pt III, Ch. III, 'Dévotions, superstitions, mentalités', has sections on confraternities and the cult of the Virgin and saints.

1248. Thomas Albert Kselman, *Miracles and Prophecies, Popular Religion in Nineteenth-Century France*, Ph.D. dissertation, Michigan (Ann Arbor, 1979). Interesting study of both 'folkloric' and 'revivalist' cults.

1249. M. -H. Froeschlé-Chopard, *La Religion populaire en Provence orientale au XVIIIe siècle* (Paris, 1980). Of especial interest for its discussion of devotions linked to chapels, of iconography and of confraternities.

(B) CULTS OF STONES AND ROCKS

1250. Edouard Piette and Julien Sacaze, 'La Montagne d'Espiaup', *Bulletins de la Société d'Anthropologie de Paris*, 2nd series, XII (1877), pp. 225–51. Valuable local study cited by Hertz.

1251. S. Reinach, *Cultes, mythes et religions* (**139**), III (1908), Ch. XXIII, 'Les Monuments de pierre brute dans le langage et les croyances populaires', pp. 364–433. Good study of cult and its christianization, by historian of religions; first published in 1893.

1252. P. Sébillot, *Le Folk-lore de France* (Paris, 1904–7 and 1968), 4 vols, Vol. I, Book III.

See also **685**.

(C) CULTS OF WELLS AND SPRINGS

1253. A. van Gennep, *Le Folklore de la Bourgogne (Côte d'Or)* (Gap, 1934), Pt III, Ch. II.

1254. Paul Gruyer, *Les Fontaines bretonnes* (Paris, 1943). Small collection of photographs with brief introduction.

1255. Francis Jones, *The Holy Wells of Wales* (Cardiff, 1954). The definitive work.

1256. P. Sébillot, *Le Folk-lore de France* (**1252**), Vol. II, Book II.

See also **685, 974**.

(D) HAGIOGRAPHY, FOLKLORE AND POPULAR LITERATURE

(See also XI (E) (iii) and (iv).)

(i) Primary sources

1257. Manfredi Del Donno, *Poesía popolare religiosa, Studi e testi di leggende agiografiche e moraleggianti del Sannio Beneventano* (Florence, 1964), Biblioteca di *Lares*, XIII. Study of popular hagiographical songs from region in South Italy; with texts.

1258. M. Del Donno, *Poesía popolare religiosa, Canti narrativi del Sannio Beneventano* (Florence, 1964), Biblioteca di *Lares*, XV. Further texts, with introduction.

1259. Katharine M. Briggs, *A Dictionary of British Folk-Tales* (London, 1970–2), 4 vols., Pt B, vol. 2, Ch. XI.

(ii) Secondary works

1260. Gordon Hall Gerould, *Saints' Legends* (Boston and New York, 1916).

1261. A. -J. Festugière, 'Lieux communs littéraires et thèmes de folk-lore dans l'hagiographie primitive', *Wiener Studien, Zeitschrift für Klassische Philologie*, LXXIII (1960), pp. 123–52.

1262. Paul Canart, 'Le Nouveau-né qui dénonce son père, Les avatars d'un conte populaire dans la littérature hagiographique', *AB*, 84 (1966), pp. 309–333. Interesting example of 'mythical' or folkloric element in hagiography.

See also 746, 748, 772, 832, 837, 838, 841, 843, 872, 886, 904, 924, 1095, 1142, 1272, 1275.

XVIII NON-CHRISTIAN CULTS

(A) PILGRIMAGE AND CULTS OF SAINTS IN ISLAM

1263. Ignace Goldziher, 'Le Culte des saints chez les Musulmans', *RHR*, II (1880), pp. 257–351. Still valuable study by the great Islamist.

1264. Edward William Lane, *Arabian Society in the Middle Ages, Studies from The Thousand and One Nights* (London, 1883). Ch. III on 'Saints'.

1265. Richard Burton, *Personal Narrative of a Pilgrimage to Al-Madinah and Meccah* (London, 1893), 2 vols. Classic first-hand account by European.

1266. G. A. Herklots and Ja'far Sharîf, *Islam in India* (Oxford, 1921), Revised edition by W. Crooke. Several chapters on saints and their festivals, and on vows.

1267. René Brunel, *Essai sur la confrérie religieuse des 'Aissâoûa au Maroc* (Paris, 1926). Study of order based on cult of founder saint.

1268. Edward Westermarck, *Ritual and Belief in Morocco* (London, 1926), 2 vols. Vol. I, Chs. I–III on saints and 'baraka'.

1269. Murray T. Titus, *Indian Islam, A Religious History of Islam in India* (London, 1930). Ch. VII is a short but valuable account of 'saint-worship'.

1270. E. Westermarck, *Pagan Survivals in Muhammedan Civilisation* (London, 1933). Chs. IV and V on saints and 'holiness'; compare generally with assimilation of Christianity and paganism (III (A) (iii)).

1271. John A. Subhan, *Sufism, Its Saints and Shrines, An Introduction to the Study of Sufism with Special Reference to India* (Lucknow, 1938), esp. Ch. VI. Thorough factual study by Methodist, with lists of saints and calendar of anniversaries.

1272. Louis Massignon, 'Les "Sept Dormants", Apocalypse de l'Islam', *AB*, 68 (1950), pp. 245–60. On important legend.

1273. G. E. von Grunebaum, *Muhammadan Festivals* (New York, 1951). Short study of festivals, pilgrimage and saints' cults.

1274. E. Dermenghem, *Le Culte des saints dans l'Islam maghrébin* (Paris, 1954). Comprehensive account for 'French' north Africa.

1275. E. Dermenghem *et al.*, 'Les Sept Dormants d'Ephèse (Ahl-al-Kahf) en Islam et en Chrétienté, Recueil documentaire et iconographique', *Revue des Etudes Islamiques*, XXIII (1954–5), pp. 59–112 (and XV Plates); XXIV (1956), pp. 93–106; and XXV (1957), pp. 1–11. Cross-cultural hagiographical study. See also **746, 772, 904, 1142, 1272**.

1276. Richard J. McCarthy (ed.), Abū Bakr Muhammed ibn at-tayyib Al-Bāqillānī, *Miracle and Magic, A Treatise on the Nature of the Apologetic Miracle and its Differentiation from Charisms, Trickery, Divination, Magic and Spells* (Beirut, 1958), Publications of Al-Hikma University of Baghdad, Kalam Series 2. Arabic text; short introduction and analytical summary in English; valuable for comparison with Christian apologetic; see XII (E).

1277. Arthur J. Arberry, *Shiraz, Persian City of Saints and Poets* (Norman, Okla. 1960). On Shīᶜite cults; see esp. Chs. III and IV on shrines of Ibn Khafif and Ruzbihan.

1278. G. Levi Della Vida, 'Leggende agiografiche cristiane nell'Islam', *ANLP*, 62 (1964), pp. 139–51. On representation of Islam in Christian hagiography.

1279. Marshall G. S. Hodgson, 'Islâm and Image', *HR*, III (1964), pp. 220–60. Important.

1280. A. J. Arberry (ed.), *Muslim Saints and Mystics, Episodes from the Tadhkirat al-Auliyaʾ* ('*Memorial of the Saints*') *by Farid al-din Attar* (London, 1966), Persian Heritage series. Valuable example of Sufi popular hagiography in English translation.

1281. Adrian C. Mayer, '*Pīr* and *Murshid*: an Aspect of Religious Leadership in West Pakistan', *Middle Eastern Studies*, III (1966–7), pp. 160–9. On aspects of living saints.

1282. I. Goldziher, 'On the Veneration of the Dead in Paganism and Islam', in S. M. Stern (ed.), *Muslim Studies*, I (Chicago, 1967), pp. 209–38. Translation of study in German dating from 1889–90.

1283. Virginia Vacca, *Vite e detti di santi musulmani* (Turin, 1968). Comprehensive historical account.

1284. Ernest Gellner, *Saints of the Atlas* (London and Chicago, 1969). Study of saintly lineages in south Morocco and of their function as mediators between lay tribes.

1285. Martin Lings, *A Sufi Saint of the Twentieth Century, Shaikh Ahmad al-'Alamī* (London, 1971), 2nd edition. Important.

1286. Nikki R. Keddie (ed.), *Scholars, Saints and Sufis, Muslim Religious Institutions* *in the Middle East since 1500* (Berkeley, Los Angeles and London, 1972 and 1978). Includes papers by B. G. Martin on the Khalwati Order of Dervishes, by V. Crapanzano on the Hamadsha, and by John Voll on *walis* in the Sudan.

1287. V. Crapanzano, *The Hamadsha, A Study in Moroccan Ethnopsychiatry* (Berkeley, Los Angeles and London, 1973). Study of lineage saints: legends, pilgrimage and cures.

1288. Michael Gilsenan, *Saint and Sufi in Modern Egypt, An Essay in the Sociology of Religion* (Oxford, 1973). Important study of a Sufi order and of the saint who founded and posthumously inspired it.

1289. Marc Gaborieau, 'Légende et culte du saint musulman Ghâzî Miyâ au Népal occidental et en Inde du nord', *Objets et Mondes*, XV (1975), pp. 289–318. Reveals discrepancy between nature of an Islamic saint as represented in legends (emphasis on chastity) and in festivals (emphasis on fertility); well illustrated.

1290. Dale F. Eickelman, *Moroccan Islam, Tradition and Society in a Pilgrimage Center* (Austin, Texas and London, 1976), Modern Middle East Series, I.

1291. Fatima Mernissi, 'Women, Saints and Sanctuaries', *Signs*, 3 (1977), pp. 101–12. Brief account of function of saints' cults for Moroccan women.

1292. Hava Lazarus-Yafeh, *Some Religious Aspects of Islam, A Collection of Articles* (Leiden, 1981). Includes studies of festivals and of 'The Sanctity of Jerusalem in Islam'.

See also **581**, and **582**.

(B) HINDUISM

1293. W. Crooke, *The Popular Religion and Folk-Lore of Northern India* (London, 1896), 2 vols. Important study of cults of ancestors and of Hindu 'godlings', and of festivals.

1294. John Campbell Oman, *The Mystics, Ascetics, and Saints of India, A Study of Sadhuism, with an Account of the Yogis, Sanyasis, Bairagis, and other strange Hindu sectarians* (London, 1903). On living Hindu saints, their ascetic practices and miracles.

1295. Léonce de Grandmaison, 'Le Sadhu Sundar Singh et le problème de la sainteté hors de l'Eglise catholique', *Recherches de Science Religieuse*, 12 (1922), pp. 1–29. Study of living saint, raising fundamental ecumenical issues.

1296. L. S. S. O'Malley, *Popular Hinduism, The Religion of the Masses* (Cambridge, 1935). Important little book.

1297. Alain Daniélou, *Hindu Polytheism* (London, 1964). Translated from French edition of 1960; standard work.

1298. Lawrence A. Babb, *The Divine Hierarchy, Popular Hinduism in Central India* (New York and London, 1975).

1299. Albert C. Moore, *Iconography of Religions, An Introduction* (London, 1977). Comparative reference work; Ch. 5 on 'Sages and Saints from India'.

1300. Barron Holland (ed.), *Popular Hinduism and Hindu Mythology, An Annotated Bibliography* (Westport, Conn. and London, 1979). See particularly Sections III (B) 3 and (C) 2 on lesser gods and goddesses, and V on festivals and pilgrimages.

See also **581, 583, 584, 1073**.

(C) MISCELLANEOUS RELIGIONS

1301. E. E. Evans-Pritchard, *Nuer Religion* (Oxford, 1956). Classic study of African religion; final chapter esp. raises comparative issues.
1302. W. Owen Cole and Piara Singh Sambhi, *The Sikhs, Their Religious Beliefs and Practices* (London, 1978). Esp. Ch. 2, 'The Place of the Ten Gurus in the Sikh Religion'.
1303. Christian Deschamps, 'Les "Fêtes" du village en Corée et leur signification sociale', *SC*, XXV (1978), pp. 191–208. Village festivals as rituals to propitiate local patron spirits and as manifestations of community.

See also **581, 586**.

(D) MODERN SECULAR CULTS AND BELIEFS

(i) Cults and festivals of the French Revolution

1304. Mona Ozouf, *La Fête révolutionnaire 1789–1799* (Paris, 1976). Comprehensive.
1305. Marie-Louise Biver, *Fêtes révolutionnaires à Paris* (Paris, 1979). Contemporary accounts with illustrations; including the 'translations' of the bodies of Voltaire and Rousseau to the Pantheon in 1791 and 1794.

See also **1066**.

(ii) National festivals

1306. Rosemonde Sanson, *Les 14 Juillet (1789–1795), Fête et conscience nationale* (Paris, 1976). Good example.

(iii) Miscellaneous

1307. Henry Nash Smith, *Virgin Land, The American West as Symbol and Myth* (New York, 1957). Chs. VIII–IX on 'The Western Hero'; origins of a powerful modern myth.
1308. Edgar Morin, *The Stars* (New York and London, 1960). Short sociological study of cinema 'stars', translated from French; Ch. III on 'fan' clubs and letters, and other 'liturgical' aspects, is of special interest.
1309. Philip French, *Westerns, Aspects of a Movie Genre* (London, 1977), Revised edition. Deals mainly with post-1950 Westerns; with bibliography.

Index

419